WORTH A THOUSAND WORDS

WORTH A THOUSAND WORDS

THOUSAND WORDS

Cultural, Literary, and Political Proverb Studies

Wolfgang Mieder

University Press of Mississippi / Jackson

The University Press of Mississippi is the scholarly publishing agency of
the Mississippi Institutions of Higher Learning: Alcorn State University,
Delta State University, Jackson State University, Mississippi State University,
Mississippi University for Women, Mississippi Valley State University,
University of Mississippi, and University of Southern Mississippi.

www.upress.state.ms.us

The University Press of Mississippi is a member
of the Association of University Presses.

Any discriminatory or derogatory language or hate speech regarding race,
ethnicity, religion, sex, gender, class, national origin, age, or disability
that has been retained or appears in elided form is in no way an endorsement
of the use of such language outside a scholarly context.

Copyright © 2025 by University Press of Mississippi
All rights reserved
Manufactured in the United States of America

∞

Publisher: University Press of Mississippi, Jackson, USA
Authorised GPSR Safety Representative: Easy Access System Europe -
Mustamäe tee 50, 10621 Tallinn, Estonia, gpsr.requests@easproject.com

Library of Congress Cataloging-in-Publication Data available

Print LCCN 2025020904
ISBN 9781496858283 (hardback)
ISBN 9781496858290 (trade paperback)
ISBN 9781496858306 (EPUB single)
ISBN 9781496858313 (EPUB institutional)
ISBN 9781496858320 (PDF single)
ISBN 9781496858337 (PDF institutional)

British Library Cataloging-in-Publication Data available

In Memoriam
Dan Ben-Amos
(1934–2023)

CONTENTS

Introduction 3

American Proverbs

1. "Think Outside the Box"
   The Wisdom and Nature of American Proverbs 19
2. "Proverbs Are Worth a Thousand Words"
   The Global Spread of American Proverbs 46
3. "A Friend (Not) in Need Is a Friend Indeed"
   Friendship in Old, Modern, and Anti-Proverbs 59
4. "Freedom Is Not Given, It Is Won"
   Democratic Principles in Modern American Proverbs 73

Proverbs in Politics

5. "Do unto Others as You Would Have Them Do unto You"
   The Humanistic Value of Proverbs in Sociopolitical Discourse 89
6. "Freedom Is Indivisible"
   John F. Kennedy's Reliance on Proverbs 122
7. "Concordia Domi, Foris Pax"
   Willy Brandt's Non-German Proverbial Rhetoric 161

Proverbs in Literature

8. "Stringing Proverbs Together"
   The Proverbial Language in Miguel de Cervantes's *Don Quixote* 195
9. "All Roads Lead to 'Perverbs'"
   Harry Mathews's *Selected Declarations of Dependence* (1977). 235

10. "Black Is Beautiful"
Hans-Jürgen Massaquoi's Proverbial Autobiography
Destined to Witness (1999) 264

Proverbs in Culture

11. "You Have to Kiss a Lot of Frogs Before You Meet Your
Handsome Prince"
From Fairy-Tale Motif to Modern Proverb. 311
12. "The Word (and Phrase) Detective"
A Proverbial Tribute to *OED* Editor John A. Simpson. 332
13. "Injustice Anywhere Is a Threat to Justice Everywhere"
From Classical to Modern Law Proverbs 366

Proverb Index. 391

WORTH A THOUSAND WORDS

INTRODUCTION

During my more than fifty years of tilling the rich field of paremiology (proverb studies), I have published my share of books, articles, and bibliographies both in my native language of German and my acquired language of English as a so-called German American here in the United States. As time passed, I had the opportunity to assemble some articles into cohesive essay volumes in several countries, with the titles of such books as *The Politics of Proverbs: From Traditional Wisdom to Proverbial Stereotypes* (1997), *Strategies of Wisdom: Anglo-American and German Proverb Studies* (2005), *Proverbs Are the Best Policy: Folk Wisdom and American Politics* (2005), *"Proverbs Speak Louder Than Words": Folk Wisdom in Art, Culture, Folklore, History, Literature, and Mass Media* (2008), and *"Right Makes Might": Proverbs and the American Worldview* (2019) revealing to a certain degree their multifaceted contents. Ten years ago, I had the welcome chance to publish the rather large volume *Behold the Proverbs of a People: Proverbial Wisdom in Culture, Literature, and Politics* (2014) with the University Press of Mississippi, which has made a name for itself for its books dealing with folkloric matters including proverbs. It is then with much joy that I accepted the kind invitation to put together another book once again containing thirteen essays with the title *Worth a Thousand Words: Cultural, Literary, and Political Proverb Studies* as a companion volume.

As in the preceding essay collection of 2014, I have divided the essays into four groups, with the first containing four of them under the heading "American Proverbs." They present a discussion of the wisdom and nature of American proverbs, the global spread of American proverbs, the theme of friendship in such proverbs and their anti-proverbs, and the expression of democratic principles in modern American proverbs. This is followed by three chapters making up the group "Proverbs in Politics." The first looks at the humanistic value of proverbs in sociopolitical discourse in the United States over time. This quite naturally leads to a discussion of President John F. Kennedy's reliance on proverbs for his important messages. Former chancellor Willy Brandt's proverbial rhetoric, often citing proverbs in English or their German translation, is quite similar to that of his American contemporary. For obvious personal reasons—Brandt and I both stem from the old Hanseatic town of Lübeck—I was eager to undertake this study and to include it in this volume. The third section is dedicated to "Proverbs in Literature" and begins with a chapter on the rich proverbial language in Miguel de Cervantes's famous novel *Don Quixote* (1605, 1615). Moving on to more modern times is a chapter on proverb manipulations by the American author Harry Mathews, who was an artist in creating prose and poetry based on anti-proverbs. The third chapter of this section discusses Hans-Jürgen Massaquoi's proverbial autobiography *Destined to Witness* (1999). He grew up in Nazi Germany as a biracial child, immigrated to the United States, and became the editor of *Ebony* magazine. Finally, then, the fourth section is dedicated to "Proverbs in Culture," with the first chapter showing how a fairy tale motif has become the modern proverb "You have to kiss a lot of frogs before you meet your handsome prince." The following chapter is a proverbial tribute to John A. Simpson, former editor of the *Oxford English Dictionary*, who in the early 1990s was instrumental in convincing Oxford University Press to publish *A Dictionary of American Proverbs* (1992). The last chapter, with its titular proverb "Injustice anywhere is a threat to justice everywhere," which originated with Martin Luther King Jr. in 1958, includes a discussion of numerous classical and modern proverbs expressing legal concepts.

It might already have become clear from just these cursory remarks that some chapters have a personal meaning for me. As I have reached the age of an octogenarian, I have become aware of the fact that during the past ten years I have ever more chosen topics to work on that have some special meanings to me personally, to wit my thankfulness as an immigrant to the United States to have been able to work for half a century as a professor of German and folklore at the University of Vermont. My deep and lasting interest in American proverbs in particular can hardly be a surprise, to wit the already mentioned dictionary and my more recent books *The Worldview of Modern American Proverbs* (2020) and *Dictionary of Authentic American Proverbs* (2021). Of course, both John F. Kennedy and his proclamation "Ich bin ein Berliner" in the presence of the then mayor of West Berlin Willy Brandt have a special meaning to me. And my studies of the proverbial rhetoric of celebrated Americans have instilled in me a sincere commitment to civil rights and the two American triads "Life, liberty, and the pursuit of happiness" and "Freedom, justice, and democracy" for all people, which comes to the fore in my books *The Proverbial Abraham Lincoln: An Index to Proverbs in the Works of Abraham Lincoln* (2000), *"No Struggle, No Progress": Frederick Douglass and His Proverbial Rhetoric for Civil Rights* (2001), *"Yes We Can": Barack Obama's Proverbial Rhetoric* (2009), *"Making a Way Out of No Way": Martin Luther King's Sermonic Proverbial*

Rhetoric (2010), *"All Men and Women Are Created Equal": Elizabeth Cady Stanton's and Susan B. Anthony's Proverbial Rhetoric Promoting Women's Rights* (2014), and *A Rising Tide Lifts All the Boats: The Proverbial Rhetoric of John F. Kennedy* (2023). Related to this, I might mention my three favorite proverbs with which I used to conclude my large lecture course "'Big Fish Eat Little Fish': The Nature and Politics of Proverbs," sending my students on their way with some proverbial wisdom to live by: the modern American proverb "Different strokes for different folks," the older American proverb popularized by Martin Luther King Jr. "Making a way out of no way," and the golden rule that is part of all world religions: "Do unto others as you would have them do unto you."

But to return to our proverbial muttons, let me make the following somewhat more detailed remarks about the thirteen chapters and their relevance for proverb studies and far beyond that, for a deeper understanding of a humane existence informed by equality and freedom. When speaking of American proverbs, it is important to keep in mind that the United States is a land of immigrants who for centuries have brought their native proverbs with them of which some have been translated into the English language that dominates the American landscape. Naturally, the majority of proverbs spoken and written in English have their roots in Great Britain and have thus not originated in North America. And yet, as can be imagined, there are plenty of proverbs that can be shown to have been coined in the English language in the United States and to a lesser degree in Canada. There is then a considerable repertoire of authentic American proverbs dating back to the early beginnings and certainly up to the present day. This is not forgetting that there do exist some proverbs in the Native American languages, but as has been shown by anthropologists, folklorists, and linguists, there is a dearth of them, a conundrum indeed considering the plethora of proverbs in the languages of other Native populations of the world. While it is not easy to determine which proverbs have in fact grown on American soil, detailed historical research of individual proverbs based on written sources and ever more on electronic databases makes this possible. Here are a few American proverbs with the dates of their earliest appearance in writing and for some even with their actual originator: "Facts don't lie" (1748), "Three removes are as bad as a fire" (1758, Benjamin Franklin), "Good fences make good neighbors" (1834), "Equal pay for equal work" (1869, Susan B. Anthony), "Crime does not pay" (1874), "Speak softly and carry a big stick" (1900, Theodore Roosevelt), "It's not over till it's over" (1921, Yogi Berra), "Life is not a spectator sport" (1958), and "Life is a box of chocolates" (1994, from the film *Forrest Gump*). As can be seen, the time of proverb making is by no means over! The modern age continues to create proverbs that might be based on such old proverb structures as "Better X than Y" (Better a big fish in a little pond than a little fish in a big pond, 1903), "One man's X is another man's Y" (One man's trash is another man's treasure, 1924), or "No X, no Y" (No guts, no glory, 1945). These proverbs come from all walks of life and are widely as well as quickly disseminated through the media and the internet. As they comment on life, finance, sports, politics, age, sex, and whatever, they do at least to a certain degree reflect somewhat of a general worldview of modern society. This book's first chapter, "The Wisdom and Nature of American Proverbs," deals with this in considerable detail, showing once and for all that proverbs are very much alive in oral and written communications including the realms of entertainment, business, politics, and justice.

Proverbs have long been loan translated from one language and culture to another. Many Greek and Latin proverbs from ancient times have appeared in translation in other languages, as is also the case with proverbs from the various religions of the world. Medieval Latin proverbs also were disseminated widely throughout Europe, as they were used for translation exercises in schools. No wonder that such proverbs as "Strike while the iron is hot," "When the cat's away, the mice will play," and "Not all that glitters is gold" appear in identical form in numerous languages. This process is very much alive today, but with one major change. It is the English language with its linguistic dominance throughout the world that is spreading proverbs elsewhere. And to be sure, it is American culture that dominates this international spread of proverbs. Thus, the two nineteenth-century proverbs "Don't swap (switch) horses in midstream (in the middle of the stream)" (1834) and "An apple a day keeps the doctor away" (1870) are now current in loan translations in many European countries but also in China, India, Japan, and doubtlessly elsewhere. But it is the modern American proverbs that have conquered the world, so to speak, to wit the appearance of such proverbs as "One picture is worth a thousand words" (1911), "The grass is always greener on the other side of the fence" (1913), and "It takes two to tango" (1952). As shown in the second chapter, "The Global Spread of American Proverbs," such proverbs often become current in other countries both as translations but also in their original English language. After all, many speakers in Germany or Israel, for example, have no difficulties citing English texts to make an important point by way of a proverb. The fact that American proverbs can so easily be transferred to other cultures can well be understood as a sign that their wisdom is globally relevant and certainly not restricted to only an American worldview.

Of late it has become somewhat of a fad in paremiological scholarship to study various proverbs belonging to the same concept. There are studies on bread, dogs, peace, war, wine, women, and so on, showing what the folk has thought about these matters over time. Care must however be taken that historical and cultural issues not be mixed up too much by ignoring that some of the proverbs have long disappeared from common use and cannot be considered as a general worldview of the modern age. Cognizant of this issue, I have attempted to look at "Friendship in Old, Modern, and Anti-Proverbs" in the third chapter, paying attention to the different views of friends and friendship over time. I also include a discussion of the seventeenth-century English proverb "A friend (not) in need is a friend indeed" (1665), which presents its own semantic difficulties that might have been instrumental in leading to such modern anti-proverbs as "A friend that ain't in need is a friend indeed" (1955), "A friend in need is a friend you don't need" (1968), and "A friend in deed is the friend you need" (1999). Be that as it may, there is also the well-known proverb "A dog is man's best friend" (1843), which has resulted in anti-proverbs of which "A book is man's [woman's] best friend" might just reach its own proverbial status. In other words, anti-proverbs can well become new proverbs with general currency and frequency. To be sure, I cite many friendship proverbs and observe that it is amazing that, considering the hundreds of proverbs that exist on this theme, still new ones can be coined. And yet, they make their point, especially about modern society and its mores, to wit: "Your best friend might be your worst enemy" (1970), "Friends don't let friends drive drunk" (1976), and "A (true, good) friend walks in when (all) others walk out" (1994). Human relations, being what they are, continue to be expressed in concise bits of wisdom that might be intended as cautionary advice, hopeful rationalization, and other concerns, showing that the sky is the limit for new proverb inventions.

The fourth chapter, "Democratic Principles in Modern American Proverbs," is somewhat related to the "friend" discussion in that it looks at uplifting modern proverbs that underpin invaluable concepts of democracy and freedom. Of fundamental importance is, of course, the triadic definition of democracy that Abraham Lincoln, influenced by some similar precursors, expressed at the end of his famous Gettysburg Address on November 19, 1863, as "government of the people, by the people, for the people." There are other presidential statements dealing more or less directly with democratic principles, for example "Eternal vigilance is the price of liberty" (1837, Andrew Jackson) and "Freedom is indivisible" (1960, John F. Kennedy). But there are also Frederick Douglass's legitimate claims as a former slave and engaged abolitionist that "Who would be free themselves must strike the blow" and "Better even die free, than to live slaves" that he repeated so frequently after 1863 that they have taken on a proverbial claim indeed. Some hundred years later, Martin Luther King Jr. coined the proverb "Freedom is not given, it is won" in his book *Where Do We Go from Here: Chaos or Community?* (1967). But there are also fascinating modern "freedom" proverbs that gained currency without famous people having coined and spread them, for instance "Freedom is not free" (1943) and "Freedom is not for sale" (1949). Such proverbial wisdom can and should continue to serve as guideposts for a free world based on the proverbial triad "Freedom, justice, democracy" for all!

The three chapters of the section "Proverbs in Politics" continue these deliberations. The fifth chapter, "The Humanistic Value of Proverbs in Sociopolitical Discourse," illustrates by way of contextualized examples that proverbs as strategic signs for recurrent situations have long played a significant communicative role in political rhetoric. Bible proverbs as well as folk proverbs appear as concise expressions of wisdom and common sense, adding authority and didacticism to the multifaceted aspects of societal discourse. Some proverbs like the golden rule "Do unto others as you would have them do unto you" (Matthew 7:12) or the American (not African) proverb "It takes a village to raise a child" (1981), popularized by way of Hillary Rodham Clinton's influential book *It Takes a Village, and Other Lessons Children Teach Us* (1996), can function as traditional leitmotifs while other well-known proverbs might be changed into anti-proverbs to express innovative insights. The moralistic, evaluative, and argumentative employment of proverbs can be seen in the letters, speeches, and writings of Lord Chesterfield from Great Britain, Abigail Adams, and Benjamin Franklin in the eighteenth century. Abraham Lincoln, Frederick Douglass, Elizabeth Cady Stanton, and Susan B. Anthony stand out in their repeated use of proverbs for civil and women's rights during the nineteenth century. This effective preoccupation with proverbs for social and political improvements can also be observed in the impressive oratory of Martin Luther King Jr., Barack Obama, Hillary Rodham Clinton, and Bernie Sanders in the modern age. And it might be added here that Congressman John Lewis also employed proverbs frequently in his emotional speeches and writings about freedom and equality. In opposition to all of this, Donald Trump's confrontational and aggressive rhetoric is devoid of proverbial language. His bombastic speeches and "writings," delivered as soundbites and tweets, have no room for metaphorical language or the indirection of proverbs. But never mind, the many proverb references cited throughout this chapter illustrate beyond any doubt that the ubiquitous proverbs underscore various political messages and add metaphorical as well as folkloric expressiveness to the worldview that social reformers and engaged politicians wish to communicate. As commonly held wisdom, the proverbs clearly add humanistic value to political communications as they argue for an improved world order.

As the title indicates, the sixth chapter, "John F. Kennedy's Reliance on Proverbs," takes a detailed look at the former president's rhetorical eloquence. There is no doubt that Kennedy's discursive prowess is based to a considerable degree on his ingenious employment of biblical and folk proverbs and his impressive ability to coin sententious remarks that have become proverbial, to wit "Ask not what your country can do for you, ask what you can do for your country," which he cited in his memorable inaugural address of January 20, 1961. His oral and written messages are replete with proverbial wisdom that adds a certain traditional authority to his speeches and writings. At times he draws special attention to the sayings, citing them as commonly accepted truths. But he also integrates well-known proverbs by merely alluding to them or changing them into anti-proverbs. Bible proverbs like "A soft answer turneth away wrath" (Proverbs 15:1) or "The truth shall make you free" (John 8:32) add a certain prophetic and didactic tone to his communications on both the national and the international stage. Folk proverbs like "Don't take down the fence until you know why it was put up" and "Practice what you preach" are employed as warnings or as imperatives for appropriate political and social behavior. The maritime proverb "A rising tide lifts all the boats" is clearly one of his favorite expressions. Its metaphor serves him well to express his optimistic worldview and his commitment to the well-being of not only the American nation but the world community, where everybody is in the same boat and rowing as a team toward a future of equality, freedom, and peace. To be sure, Kennedy also coined the claim that "Freedom is indivisible" in a campaign speech of October 12, 1960, repeating it at the momentous occasion of his speech in West Berlin on June 26, 1963, which closed with his claim that he felt like a citizen of that divided city: "Freedom is indivisible, and when one man is enslaved, all are not free. When all are free, then we can look forward to that day when this city will be joined as one [. . .]. All free men, wherever they may live, are citizens of Berlin, and, therefore, as a free man, I take pride in the words *Ich bin ein Berliner*."

As mentioned earlier, West Berlin's mayor and later German chancellor Willy Brandt was present at this memorable event and, being fluent in English as many Germans were and are, had no problem understanding Kennedy's revolutionary words. As a conscious stylist, he paid careful attention to his rhetoric, and as other world-class politicians he drew on folk speech in the form of proverbs to add to the expressive and emotional nature of his language. While he employed numerous German proverbs and proverbial expressions, he was also quite keen to integrate foreign proverbs into his verbal and written texts. Being one of the most polyglot politicians of the twentieth century, he cited various proverbs in German translation from African, Asian, and European cultures. But he was especially apt at integrating Anglo-American proverbs in English or more frequently in German translation into his discourse, notably "You can't unscramble eggs," "There are no atheists in foxholes," "Charity begins at home," "You cannot have your cake and eat it too," "Ask not what your country can do for you, ask what you can do for your country" (John F. Kennedy), "Don't change horses in the middle of the stream," "The glass is either half full or half empty," and "Think globally, act locally." In fact, having learned the Bible proverb "A house divided against itself cannot stand" (Mark 3:25) by way of Lincoln's frequent use of it, he started using it both in English and his very own German translation so frequently during the time of German unification that his wording has become proverbial among Germans. The analysis of numerous contextualized examples in this seventh chapter shows that Brandt was indeed a magisterial speaker and writer who was keenly aware of the rhetorical importance of proverbs as linguistic signs of human behavior and experiences as well as of proverbs as metaphors of national and international relations in the world of politics.

My interest in studying the use and function of proverbs and proverbial expressions in all forms of literature, from novels, plays, and poems (including songs) to aphorisms, began with my dissertation in 1970 about the appearance of proverbial language in the voluminous works of the nineteenth-century Swiss novelist Jeremias Gotthelf. Several German books followed about the proverbial language in Johann Wolfgang von Goethe, Friedrich Schiller, Friedrich Nietzsche, and Bertolt Brecht, with parallel English publications about Charles Dickens, George Bernard Shaw, and Eugene O'Neill. These three books were written together with my departed colleague and friend George B. Bryan (1939–1996), with whom I was going to undertake many more proverbial projects. But in any case, in the year of his untimely death we did publish *Proverbs in World Literature: A Bibliography* (1996), whose 2,654 titles document the importance of proverbial language in regional, national, and so-called world literature, as for example in Miguel de Cervantes Saavedra's celebrated novel *Don Quixote*. Even though I am by no means a specialist in Spanish literature, I undertook the work on this book's eighth chapter at the request of my colleague and friend Juan Maura, former professor of Spanish at the University of Vermont. It provided me with the welcome opportunity to finally read and study this significant novel, which contains a plethora of proverbs. While Sancho Panza, as a folk hero of sorts, has "a sack filled with proverbs" at his disposal, other characters also employ proverbs, including even Don Quixote himself, who mocks Sancho because of his proverb tirades. In other words, proverbs are part of the discursive strategy of the novel, with the amassment of this folk language amounting to splendid proverb duels that illustrate various points of view while at the same time underscoring the complexities of life by way of metaphorical indirection. Proverbs function as strategically placed verbal signs that take on the role of discursive indirection in their literary context. They are of common use in this masterful novel, showing that folk wisdom permeates human communication no matter what the background of the characters might be. Proverbs in this fascinating novel act as performed wisdom of everyday life in conversational situations, and it is at least in part this dynamic quality of proverbs in performance that makes this novel such a special treat still today after four hundred years.

When Don Quixote accuses Sancho Panza of unceasingly "stringing proverbs together" to the point of absurdity, one might also make a similar claim in what the American modernist writer Harry Mathews does in his tour-de-force prose and poetic book *Selected Declarations of Dependence* (1977), albeit with the major difference that he manipulates dozens of proverbs into never-ending collages of mixed-up proverbs and anti-proverbs. His creation of "All Roads Lead to 'Perverbs'" can thus serve perfectly as the title of the ninth chapter, which looks at the intricate workings of this innovative author. To be sure, the manipulative change of traditional proverbs into innovative anti-proverbs is nothing new. In fact, the playful rearrangement of proverb halves into insightful or nonsensical creations has been practiced by such aphoristic writers and poets as Friedrich Nietzsche, Bertolt Brecht, Paul Éluard, Franz Fühmann, Paul Muldoon, and others. This art of scrambling proverbs was executed in particular by several members of the French avant-garde group of writers and intellectuals called Oulipo (Ouvroir de Littérature Potentielle). Harry Mathews (1930–2017) was one of its prolific members who excelled with his enumerative poems based on various patterns of proverb fragments. While he published such tour-de-force poetic texts in French, he also wrote a unique book in English with the title *Selected Declarations of Dependence* (1977). The first part is a love story of sorts based on the 185 words that appear in forty-six common English proverbs. Proverb halves are interspersed in this prose, but there are also multiple poetic texts that employ parts of proverbs in certain patterns and as anaphora and leitmotifs. The second half is made up of 106 paraphrases of what he calls "perverbes," anti-proverbs made up of two proverb halves. It is up to readers to find which perverb (the English spelling) belongs to which paraphrase. All of this is meant to entertain and challenge readers into becoming active participants in these texts, which at times make sense but also remain without any meaning. The entire book is conceived as an intellectual game with its own riddles and perplexities but also with playful humor that should intrigue and delight paremiologists everywhere.

With the tenth chapter, "Hans-Jürgen Massaquoi's Proverbial Autobiography *Destined to Witness* (1999)," with its rich proverb repertoire, I undertook a study that has considerable meaning to me personally. After all, I grew up next to Massaquoi's native Hamburg in Lübeck after the war and am an immigrant to the United States just as he was. But his account of being a biracial child surviving the harassment and dangers of Nazi Germany with his German mother, whose Liberian husband left her to fend for herself and raise his son; his travel on to Africa to meet his estranged father; and eventually his successful career and life in the United States with his family is considerably more revealing and enriching than my life's story could be. Be that as it may, Massaquoi tells of his growing up in a working-class neighborhood during and after the severe bombing of Hamburg, describing his and his mother's struggle to survive Nazi Germany in numerous short chapters that are informed by the journalistic as well as literary style that Massaquoi became accustomed to once he established himself in the United States as managing editor of the African American magazine *Ebony*. The book is replete with proverbs and proverbial expressions that add metaphorical expressiveness to this emotional and informative account of survival among prejudice, stereotypes, and racism. Many proverbs, often quoted by Massaquoi's mother, are cited in German with English translations, and others only in English. Thus, the book is a telling example of how proverbs function in a family and beyond as social strategies, in this case to carve out a marginalized existence between 1926 and the early 1950s in Germany, Liberia, and the United States. And yet, later in life, when Massaquoi returned to Germany as an established journalist, he felt no animosity toward his hometown, recalling the proverbs that he had learned from his special mother, whose wisdom he instilled in his two successful sons about whom he was justifiably proud as a "self-made" man of color in his new homeland of America.

The last section of this volume is dedicated to "Proverbs in Culture"; the eleventh chapter, subtitled "From Fairy-Tale Motif to Modern Proverb," presents the intriguing history of the by now well-known American proverb "You have to kiss a lot of frogs (toads) before you meet your handsome prince." This investigation is a telling example of the interrelationship of folk narrative research and paremiology, remembering that many proverbs are reduced expressions of fables, legends, and fairy tales, while proverbs on the other hand can also be expanded into longer narratives exemplifying them. In this particular case, the question is simply put whether the modern American proverb that has long been loan translated into German and other languages is in fact a reduction of "The Frog King" fairy tale of the Brothers Grimm or whether it was coined more or less independently. The vexing problem in this developmental story is, of course, the fact that there is no kiss scene in the German tale; the princess liberates herself from the sexually implicit advances of the slippery frog by throwing it against the wall—not exactly a romantic encounter. The chapter presents a number of German variants, some in dialect, as well as more modern English and American retellings of the tale in which, slowly but surely, a kiss scene appears! An "invented" kiss also takes place in German and English poems based on the old fairy tale, and the recent Walt Disney animated musical fantasy comedy *The Princess and the Frog* (2009) did its part in spreading the "rumor" that there is in actuality a kiss between the frog and the princess in the Grimm tale. Cartoons and comic strips, including rather sexually explicit ones, play their part in all of this. And what are we to make of all of this in the end? I have no choice but to conclude that the frequently cited proverb, also found on greeting cards, came into being not as the reduction of a fairy tale but most likely as an imaginative allusion to one of the most popular fairy tales. In other words, people want a kiss scene to be there, somewhat in connection with the "Beauty and the Beast" narrative cycle, and thus the proverb was coined. Perhaps a fairy tale variant of "The Frog King" existed in earlier times with a kiss scene that was later eradicated by more puritan collectors and editors in order to avoid sexual implications, as stories were adapted from adult literature to become stories for innocent children. I might also mention here that this entire phenomenon is of special interest to me as a German American scholar of fairy tales and proverbs, as can be seen from my subsequent book-length study with 177 illustrations, *Der Froschkönig: Das Märchen in Literatur, Medien und Karikaturen* (2019).

The twelfth chapter of this volume, "A Proverbial Tribute to *OED* Editor John A. Simpson," also has somewhat of a personal story behind it. I wrote it in response to Simpson's fascinating scholarly autobiography *The Word Detective: Searching for the Meaning of It All at the "Oxford English Dictionary"* (2016), which touched me deeply because of its erudite content as well as its emotional depth. Of course, I also remembered my indebtedness to him, who, as the editor of the acclaimed *Concise Oxford Dictionary of Proverbs* (1982), pretty much had the last word in getting Oxford University Press to publish *A Dictionary of American Proverbs* (1992), which I edited together with my friends Stewart A. Kingsbury and Kelsie B. Harder. I still remember fondly our meeting at the OUP office in New York City many years ago and remain thankful for Simpson's positive approval of our work. As I read his informative account of his odyssey as a first-class lexicographer with obvious interest in proverbial language, I noticed that he frequently interspersed his prose with that formulaic language. As is my custom, I marked all the proverbial references, in total numbering 260 phrases in 350 pages, demonstrating clearly that his work on phraseological units had rubbed off on his narrative style. I might add here that I have noticed a similar modus operandi as I catch myself quoting proverbs and proverbial expressions in my e-mails, letters, and even scholarly writings. John Simpson must certainly have been aware of what he was doing. Some of the proverbial phrases he quite naturally intersperses in his prose, but there are also instances when his paremiographical and paremiological interests come to the fore as he explains particular proverbs or proverbial expressions, for example "When the cat's away, the mice will play" and "By a long chalk." The book also tells the history of his proverb dictionary, showing how we proverb scholars do our work. In any case, writing about John Simpson and his incredible work as a leading lexicographer gave me much pleasure indeed. And let me cite here the last few lines of this chapter as a personal comment: "I like the last sentence of the book, thinking that my wife Barbara might say something similar about me as my own retirement is approaching: 'Hilary says I'm just an ordinary bloke who's been lucky enough to do an extraordinary job. I suppose she's right. She usually is.' I am, of course, not putting myself on the same pedestal with John Simpson, and Barbara might well simply state that I have done a 'good' job for my students and my paremiological work. John Simpson's shoes are a very special size and can't be filled by another person. He is a model for us all, and I am thankful that many years ago he helped me to get my paremiological feet on the ground."

Following this somewhat emotional comment (I am now retired since 2021), I finished the thirteenth chapter, subtitled "From Classical to Modern Law Proverbs," in early 2024 and planned to deliver it at the Hebrew University of Jerusalem to inaugurate the Dan Ben-Amos Memorial Lecture Series in April 2024 as part of the annual meeting of the Jewish Folklore Society dedicated to the theme of folklore and the law. Receiving kind words about this invitation from Dan's widow Batsheva Ben-Amos was one of the greatest honors of my life. Dan and I had been friends for decades, and shortly after his death I published the book *"A Good Friend Is a Treasure": Five Decades of Correspondence Between the Folklorists Dan Ben-Amos and Wolfgang Mieder* (2023), presenting parts of it as the keynote speaker at his memorial symposium on November 19, 2023, on the campus of the University of Pennsylvania, where he had taught for more than fifty years until his death. Not knowing when I will be able to travel to Israel with the war raging in Gaza, I am including my essay here, realizing that I will prepare something different when I can eventually travel to Israel, a long-held dream coming true whenever it will occur. I am sure that Dan would have agreed with the modern American proverb "Injustice anywhere is a threat to justice everywhere," which was coined by Martin Luther King Jr. in his book *Stride Toward Freedom: The Montgomery Story* (1958) and which I chose as the titular proverb for this final chapter. My discussion starts with such legal proverbs from Roman times as "Ignorantia juris non excusat" (Ignorance of the law is no excuse), "Caveat emptor" (Buyer beware), "Necessitas non habet legem" (Necessity knows no law), and "Summum ius, summa iniuria" (Extreme law is extreme injustice). As an example of the many medieval Latin proverbs expressing legal concepts, I cite the proverb "Qui capit ante molam, merito molit ante farinam" (Who gets to the mill first, rightfully grinds his flower first), showing that it was shorted over time to the proverb "First come, first served," which certainly is understood as a very basic legal principle in the ordinary situation of standing in line. That things are never simple in legal matters is shown by the contradictory proverb pair "Right makes might" and "Might makes right," which goes back to the fourteenth century. Of newer coinage are such proverbs as "My house is my castle," "Possession is nine points of the law," and "Good fences make good neighbors," and modern proverbs such as "You break it, you buy it" (1952), "No victim, no crime" (1971), and "My body, my choice" (1989). Finally, then, there is also the proverb "No man is above the law" (1734), which has gained considerable popularity in the media recently as it relates to Donald Trump. One thing is for certain: as with other well-established proverbs, those commenting on legal matters enjoy frequent use in the modern litigious society—yet another sign that proverbs, both old and new, are never out of season!

All that remains is for me to express my thanks to the publishers in Portugal, Russia, and the United States for granting me their kind permission to reprint eleven of the chapters in this volume. Their original publications are listed at the beginning of the chapter bibliographies, with chapters 6 and 13 appearing for the first time in this book. I also wish to thank my colleagues and friends from the Interlibrary Loan Office at the Howe Library of the University of Vermont for their incredible support over my many years of depending on them for various materials. I also wish to thank my colleagues, friends, and students here and abroad for their interest in my proverb studies. While there are too many to name individually, I do want to mention at least Melita Aleksa Varga, Simon J. Bronner, Charles Clay Doyle, Christian Grandl, Hrisztalina Hrisztova-Gotthardt, Anna T. Litovkina, Dennis Mahoney, Valerii Mokienko, Andreas Nolte, Elliott Oring, Raymond Summerville, Pat Turner, and Harry Walter. Finally, I am thankful to the colleagues at the University Press of Mississippi for accepting this book into their folklore program.

As can be seen from these introductory comments and other statements in various chapters, my fellow folklorist and special friend Dan Ben-Amos (1934–2023) has been present in my mind and heart throughout the work on this book. I would so much have liked to present it to him while he was still alive. Instead, I now dedicate this volume in fond memory to my treasured friend Dan.

Wolfgang Mieder

American Proverbs

1

"THINK OUTSIDE THE BOX"

The Wisdom and Nature of American Proverbs

It might appear as if proverbs are of little relevance in the modern society of the United States. In fact, there are scholars who have claimed that proverbs have no place in this technologically advanced society (Albig 1931; Stewart 1991, 17–19), and the mass media repeatedly declares in popular magazine and newspaper articles that traditional proverbs with their didactic and moralistic messages are no longer of any value (Mieder and Sobieski 2006). Nothing could be further from the truth, as can be seen from the literally thousands of studies on proverbs and such related sayings as proverbial expressions, proverbial comparisons, proverbial exaggerations, twin formulas (traditional word pairs linked together by alliteration and/or rhyme), and wellerisms (sayings of a triadic structure: a statement, a speaker, and an unexpected situation) that continue to thrive throughout the world (Mieder 2009a). New proverb collections are also appearing for major and minor languages, with comparative international compendia showing that people everywhere distill their observations and experiences into ready-made bits of wisdom (Mieder 2011a).

The collection (paremiography) and study (paremiology) of proverbial language experienced an apex with two American scholars of the twentieth century, whose studies and collections continue to be of international importance. The renowned folklorist and philologist Archer Taylor (1890–1973) published the classic study *The Proverb* (1931), which surveys the multifaceted origins of proverbs (antiquity, the Bible, narratives, literature, individual authors, etc.), the content of proverbs (customs and superstitions, history, law, stereotypes, weather, medicine, etc.), the style of proverbs (poetics, ethics, literature, etc.), and the various subgenres (proverbial phrases and wellerisms). At about the same time, his friend Bartlett Jere Whiting (1904–1995) published three lengthy articles on the origin, nature, and study of proverbs that have been edited together as *"When Evensong and Morrowsong Accord": Three Essays on the Proverb* (1994). This volume serves as a parallel comprehensive survey of the proverb from the 1930s. Together they published *A Dictionary of American Proverbs and Proverbial Phrases, 1820–1880* (1958), with Whiting adding two massive collections that complete the historical survey of proverbs found in the United States: *Early American Proverbs and Proverbial Phrases* (1977) and *Modern Proverbs and Proverbial Sayings* (1989). These volumes are models of paremiographical scholarship in that they register for each individual phrase contextualized historical references and provide cross-references to other collections.

This deep-rooted interest in proverbs by American scholars continued into the late twentieth and early twenty-first century, with Wolfgang Mieder, Stewart A. Kingsbury, and Kelsie B. Harder having edited *A Dictionary of American Proverbs* (1992), whose fifteen thousand texts were collected throughout the United States between 1945 and 1985. I had previously presented an interpretive volume, *American Proverbs: A Study of Texts and Contexts* (Mieder 1989a), and fifteen years later faced the challenge of writing a new comprehensive book on paremiology. Standing on the broad shoulders of Taylor, Whiting, and many other international paremiologists I published *Proverbs: A Handbook* (Mieder 2004), which stresses interdisciplinary and multiethnic approaches to proverbial language; such language is characterized by its polyfunctionality, polysituativity, and polysemanticity—proverbs can take on different strategic functions and shades of meaning depending on various contexts in which they may appear (Krikmann 2009, 15–50). The book deals with the scholarly accomplishments of anthropological, cultural, empirical, folkloric, historical, iconographic, linguistic, literary, pedagogical, religious, and sociological approaches to proverbs, and there is now also the superb *Introduction to Paremiology: A Comprehensive Guide to Proverb Studies* (2015) edited by Hrisztalina Hrisztova-Gotthardt and Melita Aleksa Varga. The international accomplishments of paremiography and paremiology are indeed impressive, as can also be seen from the hefty volumes of *Proverbium: Yearbook of International Proverb Scholarship* (since 1984).

Turning to proverbs in American culture, much more work is needed on establishing what the truly indigenous American proverbs are; the proverbs of various ethnic groups from Native Americans to the newest immigrants deserve attention, and the identification and interpretation of modern proverbs must be continued. New field research resulting in collections of proverbs that have hitherto not been registered from various folk groups is a necessity, and it is high time to expand our examination of the use and function of proverbs in modern literature, film, music, mass media, cartoons, and the memes that employ proverbs on the internet. The time of proverb making and the effective use of them in all modes of oral and written communication is not over, and the traditional as well as the innovative employment of proverbs, quite often in the form of anti-proverbs (intentionally changed proverbs with a new meaning), is alive and well in modern American society (Mieder 1993). The fascinating field of proverbs is still plenty untilled, giving scholars and students a challenging opportunity to study old and new proverbs in a multitude of contexts as formulaic expressions or "sound bites," to use a modern term, of their attitudes, beliefs, mores, and values that contain aspects of a complex American worldview (Mieder 1996; Mieder 2006). The interplay of tradition and innovation that is characteristic of folklore in general is also evident in the all-encompassing world of proverbs. The modern American proverb "Think outside the box" (earliest reference thus far from 1971) should be the guiding principle as paremiographers and paremiologists encourage folklore students to return to proverb studies with the vigor and passion that made the United States the paremiological hub from the 1930s through the 1980s.

One of the basic problems remaining despite the numerous collections and studies on various aspects of American proverbs is the vexing question of what makes an "American" proverb (Jente 1931–1932; Bryant 1945). Many of the most popular proverbs found in the United States are much older than colonial times. Such proverbs as "Big fish eat little fish" and "One swallow does not make a summer" go back to antiquity, the proverbs "Pride goes before a fall" (Proverbs 16:18) and "Man does not live by bread alone" (Deuteronomy 8:3; Matthew 4:4) come from the Bible, and such favorite proverbs as "Strike while the iron is hot" and "All that glitters is not gold" originated in the Latin of the Middle Ages. They were loan translated into European languages and belong to an international stock of proverbial wisdom (Paczolay 1997). Early English-speaking settlers brought them to North America together with favorite English proverbs like "The early bird catches the worm" and "A stitch in time saves nine," but they are most certainly not of American origin. This is also true for the proverbial phrase "To be in the same boat," which goes back to Cicero's Latin phrase "In eadem es navi," as well as the twin formula "Men and mice" and the wellerism "'Each to his own,' as the farmer said, when he kissed the cow" with their wide dissemination (Mieder and Kingsbury 1994). Collections of proverbial language should indeed be more careful in using the "American" designation. British-American would be a better term, but even that will not reflect the actual situation. Since such terms are not really avoidable for practical reasons, introductions to books on proverbs should explain that these linguocultural terms actually refer to proverbs known, used, and common in the United States.

This does not, of course, mean that there are no bona fide American proverbs. To start with, there are Native American proverbs, but despite scholarly efforts by anthropologists, folklorists, and linguists, few proverbs have been registered. In fact, it remains a conundrum why there is such a dearth of proverbs in the Native American languages, among them "A deer, although toothless, may accomplish something" (Tsimshian from British Columbia; one should not judge another person by outward appearances) and "If one talks loudly, the cave will answer" (Tzotzil from Chamula in southern Mexico; anybody who acts antisocially does not deserve to live in a house but rather in a cave). Regrettably, as far as is known, the few proverbs that have been found in Native American languages have not entered the English language. It appears that Native Americans communicate their generational wisdom by way of metaphors and narratives and not by formulaically expressed proverbs (Boas 1940, 232–39; Gossen 1973; Basso 1976, 93–121; Mieder 1989a, 99–110). There have been calls for a renewed effort trying to find Native American proverbs (Mieder 1989b), but not even Keith Basso's excellent book *Wisdom Sits in Places: Landscape and Language Among the Western Apache* (1996) deals with proverbial matters because of their rare occurrence.

Considering the complex composition of the United States as a country of immigrants and refugees of many linguocultural backgrounds, it is important to observe that all of these different folk groups brought their proverbial wisdom with them in their native languages, of which some have become current in the form of English loan translations. Enslaved Africans carried proverbs with them and created their own proverbs, a phenomenon that can be observed in the richly documented proverbial tradition among African Americans (Daniel 1973; Mieder 1989a, 111–28; Prahlad 1996; Prahlad 2006). Such significant modern proverbs as "Different strokes for different folks" (1945) and "What goes around comes around" (1961) have quickly entered mainstream American culture from their African American origin (Mieder 1989a, 317–32; McKenzie 1996). Expectedly, Spanish-language proverbs are current in the United States, with those of Mexican Americans having been studied more extensively than others (Arora 1982; Briggs 1985; Glazer 1987; Domínguez Barajas 2005). Proverbs have also been collected from Chinese, German, Irish, Italian, Jewish (Yiddish language), Polish, Russian, and other immigrant groups (Mieder 1989a, 47–70). And there is even a study on the proverbs of the Hmong refugees who fled Laos after the Vietnam War came to an end and settled primarily in California and Minnesota (Mitchell 1992). New tides of immigrants, notably from the Middle East, are arriving in this country, providing excellent opportunities for anthropologists, folklorists, and linguists to undertake modern field research about their proverbs. But this is only one side of the coin when considering the proverbs of immigrants. The other side is the question of whether any of their foreign-language proverbs become established in American culture as loan translations. For example, it has been shown that the German proverbs "Man muß das Kind nicht mit dem Bade ausschütten" and "Der Apfel fällt nicht weit vom Stamm" have become the common English-language proverbs "Don't throw the baby out with the bathwater" and "The apple doesn't fall far from the tree" (Fogel 1929; Mieder 1993, 193–224; Mieder 2000b, 109–44). But much more research is needed to determine how proverbs from other linguistic cultures have entered the rich and diverse treasure trove of proverbs current in the United States.

But this is a two-way street if one considers so-called American proverbs as national/regional, transnational, and global phenomena (Mieder 2005b, 1–14). They demand international analysis, because of all those proverbs that have been absorbed into the American idiom and culture from antiquity, the Bible, medieval Latin, Great Britain, and wave after wave of immigrants and refugees. "National/regional" refers to those generally known proverbs that are indigenous to the United States and that were coined in various regions of the country. Identifying anonymous proverbs or proverbial expressions by region or even individual state is, however, a difficult if not impossible undertaking. Popular collections of Texas or Vermont proverbs and phrases must be taken with a grain of salt (Mieder 1993, 173–92). Even if the expressions were collected by way of serious field research in a specific area, that does not mean that they were definitely coined there or that they are not in use elsewhere. It would be best to state in the introduction of such collections that these proverbs were found in a specific location with a special frequency (Hendrickson 2000). The third aspect, the global distribution of true American proverbs, is a matter that has received only little attention by paremiologists. When one considers that the English language is the lingua franca of the world, which plays an international role that centuries ago was partly handled by classical and medieval Latin, it should not come as a surprise that British and American proverbs in particular are spread to other languages and cultures of the world. A fine example is the British proverb "The early bird catches the worm" (1636), which for centuries has been considered the equivalent of the German proverb "Morgenstunde hat Gold im Munde" (1570; The morning hour has gold in its mouth). Both national proverbs have existed side by side for a long time, but since about 1980 the German translation "Der frühe Vogel fängt den Wurm" of the English proverb has gained steady currency in the German-speaking countries, and frequency studies have shown that especially young German speakers in the twenty-first century prefer the loan translation over the German proverb (Mieder 2015c). All of this has happened because of the incredible influence of British and American culture and language in Europe.

American proverbs are clearly conquering the world market as well, with the proverb "Good fences make good neighbors" (1834), popularized by way of Robert Frost's famous poem "Mending Wall" (1914), having been loan translated into German and other languages during the second half of the twentieth century. Many contextualized references in literary works and the mass media deal with fences as positive and aesthetic structures, housing feuds over fences, metaphorical fences, the law and fences, international politics and fences, and the need for fences in the modern sociopolitical world. All of this shows that the American proverb "Good fences make good neighbors" is by no means a simple piece of folk wisdom. The proverb certainly takes on an ambiguous role as it is applied to the political ramifications of building walls at the border between Mexico and the United States or between Israel and the Palestinian territories. As such, this American proverbial insight has become a global metaphor for the divisive sociopolitical world (Mieder 2005b, 210–43). The medical folk proverb "An apple a day keeps the doctor away" (1870) and some other modern American proverbs have also been adopted in other countries in their original English language or in translation; other examples include "One picture is worth a thousand words" (1911), "The glass is either half empty or half full" (1930), "Think globally, act locally" (1942), and "It takes two to tango" (1952) (Mieder 1993, 135–51; Mieder 1994, 515–42; Mieder 2010b, 297–340). The fact that such proverbs are globally distributed and accepted as general truths shows that the observations and experiences found in American culture are transposable to other peoples of the world (Mieder 2011b). Stated slightly differently, these proverbs reveal that the formerly heterogeneous worldviews of different nationalities or ethnicities are becoming more homogeneous in a globalized environment.

While the number of American proverbs gaining international currency is slowly but steadily increasing, there is, of course, a plethora of indigenous American proverbs that were coined in the English language. It is just that little attention has been paid to differentiating among English-language proverbs, with collections simply referring to English, American, or at least Anglo-American proverbs, which still excludes proverbs in English from Australia, Canada, New Zealand, India, and other countries where English is spoken. In any case, collections of "American" proverbs have not made any distinctions as far as actual origin is concerned, but there now is a first attempt at identifying true American proverbs based on historical research, to wit my annotated collection—albeit written for a German readership—*"Different Strokes for Different Folks": 1250 authentisch amerikanische Sprichwörter* (2015a). The number of 1,250 authentic American proverbs could easily be increased by a few thousand texts if researched on historical principles, but this is a fair beginning. Here is a small chronologically arranged sampler of particularly popular truly American proverbs:

> It is harder to use victory than to get it. (1633, the earliest proverb in the collection)
> Time and chance happen to all men. (1677)

A friend nearby is better than a brother far off. (1682)
Money is power. (1741)
Facts don't lie. (1748)
Lost time is never found again. (1748)
Three removes is as bad as a fire. (1758, Benjamin Franklin)
All men are created equal. (1776, Thomas Jefferson)
Paddle your own canoe. (1802)
Don't kick a fellow when he is down. (1809)
Competition is the life of trade. (1816)
Safety first. (1818)
Good fences make good neighbors. (1834)
Talk is cheap. (1843)
All men and women are created equal. (1848, Elizabeth Cady Stanton)
Hitch your wagon to a star. (1862, Ralph Waldo Emerson)
Nothing succeeds like success. (1867)
It pays to advertise. (1868)
Equal pay for equal work. (1869, Susan B. Anthony)
Crime does not pay. (1874)
If you can't beat them, join them. (1882)
You can't have everything. (1893)
Speak softly and carry a big stick. (1900, President Theodore Roosevelt)
You get out of life what you put into it. (1901)
Three strikes and you're out. (1901)
The customer is always right. (1905)
Another day, another dollar. (1907)
When it rains, it pours. (1914, Morton Salt advertisement slogan)
You can't win them all. (1918)
It's not over till it's over. (1921, baseball player Yogi Berra)
The blacker the berry, the sweeter the juice. (1929)
You can't fight city hall. (1933)
Shit happens. (1944)
No guts, no glory. (1945)
You can run but you can't hide. (1946, boxer Joe Louis)
Freedom is not for sale. (1949)
If it looks like a duck, walks like a duck, and quacks like a duck, it's a
    duck. (1948)
Life is not a spectator sport. (1958)
Go with the flow. (1962)
If you've got it, flaunt it. (1968)
When you are up to your ass in alligators, it's hard to remember you're
    there to drain the swamp. (1971)

No glove, no love. (1982, from the film *The World According to Garp*)
My house, my rules. (1983)
Life is a box of chocolates. (1994, from the film *Forrest Gump*; Winick 2013)

Taken as a whole, these proverbs occupy themselves with business, sports, time, life, success, independence, freedom, and a few additional general themes. Do they then represent the American worldview (White 1987; Nussbaum 2005)? Proverbs have been studied to draw conclusions about certain national character traits and to establish the worldview (shared mentality) of certain folk groups. Alan Dundes has dealt extensively in extrapolating worldview from folkloric texts (including proverbs), but always with the caveat that these are generalizations at best with some kernel of truth nevertheless (Dundes 1969; Dundes 1972a; Dundes 1972b; Dundes 2004; see also Bronner 1982). A much larger sample of proverbs would be needed, and it behooves scholars to keep in mind whether the proverbs are in fact still current today. I tried to deal with this problem in my essay on "Yankee Wisdom: American Proverbs and the Worldview of New England" (Mieder 2007), showing that such generalizations must be taken with a proverbial grain of salt. In other words, one could take all American proverbs current in the eighteenth century and then see whether a certain worldview can be ascertained from those proverbs found in actual written contexts.

A fine example for this is Benjamin Franklin (1706–1790), the ultimate proverbialist of American culture. He incorporated about forty proverbs into each of his *Poor Richard's Almanack*s, which appeared in twenty-five issues between 1733 and 1758. To top this, he published his famous essay "The Way to Wealth" (1758) in the last issue, which comprises 105 English proverbs taken from the almanacs with some of them coined by Franklin himself, to wit: "By diligence and patience the mouse bit in two the cable (1735), "Some are weatherwise, some are otherwise" (1735), "Industry need not wish" (1739), "There will be sleeping enough in the grave" (1741), "Experience keeps a dear school, but fools learn in no other" (1743), "Drive thy business, or it will drive thee" (1744), "If passion drives, let reason hold the reins" (1749), "Laziness travels so slowly, that poverty soon overtakes it" (1756), "Sloth makes all things difficult, but industry all easy" (1758), and "Three removes is as bad as a fire" (Gallacher 1949; Newcomb 1957; Barbour 1974; Mieder 2004, 216–24). Some of these creations have not survived, but it is fair to say that the almanacs and especially "The Way to Wealth" were instrumental in establishing the so-called Puritan ethics that have been part of the general American worldview of a capitalistic society based on diligent work and steady progress ever since. Franklin's obsession with proverbs as sapiential laws for a proper life (Templeton 1997) went so far that "his" proverbs entered American material culture in the form of cups and saucers inscribed with "Poor Richard's" proverbs accompanied by appropriate educational illustrations (Riley 1991). The influence of Franklin on the social life of this country by way of the good advice of proverbs is still to be felt, but the often repeated claim that he originated the quintessential "American" proverb "Time is money" has been proven wrong. He did cite it in his important essay "Advice to a Young Tradesman" (1748) as a solid piece of wisdom: "Remember that Time is Money." In his *Poor Richard's Almanack* for 1751 he included the proverb again in a short article: "In vain did she [a wife] inculcate him [her husband] *That Time is Money.*" But alas, it has now been shown that this short prose piece appeared first on May 18, 1719, in the London-based newspaper *Free Thinker*. It was republished in 1723 and 1739 in essayistic compilations, and Franklin must have come across the earlier reprint when he lived and worked as a typesetter during 1725 in London. When he republished the essay almost completely verbatim in America some twenty-five years later, he failed to disclose his source, an omission that by contemporary standards would be considered plagiarism (Villers and Mieder 2017). The rest is history, as the saying goes. Franklin's name became attached to the proverb, and he has universally been considered as its originator for more than two centuries. It is, however, originally a British proverb with Franklin deserving the credit for having popularized it in the United States, where it became the underpinning of the American capitalistic work ethic (Manders 2006, 148–54). Franklin played the same role of popularizer with the fifteenth-century English proverb "Early to bed and early to rise, makes a man healthy, wealthy, and wise," which in the mind of most Americans is considered to be his own creation (Mieder 1993, 98–134).

It should also be mentioned that Franklin found an unlikely proponent of his high esteem of proverbs as ethical guideposts for a good and prosperous American life in the transcendentalist Ralph Waldo Emerson (1803–1882). Emerson appears to have bought into the idea of Puritan ethics hook, line, and sinker, and in so doing, he became one of America's early paremiologists, with valuable things to say about the significance of proverbs for a solid American life. He assembled small proverb collections in his journals and employed plenty of them in his letters, lectures, sermons, and essays (Mieder 2014b, 261–83). On February 16, 1822, at the young age of nineteen, he wrote the following remarks into a notebook entitled "Wide World," since it includes old ideas and new thoughts on an all-encompassing and global scope:

> [T]he proverbs and familiar sayings of all nations [. . .] are the first generalizations of the mind and have been repeated by the mouth of the million. As the peculiar language of experience, altogether independent

of other purposes than as tried guides of life, proverbs demand notice. It was early found that there were a few principles which controlled society; that the mother of all arts, the nurse of social feelings, the impeller of individual energies—was Necessity [an allusion to the proverb "Necessity is the mother of invention"]. These truths, ascertained by the progress of society, and corroborated by the observation of each succeeding generation, were incorporated into these short maxims as rules for youth which maturity would establish. (Gilman and Orth 1960–1982, 1:87)

Emerson was certainly aware that proverbs are generalizations, that they are repeated by the folk, and that they usually serve as moral rules of life. What he could not have known is that proverb scholars have now advanced an empirical and statistical approach to proverbs to ascertain what proverbs are in fact in use today and with what frequency. Thus, so-called paremiological minima of about three hundred texts have been established by way of questionnaires and now also the internet to ascertain the most commonly employed proverbs (Mieder 1992; Lau 1996). The most extensive investigation was undertaken by Heather A. Haas and published in her seminal article "Proverb Familiarity in the United States: Cross-Regional Comparisons of the Paremiological Minimum" (2008) in the prestigious *Journal of American Folklore*. As expected, it includes a list of the 313 most familiar proverbs in the United States, with the first two dozen in order of decreasing familiarity being the following texts:

Practice makes perfect.
There's no place like home.
Easier said than done.
Like father, like son.
Actions speak louder than words. (1736)
Don't judge a book by its cover. (1897)
Better safe than sorry. (1882)
Finders keepers, losers weepers.
Better late than never.
Mind your own business.
An apple a day keeps the doctor away. (1870)
Two wrongs do not make a right. (1814)
Where there's a will, there's a way.
Opposites attract.
The more the merrier.
The grass is always greener on the other side of the fence. (1913)
If at first you don't succeed, try, try, again. (1838)

First come, first served.
A penny saved is a penny earned.
Boys will be boys. (1832)
Beauty is in the eye of the beholder.
Beggars can't be choosers.
April showers bring May flowers.
The early bird catches the worm. (Haas 2008, 337–38)

Most of the proverbs are of British origin, but "First come, first served" actually had its origin in the longer medieval Latin "Qui ad molendinum prior venit, prius molit" (Who first came to the mill, grinds first) and its numerous variants. The mill connection still survives in many of the European languages, and Geoffrey Chaucer has "Whoso that first to mille comth, first grynt" in *The Wife of Bath's Prologue* (c. 1386). While the proverb survived for another three centuries, it had to compete with the shortened version "First come, first served" since the latter's first appearance in Henry Porter's *Two Angry Women of Abington* (1599). Not surprisingly, English speakers today have generally no idea that the short proverb goes back to a legal concept of the Middle Ages (Mieder 2004, 43–52). Be that as it may, it is of interest to note that eight (with dates provided) of the twenty-four proverbs are of definite American origin, with the proverb "The grass is always greener on the other side of the fence" (1913) being an example of a modern proverb if one considers the year 1900 as the beginning of what can be considered the proverbial wisdom of modernity.

This is the paremiographical modus operandi followed by Charles Clay Doyle, Wolfgang Mieder, and Fred R. Shapiro in their unique *Dictionary of Modern Proverbs* (2012), which registers more than 1,400 English-language proverbs with detailed historical contextualized references and bibliographical information. Considering the dominating role that the United States plays as a world power by way of modern communicative ways of the mass media and the internet, it should not be surprising that American cultural values are disseminated globally by way of English as a lingua franca throughout the world. To be sure, the collection contains proverbs of British, Canadian, and Australian origin, but the majority of them clearly have their start in the United States. But it might come as a surprise that such American proverbs as "The camera does not lie" (1889), "You are what you eat" (1887), "An elephant never forgets" (1886), "Behind every great man there is a great woman" (1886), "Money isn't everything" (1870), "You can prove anything with statistics" (1852), "The best things in life are free" (1881), and even the extremely popular "Use it or lose it" (1838) are all from the nineteenth century. This shows that diachronic research is absolutely necessary before making cultural generalizations by way of proverbs (Doyle 1996). The problem with many proverb studies, especially those that wish to draw conclusions about values, mentality, and worldview, is that they often look at proverbs merely as texts without contexts and ignore any consideration of cultural, folkloric, and linguistic developments. This is evident in the many studies concerning the misogynous nature of many proverbs throughout the world, to wit on the global level Mineke Schipper's massive *Never Marry a Woman with Big Feet: Women in Proverbs from Around the World* (2003) and specifically for the United States Lois Kerschen's *American Proverbs About Women: A Reference Guide* (1998). Both books are of great importance to demonstrate the stereotypical view of women in so many proverbs, but fortunately many of these misogynous proverbs, at least in Anglo-American culture, are no longer in frequent use today. Regarding Kerschen's book in particular, it must be said again that the reference to "American Proverbs" in the title is misleading, since she really is dealing with proverbs in the English language for the most part, of which a considerable amount happen to be known and in use in the United States. In any case, looking at proverbs primarily synchronically without historical considerations and citing such texts without any context is problematic. But it is good and it continues to be necessary to combat proverbial stereotypes against women and others.

It is shameful that the American proverbs "The only good Indian is a dead Indian" against Native Americans and "No tickee, no washee" against Chinese Americans became current in the second half of the nineteenth century, and it is even more upsetting to come across them occasionally in oral and written communication still today (Mieder 1997, 138–59, 160–89). Such stereotypical matters can be quite complex indeed, as I have shown in the monograph *"Call a Spade a Spade": From Classical Phrase to Racial Slur* (2002). The book traces the origin, history, dissemination, and meaning of the well-known proverbial expression "to call a spade a spade" from Aristophanes in classical antiquity via Erasmus of Rotterdam to loan translations into various European languages. It is actually an innocuous phrase stating by way of the "spade" metaphor that one should call or name things the way they are. However, in the United States the spade became associated with the black color of the spade card suit. Add to this that in American slang "spade" took on a negative connotation for African Americans, and a proverbial slur was born. The phrase is still employed in contexts that could not possibly be interpreted as a racial slur, but since it is taken that way by many Americans, it is best not to use it any longer. Nevertheless, this is a linguocultural development specific to the United States, and the phrase is used without its racial implications in other English-speaking countries.

But to return to our modern proverbial muttons (Mieder 2014b, 80–130), it can be stated that most modern American proverbs are straightforward, indicative sentences with little formulaic or poetic characteristics, such as "They don't make things like they used to" (1959). A considerable number of proverbs follow the pattern "You can't (cannot) [verb] ...," thereby continuing an established proverbial way of expressing the impossibility of a situation or action: "You can't put toothpaste back in the tube." There are also those proverbs that state their messages by way of the "Don't (Do not) / [verb] ..." or "Never ..." imperatives, which certainly are well-established proverbial formulas: "Don't get caught with your pants down" (1944) and "Never give anything away that you can sell" (1953). But such proverbial imperatives are rather rare, indicating that people today are less willing to be told directly what to do or not to do. In other words, the obvious didactic nature of many traditional proverbs appears to be on the decline.

The most prevalent structures of these new American proverbs actually follow well-established patterns, clearly helping in committing them to memory:

"If you can X, you can Y"
> If you can dream it, you can do it. (1970)

"Better X than Y"
> Better a big fish in a little pond than a little fish in a big pond. (1903)

"No X, no Y"
> No guts, no glory. (1945)

"X is (are) X" (tautologies)
> A deadline is a deadline. (1933)

"There is no such thing as X"
> There is no such thing as a free lunch. (1917)

"There are no X, only (just) Y"
> There are no bad dogs, only bad owners. (1949)

"One man's X is another man's Y"
> One man's trash is another man's treasure. (1924)

As English-language proverbs in general, modern American proverbs also have an average length of seven words. As one would expect, a minimum of two words (a topic and a comment) are required for a bona fide proverb (Dundes 1975). While they are relatively rare, they range from "Manners matter" (1909) to the slang proverb "Life sucks" (1979) all the way to scatological images as in "Shit happens" (1944). Proverbs consisting of four monosyllabic words are quite popular as short pieces of rather directly expressed insights that often lack any metaphorical element: "Go with the flow" (1962). However, many of them follow a parallel structure with or without rhyme: "Make love, not war" (1965) and "Last hired, first fired" (1918). Regarding rhyme, it should, however, be noted that this proverbial marker does not play a major role in modern proverbs, among them "Move your feet, lose your seat" (1987) and "Different ways for different days" (1971). Of course, there are also proverbs of much greater length, reaching up to more than twenty words, for example "It is not the size of the dog in the fight that matters; it's the size of the fight in the dog" (1911).

As has been the case for centuries, the originators of modern proverbs are also generally not known. However, as has also been the case with earlier proverbs, some modern proverbs have simply been attributed to certain well-known persons. Research has shown that such attributions can usually not be proven, even though people will cling to these claims when citing such proverbs. For example, "A woman without a man is like a fish without a bicycle" (1976) has been attributed to the American feminist Gloria Steinem even though she has denied it publicly. In fact, it might not be an American proverb after all, since the Australian political journalist Irina Dunn claims to have coined it in 1970 (Mieder 2015a, 247). But there are modern proverbs for which it is known precisely who originated them when and where. Such original citations by known persons begin as statements in books, articles, speeches, motion pictures, songs, and the like. As they are repeated, they become quotations, and with ever more frequent use, often without awareness of the originator, these memorable texts can become proverbs. A perfect example is "Ask not what your country can do for you, ask what you can do for your country," which began with President John F. Kennedy's inaugural address of January 20, 1960. Another popular proverb comes from Erich Segal's novel *Love Story* (1970): "Love means never having to say you're sorry" (or, as John Lennon tweaked this easily lampooned sentiment, "Love means having to say you're sorry every fifteen minutes"). It has also long been established that advertising slogans have given rise to new proverbs, for example "When you're number two, you try harder" (1962), which started as an advertising campaign for Avis Car Rental.

With music playing such a large role in the modern entertainment scene, it should not be surprising that songs have given rise to ample modern proverbs. It should be noted, however, that this is nothing new as far as the creation of proverbs is concerned. Religious hymns, anonymous folksongs, operettas, and musicals have long given rise to proverbs, and this is also true for country songs, blues, reggae, and rap music. An example would be "It takes two to tango" (1952), which is the title and refrain of a song by Al Hoffman and Dick Manning made famous by the African American singer Pearl Bailey. Movies are not surprisingly also a fruitful ground for spreading laconic insights to large segments of the population, who in turn help to distribute them by frequent

THE WISDOM AND NATURE OF AMERICAN PROVERBS 33

repetition as new proverbs of the folk, to wit "If you've got it, flaunt it" from the motion picture *The Producers* (1967).

Turning now to the realia of modern American proverbs, it is perhaps unexpected that various animals continue to appear with considerable frequency. The modern age still relates well to animals, especially such domesticated animals as cats, cows, dogs, horses, and pigs. But wild animals such as birds, elephants, fish, frogs, monkeys, and others are also employed to express human behavior and attitudes via animal metaphors, for example the proverbial interrogative "A bird may love a fish, but where would they live?" from Joseph Stein's play *Fiddler on the Roof* (1964), and the by now internationally disseminated "You have to kiss a lot of frogs to find a prince" (1976), which did not originate from the fairy tale "The Frog Prince" (Mieder 2014e). Just as animal metaphors have not disappeared from modern proverbs, the same is also true for proverbial somatisms with such nouns as eye, foot, hand, head, heart, mouth, and nose, for example "Busy hands are happy hands" (1956) and "You can't measure heart" (1967).

America's preoccupation with business, finance, and specifically money has left its mark on modern proverbs as well. They all reflect the pecuniary aspects of modern American life, stressing the importance of business, the power of money, the rights and expectations of customers, the hope for prosperity, and so on: "The business of America is business" (1925, coined by President Calvin Coolidge), "Put your money where your mouth is" (1913), and "If you have to ask the price, you can't afford it" (1926). But speaking of modern preoccupations, it certainly comes as no surprise that quite a few modern American proverbs relate to the ever-present and fascinating world of sports: "You can't steal first base" (1915), "It isn't whether you win or lose that counts; it's how you play the game" (1913), and "You can't score if you don't shoot" (1965). It is, however, strange that only a very few proverbs have been registered that exhibit at least some relationship to technology by way of certain words. It is here where proverb scholars might want to look for new proverbs in the future. Of course, there are some modern proverbs like "Garbage in, garbage out" from 1957 that come from the world of computers, but they do not show by the choice of words any immediate relationship to technology: "Speed kills" (1939), "You cannot tell which way the train went by looking at the tracks" (1977), and "Nobody washes a rental car" (1985). In any case, the newest proverb from technology is "There's an app for everything," with its first recorded reference in the British newspaper *The Guardian* on August 10, 2009. But proverbial news travels fast and wide, and the first American reference found thus far is in the *St. Louis Post-Dispatch* from October 17, 2009 (Doyle and Mieder 2016, 86–87). The proverb is therefore likely of British origin, but with ever more computer databases an earlier American source might just be found. With more and more search possibilities, it is possible to trace the origin of many proverbs further back than has hitherto been established.

As expected, there are some keywords of particular frequency in these relatively new proverbs. The most popular word is "life," indicating that modern humankind has much wisdom about existence. Many of them follow the definitional pattern "Life is X." While some refer in but a few words to life as being problematic, as in "Life is a bitch" (1940) and "Life sucks" (1979), others look at life more positively, as in "If life hands you lemons, make lemonade" (1910) and "Life begins at forty" (1932, a book title by Walter Pitkin). Proverbs about friends, time, age, love, beauty, pain, and success are nothing new as far as Anglo-American proverbs and those of other languages and cultures are concerned, but it should be noticed that most of the American proverbs are rather literal statements of basic truths of modern life without couching them in expressive metaphors:

> You cannot use your friends and have them too. (1954)
> Time flies when you're having fun. (1939)
> Old age is better than the alternative. (1960)
> Love is where you find it. (1938)
> Beauty does not buy happiness. (1989)
> Pain is nature's way of telling you to slow down. (1920)
> Success is never final. (1920)

Quite a few additional proverbs with these dominant keywords could be added to this list, and perhaps they show at least in a generalized way some of the preoccupations or even worldview of modern American society. People are preoccupied or obsessed with time, age, love, and success, and these concerns find their expression in proverbial wisdom.

With this said, yet one more group of proverbs from the realms of sexuality, obscenity, and scatology needs to be mentioned. Looking at earlier proverb collections, one might well get the impression that the folk has no so-called dirty proverbs. Even though paremiographers usually have included at least some such proverbs in their collections, they have in general been reluctant to collect them, or their publishers did not consent to publish them. But they do exist and can be found in such journals as *Anthropophyteia* (1904–1913) and *Maledicta* (1977–2004), which specialized in folklore from the underground. The word "shit," less taboo in fine society than in former times, is quite prevalent in modern proverbs, for example "Don't shit where you eat" (1953) and "If you stir shit, it will stink" (1982). Other proverbs dealing with urination, flatulence, and feces are clear indications that people at least at times rely on this more or less crassly expressed wisdom as a summary of some of the unpleasant aspects of human interaction: "The one who smelt it dealt it" (1971), "It's better to be pissed off than pissed on" (1974), and "You can't polish a turd" (1976).

It is also a well-known fact that males as well as females have had their questions about the matter of penis size, and this concern has found its way into modern proverbs as well. As sex surveys have shown, the feeling about the importance of penis size for sexual satisfaction differs considerably, and this is mirrored in the conflicting proverbs about this topic as well: "Size doesn't matter (it's what you do with it, it's how you use it)" (1903) and "It's not the size of the boat but the motion of the ocean (that matters)" (1968). Little wonder that modern American proverbs also include cautionary texts that warn against sex at an early age, advocate safe sex, and also declare that people have the right to refuse a sexual encounter: "Keep your dress down and your panties up" (1975), "No glove, no love" (1982), and "*No* means 'no'" (1980). And there is also proverbial wisdom on sex in general, expressing once again conflicting attitudes: "Everybody lies about sex" (1973) and "There is no such thing as bad sex (a bad fuck, a bad piece)" (1971). As the extremely short proverb "Sex sells" (1926) states, sexuality has become a commodity in the modern world obsessed with this topic.

But "Man does not live by sex alone," to cite a so-called anti-proverb based on the biblical claim that "Man does not live by bread alone." The humorous, ironic, or satirical alteration of proverbs has a long tradition, indicating that the folk is perfectly capable of liberating itself from the at times too didactic or moralistic proverbs. Such anti-proverbs as "Absence makes the heart grow wander," "Beauty is only skin deep," or "No body is perfect" abound, and there are also plenty of modern wellerisms that play with traditional proverbs: "'Business before pleasure,' as the man said when he kissed his wife before calling on his sweetheart" (Litovkina and Mieder 2006; Mieder 2008b, 87–119). This kind of manipulation of proverbs is also popular in journalistic headlines, advertisements are frequently based on the innovative reworking of traditional proverbs, and proverbs play a definite role in cartoons and comic strips (Mieder 2005a; Winick 2011; Winick 2014). But as is the case with today's folklore studies in general, proverb scholars are also turning to the internet to see what role proverbs play in electronic communication. Proverbs and proverbial expressions as metaphors are usually too long for tweets, but they find considerable use as verbalizations of memes, where they might be cited in their original wording or in striking variations (Szpila 2017; Tosina Fernández 2017). This is but the beginning of a most fascinating new stomping ground for proverbs, showing once and for all that they are not outdated or archaic but perfectly capable of adapting to ever more advanced communicative methods. The fact that traditional proverbs are often varied serves as more proof that they continue to be current in modern society. After all, it is the juxtaposition of the original proverb with the innovative rewording that is part of the communicative effect. Of course, the search for new proverbs should also definitely include the internet, which helps to spread such new creations in ever greater speed all over the world.

Proverbs in their ubiquity can also be found in the health science community. So-called self-help books are replete with proverbial wisdom, where they appear in the traditional role of solid advice for achieving the American dream of a successful life (Arthurs 1994; Eret 2001; Dolby 2005). Unfortunately, such dreams can be destroyed by various addictions and the serious health issue of mental disease ranging from schizophrenia to dementia. Proverbs have been employed to study these issues in various types of proverb tests. Scholars have discovered that proverbs are useful tools in studying the brain processes involved in understanding metaphorical proverbs. As the combined fields of psychology, linguistics, and neuroscience are making astounding progress in the area of cognition and comprehension, proverbs have become important scientific indicators (Van Lancker 1990; Gibbs and Beitel 1995; Honeck 1997). This is without doubt cutting-edge psycholinguistic research in which proverbs play an important role in determining the causes of mental illnesses and hopefully also finding cures for them. It needs to be said, however, that when folklorists or paremiologists read the extensive literature available on the neurology of proverbs, they do at times wish that these scientists would occupy themselves a bit more with their proverbial scholarship.

Proverbs, being a verbal device, obviously are to be found in literally all types of oral and written communication. There is a long tradition of looking at proverbs in literary works, but such studies have concentrated on such older English authors as Chaucer, Shakespeare, Dickens, and others (Mieder and Bryan 1996). However, scholars have investigated American authors such as Emily Dickinson, Ralph Waldo Emerson, Eugene O'Neill, Carl Sandburg, and more recently Zora Neale Hurston and have shown that novels, dramas, and poems include proverbial materials that add to their cultural, folkloric, linguistic, and stylistic value (Barnes 1979; Bryan and Mieder 1995; Bryan and Mieder 2003; Williams 1997; Mieder 2014b, 261–83). While these literary works contain primarily traditional English proverbs, they also register indigenous American proverbs and proverbial phrases, with Sandburg's epic poem *The People, Yes* (1936) being a goldmine for American proverbial language. But there are many additional authors, notably also those of popular fiction, who ought to be studied. Both Archer Taylor and Bartlett Jere Whiting pioneered excerpting proverbial language from literary works, an effort that resulted in superb historical proverb collections. There is no reason why such dictionaries should not be published any longer, and one contemporary example is George B. Bryan and Wolfgang Mieder's *A Dictionary of Anglo-American*

Proverbs and Proverbial Phrases Found in Literary Sources of the Nineteenth and Twentieth Centuries (2005). Furthermore, in order to obtain a complete picture of any particular author's proverbiality, it is necessary to read his or her complete works.

The same is true for the considerable interest in the proverbial rhetoric of major political figures. Paremiologists have investigated the complete works of Presidents Abraham Lincoln, Harry S. Truman, and Barack Obama (Mieder 2000a; Mieder 2009b; Mieder and Bryan 1997) as well as the works of great American civil rights champions and social reformers such as Frederick Douglass, Elizabeth Cady Stanton, Susan B. Anthony, and Martin Luther King Jr. (Mieder 2001; Mieder 2010a; Mieder 2014a). The relationship of proverbs and politics is a wide-open field, and it behooves folklorists to pay more attention to political rhetoric, as Cameron Louis has shown in his fascinating article "Proverbs and the Politics of Language" (2000; see also Raymond 1956). American presidents are well aware of the effectiveness of proverbs and quotations, as can be seen from their inclusions in their inaugural addresses (Mieder 2005b, 147–86). General George Marshall used them as he executed the Marshall Plan after the Second World War to put European countries back on their feet (Mieder 2017), and Hillary Clinton made plenty of use of proverbs in her struggle to become the first female president of the United States (Mieder 2015d). Just like literary authors, politicians are well aware of the fact that folk proverbs with their colorful metaphors can serve them well to bring their message across. There can be no doubt that proverbs are part and parcel of modern proverbial rhetoric, thus maintaining a tradition that goes back to Greek and Roman antiquity. In American proverbial rhetoric, the proverb "All men are created equal," and the proverbial triads "Life, liberty, and the pursuit of happiness" and "Government of the people, by the people, and for the people," are democratic leitmotifs (Mieder 2005b, 15–55; Aron 2008, 91–96), along with the biblical golden rule "Do unto others as you would have them do unto you" (Matthew 7:12), which is known in other religions as well, adding a humanistic touch (Griffin 1991, 67–69). The sociopolitical importance of proverbs cannot be overstated, as can be seen by way of Abraham Lincoln's use of the Bible proverb "A house divided cannot stand" (Mark 3:25) to attempt to avoid the Civil War (Mieder 1998; Mieder 2005b, 90–117) and his use of the fourteenth-century proverb "Right makes might" with its unfortunate antipode "Might makes right" going back to the same time (Mieder 2008a; Mieder 2014d). Abraham Lincoln did not originate these two proverbs, but they are ingrained in the American worldview as a reminder that people must work together and that right must prevail.

Several decades ago, the American folklorist Richard Jente (1888–1952) published a short article entitled "The Untilled Field of Proverbs" (1945) that listed various research desiderata for paremiologists with an emphasis on American proverbial matters. Much has been accomplished since this call to action, but there is much more work to be done that can build on previous accomplishments (Mieder 2014c). Here are but a few suggestions specifically regarding bona fide American proverbs: (1) compiling an annotated historical collection of indigenous American proverbs, (2) further collecting and studying modern proverbs, (3) identifying proverbs in popular culture and the mass media (advertisements, cartoons, songs, films, graffiti, etc.), (4) looking for more proverbs of Native Americans, (5) collecting proverbs from various ethnic and immigrant groups, (6) identifying foreign-language proverbs that have been translated into American English, (7) finding proverbs dealing with modern technology, (8) registering proverbs from various professions, (9) investigating the origin, history, dissemination, and meaning of individual proverbs, (10) identifying proverbs in modern literature, (11) identifying proverbs in sociopolitical rhetoric, (12) identifying proverbs in neuroscience, (13) identifying proverbs in teaching English as a second language, (14) identifying proverbs in child rearing, (15) identifying proverbs in oral communication (field research), and (16) including proverbs in folklore courses (Mieder 2015b; Domínguez Barajas 2017). This last point is of importance since students need to be introduced to the fascinating and challenging world of proverbs if paremiology and paremiography want to make further advances.

Be that as it may, one thing is for certain: English-language proverbs and specifically American proverbs are alive and well in the modern age, which is surely creating its own new proverbs. As folk wisdom, they express the attitudes, beliefs, mores, and values of the people who use them. Not only do they play an important communicative role in the United States, but with English being the lingua franca of the world, they are also a global phenomenon. As verbal "monumenta humana," they warrant the attention of cultural historians, folklorists, and other scholars interested in the social sciences and the humanities. Proverbs are indeed very much in season in America today, and the proverbial statement that "A proverb is worth a thousand words" will doubtlessly remain true for generations to come.

BIBLIOGRAPHY

This chapter was first published with the title "American Proverbs and Related Sayings" in *The Oxford Handbook of American Folklore and Folklife Studies*, edited by Simon J. Bronner (New York: Oxford University Press), 146–68.

Albig, William. 1931. "Proverbs and Social Control." *Sociology and Social Research* 15: 527–35.

Aron, Paul. 2008. *We Hold These Truths . . . and Other Words That Made America*. Lanham, MD: Rowman and Littlefield.

Arora, Shirley L. 1982. "Proverbs in Mexican American Tradition." *Aztlán* 13, nos. 1–2 (Spring–Fall): 43–69.

Arthurs, Jeffrey D. 1994. "Proverbs in Inspirational Literature: Sanctioning the American Dream." *Journal of Communication and Religion* 17, no. 2: 1–15. Also in *Cognition, Comprehension, and Communication: A Decade of North American Proverb Studies (1990–2000)*, edited by Wolfgang Mieder, 37–52. Baltmannsweiler, Germany: Schneider Verlag Hohengehren, 2003.

Barbour, Frances M. 1974. *A Concordance to the Sayings in Franklin's "Poor Richard."* Detroit: Gale Research Company.

Barnes, Daniel R. 1979. "Telling It Slant: Emily Dickinson and the Proverb." *Genre* 12: 219–41. Also in *Wise Words: Essays on the Proverb*, edited by Wolfgang Mieder, 439–65. New York: Garland Publishing, 1994.

Basso, Keith H. 1976. "'Wise Words' of the Western Apache: Metaphor and Semantic Theory." In *Meaning in Anthropology*, edited by Keith H. Basso and Henry A. Selby, 93–121. Albuquerque: University of New Mexico Press.

Basso, Keith H. 1996. *Wisdom Sits in Places: Landscape and Language Among the Western Apache*. Albuquerque: University of New Mexico Press.

Boas, Franz. 1940. *Race, Language and Culture*. New York: Macmillan.

Briggs, Charles L. 1985. "The Pragmatics of Proverb Performances in New Mexican Spanish." *American Anthropologist* 87, no. 4 (December): 793–810. Also in *Wise Words: Essays on the Proverb*, edited by Wolfgang Mieder, 317–49. New York: Garland Publishing, 1994.

Bronner, Simon J. 1982. "The Haptic Experience of Culture." *Anthropos* 77, nos. 3–4: 351–62.

Bronner, Simon J., ed. 1992. *Creativity and Tradition in Folklore: New Directions*. Logan: Utah State University Press.

Bryan, George B., and Wolfgang Mieder. 1995. *The Proverbial Eugene O'Neill: An Index to Proverbs in the Works of Eugene Gladstone O'Neill*. Westport, CT: Greenwood Press.

Bryan, George B., and Wolfgang Mieder. 2003. "The Proverbial Carl Sandburg (1878–1967): An Index of Folk Speech in His American Poetry." *Proverbium* 20: 15–49.

Bryan, George B., and Wolfgang Mieder. 2005. *A Dictionary of Anglo-American Proverbs and Proverbial Phrases Found in Literary Sources of the Nineteenth and Twentieth Centuries*. New York: Peter Lang.

Bryant, Margaret M. 1945. *Proverbs and How to Collect Them*. Greensboro, NC: American Dialect Society.

Daniel, Jack L. 1973. "Towards an Ethnography of Afroamerican Proverbial Usage." *Black Lines* 2: 3–12.

Dolby, Sandra K. 2005. "Proverbs, Quotes, and Insights." In *Self-Help Books: Why Americans Keep Reading Them*, 135–46. Urbana: University of Illinois Press.

Domínguez Barajas, Elías. 2005. "Sociocognitive Aspects of Proverb Use in a Mexican Transnational Social Network." In *Latino Language and Literacy in Ethnolinguistic Chicago*, edited by Marcia Farr, 67–95. Mahwah, NJ: Lawrence Erlbaum Associates.

Domínguez Barajas, Elías. 2017. "Proverbs in the Academy: A Folklore Studies Activity for the Writing Classroom." *Journal of American Folklore* 130, no. 517 (Summer): 335–52.

Doyle, Charles Clay. 1996. "On 'New' Proverbs and the Conservativeness of Proverb Dictionaries." *Proverbium* 13: 69–84. Also in *Cognition, Comprehension, and Communication: A Decade of North American Proverb Studies (1990–2000)*, edited by Wolfgang Mieder, 85–98. Baltmannsweiler, Germany: Schneider Verlag Hohengehren, 2003.

Doyle, Charles Clay, and Wolfgang Mieder. 2016. "*The Dictionary of Modern Proverbs*: A Supplement." *Proverbium* 33: 85–120.

Doyle, Charles Clay, Wolfgang Mieder, and Fred R. Shapiro, eds. 2012. *The Dictionary of Modern Proverbs*. New Haven, CT: Yale University Press.

Dundes, Alan. 1969. "Thinking Ahead: A Folkloristic Reflection of the Future Orientation in American Worldview." *Anthropological Quarterly* 42, no. 2 (April): 53–72.

Dundes, Alan. 1972a. "Folk Ideas as Units of Worldview." In *Toward New Perspectives in Folklore*, edited by Américo Paredes and Richard Bauman, 93–103. Austin: University of Texas Press. Also in *The Meaning of Folklore: The Analytical Essays of Alan Dundes*, edited by Simon J. Bronner, 179–92. Logan: Utah State University Press, 2007.

Dundes, Alan. 1972b. "Seeing Is Believing." *Natural History*, no. 5 (May): 814, 86. Also in *Interpreting Folklore*, by Alan Dundes, 86–92. Bloomington: Indiana University Press, 1980.

Dundes, Alan. 1975. "On the Structure of the Proverb." *Proverbium* 25: 961–73. Also in *Analytical Essays in Folklore*, by Alan Dundes, 103–18. The Hague: Mouton, 1975. Also in *The Wisdom of Many: Essays on the Proverb*, edited by Wolfgang Mieder and Alan Dundes, 43–64. New York: Garland Publishing, 1981.

Dundes, Alan. 2004. "As the Crow Flies: A Straightforward Study of Lineal Worldview in American Folk Speech." In *What Goes Around Comes Around: The Circulation of Proverbs in Contemporary Life; Essays in Honor of Wolfgang Mieder*, edited by Kimberly J. Lau, Peter Tokofsky, and Stephen D. Winick, 171–87. Logan: Utah State University Press. Also in *The Meaning of Folklore: The Analytical Essays of Alan Dundes*, edited by Simon J. Bronner, 196–210. Logan: Utah State University Press, 2007. Also in *"The Kushmaker" and Other Essays on Folk Speech and Folk Humor*, edited by Wolfgang Mieder, 93–108. Burlington: University of Vermont, 2008.

Eret, Dylan. 2001. "'The Past Does Not Equal the Future': Anthony Robbins Self-Help Maxims as Therapeutic Forms of Proverbial Rhetoric." *Proverbium* 18: 77–103.

Fogel, Edwin Miller. 1929. *Proverbs of the Pennsylvania Germans*. Lancaster, PA: Pennsylvania-German Society. Rpt., edited by Wolfgang Mieder. Bern: Peter Lang, 1995.

Gallacher, Stuart A. 1949. "Franklin's *Way to Wealth*: A Florilegium of Proverbs and Wise Sayings." *Journal of English and Germanic Philology* 48, no. 2 (April): 229–51.

Gibbs, Raymond W., and Dianara Beitel. 1995. "What Proverb Understanding Reveals About How People Think." *Psychological Bulletin* 118, no. 1: 133–54. Also in *Cognition, Comprehension, and Communication: A Decade of North American Proverb Studies (1990–2000)*, edited by Wolfgang Mieder, 109–62. Baltmannsweiler, Germany: Schneider Verlag Hohengehren, 2003.

Gilman, William H., and Ralph H. Orth, eds. 1960–1982. *The Journals and Miscellaneous Notebooks of Ralph Waldo Emerson*. 16 vols. Cambridge, MA: Harvard University Press.

Glazer, Mark. 1987. *A Dictionary of Mexican American Proverbs*. Westport, CT: Greenwood Press.

Gossen, Gary H. 1973. "Chamula Tzotzil Proverbs: Neither Fish nor Fowl." In *Meaning in Mayan Languages: Ethnolinguistic Studies*, edited by Munro S. Edmonson, 205–33. The Hague: Mouton. Also in *Wise Words: Essays on the Proverb*, edited by Wolfgang Mieder, 351–92. New York: Garland Publishing, 1994.

Griffin, Albert Kirby. 1991. *Religious Proverbs: Over 1600 Adages from 18 Faiths Worldwide*. Jefferson, NC: McFarland.

Haas, Heather A. 2008. "Proverb Familiarity in the United States: Cross-Regional Comparisons of the Paremiological Minimum." *Journal of American Folklore* 121, no. 481 (Summer): 319–47.

Hendrickson, Robert. 2000. *The Facts on File Dictionary of American Regionalisms: Local Expressions from Coast to Coast*. New York: Facts on File.

Honeck, Richard P. 1997. *A Proverb in Mind: The Cognitive Science of Proverbial Wit and Wisdom*. Mahwah, NJ: Lawrence Erlbaum Associates.

Hrisztova-Gotthardt, Hrisztalina, and Melita Aleksa Varga, eds. 2015. *Introduction to Paremiology: A Comprehensive Guide to Proverb Studies*. Berlin: Walter de Gruyter.

Jente, Richard. 1931–1932. "The American Proverb." *American Speech* 7: 342–48.

Jente, Richard. 1945. "The Untilled Field of Proverbs." In *Studies in Language and Literature*, edited by George R. Coffman, 112–19. Chapel Hill: University of North Carolina Press.

Kerschen, Lois. 1998. *American Proverbs About Women: A Reference Guide*. Westport, CT: Greenwood Press.

Krikmann, Arvo. 2009. *Proverb Semantics: Studies in Structure, Logic, and Metaphor*. Burlington: University of Vermont.

Lau, Kimberly J. 1996. "'It's About Time': The Ten Proverbs Most Frequently Used in Newspapers and Their Relation to American Values." *Proverbium* 13: 135–59. Also in *Cognition, Comprehension, and Communication: A Decade of North American Proverb Studies (1990–2000)*, edited by Wolfgang Mieder, 231–54. Baltmannsweiler, Germany: Schneider Verlag Hohengehren, 2003.

Litovkina, Anna T., and Wolfgang Mieder. 2006. *Old Proverbs Never Die, They Just Diversify: A Collection of Anti-Proverbs*. Burlington: University of Vermont.

Louis, Cameron. 2000. "Proverbs and the Politics of Language." *Proverbium* 17: 173–94. Also in *Cognition, Comprehension, and Communication: A Decade of North American Proverb Studies (1990–2000)*, edited by Wolfgang Mieder, 271–92. Baltmannsweiler, Germany: Schneider Verlag Hohengehren, 2003.

Manders, Dean Wolfe. 2006. *The Hegemony of Common Sense: Wisdom and Mystification in Everyday Life*. New York: Peter Lang.

McKenzie, Alyce M. 1996. "'Different Strokes for Different Folks': America's Quintessential Postmodern Proverb." *Theology Today* 53, no. 2 (July): 201–12. Also in *Cognition, Comprehension, and Communication: A Decade of North American Proverb Studies (1990–2000)*, edited by Wolfgang Mieder, 311–24. Baltmannsweiler, Germany: Schneider Verlag Hohengehren, 2003.

Mieder, Wolfgang. 1989a. *American Proverbs: A Study of Texts and Contexts*. Bern: Peter Lang.

Mieder, Wolfgang. 1989b. "Proverbs of the Native Americans: A Prize Competition." *Western Folklore* 48, no. 3 (July): 256–60.

Mieder, Wolfgang. 1992. "Paremiological Minimum and Cultural Literacy." In *Creativity and Tradition in Folklore: New Directions*, edited by Simon J. Bronner, 185–203. Logan: Utah

State University Press. Also in *Proverbs Are Never Out of Season: Popular Wisdom in the Modern Age*, by Wolfgang Mieder, 41–57. New York: Oxford University Press, 1993.

Mieder, Wolfgang. 1993. *Proverbs Are Never Out of Season: Popular Wisdom in the Modern Age*. New York: Oxford University Press.

Mieder, Wolfgang, ed. 1994. *Wise Words: Essays on the Proverb*. New York: Garland Publishing.

Mieder, Wolfgang. 1996. "Proverbs." In *American Folklore: An Encyclopedia*, edited by Jan Harold Brunvand, 597–601. New York: Garland Publishing.

Mieder, Wolfgang. 1997. *The Politics of Proverbs: From Traditional Wisdom to Proverbial Stereotypes*. Madison: University of Wisconsin Press.

Mieder, Wolfgang. 1998. *"A House Divided": From Biblical Proverb to Lincoln and Beyond*. Burlington: University of Vermont.

Mieder, Wolfgang. 2000a. *The Proverbial Abraham Lincoln: An Index to Proverbs in the Works of Abraham Lincoln*. New York: Peter Lang.

Mieder, Wolfgang. 2000b. *Strategies of Wisdom: Anglo-American and German Proverb Studies*. Baltmannsweiler, Germany: Schneider Verlag Hohengehren.

Mieder, Wolfgang. 2001. *"No Struggle, No Progress": Frederick Douglass and His Proverbial Rhetoric for Civil Rights*. New York: Peter Lang.

Mieder, Wolfgang. 2002. *"Call a Spade a Spade": From Classical Phrase to Racial Slur; A Case Study*. New York: Peter Lang.

Mieder, Wolfgang, ed. 2003. *Cognition, Comprehension, and Communication: A Decade of North American Proverb Studies (1990–2000)*. Baltmannsweiler, Germany: Schneider Verlag Hohengehren.

Mieder, Wolfgang. 2004. *Proverbs: A Handbook*. Westport, CT: Greenwood Press.

Mieder, Wolfgang. 2005a. "'A Proverb Is Worth a Thousand Words': Folk Wisdom in the Modern Mass Media." *Proverbium* 22: 167–233.

Mieder, Wolfgang. 2005b. *Proverbs Are the Best Policy: Folk Wisdom and American Politics*. Logan: Utah State University Press.

Mieder, Wolfgang. 2006. "Proverbs and Sayings." In *Encyclopedia of American Folklife*, edited by Simon J. Bronner, 3:996–99 Armonk, NY: M. E. Sharpe.

Mieder, Wolfgang. 2007. "Yankee Wisdom: American Proverbs and the Worldview of New England." In *Phraseology and Culture in English*, edited by Paul Skandera, 205–34. Berlin: Walter de Gruyter.

Mieder, Wolfgang. 2008a. "'Let Us Have Faith that Right Makes Might': Proverbial Rhetoric in Decisive Moments of American Politics." *Proverbium* 25: 319–52.

Mieder, Wolfgang. 2008b. *"Proverbs Speak Louder Than Words": Folk Wisdom in Art, Culture, Folklore, History, Literature, and Mass Media*. New York: Peter Lang.

Mieder, Wolfgang. 2009a. *International Bibliography of Paremiology and Phraseology*. 2 vols. Berlin: Walter de Gruyter.

Mieder, Wolfgang. 2009b. *"Yes We Can": Barack Obama's Proverbial Rhetoric*. New York: Peter Lang.

Mieder, Wolfgang. 2010a. *"Making a Way Out of No Way": Martin Luther King's Sermonic Proverbial Rhetoric*. New York: Peter Lang.

Mieder, Wolfgang. 2010b. *"Spruchschlösser (ab)bauen": Sprichwörter, Antisprichwörter und Lehnsprichwörter in Literatur und Medien*. Vienna: Praesens Verlag.

Mieder, Wolfgang. 2011a. *International Bibliography of Paremiography: Collections of Proverbs, Proverbial Expressions and Comparisons, Quotations, Graffiti, Slang, and Wellerisms.* Burlington: University of Vermont.

Mieder, Wolfgang. 2011b. "'It Takes a Village to Change the World': Proverbial Politics and the Ethics of Place." *Journal of American Folklore* 124, no. 492 (April): 4–28.

Mieder, Wolfgang. 2014a. *"All Men and Women Are Created Equal": Elizabeth Cady Stanton's and Susan B. Anthony's Proverbial Rhetoric Promoting Women's Rights.* New York: Peter Lang.

Mieder, Wolfgang. 2014b. *Behold the Proverbs of a People: Proverbial Wisdom in Culture, Literature, and Politics.* Jackson: University Press of Mississippi.

Mieder, Wolfgang. 2014c. "Futuristic Paremiography and Paremiology: A Plea for the Collection and Study of Modern Proverbs." *Folklore Fellows' Network Bulletin*, no. 44: 13–17, 20–24.

Mieder, Wolfgang. 2014d. "'M(R)ight Makes R(M)ight': The Sociopolitical History of a Contradictory Proverb Pair." In *Proceedings of the Seventh Interdisciplinary Colloquium on Proverbs*, Tavira, Portugal, November 3–10, 2013, edited by Rui J. B. Soares and Outi Lauhakangas, 107–31. Tavira, Portugal: Tipografia Tavirense.

Mieder, Wolfgang. 2014e. "'You Have to Kiss a Lot of Frogs (Toads) Before You Meet Your Handsome Prince': From Fairy-Tale Motif to Modern Proverb." *Marvels and Tales: Journal of Fairy-Tale Studies* 28, no. 1: 104–26.

Mieder, Wolfgang. 2015a. *"Different Strokes for Different Folks": 1250 authentisch amerikanische Sprichwörter.* Bochum, Germany: Norbert Brockmeyer.

Mieder, Wolfgang. 2015b. "'Different Ways to Make Life's Gold': Three Valedictory Messages of a University Course on Proverbs." In *Proceedings of the Eighth Interdisciplinary Colloquium on Proverbs*, Tavira, Portugal, November 2–9, 2014, edited by Rui J. B. Soares and Outi Lauhakangas, 122–47. Tavira, Portugal: Tipografia Tavirense.

Mieder, Wolfgang. 2015c. *"Goldene Morgenstunde" und "Früher Vogel": Zu einem Sprichwörterpaar in Literatur, Medien und Karikaturen.* Vienna: Praesens Verlag.

Mieder, Wolfgang. 2015d. "'Politics Is Not a Spectator Sport': Proverbs in the Personal and Political Writings of Hillary Rodham Clinton." *Tautosakos Darbai / Folklore Studies* (Vilnius) 50: 43–74.

Mieder, Wolfgang. 2017. "'The American People Rose to the Occasion': A Proverbial Retrospective of the Marshall Plan After Seventy Years." *Western Folklore* 76, no. 3 (Summer): 261–92.

Mieder, Wolfgang, and George B. Bryan. 1996. *Proverbs in World Literature: A Bibliography.* New York: Peter Lang.

Mieder, Wolfgang, and George B. Bryan. 1997. *The Proverbial Harry S. Truman: An Index to Proverbs in the Works of Harry S. Truman.* New York: Peter Lang.

Mieder, Wolfgang, and Alan Dundes, eds. 1981. *The Wisdom of Many: Essays on the Proverb.* New York: Garland Publishing.

Mieder, Wolfgang, and Stewart A. Kingsbury. 1994. *A Dictionary of Wellerisms.* New York: Oxford University Press.

Mieder, Wolfgang, Stewart A. Kingsbury, and Kelsie B. Harder. 1992. *A Dictionary of American Proverbs.* New York: Oxford University Press.

Mieder, Wolfgang, and Janet Sobieski, eds. 2006. *"Gold Nuggets or Fool's Gold?" Magazine and Newspaper Articles on the (Ir)relevance of Proverbs and Proverbial Phrases*. Burlington: University of Vermont.

Mitchell, Roger E. 1992. "Tradition, Change, and Hmong Refugees." In *Creativity and Tradition in Folklore: New Directions*, edited by Simon J. Bronner, 263–75. Logan: Utah State University Press.

Newcomb, Robert. 1957. "The Sources of Benjamin Franklin's Sayings of Poor Richard." PhD diss., University of Maryland.

Nussbaum, Stan. 2005. *American Cultural Baggage: How to Recognize and Deal with It*. Maryknoll, NY: Orbis Books.

Paczolay, Gyula. 1997. *European Proverbs in 55 Languages with Equivalents in Arabic, Persian, Sanskrit, Chinese and Japanese*. Veszprém, Hungary: Veszprémi Nyomda.

Prahlad, Sw. Anand. 1996. *African-American Proverbs in Context*. Jackson: University Press of Mississippi.

Prahlad, Sw. Anand. 2006. "Proverbs." In *The Greenwood Encyclopedia of African American Folklore*, edited by Sw. Anand Prahlad, 2:1022–27. Westport, CT: Greenwood Press.

Raymond, Joseph. 1956. "Tensions in Proverbs: More Light on International Understanding." *Western Folklore* 15, no. 3 (July): 153–58. Also in *The Wisdom of Many: Essays on the Proverb*, edited by Wolfgang Mieder and Alan Dundes, 300–308. New York: Garland Publishing, 1981.

Riley, Noël. 1991. "Benjamin Franklin's Maxims." In *Gifts for Good Children: The History of Children's China*, part 1, *1790–1890*, 270–83. Ilminster, Somer., England: Richard Dennis.

Schipper, Mineke. 2003. *Never Marry a Woman with Big Feet: Women in Proverbs from Around the World*. New Haven, CT: Yale University Press.

Stewart, Susan. 1991. "Notes on Distressed Genres." *Journal of American Folklore* 104, no. 411 (Winter): 5–31. Also in *Crimes of Writing: Problems in the Containment of Representation*, by Susan Stewart, 66–101. Durham, NC: Duke University Press, 1994.

Szpila, Grzegorz. 2017. "Polish Paremic Demotivators: Tradition in an Internet Genre." *Journal of American Folklore* 130, no. 517 (Summer): 305–34.

Taylor, Archer. 1931. *The Proverb*. Cambridge, MA: Harvard University Press. Rpt. as *The Proverb and an Index to The Proverb*. Hatboro, PA: Folklore Associates, 1962. Rpt. as *The Proverb and an Index to The Proverb*, with an introduction, bibliography, and photograph of Archer Taylor by Wolfgang Mieder. Bern: Peter Lang, 1985.

Taylor, Archer, and Bartlett Jere Whiting. 1958. *A Dictionary of American Proverbs and Proverbial Phrases, 1820–1880*. Cambridge, MA: Harvard University Press.

Templeton, John Mark. 1997. *Worldwide Laws of Life: 200 Eternal Spiritual Principles*. Philadelphia: Templeton Press.

Tosina Fernández, Luis J. 2017. "Proverbs in Present-Day Media: An Analysis of Television Fictions and Internet Memes and Their Contributions to the Spread of Proverbs." *Proverbium* 34: 359–89.

Van Lancker, Diana. 1990. "The Neurology of Proverbs." *Behavioural Neurology* 3, no. 3: 169–87. Also in *Cognition, Comprehension, and Communication: A Decade of North American Proverb Studies (1990–2000)*, edited by Wolfgang Mieder, 531–54. Baltmannsweiler, Germany: Schneider Verlag Hohengehren, 2003.

Villers, Damien, and Wolfgang Mieder. 2017. "*Time Is Money*: Benjamin Franklin and the Vexing Problem of Proverb Origins." *Proverbium* 34: 391–404.

White, Geoffrey M. 1987. "Proverbs and Cultural Models: An American Psychology of Problem Solving." In *Cultural Models in Language and Thought*, edited by Dorothy Holland and Naomi Quinn, 151–72. Cambridge: Cambridge University Press.

Whiting, Bartlett Jere. 1977. *Early American Proverbs and Proverbial Phrases*. Cambridge, MA: Harvard University Press.

Whiting, Bartlett Jere. 1989. *Modern Proverbs and Proverbial Sayings*. Cambridge, MA: Harvard University Press.

Whiting, Bartlett Jere. 1994. *When Evensong and Morrowsong Accord: Three Essays on the Proverb*. Edited by Joseph Harris and Wolfgang Mieder. Cambridge, MA: Harvard University Press.

Williams, Derek Antonio. 1997. "The Proverbial Zora Neale Hurston: A Study of Texts and Contexts." PhD diss., Emory University.

Winick, Stephen D. 2011. "Fall into the (Intertextual) Gap: Proverbs, Advertisements and Intertextual Strategies." *Proverbium* 28: 339–80.

Winick, Stephen D. 2013. "Proverbs Is as Proverb Does: *Forrest Gump*, the Catchphrase, and the Proverb." *Proverbium* 30: 377–428.

Winick, Stephen D. 2014. "Insights from the Middle of Nowhere: Proverbial Language and Intertextuality in Gary Larson's *The Far Side*." *Proverbium* 31: 409–60.

2

"PROVERBS ARE WORTH
A THOUSAND WORDS"

The Global Spread of American Proverbs

While the vast folkloric scholarship of Dan Ben-Amos contains occasional references to proverbial matters, there is also his magisterial essay "Meditation on a Russian Proverb in Israel" (1995), which I had the honor of including in the journal *Proverbium*. Its unassuming title might well have kept paremiologists from appreciating its scholarly significance, and it is thus a special delight for me to introduce the following deliberations with a few comments about it. It begins with an account of how Dan learned the Russian proverb "Ne skazhi gop poka ne pereskochish" (Don't say "hop" before you jumped and landed) from his father, who had emigrated from Russia to Israel and who was keen to admonish his son by way of the proverb's wisdom not to count his chickens before they are hatched. This touching account should remind proverb scholars to pay more attention to verbal family traditions, as Dennis Folly (Anand Prahlad) has done for the use of proverbs in his African American family (Folly 1982, 232–41). As one would expect, Dan's personal narrative is augmented by a detailed analysis of this proverb and its variants, explaining that it spread from Russia to the Baltic and Scandinavian countries, including Finland and also Germany (Kuusi 1985, 298; Wander 1867–1880, 2:774, 2:1027–28). I might add here that the proverb not surprisingly also spread from Russian to the Slavic languages of Croatian, Czech, Polish, and Slovak (Düringsfeld 1866, 86; Strauss 1994, 1:594, 2:950). Strangely enough, however, it does not appear to have entered the Romance languages with the exception that it was loan translated from German into the French spoken in areas of Switzerland (Düringsfeld and Reinsberg-Düringsfeld 1871–1872, 120). More importantly for Dan's acquaintance with the proverb is, of course, that it entered the Yiddish spoken in eastern Europe, with Jewish immigrants carrying it to Israel, where it was also translated into Hebrew (Ben-Amos 1995, 14–15). Interestingly enough, the

46

proverb did not find its way from German into British English, but it would be my conjecture that Jewish immigrants carried it to the United States, where it was recorded in the middle of the twentieth century in New York State as "Don't say 'hop' until you jumped over" (Mieder, Kingsbury, and Harder 1992, 308). It did not, however, gain any common currency, with the older equivalent "Do not halloo (shout) until you are out of the woods" from the eighteenth century being dominant (Wilson 1970, 345; Mieder, Kingsbury, and Harder 1992, 538). Be that as it may, the rest of Dan's illuminating article is an insightful analysis of such paremiological issues as the definition, structure, and variants of proverbs with an emphasis on the question of proverbiality, which most certainly encompasses traditionality as well as context, function, and semantics (see also Ben-Amos 1993, 213–14, 218). What appears to be just a small comment on a single proverb becomes in typical Ben-Amos fashion a precise and revealing discussion of the nature of proverbs.

But having added the fact that the Russian/Yiddish proverb has made it into American English provides me with the segue to how relatively modern American proverbs in turn are finding their way into other languages. While it has long been established that classical proverbs, Bible proverbs, and medieval Latin proverbs were translated into European languages in particular but also beyond (Mieder 2004, 10–13), to wit Gyula Paczolay's invaluable compendium *European Proverbs in 55 Languages with Equivalents in Arabic, Persian, Sanskrit, Chinese and Japanese* (1997) and numerous other comparative proverb collections (Mieder 2011, 17–36), the time has surely come to take a closer look at what proverbs English as the lingua franca of the modern world is distributing globally. In fact, ever more older Anglo-American proverbs are loan translated into foreign languages by way of the incredible influence of the mass media and the internet in all of their occurrences (Mieder 2010b, 43–59). A particularly telling example is the relatively new German takeover of the English proverb "The early bird catches the worm," with its earliest reference from 1636. The German equivalent "Morgenstunde hat Gold im Munde" (The morning hour has gold in its mouth), from 1570, one of the most popular German proverbs, is since about 1980 fighting for its survival. The word-for-word translation of "The early bird catches the worm" into the German "Der frühe Vogel fängt den Wurm" has been adopted to such a degree in a matter of about four decades that it is in fact replacing the older German proverb. Young Germans are barely employing the older proverb any longer. And this development is not just taking place in Germany, with the "bird" proverb conquering its world market in translations (Mieder 2015b).

With the first collection of 1,250 historically documented authentic American proverbs for German readers, *"Different Strokes for Different Folks": 1250 authentisch amerikanische Sprichwörter* (Mieder 2015a), we can now

48 AMERICAN PROVERBS

demonstrate, for at least a few American proverbs, how they are spreading more or less worldwide just as old and new idioms have done (Mieder 2010a, 35–54; Piirainen 2012–2016). Since these loan processes are relatively new, the translated proverbs have for the most part not yet appeared in the printed proverb collections of various national languages. I thus engaged many of my paremiological friends around the world with a questionnaire asking them to check with native speakers and on the internet to see whether certain American proverbs had gained some currency in their native languages. I am aware that much more diachronic and synchronic work is necessary, and it would be good to have the proverbs in actual contexts. But this would entail much longer individual studies and more space to present such findings, as I have provided them for several American proverbs that have entered the German language (Mieder 2010c, 285–340). All that I can do for now is to present the translated texts, and I thank all the international contributors for their invaluable help and support. I am also aware that the following lists are dominated by European languages, but I have tried to include languages from Asia and the Middle East, with African languages still sorely missing. In any case, here are the twenty-nine languages represented thus far with the names of the kind informants:

Ara: Arabic (Hilda Matta)
Bul: Bulgarian (Hrisztalina Hrisztova-Gotthardt, Roumyana Petrova)
Chi: Chinese (Xu Jinlong, Wei Liu, Wenyuan Shao)
Cro: Croatian (Melita Aleksa Varga)
Cze: Czech (František Čermák)
Dut: Dutch (Marinus van den Broek)
Est: Estonian (Anneli Baran)
Fin: Finnish (Liisa Granbom-Herranen, Outi Lauhakangas)
Fre: French (Damien Villers)
Ger: German (my responsibility)
Gre: Greek (Minas Alexiadis, Aristeidis Doulaveras)
Heb: Hebrew (Galit Hasan-Rokem)
Hun: Hungarian (Hrisztalina Hrisztova-Gotthardt, Anna T. Litovkina)
Ind: Indonesian (Rebecca Fanany)
Ita: Italian (Adriana Borra, Julia Sevilla Muñoz)
Jap: Japanese (Yoko Mori, Masamizu Tokita, Masanobu Yamaguchi)
Lat: Latvian (Anita Naciscione)
Lit: Lithuanian (Dalia Zaikauskienė)
Mal: Malay (Rebecca Fanany)
Per: Persian (Ahmad Abrishami)
Pol: Polish (Joanna Szerszunowicz)

Por:	Portuguese (Rui J. B. Soares)
Rom:	Romanian (Daniela Ionescu)
Rus:	Russian (Valerii Mokienko, Harry Walter)
Slk:	Slovak (Peter Ďurčo)
Slv:	Slovenian (Vida Jesenšek)
Spa:	Spanish (Julia Sevilla Muñoz)
Swe:	Swedish (Anders Widbåck)
Tur:	Turkish (Öznur Tuzcu)

Beginning with three American proverbs from the nineteenth century, let me first turn to the proverb "Don't swap horses in the middle of the stream," which most Americans associate with President Abraham Lincoln, who used it on June 9, 1864, in a short statement regarding his possible candidacy for a second presidential term (Mieder 2000, 34–35). It has now been shown that the proverb was already in circulation by 1834 (Mieder 2007, 3–40), but it is nevertheless of interest that my informants have stated that Lincoln's name usually remains attached to its loan translation and that it is most often cited in cases of attempted political reelections. Here is this well-known proverb appearing in twelve languages:

Don't swap (switch) horses in midstream (the middle of the stream) (12)

Bul:	Ne smenyay konete po sredata na rekata.
Chi:	Xing zhi zhong liu bu huan ma.
Est:	Poolel teel hobuseid ei vahetata.
Fre:	Il ne faut pas changer de cheval au milieu de la rivière.
Hun:	Ne cserélj lovat a víz sodrában.
Ind:	Jangan berganti kuda selagi nyebrang kali.
Ita:	Non cambiare i cavalli in mezzo alla corrente.
Jap:	Kawa no mannaka de uma wo norikaeruna.
Lit:	Perkėloje arklių niekas nekeičia.
Pol:	Nie zmienia się koni podczas przeprawy przez rzekę.
Por:	Não troques de cavalo no meio da corrida.
Tur:	Irmaktan geçerken at değişirilmez.

The earliest reference found thus far for the extremely popular American proverb "Good fences make good neighbors" also stems from 1834, gaining wide currency because of its use as a leitmotif in Robert Frost's celebrated poem "Mending Wall" (1914), which delineates the ambivalent value of building fences or walls. It is a very appropriate metaphor to express the perplexities not only of human relations but also of modern issues, with illegal immigration and the building of walls between countries (Mieder 2003, 155–79). It causes no problem in translating, and due to its multiple applicability it has gained considerable international dissemination:

Good fences make good neighbors. (10)
Bul: Dobrite ogradi pravyat dobri sasedi.
Cro: Dobre ograde čine dobre susjede.
Fre: Les bonnes clôtures font les bons voisins.
Ger: Gute Zäune machen gute Nachbarn.
Hun: A jó szomszédság záloga a jó kerítés.
Ita: I buoni recinti fanno buoni vicini.
Lit: Gera tvora—geri kaimynai.
Pol: Gdzie dobre płoty, tak dobrzy sąsiedzi.
Por: Os bons muros fazem os bons vizinhos.
Slk: Vysoké ploty robia dobrých susedov.

A third American proverb from 1870 also presents no translation problem, making it possible for the "medical" or at least nutritional piece of wisdom "An apple a day keeps the doctor away" to become established in other languages (Mieder 1993a, 162–68):

An apple a day keeps the doctor away. (19)
Bul: Edna yabalka na den darzhi doktora dalech ot men.
Chi: Ri shi yi ping guo, yi sheng yuan li wo.
Cro: Jedna jabuka na dan tjera doktora iz kuće van.
Est: Üks õun päevas hoiab arsti eemal.
Fin: Omena päivässä pitää lääkärin loitolla.
Fre: Une pomme par jour éloigne le médecin (pour toujours).
Ger: Ein Apfel pro Tag hält den Arzt fern.
Gre: Ena milo tin inera / ton giatro ton kani pera.
Hun: Naponta egy alma a doktort távol tartja.
Ita: Una mela al giorno toglie il medico di torno.
Jap: Ichinichi ikko no ringo wa isha irazu.
Per: Kordane yek sib dar ruz doctor ra dur negahmidard.
Pol: Jedno jabłko dziennie trzyma lekarza z daleka.
Por: Uma maçã por dia afasta o medico.
Rus: Po iabloku v den'—i doktor ne nuzhen.
Slk: Jedno jablko denne udrží doktora ďaleko.
Slv: Eno jabolko na dan prežene zdravnika stran.
Swe: Ett äpple om dagen håller doktorn borta från magen.
Tur: Günde bir elma doktoru uzak tutar.

What has been shown for three somewhat older American proverbs thus far can also be observed for some more modern proverbs that originated in the United States and that are registered with detailed historical and contextualized materials in *The Dictionary of Modern Proverbs* (Doyle, Mieder, and Shapiro 2012; Mieder 2014a, 80–130). While it has at times been claimed that the proverb "One picture is worth a thousand words" is of Chinese or Japanese origin, this is definitely not the case, with the proverb actually having its start in 1911 in the American advertising magazine *Printers' Ink* (Mieder 1993a, 135–51). Realizing that American society is ever more flooded by images of all sorts, and with the rest of the world also being influenced by visual representations ranging from printed illustrations to television, film, and the internet, it can hardly be surprising that this proverb, once again being easily translated, has found the widest acceptance throughout the world of the proverbs discussed here as a most fitting expression for the visual dominance in modern life:

One picture is worth a thousand words. (26)

Ara:	El-ṣura ablaġ min alf kelma.
Bul:	Edna snimka kazva / govori poveche ot hilyadi dumi.
Chi:	Yi fu hua ding yi qian ge ci.
Cro:	Slika vrijedi tisuću riječi.
Est:	Üks pilt ütleb rohkem kui tuhat sõna.
Fin:	Yksi kuva kertoo enemmän kuin tuhat sanaa.
Fre:	Une image vaut mille mots.
Ger:	Ein Bild sagt mehr als tausend Worte.
Gre:	Mia ikona axizi xilies lexis.
Heb:	Tmuna ahat shava elef milim.
Hun:	Egy kép többet mond ezer szónál.
Ind:	Gambar lebih berarti dari seribu kata.
Ita:	Un'immagine vale mille parole.
Jap:	Ichimai no e wa ichimango ni ataisuru.
Lit:	Vaizdas vertas tūkstančio žodžių.
Mal:	Sebuah gambar senilai seribu kata.
Per:	Yek aks guyatar az hezar kelameh ast.
Pol:	Jeden obraz jest więcej wart niż tysiąc słów.
Por:	Uma imagem vale mais do que mil palavras.
Rom:	O imagine face mai mult decat o mie de cucinte.
Rus:	Odna kartina luchshe tysiachi slov.
Slk:	Obraz je viac ako tisíc slov.
Slv:	Slika pove več kot tisoč besed.
Spa:	Una imagen vale más que mil palabras.

Swe: En bild är värd mer än tusen ord.
Tur: Bir resim, bin kelimeye bedeldir.

In a study of the proverb "The grass is always greener on the other side of the fence" dating from 1913, I called this insight "an American proverb of discontent" (Mieder 1993b, 151–84). The fact that grazing animals favor the fresh grass on the other side of a fence is a natural phenomenon that can be observed in most countries, and it is an easy step to transpose this image to the greed and dissatisfaction of human beings anywhere. It is then understandable that this natural metaphor could establish itself in other languages in a rather short amount of time. After all, this desire for better things is by no means just an American social problem:

The grass on the other side of the fence always looks greener. (19)
Bul: Trevata vinagi e po-zelena ot drugata strana na ogradata.
Chi: Li ba na tou (bian) de cao zong shi geng lu xie.
Cro: Trava je zelenija s druge strane ograde.
Dut: Het gras bij de buren is altijd groener.
Est: Teisel pool aeda on muru rohelisem.
Fin: Ruoho on aina vihreämpää aidan toisella puolella.
Fre: L'herbe est toujours plus verte ailleurs.
Ger: Das Gras auf der anderen Seite des Zaunes ist immer grüner.
Heb: Ha-deshe shel hashakhen yaroq yoter.
Ind: Rumput di sebelah pagar selalu kelihatan lebih hijau.
Ita: L'erba è sempre più verde dall'altro lato della recinzione.
Jap: Tonari no shibafu wa aoi.
Lit: Žolė visada žalesnė anapus tvoros.
Pol: Trawa jest zawsze bardziej zielona / zieleńsza po drugiej stronie płotu.
Por: A relva da minha vizinha é sempre mais verde que a minha.
Slk: Tráva na druhej strane hory je zelenšia.
Slv: Trava na drugi strani ograje je vedno bolj zelena.
Swe: Gräset är alltid grönare på andra sidan.
Tur: Çimenler tepenin diğer tarafında her zaman daha yeşildir.

Regarding the next text, it might come as somewhat of a surprise to learn that the proverb "Think globally, act locally" had its origin already in 1942, with its first reference found thus far indicating clearly that global awareness of various issues is not really that new: "Our vision of a better world is limited to our vision of better communities. We must think globally, but first act locally" (Doyle, Mieder, and Shapiro 2012, 256). The proverb's shortness, parallel structure, and lack of a metaphor together with its deep insight into global concerns makes it a perfect candidate to gain worldwide currency. Things are quite different concerning my favorite modern American proverb, "Different strokes for different folks," which had its beginning among the African American population around 1945 (Doyle, Mieder, and Shapiro 2012, 241–42). A translation might well lose the rhyme and parallel structure, but the main problem would be rendering the word "strokes" into another language. I have tried to translate it into German as "Andere Leute, andere Kniffe (Wege, Züge)," which would amount in English to "Other people, other tricks (ways, means)," but I am not at all satisfied with this (Mieder 2015a, 217). This liberating American proverb has a nonmetaphorical precursor in the classical "Suum quique," which in turn was translated into English as "To each his own" and into German as "Jedem das Seine." The latter, however, is not acceptable in German any longer since the phrase was part of the gate to the Buchenwald concentration camp. For the same reason, Germans should refrain from using the proverb "Arbeit macht frei" (Work makes you free), which is known from the gate at Auschwitz (Brückner 1998; Doerr 2000, 71–90). All of this shows why I would like to render the proverb "Different strokes for different folks" into my native German. And yet, as I always tell my proverb students, the proverb does not give them absolute freedom to do whatever they wish. There is an ethical component to the proverb that can best be expressed by the proverbial golden rule: "Do unto others as you would have them do unto you" (Matthew 7:12; Mieder 1989, 317–32; McKenzie 1996, 201–12). In any case, the problems mentioned in this short diversion do not exist with the uncomplicated translation of the "global/local" proverb:

Think globally, act locally. (18)

Bul:	Misli globalno, deystvay localno.
Chi:	Quan qiu si wei, ben tu xing dong.
Cro:	Misli globalno, djeluj lokalno.
Cze:	Mysli globálně, jednej lokálně.
Est:	Mõtle globaalselt, tegutse lokaalselt.
Fin:	Ajattele globaalisti, toimi paikallisesti.
Fre:	Penser global, agir local.
Ger:	Global denken, lokal handeln.
Hun:	Gondolkodj globálisan, cselekedj lokálisan.
Ind:	Berpikir global, bertindak lokal.
Ita:	Pensa globale, agisci locale (Pensare globale, agire locale).
Lit:	Galvok globaliai—veik lolakiai!
Pol:	Myśl globalnie, działaj lokalnie.
Por:	Pensar global, agir local.

Rus:	Myslit' global'no—deistvovat' lokal'no.
Slk:	Mysli globálne, konaj lokálne.
Slv:	Misli globalno, deluj lokalno.
Tur:	Global düşün, lokal davran.

Matters are also quite simple with the international distribution of the modern proverb "It takes two to tango," from the song "Takes Two to Tango" (1952) by Al Hoffman and Dick Manning, which became an international hit by way of the famous African American singer Pearl Bailey. It is probably fair to assume, however, that the new proverb is based on the old English proverb "It takes two to quarrel" from 1706, changing that regrettable insight into the positive statement that people can and should get along. The image of two partners dancing the intimate tango becomes a great metaphor for any two parties, including political leaders:

It takes two to tango. (17)

Bul:	Za tantz sa nuzhni dvama.
Cro:	Za tango treba dvoje.
Est:	Tangoks on vaja kaht.
Fin:	Tangoon tarvitaan kaksi.
Fre:	It faut être deux pour danser le tango.
Ger:	Zum Tango gehören zwei.
Gre:	Hriazonte dio gia to tango.
Heb:	Tsarikh shnayim le-tango.
Hun:	A tangóhoz két ember kell.
Ita:	Bisogna essere in due per ballare il tango.
Lit:	Tango šokoma dviese.
Pol:	Do tanga trzeba dwojga.
Por:	São precisas duas pessoas para dançar o tango.
Rus:	Dlia tango nuzhny dvoe.
Slk:	Na tango treba dvoch.
Slv:	Za tango sta potrebna dva.
Tur:	Tango iki kişiyle yapilir.

Knowing that the truly modern American proverb "You have to kiss a lot of frogs (toads) to find a (your handsome) prince" had its beginning in 1976, and that by 1984 it had also become current in Germany as a loan translation (Doyle, Mieder, and Shapiro 2012, 89), I decided to include it in my questionnaire as somewhat of a shot in the dark. I had traced the origin of the proverb in my article "'You Have to Kiss a Lot of Frogs (Toads) Before You Meet Your Handsome Prince': From Fairy-Tale Motif to Modern Proverb" (Mieder

THE GLOBAL SPREAD OF AMERICAN PROVERBS   55

2014b), showing that it is not based on "The Frog King" fairy tale of the Brothers Grimm. As we remember, the folk narrative does not have a liberating kiss scene. Instead, the young princess throws the ugly frog against the wall, whereupon it turns into a handsome prince. But the "Beauty and the Beast" narratives do at times include the kiss, and the new proverb might allude to one of them. The proverb, being relatively long, exists in a number of variants, but despite this, it has rather quickly gained considerable dissemination throughout Europe. Obviously, people of various nationalities can relate to a metaphor that deals with the complex aspects of finding a suitable partner:

You have to kiss a lot of frogs (toads) to find a (your handsome) prince. (13)
Bul: Tryabva da tzelunesh mnogo zhabi, predi da / dokato otkriesh / namerish svoya printz.
Cze: Aby si našla prince, musí políbit spoustu žabáků.
Est: Pead suudlema palju konnasid, enne kui oma printsi leiad.
Fre: Il faut embrasser beaucoup de crapauds avant de trouver le (son) prince (charmant).
Ger: Man muß viele Frösche küssen, bevor man einen Prinzen findet.
Hun: Sok békát meg kell csókolnod, mielőtt megatalálod a herceged.
Ita: Bisogna baciare molti rospi prima di trovare il principe.
Lit: Dažnai turime pabučiuoti ne vieną varle, kol surandame savo Žavųjų princą.
Pol: Trzeba pocałować wiele żab, aby trafić na księcia / zanin trafi się na księcia.
Por: Tens de beijar muitos sapos para encontrares un principe.
Rus: Vam pridetsia potselovat' mnogo liagushek prezhde, chem vy naidete svoego prekrasnogo printsa.
Slv: Preden najdeš svojega princa, moraš poljubiti veliko žab.
Tur: Prensini bulmadan önce çok kurbağa öpmen gerekir.

What took decades if not centuries in former times can be achieved today in truly a short time span. By way of oral and written communication, including the mass media in all its forms together with the internet, proverbs can be disseminated regionally, nationally, and internationally. Older proverbs and also very new proverbs can very quickly gain widespread currency, and with English as the lingua franca of the world, British proverbs in general and American proverbs in particular will doubtlessly continue to be loan translated into other languages. This limited glance at but eight American proverbs from the nineteenth and twentieth centuries represents but a beginning of the fascinating study of the process of loan translations. More detailed studies of individual proverbs in actual contexts are needed. But these short deliberations show that proverbs as "monumenta humana" (Kuusi 1957, 52) contain general wisdom that in many cases does not know any geographical or linguistic boundaries. As very basic insights and valuable wisdom, they show that people are much more alike than different, and American proverbs will doubtlessly play an important role in this globalization process. As proverbs take on their own lives in the form of loan translations, people will most likely not even be aware of their foreign origin, just as they today think of proverbs like "One hand washes the other," "Man does not live by bread alone," and "Strike while the iron is hot" as their very own wisdom even though they started as classical, biblical, and medieval Latin proverbs, respectively, that were translated into many languages. Like the widespread Russian proverb "Don't say 'hop' before you jumped and landed" used by Dan Ben-Amos's father, these globalized American proverbs contain humanistic values that tie the people of the world together into a common web of mutual respect and support.

BIBLIOGRAPHY

This chapter was first published with the same title in *Contexts of Folklore: Festschrift for Dan Ben-Amos on His Eighty-Fifth Birthday*, edited by Simon J. Bronner and Wolfgang Mieder (New York: Peter Lang), 217–29.

Ben-Amos, Dan. 1993. "'Context' in Context." *Western Folklore* 52, nos. 2–4 (April–October): 209–26.

Ben-Amos, Dan. 1995. "Meditation on a Russian Proverb in Israel." *Proverbium* 12: 13–26.

Brückner, Wolfgang. 1998. *"Arbeit macht frei": Herkunft und Hintergrund der KZ-Devise.* Opladen, Germany: Leske und Budrich.

Doerr, Karin. 2000. "'To Each His Own' (Jedem das Seine): The (Mis-)Use of German Proverbs in Concentration Camps and Beyond." *Proverbium* 17: 71–90.

Doyle, Charles Clay, Wolfgang Mieder, and Fred R. Shapiro, eds. 2012. *The Dictionary of Modern Proverbs.* New Haven, CT: Yale University Press.

Düringsfeld, Ida von. 1866. *Das Sprichwort als Kosmopolit.* Leipzig: Hermann Fries. Rpt., edited by Wolfgang Mieder. Hildesheim, Germany: Georg Olms, 2004.

Düringsfeld, Ida von, and Otto von Reinsberg-Düringsfeld. 1871–1872. *Sprichwörter der germanischen und romanischen Sprachen.* 2 vols. Leipzig: Hermann Fries.

Folly, Dennis W. [Anand Prahlad]. 1982. "Getting the Butter from the Duck: Proverbs and Proverbial Expressions in an Afro-American Family." In *A Celebration of American Family Folklore: Tales and Traditions from the Smithsonian Collection*, edited by Stephen J. Zeitlin, Amy J. Kotkin, and Holly Cutting Baker, 232–41, 290–91. New York: Pantheon Books.

Kuusi, Matti. 1957. *Parömiologische Betrachtungen.* Helsinki: Suomalainen Tiedeakatemia.

Kuusi, Matti. 1985. *Proverbia septentrionalia: 900 Balto-Finnic Proverb Types with Russian, Baltic, German and Scandinavian Parallels.* Helsinki: Suomalainen Tiedeakatemia.

McKenzie, Alyce M. 1996. "'Different Strokes for Different Folks': America's Quintessential Postmodern Proverb." *Theology Today* 53, no. 2 (July): 201–12.

Mieder, Wolfgang. 1989. *American Proverbs: A Study of Texts and Contexts*. Bern: Peter Lang.

Mieder, Wolfgang. 1993a. *Proverbs Are Never Out of Season: Popular Wisdom in the Modern Age*. New York: Oxford University Press.

Mieder, Wolfgang. 1993b. "'The Grass Is Always Greener on the Other Side of the Fence': An American Proverb of Discontent." *Proverbium* 10: 151–84.

Mieder, Wolfgang. 2000. *The Proverbial Abraham Lincoln: An Index to Proverbs in the Works of Abraham Lincoln*. New York: Peter Lang.

Mieder, Wolfgang. 2003. "'Good Fences Make Good Neighbours': History and Significance of an Ambiguous Proverb." *Folklore* (London) 114, no. 2 (August): 155–79.

Mieder, Wolfgang. 2004. *Proverbs: A Handbook*. Westport, CT: Greenwood Press. Rpt., New York: Peter Lang, 2012.

Mieder Wolfgang. 2007. "'Don't Swap Horses in the Middle of the Stream': An Intercultural and Historical Study of Abraham Lincoln's Apocryphal Proverb." *Folklore Historian* 24: 3–40.

Mieder, Wolfgang. 2010a. "American Proverbs: An International, National, and Global Phenomenon." *Western Folklore* 69, no. 1 (Winter): 35–54.

Mieder, Wolfgang. 2010b. "'Many Roads Lead to Globalization': The Translation and Distribution of Anglo-American Proverbs in Europe." In *Phraseologie, global—areal—regional: Akten der Konferenz Europhras 2008*, Helsinki, August 13–16, 2008, edited by Jarmo Korhonen, Wolfgang Mieder, Elisabeth Piirainen, and Rosa Piñel, 43–59. Tübingen, Germany: Gunter Narr.

Mieder, Wolfgang. 2010c. *"Spruchschlösser (ab)bauen": Sprichwörter, Antisprichwörter und Lehnsprichwörter in Literatur und Medien*. Vienna: Praesens Verlag.

Mieder, Wolfgang. 2011. *International Bibliography of Paremiography: Collections of Proverbs, Proverbial Expressions and Comparisons, Quotations, Graffiti, Slang, and Wellerisms*. Burlington: University of Vermont.

Mieder, Wolfgang. 2014a. "'Think Outside the Box': Origin, Nature, and Meaning of Modern Anglo-American Proverbs." In *Behold the Proverbs of a People: Proverbial Wisdom in Culture, Literature, and Politics*, 80–130. Jackson: University Press of Mississippi.

Mieder, Wolfgang. 2014b. "'You Have to Kiss a Lot of Frogs (Toads) Before You Meet Your Handsome Prince': From Fairy-Tale Motif to Modern Proverb." *Marvels and Tales: Journal of Fairy-Tale Studies* 28, no. 1: 104–26.

Mieder, Wolfgang. 2015a. *"Different Strokes for Different Folks": 1250 authentisch amerikanische Sprichwörter*. Bochum, Germany: Norbert Brockmeyer.

Mieder, Wolfgang. 2015b. *"Goldene Morgenstunde" und "Früher Vogel": Zu einem Sprichwörterpaar in Literatur, Medien und Karikaturen*. Vienna: Praesens Verlag.

Mieder, Wolfgang, Stewart A. Kingsbury, and Kelsie B. Harder. 1992. *A Dictionary of American Proverbs*. New York: Oxford University Press.

Paczolay, Gyula. 1997. *European Proverbs in 55 Languages with Equivalents in Arabic, Persian, Sanskrit, Chinese and Japanese*. Veszprém, Hungary: Veszprémi Nyomda.

Piirainen, Elisabeth. 2012–2016. *Widespread Idioms in Europe and Beyond: Toward a Lexicon of Common Figurative Units*. 2 vols. New York: Peter Lang.

Strauss, Emanuel. 1994. *Dictionary of European Proverbs.* 3 vols. Abingdon, Oxon., England: Routledge.

Wander, Karl Friedrich Wilhelm. 1867–1880. *Deutsches Sprichwörter-Lexikon.* 5 vols. Leipzig: F. A. Brockhaus.

Wilson, F. P. 1970. *The Oxford Dictionary of English Proverbs.* 3rd ed. Oxford: Oxford University Press.

3

"A FRIEND (NOT) IN NEED IS A FRIEND INDEED"

Friendship in Old, Modern, and Anti-Proverbs

One of my fondest memories of working on proverbial matters goes back more than fifty years when my dear wife and I were newlywed PhD students in 1969 at Michigan State University in East Lansing, Michigan. One day, Barbara told me that there was a well-known proverb that she really never understood as a native speaker of English. When she identified the proverb as "A friend in need is a friend indeed," I responded by inquiring what could possibly be so difficult about understanding this piece of folk wisdom. As we continued our discussion of the proverb, it became clear that she was interpreting it as referring to "a needy friend" being a good friend and consequently questioned its wisdom. Once I explained that the proverb refers to a person who actually needs help from a friend, it made sense to her, of course, but we periodically remember this event half a century ago when we encounter the proverb anew. But suffice it to say, I took home from this once and for all that proverbs are by no means simplistic statements whose messages are at all times easily accessible. The metaphors that are often part of their wording add to this complexity, especially if they appear without any context. Many proverbs make little sense in collections, but once they are employed in different situations for various purposes, they exhibit shades of meaning. Stated in more scholarly terms, proverbs must be studied in their polysituativity, polyfunctionality, and polysemanticity (Mieder 2004b, 9).

About four years after this memorable discussion with my young bride, I came across a significant article by my now longtime friend Barbara Kirshenblatt-Gimblett, "Toward a Theory of Proverb Meaning" (1973), which Alan Dundes and I republished in our essay volume *The Wisdom of Many: Essays on the Proverb* (1981). She published her seminal paper originally in the "old" *Proverbium* journal in Helsinki. Its twenty-five issues were edited by Matti

Kuusi between 1965 and 1975, and it published articles by such great twentieth-century paremiologists as Roger D. Abrahams, Shirley Arora, Charles Doyle, Kazys Grigas, Galit Hasan-Rokem, Bengt Holbek, Arvo Krikmann, Pentti Leino, Isidor Levin, Démétrios Loukatos, Katherine Luomala, Otto Moll, Siegfried Neumann, Grigorii L'vovich Permiakov, Lutz Röhrich, Agnes Szemerkényi, Archer Taylor, Bozor Tilavov, Vilmos Voigt, Bartlett Jere Whiting, and many others. The entire run of the journal amounted to but one thousand pages, but they represent the foundation of modern theoretical paremiology. It was my great honor to receive Matti Kuusi's blessing in bringing out a two-volume reprint of the journal run in 1987 with the Peter Lang publishing house in Bern, Switzerland. It behooves proverb scholars today to pay heed to these pages, among them the article by Barbara Kirshenblatt-Gimblett.

Imagine my surprise and joy in 1973 when I read her erudite treatise about proverb semantics! But not just that, for she includes a detailed discussion of the proverbs "A rolling stone gathers no moss" and "A friend in need is a friend indeed," which perplexed her students at the University of Texas at Austin. Here are the four interpretations that the students came up with:

A friend in need is a friend indeed (in deed)
1. Someone who feels close enough to you to be able to ask you for help when he is in need is really your friend.
2. Someone who helps you when you are in need is really your friend.
3. Someone who helps you by means of his actions (deeds) when you need him is a real friend as opposed to someone who just makes promises.
4. Someone who is only your friend when he needs you is not a true friend.

The students' professor explains the sources of this ambiguity as follows: "(1) syntactic ambiguity (Is your friend in need or are you in need?); (2) lexical ambiguity (indeed or in deed); and (3) key issue (Is the proverb being stated 'straight' or 'sarcastically'? Does 'a friend indeed' mean 'true friend' or 'not a true friend'?)." The readings provided here and the ambiguities they are based on do not exhaust the possibilities but merely pinpoint the most common ones (Kirshenblatt-Gimblett 1973, 822–23). All of this is ample proof that proverbs communicate by indirection and that they have to be disambiguated in actual performance situations, be that in spoken or written form, or for that matter drawn (e.g., as cartoons).

But ambiguous or not, this proverb belongs to the paremiological minimum of the English language (Haas 2008: 339), and its popularity and perhaps also its complexity as well as its parallel structure and rhyme have led to numerous parodying anti-proverbs. Here are but a few, with the dates of their first occurrence in print:

A friend in need is a friend to avoid. (1949)
A friend that ain't in need is a friend indeed. (1955)
A friend in need is a friend to keep away from. (1967)
A friend not in need is a friend indeed. (1967)
A friend in need is a friend you don't need. (1968)
A friend in need is a pest indeed. (1976)
A friend in need is a drain on the pocketbook. (1980)
A friend in need is a fiend indeed. (1996)
A friend in deed is the friend you need. (1999)
(Litovkina and Mieder 2006, 64)

But there is more to this story: of the 1,617 modern proverbs (proverbs that were coined after the year 1900) registered with dates and contexts in *The Dictionary of Modern Proverbs* (2012; hereafter *DMP*), edited by Charles Clay Doyle, Wolfgang Mieder, and Fred R. Shapiro, and its three supplements (Doyle and Mieder 2016; Doyle and Mieder 2018; Doyle and Mieder 2020), about 145, or 9 percent, originated as anti-proverbs and subsequently gained such general acceptance and frequency of use that they have become proverbs in their own right. In other words, while not all anti-proverbs gain traditional proverbiality, some in fact do make this jump. Anti-proverbs definitely need to be studied if paremiography is to go beyond repeating long-established proverbs without paying attention to modern proverbs! In any case, one such anti-proverb turned modern proverb is "A friend with weed is a friend indeed." The American folklorist Roger D. Abrahams, in his short but pregnant article "Such Matters as Every Man Should Know, and Descant Upon" (1970) in *Proverbium*, registered its appearance in the youth culture fifty years ago: "Witness the recent use of the proverb 'A friend in need is a friend indeed.' The force of the proverb in this form is underlined yet particularized in the rephrasing, 'A friend with weed is a friend indeed.' ('Weed' is a slang term for marijuana.)." In 1970, Abrahams did not know the term "anti-proverb," which I coined a few years later (Röhrich and Mieder 1977, 115). Anna Litovkina and I registered the text in minor variants a few years later as "A friend with a weed is a friend indeed" (1977) and "A friend in weed is a friend indeed" (1989), an indication that the anti-proverb was finding its way slowly but surely to standard form (Litovkina and Mieder 2006, 64). Many years later Charles Doyle, Fred Shapiro, and I, searching online, located it in the journal *Evergreen Review* of March 12, 1968, as "A friend with weed is a friend indeed," and by now, some fifty years later, the variant has become a true modern proverb (Doyle, Mieder, and Shapiro 2012, 86).

If there were time and space, this short study could now move on to trace the origin, development, and dissemination of the proverb "A friend in need is a friend indeed," starting with its rudimentary form in the eleventh century to its appearance in its precise and standard wording in John Ray's *Collection of English Proverbs* in 1678 and so on to the present (Mieder, Kingsbury, and Harder 1992, 233; Speake 2015, 121). The next step would be to see how the proverb and its basic idea appears in other languages. My longtime Hungarian friend Gyula Paczolay, renowned polyglot paremiographer, has registered it with detailed annotations in forty-five languages under the lemma "A true friend is known in need/adversity" in his unsurpassed dictionary, *European Proverbs in 55 Languages with Equivalents in Arabic, Persian, Sanskrit, Chinese and Japanese* (1997, 159–64). At such expanse of coverage of individual proverbs, it is understandable that Paczolay could present "only" 106 proverbs and their international occurrence, with this particular proverb representing the hundreds of other proverbs from around the world dealing with friendship. They are listed in valuable international proverb collections that usually amass texts without any historical annotations (Gluski 1971; Mieder 1986; Strauss 1994; Cordry 1997; Stone 2006; Rosen 2020; for more titles, see Mieder 2011, 17–36). Of course, innumerable proverb collections for individual languages also contain many "friend" proverbs, with the *Dictionary of American Proverbs* (Mieder, Kingsbury, and Harder 1992, 233–40) listing 195 texts with some annotations just under the keyword "friend," with more proverbs dealing with friendship appearing throughout the volume. As one would have expected, people everywhere have summarized their opinions, feelings, and experiences with this all-too-human matter in proverbial wisdom. Little wonder then that Alan E. Cheales included a delightfully readable chapter on "Friendship" in his book *Proverbial Folk-Lore* (1874, 91–97) that ought not to be forgotten.

With such a plethora of proverbs worldwide dealing with friendship, it is somewhat surprising that new proverbs can still be created on this so richly covered subject matter. But friendship is a basic human phenomenon, and new insights can indeed still be crystallized into proverbial form. For example, there is the Jamaican proverb "Mek fren' when you no need dem" from 1927, which was recorded in 1946 in standard English as "Make friends when you don't need them" and its variant, "Make friends before you need them" (*DMP* 87). It is somewhat related to the proverb "A friend in need is a friend indeed" discussed above. But since its anti-proverbs have been cited, it is well to mention two additional modern proverbs that started as anti-proverbs of older proverbs from the sixteenth century. Thus, the proverb "A friend's frown is better than a fool's smile" mutated into the anti-proverb "A friend's frown is better than a foe's smile" by 1922 (*DMP* 86), which is now current as a new proverb. And a witty soul changed the well-known proverb "You cannot have your cake and eat it too" to the anti-proverb "You cannot use your friends and have them too" (*DMP* 88) by 1954, which in turn has attained a proverbial status as an insightful piece of wisdom about human nature.

Another example of how some modern proverbs originate as anti-proverbs based on the same structure as an older proverb is the proverb "You can choose your friends, but you cannot choose your family" (Mieder, Kingsbury, and Harder 1992, 240). One might well wonder what brought about the following two modern proverbs based on it, but the motivation for these somewhat crass proverbs was most likely a bit of somatic folk humor to add some expressiveness to it all: "You can pick your friends, and you can pick your nose, but you can't pick your friend's nose" (1975, *DMP* 88); and "You can pick your nose, but you can't pick your family (relatives)" (1997, *DMP* 179).

In this regard, we might point out that the modern proverb "Keep your nose clean" (1903, *DMP* 179) has nothing to do with picking or blowing one's nose but is merely a somatic metaphor to admonish people to keep things in proper perspective. But as I have shown in my book *The Worldview of Modern American Proverbs* (2020), various parts and functions of the body including scatology and sexuality play a considerable role in modern proverbs.

So do animals, and as a dog lover—my wife and I have Labradors, one white and one black—I have always felt akin to the proverb "A dog is man's best friend," whose first printed reference I have found thus far stems from 1843. This might be a bit surprising, but we must remember that dogs in former times were not so much pets as working animals—a far cry from being a good friend! In any case, the English proverb has been loan translated into other languages and is extremely popular as a loving tribute to our four-legged friends. In fact, animals, and especially cats and dogs, continue to bring about new proverbs due to their status as beloved family members (Mieder 2020, 185–214). As would be expected, the popular proverb has led to numerous anti-proverbs, to wit:

> A dog is man's best friend, and vice versa. (1968)
> If a dog could talk, he wouldn't long remain man's best friend. (1968)
> If my dog could talk, would he still be my best friend? (1975)
> A man's best friend is his dogma. (1985)
> The remote control is man's best friend. (1996)
> The wastepaper basket is a writer's best friend. (1997)
> Outside of a dog, a book is man's best friend. Inside a dog, it's too dark
>   to read. (2000)
> (Litovkina and Mieder 2006, 59–60)

None of these anti-proverbs have attained proverbial status, but perhaps "A book is man's (woman's) best friend" might make it to a new modern proverb one day—at least among happy readers like my wife and me. Realizing that metaphorical proverbs could be defined as "verbal images" (Mieder 2004b, 148–50), it is only natural that artists from the Middle Ages to the present day have illustrated them in woodcuts, emblems, and oil paintings, including Pieter Bruegel's famous *Netherlandish Proverbs* from 1559 (Dundes and Stibbe 1981; Mieder 2004a). This proverb iconography also includes sculptures, plaques, pottery, and, to be sure, the whole media world of broadsheets, caricatures, cartoons, and comic strips (Mieder and Sobieski 1999). In my International Proverb Archives, which I have built during the past fifty years at the University of Vermont, there are three cartoons that might serve as examples:

> "I find it increasingly difficult to remain man's best friend."
> *New Yorker*, February 22, 1988, 96.

> "Glen, I'm not just your editor. I'm also your best friend, and I'm telling you, lose the cat."
> *New Yorker*, November 26, 2018, 42.

> "They say that dogs are man's best friend, but I've always said that man is dog's fourth-favorite food."
> *New Yorker*, November 25, 2019, 59.

Another *New Yorker* cartoon, which has generated its own Wikipedia page, has the caption "On the Internet, nobody knows you're a dog" (July 5, 1993). But the "dog" proverb has also led to an anti-proverb that has become a proverb albeit a somewhat antifeminist one: "A diamond is a girl's best friend" and its plural variant "Diamonds are a girl's best friend" (*DMP* 55). It originated in 1949 with the title and refrain of a song by Leo Robin, famously sung by Marilyn Monroe in the film *Gentlemen Prefer Blondes* (1953):

> The French are glad to die for love
> They delight in fighting duels
> But I prefer a man who lives
> And gives expensive jewels
> A kiss on the hand
> May be quite continental
> But diamonds are a girl's best friend.

With the glamour of Marilyn Monroe and the popularity of the film, thousands came in touch with the invented anti-proverb of the song, which caught on to such a degree that it counts as a modern proverb. And there is one more interesting "friend-dog" proverb, namely, "If you want a friend, get (buy) a dog" (1941). Here is what we say in our *Dictionary of Modern Proverbs* about it: "The proverb alludes to the old saying 'A dog is man's best friend.' It usually suggests that, in some particular hostile or competitive setting (Hollywood, Washington DC, Wall Street), a dog will be the *only* friend that a person can hope to find—and that (human) friendship itself is a quality not only improbable but even undesirable" (*DMP* 86–87).

Many other friendship proverbs from the nineteenth century or earlier could be discussed here, but it must suffice to mention just a few of the most popular ones out of the *Dictionary of American Proverbs* (Mieder, Kingsbury, and Harder 1992, 233–40) as a contrast to modern proverbs with that theme:

Old friends are best. (1565)
Don't trade old friends for new. (1575)
A good friend is a great treasure. (1580)
A friend is not so soon gotten as lost. (1599)
The best of friends must part. (1602)
They are rich who have friends. (1608)
When a friend asks, there is no tomorrow. (1611)
A friend to all is a friend to none. (1623)
A good friend never offends. (1659)
A friend in the market is better than money in the purse. (1664)
Friends are to be preferred to relatives. (1732)
Be slow in choosing a friend, but slower in changing him. (1735)
The way to gain a friend is to be one. (1841)

The last two texts are first found in Benjamin Franklin's and Ralph Waldo Emerson's works, respectively, both of whom employed proverbs frequently and coined some of them (Barbour 1974; Mieder 1989). But it is the proverb "A friend is a (very) precious gift" from the early nineteenth century that might be singled out here as a heartwarming and humane piece of folk wisdom. The great former slave, later abolitionist, and towering human rights champion Frederick Douglass (1818–1896), friend of President Abraham Lincoln and his equal in rhetorical prowess, employed it in a speech of January 5, 1854:

The term friend is a delightful one, filled with a thousand sweet harmonies. In journeying through this vale of tears, life is desolate indeed, if unblest by friendship. A friend is a very precious gift. A brother is not always a friend—a sister is not always a friend, and even a wife may not always be a friend, nor a husband always a friend. The central idea of friendship, and the main pillar of it is *trust*. Where there is no *trust*, there is no friendship. We cannot love those whom we cannot trust. The basis of all *trust* is truth. There cannot be trust—lasting trust—where the truth is not. Men must be true to each other, or they cannot trust each other. (Mieder 2001, 231)

Friends are indeed special gifts, and so are proverbs about them! Among the almost two hundred texts listed under the keyword "friend" in *A Dictionary of American Proverbs* are many for which we could not find any references in other proverb collections. They were collected during field research under the direction of Margaret M. Bryant of the American Dialect Society between the years 1945 and 1985 from people throughout the United States and Canada (Bryant 1945). Stewart Kingsbury, Kelsie Harder, and I inherited the files in the mid-1980s, amounting to about 250,000 (!) slips of paper. It took several years to work through them, to delete nonproverbial texts, to sort variants, and so on. The uniqueness of the published collection is therefore the fact that the proverbs were collected and not copied from written sources. Since the slips also included the geographical location of the person writing the proverb down, we were able to attach distribution areas by state after each text. Texts that only appeared once or a couple of times on the slips were not included, since we wanted to make sure that they had actual currency among the folk. What we could not do was use the various databases available now to establish dates of origin. Often, that might not have been possible in any case since they might have been current only regionally or even just locally. To be sure, I could now check each text on the internet to see what might be found. More importantly, I am mentioning all of this to point out that proverb scholars should do more field research! There are many proverbs, especially modern ones, that have never been recorded, and we should not restrict our paremiographical work only to written sources. In any case, here are a few proverbs of the structure "A friend . . ." that were identified by way of field research procedures:

A friend at hand is better than a relative at a distance.
A friend in power is a friend lost.
A friend is a present you give yourself.
A friend is easier lost than found.
    (I have now found this in a written source from 1889.)
A friend is not known until he is lost.
A friend is to be taken with his faults.
A friend married is a friend lost.
A friend whom you can buy can be bought from you.
A friend won with a feather can be lost with a straw.
(Mieder, Kingsbury, and Harder 1992, 233–34)

Additional work could now attempt to find these texts in written sources, to establish some historical dates. But more important is the fact that they have been collected at all and were included in a large proverb dictionary with over 15,000 Anglo-American proverbs and variants collected through field research in North America!

All of this leads to the last section of this chapter, namely the discovery and registration of modern proverbs. In order to prepare our *Dictionary of Modern Proverbs* and its three supplements, we culled though our own proverb archives, which we had established over many years as paremiologists, folklorists, and philologists; we relied on our own vast reading of modern literature, journals, magazines, newspapers, and websites; and we solicited help from relatives, friends, colleagues, and above all our students. Recalling the collecting effort of the American Dialect Society, we could now also use questionnaires that we could distribute electronically! Each newly discovered text needs to be researched to see whether it in fact qualifies as a new proverb. If certain standard proverbial markers such as alliteration, rhyme, parallelism, metaphor, and some apparent truth are present, that is a good start. But many modern proverbs are straightforward indicative sentences without a metaphor. Database work will help to find references in print and to establish at least some currency over time, and usually we will also discover that the identified proverb exists in variants that should be recorded as well.

But to return to our proverbial muttons, let me turn to a few more modern "friend" proverbs that we have identified and registered. While *A Dictionary of American Proverbs* includes twelve proverbs following the structure "Friends . . .," there is not one text that starts with the negative "Friends don't . . ." But here are two modern proverbs with that pattern stating rather directly what is not necessary or what should not be done:

> Friends don't need explanation. (1912, *DMP* 86)
>> Variant: You do not need to explain to a friend.
> Friends don't let friends drive drunk. (1976, *DMP* 86)
>> Variant: Friends don't let friends ride drunk (on motorcycles).
>> Variant: Friends don't let friends drink and drive.

In American society, where the automobile plays a dominant role, it is natural that a proverb against drunk driving would come about. It is only surprising that we have not found an earlier reference than the one from the mid-1970s.

A Dictionary of American Proverbs contains eight proverbs that deal with the question of what makes "a true friend" that have not been registered in any other proverb collection:

68 AMERICAN PROVERBS

A true friend is forever a friend.
A true friend is one that steps in when the rest of the world steps out.
A true friend is one who knows all your faults and loves you still.
> (We have now established that its earliest written reference is from
> 1917 and consequently have included it in *DMP* 87–88.)

A true friend is the wine of life.
A true friend is your second half.
A true friend loves at all times.
A true friend worries more over your success than your failure.
(Mieder, Kingsbury, and Harder 1992, 234)

As a red wine drinker, I like the proverb that a good friend is like wine! But what else can a true friend possibly be? Well, here is one more modern proverb following this pattern. Our short listing is quite revealing for this relatively recent text:

> A (true, good) friend walks in when (all) others walk out. 1994 *The Advertiser* 24 Oct.: "From Skyman in cyberspace, this thought: A true friend walks in when others walk out." 2002 Greg Laurie, *The God of Second Chance* (Wheaton IL: Tyndale House) 201: "An old adage says that a true friend walks in when others walk out." (Doyle, Mieder, and Shapiro 2012, 86)

As can be seen, we indicate that the proverb is current in a number of variants, with "A true friend walks in when others walk out" being the dominant one by now. Of interest is also the introductory formula "an old adage says," a very established way of adding authority to a cited proverb (Mieder 2004b, 132), even though in this case its first reference from 1994 hardly justifies its identification as being "old."

Many traditional proverbs are based on the contrast of two entities, and it stands to reason that there are proverbs that contrast friends with enemies. Seven of them appear in *A Dictionary of American Proverbs*:

> A man's best friend and worst enemy is himself.
> A reconciled friend is a double enemy.
> Cherish your friend, and temperately admonish your enemy.
> False friends are worse than open enemies.
> God protect me from my friends; my enemies I know enough to watch.
> Speak well of your friends; of your enemies say nothing.
> Trust not a new friend nor an old enemy.
> (Mieder, Kingsbury, and Harder 1992, 234–36, 238–39)

But here are two proverbs from the mid-1970s that add a new spin to this older wisdom about the relationship of friends and enemies.

> Your best friend might be your worst enemy. (1970, *DMP* 69)
>> Variant: Your worst enemy could be your best friend.
> Keep your friends close and (but) your enemies closer. (1974, *DMP* 87)

The second proverb is a little strange, but since it became popular by way of the motion picture *The Godfather Part II*, it might be underworld advice to be constantly aware of one's enemies. The first text, however, is of special interest since its variant exactly reverses the proverb and thus contradicts its truth value. This phenomenon of contradicting or dueling proverbs is not that rare, with the best example being the fourteenth-century proverb pair "Might makes right" (1311) and "Right makes might" (1375), which exists in German and most likely other languages as well (Mieder 2019, 263–86). In any case, the two "friend-enemy" proverbs advise cautionary behavior, as do the older ones as well.

It is always good to see how further scholarship can lead to welcome discoveries. This is the case with the proverb "Little friends may prove great friends," which is listed in *A Dictionary of American Proverbs* (Mieder, Kingsbury, and Harder 1992, 237) as having been recorded in the states of California, Indiana, and New York and also in Ontario, Canada. At the time, no written record could be found, but with new electronic research possibilities we were now able to piece together the following entry in *The Dictionary of Modern Proverbs*, which cites the year 1903 as its first occurrence in print. All of this is especially interesting since it links the proverb to a modern rendering of an Aesopian fable, with the interrelationship of proverbs and fables having a long tradition (Carnes 1988):

> Little friends may prove (become) great friends. 1903 *First Book of Song and Story*, introduction by Cynthia Westover Alden (New York: P. F. Collier & Son) 455: "Little friends may prove great friends," given as the "moral" to the Aesopic fable "The Lion and the Mouse." That text found its way into the Harvard Classics volume *Folk-lore and Fable* (New York: P. F. Collier & Son, 1909) 14. 1903 Huber Gray Buehler and Caroline Hotchkiss, *Modern English Lessons* (New York: Newson) 133 (the conclusion of the fable): "In a few moments the lion was free. 'I have learned,' said he, 'that little friends may become great friends.'" (Doyle, Mieder, and Shapiro 2012, 87)

Things are a bit similar with the proverb "If you want a friend, you will have to be one" and its variant "To have a friend, be one," listed without dates or references in *A Dictionary of American Proverbs* (Mieder, Kingsbury, and Harder 1992, 236–37). Again with the help of modern database searches, it has been found as the variant "To make a friend, be a friend" in the *Oakland Post* of January 26, 1977, and has thus been established for certain as a modern proverb (Doyle and Mieder 2018, 22). And here is yet another example: in *A Dictionary of American Proverbs* we registered the proverb "The more arguments you win, the less friends you will have," which had been recorded only in the state of Illinois (Mieder, Kingsbury, and Harder 1992, 26). But it obviously must have spread beyond that region and gained more currency, since its earliest written record has been found in an issue of *Public Relations Journal* from 1945 (*DMP* 7).

This brings these deliberations to two relatively recent proverbs from the 1980s that belong to the pecuniary worldview of American society (see Mieder 2020, 155–84): "Fast pay (payment) makes (for) fast friends" (1980, *DMP* 85–86) and "The trend is your friend" with its even shorter variant "Trend is friend" (1983, *DMP* 263). They might just be a little difficult to decipher for the uninitiated, but in the financial world they are well known. The first advises one to pay bills when due or even before in order to establish good business relations. The second text advises investors to follow the movement of the stock market.

Finally, there is the fascinating proverb "Only your friend knows your secret" (1976, *DMP* 87), which took on a life of its own from the popular song "Who the Cap Fit" on Bob Marley's reggae album *Rastaman Vibration* (1976). The title in its Jamaican English is a play on the old British proverb "If the cap fits, wear it" from 1600, with the modern proverb together with the "friend-enemy" proverb pair discussed above appearing in the song's first two stanzas:

> Man to man is so unjust, children
> You don't know who to trust
> Your worst enemy could be your best friend
> And your best friend, your worst enemy
>
> Some will eat and drink with you
> Then behind them su-su 'pon you
> Only your friend know[s] your secrets
> So only he could reveal it

"Spoon" refers to two people cuddling each other facing the same direction, mimicking the position of spoons stacked in a cutlery drawer. The proverb pair in the first stanza together with the proverb "Only your friend knows your secret" in the second underscore the message of the second line that one doesn't know whom one can trust. In other words, the friend who knows one's secret might well be the person who will betray the friend. The proverb is then another cautionary saying, somewhat along the lines of yet another modern proverb, "Trust but verify" (1966, *DMP* 264), the Khrushchevian motto "dovierat no provierat" that belatedly has often been attributed to Ronald Reagan, who in turn stated that he learned it from Mikhail Gorbachev. Be that as it may, there is no doubt that old, modern, and anti-proverbs about friends will continue to play a significant role as sapiential insights into human relationships.

BIBLIOGRAPHY

This chapter was first published with the same title in *Frazeologicheskie edinitsy: Semantika, pragmatika, lingvokul'turologiia*, edited by Tatiana A. Shiriaeva, Anatolii P. Vasilenko, and Wolfgang Mieder (Moscow: Akademiia Estestvoznaniia, 2022), 132–46.

Abrahams, Roger D. 1970. "Such Matters as Every Man Should Know, and Descant Upon." *Proverbium* (Helsinki) 15: 425–27.

Barbour, Frances M. 1974. *A Concordance to the Sayings in Franklin's "Poor Richard."* Detroit: Gale Research Company.

Bryant, Margaret M. 1945. *Proverbs and How to Collect Them.* Greensboro, NC: American Dialect Society.

Carnes, Pack. 1988. *Proverbia in Fabula: Essays on the Relationship of the Fable and the Proverb.* Bern: Peter Lang.

Cheales, Alan B. 1874. *Proverbial Folk-Lore.* London: Simpkin, Marshall and Company. Rpt., Folcroft, PA: Folcroft Library Editions, 1976.

Cordry, Harold V. 1997. *The Multicultural Dictionary of Proverbs.* Jefferson, NC: McFarland.

Doyle, Charles Clay, and Wolfgang Mieder. 2016. "*The Dictionary of Modern Proverbs*: A Supplement." *Proverbium* 33: 85–120.

Doyle, Charles Clay, and Wolfgang Mieder. 2018. "*The Dictionary of Modern Proverbs*: Second Supplement." *Proverbium* 35: 15–44.

Doyle, Charles Clay, and Wolfgang Mieder. 2020. "*The Dictionary of Modern Proverbs*: Third Supplement." *Proverbium* 37: 53–86.

Doyle, Charles Clay, Wolfgang Mieder, and Fred R. Shapiro. 2012. *The Dictionary of Modern Proverbs.* New Haven, CT: Yale University Press.

Dundes, Alan, and Claudia A. Stibbe. 1981. *The Art of Mixing Metaphors: A Folkloristic Interpretation of the "Netherlandish Proverbs" by Pieter Bruegel the Elder.* Helsinki: Suomalainen Tiedeakatemia.

Gluski, Jerzy. 1971. *A Comparative Book of English, French, German, Italian, Spanish and Russian Proverbs with a Latin Appendix.* Amsterdam: Elsevier.

Haas, Heather A. 2008. "Proverb Familiarity in the United States: Cross-Regional Comparisons of the Paremiological Minimum." *Journal of American Folklore* 121, no. 481 (Summer): 319–47.

Kirshenblatt-Gimblett, Barbara. 1973. "Toward a Theory of Proverb Meaning." *Proverbium* (Helsinki) 22: 821–27. Also in *The Wisdom of Many: Essays on the Proverb*, edited by

Wolfgang Mieder and Alan Dundes, 111–21. New York: Garland Publishing, 1981. Rpt., Madison: University of Wisconsin Press, 1994.

Litovkina, Anna T., and Wolfgang Mieder. 2006. *Old Proverbs Never Die, They Just Diversify: A Collection of Anti-Proverbs*. Burlington: University of Vermont; Veszprém, Hungary: University of Pannonia.

Mieder, Wolfgang. 1986. *The Prentice-Hall Encyclopedia of World Proverbs: A Treasury of Wit and Wisdom Through the Ages*. Englewood Cliffs, NJ: Prentice-Hall.

Mieder, Wolfgang, ed. 1987. *Proverbium, 1 (1965)–25 (1975)*. Edited by Matti Kuusi et al. 2 vols. Bern: Peter Lang.

Mieder, Wolfgang. 1989. *American Proverbs: A Study of Texts and Contexts*. Bern: Peter Lang.

Mieder, Wolfgang. 2001. *"No Struggle, No Progress": Frederick Douglass and His Proverbial Rhetoric for Civil Rights*. New York: Peter Lang.

Mieder, Wolfgang, ed. 2004a. *The Netherlandish Proverbs: An International Symposium on the Pieter Brueg(h)els*. Burlington: University of Vermont.

Mieder, Wolfgang. 2004b. *Proverbs: A Handbook*. Westport, CT: Greenwood Press. Rpt., New York: Peter Lang, 2012.

Mieder, Wolfgang. 2011. *International Bibliography of Paremiography: Collections of Proverbs, Proverbial Expressions and Comparisons, Quotations, Graffiti, Slang, and Wellerisms*. Burlington: University of Vermont.

Mieder, Wolfgang. 2019. *"Right Makes Might": Proverbs and the American Worldview*. Bloomington: Indiana University Press.

Mieder, Wolfgang. 2020. *The Worldview of Modern American Proverbs*. New York: Peter Lang.

Mieder, Wolfgang, Stewart A. Kingsbury, and Kelsie B. Harder. 1992. *A Dictionary of American Proverbs*. New York: Oxford University Press.

Mieder, Wolfgang, and Janet Sobieski. 1999. *Proverb Iconography: An International Bibliography*. New York: Peter Lang.

Paczolay, Gyula. 1997. *European Proverbs in 55 Languages with Equivalents in Arabic, Persian, Sanskrit, Chinese and Japanese*. Veszprém, Hungary: Veszprémi Nyomda.

Röhrich, Lutz, and Wolfgang Mieder. 1977. *Sprichwort*. Stuttgart: J. B. Metzler.

Rosen, Henry. 2020. *Vox Populi: Proverbs and Sayings; A Comparative Collection of English, French, Spanish, Portuguese, German, Italian, Romanian, Esperanto, Latin, Russian, Yiddish and Hebrew Proverbs*. Columbus, OH: Gatekeeper Press.

Speake, Jennifer. 2015. *Oxford Dictionary of Proverbs*. 6th ed. Oxford: Oxford University Press.

Stone, Jon R. 2006. *The Routledge Book of World Proverbs*. New York: Routledge.

Strauss, Emanuel. 1994. *Dictionary of European Proverbs*. 3 vols. Abingdon, Oxon., England: Routledge.

4

"FREEDOM IS NOT GIVEN, IT IS WON"

Democratic Principles in Modern American Proverbs

There are a number of older proverbs that belong to the American political worldview. It so happens that several of them are attributed to Abraham Lincoln, the country's most revered and quite proverbial president (Mieder 2000). Before the Civil War, he made the biblical proverb "A house divided against itself cannot stand" (Mark 3:25) a slogan in his plea to keep the young union intact (Mieder 2005, 90–117). When he ran for reelection, he employed the proverb "Don't change horses in midstream" on June 4, 1864, as an argument for staying in office, but it has been found in print as early as 1834 (Mieder 2008, 205–50). And there is also the lengthy, tongue-twisting proverb "You can fool all of the people some of the time; you can fool some of the people all of the time; but you can't fool all of the people all of the time," which the witty president is supposed to have uttered during the late 1850s. However, the earliest published record of this proverb dates from 1887, with many humorous anti-proverbs having followed ever since (Litovkina and Mieder 2006, 340–41; Litovkina 2013, 99–100; Litovkina 2015). And more importantly, there is the proverbial triad "Government of the people, by the people, and for the people," with some slightly different precursors. Most significant is clearly the rendering with the emphasis on "all" by the abolitionist Theodore Parker from May 29, 1850: "Government of all the people, by all the people, for all the people." President Lincoln cited it at the end of his famous Gettysburg Address of November 19, 1863: "Government of the people, by the people, for the people, shall not perish from the earth." He unfortunately dropped the all-inclusiveness from his statement, realizing that the country was by far not ready to include African American men, let alone women, in the political process (Mieder 2005, 15–55). But just the same, his variant represents perhaps the best short definition of democracy!

Even though Archer Taylor, the doyen of international paremiology, argued already in his classic study *The Proverb* (1931) that "all ascriptions [of proverbs] to definite persons must be looked at with suspicion" (38), it remains a fact that Lincoln's name will remain affixed to these proverbs. A more modern case is President Harry S. Truman's repeated use of the proverb "The buck stops here" (Doyle, Mieder, and Shapiro 2012, 28; hereafter *DMP*, for references to *The Dictionary of Modern Proverbs*), of which he had a sign on his desk, as most Americans know, to remind him since 1945 that as president following the sudden death of Franklin Delano Roosevelt he carried the ultimate responsibility for major government decisions. As one of the most proverbial American presidents (Mieder and Bryan 1997), Truman referred to this sign in two speeches in the early 1950s. His utterance of the proverb (here cited as the proverbial phrase "to pass the buck") during a speech on October 14, 1948, stands out, since he employed it as an answer to the omnipresent question of why he decided to drop the atomic bomb at the end of World War II:

> As President of the United States, I had the fateful responsibility of deciding whether or not to use this weapon for the first time. It was the hardest decision that I ever had to make. But the President cannot duck hard problems—he cannot pass the buck. [. . .] I decided that the bomb should be used in order to end the war quickly and save countless lives—Japanese as well as American. But I resolved then and there to do everything I could to see that this awesome discovery was turned into a force for peace and the advancement of mankind. (Mieder 1997, 96–97)

More often than not, this proverb, with its earliest appearance in print in 1942, is stated with the introductory formula "as Truman said," ensuring that his name will remain attached to it, even though he most certainly did not originate it.

Things are much more straightforward with President Theodore Roosevelt's imperialistic proverb "Speak softly and carry a big stick," which he coined in a letter of January 26, 1900: "I have always been fond of the West African proverb: 'Speak softly and carry a big stick; you will go far'" (*DMP* 238). On several later occasions Roosevelt repeated the proverb, without the last clause and without the West African ascription. Not having found the proverb in numerous African proverb collections, we must assume that Roosevelt, who had traveled to Africa, added the ascription to add clout to his invention. It, too, is often used with Roosevelt's name attached to it, varying the first verb with "talk" or "walk," expressing a controlling mentality or worldview (Dundes 1972; Hakamies 2002; Mieder 2004, 137–39). A quarter century later, President Calvin Coolidge said on January 18, 1925: "After all, the chief business of the American people is business." He repeated it shortly before the beginning of the Great Depression on August 28, 1928, in a slightly varied formulation, as "The business of America is business" (*DMP* 30), which quickly became proverbial.

DEMOCRATIC PRINCIPLES IN MODERN AMERICAN PROVERBS   75

The next president who came up with a memorable statement was John F. Kennedy, who in his inaugural address on January 20, 1960, uttered the following words with enthusiastic vigor: "Ask not what your country can do for you, ask what you can do for your country" (*DMP* 45–46). He most likely had help from his sophisticated speechwriter, Theodore C. Sorensen, who might have based the statement on a remark by Oliver Wendell Holmes Jr. of May 30, 1884: "It is now the moment [. . .] to recall what our country has done for each of us, and to ask ourselves what we can do for our country in return" (Mieder 2005, 172–73). Just the same, Kennedy coined the proverbial motto as it is known today. However, his father, Joseph P. Kennedy, did not invent the popular "When the going gets tough, the tough get going" (*DMP* 106), yet another proverbial slogan for energetic action. It has been attributed to him since about 1960, after having its start with the football coach Frank Leahy in 1954. Such motivating phrases bring to mind the modern proverbs "Push, pull, or get out of the way" (1909, *DMP* 273) and "Lead, follow, or get out of the way" (1912, *DMP* 273), which were not picked up by the presidents. That leaves the modern Russian proverb "Trust but verify" (*DMP* 264), which appeared in English translation in 1966 and was quoted by President Ronald Reagan at a campaign rally in Springfield, Missouri, on October 23, 1986 (Shapiro 2021, 676). It continues to be attributed to Reagan, even though he stated that he had learned it from Mikhail Gorbachev. And President Donald Trump? Nothing at all from him, as his talks and Twitter messages are basically void of metaphorical language. But there is the relatively new proverb "Love trumps hate" (Doyle and Mieder 2018, 30–31) from 1996, which has acquired a special satiric application in light of "Trump" as a menacing political phenomenon.

With this, a phase of American politics with its intricacies has been reached for which the nineteenth-century proverb "Politics makes strange bedfellows" (1832; Shapiro 2021, 662) is the appropriate descriptor, which originally might well have been an anti-proverb of "Misery makes strange bedfellows" from the seventeenth century, which in turn probably goes back to Shakespeare's "Misery acquaints a man with strange bedfellows" from *The Tempest* (1611; Mieder, Kingsbury, and Harder 1992, 413, 472). This old proverb is as popular today as ever, but of much greater significance for a democracy is the relatively recent proverb "Politics is not a spectator sport," from Nelson Rockefeller's statement on November 17, 1963: "And I think we would arouse a lot of participation on the part of the public. Politics is not a spectator sport. We need public participation" (*DMP* 113). It is possible that Rockefeller based his remark on the slightly earlier "Life is not a spectator sport. We are all on the team" (1958, *DMP* 143), which shows that the "spectator sport" metaphor alludes to the ever-present world of sports. As if to prove this obvious point, there is the proverb "Politics is a contact sport" (1960, *DMP* 203), expressing that it takes serious involvement to make democracy work. Frederick Douglass, the renowned former slave and abolitionist, clearly had this in mind when he uttered the proverbial words "No struggle, no progress" (Mieder 2021a, 172) during one of his memorable antislavery speeches on August 3, 1857:

> The whole history of the progress of human liberty shows that all concessions yet made to her august claims, have been born of earnest struggle. The conflict has been exciting, agitating, all-absorbing, and for the time being, putting all other tumults to silence. It must do this or it does nothing. If there is no struggle, there is no progress. Those who profess to favor freedom and yet depreciate agitation, are men who want crops without plowing up the ground, they want rain without thunder and lightning. They want the ocean without the awful roar of its many waters. This struggle may be a moral one, or it may be a physical one, and it may be both moral and physical, but it must be a struggle. Power concedes nothing without a demand. It never did and it never will. (Mieder 2001, 456–57)

It should be noted that "Power concedes nothing without a demand" (Mieder 2021a, 149) has also become proverbial—and it is quite an accomplishment by Douglass, in rhetorical prowess Lincoln's equal, to create two proverbs within a short paragraph!

Yet this moral high road is clearly lacking in the more pragmatic proverbs from the modern world of American politics. Thus, the proverb "In politics a man must learn to rise above principle" (1927, *DMP* 202–3) seems to argue that in certain situations politicians have to push ethics aside to gain the upper hand. This probably applies especially to political campaigns, with their aggressive and at times questionable tactics. Of course, such behavior and also the fair play in politics are subject to the vicissitudes of political life, which are fittingly expressed in the proverb "A week is a long time in politics" (1961, *DMP* 274). This has been attributed to former British prime minister Harold Wilson, but he appears not to have used it until several years after its first appearance in the *New York Times* of December 3, 1961. How much the media influences politics especially during important election campaigns is tellingly expressed in the proverb "In politics perception is reality" (1975, *DMP* 203). That is not exactly a very uplifting piece of wisdom, but there is plenty of truth to it. Maybe the proverb "(All) Politics is local" (1905, *DMP* 203) puts a more positive spin on the matter, since events are more easily controlled on a regional level. The proverb has come to be associated with the popular Massachusetts congressman Thomas P. "Tip" O'Neill Jr., who was known for his straight-shooting politics. Of course, there is also the proverb "You can't fight city hall" (1933, *DMP* 40), indicating that local politics can also go awry. But the proverb can also be interpreted more broadly in that "city hall" can stand for any controlling organization. Informed voters make democracy function properly, and in this regard the proverb "Signs don't vote" (1981, *DMP* 231) is a solid piece of folk wisdom against voter coercion, arguing that campaign signs posted on roadsides and front yards do not vote, but people do! Finally, there is the proverb "The personal is political" (1970, *DMP* 196) and its anti-proverb "The political is personal" (1975, *DMP* 202), which are often cited in tandem as a chiasmus, indicating how intertwined the individual is or should be with the political process in a democratic society.

The mention of local proverbs brings to mind a few modern texts that refer to specific states. Unfortunately, there is the negative stereotype "Thank God for Mississippi" (1929). That southern state has the misfortune of being one of the poorest and most underprivileged in the United States, as can be seen from these three references:

> 1929: "They used to say whenever a list of illiteracy according to States was published, in which North Carolina ranged next to the bottom, 'Thank God for Mississippi.'"
>
> 1947: "'Thank God for Mississippi' was a favorite expression formerly used by some educators in Florida, the thanks being due to the fact that Mississippi kept Florida from being at the bottom of the education system in the United States by occupying that lowly position itself."
>
> 1976: "'Thank God for Mississippi,' they say up North, meaning that no matter how bad things get up there, there's at least one place that's worse." (Doyle and Mieder 2016, 100–101)

The invective is still heard today, and it is an indication of the still lingering feeling of superiority of the northern states toward the Deep South. And it should be noted that within states, for example my state of Vermont, such local stereotypes also exist, for example "Thank God for Winooski," by which other low-income towns like Milton, Vermont, claim that they are not at the very bottom because things are even worse in Winooski. Such unkind and prejudiced proverbs die hard, and it behooves people to avoid using them.

As is well known, the large state of Texas considers itself to be a special powerhouse and enjoys playing out its trump card with the proverbial slogan "Don't mess with Texas" (1985, *DMP* 251). It started as a slogan in a campaign for a clean environment, but it was reinterpreted as a somewhat belligerent declaration of state pride and can also be cited to refer to the insistence on the part of Texans that outsiders not raise problematic issues affecting their state. This somewhat obnoxious self-promotion is also expressed in the proverb "You can take the man out of Texas, but you can't take Texas out of the man" (1944, *DMP* 162), which is an adaptation of the considerably older proverb "You can take the man (a boy) out of the country, but you can't take the country out of the man (a boy)" (Mieder, Kingsbury, and Harder 1992, 119). Of special interest also are three proverbs that express how the political decisions of one state affect another. An early proverb is "As Maine goes, so goes the union" from around 1840, which was changed to "As Maine goes, so goes Vermont" (Shapiro 2021, 263) during Franklin D. Roosevelt's first reelection of November 4, 1936, since only these two states did not vote for him that year. With Pennsylvania gaining more importance nationally in the late 1850s, the variant "As Pennsylvania goes, so goes the union" took hold on the political scene. But since California dominates the United States as an economic power and a trendsetter in modern life, it comes as no surprise that the modern proverb "As California goes, so goes the nation" (1940, *DMP* 32) appeared on the horizon shortly after the beginning of World War II. Finally then, there is the quite new proverb "What happens (goes on) in Las Vegas stays at Las Vegas" (2002, *DMP* 137; Bock 2014). It started as an advertising slogan as described on November 25, 2002, in the *Las Vegas Review-Journal* to lure visitors to the infamous casinos of that city:

> The Las Vegas Visitors and Convention Authority, meanwhile, continued its saucy come-to-Vegas-baby advertising campaign with six new spots filmed over a three-day period last week. Depicting the theme "what happens in Las Vegas stays in Las Vegas," the national commercials, produced by Hungry Man Productions, feature Vegas visitors indulging in fantasies in locations ranging from a limousine to a tattoo parlor.

By now, the structure underlying the slogan-turned-proverb has produced many anti-proverbs, for example "What happens at home, stays at home," or more generally "What happens in the group (at the meeting, in the bar) stays . . ." Actually, the original proverb has become the proverbial structure "What happens at X, stays at X," and there is literally no limit to creating ever-new variants; it might well be that one of them can eventually become a new proverb (Doyle 1996).

Speaking of cities or even just towns, there is the heart-warming proverb "Small town, big heart" (1982; Doyle and Mieder 2016, 118). Since I live in the small town of Williston in Vermont, I feel there is some basic truth to this observation, even though the anti-proverb "Small town, big ears" puts a negative spin on it all by referring to the fact that people will too often listen to gossip and rumors. In any case, it must not be forgotten that the United States does not consist only of major, large cities known throughout the world but rather of many average-sized cities, small towns, villages, and hamlets of but a few families. This leads to the insightful proverb "It takes a (whole) village to raise a child" (1981, *DMP* 268). This is not of African origin, as has often been claimed, but had its start with the African American author Toni Morrison during the early 1980s (Speake 2008, 336; Mieder 2014b, 201–3). It was popularized by way of former US senator and secretary of state Hillary Rodham Clinton's book *It Takes a Village, and Other Lessons Children Teach Us* (1996), with the first chapter being titled "It Takes a Village" and including the following comments:

> Children exist in the world as well as in the family. From the moment they are born, they depend on a host of other "grown-ups"—grandparents, neighbors, teachers, ministers, employers, political leaders and untold others who touch their lives directly and indirectly. Adults police their streets, monitor the quality of their food, air, and water, produce the programs that appear on their television, run the businesses that employ their parents, and write the laws that protect them. Each of us plays a part in every child's life: It takes a village to raise a child. (Mieder 2019, 214–17)

In a way, the proverb "Think globally, act locally" (1942, *DMP* 256) relates to these thoughts. Having originated in the early 1940s, it is older than one might have expected. Also current in the still shorter variant "Think global, act local," it has gained international distribution in English and loan translations due to globalization and an ever more interconnected world with people being concerned about migration, the environment, natural resources, and quality of life in general. The world and certainly America face an ever-increasing gap between the rich and the poor, leading the socially conscious US senator from Vermont Bernie Sanders to state:

> Let's take a hard look at some of America's major problems: While the rich get richer, almost everyone else gets poorer; the standard of living of most Americans is in decline; democracy is in crisis, and oligarchy looms; what we know is determined by the corporate media; our health care system is in shambles; our educational system is facing a crisis. (Mieder 2019, 236)

There is still hope that the American proverb "The rich get richer, and the poor get poorer" from the early 1840s and more recently popularized by Sanders will one day be invalidated (Mieder 2019, 235–39). In the meantime, most Americans, with their generally positive worldview expressed in numerous modern proverbs (Mieder 2020; Mieder 2021b), might well respond to Sanders with the proverb "Never (Don't) sell America short" (1922, *DMP* 5–6) or even the jingoistic proverbial slogan "Love it [America] or leave it" (1901, *DMP* 152). This type of nationalistic viewpoint comes to the fore whenever there is a political or economic crisis. In addition, it is also coupled with the claim that the United States is simply an exceptional country in all respects. Unfortunately, there often is the insistence that America is the best, and the rest of the world is a few notches below. A proverb that expresses this viewpoint in a number of variants is "When the United States (the U.S., America, Wall Street, etc.) sneezes, the world catches (a) cold (pneumonia)." It is interesting to note that the earliest reference to this proverb found actually contradicts the America-centeredness: "It was once said that 'when the United States sneezes, the world catches pneumonia.' A more fitting expression would perhaps be that 'the world is like the human body; if a part aches, the rest will feel it" (1977; Doyle and Mieder 2020, 84). In any case, the proverb appears primarily in financial contexts, and it is noteworthy that quite a few modern American proverbs relate to monetary matters, as I have shown in my study "'Money Makes the World Go Round': The Pecuniary Worldview of Modern American Proverbs" (Mieder 2020, 155–84). Capitalist society is reflected in such proverbs as "Another day, another dollar" (1907, *DMP* 50), "You can only spend a dollar (spend money, spend earnings) once" (1913, *DMP* 60), and "A dollar in the bank is worth two in the hand" (1904, *DMP* 59), with the latter having originated as an anti-proverb based on the fifteenth-century English proverb "A bird in the hand is worth two in the bush," which has been known since the Middle Ages in most European languages (Paczolay 1997, 194–202). Nevertheless, speaking of capitalism, there is the corporate proverb "What is good for General Motors is good for America (the country)" (1953, *DMP* 95). This had its start as a misquotation of testimony that Charles E. Wilson, former president of General Motors, gave at a US Senate hearing: "For years I thought what was good for the country was good for General Motors, and vice versa. The difference did not exist." In its later use, the proverb usually satirizes the idea that the flourishing of large corporations is related in a positive way to the well-being of the county and its population.

A similar concept is expressed in the newer proverb "What's good for Main Street is good for Wall Street" (1995; Doyle and Mieder 2016, 107), which sometimes is expanded to "What's good for Main Street is good for Wall Street is good for America" (1995; Doyle and Mieder 2016, 118–19). Money managers and hedge fund investors came up with the reversal of this proverb emphasizing the importance of the financial world: "What's good for Wall Street is good for Main Street." The variant "If it's good for Wall Street, it's good for Main Street" seems to argue even more strongly that the well-being of the population is dependent on the success of the financial markets. But is this really true, or, to speak with Bernie Sanders one more time, are the rich getting richer and the poor poorer? Barack Obama used both proverbs repeatedly during speeches as he campaigned for the presidency. On November 24, 2008, in Chicago, now already as president, he paraphrased the first proverb in emphasizing the need for a joint effort by members of both streets to stand on solid and fair financial footing: "Even as we are doing whatever's required to stabilize the financial system [. . .] we [must] also recognize that a strong Main Street will reinforce and help a strong Wall Street, and [. . .] we can't separate those two things" (Mieder 2009, 259). And in the same speech, he also alluded to the second proverb, stressing once again the need for people of both streets to work hand in glove for the benefit of all: "I've sought leaders who [. . .] share my fundamental belief that we cannot have a thriving Wall Street without a thriving Main Street; that in this country, we rise and fall as one nation, as one people" (Mieder 2009, 334). What a delight to reread these words of the remarkable President Barack Obama, whose uplifting sociopolitical and humane ideals are expressed so convincingly in his book with the appropriate title *The Audacity of Hope: Thoughts on Reclaiming the American Dream* (2006). It is there where he stated: "There are some things I'm absolutely sure about—the Golden Rule, the need to battle cruelty in all its forms, the value of love and charity, humility and grace" (224). Indeed, an adherence to the golden rule "Do unto others as you would have them do unto you" (Matthew 7:12), which appears in all the major religions of the world, should be the foundation of all human interaction and should guide us to a better world for everybody. Here are President Obama's unforgettable words, spoken on June 4, 2009, in front of thousands of students at Cairo University in Egypt:

> It's easier to start wars than to end them. It's easier to blame others than to look inward. It's easier to see what is different about someone than to find the things we share. But we should choose the right path, not just the easy path. There's one rule that lies at the heart of every religion— that we do unto others as we would have them do to us. This truth transcends nations and peoples—a belief that isn't new; that isn't black or white or brown; that isn't Christian or Muslim or Jew. It's a belief that pulsed in the cradle of civilization, and that still beats in the hearts of billions around the world. It's a faith in other people, and it's what brought me here today. (Mieder 2014b, 193)

Many American presidents have cited this humane rule, but, not at all surprising, it has not been heard from Donald Trump.

In a world that is plagued by wars, terrorism, and ill-suited leaders, it is difficult at times to keep up Obama's high spirit. The modern American proverb "One man's terrorist is another man's freedom fighter" and its reversal "One man's freedom fighter is another man's terrorist" (1970, *DMP* 162), originally anti-proverbs of the sixteenth-century proverb "One man's meat is another man's poison" (Mieder, Kingsbury, and Harder 1992, 408; Litovkina and Mieder 2006, 250–51), illustrate the complex power struggles that overshadow valiant attempts at making sure that we are our bothers' and sisters' keepers (Genesis 4:9), as Obama stressed repeatedly (Mieder 2009, 180–81). Of course, this presumes a willingness to see where change and improvement are necessary and then to act upon such recognition. This is well expressed in the interesting proverb "Seeing is freeing" (1942, *DMP* 225), which clearly had its start as an anti-proverb of "Seeing is believing" from the early seventeenth century (Mieder, Kingsbury, and Harder 1992, 530). It appeared as a headline of a short article in the *Washington Post* of May 2, 1942: "Seeing is freeing: Before Pearl Harbor, Ray and Robert Graham, twins, tried to join the Navy to 'see the world.' [. . .] On their seventeenth birthday, the twins returned. 'This time we want to help free, not just see, the world,' they chorused." This brings to mind the proverb "Eternal vigilance (by the people) is the price of liberty" (Mieder 2021a, 188), which was coined by President Andrew Jackson in his farewell speech of March 4, 1837. It is also current in the variant "Eternal vigilance is the price of freedom" (Mieder, Kingsbury, and Harder 1992, 232), and it is four modern American "freedom" proverbs that will bring these deliberations to a conclusion.

There is first of all the proverb "Freedom is not free" (1943, *DMP* 85), which had its start as an explicit advertisement for war bonds in the midst of World War II: "Freedom is not free—It is priceless." A few months later, the *New York Times* of September 23, 1943, printed a similar call for the purchase of war bonds: "Freedom is not free. We must fight for it." These calls for financial support of the war effort and a call to arms for freedom are today lost in the employment of the short proverb "Freedom is not free," which signifies rather generally that freedom has a price of engagement, commitment, and belief in democracy. The proverb "Freedom is not for sale" (1949, *DMP* 85) and its older wording "Freedom cannot be bought" expressing the same idea as early as 1830 contain the message that money is not or should not be the determining factor in a free and democratic society. While this uplifting proverb has gained general currency, this is not so much the case with the rather depressing proverb "Freedom's just another word for nothing left to lose" (1969, *DMP* 85), which stems from the song "Me and Bobby McGee" by Kris Kristofferson and Fred Foster: "Freedom's just another word for nothin' left to lose, / Nothin' ain't worth nothin', but it's free" (Shapiro 2021, 464).

Three African American voices have perhaps expressed best what the eternal struggle for freedom entails. In the nineteenth century, Frederick Douglass, as a freed slave, repeated his claims that "Who would be free themselves must strike the blow" and "Better die free, than to live slaves" numerous times during his long life to call for the freedom of all people. Here is but one example from a speech of March 21, 1863:

> Action! Action! not criticism, is the plain duty of this hour. Words are now useful only as they stimulate to blows. The office of speech now is only to point out when, where, and how to strike to the best advantage. There is no time to delay. The tide is at its flood that leads on to fortune. From East to West, from North to South, the sky is written all over: "Now or never." Liberty won by the white men would lose half its luster. "Who would be free themselves must strike the blow." "Better even die free, than to live slaves." This is the sentiment of every brave colored man amongst us. (Mieder 2001, 230)

This somewhat belligerent outburst does not mean that Douglass took up arms as a violent revolutionary. His weapon remained his voice, which led to friendships with Abraham Lincoln and the two early American feminists Elizabeth Cady Stanton and Susan B. Anthony (Mieder 2014a), who like Douglass all used proverbs and proverbial expressions to add expressiveness to their political agitation.

No wonder that later civil rights champions took rhetorical lessons from them. A. Philip Randolph, African American compatriot of Martin Luther King Jr., is generally credited with having coined the proverb "Freedom is never granted: it is won" in his speech "A Vision of Freedom," delivered on his eightieth birthday on April 15, 1969, in New York:

> Salvation for the Negro masses must come from within. Freedom is never granted: it is won. Justice is never given: it is exacted. But in our struggle we must draw for strength upon something that transcends the boundaries of race. We must draw for strength upon the capacity of human beings to act with humanity towards one another. (Summerville 2020, 305)

However, Martin Luther King Jr., known for his proverbial prowess, had actually written less than two years earlier "Freedom is not given, it is won" in his book *Where Do We Go from Here: Chaos or Community?* (1967, 19; Mieder 2010, 313; Mieder 2021a, 88), a widely distributed book that Randolph most assuredly had read. Clearly King coined the proverb, with Randolph as his comrade and friend in the struggle for freedom throughout America helping to spread the good word. In any case, the prophetic voice of Martin Luther King Jr., who popularized the proverb "God can make a way out of no way" and its secular variant "Making a way out of no way" (Mieder 2010, 171–86; Mieder 2021a,

95; Doyle 2014) from the concluding message of his famous "I Have a Dream" speech on August 28, 1963, at the Lincoln Memorial in Washington, DC, is best suited to end these proverbial deliberations:

> Let freedom ring. [. . .] And when we allow freedom to ring, when we let it ring in every village and every hamlet, from every state and every city, we will be able to speed up that day when all of God's children—black men and white men, Jews and Gentiles, Protestants and Catholics—will be able to join hands and to sing in the words of the old Negro spiritual, "Free at last, free at last, thank God Almighty, we are free at last."

BIBLIOGRAPHY

This chapter was first published with the same title in *Diligence Brings Delight: A Festschrift in Honour of Anna T. Litovkina on the Occasion of Her 60th Birthday*, edited by Hrisztalina Hrisztova-Gotthardt, Melita Aleksa Varga, and Wolfgang Mieder (Osijek, Croatia: Faculty of Humanities and Social Sciences, Josip Juraj Strossmayer University of Osijek, 2023), 65–82.

Bock, Sheila. 2014. "'What Happens Here, Stays Here': Selling the Untellable in a Tourism Advertising Campaign." *Western Folklore* 73, nos. 2–3 (Spring): 216–34.

Clinton, Hillary Rodham. 1996. *It Takes a Village, and Other Lessons Children Teach Us.* New York: Simon and Schuster.

Doyle, Charles Clay. 1996. "On 'New' Proverbs and the Conservativeness of Proverb Dictionaries." *Proverbium* 13: 69–84.

Doyle, Charles Clay. 2014. "'A Way Out of No Way': A Note on the Background of the African American Proverbial Saying." *Proverbium* 31: 193–98.

Doyle, Charles Clay, and Wolfgang Mieder. 2016. "*The Dictionary of Modern Proverbs*: A Supplement." *Proverbium* 33: 85–120.

Doyle, Charles Clay, and Wolfgang Mieder. 2018. "*The Dictionary of Modern Proverbs*: Second Supplement." *Proverbium* 35: 15–44.

Doyle, Charles Clay, and Wolfgang Mieder. 2020. "*The Dictionary of Modern Proverbs*: Third Supplement." *Proverbium* 37: 53–86.

Doyle, Charles Clay, Wolfgang Mieder, and Fred R. Shapiro, eds. 2012. *The Dictionary of Modern Proverbs.* New Haven, CT: Yale University Press.

Dundes, Alan. 1972. "Folk Ideas as Units of Worldview." In *Toward New Perspectives in Folklore*, edited by Américo Paredes and Richard Bauman, 93–103. Austin: University of Texas Press.

Hakamies, Pekka. 2002. "Proverbs and Mentality." In *Myth and Mentality: Studies in Folklore and Popular Thought*, edited by Anna-Leena Siikala, 222–30. Helsinki: Finnish Literature Society.

King, Martin Luther, Jr. 1967. *Where Do We Go from Here: Chaos or Community?* Boston: Beacon Press.

Litovkina, Anna T. 2013. "Politicians in Anglo-American Anti-Proverbs." In *International Issues from Wars to Robots*, edited by Erika Grodzki, Sharaf Rehman, Clarinda Calma, and Karyn Colombo, 95–109. Ronkonkoma, NY: Linus Learning.

Litovkina, Anna T. 2015. "Anti-Proverbs." In *Introduction to Paremiology: A Comprehensive Guide to Proverb Studies*, edited by Hrisztalina Hrisztova-Gotthardt and Melita Aleksa Varga, 326–52. Berlin: Walter de Gruyter.

Litovkina, Anna T., and Wolfgang Mieder. 2006. *Old Proverbs Never Die, They Just Diversify: A Collection of Anti-Proverbs*. Burlington: University of Vermont; Veszprém, Hungary: University of Pannonia.

Mieder, Wolfgang. 1997. *The Politics of Proverbs: From Traditional Wisdom to Proverbial Stereotypes*. Madison: University of Wisconsin Press.

Mieder, Wolfgang. 2000. *The Proverbial Abraham Lincoln: An Index to Proverbs in the Works of Abraham Lincoln*. New York: Peter Lang.

Mieder, Wolfgang. 2001. *"No Struggle, No Progress": Frederick Douglass and His Proverbial Rhetoric for Civil Rights*. New York: Peter Lang.

Mieder, Wolfgang. 2004. *Proverbs: A Handbook*. Westport, CT: Greenwood Press.

Mieder, Wolfgang. 2005. *Proverbs Are the Best Policy: Folk Wisdom and American Politics*. Logan: Utah State University Press.

Mieder, Wolfgang. 2008. *"Proverbs Speak Louder Than Words": Folk Wisdom in Art, Culture, Folklore, History, Literature, and Mass Media*. New York: Peter Lang.

Mieder, Wolfgang. 2009. *"Yes We Can": Barack Obama's Proverbial Rhetoric*. New York: Peter Lang.

Mieder, Wolfgang. 2010. *"Making a Way Out of No Way": Martin Luther King's Sermonic Proverbial Rhetoric*. New York: Peter Lang.

Mieder, Wolfgang. 2014a. *"All Men and Women Are Created Equal": Elizabeth Cady Stanton's and Susan B. Anthony's Proverbial Rhetoric Promoting Women's Rights*. New York: Peter Lang.

Mieder, Wolfgang. 2014b. *Behold the Proverbs of a People: Proverbial Wisdom in Culture, Literature, and Politics*. Jackson: University Press of Mississippi.

Mieder, Wolfgang. 2019. *"Right Makes Might": Proverbs and the American Worldview*. Bloomington: Indiana University Press.

Mieder, Wolfgang. 2020. *The Worldview of Modern American Proverbs*. New York: Peter Lang.

Mieder, Wolfgang. 2021a. *Dictionary of Authentic American Proverbs*. New York: Berghahn Books.

Mieder, Wolfgang. 2021b. *"There's No Free Lunch": Six Essays on Modern Anglo-American Proverbs*. Burlington: University of Vermont.

Mieder, Wolfgang, and George B. Bryan. 1997. *The Proverbial Harry S. Truman: An Index to Proverbs in the Works of Harry S. Truman*. New York: Peter Lang.

Mieder, Wolfgang, Stewart A. Kingsbury, and Kelsie B. Harder. 1992. *A Dictionary of American Proverbs*. New York: Oxford University Press.

Obama, Barack. 2006. *The Audacity of Hope: Thoughts on Reclaiming the American Dream*. New York: Crown Publishers.

Paczolay, Gyula. 1997. *European Proverbs in 55 Languages with Equivalents in Arabic, Persian, Sanskrit, Chinese and Japanese*. Veszprém, Hungary: Veszprémi Nyomda.

Shapiro, Fred R., ed. 2021. *The New Yale Book of Quotations*. New Haven, CT: Yale University Press.

Speake, Jennifer. 2008. *The Oxford Dictionary of Proverbs*. 5th ed. Oxford: Oxford University Press.

Summerville, Raymond M. 2020. "'Winning Freedom and Exacting Justice': A. Philip Randolph's Use of Proverbs and Proverbial Language." *Proverbium* 37: 281–310.

Taylor, Archer. 1931. *The Proverb*. Cambridge, MA: Harvard University Press. Rpt. as *The Proverb and an Index to The Proverb*, with an introduction, bibliography, and photograph of Archer Taylor by Wolfgang Mieder. Bern: Peter Lang, 1985.

Proverbs in Politics

5

"DO UNTO OTHERS AS YOU WOULD HAVE THEM DO UNTO YOU"

The Humanistic Value of Proverbs in Sociopolitical Discourse

At first glance, it might well appear that proverbs as the most concise form of such verbal folklore genres as fairy tales, legends, jokes, and riddles would also have to be the simplest (Permiakov 1970; Koch 1994; Abrahams 2005, 39–69). That assumption is quickly shown to be utterly false when we consult comprehensive international bibliographies listing annotated proverb collections and the multifaceted scholarship on proverbs (Moll 1958; Mieder 2009a). The collection and study of proverbs goes back to antiquity, with comprehensive studies existing in various languages. Archer Taylor's *The Proverb* (1931) is considered the classic survey of the origin, content, and style of proverbs, including a final section on such subgenres as proverbial expressions, proverbial comparisons, and wellerisms. The more recent *Proverbs: A Handbook* (Mieder 2004) presents an update of sorts by including modern paremiological scholarship with a special section on the various scholarly approaches to the study of proverbs: (1) proverb journals, essay volumes, and bibliographies; (2) proverb collections and future paremiography; (3) comprehensive overviews of paremiology; (4) empiricism and paremiological minima (the most frequent three hundred proverbs for a given language; see Mieder 1992; Haas 2008); (5) linguistic and semiotic considerations; (6) performance (speech acts) in social contexts; (7) issues of culture, folklore, and history; (8) politics, stereotypes, and worldview; (9) sociology, psychology, and psychiatry; (10) use in folk narratives and literature; (11) religion and wisdom literature; (12) pedagogy and language teaching; (13) iconography: proverbs in art; and (14) mass media and popular culture (Mieder 2004, 117–59; see also Norrick 1985; Honeck 1997; Hrisztova-Gotthardt and Varga 2015). The book also includes sections on definition and classification, proverbs from different cultures and languages, several historical studies of individual proverbs, and a number of case studies on the use and function of proverbs by literary authors and public figures. Altogether, this handbook presents ample proof that the ubiquitous proverbs always have been and most certainly continue to be part of oral and written communication. They serve the human inclination to summarize observations and experiences into generalized nuggets of wisdom, which in turn can be employed as ready-made comments on everyday relationships and sociopolitical affairs of various types. The polysituativity, polyfunctionality, and polysemanticity (Krikmann 2009, 15–50) of the only seemingly rigid proverbs—their textual fixidity can easily be broken in context—renders them incredibly adaptable to changing times and mores. And, very importantly, it must not be forgotten that proverbs, as everything else in life, come and go. Proverbs whose imagery or message do not fit into the modern age disappear—as can be seen from the "dead wood" in proverb collections (Mieder, Kingsbury, and Harder 1992)—and new proverbs gain general currency, to wit such favorites as "Different strokes for different folks" or "If life hands you lemons, make lemonade" (Mieder 1989, 317–32; McKenzie 1996a; Doyle, Mieder, and Shapiro 2012). They are also not always didactic, authoritative, or proscriptive but can take on many indirectly expressed (usually by way of metaphors) intents and meanings.

One thing is for certain: proverbs have not outlived their communicative usefulness in sophisticated technological societies, as has falsely been claimed by scholars (Albig 1931; Stewart 1991, 17–19) and as can be read again and again in articles debunking the truth value of proverbs in the popular press (Mieder and Sobieski 2006). The fact that such contradictory proverb pairs as "Out of sight, out of mind" and "Absence makes the heart grow fonder," or "Look before you leap" and "He who hesitates is lost," exist makes it perfectly clear that proverbs are not based on a logical philosophical system. Proverbs are as contradictory as life itself, and depending on their use in a certain context, they prove to be either true or false. The art of proverb employment lies in citing the perfectly fitting one on the right occasion. And while the frequency of their employment might vary among speakers and writers, proverbs remain an effective discursive force in various communicative modes, from sermons to gossip, from lyrical poetry to dramatic dialogue, from short stories to novels, from conversational chatter to forceful political rhetoric, and from rap music to slogans and headlines in the mass media. Proverbs are indeed everywhere and have been studied from a multitude of perspectives, from the classical philosophers such as Aristotle to the humanists like Erasmus of Rotterdam and on to such great minds as Ralph Waldo Emerson and Bertolt Brecht in more modern times, who both not only used proverbs but also showed great theoretical interest in them (Mieder 2014b, 261–83; Mieder 2000b, 237–64). There is no need for concern about the possible demise or death of proverbs today, as can easily be seen from the content of a book with the absolutely appropriate title *Proverbs Are Never Out of Season: Popular Wisdom in the Modern Age* (Mieder 1993). And, to be sure, yet another book title claims proverbially that *"Proverbs Speak Louder Than Words": Folk Wisdom in Art, Culture, Folklore, History, Literature, and Mass Media* (Mieder 2008), indicating that it behooves humanists to pay close attention to proverbs. Their steady appearance in the epideictic inaugural addresses of American presidents is certainly proof positive that they continue to be of considerable humanistic value in sociopolitical discourse (Mieder 2005, 147–86). In his enlightening article "Maxims, 'Practical Wisdom,' and the Language of Action: Beyond Grand Theory," political scientist Ray Nichols argues convincingly that political rhetoric must be characterized by "'practical wisdom,' 'practical knowledge,' 'practical reason,' [and] 'practical judgment'" (Nichols 1996, 687), literally calling for proverbial praxis in the rhetoric of politics. After all, a well-chosen maxim (a memorable phrase) or a well-known proverb add considerable communicative and emotional quality to political discourse and might well underscore the value system and mentality of the people (Raymond 1956; Mieder 1997).

It would be a welcome task to trace the humanistic value of proverbs in sociopolitical discourse throughout the centuries, including the proverbial rhetoric of Cicero, Thomas More, Martin Luther, Otto von Bismarck, and Franklin Delano Roosevelt, to name but a few of many candidates (Mieder and Bryan 1996). For now it must suffice to look at several representative figures from the Anglo-American world of the eighteenth century to the present. Realizing that social politics not only are part of the national scene but can play out in family interactions as well, one Philip Dormer Stanhope, fourth Earl of Chesterfield (1694–1773), and his relationship to his illegitimate son Philip Stanhope (1732–1768) come to mind (Mieder 2000b, 37–68). Lord Chesterfield, as the father is generally known, was a well-educated British diplomat and a perfect example of the Age of Reason who felt that life in general and that of his son in particular could and should be controlled by reason. As somewhat of an intellectual snob, he had no use for proverbs, and he stressed the importance of proper social behavior in a letter of July 25, 1741, to his son:

> There is an awkwardness of expression and words, most carefully to be avoided: such as false English, bad pronunciation, old sayings, and common proverbs; which are so many proofs of having kept bad or low company. For example, if, instead of saying that tastes are different, and that every man has his own peculiar one, you should let off a proverb, and say, That what is one man's meat is another man's poison; or else, Everyone as they like, as the good man said when he kissed his cow, everybody would be persuaded that you had never kept company with anybody above footmen and housemaids. (Stanhope 1901, 2:401)

92   PROVERBS IN POLITICS

Such tirades against proverbs find their summum bonum in a lengthy letter to his son of September 27, 1749, with Lord Chesterfield standing on his rhetorical soapbox for proper linguistic and social behavior:

> Vulgarism in language is the next and distinguishing characteristic of bad company and bad education. A man of fashion avoids nothing with more care than that. Proverbial expressions and trite sayings are the flowers of the rhetoric of a vulgar man. Would he say that men differ in their tastes; he both supports and adorns that opinion by the good old saying, as he respectfully calls it, that *What is one man's meat, is another man's poison.* A man of fashion never has recourse to proverbs and vulgar aphorisms; uses neither favorite words nor hard words; but takes great care to speak very correctly and grammatically, and to pronounce properly; that is, according to the usage of the best companies. (Stanhope 1901, 1:218)

The basis of Lord Chesterfield's educational philosophy and pedagogical program for his son consisted of the conviction that certain social graces must be maintained, including good manners, proper speech, moderation, civility, self-control, and politeness. Proverbs were too vulgar, that is too low and common, to be of any use in upper society. And yet, when one reads his entire massive correspondence with his son, it becomes clear that Lord Chesterfield could not escape proverbs in his self-righteous tirades. Some proverbs are simply too good at driving home an important point or message, as can be seen from his repeated use of the proverb "Never put off till tomorrow what you can do today" as an expression of a solid work ethic. Just imagine the vexed reaction of his son receiving the following statement from his didactic father:

> Use yourself, therefore, in time to be alert and diligent in your concerns; never procrastinate, never put off till to-morrow what you can do to-day; and never do two things at a time; pursue your object, be what it will, steadily and indefatigably; and let any difficulties (if insurmountable) rather animate than slacken your endeavors. Perseverance has surprising effects. (Stanhope 1901, 2:185)

It appears that Lord Chesterfield would have had strong objections to modern multitasking. Be that as it may, he definitely had a proverb that served him as a leitmotif for teaching his son the basic principle of proper human behavior, namely the biblical golden rule "Do unto others as you would have them do unto you" (Matthew 7:12) in its many variants (Hertzler 1933–1934; Burrell 1997, 13–27; Templeton 1997, 8–12). The following excerpt from his letter of

September 27, 1748, represents the summary of his entire moral teaching to his son: "Pray let not quibbles of lawyers, no refinements of casuists, break into the plain notions of right and wrong, which every man's right reason and plain common sense suggest to him. To do as you would be done by, is the plain, sure, and undisputed rule of morality and justice. Stick to that" (Stanhope 1901, 1:117). One thing is for certain: despite Lord Chesterfield's apparent dislike of proverbs, they repeatedly enter his educational epistles automatically as preformulated rules of proper conduct. No wonder that his son escaped this constant barrage of proverbial etiquette by fleeing his domineering father to live with his wife away from England. Clearly neither Lord Chesterfield nor his Age of Enlightenment could avoid the social use of metaphorical proverbs (Seitel 1969), and this is also evident by their appearance in the writings of such greats of his age as Goethe, Voltaire, and Kant.

Across the ocean, there is another epistolary example of proverbs being employed as a didactic tool, but this time by the intelligent, diligent, resourceful, and quite independent Abigail Adams (1744–1818), who was perfectly capable of raising her children and running the farm while her husband John was off in France and England in the service of his country before becoming the second president of the United States. She had no quibbles with the value of proverbs but considered them the perfect instrument to teach by way of experienced common sense (Mieder 2005, 56–89). Her letter of March 2, 1780, to her son John Quincy Adams, sixth president of the United States, is reminiscent of some of Lord Chesterfield's letters. In fact, she had read an early edition of his correspondence and surely came across his frequent use of the proverb "If it is worth doing at all, it is worth doing well." So, like the father to his son, it is now the well-intending mother preaching to her son in sound proverbial language:

> You have great reason for thankfulness to your kind preserver, who hath again carried you through many dangers, preserved your Life and given you an opportunity of making further improvements in virtue and knowledge. You must consider that every Moment of your time is precious, if trifled away never to be recalled. Do not spend too much of it in recreation, it will never afford you that permanent satisfaction which the acquisition of one Art or Science will give you, and whatever you undertake aim to make yourself perfect in it, for if it is worth doing at all, it is worth doing well. (Butterfield 1963–1993, 3:293)

Indeed, Abigail at times comes across as a female Chesterfield, never lacking the words to give advice for proper social conduct, but there is much more to her proverbial use as a concerned matriarch during the long absences of her politically engaged husband. Proverbs like "God helps them who help themselves," "Necessity has no law," and "Hope springs eternal" help her to cope, but her proverbial letters do not only preach the puritan life. Even though as a woman she had no public political voice, she was heavily involved in the sociopolitical affairs of her day by way of strong and influential letters to her husband. Thus, her letter of November 27, 1775, contains a powerful statement about human nature at the time of American revolutionary reactions against the British abuse of power. The proverb "Big fish eat little fish" has served as a metaphor to describe human power struggles since ancient times (Mieder 1987, 178–228), and it is the perfect expression for the politics of her time and a clear indication that humanity in the Age of Reason and the Enlightenment had not advanced much beyond the rapacious fish world:

> I am more and more convinced that Man is a dangerous creature, and that power whether vested in many or a few is ever grasping, and like the grave cries give, give. The great fish swallow up the small, and he who is most strenuous for the Rights of the people, when vested with power, is as eager after the prerogatives of Government. You tell me of degrees of perfection to which Humane Nature is capable of arriving, and I believe it, but at the same time lament that our admiration should arise from the scarcity of the instances. (Butterfield 1963–1993, 1:329)

What a devastating indictment of humanity with respect to the corruptness of governmental power! And she even condemns slavery, albeit indirectly, in her letter of March 31, 1776, to John, with whom she shared the distinction of not owning slaves: "I have sometimes been ready to think that the passion for Liberty cannot be Equally Strong in the Breasts of those who have been accustomed to deprive their fellow Creatures of theirs. Of this I am certain that it is not founded upon that generous and Christian principal of doing to others as we would that others should do unto us" (Butterfield 1963–1993, 1:359).

Clearly the proverbial golden rule was the perfect expression to give authority to her argument against slavery, and it should not be surprising that this Bible proverb became a leitmotif about seven decades later in the powerful antislavery rhetoric of Frederick Douglass. Reading many more proverbial observations of this type by both Abigail and John Adams, it seems strange that scholars have repeatedly argued that proverbs were of little value during the eighteenth century (Jente 1945, 116; Obelkevich 1987, 57).

Of course, one only needs to turn to Benjamin Franklin (1706–1790), the printer, inventor, scientist, businessman, diplomat, and one of the founding fathers of the United States, to dispel any notion that proverbs might have become irrelevant in his age. In twenty-five years of his annual *Poor Richard's*

Almanack (1733–1758), he included 1,044 proverbs (about 40 each year), of which he chose 105 to be part of his celebrated essay "The Way to Wealth" (1758), which became a secular Bible of sorts in America (Barbour 1974; Mieder 2004, 216–24). Most of the proverbs, he copied from earlier English proverb collections (Newcomb 1957), with only very few proverbs like "Three removes is (are) as bad as a fire" and "There will be sleeping enough in the grave" being his very own inventions (Gallacher 1949). His famous essay is a literal cannonade of proverbial wisdom, as just this short excerpt amply illustrates:

> If time be of all things the most precious, wasting time must be, as Poor Richard says, the greatest prodigality; since, as elsewhere he tells us, Lost time is never found again; and what we call time enough, always proves little enough. Let us then up and be doing, and doing to the purpose; so by diligence shall we do more with less perplexity. Sloth makes all things difficult, but industry all easy, and He that riseth late must trot all day, and shall scarce overtake his business at night; while Laziness travels so slowly, that Poverty soon overtakes him. Drive thy business, let not that drive thee, and Early to bed, and early to rise, makes a man healthy, wealthy, and wise, as Poor Richard says. (Sparks 1840, 2:94–103)

With Franklin's almanacs selling as many as ten thousand copies each year in the early colonies, his essay "The Way to Wealth" became an absolute international "hit" with translations into numerous languages. Many of the proverbs became associated with either the fictional "Poor Richard" or with Franklin himself. This continues to the present day, so that people for example cite the proverb "Early to bed, and early to rise, makes a man healthy, wealthy, and wise" with the authoritative introductory formula "as Benjamin Franklin says." And yet, this very proverb has been traced back to the late fifteenth century with Franklin at best being able to claim that he helped to popularize it in the United States (Mieder 1993, 98–134). In any case, Franklin's obsession with proverbs led to what today are called Puritan ethics, with their emphasis on virtue, prosperity, prudence, and economic common sense. As such, "The Way to Wealth," with its Puritan ethics expressed in a hundred proverbs, especially helped to shape the worldview of the young American nation and continues to have an indirect influence to this very day. Franklin and "his" proverbs were everywhere, including broadsheets, plates, and cups featuring the proverbial texts with illustrations. If one is lucky enough to find such paraphernalia in an antique shop today, any such item will not be had for less than two hundred dollars. The influence of Franklin on the social life of the United States by way of the humanistic value of the good advice of proverbs is surely very considerable indeed.

Moving on to the nineteenth century leads to the former slave and renowned abolitionist Frederick Douglass (1818–1895), who as an African American dominated sociopolitical discourse in the United States and Europe for fifty years! Without any formal education whatsoever, he became a most impressive rhetorician, whose *Narrative of the Life of Frederick Douglass, Written by Himself* (1845, expanded twice in 1855 and 1893) became a classic in his lifetime. Two sets of five massive volumes each of his speeches and writing bear witness to his rhetorical skills and moral courage in the service of abolitionism and civil rights. He doubtlessly was a social and political agitator par excellence, always arguing for morality, equality, and democracy. His rhetorical prowess is legendary, but it has taken a long time to recognize that a major element of his oratorical power was his repeated use of biblical and folk proverbs, which added authoritative and traditional wisdom to his engaged arguments (Mieder 2001; Mieder 2005, 118–46). He was so keenly aware of proverbs that he summarized his life's philosophy in a speech delivered on August 3, 1857, in Canandaigua, New York, into a proverb-like utterance that by now has become proverbial in the slightly shorted form of "No struggle, no progress":

> Let me give you a word of the philosophy of reform. The whole history of the progress of human liberty shows that all concessions yet made to her august claims, have been born of earnest struggle. The conflict has been exciting, agitating, all-absorbing, and for the time being, putting all other tumults to silence. It must do this or it does nothing. If there is no struggle there is no progress. Those who profess to favor freedom and yet deprecate agitation, are men who want crops without plowing up the ground, they want rain without thunder and lightning. They want the ocean without the awful roar of its many waters. This struggle may be a moral one, or it may be a physical one, and it may be both moral and physical, but it must be a struggle. Power concedes nothing without a demand. It never did and it never will. (Blassingame 1985–1992, 3:204)

Douglass saw his struggle as an enlightened progress based on nonviolent moral suasion, but he was well aware that the mistreatment of Blacks could result in violence. As a warning, he relied several times on the sixteenth-century English proverb "Tread on a worm and it will turn," where the worm becomes a metaphor for the miserable life of the slaves. The following incredibly powerful utterance stems from an antislavery speech that he delivered on December 8, 1850, in his hometown of Rochester, New York:

> I would warn the American people, and the American government, to be wise in their day and generation. I exhort them to remember the history

of other nations; and I remind them that America cannot always sit "as a queen," in peace and repose; that prouder and stronger governments than this have been shattered by the bolts of a just God. [. . .] There is a point beyond which human endurance cannot go. The crushed worm may yet turn under the heel of the oppressor. I warn them, then, with all solemnity, and in the name of retributive justice, to look to their ways; for in an evil hour, those sable arms that have, for the last two centuries, been engaged in cultivating and adorning the fair fields of our country, may yet become the instruments of terror, desolation, and death, throughout our borders. (Blassingame 1985–1992, 2:271)

Anybody who witnessed in person or on film the civil rights marches and the struggles to keep them peaceful under the leadership of Martin Luther King Jr., who certainly was influenced by Douglass, will be experiencing déjà vu here. Douglass is drawing attention to a very precarious situation by way of the somewhat changed proverb, thus rendering its metaphorical language even more powerful.

Again and again Douglass turned to the proverbs of the Bible (Fontaine 1982; Winton 1990; McKenzie 1996b; Dundes 1999) to underpin his antislavery arguments, making the proverbial golden rule his often repeated leitmotif, as in this early speech of January 6, 1846:

[The Bible] is filled with the Wisdom from above, which is pure, and peaceable, and full of mercies and good fruits, without prolixity, and without hypocrisy. It knows no one by the color of his skin. It confers no privilege upon class, which it does not confer upon another. The fundamental principle running through and underlying the whole, is this—"Whatsoever ye would that men should do unto you, do you even so unto them." If you claim liberty for yourself, grant it to your neighbor. If you, yourself, were a slave, and would desire the aid of your fellowman to rescue you from the clutch of the enslaver, you surely are bound by that very desire to labor for the freedom of those whom you know to be in bonds. (Blassingame 1985–1992, 1:129)

The golden rule, which exists in close variants in all major religions (Griffin 1991, 67–69), is clearly the most prevalent proverb in sociopolitical discourse, and it should not come as a surprise that President Abraham Lincoln (1809–1865), clearly influenced by Douglass's rhetoric, also made effective emotional use of its message. But while Douglass was more verbose or even long-winded in his eloquent sociopolitical rhetoric, Lincoln, except in his lengthy public debates with Stephen Douglas, is much more precise in his speeches and letters.

98   PROVERBS IN POLITICS

So much more reason for him to integrate folk and Bible proverbs into his weighty utterances (Mieder 2000a; Mieder 2005, 90–117). His preoccupation with biblical proverbs could take on overpowering proportions, as in the following satirical masterpiece written to a delegation of Baptists on May 30, 1864:

> I can only thank you for adding to the effective and almost unanimous support which the Christian communities are so zealously giving to the country, and to liberty. Indeed, it is difficult to conceive how it could be otherwise with any one professing Christianity, or even having ordinary perceptions of right and wrong. To read the Bible, as the word of God himself, that "in the sweat of thy face shalt thou eat bread" [Genesis 3:19], and to preach there from that "In the sweat of other mans [*sic*] faces shalt thou eat bread," to my mind can scarcely be reconciled with honest sincerity. When brought to my final reckoning, may I have to answer for robbing no man of his goods; yet more tolerable even this, than for robbing one of himself, and all that was his. When, a year or two ago, those professedly holy men of the South, met in the semblance of prayer and devotion, and, in the Name of Him who said "As ye would all men should do unto you, do even ye so unto them" [Matthew 7:12] appeal to the Christian world to aid them in doing to a whole race of men, as they would have no man do unto themselves, to my thinking they contemned and insulted God and His church, far more than Satan when he tempted the Saviour with the Kingdoms of the earth. The devil's attempt was no more false, and far less hypocritical. But let me forbear, remembering it is also written "Judge not, lest ye be judged" [Matthew 7:1]. (Basler 1953, 7:368)

What a paragraph, with its three well-known proverbs from the Bible! Without mentioning the word "slavery," Lincoln ridicules the southern ministers and the slaveholders of the South who earned their bread through the hard work of their slaves. He also points out that they have all forgotten the humane message of the golden rule. And then, with his typical humility, he quotes the third proverb about judging others, warning that self-righteousness will not do to overcome slavery. The satirical message is direct, clear, and authoritative, with the didactic Bible proverbs adding ethical persuasiveness to this masterful paragraph.

But it would be a mistake to conclude that Lincoln forgot about the rhetorical effectiveness of folk proverbs. That this is absolutely not the case can be seen from the last paragraph of his famous Cooper Union speech on February 27, 1860, in New York City. Lincoln had outlined his solid commitment to maintaining the Union and to keeping slavery from spreading beyond where it existed, concluding his speech with an unforgettable oratorical crescendo: "Neither let us be slandered from our duty by false accusations against us, nor frightened from it by menaces of destruction to the Government nor of dungeons to ourselves. Let us have faith that right makes might, and in that faith, let us, to the end, dare to do our duty as we understand it" (Basler 1953, 3:550). This is indeed a powerful peroration, with "Right makes might" often being cited as a Lincoln quotation today (Shapiro 2006, 461). However, he was in fact quoting the fourteenth-century proverb "Right makes might," whose antipode "Might makes right" is just as old (Mieder 2014c). In any case, the proverb adds conviction and authority to Lincoln's argument. It summarizes everything he had said in his speech, namely that the preservation of the Union and the geographical control of slavery are just and "right" goals. Believing in these two goals will give people the "might" to keep the sociopolitical status quo under control.

Of course, Lincoln's faith in this was broken when he was unable to prevent the start of the Civil War as president a year later. It was a gloomy time when he left Springfield, Illinois, on February 11, 1861, on his way to Washington to assume the presidency. Stopping at Tolono, Illinois, here is what this quiet, humble, and noble man said: "I am leaving you on an errand of national importance, attended, as you are aware, with considerable difficulties. Let us believe, as some poet has expressed it: 'Behind the cloud the sun is still shining.' I bid you an affectionate farewell" (Basler 1953, 4:191). Today he would have cited the more common proverb "Every cloud has a silver lining," but the people who had met his train to see him off certainly knew the variant "Behind the cloud the sun is shining" and were able to appreciate its hopeful message on the eve of the Civil War. It was the perfect piece of folk wisdom to use in this short, impromptu statement intended to calm an anxious citizenship.

And here is one final example for Lincoln's employment of folk proverbs to underscore his determination to do the right and moral thing. He had finally issued the Emancipation Proclamation on January 1, 1863, among plenty of opposition and calls for its retraction. But the president was committed to this noble act, as he explained in a letter of January 8, 1863, to Major General John A. McClernand. As can be seen, he very consciously chose the metaphorical proverb "Broken eggs cannot be mended" to express his determination to keep the proclamation intact:

> I never did ask more, nor ever was willing to accept less, than for all the States, and the people thereof, to take and hold their places, and their rights, in the Union under the Constitution of the United States. For this alone have I felt authorized to struggle; and I seek neither more nor less now. Still, to use a coarse, but an expressive figure, broken eggs can not

be mended. I have issued the emancipation proclamation, and I can not retract it. (Basler 1953, 6:48)

This is but one of many such proverbial paragraphs in Lincoln's statements. In this particular case—it is strange that he does not use the term "proverb" here—this "coarse" (in the sense of common, folksy) proverb expresses in simple metaphorical language his strong will to maintain the humane emancipation of the slaves. The proverb proves itself not to be just a trite remark but becomes of much humanistic value in this context.

Clearly the friends Frederick Douglass and Abraham Lincoln will forever be two shining lights of the sociopolitical history of the United States. But to be sure, two remarkable women of the nineteenth century can stand as their distinguished equals in their fifty years of committed struggle for women's rights in particular and civil rights in general. And expectedly by now, early feminists Elizabeth Cady Stanton (1815–1902) and her dear friend Susan B. Anthony (1820–1906) both relied heavily on proverbs from the Bible and the folk to add authority, expressiveness, and humanistic value to their multitude of speeches, essays, and letters (Mieder 2014a; Mieder 2015c). More importantly, they are any time the equals of the male political giants when it comes to the employment of proverbial language in their unceasing, emotive, and aggressive struggle for women's rights. They called on proverbs to add generational wisdom to their arguments, realizing that proverbs are strategies for dealing with recurrent social situations (Burke 1941) that need to be questioned and changed as far as the sociopolitical role of women is concerned.

Just like their friend Frederick Douglass with his "No struggle, no progress," each of these two grand ladies has one unique utterance that has become proverbial as an invaluable sociopolitical statement. In the case of Elizabeth Cady Stanton, it is what she did with the proverb "All men are created equal" from the Declaration of Independence (Mieder 2015a). As is well known, the women's rights convention held on July 19–20, 1848, at Seneca Falls, New York, ushered in the birth of the movement for gender equality and women's suffrage. With about three hundred people in attendance, Stanton presented her magisterial manifesto "Declaration of Sentiments," which begins with a rhetorical stroke of genius that brought the audience to their feet. Its beginning was so very familiar, but then came that unexpected revolutionary alteration of the male-oriented proverb:

When, in the course of human events, it becomes necessary for one portion of the family of man to assume among the people of the earth a position different from that which they have hitherto occupied, but one to which the laws of nature and of nature's God entitle them, a decent respect to the opinions of mankind requires that they should declare the causes that impel them to such a course.

We hold these truths to be self-evident: that all men and women are created equal; that they are endowed by their Creator with certain inalienable rights; that among these are life, liberty, and the pursuit of happiness; that to secure these rights governments are instituted, deriving their just powers from the consent of the governed. Whenever any form of Government becomes destructive of these ends, it is the right of those who suffer from it to refuse allegiance to it, and to insist upon the institution of a new government, laying its foundation on such principles, and organizing its powers in such form as to them shall seem most likely to effect their safety and happiness. (Gordon 1997–2013, 1:78–79)

The expansion of "all men" to "all men and women" is, of course, not the only change in this obvious parody that leaves no room for humor. Stanton and the other women clearly meant business, because it was high time that the female "portion of the family of man" claimed its natural rights and demanded "the equal station to which they are entitled." And to be sure, as stated in the original Declaration and repeated verbatim in this manifesto, this includes the proverbial triad "life, liberty, and the pursuit of happiness" (Aron 2008, 91–96).

Susan B. Anthony's call to proverbial fame stems from her strong argument for women entering various professions without being discriminated against because of their gender. The ever agitating Anthony was also protesting against the salary discrepancy between men and women as early as October 8, 1869, when she wrote in *The Revolution*: "Join the union, girls, and together say, 'Equal Pay for Equal Work'" (Shapiro 2006, 23). Some thirty years later, in a speech on July 29, 1897, Anthony returned to her sententious remark–turned–proverb by then and became—how could it be otherwise!—an outspoken champion of its significant message:

What I have been working for all these years is just this—when Sally Ann [Hyatt] does know more and does better work than [her brother] James [Hyatt], the superintendent, she shall be put in the position of the superintendent and have a superintendent's salary. That is the whole question. Equal pay for equal work. There isn't a woman in the sound of my voice, who does not want this justice. There never was one— there never will be one who does not want justice and equality. But they have not yet learned that equal work and equal wages can come only through the political equality, represented by the ballot. (Gordon 1997–2013, 6:155)

102 PROVERBS IN POLITICS

It is of interest to note that in 1897 Anthony had no choice but to argue that the demand of "Equal pay for equal work" would have no way of becoming law as long as women did not have the right to cast their vote. Finally then, there is this short excerpt from a letter of July 6, 1903, to unionist Margaret Haley: "Women must have equal pay for equal work, and they must be considered equally eligible to the offices of principal and superintendent, professor and president. The saying that women have equal pay is absurd while they are not allowed to have the highest positions which their qualifications entitle them to; so you must insist that qualifications, not sex, shall govern the appointments to the highest positions" (Gordon 1997–2013, 6:482–83). More than a hundred years later, the struggle for equal pay for equal work is still ongoing, but great progress has indeed been made, and it behooves modern women to give considerable credit for these advances to Susan B. Anthony in particular.

As do most social reformers, both women employed the golden rule as a proverbial sign of equality. In her address to the legislature of New York on February 14, 1854, Stanton pointed to the misogyny in the legal system and argued that women deserved the same protection under the law that is granted to men:

> But if, gentlemen [the legislators], you take the ground that the sexes are alike, and, therefore, you are our faithful representatives—then why all these special laws for woman? Would not one code answer for all of like needs and wants? Christ's golden rule is better than all the special legislation that the ingenuity of man can devise: "Do unto others as you would have others do unto you." This, men and brethren, is all we ask at your hands. We ask no better laws than those you have made for yourselves. We need no other protection than that which your present laws secure to you. (Gordon 1997–2013, 1:254)

And her friend Anthony also took the Bible proverb into the realm of government during a speech on September 10, 1989, in her hometown of Rochester, New York:

> As a representative of the most radical and hence the most unpopular demand for the practical application of the Golden Rule as the basis of our religion, and the Declaration of Independence as the basis of our Government, I esteem the invitation to address this class [of young men] not only a high honor but a most significant "sign of the times." I shall take it for granted that the members of it are believers in good government. To acquire this we must have good citizens. The old maxim that the fountain can rise no higher than its head, is no truer in the law

of physics than in the law of political ethics, that the government can be no higher than the majority of its constituents. Hence, if our city, State or national government is not what we wish, the remedy is not in securing new officials but larger numbers of good constituents—in other words make the source higher. (Harper 1898–1908, 3:1148–49)

What a rhetorical coup to combine her allusions to the Bible proverb "Do unto others as you would have them do unto you" and the quotation-long-turned-proverb "All men are created equal" with the folk proverb "The fountain can rise no higher than its head," and turn them into "radical" demands for "good government" on all levels that accepts women as equal partners. The fact that she delivered this proverbial manifesto in front of young men was indeed a hopeful "sign of the times."

Of course, Elizabeth Cady Stanton was equally adapt at integrating folk proverbs into her verbal agitations as she addressed large crowds throughout the United States. Here is an example of her use of the proverb "Two dogs over one bone seldom agree" in a speech of May 30, 1874, that also deals with the issue of voting rights:

There is no danger that women will corrupt politics or that politics will corrupt them. But when the women vote they will be pretty sure to demand better and cleanlier [*sic*] places for voting. Law should be a holy thing and the ballot box the holy of holies. It is claimed that the ballot for women will divide the family, or merely duplicate the voting. But it produces unpleasantness in the family now. Give two dogs a bone and they will fight over it. But give them two bones and there is peace immediately. Woman would not be so bothered and perplexed over the finance question as men are. (Gordon 1997–2013, 3:83)

As these few contextualized references show, Elizabeth Cady Stanton and Susan B. Anthony championed women's rights and equality for all people by way of their engaged, courageous, and expressive rhetoric, which was informed to a considerable degree by proverbial wisdom based on humane values.

No doubt Martin Luther King Jr. (1929–1968) would have admired these two exemplary social reformers who knew that social change would not come by way of lip service but must be accomplished through words and deeds, something that King did with unwavering commitment. Trained in the Baptist sermonic tradition with its Bible proverbs and having grown up with folk proverbs in his African American community (Prahlad 1996), he realized that proverbial language would serve him extremely well in his sermons, speeches, and writings to bring his nonviolent civil rights message across to the American people. In fact, his frequent use of proverbs can be seen as the quintessential example of the humanistic value of proverbs in modern sociopolitical discourse. His repertoire of proverbs is truly astounding, and there can be no doubt that this traditional wisdom from the Bible and the folk added considerable metaphorical expressiveness to his rhetoric, which in turn made it possible for him to reach and touch millions of people (Mieder 2010; Mieder 2014b, 133–71).

As expected, King as a minister relied heavily on Bible proverbs in his many emotionally charged sermons. When he delivered one of the versions of his well-known sermon "The Three Dimensions of a Complete Life" on April 9, 1967, at New Covenant Church in Chicago, he included the proverb "Love your neighbor as you love yourself" as an expression of reciprocal love, and two additional proverbial Bible passages from Amos and Isaiah. Above all, he summarized the three dimensions of a complete life—how could it be otherwise?—by way of the golden rule "Do unto others as you would have them do unto you." But here then is King's rhetorical masterpiece, which amasses four Bible proverbs into a powerful statement of love, justice, peace, and morality:

> Go out this morning. Love yourself, and that means rational and healthy self-interest. You are commanded to do that. That's the length of life. Then follow that: Love your neighbor as you love yourself [Galatians 5:14]. You are commanded to do that. That's the breadth of life. And I'm going to take my seat now by letting you know that there's a first and even greater commandment: "Love the Lord thy God with all thy heart, [*yeah*] with all thy soul, with all thy strength." I think the psychologist would just say "with all thy personality." And when you do that, you've got the breadth [King meant to say "height"] of life.
>
> And when you get all three of these together, you can walk and never get weary. You can look up and see the morning stars singing together, and the sons of God shouting for joy. When you get all of these working together in your very life, judgment will roll down like waters, and righteousness like a mighty stream [Amos 5:24].
>
> When you get all the three of these together, the lamb will lie down with the lion [Isaiah 11:6]. [. . .]
>
> When you get all three of these working together, you will do unto others as you'd have them do unto you [Matthew 7:12].
>
> When you get all three of these together, you will recognize that out of one blood God made all men to dwell upon the face of the earth. (Carson and Holloran 1998, 139)

And yet, despite its grand biblical and moral rhetoric, this passage says nothing about racial and social matters. But such exclusion is relatively rare, with

King's usual modus operandi being to combine the religious *and* sociopolitical implications of proverbial wisdom in his sermons and speeches. A fine example involves the widely known Bible proverb "Man does not live by bread alone" (Deuteronomy 8:3; Matthew 4:4), which appears in both the Old and the New Testaments. King used it in a sermon, "The Christian Doctrine of Man," on March 12, 1958, in Detroit, stating that he as a minister has a moral and social obligation to his parishioners and the world at large. But there is also an extremely important interpretive twist of the proverb in this text when King states that the word "alone" in the proverb implies that Jesus was very well aware that man cannot live without bread nor by it alone. And this in turn gives King the proverbial argument that poverty must be combated in the United States and throughout the world:

> And so in Christianity the body is sacred. The body is significant. This means that in any Christian doctrine of man we must forever be concerned about man's physical well-being. Jesus was concerned about that. He realized that men had to have certain physical necessities. One day he said, "Man cannot live by bread alone" [Deuteronomy 8:3; Matthew 4:4]. [*Yeah*] But the mere fact that the "alone" was added means that Jesus realized that man could not live without bread. [*Yes*] So as a minister of the gospel, I must not only preach to men and women to be good, but I must be concerned about the social conditions that often make them bad. [*Yeah*] It's not enough for me to tell men to be honest, but I must be concerned about the economic conditions that make them dishonest. [*Amen*] I must be concerned about the poverty in the world. I must be concerned about the ignorance in the world. I must be concerned about the slums in the world. (Carson et al. 1992–2007, 6:332)

Usually relying on the proverbial wisdom of Jesus (Winton 1990), King found the perfect metaphor for his social agenda in the New Testament proverb "He who lives by the sword shall perish by the sword" (Matthew 26:52). It became *the* symbolic argument against all the ills of violent mistreatment of others. In his address "The Montgomery Story" at the annual National Association for the Advancement of Colored People (NAACP) Convention on June 27, 1956, in San Francisco, he cited the Bible proverb as a metaphorical sign of violence that must be overcome by a philosophy of nonviolence:

> From the beginning there has been a basic philosophy undergirding our movement. It is a philosophy of nonviolent resistance. It is a philosophy which simply says we will refuse on a nonviolent basis, to cooperate with the evil of segregation. In our struggle in America we cannot

fret with the idea of retaliatory violence. To use the method of violence would be both impractical and immoral. We have neither the instruments nor the techniques of violence, and even if we had it, it would be morally wrong. There is the voice crying, [*applause*] there is a voice crying through the vista of time, saying: "He who lives by the sword will perish by the sword" [Matthew 26:52]. [*Applause*] History is replete with the bleached bones of nations who failed to hear these words of truth, and so we decided to use the method of nonviolence, feeling that violence would not do the job. (Carson et al. 1992–2007, 3:305)

But King is equally well versed in the wisdom of folk proverbs. For example, in his stirring address of June 23, 1963, at the Freedom Rally in Cobo Hall in Detroit, he cited the modern proverb "Last hired, first fired" (Doyle, Mieder, and Shapiro 2012, 121) as an unfortunate truism especially regarding the employment injustice that African Americans face in light of racial discrimination:

We've been pushed around so long; we've been the victims of lynching mobs so long; we've been the victims of economic injustice so long— still the last hired and the first fired all over this nation. And I know the temptation. I can understand from a psychological point of view why some caught up in the clutches of the injustices surrounding them almost respond with bitterness and come to the conclusion that the problem can't be solved within, and they talk about getting away from it in terms of racial separation. But even though I can understand it psychologically, I must say to you this afternoon that this isn't the way. Black supremacy is as dangerous as white supremacy. [*Applause*] And oh, I hope you will allow me to say to you this afternoon that God is not interested merely in the freedom of black men and brown men and yellow men. God is interested in the freedom of the whole human race. [*Applause*] And I believe that with this philosophy and this determined struggle we will be able to go on in the days ahead and transform the jangling discords of our nation into a beautiful symphony of brotherhood. (Carson and Shepard 2001, 68–69)

In his constant concern for progress in the fight for civil rights, King found another proverb to express that there is no easy way or quick fix, namely "No pain, no gain." King cited the less frequent variant "No gain without pain" at the same Freedom Rally in Cobo Hall (1963) to explain that there is a heavy price to pay (an additional proverbial phrase) for social advancement:

And I do not want to give you the impression that it's going to be easy [to get civil rights]. There can be no great social gain without individual pain. And before the victory for brotherhood is won, some will have to get scarred up a bit. Before the victory is won, some more will be thrown into jail. Before the victory is won, some, like Medgar Evers, may have to face physical death. But if physical death is the price that some must pay to free their children and their white brothers from an eternal psychological death, then nothing can be more redemptive. Before the victory is won, some will be misunderstood and called bad names, but we must go on with a determination and with a faith that this problem can be solved. [*Yeah*] [*Applause*] (Carson and Shepard 2001, 70–71)

What a sociopolitical message based on proverbial wisdom! And King's speeches and writings are filled with such statements, showing once and for all that proverbs are of much relevance and value in humankind's sociopolitical attempt to construct a more humane world.

By his own admission, former president Barack Obama (b. 1961) has been deeply influenced by his extensive reading of Abraham Lincoln and Martin Luther King Jr., and it might well be conjectured that he read at least Frederick Douglass's autobiography as well. As all of them, he is conscious of his use of language, as can be seen from the exquisite style of his autobiography *Dreams from My Father* (1995). It is replete with proverbial language, as are his speeches and other writings that set forth his political agenda. Having a better education than his abovementioned predecessors, he, too, is well versed in Bible and folk proverbs, using them at key points in his various sociopolitical communications. As such, they become metaphorical expressions of his humane and ethical worldview based on fairness, empathy, and, yes, the proverbial golden rule (Mieder 2009b; Mieder 2014b, 172–97).

As a matter of fact, in his political and personal manifesto *The Audacity of Hope* (2006), Obama states unequivocally that he is guided by the proverb "Do unto others as you would have them do unto you" (Matthew 7:12). Being well aware of the general knowledge and currency of this law of life expressed either in its longer proverbial form or simply its "golden rule" designation, Obama can assume that his readers or audience will be able to understand and hopefully identify with his subjective statement that "a sense of empathy [. . .] is at the heart of my moral code, and it is how I understand the Golden Rule—not simply as a call to sympathy or charity, but as something more demanding, a call to stand in somebody else's shoes and see through their eyes" (Obama 2006, 66). Always the proverbialist, he is quick to add the two proverbial expressions "to put oneself into somebody else's shoes" and "to see through someone else's eyes" to the not directly stated proverbial law, thereby stressing that this golden rule will only be fulfilled if people have understanding and compassion for each other. Later in this book, he reiterates his personal commitment to this high moral principle: "There are some things that I'm absolutely sure about—the Golden Rule, the need to battle cruelty in all its forms, the value of love and charity, humility and grace" (Obama 2006, 224).

Not long after his inauguration, President Obama undertook a trip abroad to Egypt, Germany, and France. It was on June 4, 2009, at Cairo University where he gave a major address reaching out to the Muslim world. During this speech, Obama argued forcefully "against negative stereotypes of Islam," but he was quick to point out that eradicating the world of stereotypes must involve people everywhere, who, after all, were all created equal, as Obama never tires to point out proverbially:

> Just as Muslims do not fit a crude stereotype, America is not the crude stereotype of a self-interested empire. The United States has been one of the greatest sources of progress that the world has ever known. We were born out of revolution against an empire. We were founded upon the ideal that all [men] are created equal, and we have shed blood and struggled for centuries to give meaning to those words—within our borders, and around the world. We are shaped by every culture, drawn from every end of the Earth, and dedicated to a simple concept: E pluribus unum—"Out of many, one." (Mieder 2014b, 191–92)

The old classical proverb "E pluribus unum," which appears on the seal of the United States, embodies Obama's vision of a world in which people emphasize their similarities rather than stress their differences (Fields 1996, 1–25; Aron 2008, 23–25). And this view includes a democratic form of government, of course, as Obama stresses by citing part of the proverbial triad of a "government of the people, by the people, for the people," popularized as the shortest definition of democracy by way of Abraham Lincoln's Gettysburg Address of November 19, 1863, when he said at the end of his oration: "that this nation, under God, shall have a new birth of freedom—and that government of the people, by the people, for the people, shall not perish from the earth" (Mieder 2005, 15–55). But here is what Obama said about democracy at Cairo:

> There are some who advocate for democracy only when they're out of power; once in power, they are ruthless in suppressing the rights of others. [*Applause*] So no matter where it takes hold, government of the people and by the people sets a single standard for all who would hold power: you must maintain your power through consent, not coercion;

you must respect the rights of minorities, and participate with a spirit of tolerance and compromise; you must place the interests of your people and the legitimate workings of the political process above your party. Without these ingredients, elections alone do not make a true democracy. (Mieder 2014b, 192)

It is not clear why Obama did not cite the third element "for the people" of this proverbial definition, but what he did say surely refers to the fact that the government is there for the people whom it serves! And then, very close to the end of this moving and inspiring speech to thousands of Arabic students, he asked them "to reimagine the world, to remake this world." Little wonder that there was repeated applause, that there were calls such as "Barack Obama, we love you!" during the speech. The president reached the climax of the speech when he called for a new world of brother- and sisterhood informed by empathy and mutual respect, with the center of his powerful statement being occupied by the proverbial golden rule once again:

All of us share this world for but a brief moment in time. The question is whether we spend that time focused on what pushes us apart, or whether we commit ourselves to an effort—a sustained effort—to find common ground, to focus on the future we seek for our children, and to respect the dignity of all human beings.

It's easier to start wars than to end them. It's easier to blame others than to look inward. It's easier to see what is different about someone than to find the things we share. But we should choose the right path, not just the easy path. There's one rule that lies at the heart of every religion—that we do unto others as we would have them do unto us. [*Applause*] This truth transcends nations and peoples—a belief that isn't new; that isn't black or white or brown; that isn't Christian or Muslim or Jew. It's a belief that pulsed in the cradle of civilization, and that still beats in the hearts of billions around the world. It's a faith in other people, and it's what brought me here today. (Mieder 2014b, 192–93)

That is rational and emotional rhetoric, coming from both the mind and the heart, as it calls for a new world based on ethical values that bind humankind together. One certainly can hear echoes of Abraham Lincoln, Frederick Douglass, and Martin Luther King Jr. in this deeply moral worldview.

Of course, Barack Obama's oral and written words also include plenty of folk proverbs to underscore the vision of a more humane world order. He usually incorporates them without any introductory formulas into his rhetorical flow so that they in a way become his "own" words of wisdom without coming across like timeworn clichés. He might also add a word or two to break up the formulaic nature of proverbs, to lessen the apparent didactic tone while at the same time maintaining the intended deeper message of bringing about positive change. On May 7, 2005, in Rockford, Illinois, he made good use of the proverb "Knowledge is power":

> See, in this new world, knowledge really is power. A new idea can lead not just to a new product or a new job, but [to] entire new industries and a new way of thinking about the world. And so you need to be the Idea Generation. The generation who's always thinking on the cutting edge, who's wondering how to create and keep the next wave of American jobs and American innovations. (Mieder 2009b, 82)

On another occasion, on July 25, 2005, in Chicago, he underscored his commitment to health care with the ethical proverb "A promise made is a promise kept": "We'll never rise together if we allow medical bills to swallow family budgets or let people retire penniless after a lifetime of hard work, and so today we must demand that when it comes to commitments made by working men and women on health care and pensions, a promise made is a promise kept" (Mieder 2009b, 82). And here is yet a third example of the encouragement that Obama was able to give graduating students by the use of the proverb "Time will tell" in a speech of June 26, 2006, in Evanston, Illinois: "Time will tell. You will be tested by the challenges of this new century, and at times you will fail. But know that you have it within your power to try. That generations who have come before you faced these same fears and uncertainties in their own time" (Mieder 2009b, 82). He might just as well have spoken of the "audacity of hope" in this last reference, but the simple proverb suffices to encourage his young audience to look with confidence and good will into the future. There is no doubt that President Obama was especially skillful in his sociopolitical employment of proverbial wisdom as valid expressions of moral, ethical, and humane values.

Judging by the writings and speeches of former first lady, senator from New York, secretary of state under Barack Obama, and unsuccessful presidential candidate Hillary Rodham Clinton (b. 1947), she would have carried on many of Obama's policies had she succeeded in her presidential run, albeit with a more pragmatic and less idealistic approach. While she certainly does not have the oratorical flare and appeal of her friend Obama, her commitment to sociopolitical issues finds solid expression in her writings, where she appears more proverbial than in her too-factual speeches, which lack emotive warmth. Her approach is completely different when it comes to the at times passionate and certainly emotional as well as natural style of her three books *It Takes a Village, and Other Lessons Children Teach Us* (1996), *Living History* (2003), and *Hard*

Choices (2014). The "cool" or "icy" and certainly intellectual Hillary Clinton is perfectly capable of letting her official hair down, to put it proverbially. And, yes, her books show Hillary Clinton to be quite the proverbialist (Mieder 2015b).

It comes as no surprise that Clinton's personal and political ethics are informed by the proverbial golden rule as well. Always interested in the children of the world, Clinton writes: "I wish more churches—and parents—took seriously the teachings of every major religion that we treat one another as each of us would want to be treated. If that happened, we could make significant inroads on the social problems we confront" (Clinton 1996, 164). And that people really get the message, she chose Barbara Reynolds's aphorism "The Golden Rule does not mean that gold shall rule" (Clinton 1996, 265) as the epigraph for her chapter "Every Business Is a Family Business" (Clinton 1996, 265–79). After all, it is humanitarian engagement rather than mercantile success that makes the world a better place for humankind.

There is a proverbial metaphor that has served Hillary Clinton well on her long and engaged political and social journey. It all has to do with the proverbial title of her extremely successful first book *It Takes a Village, and Other Lessons Children Teach Us* (1996), which begins with a chapter also entitled "It Takes a Village" (Clinton 1996, 1–11). A few pages into the chapter, she makes the following comments around the proverb "It takes a village to raise a child" that encapsulate the entire thrust of this book on the raising and educating of children. As can be seen from her remarks, she very astutely incorporates the village with its familial and social structures, traditions, and values as a small place into the nation as a whole, and beyond that into the world. After all, the child of today is a citizen not only of a particular village or country but of the interconnected world:

> Children exist in the world as well as in the family. From the moment they are born, they depend on a host of other "grown-ups"—grandparents, neighbors, teachers, ministers, employers, political leaders, and untold others who touch their lives directly and indirectly. Adults police their streets, monitor the quality of their food, air, and water, produce the programs that appear on their television, run the businesses that employ their parents, and write the laws that protect them. Each of us plays a part in every child's life: It takes a village to raise a child.
>
> I chose that old African proverb to title this book because it offers a timeless reminder that children will thrive only if their families thrive and if the whole of society cares enough to provide for them. [. . .]
>
> In earlier times and places—and until recently in our own country— the "village" meant an actual geographic place where individuals and families lived and worked together. [. . .] For most of us, though, the

village doesn't look like that anymore. [. . .] The horizons of the contemporary village extend well beyond the town line. From the moment we are born, we are exposed to vast numbers of other people and influences through radio, television, newspapers, books, movies, computers, compact discs, cellular phones, and fax machines. Technology connects us to the impersonal global village it has created. [. . .]

The sage who first offered that proverb would undoubtedly be bewildered by what constitutes the modern village. [. . .] The village can no longer be defined as a place on a map, or a list of people or organizations, but its essence remains the same: it is a network of values and relationships that support and affect our lives. (Clinton 1996, 5–7; see also 11)

The proverb is not actually of African origin, even though there is a somewhat similar Swahili proverb, "One hand (person) cannot bring up (nurse) a child." Rather, it might well have had its start from a statement made by Toni Morrison in 1981 (Mieder 2014b, 201–2; see also Shapiro 2006, 529). The fact that Morrison is a well-known African American writer might have led Clinton erroneously to conclude that she was using an African proverb. Employing it with the introductory formula "that old African proverb" certainly added authoritative expressiveness to her significant sociopolitical comment regarding the life of children.

There is also Clinton's famous remark "Human rights are women's rights and women's rights are human rights" (Clinton 2014, 585), which has become quotational if not proverbial by now (Foss 1999, 124; Bartlett 2012, 864). Here is what Hillary Rodham Clinton, as an effective advocate for women's rights worldwide, actually said at the end of a powerful anaphora during a major address at the United Nations Fourth World Conference on Women on September 5, 1995, in Beijing:

It is a violation of *human* rights when babies are denied food, or drowned, or suffocated, or their spines broken, simply because they are born girls.

It is a violation of *human* rights when women and girls are sold into the slavery of prostitution.

It is a violation of *human* rights when women are doused with gasoline, set on fire and burned to death because their marriage dowries are deemed too small.

It is a violation of *human* rights when individual women are raped in their own communities and when thousands of women are subjected to rape as a tactic or prize of war.

It is a violation of *human* rights when a leading cause of death worldwide among women ages 14 to 44 is the violence they are subjected to in their own homes.

> It is a violation of *human* rights when young girls are brutalized by the painful and degrading practice of genital mutilation.
>
> It is a violation of *human* rights when women are denied the right to plan their own families, and that includes being forced to have abortions or being sterilized against their will.
>
> If there is one message that echoes forth from this conference, it is that human rights are women's rights—and women's rights are human rights. Let us not forget that among those rights are the right to speak freely—and the right to be heard.
>
> Women must enjoy the right to participate fully in the social and political lives of their countries if we want freedom and democracy to thrive and endure. [. . .]
>
> Let this Conference be our—and the world's—call to action. (Clinton 1995, 5–7)

Indeed, her statement about human rights also being women's rights and vice versa deserves to be quoted, remembered, and adhered to as a piece of quintessential wisdom, especially in light of the fact that the world is full of painful, misogynous proverbs denying women their equal rights (Kerschen 1998; Schipper 2003). The entire speech showed Clinton's fighting spirit, which on a personal level could also be seen in her two attempts to become the first woman president in the United States during the presidential campaigns of 2008 and 2016.

Clearly, Hillary Clinton is tuned into proverbs, frequently directly calling attention to them with introductory formulas that help to strengthen the proverbial point she wishes to make. In this example, she even declares her "love" for a particular proverb! No proverb scholar could ask for more:

> There's an old saying I love: You can't roll up your sleeves and get to work if you're still wringing your hands. So, if you, like me, are worrying about our kids; if you, like me, have wondered how we can match our actions to our words, I'd like to share with you some of my convictions I've developed over a lifetime—not only as an advocate and a citizen but as a mother, daughter, sister, and wife—about what children need from us and what we owe to them. (Clinton 1996, 10)

No matter what sociopolitical issues she has been fighting for—proper care for children, women's rights, health care, welfare reform, and many others— she has struggled on against all odds and obstacles, being well aware of the modern proverbial truth that "In politics, as in life, the devil is in the details" (Clinton 2003, 290).

When Senator Bernie Sanders (b. 1941) from Vermont challenged his friend Hillary Clinton for the Democratic nomination for president in 2016, he put up a valiant fight and came close to defeating her. The reasons for his good showing are many, but one of them is doubtlessly his engaging grassroots rhetoric, which excited young people in particular to accept his revolutionary stance as a democratic socialist. His speeches and two books *Outsider in the White House* (with Huck Gutman, 2015, updated from 1997) and *Our Revolution: A Future to Believe In* (2016) contain a steady reiteration of his progressive politics, which swept the country like a fresh breeze. Since he is unwavering from his socialist agenda, Sanders's political message is steadfast and clear, with a number of proverbial leitmotifs making up his sociopolitical agenda. The tautological proverb "Enough is enough" is his often repeated slogan for his dissatisfaction with the American political status quo in need of a truly revolutionary change:

> I believe that Americans, battered by job losses and wage stagnation, angered by inequality and injustice, have come to this understanding [that a political revolution is necessary]. I hear Americans saying loudly and clearly: enough is enough. This great nation and its government belong to all of the people, and not solely to a handful of billionaires, their super PACs, and their lobbyists. (Sanders and Gutman 2015, vii; similarly in Sanders 2016, 117, 136)

With his populist arguments for a more equalitarian government, Sanders frequently references the proverbial definition of democracy that includes all people, adding much authority to the phrase by mentioning Abraham Lincoln's use of it:

> At the conclusion of his Gettysburg Address, Lincoln stated "that we here highly resolve that these dead shall not have died in vain . . . that this nation, under God, shall have a new birth of freedom . . . and that government of the people, by the people, for the people, shall not perish from the earth." In the year 2016, with a political campaign finance system that is corrupt and increasingly controlled by billionaires and special interests, I fear very much that, in fact, "government of the people, by the people, for the people" will perish in the United States of America. We cannot allow this to happen. (Sanders 2016, 203; see also 81, 187)

Again and again, Sanders attacks America's unfortunate move toward an oligarchy with the most inequitable distribution of wealth in the entire world. The proverb "The rich get richer and the poor get poorer" serves him perfectly to add emotive power to his steady warnings: "While the rich get richer, almost everyone else gets poorer; the standard of living of most Americans is in decline; democracy is in crisis, and oligarchy looms; what we know is determined by the corporate media; our health care system is in shambles, our educational system is facing a crisis" (Sanders and Gutman 2015, 274; see also 31, 107). But here is Sanders's most powerful sociopolitical use of this proverb, bookended by the proverbs "It takes money to make money" to describe the modus operandi of billionaires and "You can't have it all" to tell them that their pecuniary greed must come to a stop in a more equitable world order:

> Add in a whole slew of other credits and deductions that advantage the wealthy, and a billionaire hedge fund manager can pay a lower effective tax rate than a truck driver, teacher, or nurse. The old adage "It takes money to make money" is alive and well. The tax code is helping the very rich get insanely richer, while the middle class is disappearing and the poor are getting poorer. It is the Robin Hood principle in reverse.
>
> In my view, we have got to send a message to the billionaire class: "You can't have it all." You can't continue getting huge tax breaks by shipping American jobs to China. You can't hide your profits in the Cayman Islands and other tax havens while there are massive unmet needs in every corner of this nation. Your greed has to end. You cannot take advantage of all the benefits of America if you refuse to accept your responsibilities as Americans. We need a tax system that is fair and progressive. (Sanders 2016, 266–67; see also 121, 217, 315, 410)

And here is yet another attack on this grotesque situation, this time warning the nation that the proverbial beginning of the Declaration of Independence is in danger of being subverted:

> The ideas that all Americans are created equal and that all of us are entitled to life, liberty, and the pursuit of happiness were, according to the founders, supposed to be "self-evident truths." But those foundational notions about what this country is supposed to be all about are seriously imperiled by the grotesque level of wealth and income inequality that exists in America today. (Sanders 2016, 277; see also 186)

Clearly supportive of pay equity for women, Sanders includes a chapter with the proverbial title "Equal Pay for Equal Work" in *Our Revolution* (2016, 228–32) that certainly would have earned him the respect and admiration of Susan B. Anthony.

What is so fascinating about Sanders's effective use of proverbs is that they serve as subversive instruments to bring about a change of political power structures that are to a degree maintained by the authority of traditional proverbs. In his seminal article "Proverbs and the Politics of Language" (2000), Cameron Louis observes that in politics "proverbs are attempts to give automatic authority and legitimacy to one's perceptions or advice. When one uses a proverb, one is attempting to invoke self-evident social truths and social norms to support one's point of view" (Louis 2000, 178; see also Manders 2006). Sanders is well aware of this as he employs proverbs not so much to keep matters as they are but rather to bring about revolutionary social change. And for him also, this includes the proverbial golden rule, which appears to have fallen by the wayside in light of recent social behavior:

> America has always been a haven for the oppressed. We cannot and must not shirk our historic role as a protector of vulnerable people fleeing persecution. We must, as President Lincoln urged in his first inaugural address, appeal to the better angels of our nature. We must treat others as we would like to be treated.
>
> Sadly, in 2016, we had a major party candidate for president spending endless hours doing the exact opposite, appealing to our worst human traits—bigotry and racism. It is way past time to stop peddling hatred for political gain. We need real solutions to the real problems facing our country, including immigration. (Sanders 2016, 398; see also 149–50)

Here, then, is the final proof of the humanistic value of proverbs in sociopolitical discourse. And, no, Bernie Sanders is not talking about his Democratic opponent Hillary Clinton here but rather about President Donald Trump (b. 1946), a perplexing enigma in the proud history of the United States. Having discussed three centuries of proverbs as valued wisdom for proper social behavior, it should be of interest that Trump's confrontational and ill-conceived rhetoric is void of proverbial language. In fact, he does not even use metaphors, which usually permeate verbal and written communication. He is too straightforward in his length-restricted tweets, where there is no room for metaphors or proverbs that would help him to overcome his direct and often insulting language. After all, there is no doubt that the folkloric indirection of proverbs has always carried considerable humanistic value in effective, considerate, and ethical sociopolitical discourse.

BIBLIOGRAPHY

This chapter was first published with the same title in *Humanities* 7, no. 1 (March 2018), special issue, *The Challenge of Folklore to the Humanities*, edited by Dan Ben-Amos.

Abrahams, Roger D. 2005. *Everyday Life: A Poetics of Vernacular Practices*. Philadelphia: University of Pennsylvania Press.

Albig, William. 1931. "Proverbs and Social Control." *Sociology and Social Research* 15: 527–35.

Aron, Paul. 2008. *We Hold These Truths . . . and Other Words That Made America*. Lanham, MD: Rowman and Littlefield.

Barbour, Frances M. 1974. *A Concordance to the Sayings in Franklin's "Poor Richard."* Detroit: Gale Research Company.

Bartlett, John. 2012. *Bartlett's Familiar Quotations*. Edited by Geoffrey O'Brien. 18th ed. New York: Little, Brown.

Basler, Roy P., ed. 1953. *The Collected Works of Abraham Lincoln*. 8 vols. New Brunswick, NJ: Rutgers University Press.

Blassingame, John, ed. 1985–1992. *The Frederick Douglass Papers*. 5 vols. New Haven, CT: Yale University Press.

Burke, Kenneth. 1941. "Literature as Equipment for Living." In *The Philosophy of Literary Form: Studies in Symbolic Action*, 253–62. Baton Rouge: Louisiana State University Press.

Burrell, Brian. 1997. *The Words We Live By: The Creeds, Mottoes, and Pledges That Have Shaped America*. New York: Free Press.

Butterfield, L. H., ed. 1963–1993. *Adams Family Correspondence (1761–1785)*. 6 vols. Cambridge, MA: Belknap Press of Harvard University Press.

Carson, Clayborne, et al., eds. 1992–2007. *The Papers of Martin Luther King, Jr.* 6 vols. Berkeley: University of California Press.

Carson, Clayborne, and Peter Holloran, eds. 1998. *A Knock at Midnight: Inspiration from the Great Sermons of Reverend Martin Luther King, Jr.* New York: Warner Books.

Carson, Clayborne, and Kris Shepard, eds. 2001. *A Call to Conscience: The Landmark Speeches of Dr. Martin Luther King, Jr.* New York: Warner Books.

Clinton, Hillary Rodham. 1995. "Remarks by First Lady Hillary Rodham Clinton." United Nations Fourth World Conference on Women, September 5–6, 1995, Beijing. Executive Office of the President, Washington, DC.

Clinton, Hillary Rodham. 1996. *It Takes a Village, and Other Lessons Children Teach Us*. New York: Simon and Schuster.

Clinton, Hillary Rodham. 2003. *Living History*. New York: Simon and Schuster.

Clinton, Hillary Rodham. 2014. *Hard Choices*. New York: Simon and Schuster.

Doyle, Charles Clay, Wolfgang Mieder, and Fred R. Shapiro. 2012. *The Dictionary of Modern Proverbs*. New Haven, CT: Yale University Press.

Dundes, Alan. 1999. *Holy Writ as Oral Lit: The Bible as Folklore*. Lanham, MD: Rowman and Littlefield.

Fields, Wayne. 1996. *Union of Words: A History of Presidential Eloquence*. New York: Free Press.

Fontaine, Carole R. 1982. *Traditional Sayings in the Old Testament: A Contextual Study*. Sheffield, England: Almond Press.

Foss, William O., ed. 1999. *First Ladies Quotation Book: A Compendium of Provocative, Tender, Witty, and Important Words from the Presidents' Wives*. New York: Barricade Books.

Gallacher, Stuart A. 1949. "Franklin's *Way to Wealth*: A Florilegium of Proverbs and Wise Sayings." *Journal of English and Germanic Philology* 48, no. 2 (April): 229–51.

Gordon, Ann D., ed. 1997–2013. *The Selected Papers of Elizabeth Cady Stanton and Susan B. Anthony.* 6 vols. New Brunswick, NJ: Rutgers University Press.

Griffin, Albert Kirby. 1991. *Religious Proverbs: Over 1600 Adages from 18 Faiths Worldwide.* Jefferson, NC: McFarland.

Haas, Heather H. 2008. "Proverb Familiarity in the United States: Cross-Regional Comparisons of the Paremiological Minimum." *Journal of American Folklore* 121, no. 481 (Summer): 319–47.

Harper, Ida Husted. 1898–1908. *The Life and Work of Susan B. Anthony, Including Public Addresses, Her Own Letters and Many from Her Contemporaries During Fifty Years: A Story of the Evolution of the Status of Women.* 3 vols. Indianapolis: Hollenbeck Press.

Hertzler, Joyce. 1933–1934. "On Golden Rules." *International Journal of Ethics* 44, no. 4 (July): 418–36.

Honeck, Richard P. 1997. *A Proverb in Mind: The Cognitive Science of Proverbial Wit and Wisdom.* Mahwah, NJ: Lawrence Erlbaum Associates.

Hrisztova-Gotthardt, Hrisztalina, and Melita Aleksa Varga, eds. 2015. *Introduction to Paremiology: A Comprehensive Guide to Proverb Studies.* Berlin: Walter de Gruyter.

Jente, Richard. 1945. "The Untilled Field of Proverbs." In *Studies in Language and Literature,* edited by George R. Coffman, 112–19. Chapel Hill: University of North Carolina Press.

Kerschen, Lois. 1998. *American Proverbs About Women: A Reference Guide.* Westport, CT: Greenwood Press.

Koch, Walter A., ed. 1994. *Simple Forms: An Encyclopaedia of Simple Text-Types in Lore and Literature.* Bochum, Germany: Norbert Brockmeyer.

Krikmann, Arvo. 2009. *Proverb Semantics: Studies in Structure, Logic, and Metaphor.* Edited by Wolfgang Mieder. Burlington: University of Vermont.

Louis, Cameron. 2000. "Proverbs and the Politics of Language." *Proverbium* 17: 173–94. Also in *Cognition, Comprehension, and Communication: A Decade of North American Proverb Studies (1990–2000),* edited by Wolfgang Mieder, 271–92. Baltmannsweiler, Germany: Schneider Verlag Hohengehren, 2003.

Manders, Dean Wolfe. 2000. *The Hegemony of Common Sense: Wisdom and Mystification in Everyday Life.* New York: Peter Lang.

McKenzie, Alyce M. 1996a. "'Different Strokes for Different Folks': America's Quintessential Postmodern Proverb." *Theology Today* 53, no. 2 (July): 201–12. Also in *Cognition, Comprehension, and Communication: A Decade of North American Proverb Studies (1990–2000),* edited by Wolfgang Mieder, 311–24. Baltmannsweiler, Germany: Schneider Verlag Hohengehren, 2003.

McKenzie, Alyce M. 1996b. *Preaching Proverbs: Wisdom for the Pulpit.* Louisville, KY: Westminster John Knox Press.

Mieder, Wolfgang. 1987. *Tradition and Innovation in Folk Literature.* Hanover, NH: University Press of New England.

Mieder, Wolfgang. 1989. *American Proverbs: A Study of Texts and Contexts.* Bern: Peter Lang.

Mieder, Wolfgang. 1992. "Paremiological Minimum and Cultural Literacy." In *Creativity and Tradition in Folklore: New Directions,* edited by Simon J. Bronner, 185–203. Logan: Utah State University Press. Also in *Wise Words: Essays on the Proverb,* edited by Wolfgang Mieder, 297–316. New York: Garland Publishing, 1994.

Mieder, Wolfgang. 1993. *Proverbs Are Never Out of Season: Popular Wisdom in the Modern Age*. New York: Oxford University Press. Rpt., New York: Peter Lang, 2012.

Mieder, Wolfgang, ed. 1994. *Wise Words: Essays on the Proverb*. New York: Garland Publishing. Rpt., Abingdon, Oxon., England: Routledge, 2015.

Mieder, Wolfgang. 1997. *The Politics of Proverbs: From Traditional Wisdom to Proverbial Stereotypes*. Madison: University of Wisconsin Press.

Mieder, Wolfgang. 2000a. *The Proverbial Abraham Lincoln: An Index to Proverbs in the Works of Abraham Lincoln*. New York: Peter Lang.

Mieder, Wolfgang. 2000b. *Strategies of Wisdom: Anglo-American and German Proverb Studies*. Baltmannsweiler, Germany: Schneider Verlag Hohengehren.

Mieder, Wolfgang. 2001. *"No Struggle, No Progress": Frederick Douglass and His Proverbial Rhetoric for Civil Rights*. New York: Peter Lang.

Mieder, Wolfgang, ed. 2003. *Cognition, Comprehension, and Communication: A Decade of North American Proverb Studies (1990–2000)*. Baltmannsweiler, Germany: Schneider Verlag Hohengehren.

Mieder, Wolfgang. 2004. *Proverbs: A Handbook*. Westport, CT: Greenwood Press. Rpt., New York: Peter Lang, 2012.

Mieder, Wolfgang. 2005. *Proverbs Are the Best Policy: Folk Wisdom and American Politics*. Logan: Utah State University Press.

Mieder, Wolfgang. 2008. *"Proverbs Speak Louder Than Words": Folk Wisdom in Art, Culture, Folklore, History, Literature, and Mass Media*. New York: Peter Lang.

Mieder, Wolfgang. 2009a. *International Bibliography of Paremiology and Phraseology*. 2 vols. Berlin: Walter de Gruyter.

Mieder, Wolfgang. 2009b. *"Yes We Can": Barack Obama's Proverbial Rhetoric*. New York: Peter Lang.

Mieder, Wolfgang. 2010. *"Making a Way Out of No Way": Martin Luther King's Sermonic Proverbial Rhetoric*. New York: Peter Lang.

Mieder, Wolfgang. 2014a. *"All Men and Women Are Created Equal": Elizabeth Cady Stanton's and Susan B. Anthony's Proverbial Rhetoric Promoting Women's Rights*. New York: Peter Lang.

Mieder, Wolfgang. 2014b. *Behold the Proverbs of a People: Proverbial Wisdom in Culture, Literature, and Politics*. Jackson: University Press of Mississippi.

Mieder, Wolfgang. 2014c. "'M(R)ight Makes R(M)ight': The Sociopolitical History of a Contradictory Proverb Pair." *Proceedings of the Seventh Interdisciplinary Colloquium on Proverbs*, Tavira, Portugal, November 3–10, 2013, edited by Rui J. B. Soares and Outi Lauhakangas, 107–31. Tavira, Portugal: Tipografia Tavirense.

Mieder, Wolfgang. 2015a. "'All Men Are Created Equal': From Democratic Claim to Proverbial Game." *Scientific Newsletter, Series: Modern Linguistic and Methodical-and-Didactic Researches* (Voronezh State University of Architecture and Civil Engineering, Voronezh, Russia), no. 1: 10–37.

Mieder, Wolfgang. 2015b. "'Politics Is Not a Spectator Sport': Proverbs in the Personal and Political Writings of Hillary Rodham Clinton." *Tautosakos Darbai / Folklore Studies* (Vilnius) 50: 43–74.

Mieder, Wolfgang. 2015c. "'These Are the Times That Try Women's Souls': The Proverbial Rhetoric for Women's Rights by Elizabeth Cady Stanton and Susan B. Anthony." *Proverbium* 32: 261–330.

Mieder, Wolfgang, and George B. Bryan. 1996. *Proverbs in World Literature: A Bibliography.* New York: Peter Lang.

Mieder, Wolfgang, and Alan Dundes, eds. 1981. *The Wisdom of Many: Essays on the Proverb.* New York: Garland Publishing. Rpt., Madison: University of Wisconsin Press, 1994.

Mieder, Wolfgang, Stewart A. Kingsbury, and Kelsie B. Harder. 1992. *A Dictionary of American Proverbs.* New York: Oxford University Press.

Mieder, Wolfgang, and Janet Sobieski, eds. 2006. *"Gold Nuggets or Fool's Gold?" Magazine and Newspaper Articles on the (Ir)relevance of Proverbs and Proverbial Phrases.* Burlington: University of Vermont.

Moll, Otto E. 1958. *Sprichwörterbibliographie.* Frankfurt am Main: Vittorio Klostermann.

Newcomb, Robert. 1957. "The Sources of Benjamin Franklin's Sayings of Poor Richard." PhD diss., University of Maryland.

Nichols, Ray. 1996. "Maxims, 'Practical Wisdom,' and the Language of Action: Beyond Grand Theory." *Political Theory* 24, no. 4 (November): 687–705.

Norrick, Neal R. 1985. *How Proverbs Mean: Semantic Studies in English Proverbs.* Berlin: Mouton.

Obama, Barack. 2006. *The Audacity of Hope: Thoughts on Reclaiming the American Dream.* New York: Crown Publishers.

Obelkevich, James. 1987. "Proverbs and Social History." In *The Social History of Language,* edited by Peter Burke and Roy Porter, 43–72. Cambridge: Cambridge University Press. Also in *Wise Words: Essays on the Proverb,* edited by Wolfgang Mieder, 211–52. New York: Garland Publishing, 1994.

Permiakov, Grigorii L'vovich. 1970. *Ot pogovorki do skazki (Zametki po obshchei teorii klishe).* Moscow: Nauka Publishing House. Also in English as *From Proverb to Folk-Tale: Notes on the General Theory of Cliché.* Moscow: Nauka Publishing House, 1979.

Prahlad, Sw. Anand. 1996. *African-American Proverbs in Context.* Jackson: University Press of Mississippi.

Raymond, Joseph. 1956. "Tensions in Proverbs: More Light on International Understanding." *Western Folklore* 15, no. 3 (July): 153–58. Also in *The Wisdom of Many: Essays on the Proverb,* edited by Wolfgang Mieder and Alan Dundes, 300–308. New York: Garland Publishing, 1981.

Sanders, Bernie. 2016. *Our Revolution: A Future to Believe In.* New York: St. Martin's Press.

Sanders, Bernie, with Huck Gutman. 2015. *Outsider in the White House.* London: Verso. First published as *Outsider in the House,* 1997.

Schipper, Mineke. 2003. *Never Marry a Woman with Big Feet: Women in Proverbs from Around the World.* New Haven, CT: Yale University Press.

Seitel, Peter. 1969. "Proverbs: A Social Use of Metaphor." *Genre* 2: 143–61. Also in *The Wisdom of Many: Essays on the Proverb,* edited by Wolfgang Mieder and Alan Dundes, 122–39. New York: Garland Publishing, 1981.

Shapiro, Fred R., ed. 2006. *The Yale Book of Quotations.* New Haven, CT: Yale University Press.

Sparks, Jared, ed. 1840. *The Works of Benjamin Franklin.* 10 vols. Philadelphia: Childs and Peterson.

Stanhope, Philip Dormer, Earl of Chesterfield. 1901. *Letters to His Son: On the Fine Art of Becoming a Man of the World and a Gentleman.* Edited by Oliver H. G. Leigh. 2 vols. London: M. Walter Donne.

Stewart, Susan 1991. "Notes on Distressed Genres." *Journal of American Folklore* 104, no. 411 (Winter): 5–31.

Taylor, Archer. 1931. *The Proverb*. Cambridge, MA: Harvard University Press. Rpt. as *The Proverb and an Index to The Proverb*. Hatboro, PA: Folklore Associates, 1962. Rpt. as *The Proverb and an Index to The Proverb*, with an introduction, bibliography, and photograph of Archer Taylor by Wolfgang Mieder. Bern: Peter Lang, 1985.

Templeton, John Mark. 1997. *Worldwide Laws of Life: 200 Eternal Spiritual Principles*. Philadelphia: Templeton Press.

Winton, Alan P. 1990. *The Proverbs of Jesus: Issues of History and Rhetoric*. Sheffield, England: Sheffield Academic Press.

6

"FREEDOM IS INDIVISIBLE"

John F. Kennedy's Reliance on Proverbs

There is general agreement that President John F. Kennedy (1917–1963) was a wordsmith par excellence in his multitude of oral and written communications. He took great pride in his rhetorical prowess in his books *Why England Slept* (1940), *Profiles in Courage* (1956), and *A Nation of Immigrants* (1958 [1964]). *Profiles in Courage*, his acclaimed historical depiction of nine courageous American politicians for which he had obtained considerable help in the research and writing process by his influential speechwriter Theodore C. Sorensen, earned him a Pulitzer Prize in 1957 (Sorensen 1965, 66–70; Wills 1982, 134–39). *The Strategy of Peace* (1960), edited by Allan Nevins, might well be considered a fourth book by Kennedy. It contains a collection of his Senate speeches delivered between 1953 and 1960 together with his explanatory remarks. The very first paragraph of Kennedy's introduction to the book, written on January 1, 1960, in Washington, DC, is a revealing statement of Kennedy's view about the importance of verbal communication in a democratic society:

> This volume is born of the reminder that "in the beginning is the word"—and particularly so, in the case of a democratic government. For in such a government it is the freely spoken and freely challenged word that is meant to lay open a vision of the realities lying beyond the sweep of naked eyesight. Surely, then, the first duty of an officer in a democratic government is to uphold the integrity of words used in public debate; and to do this by himself using them in ways that they will stand as one with the things they are meant to represent. (IX, 3)

It is of linguistic interest that Kennedy changed the past tense of the Bible quotation "In the beginning was the word (John 1:1) to the present, thereby emphasizing that the proper and honest employment of words is of utmost significance in a democratic society.

Of course, the following declaration from the third short paragraph of the new president's inaugural address reiterates the programmatic value of the word in international affairs:

> Let the word go forth from this time and place, to friend and foe alike, that the torch has been passed to a new generation of Americans—born in this century, tempered by war, disciplined by hard and bitter peace, proud of our ancient heritage—and unwilling to witness or permit the slow undoing of those human rights to which this nation has always been committed, and to which we are committed today at home and around the world. (I, 1)

Not surprisingly, this memorable sentence has made it into the two seminal quotation dictionaries (Bartlett 2012, 785; Shapiro 2021, 446, no. 7). The uncommon formulation "Let the word go forth" has a somewhat biblical ring to it, and perhaps Kennedy had the following passage from the Old Testament in mind: "So shall my word be that goeth forth out of my mouth: it shall not return unto me void, but it shall accomplish that which I please, and it shall prosper in the thing whereto I sent it" (Isaiah 55:11). My supposition might not be too far-fetched, since Kennedy with his solid Catholic upbringing had "a genuine interest in and working knowledge of the Bible. He delighted in several Biblical passages and his public addresses were replete with Biblical references" (Menendez 1978, 72).

To say that "John Kennedy's authority rested in large part on his charisma and style" (Murphy 2000, 580) is an oversimplification of his rhetorical effectiveness. It is his visionary idealism as expressed in the slogan "New Frontier" delineated in his nomination acceptance speech of July 15, 1960, at the Democratic National Convention in Los Angeles (XVI, 96–102) and in countless other oral and written communications that excited and motivated people in the United States and far beyond to follow his dream of a peaceful world. Befittingly, he returned to his "word go forth" phrase barely two weeks before his untimely death during his remarks upon receiving the annual Family of Man Award on November 8, 1963, in New York City: "It is essential, in short, that the word go forth from the United States to all who are concerned about the future of the Family of Man; that we are not weary in well-doing. And we shall, I am confident, if we maintain the pace, in due season reap the kind of world we deserve and deserve the kind of world we will have" (XVI, 350).

Little wonder that Ted Sorensen, who knew Kennedy's rhetorical excellence better than anybody, entitled his edition of his friend's major communications as *"Let the Word Go Forth": The Speeches, Statements, and Writings of John F. Kennedy* (1988).

Kennedy's most memorable speech was his inaugural address of January 20, 1961, which has been analyzed in numerous scholarly publications that include Thurston Clarke's book-length study *Ask Not: The Inauguration of John F. Kennedy and the Speech That Changed America* (2004). In his seminal work *Kennedy* (1965), Sorensen, as Kennedy's major speechwriter, clearly states that despite his help Kennedy is the author of the final delivered version of his inaugural address:

> He asked me to read all the past Inaugural Addresses. [. . .] He asked me to study the secret of Lincoln's Gettysburg Address. [. . .] Actual drafting did not get under way until the week before it was due. As had been true of his acceptance speech at Los Angeles, pages, paragraphs, and complete drafts had poured in. [. . .] The final text included several phrases, sentences and themes suggested by these sources. [. . .] But however numerous the assistant artisans, the principal architect of the Inaugural Address was John Fitzgerald Kennedy. (Sorensen 1965, 240–41)

Help he did receive, but the final product was of his own making (Windt 1993, 183–85). The young, handsome, and vigorous Kennedy could in fact stand tall and proud at the lectern on that cold, wintery day in Washington, DC, and pronounce his optimistic vision for a new America in concert with a peaceful world.

Kennedy's delivery of his inaugural address, with its 1,355 words amounting to one of the shortest inaugural addresses, lasting but fourteen minutes, was an oratorial masterpiece (Wolfarth 1961). He certainly had found the perfect demeanor and tone for his epideictic message (Meyer 1982). In fact, there is no doubt that with his speech "he re-established the tradition of political eloquence" (Corbett 1965, 508) that was marked by emotional and ethical persuasion including figures of speech, metaphors, personification, antithesis, anaphora, and other rhetorical devices (Corbett 1965, 508; Kenny 1965). Putting it somewhat poetically, Theodore Otto Windt states that Kennedy's rhetorical eloquence was a "majestic march of language" (Windt 1993, 188).

As the speech shows, Kennedy was clearly fond of formulaic statements based on parallelism and antithesis. He couched his uplifting message into such structures which as sentamous remarks are poignant and memorable, if not almost proverbial due to the lingering high popular esteem for the former president. The insightful observation "If a free society cannot help the many who are poor, it cannot save the few who are rich" (I, 1; January 20, 1961) is but one example. Of special interest is Kennedy's generally known sententious remark "Let us never negotiate out of fear. But let us never fear to negotiate" in his inaugural address. It was an indirect signal to Nikita Khrushchev and the Soviet Union that the new president was willing to start serious negotiations across the Iron Curtain. Rightfully so, it has been registered in the two major quotation dictionaries (Bartlett 2012, 785; Shapiro 2021, 446, no. 11): "So let us begin anew—remembering on both sides that civility is not a sign of weakness, and sincerity is always subject to proof. Let us never negotiate out of fear. But let us never fear to negotiate. Let both sides explore what problems unite us instead of belaboring those problems which divide us" (I, 2; January 20, 1961).

Kennedy speaks of "both sides," employing diplomatic indirection to let it be known that he is prepared and willing to start serious negotiations between the two superpowers. What a powerful tiny paragraph that speaks volumes in stressing sincerity and civility between East and West! And yet, the Cuba and Berlin crises during Kennedy's short presidency brought the world close to war. Having diffused them by "sincere" and "civil" negotiations with Khrushchev, Kennedy was able to get the nuclear test ban treaty ratified—an achievement that he rightfully considered a pivotal landmark on the international scene.

With that, John F. Kennedy is reaching the ultimate crescendo of his magnificent inaugural address with a dual call for responsible action by Americans and citizens of the world. It obviously speaks for Kennedy that he includes humanity everywhere in his prophetic image of a better world order. He had worked toward the sententious remark "Ask not what your country can do for you, ask what you can do for your country" in previous speeches before and during his presidential campaign in 1960:

> We stand today on the edge of a New Frontier—the frontier of the 1960s—a frontier of unknown opportunities and perils—a frontier of unfulfilled hopes and unfilled threats. [. . .] The New Frontier of which I speak is not a set of promises—it is a set of challenges. It sums up not what I intend to offer the American people, but what I intend to ask of them. (XVI, 100–101; July 15, 1960; acceptance of presidential nomination)

> I run for the office of the Presidency not because I think it is an easy job. In many ways I think the next years are going to be the most difficult years in our history. I don't run for the office of the Presidency telling you that if you elect me life is going to be easy, because I don't think that life is going to be easy for Americans in the next decade. But I run for the Presidency because I do not want it said in the years when our generation held political power that those were the years when America began to slip, when America began to slide. [. . .] The New Frontier is not what I promise I am going to do for you. The New Frontier is what I

ask you to do for our country. Give me your help, your hand, your voice, and this country can move again. (XVI, 29; September 5, 1960)

I do not pretend that we in the Democratic Party have all the answers to most difficult questions. Senator [Lyndon] Johnson and I do not run for the office of the Presidency and Vice Presidency promising that life is going to be easy in the future. We do not campaign stressing what our country is going to do for us as a people. We stress what we can do for the country, all of us. [*Applause*] We stress the point that if we meet our public and our private responsibilities and obligations, if we recognize that self-government requires qualities of self-denial and restraint, then future historians will be able to say, "These were the great years of the American Republic, these were the years when America began to move again." (IV, 298; September 20, 1960; also registered in Shapiro 2021, 446, no. 5)

As Sorensen points out, Kennedy "worked and reworked the 'ask not' sentence, with the three campaign speeches containing a similar phrase (Anchorage, Detroit, Washington) spread out on a low glass coffee table beside him" (Sorensen 1965, 243). Clearly he wanted the perfect summation for winding up his inaugural speech in front of America and the world listening to him. He starts with a call to his fellow citizens to follow his trumpet to new action in the name of his New Frontier, but then ingeniously goes beyond the national view by repeating his sententious statement with a call for the citizens of the world. That is indeed a moment of oratory grandeur expressing hope for all people on earth:

And so, my fellow Americans: ask not what your country can do for you—ask what you can do for your country. My fellow citizens of the world: ask not what America will do for you, but what together we can do for the freedom of man. Finally, whether you are citizens of America or citizens of the world, ask of us here the same high standards of strength and sacrifice which we ask of you. (I, 3; January 20, 1961)

Rightfully so, this call for responsible civic action has gone down in the annals of great rhetoric (Bartlett 2012, 785; Shapiro 2021, 447, no. 16). There is no analysis of the inaugural address that does not address the source of the by now proverbial statement "Ask not what your country can do for you, ask what you can do for your country." This antithetical statement with its parallel structure has even more precisely been categorized as containing "a figure of repetition known as antimetabole (repetition of words in converse order)"

(Corbett 1965, 515; see also Carter 1963, 36–37; Windt 1993, 188–89). Thurston Clarke gives the best overview of what all might lie behind this best-known utterance of Kennedy:

> Bartlett's *Familiar Quotations* and numerous editors and authors have pointed out that "ask not" has numerous analogues. Warren Harding, for example, had told the 1916 Republican National Convention that "we must have citizenship less concerned about what the government can do for it, and more anxious about what it can do for the nation." In an 1884 Memorial Day address, the Supreme Court justice Oliver Wendell Holmes [Jr.] had said, "It is now the moment when by common consent we pause to become conscious of our national life and to rejoice in it, to recall what our country has done for each of us, and ask ourselves what we can do for our country in return." We can assume that someone as widely read and historically savvy as Kennedy would have come across these quotations. He must have also been familiar with the exhortation of his prep school headmaster that what mattered most was "not what Choate does for you, but what you can do for Choate," familiar with Cicero's "you should do something for your country once in a while instead of always thinking about what your country can do for you," and with the verse from Luke [12:48] that his mother had drilled into him, "For unto whomsoever much is given, of him shall much be required." This was a bare-bones summary of the concept behind "ask not": that because much has been given to the citizens of the prosperous and democratic nation, they are required to make sacrifices for the good of that nation. (Clarke 2004, 78–79; see Bartlett 2012, 785n2; Shapiro 2021, 447, no. 16)

When I wrote my article on all inaugural addresses of American presidents, which was originally published in 2000, I, too, had reached the conclusion after having cited the statement by Holmes that it is hard to imagine that Kennedy's famous civic slogan was not related to it (Mieder 2005, 173). But no matter what the precursors were, including Kennedy's own attempts, in the precise wording by John F. Kennedy it is *his* sententious remark that has taken on a proverbial status, often cited as the mere "ask not" formula.

There are several more phrases that indicate Kennedy's "recurrent use of antithesis" (Kenny 1965, 10) in his oral and written communications. A very powerful example in the face of the threat of nuclear war is "Mankind must put an end to war or war will put an end to mankind," which Kennedy included in his major address before the General Assembly of the United Nations of September 25, 1961:

128   PROVERBS IN POLITICS

Unconditional war can no longer lead to unconditional victory. It can no longer serve to settle disputes. It can no longer concern the great powers alone. For a nuclear disaster, spread by wind and water and fear, could well engulf the great and the small, the rich and the poor, the committed and the uncommitted alike. Mankind must put an end to war—or war will put an end to mankind. (I, 618–19)

In the same speech, indirectly addressing the Soviet Union, he also repeated his antithetical sententious "negotiation" remark from his inaugural address:

The events and decisions of the next ten months may well decide the fate of man for the next ten thousand years. There will be no avoiding those events. There will be no appeal from these decisions. And we in this hall shall be remembered either as part of the generation that turned this planet into a flaming funeral pyre or the generation that met its vow "to save succeeding generations from the scourge of war [between the United States and the Soviet Union]." In the endeavor to meet that vow, I pledge you every effort this Nation possesses. I pledge you that we shall neither commit nor provoke aggression, that we shall neither flee nor invoke the threat of force, that we shall never negotiate out of fear, we shall never fear to negotiate. (I, 625)

And indeed, in his short remarks, filled with serious commitment and clear emotion, at the Rudolph Wilde Platz in West Berlin on June 26, 1963, he twice proudly exclaimed in four short German words "Ich bin ein Berliner"— without doubt a pronouncement that is known throughout the world. He began by citing the classical boast "civis Romanus sum," which was known to many of his German listeners who had come by the thousands to greet the admired president:

I am proud to come to this city as the guest of your distinguished Mayor [Willy Brandt], who has symbolized throughout the world the fighting spirit of West Berlin. And I am proud to visit the Federal Republic with your distinguished Chancellor [Konrad Adenauer] who for so many years has committed Germany to democracy and freedom and progress, and to come here in the company of my fellow American, General [Lucius D.] Clay, who has been in this city during its great moments of crisis and will come again if ever needed. Two thousand years ago the proudest boast was "civis Romanus sum." Today, in the world of freedom, the proudest boast is "Ich bin ein Berliner." (III, 524)

Understandably, the large crowd "went wild" with appreciation and enthusiasm, but Kennedy had not yet reached the crescendo of his speech. What came next was his claim that "Freedom is indivisible," which he had earlier pronounced in a campaign speech on October 12, 1960, in New York City:

> Freedom is indivisible in all its aspects. To provide equal rights for all requires that we respect the liberties of speech and belief and assembly, guaranteed by the Constitution, and these liberties in turn are hollow mockeries unless they are maintained also by a decent economic life. Those who are too poor, uninformed, too uneducated to enjoy their constitutional freedoms of choice, do not really possess those freedoms. These are the indispensable foundations of a free society. (XII, 102)

Regarding the divided city of Berlin, it was natural that Kennedy returned to his phrase "Freedom is indivisible," which appears to be his creation and which could well become a proverb. It certainly was the perfect and succinct summary of the message that Kennedy wanted to express. Stating this wisdom was one thing, but Kennedy went on to call for a unified Berlin in a unified Germany as a member of the free world. And then he declared himself as a free man to be a Berlin citizen:

> Freedom is indivisible, and when one man is enslaved, all are not free. When all are free, then we can look forward to that day when this city will be joined as one and this country and this great Continent of Europe in a peaceful and hopeful globe. When that day finally comes, as it will, people of West Berlin can take sober satisfaction in the fact that they were in the front lines for almost two decades. All free men, wherever they may live, are citizens of Berlin, and, therefore, as a free man, I take pride in the words "*Ich bin ein Berliner.*" (III, 525; June 26, 1963)

Freedom, peace, and a better future were constantly on Kennedy's mind, as can be seen from a few additional "memorable aphorisms" (Corbett 1965, 437) that most likely were coined by Kennedy. As a pragmatist with idealistic visions, he is well aware of the proverbial price that needs to be paid to maintain or to create a free society, for "The cost of freedom is always high":

> The path we have chosen for the present is full of hazards, as all paths are—but it is the one most consistent with our character and courage as a nation and our commitments around the world. The cost of freedom is always high—but Americans have always paid it. And one path we

shall never choose, and that is the path of surrender or submission. Our goal is not the victory of might, but the vindication of right—not peace at the expense of freedom, but both peace *and* freedom, here in this hemisphere, and, we hope, around the world. God willing, that goal will be achieved. (II, 808; October 22, 1962)

It should be noted that the statement "Our goal is not the victory of might, but the vindication of right" is yet another example of his antithetical style. In addition, it is almost certainly based on the fourteenth-century English proverb "Right makes might," with its antithesis "Might makes right" stemming from the same century. This contradictory proverb pair has an impressive sociopolitical history, with one piece of wisdom negating the other in a world of confrontation (Mieder 2019, 263–86).

As an American president, Kennedy was deeply involved in the international politics of war and peace, especially regarding the relationship between the Soviet Union and the United States. The proverb-like statement "The mere absence of war is not peace" probably stems from his preoccupation with finding lasting solutions to conflicts:

But we cannot be satisfied to rest here. This is the side of the hill, not the top. The mere absence of war is not peace. The mere absence of recession is not growth. We have made a beginning—but we have only begun. Now the time has come to make the most of our gains—to translate the renewal of our national strength into the achievement of our national purpose. (III, 12; January 14, 1963)

It comes as no surprise that Kennedy also turned to the biblical injunction "Seek peace, and pursue it" from the book of Psalms (34:14), which suited him perfectly in his mission to maintain peace throughout the world:

Peace is our primary objective in the Middle East—and peace is partly our responsibility. "Seek peace, and pursue it" commands the psalmist. And that we must do. With open minds, open hearts, and the priceless asset of our American heritage, we shall seek peace in the Middle East, as elsewhere. And when history writes its verdict, let it be said that we pursued the peace with all the courage, all the strength, and all the resourcefulness at our command. (IV, 50; August 26, 1960)

There are also several statements in which Kennedy quotes "Seek peace, and pursue it" only as the truncated admonition "Pursue peace" together with an unusual employment of the proverbial expression "to beat swords into plowshares" (Isaiah 2:9) from the Old Testament (Mieder 2014b, 230–58). Normally this phrase is cited in its positive sense, but Kennedy appears not to be ready to give up the sword as a protective device, rather being willing to change more aggressive weaponry into peaceful substitutes:

> In a world of danger and trial, peace is our deepest aspiration, and when peace comes we will gladly convert not our swords into plowshares, but our bombs into peaceful reactors, and our planes into space vessels. "Pursue peace," the Bible tells us, and we shall pursue it with every effort and every energy that we possess. (IV, 134–35; September 6, 1960)

Even though John F. Kennedy attended church regularly and was a faithful Catholic, he "had no real intellectual interest in religion nor had he ever had much systematic training in theology" (Menendez 1978, 67). His interest was not strictly in Catholicism but rather in the ethical messages of different religions. In fact, he "abhorred religious divisiveness and provincialism" (Menendez 1978, 67). As his writings and speeches reveal, he was without doubt *bibelfest*, as the German language refers to being well versed in the Bible, specifically in wisdom sayings, of which many have long become proverbs in secular use (Mieder 1990a; Griffin 1991):

> John F. Kennedy had a genuine interest in and working knowledge of the Bible. [. . .] He seemed to prefer the Old Testament, especially the Psalms and Proverbs and the passage from the third chapter of Ecclesiastes, which treats of the changing seasons, the ebb and flow of human life. Courage, integrity, destiny, righteousness, and dependence on God are the items that he thought to illuminate in Biblical verse. Tenacity, endurance, and observing one's commitment appear with frequency in the scriptural allusions pervading his speeches. (Menendez 1978, 72–73)

This is indeed a befitting summary of Kennedy's use of well-known Bible verses for his "rhetorical exigence" (Warnick 1996, 185), with his "epideictic rhetoric" (Bostdorff and Ferris 2014, 411) being informed by a solid dose of ethos. Considering that Kennedy fought against being considered a Catholic president, his steady reliance on the Bible might at first be surprising, especially also in light of the fact of the so-called separation of church and state in the United States. But Kennedy employs these short biblical passages—or, better, verses or wisdom sayings—not so much as religious statements but more from the

132   PROVERBS IN POLITICS

point of view of "linguistic pragmatics" (Wilson 2015, 30), knowing only too
well that the American public in general will react positively to this language
in politics. Presidents Lincoln's and Obama's rhetoric is quite similar in that
respect (Mieder 2000, 3–10; Mieder 2009, 20–22).

As some of the following contextualized passages will show, Kennedy always
states his quotations from the Bible in a secular context informed by worldly
matters. And he does not hide his biblical messages, using such introductory
formulas as "the Bible tells us," "the Scripture tells us," "the biblical injunction,"
"the words of Isaiah," and "in the words of the Psalmist." And yet, Kennedy
does not preach as such, as can be seen from the way he integrates the Bible
proverb "Whom God has joined together, let no man put asunder" (Matthew
19:6), often cited in wedding vows, to celebrate the relationship of the United
States with Canada and Mexico as our immediate neighbors:

> Geography has made us neighbors [Canada and the United States]. His-
> tory has made us friends. Economics has made us partners. And neces-
> sity has made us allies. Those whom nature hath joined together, let no
> man put asunder. (I, 383; May 17, 1961)

> Geography has made us neighbors [Mexico and the United States],
> tradition has made us friends. Economics has made us partners. And
> necessity has made us allies—in a vast *Alianza para el Progreso*. Those
> whom nature has joined together, let no man put asunder. (II, 520;
> June 29, 1962)

The two passages were delivered about a year apart, and their almost identical wording indicates how presidential statements can be recycled for different occasions. Of course, it should also be noticed that Kennedy very
shrewdly exchanged "God" with "nature" in this secular application of the
Bible verse.

In this dangerous world, it was of utmost importance to Kennedy to retain
America's strength without any sign of weakness. This led him to render
a negative interpretation of the Bible proverb "A soft answer turneth away
wrath" (Proverbs 15:1), since the Soviet Union could not be dealt with in
gentle terms:

> We send arms to other peoples—just as we send them the ideals of
> democracy in which we believe—but we cannot send them the will to
> use those arms or to abide by those ideals. And while we believe not
> only in the force of arms but in the force of right and reason, we have
> learned that reason does not always appeal to unreasonable men—that

it is not always true that "a soft answer turneth away wrath"—and that right does not always make might. In short, we must face problems which do not lend themselves to easy or quick or permanent solutions. And we must face the fact that the United States is neither omnipotent [n]or omniscient. (I, 725–26; November 16, 1961)

It should be noted that Kennedy also points out "that right does not always make right," negating the old English proverb "Right makes might" (Mieder 2019, 263–86) in light of the fact that the humane cause of freedom pursued by the United States does not automatically translate into changing the mind of its Soviet adversary. In order to express that America is on the right side of the struggle with the Soviet Union, Kennedy calls on the Old Testament proverb "Righteousness exalteth a nation" (Proverbs 14:34):

And though the task ahead is not easy, it is exciting. For our cause is a sacred cause. Our fight is the fight of God-fearing men against godless communism. Our business is the unfinished business—not of Houston alone, not of Harris County alone, not of America alone. It is the unfinished business of the world. It is the business of making peace. For the making of peace is the noblest work of God-fearing men. It is the righteous way. And righteousness exalteth a nation. (IV, 1016; September 12, 1960)

In the fight for freedom, it is paramount that truth prevails in national and international affairs, with Kennedy being quick to cite the well-known Bible proverb "The truth shall make you free" (John 8:32) as the underpinning of fair and honest social interaction:

If we are to make the sacrifices and summon the courage that are necessary to meet the challenge of the 1960s, we need to know the truth, the bad news as well as the good. We must hold steadfastly to the Biblical injunction: "Ye shall know the truth and the truth will make ye free." (IV, 1198; October 26, 1960)

This proverb became a favorite piece of wisdom in the many addresses that Kennedy gave on university campuses, where he enjoyed "the 'teacher role' that epideictic rhetors assume" (Bostdorff and Ferris 1978, 414):

Ninety years from now I have no doubt that Vanderbilt University will still be fulfilling this mission. It will still uphold learning, encourage public service, and teach respect for the law. It will neither turn its back on proven wisdom [n]or turn its face from newborn challenge. It will still pass on to the youth of our land the full meaning of their rights and their responsibilities. And it will still be teaching the truth—the truth that makes us free and will keep us free. (III, 409; May 18, 1963)

At another university, he referred to the command "Let there be light" (Genesis 1:3) to conclude his address, encouraging students to carry forward the torch of education, which will be instrumental in improving society:

The nation was then [in 1861, at the time of the founding of the University of Washington] torn by war. This territory had only the simplest elements of civilization. And this city [Seattle] had barely begun to function. But a university was one of their earliest thoughts—and they summed it up in the motto that they adopted: "Let there be light." What more can be said today, regarding all the dark and tangled problems we face than: Let there be light. And to accomplish that illumination, the University of Washington shall still hold high the torch. (I, 728; November 16, 1961)

Kennedy was thoroughly convinced that high school and university education, together with the ethics contained in the Bible, are necessary for an improved world order, with educated students going out to spread knowledge and the idea of freedom by way of the Peace Corps to underdeveloped countries (Sorensen 1965, 357–65).

Kennedy's commitment to peace and freedom is ever present in his communications, but there is also the significant aspect of helpfulness to those nations not as fortunate as the affluent and prosperous United States. In many ways he saw himself as the caregiver, exemplified by the creation of the Peace Corps, to those less fortunate in this country and beyond. What better rhetorical way than to cite the phrase "My cup runneth over" (Psalms 23:5) to advance this social agenda:

We live in the land of abundance, the land of such great abundance of food and fiber, in fact, that our cup runneth over. At the same time we live in a world where over 60 percent of the population lives under the shadow of hunger and malnutrition. This is the great paradox of the 1950s. (XV, 48; October 31, 1960)

As one would expect, there is also the very popular Bible proverb "It is more blessed to give than to receive" (Acts of the Apostles 20:35) to underscore the need to care for others and to lend a helping hand whenever possible:

I was struck by the fact that in the far off continents Muslims, Hindus, Buddhists, as well as Christians, pause from their labors on the 25th day of December to celebrate the birthday of the Prince of Peace. There could be no more striking proof that Christmas is truly the universal holiday of all men. It is the day when all of us dedicate our thoughts to others; when all are reminded that mercy and compassion are the enduring virtues; when all show, by small deeds and large and by acts, that it is more blessed to give than to receive. (II, 888; December 17, 1962)

It is a bit strange to connect other religions with the celebration of Christmas, but Kennedy's laudable "ecumenism revealed [itself] in his private charity. He donated his entire salary to Protestant, Catholic, Jewish, and other non-sectarian charities, stipulating that his gifts be given without publicity" (Menendez 1978, 68–69).

There is another New Testament proverb, "Of those to whom much is given, much is required" (Luke 12:48), that served Kennedy well in his philanthropic mission far beyond the borders of the United States:

For of those to whom much is given, much is required. And when at some future date the high court of history sits in judgment on each of us, recording whether in our brief span of service we fulfilled our responsibilities to the state, our success or failure, in whatever office we hold, will be measured by the answers to four questions [dealing with] courage, judgment, integrity, and dedication. (XIII, 5; January 9, 1961)

Equality of opportunity does not mean equality of responsibility. All Americans must be responsible citizens, but some must be more responsible than others, by virtue of their public or their private position, their role in the family or community, their prospects for the future, or their legacy from the past. Increased responsibility goes with increased ability, for "of those to whom much is given, much is required." (III, 407; May 18, 1963)

This is a positive call to arms for Americans to become role models of charity and service to all those less fortunate.

Especially in the heat of his presidential campaign, Kennedy employed Bible proverbs as cautionary statements, with the Bible reference adding rhetorical authority to his arguments, for example with the often-heard New Testament proverb "Whatsoever a man soweth, that shall he also reap" (Galatians 6:7). He quotes it as a promise to his fellow Democrats that were they to choose to vote for him, they would definitely reap positive results:

Give me your help. Give me your hand and your heart in the week ahead [the last week of the campaign]—and remember what the Bible tells us: That "whatsoever a man soweth, that shall he also reap." If in this coming week, and in all the weeks and years that follow, we can sow the seeds of dedication and effort, we shall surely reap a great victory for our country. (IV, 837; October 31, 1960)

President Kennedy, despite his Harvard education and his intellectual prowess, had great respect for farmers, and his commitment to their hard work was by no means just political lip service. He knew well that the population of the world depends on food production. To this vital matter for the survival of humankind, Kennedy added the spread and protection of human rights. In his major address before the General Assembly of the United Nations on September 20, 1963, in New York, he included the proverb "Man does not live by bread alone" (Deuteronomy 8:3; Matthew 4:4), which appears in both the Old and New Testaments. While acknowledging the need for food, the proverb also states that there is more to life than mere nourishment. And this gives him the opportunity to talk about human rights, which are of the greatest importance for a safe and free life:

The worldwide program of farm productivity and food distribution, similar to our country's "Food for Peace" program, could now give every child the food he needs. But man does not live by bread alone—and the members of this organization [the United Nations] are committed by the Charter to promote and respect human rights. Those rights are not respected when a Buddhist priest is driven from his pagoda, when a synagogue is shut down, when a Protestant church cannot open a mission, when a Cardinal is forced into hiding, or when a crowded church service is bombed. The United States of America is opposed to discrimination and persecution on grounds of race and religion anywhere in the world, including our own Nation. We are working to right the wrongs of our own country. (III, 696–97)

It does seem strange, however, that the golden rule "Do unto others as you would have them do unto you" (Matthew 7:12), as the most basic principle of social behavior and which appears in all the major religions of the world, cannot be found in Kennedy's many communications (Griffin 1991). Other presidents, certainly Abraham Lincoln and Barack Obama, relied repeatedly on its humane message (Mieder 2014b, 172–97). But while Kennedy does not cite the proverb, there is one passage in which he at least refers to the "Golden Rule," assuming most people would know it:

Brotherhood, tolerance, enlightened relations between members of different ethnic groups—these are, after all, simply an extension of the concept upon which all free organized society is based. Some call this concept comity. Some find it in the Golden Rule, others in Rousseau's "social contract." Our Declaration of Independence calls it "the consent of the governed." The ancient Romans called it "civitatis filia," or civic friendship. (IX, 112–13; February 24, 1957)

Perhaps his intellectual mind and his inclination toward high rhetoric carried him away just a little here. But there is no reason to speculate at the end of this discussion of Kennedy's effective use of Bible proverbs. They served him well to express his vision for a free and peaceful world, perfectly expressed by the Bible proverb "Love your neighbor" (Matthew 5:43), which parallels the golden rule:

World peace, like community peace, does not require that each man love his neighbor—it requires only that they live together in mutual toler-ance, submitting their disputes to a just and peaceful settlement. And history teaches us that enmities between nations, as between individu-als, do not last forever. However fixed our likes and dislikes may seem, the tide of time and events will often bring surprising changes in the relations between nations and neighbors. (III, 461; June 10, 1963)

Theodore C. Sorensen, Kennedy's alter ego in the formulation of speeches and writings, begins the chapter "The Speech-Writing" of his seminal book *Kennedy* (1965, 59–65) with the enumerative observation that Kennedy "used little or no slang, dialect, legalistic terms, contradictions, clichés, elaborate metaphors or ornate figures of speech. He refused to be folksy or to include any phrase or image he considered corny, tasteless or trite" (Sorensen 1965, 62). Generally speaking, there is considerable truth to this statement, but it is unfortunate that Sorensen nowhere says anything about the prevalence of Bible proverbs as well as folk proverbs, proverbial expressions and comparisons, and other preformulated language. Unless, of course, he considers the term "cliché" to be an umbrella term for all types of phraseological units. But the scarcity of commentary on Kennedy's rather frequent use of Bible verses in the vast secondary literature on John F. Kennedy regrettably also pertains to his skillful and significant employment of proverbial language. Even granting that Kennedy might not have been as keen as such presidents as Abraham Lincoln, Harry Truman, and Barack Obama to rely on proverbial language in his communications, the fact that he occasionally introduces folk proverbs with such introductory formulas as "the proverb" or "the saying" shows that he was aware that such "folksy" phrases added traditional wisdom and metaphorical

138   PROVERBS IN POLITICS

expressiveness to his elevated rhetoric. Considering his high regard for Winston Churchill's linguistic prowess and Harry Truman's down-to-earth style, Kennedy can hardly have missed their memorable statements replete with proverbs and proverbial expressions (Mieder and Bryan 1995; Mieder and Bryan 1997).

It must be acknowledged that Kennedy, and probably also Sorensen, did not especially consider the term "proverb" when citing folk wisdom. They much preferred the designation "old saying" as an identifying introductory formula, thereby calling attention to the occurrence of traditional proverbs. In fact, strange as it might seem, the term *proverb* appears but three times in the vast published corpus of Kennedy's communications. Interestingly enough, he used the term only to identity two proverbs as being of Chinese origin. In the first case, the proverb "A journey of a thousand miles must begin with a single step" has become current in English translation (Mieder, Kingsbury, and Harder 1992, 340) and served Kennedy well to explain that America has been willing to take the first step to find peace and freedom everywhere and will continue to do so:

> But now, for the first time in many years, the path of peace may be open [by way of the Nuclear Test Ban Treaty]. Nobody can be certain what the future will bring. No one can say whether the time has come for an easing of the struggle. But history and our own conscience will judge us harshly if we do not now make every effort to test our hopes by action, and this is the place to begin. According to the ancient Chinese proverb, "A journey of a thousand miles must begin with a single step." My fellow Americans, let us take that first step. Let us, if we can, step back from the shadows of war and seek out the way of peace. And if that journey is a thousand miles or even more, let history record that we, in this land, at this time, took the first step. (III, 606; July 26, 1963)

This proverb has been traced back to the ancient Chinese philosopher Lao Tzu (Shapiro 2021, 471).

In his use of a second Chinese proverb, "Each generation builds a road for the next," Kennedy calls it "an old Chinese saying," thereby employing his preferred term of designation. In his second use of the proverb in a speech two days later, he does not identify it as being old or of Chinese origin, understanding it as a piece of folk wisdom that does not need an identifying marker. It is certainly prudent to point to the responsibilities that one generation has for the next:

> There is an old Chinese saying that each generation builds a road for the next. The road has been well built for us, and I believe it is incumbent upon us, in our generation, this year of 1962, to build a road for

the next generation. And I believe that this bill [on trade] is it. (II, 412; May 17, 1962)

Nevertheless, there are several instances when Kennedy introduces common Anglo-American proverbs with the "saying" designation, which signals that he is citing an accepted truth that brings with it an authoritative claim:

> Familiarity breeds contempt.
> I do not mean to imply that the relations between our two nations [Canada and the United States] are so close as to encourage domination or subservience. This has not been a case where in terms of the old saying, "familiarity breeds contempt." On the contrary, a co-operative friendship of such meaning and solidarity permits a full and frank discussion of issues of mutual interest, even when that discussion may jar sensitive ears on the other side of the border. (VII, 8; 1957)

> Victory has a hundred fathers and defeat is an orphan.
> One of the problems of a free society, a problem not met by a dictator-ship, is this problem of information. A good deal has been printed in the paper and I wouldn't be surprised if those of you who are members of the press will be receiving a lot of background briefings in the next day or two by interested people or interested agencies. There's an old saying that victory has 100 fathers and defeat is an orphan. And I wouldn't be surprised if information is poured into you in regard to all of the recent activities. (I, 312; April 21, 1961)

It is clear that Kennedy draws on familiar proverbs to strengthen the points he is making. The generally known sayings create a bond between him as the speaker and his audience, who readily accept his proverbial claims expressed with such a vigorous and self-assured voice. But Kennedy is not married to the "old saying" marker, and he is apt to drop it when he becomes aware that people know the saying well enough in any case. Thus in the case of "Things don't happen, they are made to happen," which he started to cite in the fall of 1963, he at first used the introductory formula together with the proverb, giving him the opportunity to explain that he as a man of action is making things move forward:

> There is an old saying that things don't happen, they are made to hap-pen. And we in our years have to make the same wise judgments about what policies will ensure us a growing prosperity as were made in the years before. The whole experience between two world wars, which was

so tragic for this country, should tell us that we cannot leave it to mere chance and accident. It requires the long-range judgment of all of us, the public judgment, not only the pursuit of our private interests but the public judgment of what it takes to keep 180 million people gradually rising. And anyone who thinks it can be done by accident and chance should look back on the history of 1919 to 1939 to know what can happen when we let natural forces operate completely freely. (III, 718; September 25, 1963)

Things are somewhat similar with the repeated appearance of the proverb "Don't take down the fence until you know why it was put up," which Kennedy began to use in 1958 by first ascribing it to the English writer G. K. Chesterton (1874–1936):

> G. K. Chesterton once said, "Never take down the fence until you know why it has been put up." One of the fences in the Senate has been consideration of all of these appropriate matters in committee. I think the hearing this morning indicates, and I know future hearings will indicate, the great value of having this legislation tested by the appropriate committee of the Senate. (US Senate 1958, 239; I owe this and the following two references to my friend Charles Clay Doyle.)

However, the proverb cannot be found in Chesterton's works, although the following paragraph from *The Thing: Why I Am a Catholic* (1929) contains the concept, with Kennedy perhaps having read this popular book in its 1957 edition:

> In the matter of reforming things, as distinct from deforming them, there is one plain and simple principle; a principle which will probably be called a paradox. There exists in such a case a certain institution or law; let us say, for the sake of simplicity, a fence of gate erected across a road. The more modern type of reformer goes gaily up to it and says, "I don't see the use of this; let us clear it away." To which the more intelligent type of reformer will do well to answer: "If you don't see the use of it, I certainly won't let you clear it away. Go away and think. Then, when you can come back and tell me that you *do* see the use of it, I may allow you to destroy it." (Chesterton [1929] 1957, 35)

In any case, a year later Kennedy used the proverb again in an interview, this time claiming that it stemmed from the poet Robert Frost:

[SENATOR KEN] KEATING: How do you feel about repealing the amendment that prevents a President from serving more than two terms?

KENNEDY: Well I voted for that amendment when I was first in the Congress, as I think you did. I think that, though I'm a great believer in Robert Frost's saying, "Don't take down a fence 'til you know why it's been put up," I would think that on balance we should. ("Interview of Senator John F. Kennedy" 1959)

Kennedy continued citing the insightful proverb early in his presidency. The repeated appearance of this saying—proverb—is of great paremiological interest! Our *Dictionary of Modern Proverbs* gives as its earliest recorded reference the year 1964 (Doyle, Mieder, and Shapiro 2012, 75), and now we have Kennedy using it several times before that date, between 1958 and 1963. Little did Kennedy know that one day, sixty years after he uttered it, his citations would help to correct the historical record of the proverb!

But that is not the end of the story. For some unknown reason, Kennedy moved away from stating "Don't take down the fence until you know why it was put up" as an anonymous proverb to claiming repeatedly that Robert Frost used it—perhaps even coined it—in one of his poems. Having invited Frost to read a poem at his inauguration and quoting him from time to time (St. Onge and Moore 2016), Frost was clearly often on his mind, as can be seen from his touching statement on the poet's death on January 29, 1963:

> The death of Robert Frost leaves a vacancy in the American spirit. He was the great American poet of our time. His art and his life summed up the essential qualities of the New England he loved so much: the fresh delight in nature, the plainness of speech, the canny wisdom, and the deep, underlying insight into the human soul. His death impoverishes us all; but he has bequeathed his Nation a body of imperishable verse from which America will forever gain joy and understanding. He had promises to keep, and miles to go, and now he sleeps. (III, 105; January 29, 1963)

Below are two passages showing Kennedy's association of "fence" proverbs with Robert Frost, even though the first proverb does not appear in the poet's works; the first passage is as follows:

> But recalling what Robert Frost, one of our poets, once said, "Don't take down the fence until you know why it was put up," I have a strong conviction that we should seek to strengthen the United Nations and make

it the kind of instrument which all of us hope it will be. I don't think, really, in any sense, the United Nations has failed as a concept. I think occasionally we fail it. And the more that we can do to strengthen the idea of a community of the world, to seek to develop matters by which tensions of the world and problems of the world can be solved in an orderly and peaceful way, I think that's in the common interest of us all. (I, 797; December 11, 1961)

The proverb with its fence imagery is perfect for Kennedy's explanation of the work of the United Nations and America's maintenance of a border between the free and the communist worlds. Of course, there is a second, equally befitting American "fence" proverb, namely "Good fences make good neighbors." In my lengthy historical study of the proverb, I found its earliest printed record in 1850, with my friend Fred R. Shapiro discovering three earlier references from 1834, 1846, and 1847 (Mieder 2005, 210–43; Shapiro 2021, 657, no. 125). But in a letter of January 3, 2023, Fred informed me that he had found the line "Good fences make good neighbors, and a critical watch over persons in trust makes them careful to preserve their integrity" in an issue of the *Vermont Gazette* (May 30, 1794, 2, column 4). A couple of weeks later I discovered it verbatim in *Spooner's Vermont Journal* (June 16, 1794, 1, column 4). It was surely picked up subsequently by other publications in Vermont, and it does my heart good to finally know that this proverb almost certainly had its beginnings in my beloved rural state of Vermont.

Enough of this personal detour! But there is a point to it, for Fred Shapiro and I wholeheartedly agree that President Kennedy was thinking of "Good fences make good neighbors" when he mistakenly attached Frost's name to "Don't take down the fence until you know why it was put up." After all, Kennedy certainly knew Frost's famous poem "Mending Wall" (1914), in which this proverb appears twice, once in the middle and then at the very end. And he made convincing use of it in a convocation address on October 8, 1957, at the University of New Brunswick in Fredericton, New Brunswick, Canada. In fact, the speech was published as a small pamphlet with the title "Good Fences Make Good Neighbors" (1960), a copy of which was obtained for me by colleague and longtime friend Lisa Brooks, head of our interlibrary loan staff at the University of Vermont. As expected, the proverb appears as the perfect description of the neighborly relationship between Canada and the United States:

A friendship such as ours, moreover encourages healthy competition in international trade, it requires that neither take the other for granted in international politics. "Good fences," reads a poem by one of our most distinguished New England poets, Robert Frost, "make good neighbours." Canada and the United States have carefully maintained the good fences that help make them good neighbours. (VII, 8–9)

And yet, it baffles me that Kennedy used this proverb but this one time! It would have been such a befitting proverbial metaphor in multiple national and international situations, which he dealt with day in and day out!

One thing is for certain: Kennedy was perfectly willing to ensure that people were aware that he used proverbs with ever different introductory phrases drawing attention to the wisdom expressed in them. The proverbs function primarily as concise summaries of major points that he wanted to make. They also add a certain authority to his explanations, placing Kennedy in an educational position. Here are two examples in which he draws on ancient proverbs that have been loan translated into most European languages and beyond (Paczolay 1997):

Know thyself.

In all recorded history, probably the safest bit of advice ever offered man was the ancient admonition to "know thyself." As with individuals, so with nations. Just as a man who realizes that his life has gone off course can regain his bearings only through the strictest self-scrutiny, so a whole people, become aware that things have somehow gone wrong, can right matters only by a rigidly honest look at its core of collective being, its national purpose. (X, 70; 1960)

A sound mind in a sound body.

I want to urge that this [health] be a matter of great priority. "A sound mind and a sound body" is one of the oldest slogans of the Western World. I am hopeful that we will place proper weight on intellectual achievement, but in my judgment, for the long-range happiness and well-being of all of you, for the strengthening of our country, for a more active and vigorous life, all of you as individuals and as groups will participate in strengthening the physical well-being of young American boys and girls. (I, 524; July 19, 1961)

As can be seen, Kennedy draws special attention to the fact that both proverbs go back to ancient times. When it comes to the proverb "All roads lead to Rome," he was wise not to mention its age. Most people automatically think of ancient Rome as the time when this proverb became current. However, this is a false assumption, since the proverb stems from medieval times when a visit or pilgrimage to Rome was a Christian's ultimate goal (Mieder 2004, 12). Kennedy used the proverb twice, once in its original wording while visiting Rome on a trip to Italy. But of special interest is surely his second statement, that there is "the belief that all roads lead to communism." Of course, he formulates this anti-proverb in order to argue that this is exactly not the case at all (Litovkina and Mieder 2006, 265–66). There is no doubt that this is an effective manipulation of a most popular proverb throughout the world:

> After some gains in the fifties the Communist offensive, which claimed to be riding the tide of historic inevitability, has been thwarted and turned back in recent months. Indeed, the whole theory of historical inevitability, the belief that all roads must lead to communism, sooner or later, has been shattered by the determination of those who believe that men and nations will pursue a variety of roads, that each nation will evolve according to its own traditions and its own aspirations, and that the world of the future will have room for a diversity of economic systems, political creeds, religious faiths, united by the respect for others, and loyalty to a world order. (III, 737; September 26, 1963)

On one occasion, Kennedy drew attention to his use of the proverb "The wish is father to the thought" by commenting that "we know," and in the case of "It's better to light a candle than curse the darkness" by claiming "as we know." Such phrasal units help Kennedy to pull his audience along, who most likely will agree with his assessment due to the truth value of the proverbs:

> Some have hailed his [Nikita Khrushchev's] visit [to the United States] as a prelude to a new, great era of peace—the end of the Cold War— the relaxation of tensions. This is the way Mr. Khrushchev most often talked—this is what the American people most want—and the wish, we know, is so often father to the thought. (IX, 10; October 1, 1959)

Regarding the claim of truth and authority in proverbs, Kennedy did well in introducing the proverb "For every wrong, a remedy" as "the venerable code of equity law" and "Justice delayed is justice denied" as a "legal maxim":

> Experience has shown, however, that these highly useful Acts of the 85th and 86th Congresses suffer from two major defects. One is the usual long and difficult delay which occurs between the filing of a lawsuit and its ultimate conclusion. In one recent case, for example, nineteen months elapsed between the filing of the suit and the judgment of the court. In another, an action brought in July 1961 has not yet come to trial. The legal maxim "Justice delayed is Justice denied" is dramatically applicable in these cases. (III, 223; February 28, 1963)

The legal proverb "Justice delayed is justice denied" was the perfect phrase for the president to include in his Special Message to the Congress on Civil Rights on February 28, 1963. It appeared as early as 1838 in an American magazine but was popularized by the English statesman William E. Gladstone by way of his speech in the House of Commons on March 16, 1858 (Shapiro 2010; Shapiro 2021, 327, no. 2). In more modern times, Martin Luther King Jr. cited the proverb on April 16, 1963, about three months after Kennedy. While the president connected it to the slowness of legal cases regarding discrimination, King applied it more generally to civil rights issues in his famous "Letter from Birmingham City Jail" on June 16, 1963:

> We know through painful experience that freedom is never voluntarily given by the oppressor; it must be demanded by the oppressed. Frankly, I have never yet engaged in a direct action movement that was "well-timed," according to the timetable of those who have not suffered unduly from the disease of segregation. For years now I have heard the word "Wait!" It rings in the ear of every Negro with piercing familiarity. This "Wait" has almost always meant "Never." It has been a tranquilizing thalidomide, relieving the emotional stress for a moment, only to give birth to an ill-informed infant of frustration. We must come to see with the distinguished jurist of yesterday that "justice too long delayed is justice denied." We have waited for more than 340 years for our constitutional and God-given rights. The nations of Asia and Africa are moving with jet-like speed toward the goal of political independence, and we still creep at horse-and-buggy pace toward the gaining of a cup of coffee at a lunch counter. I guess it is easy for those who have never felt the stinging darts of segregation to say, "Wait." (Mieder 2010, 369–70)

Not surprisingly, Kennedy also turned frequently to the proverb "Practice what you preach" out of concern that the country was not adhering to the principles established by the Founding Fathers in the Declaration and the Constitution. At times he changes the basic structure of the proverb, showing that he is very much at ease with integrating proverbial language into the natural flow of his messages:

> It should be clear by now that a nation can be no stronger abroad then she is at home. Only an America which practices what it preaches about equal rights and social justice will be respected by those whose choice affects our future. Only an America which has fully educated its citizens is fully capable of tackling the complex problems and perceiving the hidden dangers of the world in which we live. And only an America

146   PROVERBS IN POLITICS

which is growing and prospering economically can sustain the world-wide defenses of freedom, while demonstrating to all concerned the opportunities of our system and society. (III, 894; November 22, 1963; prepared remarks that the president was scheduled to make on the day of his assassination at the Trade Mart in Dallas)

What a loss that Kennedy was prevented from uttering these last words in Dallas! They summarize so well his commitment to justice, freedom, and peace, matters that were always on his mind. Even when he talked about American social problems, he often projected his thoughts onto the world scene. Proverbs were ready-made communication tools to add authority and truth to his statements.

Kennedy's repertoire of folk proverbs is impressive, with his somewhat humorous play with the weather proverb "Everybody talks about the weather, but nobody does anything about it" deserving a special note. Its earliest printed occurrence was in the *Hartford Courant* of August 24, 1897, with Mark Twain possibly having coined it (Mieder 2021, 192; Shapiro 2021, 843, no. 145): "Economic growth has come to resemble the Washington weather—everyone talks about it, no one says precisely what to do about it, and our only satisfaction is that it can't get any worse" (I, 87; February 13, 1961). A few additional references dealing with the economic, social, and political concerns of the United States are all proof positive that Kennedy relied on proverbs as he tried to practice what he preached right here at home:

The time to repair the roof is when the sun is shining.
    The time to repair the roof is when the sun is shining—and the time to build a sound, long-range farm program is now. (IX, 189; October 24, 1959)

Equal pay for equal work.
    Well, I'm sure we haven't done enough [for equal pay for women]. I must say I am a strong believer in equal pay for equal work, and I think we ought to do better than we're doing. (I, 709; November 8, 1961)

This is a free country.
    A free market is regulated by supply and demand. If the supply is greater than the demand, then quite obviously it can be and will be because everyone [farmers] is now free to plant what they wish. Then, of course, that knocks the price down. So that we will have a combination of lower prices and larger surpluses. We sought to avoid that. But this is a free country and the farmers were offered their choice and they

made the choice by—a great number of them voted for the free market and unlimited production. So we are going to be faced with the problem, but I don't think it will have much effect on the consumer. (III, 419; May 22, 1963)

An ounce of prevention is worth more than a pound of cure.

We must seek out the causes of mental illness and of mental retardation and eradicate them. Here, more than in any other area, an ounce of prevention is worth more than a pound of cure. For prevention is far more desirable for all concerned. It is far more economical and is far more likely to be successful. Prevention will require both selected specific programs directed especially at known causes, and the general strengthening of our fundamental community, social welfare, and educational programs which can do much to eliminate or correct the harsh environmental conditions which often are associated with mental retardation and mental illness. (III, 127; February 5, 1963)

The integration of these proverbs adds a welcome element of folk language to Kennedy's deliberations, especially "The time to repair the roof is when the sun is shining." The proverb "An ounce of prevention is worth a pound of cure" is the perfect fit for his discussion of medical matters (Mieder 1993, 155–59). And the proverb "Equal pay for equal work" was certainly appreciated by women. President Kennedy might have been interested in knowing that this proverbial slogan stems from the early feminist Susan B. Anthony, who included it in her journal *The Revolution* of March 18, 1869 (Mieder 2014a, 246–47; Shapiro 2021, 24, no. 2). This brings to mind the proverb "If you can't stand the heat, get out of the kitchen," which has been falsely attributed to President Harry Truman (Mieder 1997, 60–61). Kennedy most certainly knew that, but considering his admiration for the former president, it is surprising that he does not mention his name in this next passage, since so many of his listeners at a meeting of the American Foreign Service Association on July 2, 1962, in Washington, DC, would have been aware of Truman's association with the proverb:

If change were easy, everybody would change. But if you did not have change, you would have revolution. I think that change is what we need in a changing world, and therefore when we embark on new policies, we drag along all the anchors of old opinions and old views. You just have to put up with it. Those who cannot stand the heat should get out of the kitchen. [. . .] Personally, I think the place to be is in the kitchen, and I am sure the Foreign Service officers of the United States feel the same way. (II, 533)

Since Harry Truman has now been mentioned, it must be pointed out that President Kennedy also enjoyed quoting Truman's favorite proverb "The buck stops here" while being aware that his respected friend did not coin it. In fact, Truman himself had repeated several times that he did not originate the proverb, which so perfectly summarizes the ultimate decision-making authority and responsibility of a president (Mieder 1997, 62–65). Here is but one statement from the campaign trail, with Kennedy reflecting on the challenges he would face if elected in November 1960:

> Whoever wins, the task of governing the great Republic will not be easy. The next President's desk will not be clear, waiting for new plans and problems. It will be piled high with old problems, inherited problems, chronic problems, old bills demanding payment, Ambassadors and negotiators demanding instructions, agencies disappointed by the budget demanding relief, legislation previously submitted demanding new orders. But as the new President tries to clean out this pile, new problems and new pressures will rush in upon new areas of crisis around the world—new decisions on weapons and strategy and economic policy and a thousand other items. There, on that one desk, on his shoulders will converge all the hopes and fears of every American, and indeed all the hopes and fears of all who believe in peace and freedom anywhere in the world. Whatever the issue, however critical the problem may be, the President will sit alone at the apex. He will have his advisers, his Cabinet, his own sources of information and ideas. But the responsibility, the burden, the final decision must be his and his alone. As the legend on President Truman's desk puts it: "The buck stops here." (IV, 1229; November 1, 1960)

This is an amazing general summary of the president's chores, heaped up on the desk beyond which a final decision cannot go. Rhetorically speaking, Kennedy uses the presidential desk with Truman's sign on it as a splendid image for the ultimate decision maker in the United States. Everybody who was there on November 1, 1960, in Los Angeles to listen to Kennedy's campaign speech could identify with the proverbial metaphor "The buck stops here"—a superb employment of a modern authentic American proverb dating from 1942 (Mieder 2021, 55).

Obviously, Kennedy spoke primarily of American issues in this particular passage. And yet, he also referred in general terms to "the hopes and fears of all who believe in peace and freedom anywhere in the world." In almost all of Kennedy's speeches and writings, one finds this interconnectedness of national and international concerns. Freedom in the United States meant the search for freedom elsewhere; the concern for peace is a global matter, and American issues for the most part are similar to those of other countries as well. All of this was exasperated by the Cold War pivoting the Soviet Union against the United States, communism against democracy, dictatorship against freedom, and war against peace. These are complex issues, with the sword of Damocles hanging over the heads of decision makers. But even in these fragile world situations, John F. Kennedy relied on proverbs in some of his most important messages, especially regarding Nikita Khrushchev. Who could possibly ever argue that proverbs are trite and of little use in modern times? The following excerpts with their proverbs certainly exemplify the rhetorical effectiveness of proverbial wisdom in the complex strategies of international relations (Raymond 1956). Notice the change of the proverb "Father knows best" to the more colloquial "Papa knows best" in the first passage, where Kennedy adds a bit of irony to his remark. Of note is also his acute change of the proverb "It takes two to make a quarrel" to the innovative anti-proverb "It takes two to make peace" (Wicker 1962, 72), which could well gain true proverbial status. But Kennedy might also have had the proverb "It takes two to tango" in mind, which had its start in 1952 from a song by Al Hoffman and Dick Manning, made popular by the famous African American singer Pearl Bailey (Mieder 2004, 233; Doyle, Mieder, and Shapiro 2012, 266). But this modern proverb could possibly have originated as an anti-proverb of "It takes two to quarrel" as well:

Father knows best.

    If we take our Western Hemisphere friends for granted—if we regard them as worthy of little attention except in an emergency—if, in patronizingly referring to them as our own "back yard," we persist in a "Papa knows best" attitude, throwing a wet blanket on all of their proposals for economic co-operation and dispatching Marines at the first hint of trouble—then the day may not be far off when our own security will be far more endangered in this area than it is in the more distant corners of the earth to which we have given our attention. (IX, 136; December 15, 1958)

Only when the iron is hot can it be molded.

    The task is to do all in our power to see that the changes taking place all around us—in our cities, our countryside, our economy, within the Western world, in the uncommitted world, in the Soviet empire, on all continents—lead to more freedom for more men and to world peace. It is only when the iron is hot that it can be molded. The iron—the new world—being forged today is now ready to be molded. Our job is to shape it, so far as we can, into the world we want for ourselves and our children and for all men. (XIV, 15; January 1, 1960; the more familiar proverb "Strike while the iron is hot" comes to mind.)

It takes two to make a quarrel.
We want good will. But it takes two to make peace, and I am hopeful that the Chinese will be persuaded that a peaceful existence with [their] neighbors represents the best hope for us all. We would welcome it. But I do not see evidence of it today. (I, 436; June 2, 1961)

Once again, Kennedy returns to his leitmotifs of peace and freedom, and it is perfectly understandable that his creation of the Peace Corps literally meant the world to him, as expressed in the following passage. Here he does not cite the modern proverb "If life hands you lemons, make lemonade," whose earliest record stems from 1910 directly (Doyle, Mieder, and Shapiro 2012, 14). Instead, he personalizes the Peace Corps in order to give its founding director, Sargent Shriver, all the credit he deserved for its overwhelming international success. And not to worry, Kennedy's listeners at the headquarters of the Peace Corps surely recognized the proverb allusion:

I wanted to come over here this morning to express my very great appreciation to you for all that you have done to make the Peace Corps such an important part of the life of America and, though I hate to use this word which we have inherited from other days, the image of America overseas. I don't think it is altogether fair to say that I handed Sarge [Sargent Shriver] a lemon from which he made lemonade, but I do think that he was handed and you were handed one of the most sensitive and difficult assignments which any administrative group in Washington has been given, almost, in this century. The concept of the Peace Corps was entirely new. It was subjected to a great deal of criticism at the beginning. If it had not been done with such great care and really, in a sense, loving and prideful care, it could have defeated a great purpose and could have set back the whole cause of public service internationally for a good many years. (II, 482; June 14, 1962)

It was generous of President Kennedy to recognize the sociopolitical achievements of his brother-in-law Sargent Shriver, especially in light of the fact that the president was used to and enjoyed being the center of attention. As one reads his massive textual corpus, there are times when his self-assuredness and know-it-all attitude become a bit overbearing. But this assertiveness and dominance come with the territory of being the president of the United States as a key player in national and international affairs. And yet, there are times when he exhibits deeply felt humility and compassion, as evidenced by the appearance of the proverb "We are all mortal" in his Commencement Address at American University of June 10, 1963, in Washington, DC, just six months before his own death:

> So, let us not be blind to our differences—but let us also direct attention to our common interests and to the means by which those differences can be resolved. And if we cannot end now our differences, at least we can help make the world safe for diversity. For, in the final analysis, our most basic common link is that we all inhabit this small planet. We all breathe the same air. We all cherish our children's future. And we are all mortal. (III, 462; note the echo of Woodrow Wilson's "Make the world safe for democracy" from 1917.)

Two weeks later, in his address at the Free University of Berlin on June 26, 1963, he employed the proverb "The truth does not die" as the proverbial summary of his hope for justice, freedom, and peace everywhere: "The cause of human rights and dignity, some two centuries after its birth, in Europe and the United States, is still moving men and nations with ever increasing momentum. [. . .] The truth doesn't die" (III, 528).

And yet, Kennedy did not always appear as a modern Jeremiah, warning his country to be vigilant in face of the communist danger and other crises. He was perfectly capable of having some linguistic fun, as with this folkloric comment at a campaign event in Los Angeles: "I appreciate your welcome. As the cow said to the Maine farmer, 'Thank you for a warm hand on a cold morning'" (XI, 16; November 2, 1960). It is not known where Kennedy came across this statement, which appears to be a so-called wellerism, a folk expression based on a triadic structure: a statement, followed by a speaker, and placed into an unexpected and usually humorous situation. Kennedy's text is not included in *A Dictionary of Wellerisms* (Mieder and Kingsbury 1994), but he probably heard it during a previous visit to Maine. If it is in fact a wellerism in oral tradition, it might just as well have originated in my beloved state of Vermont, known for its cow farms.

From a domestic cow to a wild tiger is a considerable metaphoric jump, but Kennedy made it by including the cautionary phrase "to remember that, in the past, those who foolishly sought power by riding the back of the tiger ended up inside" (I, 1; January 20, 1961) in his inaugural address. The metaphor was intended to warn other nations against riding the communist tiger, since it would lead to dependence on the Soviet Union and a loss of democratic principles. It took some time to figure out how Kennedy, perhaps with the help of Theodore Sorensen, came upon this metaphor. Chances have it that the proverbs "Who has a tiger by the tail dare not let go," "Who rides the back of the tiger will end up inside," and "Who rides the tiger can never dismount" had something to do with it (Whiting 1989, 625–26; Mieder, Kingsbury, and Harder 1992, 596). In addition, there is also the variant "He who rides a tiger is afraid to dismount," registered in William Scarborough's *Collection of Chinese Proverbs* from 1875 (Speake 2015, 266; Shapiro 2021, 663, no. 254), indicating that the proverbial metaphor probably had its start in China. The following limerick could have been at play as well:

> There was a young lady of Niger
> Who smiled as she rode on a tiger;
> They returned from the ride
> With the lady inside,
> And the smile on the face of the tiger.

But since tigers are not native to Africa and certainly not to Niger, the fact that the limerick lists the West African country can only be due to the need of a rhyme with "tiger." In other words, the assumption that the metaphor stems from China appears to be on solid scholarly ground.

Attention can also be drawn to the fact that Winston Churchill made this comment in his Constituency Speech of September 24, 1921, at Carid Hall, Dundee: "Well was it said, 'The man who rides a tiger has difficulty in getting off.' Certainly, I assure you on behalf of the Government that no mere pedantry, no hair-splitting, no quibbling about words and phrases, no metaphysical perplexities, will be allowed by us to stand in the way of practical steps to peace." In his essay "Armistice—or Peace" (1937), he wrote: "Dictators ride to and fro upon tigers from which they dare not dismount. And the tigers are getting hungry." And two years later, and now doubtless having Hitler and Mussolini in mind, Churchill repeated the warning: "Neither of these Dictators can stop. Well was it said: 'He who rides a tiger cannot dismount'" in his essay "Will There Be War in Europe—and When?," which appeared in the weekly newspaper *News of the World* on June 4, 1939. "Armistice—or Peace" was reprinted in Churchill's book *Step by Step, 1936–1939* (1939), which Kennedy lists in his bibliography to *Why England Slept* (V, 247; 1940). So he probably read the "tiger" proverb in that book, and it is perhaps not unlikely that he also read "Will There Be War in Europe—and When?" in the British newspaper (for bibliographical information for these three quotations from Churchill, see Mieder and Bryan 1995, 395). Knowing that Kennedy was a prolific reader, it is also possible that he read the two volumes of Harry Truman's *Memoirs* (1956). The second volume begins with this short paragraph:

Within the first few months I discovered that being a President is like riding a tiger. A man has to keep on riding or be swallowed. The fantastically crowded nine months of 1945 taught me that a President either is constantly on top of events or, if he hesitates, events will soon be on top of him. I never felt that I could let up for a single moment. No one who has not had the responsibility can really understand what it is like to be President, not even his closest aides or members of his immediate family. There is no end to the chain of responsibility that binds him, and he is never allowed to forget that he is President. What kept me going in 1945 was my belief that there is far more good than evil in men and that it is the business of government to make the good prevail. (Mieder and Brian 1997, 224).

No wonder that Kennedy admired Harry Truman, for he was experiencing exactly this sentiment as president. In any case, with Churchill and Truman having employed the proverbial tiger image, it is not so surprising that Kennedy also made such convincing use of it. To be sure, the "tiger" metaphor was much more than a bit of colloquial language. After all, it served Kennedy well as an indirect message that peace and freedom throughout the world were threatened.

Finally, then, it can be observed that Kennedy's oral and written messages are replete with maritime proverbs and proverbial expressions. After all, it is an international linguistic phenomenon to refer to the state as a ship or boat and to the head of the government as a captain who depends on the sailors, the sea, the tide, and the wind. It is easy to imagine that a rich repertoire of maritime expressions developed over the centuries of which many have been assembled in such collections as Robert Hendrickson's *Salty Words* (1984) and my own *Salty Wisdom: Proverbs of the Sea* (Mieder 1990b). It should come as no surprise that political leaders rely on seafaring metaphors, especially if they are—as in the Anglo-American case—former navy men like Winston Churchill, Franklin D. Roosevelt (as assistant secretary of the navy), and John F. Kennedy. The latter is known to have been an experienced recreational sailor, and his wartime service as the commander of patrol torpedo boat PT-109, which was rammed by a Japanese destroyer, almost costing him his life, must also be mentioned, of course. Little wonder that he quite frequently referred to the sea even to the point of mixing metaphors, for example in this comment: "We have a long way to go in the space race. We started late. But this is the new ocean, and I believe the United States must sail on it and be in a position second to none" (II, 150; February 20, 1962).

There is a definite preoccupation with the image of the tide in Kennedy's rhetoric, and he did not tire of employing the maritime phrase "to turn the tide" as a visualization that sociopolitical matters were changing or had to move forward. John W. Garner even included the phrase in the title of his edited book *To Turn the Tide: A Selection from President Kennedy's Public Statements* (1962). Here are two statements Kennedy made while campaigning for the presidency. The fact that Kennedy employs the phrase in relation both to democracy versus despotism and to political issues at home is a sign of the differentiated applicability of the metaphor. Notice that the second passage includes an important allusion to the proverb "Speak softly and carry a big stick":

> Mr. Khrushchev has spent his life in arguments. The question is, which candidate and which political party can mobilize the resources of the United States and the resources of the entire free world to turn the tide of freedom against the Communists? That is the issue. It is not a debate. It is a matter of consistent work, setting before the American people the unfinished business of our society. (IV, 1132; October 14, 1960)

> The Democratic Party's call for a nation awakened and rededicated is evidence that the tide is turning. It is turning away from the self-satisfied delusion that time is always on the side of the righteous. It is turning away from the counsels of complacency that would have us believe that our prestige was never higher. It is turning away from the dangerous theory that bigger talk can substitute for a bigger stick. (IV, 1268; part of an "It's Up to You" statement written by Kennedy a few days before November 8, 1960, and published in *Democratic Digest*, November–December, 1960)

With this, President Kennedy's quintessential proverb has been reached. Before turning to the frequent appearance of the maritime wisdom that "A rising tide lifts all the boats" in Kennedy's published communications, let it be observed that President Barack Obama also relied repeatedly on its message, for example:

> And when we've succeeded [to be good citizens], it's made America the place where dreams are possible, where freedoms of speech and press and worship are protected, and where the rising tide lifts the boats of the many instead of just the few. (Lecture on April 11, 2005; Mieder 2009, 323)

> But through hard times and good, great challenge and great change, the promise of Jamesville [Wisconsin] has been the promise of America— that our prosperity can and must be the tide that lifts every boat; that we rise or fall as one nation; that our economy is strongest when our

middle class grows and opportunity is spread as widely as possible. (Speech on February 13, 2008; Mieder 2009, 323)

Even more than Obama, Kennedy relied on the proverb "A rising tide lifts all the boats," using it thirteen times, making it his favorite piece of folk wisdom. The proverb belongs to the set of relatively new proverbs, being registered in *The Dictionary of Modern Proverbs* with its earliest printed reference from 1915 (Doyle, Mieder, and Shapiro 2012, 258). However, the unbeatable quotation sleuth Fred R. Shapiro has now found it four years earlier in *The Missionary Voice* of May 1911 (Shapiro 2021, 447, no. 26). In any case, the proverb has been widely distributed and appears with impressive frequency. Jennifer Speake also includes it in the sixth edition of the *Oxford Dictionary of Proverbs* (2015), citing it from several sources, one being Kennedy's speech of June 25, 1963, in Frankfurt, West Germany. What is amazing about Speake's dictionary entry is her introductory comment to her four contextualized entries for the proverb: "Principally known in the U.S., this is one of several proverbs popularized by the Kennedy family. It is now generally used in economic contexts[,] the *tide* being that of prosperity" (Speake 2015, 267). In the reference mentioned by Speake, President Kennedy alludes to the fact that he most likely learned the proverb from his immediate family or at least from the surroundings of the Kennedy compound in Hyannis Port on Cape Cod, Massachusetts:

> The experience of the Common Market—like the experience of the German Zollverein [a nineteenth-century customs union]—shows an increased rise in business activity and in general prosperity resulting for all participants in such trade agreements, with no member profiting at the expense of another. As they say on my own Cape Cod, a rising tide lifts all the boats. And a partnership, by definition, serves both partners, without domination or unfair advantage. Together we have been partners in adversity—let us also be partners in prosperity. (III, 519; June 25, 1963)

Of course, he might also have picked the proverb up from talking with people involved with gathering fish, lobsters, and shrimp from the sea. The introductory formula to this passage appears to allude to this:

> New England fishermen have a saying, "The rising tide lifts all the boats." It is time to raise the American tide. This country has stood still long enough. Russia is outproducing us in steel, outflying us in the conquest of space, and out maneuvering us in feeding the world's hungry. I say we need a fresh start. And the place to start the chain reaction

156 PROVERBS IN POLITICS

of national prosperity and national greatness is on the farm. (IV, 1184; October 23, 1960)

Even though Kennedy usually quotes proverbs without marking them as a "saying," he refers to this proverb as being "an old saying" on two occasions. The purpose of this claim is to add a certain truth value to his economic comments, even though the proverb is in actuality not really particularly old:

> Many opportunities lie before us, but New Hampshire and New England cannot move ahead unless the Nation, itself, is moving ahead. Everything that we make here, which we sell throughout the country, depends upon a rising economy. There is an old saying of the New England Council, a rising tide lifts all the boats, and I believe that the boats of New Hampshire can only be raised when the boats are being raised in the rest of the country, so that markets can be developed for our goods, so that ranges and other sections of the United States will equal ours, so that the country and [we] can move together. (IV, 940; November 7, 1960)

> When we develop these resources in the Northwest United States, it is just as well that the country realizes that we are not talking about one State or two States or three States; we are talking about the United States. Our people move freely from east to west, and even once in a while from west to east, but in any case, the country becomes stronger. There is an old saying that a rising tide lifts all the boats, and as the Northwest United States rises, so does the entire country, so we are glad. (III, 731; September 36, 1963)

Kennedy is not married to integrating the proverb in its precise wording into his rhetorical flow, as can be seen in this next passage. Of importance is, of course, that while he is concerned with the American economy, he broadens his view internationally, as he did with most of his messages. America is looking out for itself, but it needs to keep in mind that the tide can best raise the boats when matters improve throughout the world:

> We are not talking about dumping our great productive resources abroad. The fact of the matter is there are enough dollars to pay for what we want to export through tourists and through all the other means. We spread a good many dollars throughout the world. We are asking that there be a rising tide in trade which will benefit all the countries, which will lift all the boats. We are not novices at export trade.

Indeed, one of the factors which led to the American Revolution was an attempt to limit our access to foreign markets. And during much of the 19th century American exports were aggressively merchandised around the globe. (III, 683; September 17, 1963)

In conclusion, then, is this short statement that President Kennedy made in Colorado, showing him as the concerned "preacher" committed to the well-being of the entire nation, where everybody is in the same boat and rowing as a team toward a future of freedom and peace: "What I preach is the interdependence of the United States. We are not 50 countries—we are one country of 50 States and one people. And I believe that those programs which make life better for some of our people will make life better for all of our people. A rising tide lifts all the boats" (II, 625–26; August 17, 1962). What a fortune it would have been if the proverbial rhetoric of President John F. Kennedy and his actions could have had a few additional years to make a difference in the United States and the world!

BIBLIOGRAPHY

JOHN F. KENNEDY'S BOOKS, ADDRESSES, ESSAYS, MESSAGES, NEWS CONFERENCES, AND SPEECHES

I. *Public Papers of the Presidents of the United States: John F. Kennedy.* January 20 to December 31, 1961. Washington, DC: United States Printing Office, 1962. 908 pp.

II. *Public Papers of the Presidents of the United States: John F. Kennedy.* January 1 to December 31, 1962. Washington, DC: United States Printing Office, 1963. 1,019 pp.

III. *Public Papers of the Presidents of the United States: John F. Kennedy.* January 1 to November 22, 1963. Washington, DC: United States Printing Office, 1966. 1,007 pp.

IV. Magnuson, Warren G., ed. *The Speeches, Remarks, Press Conferences, and Statements of Senator John F. Kennedy.* August 1 to November 7, 1960. Washington, DC: US Government Printing Office, 1961. 1,440 pp. (1,290 pp. of texts and the rest a giant index)

V. Kennedy, John F. *Why England Slept.* New York: Wilfred Funk, 1940. 252 pp.

VI. Kennedy, John F. *Profiles in Courage.* New York: Harper and Brothers, 1956. 266 pp.

VII. Kennedy, John F. "Good Fences Make Good Neighbors." Convocation, October 8, 1957, University of New Brunswick, Fredericton, New Brunswick. 11 pp.

VIII. Kennedy, John F. *A Nation of Immigrants.* New York: Anti-Defamation League, 1958. 40 pp. Expanded version with an introduction by Robert F. Kennedy, New York: Harper and Row, 1964. 160 pp.

IX. Kennedy, John F. *The Strategy of Peace.* Edited by Allan Nevins. New York: Harper and Row, 1960. 233 pp.

X. Kennedy, John F. "We Must Climb to the Hilltop." *Life,* August 22, 1960, 70–72, 77.

PROVERBS IN POLITICS

ANTHOLOGIES OF JOHN F. KENNEDY'S LETTERS, REMARKS, QUOTATIONS, AND WIT

XI.   Adler, Bill, ed. *The Kennedy Wit*. New York: Citadel Press, 1964. 83 pp.

XII.   Frost, David B., ed. *John F. Kennedy in Quotations: A Topical Dictionary, with Sources*. Jefferson, NC: McFarland, 2013. 207 pp.

XIII.   Garner, John W., ed. *To Turn the Tide: A Selection from President Kennedy's Public Statements from His Election Through the 1961 Adjournment of Congress, Setting Forth the Goals of His First Legislative Year*. New York: Harper and Brothers, 1962. 236 pp.

XIV.   Lewis, Edward, and Richard Rhodes, eds. *John F. Kennedy: Words to Remember*. Kansas City, MO: Hallmark Editions, 1967. 59 pp.

XV.   Meyersohn, Maxwell, ed. *Memorable Quotations of John F. Kennedy*. New York: Thomas Y. Crowell, 1965. 314 pp.

XVI.   Sorensen, Theodore C., ed. *"Let the Word Go Forth": The Speeches, Statements, and Writings of John F. Kennedy*. New York: Delacorte Press, 1988. 433 pp.

SECONDARY SOURCES

Bartlett, John. 2012. *Bartlett's Familiar Quotations*. Edited by Geoffrey O'Brien. 18th ed. New York: Little, Brown.

Bostdorff, Denise M., and Shawna Ferris. 2014. "John F. Kennedy at American University: The Rhetoric of the Possible, Epideictic Progression, and the Commencement of Peace." *Quarterly Journal of Speech* 100, no. 4 (October): 407–41.

Carter, Burnham, Jr. 1963. "President Kennedy's Inaugural Address." *College Composition and Communication* 14, no. 1 (February): 36–40.

Chesterton, C. K. (1929) 1957. *The Thing: Why I Am a Catholic*. London: Sheed and Ward.

Clarke, Thurston. 2004. *Ask Not: The Inauguration of John F. Kennedy and the Speech That Changed America*. New York: Henry Holt.

Corbett, Edward P. J. 1965. *Classical Rhetoric for the Modern Student*. New York: Oxford University Press.

Doyle, Charles Clay, Wolfgang Mieder, and Fred R. Shapiro, eds. 2012. *The Dictionary of Modern Proverbs*. New Haven, CT: Yale University Press.

Griffin, Albert Kirby. 1991. *Religious Proverbs: Over 1600 Adages from 18 Faiths Worldwide*. Jefferson, NC: McFarland.

Hendrickson, Robert. 1984. *Salty Words*. New York: Hearst Marine Books.

"Interview of Senator John F. Kennedy on Television Program, 'Let's Look at Congress,' New York, NY, May 31, 1959." 1959. John F. Kennedy Presidential Library and Museum. https://www.jfklibrary.org/archives/other-resources/john-f-kennedy-speeches/lets-look -at-congress-19590531.

Kenny, Edward B. 1965. "Another Look at Kennedy's Inaugural Address." *Today's Speech* 13, no. 4 (November): 17–19.

Litovkina, Anna T., and Wolfgang Mieder. 2006. *Old Proverbs Never Die, They Just Diversify: A Collection of Anti-Proverbs*. Burlington: University of Vermont; Veszprém, Hungary: University of Pannonia.

Menendez, Albert J. 1978. *John F. Kennedy: Catholic and Humanist*. Buffalo: Prometheus Books.

Meyer, Sam. 1982. "The John F. Kennedy Inauguration Speech: Function and Importance of Its 'Address System.'" *Rhetoric Society Quarterly* 12, no. 4 (Autumn): 239–50.

Mieder, Wolfgang. 1990a. *Not by Bread Alone: Proverbs of the Bible*. Shelburne, VT: New England Press.

Mieder, Wolfgang. 1990b. *Salty Wisdom: Proverbs of the Sea*. Shelburne, VT: New England Press.

Mieder, Wolfgang. 1993. *Proverbs Are Never Out of Season: Popular Wisdom in the Modern Age*. New York: Oxford University Press.

Mieder, Wolfgang. 1997. *The Politics of Proverbs: From Traditional Wisdom to Proverbial Stereotypes*. Madison: University of Wisconsin Press.

Mieder, Wolfgang. 2000. *The Proverbial Abraham Lincoln: An Index to Proverbs in the Works of Abraham Lincoln*. New York: Peter Lang.

Mieder, Wolfgang. 2004. *Proverbs: A Handbook*. Westport, CT: Greenwood Press. Rpt., New York: Peter Lang, 2012.

Mieder, Wolfgang. 2005. *Proverbs Are the Best Policy: Folk Wisdom and American Politics*. Logan: Utah State University Press.

Mieder, Wolfgang. 2009. *"Yes We Can": Barack Obama's Proverbial Rhetoric*. New York: Peter Lang.

Mieder, Wolfgang. 2010. *"Making a Way Out of No Way": Martin Luther King's Sermonic Proverbial Rhetoric*. New York: Peter Lang.

Mieder, Wolfgang. 2014a. *"All Men and Women Are Created Equal": Elizabeth Cady Stanton's and Susan B. Anthony's Proverbial Rhetoric Promoting Women's Rights*. New York: Peter Lang.

Mieder, Wolfgang. 2014b. *Behold the Proverbs of a People: Proverbial Wisdom in Culture, Literature, and Politics*. Jackson: University Press of Mississippi.

Mieder, Wolfgang. 2019. *"Right Makes Might": Proverbs and the American Worldview*. Bloomington: Indiana University Press.

Mieder, Wolfgang. 2021. *Dictionary of Authentic American Proverbs*. New York: Berghahn Books.

Mieder, Wolfgang, and George B. Bryan. 1995. *The Proverbial Winston S. Churchill: An Index to Proverbs in the Works of Sir Winston Churchill*. Westport, CT: Greenwood Press.

Mieder, Wolfgang, and George B. Bryan. 1997. *The Proverbial Harry S. Truman: An Index to Proverbs in the Works of Harry S. Truman*. New York: Peter Lang.

Mieder, Wolfgang, and Alan Dundes, eds. 1981. *The Wisdom of Many: Essays on the Proverb*. New York: Garland Publishing.

Mieder, Wolfgang, and Stewart A. Kingsbury. 1994. *A Dictionary of Wellerisms*. New York: Oxford University Press.

Mieder, Wolfgang, Stewart A. Kingsbury, and Kelsie B. Harder. 1992. *A Dictionary of American Proverbs*. New York: Oxford University Press.

Murphy, John M. 2000. "Crafting the Kennedy Legacy." *Rhetoric and Public Affairs* 3, no. 4 (Winter): 577–601.

Paczolay, Gyula. 1997. *European Proverbs in 55 Languages with Equivalents in Arabic, Persian, Sanskrit, Chinese and Japanese*. Veszprém, Hungary: Veszprémi Nyomda.

Raymond, Joseph. 1956. "Tensions in Proverbs: More Light on International Understanding." *Western Folklore* 15, no. 3 (July): 153–58. Also in *The Wisdom of Many: Essays on the Proverb*, edited by Wolfgang Mieder and Alan Dundes, 300–308. New York: Garland Publishing, 1981.

Shapiro, Fred R. 2010. "You Can Quote Them: 'Justice Delayed Is Justice Denied.'" *Yale Alumni Magazine*, May–June, 58.

Shapiro, Fred R., ed. 2021. *The New Yale Book of Quotations*. New Haven, CT: Yale University Press.

Sorensen, Theodore C. 1965. *Kennedy*. New York: Harper and Row.

Speake, Jennifer. 2015. *Oxford Dictionary of Proverbs*. 6th ed. Oxford: Oxford University Press.

St. Onge, Jeffrey, and Jennifer Moore. 2016. "Poetry as a Form of Dissent: John F. Kennedy, Amiri Baraka, and the Politics of Art in Rhetorical Democracy." *Rhetoric Review* 35, no. 4: 335–47.

US Senate. 1958. Hearings of the Subcommittee on Labor, 85th Cong., 2nd Sess. Washington, DC: US Government Printing Office.

Warnick, Barbara. 1996. "Argument Schemes and the Construction of Social Reality: John F. Kennedy's Address to the Houston Ministerial Association." *Communication Quarterly* 44, no. 2 (Spring): 183–96.

Whiting, Bartlett Jere. 1989. *Modern Proverbs and Proverbial Sayings*. Cambridge, MA: Harvard University Press.

Wicker, Tom. 1962. "Kennedy as a Public Speakah." *New York Times Magazine*, February 25, 14, 70–71.

Wills, Garry. 1982. *The Kennedy Imprisonment: A Meditation on Power*. Boston: Little, Brown.

Wilson, John. 2015. *Talking with the President: The Pragmatics of Presidential Language*. New York: Oxford University Press.

Windt, Theodore O. 1993. "President John F. Kennedy's Inaugural Address, 1961." In *The Inaugural Addresses of Twentieth-Century American Presidents*, edited by Halford Ryan, 181–93. Westport, CT: Praeger.

Wolfarth, Donald L. 1961. "John F. Kennedy in the Tradition of Inaugural Speeches." *Quarterly Journal of Speech* 47, no. 2: 124–32.

7

"CONCORDIA DOMI, FORIS PAX"

Willy Brandt's Non-German Proverbial Rhetoric

It is a commonplace contention that most politicians are not particularly skill-ful linguists or stylists in either their oral or written communications (Pelster 1966; Dieckmann 1969; Bergsdorf 1978; Girnth 2002). In fact, their language is often ridiculed and considered vague, stilted, colorless, clichéd, and certainly bad (Patzelt 1995, 47; Schwab-Felisch 1966, 230). And yet, as the rhetorically interested political scientist Dolf Sternberger has shown, world-class politicians like Abraham Lincoln, Winston Churchill, and John F. Kennedy certainly were exquisite masters of the English language, and the same is doubtlessly true for the magisterial use of the German language by Otto von Bismarck, Theodor Heuss, and Willy Brandt (Sternberger [1966] 1991). All politicians have to be aware that they address heterogeneous listeners and readers and that they need to communicate clearly, find a good balance between factual information and emotional engagement, and use colloquialisms, metaphors, and various types of phraseologisms in a controlled but effective fashion (Kienpointner 1999, 68; Zimmermann 1969, 90–91). It has been repeatedly pointed out that proverbs, proverbial expressions, and proverbial comparisons are part and parcel of good political communication (Mieder 1975, 14–22; Koller 1977, 138–54; Röhrich and Mieder 1977, 108–10; Elspaß 1998, 150–216). Articles with titles like "Tensions in Proverbs: More Light on International Understanding" (Raymond 1956), "Proverbes et pouvoir politique: Le cas de l'U.R.S.S." (Breuillard 1984), "Sprichwortgebrauch im aktuellen politischen Kontext Kroatiens" (Matulina 1995), "Empleo y función de la expresión idiomática en el discurso politico en Francia" (Reyes de la Rosa 1997), and "Phrasemes in Political Speech" (Elspaß 2007); and the two books *The Politics of Proverbs: From Traditional Wisdom to Proverbial Stereotypes* (Mieder 1997) and *Proverbs Are the Best Policy: Folk Wisdom and American Politics* (Mieder 2005) make it abundantly clear that proverbial rhetoric is a widespread phenomenon. Stephan Elspaß's assessment is basically correct:

> Propositions in the form of sentence-like phrasemes, such as proverbs, commonplaces, slogans, commandments and maxims, quotations and "winged words," are used as sparingly and effectively as idioms in political speech. By employing quotations etc. from culturally significant texts (the Bible, fictional literature, historical speeches) and proverbs, speakers evoke a mutual cultural knowledge and appeal to quasi-authorized "truths" inherent in these phrasemes, thus establishing a kind of "manifest intertextuality." Such phrasemes can serve as markers of bonding between the speaker and the audience or to support the argument of a speech. (Elspaß 2007, 288)

Proverbs and other full-sentence phrasemes are in fact used less than idioms, but it is important to stress that proverbial expressions and proverbial comparisons appear with considerable frequency albeit not as often as nonmetaphorical idioms.

This has been shown in much detail for some significant politicians and social reformers, to wit book-length studies about the proverbial rhetoric of Abraham Lincoln (Mieder 2000b), Frederick Douglass (Mieder 2001), Elizabeth Cady Stanton and Susan B. Anthony (Mieder 2014a), Winston Churchill (Mieder and Bryan 1995), Harry S. Truman (Mieder and Bryan 1997), Martin Luther King Jr. (Mieder 2010), and Barack Obama (Mieder 2009). Such detailed studies do not exist thus far for German politicians, but there are a few primarily enumerative articles on the proverbial language of Otto von Bismarck (Blümner 1891; Blümner 1894; Blümner 1895; Rogge 1899, 14–17) and Adolf Hitler (Mieder 1995), and Edmund Kammerer discusses some isolated proverbial references by such political figures as Franz Josef Strauß, Helmut Kohl, Willy Brandt, Helmut Schmidt, and Herbert Wehner in his master's thesis, "Sprichwort und Politik" (1983). But speaking of students looking at the proverbial speech of politicians, it gives me great pleasure to refer to my former undergraduate student Sonja Eggert, who wrote her honors thesis, "Willy Brandts sprichwörtliche Rhetorik" (1998), under my supervision at the University of Vermont. And my former graduate student Andreas Nolte and I published our book *"Kleine Schritte sind besser als große Worte": Willy Brandts politische Sprichwortrhetorik* (2015) investigating Brandt's proverbial prowess in all of his published speeches, interviews, and books—a vast undertaking based on over ten thousand pages of texts (see our other coauthored books Mieder and Nolte 2006; Nolte and Mieder 2012).

For me personally it was a special scholarly pleasure to have worked on Willy Brandt (1913–1992), since he was born in my beloved German hometown of Lübeck. As a journalistically inclined social democrat, an exile during the Nazi period in Norway (1933–1940) and Sweden (1940–1945), a politician in the

Social Democratic Party of Germany (SPD), mayor of West Berlin (1957–1966), head of the SPD (1964–1987), foreign minister and vice chancellor (1966–1969), member of the West German Parliament (1969–1992), chancellor of West Germany (1969–1974), *Time* magazine's "Man of the Year" (1970), recipient of the Nobel Peace Prize (1971), president of the Socialist International (1976–1992), head of the North-South Commission (1977–1983), member of the European Parliament (1979–1983), honorary head of the SPD (1987–1992), and honorary president of the first Parliament of unified Germany (1992), Willy Brandt attained an international reputation as a German and European politician, an advocate for world peace, and a humanitarian fighting against poverty (Grebing, Schöllgen, and Winkler 2002–2009 [hereafter *BA*], 1:7–9; Stern 2002, 172–73). Born into a stark environment as an illegitimate child, he became a "true 'self-made man'" (Marshall 1997, 151) who saw his role in life as alleviating social misery throughout a democratically governed world. As Germany came to terms with its Nazi past and was readmitted into the political world as a valued and respected partner, Brandt was characterized as "the other German" (Binder 1975, 282), as a German who returned Germany to civilized democracy.

His leadership style was not authoritative but rather based on free discussion and deliberate consensus building, always looking for liberal and peaceful solutions of conflicts (Zundel 1970, 22–23). He accomplished this by way of his keen and analytical mind, his vast historical knowledge, and his incredible skill of effective communication with all strata of society, from hard-working laborers to members of the established middle class and on to high-level executives and intellectuals. According to some of his biographers, Brandt was "fluent in private conversation as well as public debate" (Prittie 1974, 109); "[he] was a highly polished public speaker" (Drath 1975, 329); and some of his speeches exhibited "brilliant rhetoric" (Marshall 1997, 67). And he was a politician who did not just talk but who also thoroughly enjoyed writing his own speeches for the most part, and numerous biographies and sociopolitical books to boot (Hofmann 1988, 47). The problem with all of these acute observations is that the well-deserved praise of Brandt's linguistic abilities is seldom backed up by contextualized examples. The question that lingers is how Brandt talked and wrote and what made him into such a captivating speaker and recognized author who not only had a superb command of his native German but was also fluent in Norwegian, French, and English, with good knowledge of a number of other European languages including Latin. His residences in a number of countries and his interest in European and world politics made him ever more aware of the importance of languages, and it should not be surprising that he registered a number of significant observations regarding his own political speech habits, for example in his autobiographical reflections *Begegnungen und Einsichten* (1976) concerning his political activities between 1960 and 1975:

Ich verwandte viel Zeit auf die Arbeit an den Texten für Reden, Stellungnahmen, Artikel und schriftliche Interviews; keine noch so gute Vorarbeit, die bei der Fülle öffentlicher Äußerungen unentbehrlich war, konnte mir die eigene Arbeit an den Texten abnehmen. Wer meint, ich hätte, ohne Klärung der Substanz, der Korrekturen, Ergänzungen und Neuformulierungen selbst bei Routine-Angelegenheiten, die Texte sogenannter Ghostwriter übernommen, hat sich geirrt. Überdies macht man sich von der Technik dieser Zuarbeit und Zusammenarbeit meist ein falsches Bild. Es gab keine langen, versonnenen und versponnenen Rotweingespräche, in denen vage "Visionen" formuliert wurden—das erlaubte der Druck der Termine nicht. Aber ich versuchte sehr wohl, meine Mitarbeiter zu disziplinierter Denkarbeit über die Richtpunkte anzuregen, die durch meine politischen Ziele gesetzt wurden, und ich wünschte, es wäre mehr Zeit für die produktiven Diskussionen geblieben, die anderswo "brain storming" genannt werden. (Brandt 1976, 305)

I expended much time working on the texts of speeches, statements, articles, and printed interviews; given the abundance of unavoidable public comments, no amount of preparatory work, however good, was able to relieve me of my own work on these texts. Whoever thinks that I used ghostwriters without first discussing the substance and checking matters for accuracy and making corrections, additions, and revisions, is mistaken. Moreover, the image people have of this preparatory work and collaboration is usually completely wrong. There were no lengthy, pensive, and airy-fairy conversations over wine, in which vague "visions" were dreamed up—the pressure of the deadlines did not allow it. But, to be sure, I did attempt to stimulate my collaborators to think in a disciplined fashion about the positions and principles being established in light of my political goals, and I wished there had been more time for productive discussion, more time for what is known elsewhere as "brainstorming."

Toward the end of his life he added the following insightful comments during a lecture on February 1, 1992, at the University of Heidelberg:

Es ist gut—und in öffentlichen Angelegenheiten nahezu unverzichtbar -, daß man aus dem Stand argumentieren und replizieren kann. Aber selten läßt sich eine gute Rede aus dem Ärmel schütteln. Inhalt und Form erfordern—vorzugsweise eigene—Arbeit.

Zu festlichen Anlässen (oder überhaupt) kommen wir lieber in eigenen als in geliehenen Kleidern. Auch die Rede, die man hält, sollte die eigene sein—man sollte sie sich jedenfalls zu eigen gemacht haben. [. . .]

Professor Sternberger hat uns aus gutem Grund darauf hingewiesen, daß Sprechen Handeln sei; er hat hinzugefügt, eine Demokratie ohne Redekunst sei im Verdorren. Das Verlesen von Berichten oder Protokollen hat er damit nicht gemeint. [. . .]

Man sollte, wo es darauf ankommt, sich in freier Rede äußern können. Das Gütezeichen öffentlicher Rede bleibt der ansprechende Vortrag eines nicht anspruchslosen Textes. Eine gute Rede nachlesen zu können, bereitet im übrigen weniger Verdruß, als einer schlechten zuhören zu müssen.

Sprechen selbst sei Handeln, haben wir gelernt, zu verantwortendes Handeln. Das heißt, an der Rede—so sie nicht aus dem Stand zu halten ist—muß gearbeitet, an wichtigen Sätzen gefeilt werden. (Brandt 1993b, 146–47)

It is good—and in public life virtually indispensable—to argue and have at the ready an appropriate riposte. But seldom can you produce a good speech just like that. The content and form demand work—preferably one's own work.

We much prefer to attend festive occasions (or any other kind of occasion) in our own rather than rented clothes. The speech you give should likewise be your own—or you should at all events make it your own. [. . .]

Professor [Dolf] Sternberger has pointed out with good reason that to speak is to act; he added that a democracy without the art of speechmaking is moribund. And he did not mean the reading out loud of reports or transcripts. [. . .]

Wherever necessary you should be able to give a speech without notes. The hallmark of a good speech was and is the appealing performance of a substantial text. To read a good speech after it is given, furthermore, is less irritating than having to listen to a bad one.

To speak, we have learned, is itself to act, to act in a responsible way. That means that the speech—so long as it cannot be given extempore—must be worked on; its important sentences must be polished.

All of this points to the fact that Brandt had a very differentiated understanding of the important interrelationship of language and politics (Kölbel 2013, 1123–24), stressing repeatedly that politicians should be very conscious of the communicative power of the nuances of language. Of course, as is the case with other politicians of the stature of Willy Brandt, proverbial rhetoric is without any doubt part of this magisterial political communication. Naturally Brandt was particularly adapt at using the rich German proverbial language, but as a true cosmopolitan, he also drew on his impressive repertoire of proverbs from other languages and cultures, which he at times cited in their English or Latin original wording but which he employed more commonly in German translation. At times he explicitly introduced such proverbs as being loan translations, but he also integrated them as if they had already become current in German as well. Be that as it may, Brandt doubtlessly helped to spread such proverbs throughout the German-speaking world by way of his popularity and exposure in the mass media. As the discussion of the following contextualized examples will show, the use of these proverbs added much emotive and argumentative character to his speeches, interviews, and books.

Willy Brandt and I have a proverbial memory in common from the years when we were gymnasium students in our hometown of Lübeck on the Baltic Sea in northern Germany. We each passed by the beautiful structure of the Holsten Gate many times as we entered the city itself and often glanced at the large Latin inscription "Concordia domi, foris pax" (Bayer 1994, 71), whose message, "Harmony within, peace without," became ingrained in our young minds. For Brandt it developed into "his political credo" (Binder 1975, 353), which informed his entire political life as a leitmotif as he worked toward a unified democratic Germany at peace with the rest of the world. As he stated at a national meeting of the SPD on November 25, 1960, in Hannover and recalled in his book *Plädoyer für die Zukunft* (1961):

Ich bin in einer Hansesstadt aufgewachsen, an deren Holstentor die Worte stehen: "Concordia domi—foris pax." Es ist immer noch so. Die Eintracht im Innern fördert auch den Frieden nach außen. (Brandt 1961, 19; Brandt 1984, 34)

I grew up in one of the Hanseatic cities, whose Holsten Gate displays the words "Concordia domi—foris pax." It still does today. Harmony within, peace without.

Four years later, in a speech of November 24, 1964, he alluded to the Latin proverb once again in German translation, arguing that the German state, economy, and society needed to adhere to its wisdom:

Was brauchen wir? Was braucht unser Volk, unser Land? Ich antworte: Deutschland braucht den Frieden im Innern und nach außen, den Frieden in Deutschland und für Deutschland. (Brandt 1984, 91)

What do we need? What do our people need, our country? My answer is: Germany needs peace within, and without, peace in Germany and peace for Germany.

In a speech of February 29, 1972, on the occasion of becoming an honorary citizen of his hometown, Lübeck, he was much more direct in his high regard for this Latin proverb, which was ever present in his political mind:

> Als ich im [28.] Oktober 1969 meine erste Regierungserklärung als Bundeskanzler abzugeben hatte, schloß ich sie ab mit dem Satz: "Wir wollen ein Volk der guten Nachbarn sein [und werden] im Innern wie [und] nach außen." Ein Echo dessen, was ich in meinen jungen Jahren immer wieder am Holstentor gelesen [habe]: Concordia domi, foris pax. Ich weiß, das ist—zumal in Lübeck—kein sehr originelles Zitat. Aber selbst Thomas Mann fühlte sich unbefangen genug, hier im Rathaus im Jahre 1955 seine Dankesrede damit zu schließen. (Brandt 1973, 156; *BA* 6:246)

> When I was to give my first inaugural speech as chancellor in October [28,] 1969, I closed with the sentence: "We want to be [and become] a people of good neighbors both within as well as [and] without." An echo of what, when I was young, I used to read again and again on the Holsten Gate: Concordia domi, foris pax. I know that is not—especially in Lübeck—a particularly original quotation. But even Thomas Mann felt comfortable using it to end his acceptance speech here in the Town Hall in 1955.

But here is Brandt's ultimate statement concerning the significance of this proverb for himself and his political views for the future:

> "Concordia domi, foris pax"—das habe ich an all den Tagen lesen können, an denen ich morgens in die Schule ging oder am Abend nochmals mit dem Rad in die Stadt fuhr. Und dieses "Eintracht im Innern, Friede nach außen" (oder noch einfacher: Friede im Innern und nach außen) hat sich mir für immer eingeprägt, obwohl—oder gerade?—weil es von der Wirklichkeit so weit enfernt war. Ich nahm das Wort auf [. . .] aber ich habe damit nicht Geschichte beschrieben, sondern Ansprüche an die Zukunft angemeldet. (Brandt 1982, 34)

> "Concordia domi, foris pax"—I was able to read these words on all those days when I went to school in the morning or bicycled back into town in the evening. And this "Harmony within, peace without" (or, more simply, peace within and without) has always struck me, although—or perhaps because?—it was so far from the reality I knew. I made this

saying my own [. . .] but I was not describing history through it, but laying claim to it for the future.

The work toward a better future was constantly on Willy Brandt's mind, as can be seen from a luncheon speech on July 3, 1975, hosted by Soviet leader Leonid Brezhnev in Moscow. Here Brandt stressed that progress in international relations could only be made if the leaders of the world looked confidently and without fear into the future. To make this point, he employed a Russian proverb well known to his hosts:

> Auch künftig werden die Fortschritte mühselig sein. [. . .] Das Friedenswerk, an dem wir arbeiten, fordert, wie mir scheint, immer wieder das sabotierende Ressentiment der Kleinmütigen, Engstirnigen, der Ängstlichen heraus, die ihrer selbst und ihrer Sache nicht sicher zu sein scheinen. Ich halte mich, was dies angeht, an ein europäisches Sprichwort, von dem man mir sagte, es stamme aus Ihrem Lande: Furcht ist die Arbeit am eigenen Grab. (*BA* 9:136)

> In the future, too, progress will be laborious. [. . .] The state of peace for which we are striving continuously provokes, it seems to me, the resentful sabotage of the fainthearted, the narrow-minded, the fearful, who appear to be unsure of themselves, of what they think. In this regard I subscribe to a European proverb, which, someone told me, has its origin in your country: Fear is the work on your own grave.

Brandt was well aware that the use of a proverb can summarize an observation, and he clearly enjoyed citing proverbs from different cultures at international meetings. Thus, in his role as the president of the Socialist International, he made the following remarks on October 18, 1984, in Mexico City:

> Ich war überrascht über die Fortschritte der Demokratisierung oder die Wiedergeburt der Demokratie in Südamerika. Auch wenn sie noch immer zerbrechlich ist und dringend Unterstützung braucht, ist die Demokratie in eine Reihe von Ländern zurückgekehrt. Und wo Diktatoren noch immer regieren, sind ihre Tage endgültig gezählt. Es ist ermutigend, diesen Wandel mit eigenen Augen zu sehen. Auch das alte chinesische Sprichwort wurde wieder bestätigt: Es ist besser, etwas ein einziges Mal zu sehen, als hundertmal davon zu hören. (*BA* 8:388)

> I was surprised by the progress in the democratization or the rebirth of democracy in South America. Even though it continues to be fragile

and in urgent need of support, democracy has returned to a number of countries. And where dictators are still in power, their days are definitely numbered. It is encouraging to see this change with one's own eyes. Once again the old Chinese proverb is borne out: It is better to see something once than to hear of it a hundred times.

Of course, this proverb not being native to him, Brandt cites it somewhat differently on other occasions. In his important book *Der organisierte Wahnsinn: Wettrüsten und Welthunger* (1985), it appears as the chapter title "Sehen ist besser als hören" (To see is better than to hear), while later on he cites yet another variant: "So hat sich eine östliche Weisheit bestätigt: Einmal sehen ist besser als hundertmal von etwas reden hören" (Brandt 1985, 183, 197)—"Thus an eastern bit of wisdom holds true: It is better to see once than to hear about something a hundred times." During an interview on January 23, 1985, concerning the problem of starvation in Africa, Brandt is reminded of "eine fernöstliche Weisheit. Nämlich, dass es besser ist, eine Kerze anzuzünden, als über die Finsternis zu klagen. Das heißt auf gut Deutsch: Wenn eine ganz akute Notsituation da ist, dann bin ich der Meinung, man muss alles tun, um Menschenleben zu retten" (*BA* 8:407)—"a far eastern piece of wisdom: That is, that it is better to light a candle than to complain about the darkness. In good German that means: If an acute emergency situation exists, I am of the opinion that one must do everything to save human lives." Above all, Brandt is always forward looking, no matter what the social ills or political threats might be. Thus he cites a Tanzanian *Lebensregel* (rule of life): "Wenn du einen Löwen siehst, dann rettest du dich nicht, indem du stehenbleibst und betest. Statt dessen mußt du rennen und beten, daß du die Kraft haben wirst, weiterzulaufen" (Brandt 1985, 48)—"If you see a lion, you don't save yourself by standing still and praying. Instead you must run and pray that you will have the strength to continue running."

It will not come as a surprise, however, that Willy Brandt relied primarily on Anglo-American proverbs in his various communications. His command of the English language as well as his knowledge of Great Britain and the United States were so great that he felt quite at home with their proverbial wisdom in the original or in translation. Of special interest is his rather free German translation of the English proverb "You cannot make an omelet without breaking eggs" (Wilson 1970, 594; Mieder, Kingsbury, and Harder 1992, 438) in a major speech on May 8, 1949, at an SPD convention in Berlin. Wanting to make the point that politics and economics would definitely change as Germany was rebuilding, he said:

Auch von der wirtschaftlichen Seite her erhalten wir also eine Bestätigung unserer Behauptung, daß die alte Ordnung nicht willkürlich wiederaufgerichtet werden kann. Die Engländer haben dazu ein nettes Wort: Man kann einen Eierkuchen nicht mehr in Eier zurückverwandeln. (*BA* 4:113)

From the economic aspect, too, we have confirmation of our assertion that the old order cannot be restored arbitrarily. The English have a nice expression for such situations: You can't change an omelet back into eggs.

His translation did not catch on among the German population, but it has now gained some currency in the literal translation "Man kann kein Omelett machen, ohne Eier zu zerschlagen."

Brandt also offered a German translation of the American proverb "There are no atheists in foxholes" in his autobiography *Mein Weg nach Berlin* (with Leo Lania, 1960). That is quite amazing, since the earliest reference of the proverb found thus far stems only from a *Los Angeles Times* account of April 13, 1942 (Doyle, Mieder, and Shapiro 2012, 9–10):

Krieg empfindet nur der als aufregendes Abenteuer—das sprichwörtliche Stahlbad -, der weit vom Schuß ist, nicht die Menschen an der Front. Einem amerikanischen Sprichwort zufolge soll es keine Atheisten im Schützengraben geben; sicher ist, daß die im Schützengraben ein richtigereres Gefühl für die wahren Werte des Lebens besitzen. (Brandt and Lania 1960: 23–24)

Only those who are far away from the shooting see war as an exciting adventure—the proverbial baptism by fire—not the people at the front. According to an American proverb, there are said to be no atheists in the trenches [foxholes]; you may be sure that those in the trenches have a better feel for the true value of life.

Brandt must have been one of the first to use this relatively new proverb in German, where it now has been registered in small numbers as "Es gibt keine Atheisten im Schützengraben." Since it was barely known when Brandt offered his German translation, it was definitely appropriate that he introduced it with an introductory formula that identified it as an American proverb.

Occasionally one finds statements in which Brandt uses a German proverb in one situation and an English equivalent on another occasion. In front of his German listeners on July 22, 1961, in Munich it was perfectly natural that he employed the proverb "Das Hemd ist mir näher als die Jacke [der

Rock]" (The shirt is closer to me than the jacket [overcoat]) in a critically expanded formulation:

> In den 16 Jahren der widernatürlichen Trennung ist die Gefahr täglich größer geworden, daß wir uns nicht mehr verstehen, daß zumindest der eine Teil Deutschlands, nämlich der, dem es äußerlich besser geht, den anderen vergißt, daß uns die westeuropäische Jacke näher ist als das gesamtdeutsche Hemd, daß im Bewußtsein vieler von uns nicht nur Deutschland, sondern auch Europa an jenen Schlagbäumen aufhört, an denen Deutsche im Auftrag der sowjetischen Weltmacht den freien Zugang in den anderen Teil Deutschlands hindern. (Brandt 1962, 133)

> After sixteen years of unnatural separation, the danger grows daily that we will no longer understand each other, that at least one part of Germany, namely the one where people appear to be better off, will forget the other, that we will be closer to the West European jacket than to the all-German shirt, that deep-down for many of us it is not only Germany but also Europe that ends with the barrier that Germans at the behest of the Soviet superpower have erected to prevent free entry into the other part of Germany.

And yet, the polyglot Brandt was quite willing to cite the English equivalent "Charity begins at home" in a speech on March 21, 1971, in Cologne, while clearly addressing a German audience:

> Ich bin gegen den Zeigefinger, der vergessen läßt, wieviel Finger dabei auf uns selbst gerichtet bleiben. Ich bin gegen die Selbstgerechtigkeit, um die es sich allzuoft leicht handelt, wenn fremde und ferne Länder kritisch unter die Lupe genommen werden. "Charity begins at home"— auch mit den Menschenrechten fängt es zu Hause an. Afrika ist weit, und mancher unserer Mitbürger mag meinen, rassische Diskriminierung sei für uns kein Problem mehr oder doch höchstens ein abstraktes. (Brandt 1971a, 335; Brandt 1971b, 273)

> I am against the index finger because it makes us forget how many other fingers are pointed at us. I am against self-righteousness, which crops up all too often when we scrutinize foreign and distant lands. "Charity begins at home"—but human rights begin at home, too. Africa is far away, and many of our fellow citizens may think that racial discrimination is no longer a problem for us, or at most an abstract problem.

172   PROVERBS IN POLITICS

Perhaps Brandt went a bit far here in citing the English-language proverb in a German speech when a German proverb was ready at hand. However, in his book on *Der organisierte Wahnsinn* (1985), which addresses the arms race in juxtaposition to hunger in the world, the context necessitated the appropriate employment of the English text, which is translated in any case:

> In Genf berichtete ein afrikanischer Freund, in seinem Land heiße es neuerdings: "Menschenrechte fangen beim Frühstück an" ("Human rights begins with breakfast," in Abwandlung der englischen Redensart "Charity begins at home," Barmherzigkeit beginne zu Hause). (Brandt 1985, 47)

> In Geneva, an African friend told me of a new saying: "Human rights begin with breakfast" ("Human rights begins [*sic*] with breakfast," as a variant of the English expression "Charity begins at home"; compassion begins at home).

Brandt shows himself here almost like a paremiologist, interested in proverb manipulations or even anti-proverbs, but he should have used the genre designation "proverb" rather than proverbial "expression."

He also at times seems to think that proverbs are by nature quite old. Regarding the American proverb "What is good for General Motors is good for America (the country)," he was mistaken, since its date of origin in 1953 by the president of General Motors, Charles E. Wilson, during his testimony in front of the US Senate in Washington, is for once thoroughly established (Doyle, Mieder, and Shapiro 2012, 95). But it is once again surprising that Willy Brandt picked it up as early as 1960, and by now it has reached some currency in its German translation "Was gut ist für General Motors, ist gut für Amerika." The proverb is based on the structure "What is good for X is good for Y," and Brandt was quick to change the two variables to suit his sociopolitical messages. In his early book *Mein Weg nach Berlin* (with Leo Lania, 1960) he altered its wording to stress the importance of Berlin for Germany:

> Im Mittelpunkt steht für mich natürlich die Sorge um die Stadt, zu deren Sprecher ich berufen worden bin. Die lokale Aufgabe ist auch von entscheidender Bedeutung für die gesamtdeutsche Zukunft. Man kann es auf den einfachen Nenner bringen: Was gut ist für Berlin, ist auch gut für Deutschland. (Brandt and Lania 1960, 346)

> For me, of course, concern for the city whose voice I have been called upon to be, is central. This local assignment is of crucial significance for

the all-German future. You can reduce it to the common denominator: What is good for Berlin is good for Germany.

In this reference, Brandt did not yet mention that he was "playing" with a proverb. However, about ten years later, in a speech of November 18, 1971, he stated that he was varying an old proverb in his formulaic claim that what is good for Europe is also of benefit for the United States. Even though the adjective "old" of the introductory formula is factually incorrect, Brandt must have chosen it to add a special element of authority to his proverb variation:

Eine europäische Lösung [der Weltwirtschaftsprobleme] soll und darf keine antiamerikanische Lösung sein. Im übrigen könnte man jedoch in Abwandlung eines alten Sprichwortes sagen: Was gut ist für Europa, ist gut für die Vereinigten Staaten. Wir werden zu einem Ausgleich der deutschen und europäischen Interessen mit jenen der USA finden müssen. Diese Bundesrepublik—das möchte ich hier sagen—will eine gesunde Kraft in Europa und für Europa sein, nicht mehr, nicht weniger. Die Zeit des Feiertags-Europäertums ist vorbei; Europa ist unser Alltag. (Brandt 1971a, 176; Brandt 1973, 80)

A European solution [to global economic problems] should not and can not be an anti-American solution. But one could add as a variation of an old proverb: What is good for Europe is good for the United States. We will have to reach an accommodation of German and European interests with those of the USA. The Federal Republic—I wish to state this clearly—wants to be a healthy power in and for Europe, no more, no less. The time of vacation Europeanism is over; Europe is our everyday life.

Not quite half a year later, in a speech of April 29, 1972, in Berlin, Brandt returned to his favorite formula and expanded it from what is good for Berlin to include Germany as well as Europe, indicating that he was ever more becoming a European politician as well:

Diese unsere Stadt [Berlin] hat jetzt bessere Chancen als irgendwann nach dem Kriege. Diese Stadt weiß: was gut ist für Berlin, das ist auch gut für unser Land, und es ist gut für Europa. Deshalb nehme ich den Appell auf: Abgeordnete des Deutschen Bundestages, hört auf diese Stadt! (Brandt 1973, 219)

This city of ours [Berlin] now has better opportunities than ever before in the postwar period. This city knows: what is good for Berlin, is also good for our country, and it is good for Europe. For this reason I appeal to you: Members of the German Parliament, listen to this city!

As far as Brandt was concerned, it is the purpose of all politics to make life safer and better for all people of the world, and in a narrower sense for the Germans in both parts of the divided country. In his memoirs *Begegnungen und Einsichten* (1976), he stated categorically "Die ganze Politik sollte sich zum Teufel scheren, wenn sie nicht dazu da sei, den Menschen das Leben leichter statt schwerer zu machen: 'Was gut ist für die Menschen im geteilten Land, das ist auch gut für die Nation'" (Brandt 1976, 106–7)—"The whole of politics can go to the devil if its purpose is not to make life easier rather than more difficult for people. 'What is good for the people in a divided country is also good for the nation.'" In yet another voluminous memoir, entitled *Erinnerungen* (1989), he repeated this strong statement almost verbatim, also once again including the proverbial expression "to go to the devil," of which he was rather fond when expressing strong feelings:

> Meine Meinung war und ist: Es soll sich die Politik zum Teufel scheren, die—um welcher Prinzipien auch immer—den Menschen das Leben nicht leichter zu machen sucht. Wo eine Wahl unausweichlich ist, muß das menschliche Wohl den Vorrang haben. Denn was gut ist für die Menschen im geteilten Land, ist auch gut für die Nation. (Brandt 1989, 64)

> My opinion was and still is: to hell [to the devil] with the politics that—whatever its principles—does not attempt to make life easier for people. Where a choice is unavoidable, the welfare of the people must take precedence. Because what is good for the people in a divided nation, is also good for the nation.

It is remarkable, of course, how Brandt altered the first part of the proverb to include human beings rather than an automobile company, a city, a country, or a continent.

Obviously Brandt had many dealings with the Soviet Union regarding the divided Germany in particular and the so-called Cold War in general. The modus vivendi for many years was peaceful coexistence between the West and the East, with Brandt using an English proverb in his book *Koexistenz: Zwang zum Wagnis* (1963) to describe the difficulties in negotiating with the Soviets:

> Das Konzept einer gemeinsamen Anstrengung, die gegenseitigen Interessen zu definieren und zu respektieren, findet bei den Sowjets nur soweit Widerhall, wie ihr eigenes Interesse reicht. Sie möchten ihren Teil

des Kuchens behalten und unseren Teil dazu bekommen, oder mind-
estens dabei helfen, ihn zu verspeisen. (Brandt 1963, 27)

The concept of a common effort to define and respect common interests
only meets with a response from the Soviets when it is in their own
interest. They want to have their own piece of the cake and get our piece
too, or at least help eat it.

Karl Friedrich Wilhelm Wander lists a similar German proverb in his *Deutsches
Sprichwörter-Lexikon*: "Er möchte den Kuchen schenken, er will ihn aber für
morgen zum Frühstück behalten" (He wants to give away the cake, but he
also wants to keep it for tomorrow's breakfast), but he is quick to add that the
English say: "Man kann den Kuchen nicht essen und auch zugleich behalten"
(You cannot eat your cake and have it, too) (Wander 1867–1880, 2:1659, no. 68).
It is very doubtful that Brandt is dealing with the basically unknown German
proverb in his statement. He is in fact alluding to the sixteenth-century English
proverb "You cannot eat your cake and have it, too" (Wilson 1970, 215; Mieder,
Kingsbury, and Harder 1992, 79).

It is, of course, well known that Willy Brandt and US president John F.
Kennedy became good friends after the latter visited Berlin while Brandt
was mayor and uttered those famous words "Ich bin ein Berliner"—"I am a
Berliner"—on June 26, 1963, at the Berlin Wall, endearing him forever to all
Germans. Little wonder that Brandt created a testimony of this deep friendship
with his acclaimed book *Begegnungen mit Kennedy* (1964), in which he quotes
a famous passage from Kennedy's inaugural address of January 20, 1961, in
German translation:

Und deshalb, meine amerikanischen Mitbürger: Fragt nicht, was euer
Land für euch tun kann, sondern fragt, was ihr für euer Land tun könnt.
Meine Mitbürger in der ganzen Welt: Fragt nicht, was Amerika für euch
tun wird, sondern was wir gemeinsam für die Freiheit der Menschen
tun können. Und schließlich, ob ihr nun Bürger Amerikas seid oder der
übrigen Welt, fordert von uns hier das gleiche hohe Maß an Stärke und
Opfer, das wir von euch verlangen. (Brandt 1964, 34)

And so, my fellow Americans, ask not what your country can do for
you; ask what you can do for your country. My fellow citizens of the
world: Ask not what America will do for you, but what together we can
do for the freedom of man. Finally, whether you are citizens of America
or citizens of the world, ask of us the same high standards of strength
and sacrifice which we ask of you. (Hunt 1995, 431; Mieder 2005, 172–73)

176 PROVERBS IN POLITICS

It should not be a big surprise that Willy Brandt returned to this statement when he spoke on February 24, 1969, in New York during a ceremony honoring General Lucius D. Clay, former head of the American forces in Berlin and architect of the Berlin airlift during 1948–1949, with the Freedom Award:

> Warum sollen wir in Europa uns stets als diejenigen darstellen, die klagen und fordern? Wir sollten vielmehr zeigen, was wir uns zutrauen und zu leiten vermögen. Es geht ja nicht mehr darum, was Amerika für Europa tun kann, sondern was wir miteinander und für einander tun können. (Brandt 1970, 150)

> Why should we always portray ourselves in Europe as those who complain and demand? Rather should we demonstrate our self-confidence and leadership. It is no longer a matter of what America can do for Europe but what we can do with one another and for one another.

His American and international audience—Brandt spoke in English—will have heard Kennedy's voice behind this formulation, for his "Ask not what your country can do for you, ask what you can do for your country" had with incredible speed already entered oral tradition as a proverb in the United States. Not to take anything away from President Kennedy, it should be mentioned here that Oliver Wendell Holmes Jr. had said something quite similar in a speech of May 30, 1884, that might be regarded as a prototype of Kennedy's wording, since it anticipates the idea and the parallel phrasing, the chiasmus: "We pause to recall what our country has done for each of us, and to ask ourselves what we can do for our country in return" (Mieder 2005, 173; Doyle, Mieder, and Shapiro 2012, 45–46).

Be that as it may, Brandt, with his keen interest in improving the lot of people throughout the world, took a definite rhetorical liking to Kennedy's utterance, and he liked referring to his murdered friend when citing it. Thus, in his major address of January 26, 1973, in the West German Parliament in Bonn, he said:

> In diesem Jahr werden zehn Jahre vergangen sein, seit der Präsident Kennedy ermordet wurde. Aber was von ihm weiterlebt, ist doch nicht zuletzt der Satz, der nun einmal auch bei uns gilt, der Satz nämlich: Frage nicht nur, was der Staat für dich tun kann, sondern frage auch, was du für dein Land tun kannst! (Brandt 1973, 541)

> It is now ten years since President Kennedy was assassinated. But something of him still lives, namely the sentence that is applicable for us, too,

namely: Ask not what your country can do for you—ask what you can do for your country!

Brandt repeated this statement almost verbatim in his self-reflective book on his political achievements, *Über den Tag hinaus* (1974), which certainly helped to spread Kennedy's bon mot among Germans: "Aber was von Kennedy weiterlebt, ist doch nicht zuletzt das Wort: Frage nicht nur, was dein Land für dich tun kann, sondern frage auch, was du für dein Land tun kannst!" (Brandt 1974, 286)—"But what lives on from Kennedy is to be sure the statement: Ask not only what your country can do for you but ask also what you can do for your country." And remembering his friend once again in his autobiographical account *Begegnungen und Einsichten* (1976), Brandt reminds his readers how Kennedy had influenced Germans with his ethical claim, "daß es nicht genüge danach zu fragen, was 'Dein Land für Dich tun kann, sondern was Du für Dein Land tun kannst'" (Brandt 1976, 74)—"that it is not enough to ask 'what your country can do for you but rather what you can do for your country.'" There can be no doubt that Willy Brandt deserves much of the credit for popularizing John F. Kennedy's sociopolitical proverb in Germany, where it is by now an established translated proverb as well.

Of great paremiological interest is also Willy Brandt's effective political use of the nineteenth-century American proverb "Don't swap horses in midstream," which also exists in such variants as "Don't switch (change) horses in the middle of the stream." It was used by Abraham Lincoln on June 9, 1864, in response of having been nominated for a second term as president of the United States. With typical humility, Lincoln stated in Baltimore: "I have not permitted myself to conclude that I am the best man in the country; but I am reminded, in this connection, of a story of an old Dutch farmer, who remarked to a companion once that 'it was not best to swap horses when crossing streams'" (Basler 1953, 7:383–84; Mieder 2008, 207). While many Americans think that Lincoln originated the proverb, it actually was already current in the 1830s in the United States. Surprisingly, Wander lists the German proverb "Mitten im Strom kann man die Pferde nicht umspannen" in the fourth volume of his *Deutsches Sprichwörter-Lexikon* (1867–1880, 4:922, no. 22), albeit without any historical reference. Since he had spent the year 1851–1852 in the United States (see Wander 1852), it is possible that he had heard the proverb as a loan translation among German immigrants and then included it in his massive proverb dictionary. But it did not attain any noticeable currency in the German language and became better known in German only later by way of Lincoln's association with it (Alsleben and Scholze-Stubenrecht 2002, 206). In any case, Brandt most likely became acquainted with the proverb because of his knowledge of American history, culture, and language. Obviously he realized its metaphorical potential as an expression for dealing with the politics of elections. Reflecting on the politics of West Germany, he used the proverb in a rather innovative way in claiming that in 1966 the government had reached a point where there were not really any qualified new politicians who might be capable of standing in for the tired old guard:

> Früher sagte man, mitten im Strom dürfte man nicht die Pferde wechseln. Aber im Herbst 1966 gab es für diese Regierung keine neuen Pferde mehr. Eine Handvoll müder Reiter mußte sich ohne Gefolgschaft vom Strom treiben lassen, und mit ihnen trieb der Staat den Gefahren wirtschaftlicher Depressionen und außenpolitischer Isolierung rasch entgegen. (Brandt 1968, 39)

> In the past you used to say: don't swap horses in midstream. But in the autumn of 1966 there were for this government no new horses left. A handful of tired riders were drifting in the river with no retinue, and with them the state drifted swiftly toward the dangers of economic depression and political isolation abroad.

Four years later, in a speech on October 12, 1972, at an SPD convention in Dortmund, Brandt employed the proverb in a more traditional way, arguing that the social-liberal team of himself and Walter Scheel had proven itself to be very effective and that it would be a mistake to change these two workhorses in the middle of the political stream: "Das sozialliberale Gespann hat sich gerade auf außenpolitischem Gebiet bewährt, und man soll nicht mitten im Strom die Pferde wechseln" (Brandt 1973, 448)—"The social-liberal team has proven itself especially in the area of foreign affairs, and one is not supposed to swap horses in midstream." But there is a third especially interesting reference of the proverb in a joint election proclamation by Willy Brandt and Helmut Schmidt of August 25, 1976: "Angesichts einer weltweit schwierigen Lage darf man nicht mitten im Strom den Steuermann wechseln. Die Opposition hat weder den Mann noch das Konzept, die Aufgabe zu meistern" (*BA* 5:224–25)—"In view of the difficult situation worldwide one must not swap the helmsman in midstream. The opposition has neither the man nor the concept to master the task." Both politicians stem from northern Germany and are thus well acquainted with the language of the sea and of sailors. So it was easy to exchange the proverbial horses for the helmsman of the ship of state, who should not be replaced in the middle of the stream. This certainly was a fitting variation of the metaphor in their argument to keep the political leadership as it was.

It will come as no surprise that the eternally optimistic Willy Brandt also picked up the proverb "The glass is either half empty or half full," which has been documented in English in the United States since 1930 (Doyle, Mieder, and Shapiro 2012, 98). For him, the glass was always half full, but he realized that pessimists will immediately claim that it is half empty. There is first of all this personal statement in a speech of March 18, 1968, in which Brandt stressed his positive political outlook:

> Wieso nennt man ein Glas, das halbvoll ist, halbleer? Ich ziehe vor, es halbvoll zu nenen. Dazu braucht man kein weltfremder Optimist zu sein. Dazu braucht man nur jenes gesunde Augenmaß, ohne das ich mir keine vernünftge Politik vorstellen kann. (Brandt 1984, 142)

> Why do we call a glass that is half full half empty? I prefer to call it half full. You do not need to be an unworldly optimist to do so. All you need is that healthy way of seeing things, without which I cannot imagine rational politics.

In a handwritten note for an SPD meeting on March 3, 1972, he acknowledged that it is difficult to deal with those who far too often exhibit a negative attitude: "Kann niemand hindern, aufgrund pessimist[ischer] Grundeinstellung zu sagen: halbvolles Glas = halbleer" (*BA* 7:299)—"[I] can't prevent people, because of their fundamental pessimism, from saying: half full glass = half empty."

In yet another speech, of November 22, 1980, he admitted that mistakes had been made during past years, but he saw no reason to give in to defeatism, always preferring to look at the glass as being half full:

> Ich gehöre nicht zu denen, die meinen, alles sei in den vergangenen Jahren auf bestmögliche Weise gehandhabt worden, keine Seite habe Fehler gemacht. Trotzdem gehöre ich zu denen, die ein Glas, das halb voll ist, halb voll und nicht halb leer nennen. (*BA* 9:297)

> I am not among those who think that everything in the past few years has been handled in the best possible way, that none of the parties have made mistakes. On the contrary, I am one of those who call a glass that is half full half full and not half empty.

That Willy Brandt was quite tuned in to relatively modern proverbs can also be seen from his German use of the originally American proverb "Think globally, act locally," which was first registered in 1942 (Doyle, Mieder, and Shapiro 2012,

180   PROVERBS IN POLITICS

256). Considering his sincere commitment to safeguarding the environment in a global world, it could be expected that he employed it strategically in his speech on global challenges on November 25, 1988, at Ruhr University Bochum:

> Es ist nicht damit getan, auf Konferenzen das Fortschreiten der Wüsten zu beklagen und Sorge über den klimagefährdeten Verlust des tropischen Regenwaldes zu bekunden, vielmehr bedarf es der Erarbeitung von Entwicklungsstrategien im Weltmaßstab. Helfen kann dabei, daß die allgegenwärtigen Umweltgefahren einen explosiven Bewußtseinswandel bewirkt haben. Sehr viel Zeit zum Handeln bleibt uns nicht mehr. Sicherlich wäre schon sehr viel erreicht, wenn "global gedacht und lokal vernünftig gehandelt" würde. Die Industriegesellschaften haben die finanziellen Mittel und technischen Möglichkeiten zu ihrer ökologischen Modernisierung. (*BA* 8:458)

> It is not enough to lament the growth of deserts at conferences and to announce concern over the climate-caused loss of the tropical rainforest; rather, there is a need to work out strategies on a worldwide basis. It may help that ever-present environmental dangers have caused an explosive change in consciousness. There is not much time left for action. To be sure, we would have achieved much if people were to "think globally and act locally in a rational way." The industrial nations have the financial means and technical possibilities for ecological modernization.

It is not possible to ascertain whether Brandt is translating the English-language proverb here or citing it in its German version, which has become current by now.

It is also questionable whether he knew that he was "playing" with one of the most stereotypical American proverbs when he somewhat flippantly stated in a newspaper interview of December 14, 1989, that for German conservatives "Ein toter Sozialdemokrat ist ein guter Sozialdemokrat":

> Question: Aber Sie werden vielleicht vom Kanzler [Helmut Kohl] als der gute Sozialdemokrat hochstilisiert, damit die CDU [Christlich Demokratische Union] die anderen Sozialdemokraten etwas mehr prügeln kann.
>
> Answer: Da bin ich fein raus. Normalerweise ist für die deutsche Rechte ein toter Soialdemokrat ein guter Sozialdemokrat. Und tot bin ich ja noch nicht. (*BA* 10:416)

> Question: But you will perhaps be characterized by the chancellor [Helmut Kohl] as the good Social Democrat, so that the CDU [the

Christian Democratic Union] can beat up on the other Social Democrats even more.

Answer: That's fine by me. For the German right, it is normally a dead Social Democrat that is a good Social Democrat. And I'm not dead yet.

The underlying proverbial invective is "The only good Indian is a dead Indian," which became current in the United States during the 1860s as Native Americans were killed, displaced, and driven onto reservations (Mieder 1993b). Regrettably, this insensitive and despicable proverb has been loan translated into various languages, appearing in German as "Nur ein toter Indianer ist ein guter Indianer" (Mieder 1993a)—"Only a dead Indian is a good Indian." It is to be assumed that Brandt would not have expressed his variant if he had known that it was based on a proverbial slur that is offensive even when varied.

Finally, there is the incredible role that Willy Brandt played in the German acceptance and dissemination of the American folk proverb "A house divided against itself cannot stand," which is a shortened version of the biblical verse "And if a house be divided against itself, that house cannot stand" (Mark 3:25). Martin Luther's German translation of the same passage into "Und wenn ein Haus mit sich selbst uneins wird, kann es nicht bestehen" (And if a house becomes at odds with itself, it cannot endure) never became proverbial, but the translation of the American proverb has established this biblical wisdom in German in the form of "Ein in sich gespaltenes Haus hat keinen Bestand" as well during the past fifty years. But to be sure, the popularization of this Bible proverb brought with it a secularization of its message, in which the "house" refers at first to the United States and subsequently to Germany, to Europe, and to the entire world. And there can be no doubt that Willy Brandt was instrumental in helping to spread the American proverb from the Bible to Germany and beyond.

The story behind this development goes back to President Abraham Lincoln, who employed the proverb "A house divided against itself cannot stand" on numerous occasions starting in 1843 in order to argue for a unified nation that was being torn apart by the vexing problem of slavery (Mieder 2000b, 124–27). But it was the famous "House Divided" speech that he delivered on June 16, 1858, in Springfield, Illinois, that attached the proverb forever to this great man and helped establish it as a frequently cited piece of sociopolitical wisdom:

If we could first know where we are, and whither we are tending, we could then better judge what to do, and how to do it. [. . .]

"A house divided against itself cannot stand."

I believe this government cannot endure, permanently half slave and half free.

182 PROVERBS IN POLITICS

I do not expect the Union to be dissolved—I do not expect the house to fall—but I do expect it will cease to be divided.

It will become all one thing, or all the other.

(Basler 1953, 2:461–62; Mieder 1998, 63–74)

Of course, Lincoln's preoccupation with this proverb before the Civil War did not prevent the war's actual horrific occurrence, but the proverb without doubt was an effective leitmotif in Lincoln's struggle to avoid it and to rid the young nation of slavery. Be that as it may, a hundred years later Willy Brandt was invited to deliver a keynote address on the occasion of Lincoln's 150th birthday on February 12, 1959, in Springfield. As one can imagine, the honored Brandt—only fourteen years after the end of the Second World War—was deeply moved by this opportunity. As he prepared the address, he read much about Abraham Lincoln and also came across his "House Divided" speech. As mayor of the divided city of Berlin, he realized that this metaphor was also appropriate for the situation in Germany. In his perfect English, Brandt alluded to the proverb in the following remarks:

Abraham Lincoln spoke of the duty of the whole people never to entrust the preservation of their liberties to any hands but their own, a duty which, after bitter experience, the great majority of the German people also acknowledge. He spoke of the eternal struggle between democracy and tyranny. We know that this struggle has torn apart the European continent and that it has assumed world-wide dimensions. He quoted the passage from the Bible about the house divided against itself, and expressed his conviction that the government could not endure permanently to be half slave and half free.

The truths which Lincoln spoke here in Springfield in June 1858 are possibly even more applicable to the present situation of the German people than to the one which he faced: that is, to the arbitrary disruption of their lives, for which, of course, they themselves are not without guilt. I can only tell you that the Germans in the East and in the West do not accept this situation and that they will not accept conditions under which a son is separated from his mother, nor brothers from each other. (Brandt 1959b, 18; German translation, Brandt 1959a, 210)

Brandt never forgot the deep emotions he felt during the delivery of his memorable address (Brandt 1976, 80, 102; Brandt 1989, 64), and the proverb "A house divided against itself cannot stand" became so ingrained in his psyche that he began citing it repeatedly in his very own German translation of "Ein in sich gespaltenes Haus hat keinen Bestand" (literally, A house divided against itself has no permanency) in his speeches and writings. In fact, at the time of German unification in 1989 and also afterward, he quoted it both in English and German to such an extent in his speeches as well as radio and television addresses that the proverb in his translation took hold of the German population. And since Brandt often referred to Lincoln when citing the proverb, the latter's has somewhat become attached to the proverb in Germany as well. This can go so far that both Americans and Germans no longer associate the proverb with the Bible but rather with Abraham Lincoln and to a lesser degree with Willy Brandt (Mieder 1998, 115–25; Mieder 2000a, 192–96).

It is of interest to note that it took Brandt some time to find the "perfect" formulation of the proverb in German, and the fact that German syntax can destroy a basic proverbial structure probably had something to do with this as well. Here, for example, is an early reference from a major political address of November 25, 1960, in which the verb is forced to the end of the sentence and in which Brandt does not cite the noun *Bestand*—"permanency":

> Abraham Lincoln hat in einer tödlichen Krise für die Einheit seines Volkes das Bibelwort aufgegriffen, daß ein in sich gespaltenes Haus nicht bestehen kann. Das gilt für die Vergangenheit, das gilt auch für die Gegenwart unseres gespaltenen Volkes. [. . .] Wir sind alle *eine* Familie. Deshalb muß unser Volk endlich den Frieden mit sich selbst machen. Daran möchte ich nach besten Kräften mitwirken. (Brandt 1972, 24; Brandt 1984, 39)

> In a deadly crisis for the unity of his people Abraham Lincoln chose a phrase from the Bible, that a house divided against itself cannot stand. That was valid for the past, and that is also valid for the present of our divided people. [. . .] We are all *one* family. For that reason our people must finally make peace with themselves. I would like to work toward that with all my might.

In his book *Begegnungen mit Kennedy* (1964), a sincere testimony of the friendship of these two great politicians, Brandt refers to Lincoln's "House Divided" speech but merely alludes to the proverb, which one could easily miss:

> Ein Höhepunkt meiner damaligen Reise war der Besuch in Springfield, der Hauptstadt des Staates Illinois, wo ich die Festrede anläßlich des 150. Geburtstages von Abraham Lincoln hielt. Ich erinnerte daran, daß sich Lincoln auf das Bibelwort vom "geteilten Haus" berufen und

seiner Überzeugung Ausdruck gegeben habe, daß ein Staat nicht auf die Dauer mit einer versklavten und einer freien Hälfte bestehen kann. [...] In meinem Arbeitszimmer steht eine Büste Lincolns von Leo Cherne. (Brandt 1964, 39; Binder 1975, 167)

A high point of my journey at that time was the visit to Springfield, the state capital of Illinois, where I gave a speech on the occasion of Abraham Lincoln's 150th birthday. I drew attention to Lincoln's use of the biblical saying about the "divided house" and to his conviction that a nation cannot continue to exist for any length of time when it consists of an enslaved half and a free half. [...] In my study there is a Lincoln bust by [economist and sculptor] Leo Cherne.

Lincoln's bust in his study shows once again the admiration that Brandt had for this former president, whom he liked to cite together with the proverb, for example in his speech "Weltfriede" (world peace) delivered on December 12, 1971, in Stockholm:

Das Gleichgewicht des Schreckens darf uns nicht beruhigen. Wir brauchen zusätzliche Sicherheit. Wir brauchen die Konsequenzen aus der Erkenntnis, daß der Weltfriede zur Lebensbedingung unseres technischen Zeitalters geworden ist. Wir brauchen über die regionalen Zusammenschlüsse hinaus die vielgestaltige europäische Zusammenarbeit. Auch für Europa gilt das Wort Abraham Lincolns, daß ein in sich gespaltenes Haus nicht Bestand haben kann. (Brandt 1971a, 380; Brandt 1971b, 105–6)

The balance of terror should not leave us complacent. We need additional safety. We need to draw the consequences from the recognition that world peace has become a requirement for life in our technical age. We need above and beyond regional amalgamations a Europe that works together in a multitude of varied ways. Abraham Lincoln's conviction that a house divided against itself cannot stand works for Europe, too.

In an interview with the editors of *Der Spiegel* on August 28, 1978 (one of many that he did for that newsmagazine), Brandt pointed out that he often referred to a sentence by Lincoln with a biblical origin before citing the proverb in German translation. It is almost as if he were becoming a paremiologist, informing readers where the proverb comes from and that it has already played an important political role in America that is applicable to the German situation:

Ich habe über viele Jahre hinweg im Ausland um Verständnis dafür gebeten, daß wir auf die Dauer nicht als ein wegen der Nazi-Zeit innerlich gespaltenes Volk leben könnten. Ich habe mich häufig auf einen Satz von Lincoln, der auch nicht von ihm kommt, sondern den er aus der Bibel hat—was ja auch keine Schande ist –, bezogen, daß ein in sich gespaltenes Haus keinen Bestand haben kann. (Brandt 1993a, 279)

Over many years I have, whenever abroad, called for an understanding that we cannot go on living as a people deeply divided because of the Nazi era. I frequently drew on a sentence used by Lincoln, which does not stem from him but which he took from the Bible—which is in no way shameful—that a house divided against itself cannot stand.

As already mentioned, Willy Brandt made especially effective use of the proverb during Germany's unification, often referring to Abraham Lincoln, at times quoting it in English as "A house divided against itself cannot stand" and at other times citing it more appropriately in German as "Ein in sich gespaltenes Haus hat keinen Bestand." His arguments were always that now that the Iron Curtain had been lifted, the time had come for Germans to grow back together in a unified house. In his speech of January 31, 1990, he even stated exactly why he employed this proverbial wisdom, giving Lincoln more credit than the Bible as he uttered the proverb in German and English:

Meine Kundgebungen in der DDR schließe ich nicht von ungefähr mit den schönen Lincoln-Worten, daß ein in sich gespaltenes Haus nicht Bestand hat. "A house divided against itself cannot stand." Das gilt für die gespaltene deutsche Nation; über die aktuellen Aufregungen hinaus auch für die Zukunft der DDR, die wieder zusammenfinden muß und nicht in Haß und Rache untergehen darf. (Brandt 1993b, 82)

I close my speeches in the GDR [German Democratic Republic; East Germany] intentionally with Lincoln's beautiful words that a house divided against itself cannot stand. "A house divided against itself cannot stand." That applies to the divided German nation; and, beyond the current excitement, to the future of the GDR, too, which must find its way forward and not be allowed to decline into hatred and revenge.

Brandt continued his preoccupation with this proverb until the end of his life as he dealt with issues of German unification, which brought with it plenty of socioeconomic and political problems. Thus in an address about the future of the united Germany on February 23, 1992, in Dresden, he quoted "Lincoln's" proverb in English, arguing that it would take serious effort for the two former Germanies to grow together. It is, however, somewhat surprising that he cited the proverb only in English in the former East Germany, since English was not at all well established as a foreign language there, with students having had to study Russian:

> "A house divided against itself cannot stand"—das sagte Abraham Lincoln den Amerikanern nach dem Bürgerkrieg [eigentlich *davor* als Argument gegen die Spaltung des Landes! vgl. die Belege in Mieder 2000b, 124–27]. Das sollten auch wir uns durch den Kopf gehen lassen—und im deutschen Westen nicht vergessen, daß wir ohne ein erhebliches Maß an innerer Aussöhnung über die Jahre 1933–1945 nicht hinweggekommen wären. (Brandt 1993b, 166)

> "A house divided against itself cannot stand"—this is what Abraham Lincoln told the American people after the Civil War [actually *before* the war, as an argument against the division of the country! See the evidence in Mieder 2000b, 124–27]. We too should ponder these words— and in West Germany not forget that we would not have gotten over the years 1933–1945 without a good measure of inner reconciliation.

But in this last reference, spoken during yet another *Spiegel* interview only one day later on February 24, 1992, Brandt appears to have come to the conclusion that perhaps it would be more appropriate to add his very own proverbial translation "Ein in sich gespaltenes Haus hat keinen Bestand" with a nod to Abraham Lincoln to his discourse. As he showed much understanding for former East German politicians, believing that they should not automatically be excluded from the new German politics, he repeated a small factual mistake by once again claiming that Lincoln used the proverb after the American Civil War was over to help heal the split between the North and the South. Lincoln barely survived the end of the war, and there is no written record that he employed the proverb after he rhetorically uttered it before the war—in vain, as he was unable to prevent the outbreak of one of the worst civil wars in history. Actually, Lincoln stopped using the proverb at the end of 1860, with but one allusion to it in 1863 in the middle of the war (Mieder 2000b, 127). But here are Brandt's otherwise perfectly appropriate remarks:

> Ich will hier nicht als Lehrmeister auftreten. Aber, daß man nicht jedermann, der mal in der SED [Sozialistische Einheitspartei Deutschlands] mitgemacht hat oder in den Blockparteien, von politischen Ämtern

ausschließen kann, das scheint mir einleuchtend. Ich erinnere da an ein Wort, das Abraham Lincoln, nach [eigentlich *vor*!] dem amerikanischen Bürgerkrieg, seinen Leuten gesagt hat: Ein in sich gespaltenes Land hat keinen Bestand. (Brandt 1993a, 523)

I do not wish to appear before you as a schoolmaster. But that you cannot simply exclude everybody who was once a member of the SED [the East German Socialist Unity Party] or in the minority parties from any political office seems to me to be obvious. Let me remind you of Abraham Lincoln's words after [in fact *before*!] the American Civil War: A country divided against itself cannot stand.

It is noteworthy to recognize that Brandt quotes the proverb here exactly in the wording and structure that he gave it in his very own translation of the proverb "A house divided against itself cannot stand" that he had picked up from the admired Abraham Lincoln. The American president was instrumental in spreading this piece of folk wisdom from the Bible among the American people, and it has preoccupied the sociopolitical life in the United States ever since. Brandt's loan translation has gained considerable currency in Germany now as well, and it was indeed this important politician who made this possible by way of his many interviews, speeches, and books. He cited it in variants, he alluded to it, he mentioned it alongside Lincoln's name and attested to its biblical origin, and at times the polyglot Brandt got carried away and quoted it only in English. Both in the United States and in Germany, the biblical background of the proverb has pretty much been lost, as the Bible proverb–turned–folk proverb has taken on a secularized political meaning. But Lincoln's name continues to be attached to the proverb in both countries, and there is no reason why this extraordinary human being should not be revered in the United States and in Germany. It could, however, be argued that Willy Brandt, as a truly great German and European politician, could also be mentioned in connection with this proverb. In many ways he was a much more cosmopolitan world leader than Lincoln, and while both Brandt and Lincoln knew how to play all registers of their respective native languages, it was Willy Brandt who with his keen linguistic sensitivity and fluency in several languages played an important role in spreading especially English-language proverbs by way of translations into German. He might not necessarily have been the first to come up with these loan translations, but in his role as a great political communicator he certainly acquainted the German people with several American proverbs in particular. Without any doubt, Willy Brandt was one of the giants of German and European politics in the twentieth century, but in addition to that he can

188 PROVERBS IN POLITICS

definitely hold the candle to such world-class politicians as Abraham Lincoln, Otto von Bismarck, Winston S. Churchill, and Barack Obama when it comes to effective proverbial rhetoric.

BIBLIOGRAPHY

This chapter was first published with the same title in *Proceedings of the Ninth Interdisciplinary Colloquium on Proverbs*, Tavira, Portugal, November 1–8, 2015, edited by Rui J. B. Soares and Outi Lauhakangas (Tavira, Portugal: Tipografia Tavirense, 2016), 114–44.

Alsleben, Brigitte, and Werner Scholze-Stubenrecht. 2002. *Duden: Das große Buch der Zitate und Redewendungen*. Mannheim, Germany: Duden Verlag.

Basler, Roy P., ed. 1953. *The Collected Works of Abraham Lincoln*. 8 vols. New Brunswick, New Jersey: Rutgers University Press.

Bayer, Karl. 1994. *Nota bene! Das lateinische Zitatenlexikon*. Munich: Artemis and Winkler.

Bergsdorf, Wolfgang. 1978. *Politik und Sprache*. Munich: Günter Olzog.

Binder, David. 1975. *The Other German: Willy Brandt's Life and Times*. Washington, DC: New Republic Book Company.

Blümner, Hugo. 1891. *Der bildliche Ausdruck in den Reden des Fürsten Bismarck*. Leipzig: S. Hirzel.

Blümner, Hugo. 1894. "Der bildliche Ausdruck in den Briefen des Fürsten Bismarck." *Euphorion* 1: 590–603, 771–87.

Blümner, Hugo. 1895. "Der bildliche Ausdruck in den Ansprachen des Fürsten Bismarck." *Zeitschrift des allgemeinen deutschen Sprachvereins* 10, cols. 79–87.

Brandt, Willy. 1959a. "Amerikanische und deutsche Einheit. Abraham Lincoln zum 150. Geburtstag. Festansprache gehalten am 12. Februar 1959 in Springfield (Illinois) USA." *Außenpolitik* 10: 209–13.

Brandt, Willy. 1959b. "We Will Bend the Knee to Nobody." Speech delivered on February 12, 1959, in Springfield, Illinois. *Germany: The Magazine of the Federal Republic*, special issue on Berlin, 18–19.

Brandt, Willy. 1961. *Plädoyer für die Zukunft: Beiträge zur deutschen Politik*. Frankfurt am Main: Europäische Verlagsanstalt.

Brandt Willy. 1962. *Mit Herz und Hand: Ein Mann in der Bewährung*. Hannover, Germany: Verlag für Literatur und Zeitgeschehen.

Brandt, Willy. 1963. *Koexistenz: Zwang zum Wagnis*. Stuttgart: Deutsche Verlags-Anstalt.

Brandt, Willy. 1964. *Begegnungen mit Kennedy*. Munich: Kindler.

Brandt, Willy. 1968. *Friedenspolitik in Europa*. Frankfurt am Main: S. Fischer.

Brandt, Willy. 1970. *Reden und Interviews, 1968–1969*. Bonn: Presse- und Informationsamt der Bundesregierung.

Brandt, Willy. 1971a. *Der Wille zum Frieden: Perspektiven der Politik*. Hamburg: Hoffmann und Campe.

Brandt, Willy. 1971b. *Reden und Interviews*. Hamburg: Hoffmann und Campe.

Brandt, Willy. 1972. *Plädoyer für die Zukunft: Beiträge zur deutschen Politik*. 2nd ed. Frankfurt am Main: Europäische Verlagsanstalt.

Brandt, Willy. 1973. *Reden und Interviews II (1970–1974)*. Bonn: Presse- und Informationsamt der Bundesregierung.

Brandt, Willy. 1974. *Über den Tag hinaus: Eine Zwischenbilanz*. Hamburg: Hoffmann und Campe.

Brandt, Willy. 1976. *Begegnungen und Einsichten: Die Jahre 1960–1975*. Hamburg: Hoffmann und Campe.

Brandt, Willy. 1982. *Links und frei: Mein Weg 1930–1950*. Hamburg: Hoffmann und Campe.

Brandt, Willy. 1984. *. . . auf der Zinne der Partei: Parteitagsreden 1960–1983*. Edited by Werner Krause and Wolfgang Gröf. Bonn: J. H. W. Dietz.

Brandt, Willy. 1985. *Der organisierte Wahnsinn: Wettrüsten und Welthunger*. Cologne: Kiepenheuer und Witsch.

Brandt, Willy. 1989. *Erinnerungen*. Berlin: Wolf Jobst Siedler.

Brandt, Willy. 1993a. *Die Spiegel-Gespräche, 1959–1992*. Edited by Erich Böhme and Klaus Wirtgen. Stuttgart: Deutsche Verlags-Anstalt.

Brandt, Willy. 1993b. *". . . was zusammengehört": Über Deutschland*. 2nd ed. Bonn: J. H. W. Dietz.

Brandt, Willy, with Leo Lania. 1960. *Mein Weg nach Berlin*. Munich: Kindler.

Breuillard, Jean. 1984. "Proverbes et pouvoir politique: Le cas de L'U.R.S.S." In *Richesse du proverbe*, edited by François Suard and Claude Buridant, 2:155–66. Lille, France: Université de Lille.

Dieckmann, Walther. 1969. *Sprache in der Politik: Einführung in die Pragmatik und Semantik der politischen Sprache*. Heidelberg, Germany: Carl Winter.

Doyle, Charles Clay, Wolfgang Mieder, and Fred R. Shapiro. 2012. *The Dictionary of Modern Proverbs*. New Haven, CT: Yale University Press.

Drath, Viola Herms. 1975. *Willy Brandt: Prisoner of His Past*. Radnor, PA: Chilton Book Company.

Eggert, Sonja Brunhilde. 1998. "'Kleine Schritte sind besser als keine Schritte': Willy Brandts sprichwörtliche Rhetorik." Honors thesis, University of Vermont.

Elspaß, Stephan. 1998. *Phraseologie in der politischen Rede: Untersuchungen zur Verwendung von Phraseologismen, phraseologischen Modifikationen und Verstößen gegen die phraseologische Norm in ausgewählten Bundestagsdebatten*. Opladen, Germany: Westdeutscher Verlag.

Elspaß, Stephan. 2007. "Phrasemes in Political Speech." In *Phraseologie: Ein internationales Handbuch der zeitgenössischen Forschung*, edited by Harald Burger, Dmitrij Dobrovol'skij, Peter Kühn, and Neal R. Norrick, 1:284–92. Berlin: Walter de Gruyter.

Girnth, Heiko. 2002. *Sprache und Sprachverwendung in der Politik: Eine Einführung in die linguistische Analyse öffentlich-politischer Kommunikation*. Tübingen, Germany: Max Niemeyer.

Grebing, Helga, Gregor Schöllgen, and Heinrich August Winkler, eds. 2002–2009. *Willy Brandt: Berliner Ausgabe*. 10 vols. Bonn: J. H. W. Dietz.

Hofmann, Gunter. 1988. *Willy Brandt: Porträt eines Aufklärers aus Deutschland*. Reinbek, Germany: Rowohlt.

Hunt, John Gabriel, ed. 1995. *The Inaugural Addresses of the Presidents*. New York: Gramercy Books.

Kammerer, Edmund. 1983. "Sprichwort und Politik: Sprachliche Schematismen in Politkerreden, politischem Journalismus und Graffiti." Master's thesis, University of Freiburg.

Kienpointner, Manfred. 1999. "Metaphern in der politischen Rhetorik." *Der Deutschunterricht* 51, no. 5: 66–78.

Kölbel, Martin, ed. 2013. *Willy Brandt und Günter Grass: Der Briefwechsel*. Göttingen, Germany: Steidl.

Koller, Werner. 1977. *Redensarten: Linguistische Aspekte, Vorkommensanalysen, Sprachspiel*. Tübingen, Germany: Max Niemeyer.

Marshall, Barbara. 1997. *Willy Brandt: A Political Biography*. New York: St. Martin's Press.

Matulina, Željka. 1995. "Sprichwortgebrauch im aktuellen politischen Kontext Kroatiens." In *Von der Einwortmetapher zur Satzmetapher: Akten des Westfälischen Arbeitskreises Phraseologie/Parömiologie*, edited by Rupprecht S. Baur and Christoph Chlosta, 239–67. Bochum, Germany: Norbert Brockmeyer.

Mieder, Wolfgang. 1975. "Das Sprichwort und die politische Sprache." In *Das Sprichwort in unserer Zeit*, 14–22. Frauenfeld, Switzerland: Huber.

Mieder, Wolfgang. 1993a. "'Nur ein toter Indianer ist ein guter Indianer': Zur Geschichte eines nicht nur amerikanischen Sprichwortes." *Der Sprachdienst* 37: 137–42.

Mieder, Wolfgang. 1993b. "'The Only Good Indian Is a Dead Indian': History and Meaning of a Proverbial Stereotype." *Journal of American Folklore* 106, no. 419 (Winter): 38–60. Also in *The Politics of Proverbs: From Traditional Wisdom to Proverbial Stereotypes*, by Wolfgang Mieder, 138–59, 221–27. Madison: University of Wisconsin Press, 1997.

Mieder, Wolfgang. 1995. "Proverbial Manipulation in Adolf Hitler's *Mein Kampf*." *International Folklore Review* 10: 35–53. Also in *The Politics of Proverbs: From Traditional Wisdom to Proverbial Stereotypes*, by Wolfgang Mieder, 9–38, 193–200. Madison: University of Wisconsin Press, 1997.

Mieder, Wolfgang. 1997. *The Politics of Proverbs: From Traditional Wisdom to Proverbial Stereotypes*. Madison: University of Wisconsin Press.

Mieder, Wolfgang. 1998. *"A House Divided": From Biblical Proverb to Lincoln and Beyond*. Burlington: University of Vermont.

Mieder, Wolfgang. 2000a. "'A House Divided Cannot Stand': From Bible Proverb to Abraham Lincoln and on to Willy Brandt." In *Strategies of Wisdom: Anglo-American and German Proverb Studies*, 171–203. Baltmannsweiler, Germany: Schneider Verlag Hohengehren.

Mieder, Wolfgang. 2000b. *The Proverbial Abraham Lincoln: An Index to Proverbs in the Works of Abraham Lincoln*. New York: Peter Lang.

Mieder, Wolfgang. 2001. *"No Struggle, No Progress": Frederick Douglass and His Proverbial Rhetoric for Civil Rights*. New York: Peter Lang.

Mieder, Wolfgang. 2005. *Proverbs Are the Best Policy: Folk Wisdom and American Politics*. Logan: Utah State University Press.

Mieder, Wolfgang. 2008. "'Don't Swap Horses in the Middle of the Stream': History of Abraham Lincoln's Apocryphal Proverb." In *"Proverbs Speak Louder Than Words": Folk Wisdom in Art, Culture, Folklore, History, Literature, and Mass Media*, 205–50. New York: Peter Lang.

Mieder, Wolfgang. 2009. *"Yes We Can": Barack Obama's Proverbial Rhetoric*. New York: Peter Lang.

Mieder, Wolfgang. 2010. *"Making a Way Out of No Way": Martin Luther King's Sermonic Proverbial Rhetoric*. New York: Peter Lang.

Mieder, Wolfgang. 2014a. *"All Men and Women Are Created Equal": Elizabeth Cady Stanton's and Susan B. Anthony's Proverbial Rhetoric Promoting Women's Rights.* New York: Peter Lang.

Mieder, Wolfgang. 2014b. "'Ein in sich gespaltenes Haus hat keinen Bestand': Zur Politisierung eines Bibelsprichworts bei Abraham Lincoln, Willy Brandt und Barack Obama." In *Das Wort—ein weites Feld: Festschrift für Regina Hessky*, edited by Ida Dringó-Horváth, József Fülöp, Zita Hollós, Petra Szatmári, Anita Szentpétery-Czeglédy, and Emese Zakariás, 268–84. Budapest: L'Harmattan Kiadó.

Mieder, Wolfgang, and George B. Bryan. 1995. *The Proverbial Winston S. Churchill: An Index to Proverbs in the Works of Sir Winston Churchill.* Westport, CT: Greenwood Press.

Mieder, Wolfgang, and George B. Bryan. 1997. *The Proverbial Harry S. Truman: An Index to Proverbs in the Works of Harry S. Truman.* New York: Peter Lang.

Mieder, Wolfgang, Stewart A. Kingsbury, and Kelsie B. Harder. 1992. *A Dictionary of American Proverbs.* New York: Oxford University Press.

Mieder, Wolfgang, and Andreas Nolte. 2006. *"Ich habe den Kopf so voll": Wilhelm Heinse als sprichwortreicher Literat im 18. Jahrhundert.* Bern: Peter Lang.

Mieder, Wolfgang, and Andreas Nolte. 2015. *"Kleine Schritte sind besser als große Worte": Willy Brandts politische Sprichwortrhetorik.* Würzburg, Germany: Königshausen and Neumann.

Nolte, Andreas, and Wolfgang Mieder. 2012. *"Zu meiner Hölle will ich den Weg mit guten Sprüchen pflastern": Friedrich Nietzsches sprichwörtliche Sprache.* Hildesheim, Germany: Georg Olms.

Patzelt, Werner J. 1995. "Politiker und ihre Sprache." In *Sprache des Parlaments und Semiotik der Demokratie: Studien zur politischen Kommunikation in der Moderne*, edited by Andreas Dörner and Ludgera Vogt, 17–54. Berlin: Walter de Gruyter.

Pelster, Theodor. 1966. *Die politische Rede im Westen und Osten Deutschlands: Vergleichende Stiluntersuchung mit beigefügten Texten.* Düsseldorf: Pädagogischer Verlag Schwann.

Prittie, Terence. 1974. *Willy Brandt: Portrait of a Statesman.* New York: Schocken Books.

Raymond, Joseph. 1956. "Tensions in Proverbs: More Light on International Understanding." *Western Folklore* 15, no. 3 (July): 153–58. Also in *The Wisdom of Many: Essays on the Proverb*, edited by Wolfgang Mieder and Alan Dundes, 300–308. New York: Garland Publishing, 1981.

Reyes de la Rosa, José. 1997. "Empleo y función de la expresión idiomática en el discurso político en Francia." *Paremia* 6: 527–30.

Rogge, Christian. 1899. *Bismarck als Redner: Eine Studie.* Kiel, Germany: H. Eckardt.

Röhrich, Lutz, and Wolfgang Mieder. 1977. *Sprichwort.* Stuttgart: J. B. Metzler.

Schwab-Felisch, Hans. 1966. "Zur Sprache der Politiker." *Neue Rundschau* 77: 230–39.

Stern, Carola. 2002. *Willy Brandt.* Reinbek, Germany: Rowohlt.

Sternberger, Dolf. (1966) 1991. "Der Staatsmann als Rhetor und Literat." In *Sprache und Politik*, 33–51. Frankfurt am Main: Insel Verlag.

Wander, Karl Friedrich Wilhelm. 1852. *Auswanderungs-Katechismus: Ein Rathgeber für Auswanderer.* Glogau, Germany: E. Fleming. Rpt., edited by Wolfgang Mieder. Bern: Peter Lang, 1988.

Wander, Karl Friedrich Wilhelm. 1867–1880. *Deutsches Sprichwörter-Lexikon.* 5 vols. Leipzig: F. A. Brockhaus.

Wilson, F. P. 1970. *The Oxford Dictionary of English Proverbs*. 3rd ed. Oxford: Oxford University Press.

Zimmermann, Hans Dieter. 1969. *Die politische Rede: Der Sprachgebrauch Bonner Politiker*. Stuttgart: W. Kohlhammer.

Zundel, Rolf. 1970. "Der neue Kanzler." In *Willy Brandt: Porträt und Selbstporträt*, edited by Klaus Harpprecht, 15–26. Munich: Kindler.

Proverbs in Literature

8

"STRINGING PROVERBS TOGETHER"

The Proverbial Language in
Miguel de Cervantes's *Don Quixote*

While the amassment of proverbs and proverbial expressions in Miguel de Cervantes Saavedra's *Don Quixote* (1605, 1615) amounts to an impressive collection of proverbial lore current in Spain in his time, it must be remembered that this fascination and preoccupation with folk wisdom was evident throughout Europe. Erasmus of Rotterdam's *Adagia* (1500–1536) encouraged other humanists to publish proverb collections in Latin, but there was an equal interest in compiling proverb dictionaries in various vernacular languages as well, with Martin Luther even putting together his own collection in 1530 that served him well to render the Bible into German (Mieder 2009; Mieder 2011). But there were also iconographical illustrations of proverbs in the form of woodcuts, carvings, and illustrated broadsheets, with Pieter Bruegel's celebrated oil painting *Netherlandish Proverbs* (1559) representing the quintessential artistic accomplishment (Mieder 2004a). There can be no doubt that the sixteenth and the first half of the seventeenth centuries were the golden age for the proverb in Europe both in its oral and written form. François Rabelais in France, Hans Sachs in Germany, and William Shakespeare in England, to name but three major authors, are known for their proverbial prowess (Mieder and Bryan 1996), and the literature of the Spanish Siglo de Oro did not lag behind, as can be seen from the rich proverbial language in the works of Félix Lope de Vega y Carpio, Tirso de Molina, and Pedro Calderón de la Barca (Hayes 1936; González Martín 1997). There also appeared major Spanish proverb collections, among them Pedro Vallés, *Libro de refranes* (1549); Hernán Núñez, *Refranes o proverbios en romance* (1555); Juan de Mal Lara, *La philosophía vulgar* (1568); and Gonzalo de Correas, *Vocabulario de refranes* (1627). In fact, even though Cervantes employed proverbs from oral tradition, it has now been established that he most likely also had access to the collection by Vallés (see the comparative list in Cull 2014, 150–60). This is not the place to review the impressive

195

paremiographical work that has gone into identifying the proverbial materials in the long novel, with the most significant collections being Enrique de Cárcer y de Sobíes's massive (666 large pages printed in two columns) polyglot lexicon *Las frases del "Quijote": Su exposición, ordenación y comentarios, y su versión á las lenguas francesa, portugesa, italiana, catalana, inglesa y alemana* (1916); Jesús Cantera Ortiz de Urbina, Julia Sevilla Muñoz, and Manuel Sevilla Muñoz's *Refranes, otras paremias y fraseologismos en "Don Quijote de la Mancha"* (2005); and Hugo O. Bizzarri's *Diccionario de paremias cervantinas* (2015), with its 621 pages printed in two dense columns (see also Suñé Benages 1929; Bizzarri 2003). The identification of the rich proverbial materials in Cervantes's *Don Quixote* is but one side of the coin, with paremiologists having also looked at linguistic, stylistic, and functional aspects of the proverbs and proverbial expressions in this novel. Identification (paremiography) is after all only the first step in literary proverb investigations, with interpretation (paremiology) being the necessary second task to discover how, why, when, and by whom the proverbial language is instantiated in Cervantes's prose. Among the many publications on these aspects are several chapters in Monique Joly's book *Études sur "Don Quichotte"* (1996, 205–97); María Cecilia Colombi's *Los refranes en el "Quijote": Texto y contexto* (1989b); and numerous articles in the Spanish yearbook *Paremia* as well as articles in cultural, folkloric, and literary journals from throughout the world. (For a complete bibliography of paremiographical and paremiological studies, see Mieder 2016, 301–12.)

It is doubtful that Cervantes wrote his unequivocally Spanish novel with the idea in mind that it would be translated into at least fifty languages. But with the first part of his novel having already appeared in English translation by Thomas Shelton in 1612, he might well have thought of the possibility of at least some translations when he has Don Quixote early in the second part of the novel from 1615 (Shelton [1612–1620] 1907) make the observation that "[o]ne of the things that must give the greatest contentment to a virtuous and eminent man is to see, while he is still alive, his good name printed and published in the languages of different peoples" (475; all English texts and their page numbers are from Edith Grossman's 2003 translation). He certainly was very cognizant of the art of translation necessary to make the classics of Greek and Roman antiquity available to Spanish readers. And he was, of course, also aware of the linguistic prowess of Erasmus of Rotterdam and other humanists of his time, with the same being true for the skillful translators of the Bible into the vernacular languages of Europe. All of this clearly occupied his literary mind, in fact so much so that he included a treatise of sorts in his *Don Quixote* that is a treasure trove of commentary on an unlimited number of subjects. And typically for Cervantes, he has Don Quixote create a perfect metaphor for it all:

It seems to me that translating from one language to another, unless it is from Greek and Latin, the queens of all languages, is like looking at Flemish tapestries from the wrong side, for although the figures are visible, they are covered by threads that obscure them, and cannot be seen with the smoothness and color of the right side; translating easy languages does not argue for either talent or eloquence, just as transcribing or copying from one paper to another does not argue for those qualities. And I do not wish to infer from this that the practice of translating is not deserving of praise, because a man might engage in worse things that bring him even less benefit. (873–74)

The German novelist Thomas Mann, who describes in his account "Voyage with *Don Quixote*" (1934) how he read Cervantes's novel on the ship that carried him into exile from Nazi Germany to the United States, stated that this is an "admirable critique of the nature of translation" and that "the metaphor [of the Flemish tapestries] is striking" (Mann [1934] 2001, 29). Little wonder that Ilan Stavans titled his survey of various English translations of the novel "Flemish Tapestries" (2015, 172–204), thereby signaling that none of them are so perfect that they equal the art of the original. In general, translators have the choice of puritanically sticking to the text or in a more liberal way trying to "capture the spirit, style, and tone of the original work but not intending to replicate that work precisely in a different language" (Parr and Vollendorf 2015b, 18–19). In the case of *Don Quixote*, it has been observed that "the Spaniards are correct when they claim that *Don Quixote*, like much verbal humor, is to some extent untranslatable. Some levels of style and some chivalric archaisms and proverbs can be reproduced in English, but the vivid dialogue [. . .] can only be explained, never translated" (Eisenberg 1984, 66). And yet, translators around the world have valiantly attempted to render the novel into various target languages, with numerous such attempts in some of the major world languages (Cobelo 2009).

It is true that some proverbs, proverbial expressions, and other phraseologisms can be translated without any particular problem. Regarding proverbs as such, this is true for older texts that can be traced back to Greek and Roman antiquity that were spread via the Latin lingua franca and by humanists like Erasmus of Rotterdam throughout Europe. Such classical proverbs as "Big fish eat little fish," "One swallow does not make a summer," "One hand washes the other," and "Love is blind" were loan translated and exist in equal wording as common European proverbs. The same is true for such Bible proverbs as "He who digs a pit for others, falls in himself" (Prophets 26:27), "There is nothing new under the sun" (Ecclesiastes 1:9), "A prophet is not without honor save in his own country" (Matthew 13:57), and the golden rule "Do unto others as you would have them do unto you" (Matthew 12:7). Yet another group of common European proverbs are those that were coined during the Middle Ages in Latin and then subsequently translated into the vernacular languages, including such well-known proverbs as "New brooms sweep clean," "Strike while the iron is hot," "The pitcher goes so long to the well until at last it breaks," and "All that glitters is not gold" (Paczolay 1997; Mieder 2014, 60–63). But every language has large numbers of proverbs that are indigenous to that culture (Krauss 1946; Krauss 1959), and it is with these unique texts that translators have great problems. They can translate them literally, they can try to find equivalent proverbs in the target language, they can paraphrase them, or they can simply ignore them. Translators might well employ all four strategies in dealing with this vexing problem, depending also on whether they are at all attuned to proverbial language and its cultural background. Not only do proverbs need to be identified as "culturally marked models," they also require interpretation by the translator in order to find an appropriate wording in the target language (Zurdo Ruiz-Ayúcar 2014, 35).

It is a fascinating undertaking to take a look at how various translators have rendered the proverbial language of *Don Quixote* into their respective languages. The opinions of what modern American English translation might be "the best" differ widely (Putnam 1949; Jones and Douglas 1981; Raffel 1995; Grossman 2003; Lathrop 2005; Montgomery 2009). Michael McGrath (2006, 38) gives the nod to Jones/Douglas and Lathrop, while Daniel Eisenberg, in his "The Text of *Don Quixote* as Seen by Its Modern English Translators," appears to skirt the issue by stating that "there is no one translation that will serve every purpose" (2006, 120; see also Thacker 2015, 41–44). I chose Edith Grossman's translation, which had been recommended to me by my Spanish colleagues in the University of Vermont's Department of Romance Languages, when I, relatively late in my life, decided to read *Don Quixote* in 2005 as I began work on my book *"Tilting at Windmills": History and Meaning of a Proverbial Allusion to Cervantes' "Don Quixote"* (Mieder 2006b; see also Mieder 2006a). Grossman's translation had received glowing reviews in the media, and as a novice to *Don Quixote*, I must admit that I thoroughly enjoyed reading this translation, which as a best seller conquered its market (Lathrop 2006). Since it is the most widely distributed and available modern translation of *Don Quixote*, I felt justified in basing my proverbial study on Grossman's valiant attempt to make the novel accessible in a readable translation. For better or worse, I take her translations of proverbs, proverbial expressions, and other phraseologisms at face value, without analyzing in each case how successful the English renditions are. A comparative analysis of the proverbial material in the roughly twenty English translations must wait for a future effort by a research team. Of importance for my study is that Grossman has succeeded in maintaining the rich proverbial language especially in the dialogues between Don Quixote and Sancho Panza, thereby ensuring that this particular trademark of the novel is not lost. This certainly contradicts Vladmir Nabokov's excessively negative judgment of *Don Quixote* translations: "Proverbs: Sancho, of the second part especially, is a bursting bag of old saws and sayings. To the readers of translations this Breughelian [*sic*] side of the book is as dead as cold mutton" ([1951–1952] 1983, 29). The 714 proverbial texts (386 proverbs, 327 proverbial expressions and comparisons, and 1 wellerism; these numbers include duplicates) that I have identified and presented in a contextualized "Index of Proverbs and Proverbial Expressions" (Mieder 2016, 157–298) are ample proof that Grossman has succeeded splendidly in keeping the rich proverbial language of the novel alive in her celebrated translation.

There can be no doubt that Cervantes was very much aware of the great interest in collecting proverbs during his age, which had begun with scholars like Erasmus of Rotterdam, other humanists, Protestant reformers, and others interested in assembling the proverbs of the various developing languages in Europe. One can surely imagine that he, too, enjoyed the rich proverbial tradition of Spain, which he could see presented in such collections as Pedro Vallés's *Libro de refranes* (1549) and Juan de Mal Lara's *La philosophía vulgar* (1568), with Sancho Panza being a folksy and ridiculed mirror of this obsession with proverbs (Rosenblat 1971; Neumeister 1994, 206–7). At the same time, however, he might well have realized that such compilations are in fact filled with contradictory pieces of folk wisdom. Proverbs are not universal truths but rather limited generalizations that are valid only in certain situations. Such proverb pairs as "Nothing ventured, nothing gained" and "Look before you leap," or "Absence makes the heart grow fonder" and "Out of sight, out of mind" make clear that proverbs are not a logical philosophical system, but each proverb in itself can be employed effectively as a communicative strategy in a context where its underlying insight is appropriate (Mieder 2004b, 133–34). This basic fact must have had its special appeal to Cervantes, leading him to include numerous dialogues in his novel that enumerate proverbs as being valid or invalid. That he did in fact "theorize" about this traditional wisdom can be seen from a number of pertinent passages that draw special attention to the nature and use of proverbs.

Cervantes, as collector and interpreter of proverbs, definitely had a keen interest in and knowledge of the complexity of these traditional bits of wisdom. Just as "in structure and style, as on the level of meanings, nothing in *Don Quixote* is simple" (Gerhard 1982, 26), so it is with the proverbs that are part of Cervantes's "age of hybridity" and the "cultural polyphony [that] resonates throughout Cervantes's novel" (Jehenson and Dunn 2010, 128, 129). As the novel confronts the reader with a "barrage of adventures, encounters, speeches, and general display of humanity" (Durán and Rogg 2010, 106), the ever-present stories and proverbs "jostle each other for expression" (Riley 1962, 125). The simple fact that proverbs can contradict each other and that as metaphors they can be quite ambiguous served Cervantes well in his desire to write a new type of novel based on a multitude of antitheses (Hatzfeld 1947, 95; Durán 1974, 126; Dunn 1984, 83) and such "conceptual polarities [as] madness-sanity, illusion-reality, appearances-truth, fiction-fact, art-life, poetry-history, romance-novel, idealism-realism, theory-practice, mind-matter, spirit-flesh" (Riley 1986, 133). Things are simply not obvious or clear in this novel of duality, ambiguity, and uncertainty (Cassou 1947, 12; Serrano-Plaja 1970, 16; Gerhard 1982, 28; Russell 1985, 107–9), which in its multivalency contains wisdom (Bloom [1994] 2001, 160) that at least in part is evident in the proverbial dialogues of Don Quixote and Sancho Panza. In those cases where these two discuss the actual nature of proverbs, Cervantes as a "wisdom writer" (Bloom [1994] 2001, 145) steps forth as a bona fide paremiographical paremiologist, as Benjamin Franklin and Ralph Waldo Emerson in due course would likewise reveal themselves as multital-ented writers with their own keen interest in proverbs (Mieder 1993, 98–134; Mieder 2014, 261–83). They all enjoyed descanting upon the multifaceted and fascinating world of proverbs.

Leaving aside a discussion of the use and function of proverbs by the nar-rator and minor characters as well as the appearance of individual proverbs from Don Quixote's unexpected proverb repertoire and Sancho Panza's mes-sages as the proverbial wise fool throughout the novel, let us take a look at the enumerative proverbial wisdom employed by Teresa Panza. While nobody can possibly match Sancho Panza's proverbial prowess, there can be no doubt that his down-to-earth peasant wife Teresa does have an impressive proverb repertoire, which would be more evident if she were playing a larger role in the novel. The fifth chapter of the second part contains a particularly rich proverbial dialogue between Teresa and Sancho, with the latter telling his wife with great excitement that he will leave again with Don Quixote and that their lives will drastically change for the better once he receives the governorship of an *ínsula* in due course. It is here where two people from the lower strata of society talk in proverbs to underscore their respective arguments with the authority of tradition. It begins with Teresa stressing that her husband has so changed that she does not even understand his peasant speech any longer, to which Sancho responds with the proverb that "God understands all things":

> "Look, Sancho," replied Teresa, "ever since you became a knight errant's servant your talk is so roundabout nobody can understand you."
> "It's enough if God understands me, my wife," responded Sancho, "for He understands all things, and say no more about it for now." (486)

But the discussion does not stop there, even though Sancho says proverbially that he would fall down dead if he were not to receive his governorship. To this, Teresa retorts with the proverb "Let the chicken live even if she has the pip"; the chicken metaphor has to be understood as somewhat of a demasculinization of Sancho. As she tries to convince her husband to be happy with his lot be it ever so poor, she adds the proverb "The best sauce in the world is hunger" to conclude her argument for the status quo:

> "I'll tell you, Teresa," responded Sancho, "that if I didn't expect to be the governor of an ínsula before too much more time goes by, I'd fall down dead right here."
>
> "Not that, my husband," said Teresa, "let the chicken live even if she has the pip; may you live, and let the devil take all the governorships there are in the world; you came out of your mother's womb without a governorship, and you've lived until now without a governorship, and when it pleases God you'll go, or they'll carry you, to the grave without a governorship. Many people in the world live without a governorship, and that doesn't make them give up or not be counted among the living. The best sauce in the world is hunger, and since poor people have plenty of that, they always eat with great pleasure." (486)

The argument could have stopped there, but then the good woman reminds her husband of their children Sanchico and Mari Sancha, using the proverb "A daughter is better off badly married than happily kept" to remind him that their daughter is looking for a husband:

> "But look, Sancho: if you happen to find yourself a governor somewhere, don't forget about me and your children. Remember that Sanchico is already fifteen, and he ought to go to school if his uncle the abbot is going to bring him into the Church. And don't forget that our daughter, Mari Sancha, won't die if we marry her; she keeps dropping hints that she wants a husband as much as you want to be a governor, and when all is said and done, a daughter's better off badly married than happily kept."
>
> "By my faith, Teresa," responded Sancho, "if God lets me have any kind of governorship, I'll marry Mari Sancha so high up that nobody will be able to reach her unless they call her Señora." (486–87)

Of course, good old Sancho immediately returns to the fantasy of being a rich governor who will be able to plan the fanciest wedding for her to a noble-man. Teresa will have nothing of it, arguing that they should be content with their life as it is. In order to convince Sancho of this view, she cites a proverb and a proverbial expression, giving him some of his own folk medicine, as it were:

> "Be content with your station," responded Teresa, "and don't try to go to a higher one; remember the proverb that says: 'Take your neighbor's son, wipe his nose, and bring him into your house.' Sure, it would be very nice to marry our María to some wretch of a count or gentleman who might take a notion to insult her and call her lowborn, the daughter of peasants and spinners! Not in my lifetime, my husband! I didn't bring up my daughter for that! You bring the money, Sancho, and leave her marrying to me." (487)

But Sancho will not let go of his idée fixe and, tit for tat, continues the argument with two proverbs and a proverbial phrase. By using the introductory formula "the old folk say" with the proverbs "If you don't know how to enjoy good luck when it comes, you shouldn't complain if it passes you by" and "If luck comes knocking, don't shut the door in its face," he adds considerable traditional authority to his statement. The proverbial metaphor of the "favorable wind" that should be followed strengthens his argument even more:

> "Come here, you imbecile, you troublemaker," replied Sancho. "Why do you want to stop me now, and for no good reason, from marrying my daughter to somebody who'll give me grandchildren they'll call *Lord* and *Lady*? Look, Teresa: I've always heard the old folks say that if you don't know how to enjoy good luck when it comes, you shouldn't complain if it passes you by. It wouldn't be a good idea, now that it's come knocking, to shut the door in its face; we should let the favorable wind that's blowing carry us along." (487)

And yet, Teresa is by no means an imbecile, and she argues against a high-society marriage for their daughter by three times stating that the proverbial "to put on airs" is not for her. In her excitement, she misquotes the proverb "Where kings go laws follow" as "Where laws go kings follow" and then concludes her tirade with the antifeminist proverb "La mujer honrada, la pierna quebrada, y en casa" (To keep a woman honorable, break her leg and keep her in the house; see Bizzarri 2015, 375–76). Of course, in this particular case Teresa interprets the proverb to mean that Mari is better off staying at home than moving away from her social environment. She does not mean to insult her daughter with it, a fine example of the polysemanticity of proverbs. Besides, she also adds the somewhat less drastic proverb "For a chaste girl, work is her fiesta" to it all:

THE PROVERBIAL LANGUAGE IN CERVANTES'S *DON QUIXOTE*   203

"Do you hear what you're saying, husband?" responded Teresa. "Well, even so, I'm afraid that if my daughter becomes a countess it will be her ruin. You'll do whatever you want, whether you make her a duchess or a princess, but I can tell you it won't be with my agreement or consent. Sancho, I've always been in favor of equality, and I can't stand to see somebody putting on airs for no reason. They baptized me Teresa, a plain and simple name without any additions or decorations or trimmings of *Dons* or *Doñas*; my father's name was Cascajo, and because I'm your wife, they call me Teresa Panza, though they really ought to call me Teresa Cascajo. But where laws go kings follow, and I'm satisfied with this name without anybody adding on a *Doña* that weighs so much I can't carry it, and I don't want to give people who see me walking around dressed in a countish or governorish way a chance to say: 'Look at the airs that sow is putting on! Yesterday she was busy pulling on a tuft of flax for spinning, and she went to Mass and covered her head with her skirts instead of a mantilla, and today she has a hoopskirt and brooches and airs, as if we didn't know who she was.' If God preserves my seven senses, or five, or however many I have, I don't intend to let anybody see me in a spot like that. You, my husband, go and be a governor or an insular and put on all the airs you like; I swear on my mother's life that my daughter and I won't set foot out of our village: to keep her chaste, break her leg and keep her in the house; for a chaste girl, work is her fiesta. You go with your Don Quixote and have your adventures, and leave us with our misfortunes, for God will set them right if we're good; I certainly don't know who gave him [Don Quixote] a *Don*, because his parents and grandparents never had one." (488)

In the context of Teresa and Sancho's argument, the questionable proverb clearly "functions dialogically as a defense of Teresa, her family and also a proverbial collective authority" (Ciallella 2007, 27; see also Ciallella 2003, 278). It should, however, be noted here that Sancho uses the proverb later when he is governor of his *ínsula* in its chauvinistic sense. In fact, he adds two other antifeminist proverbs to it, making it a triadic proverbial attack on women:

"Nothing's been lost," responded Sancho. "Let's go, and we'll leave your graces [a young maiden and her brother] at your father's house; maybe he hasn't missed you. And from now on don't be so childish, or so eager to see the world; an honorable maiden and a broken leg stay in the house; and a woman and a hen are soon lost when they wander; and a woman who wants to see also wants to be seen. That's all I'll say." (781)

Perhaps readers of the seventeenth century saw some humor in this string of proverbs, but to modern students of the novel Sancho does not gain positive points with these stereotypical invectives that unfortunately are current in all cultures (Schipper 2003). But on the other hand, when Sancho uses the proverb on a third occasion as a mere allusion and changes the word "woman" to "governor," there is a certain sense of irony or humor at play. "'No,' responded Sancho, 'a good governor and a broken leg stay at home. How nice if weary merchants came to see him and he was in the woods enjoying himself! What a misfortune for the governorship!'" (686). All of this is a sign of Cervantes's mastery of the adaptability of proverbs to ever new situations where one and the same proverb can take on different functions and meanings. In paremiological terms, this very phenomenon of proverbs has been referred to as polysituativity, polyfunctionality, and polysemanticity (Krikmann [1974] 2009, 15–50; Mieder 2004b, 9, 132).

But to return to the scene between Teresa and Sancho, he is by no means letting the argument go, and like the pot calling the kettle black even reproaches his wife for her use of proverbs:

> "Now I'll say," replied Sancho, "that you must have an evil spirit in that body of yours. God save you, woman, what a lot of things you've strung together willy-nilly! What do Cascajo, brooches, proverbs, and putting on airs have to do with what I'm saying? Come here, you simple, igno-rant woman, and I can call you that because you don't understand my words and try to run away from good luck. If I had said that my daugh-ter ought to throw herself off a tower or go roaming around the way the Infanta Doña Urraca wanted to [an allusion to the ballad of Doña Urraca's desire to go wandering], you'd be right not to go along with me; but if in two shakes and in the wink of an eye I dress her in a *Doña* and put a *my lady* on her back for you, and take her out of the dirt and put her under a canopy and up on a pedestal in a drawing room with more velvet cushions than Moors in the line of the Almohadas of Morocco, why won't you consent and want what I want?" (488–89)

This question gives Teresa one final opportunity to employ a proverb in this duel that she cannot win:

> "Do you know why, Sancho?" responded Teresa. "Because of the prov-erb that says: 'Whoever *tries* to conceal you, reveals you!' Nobody does more than glance at the poor, but they look closely at the rich; if a rich man was once poor, that's where the whispers and rumors begin, and the wicked murmurs of gossips who crowd the streets like swarms of bees." (489)

THE PROVERBIAL LANGUAGE IN CERVANTES'S *DON QUIXOTE*   205

Sancho remains resolved, with Teresa in tears stating in desperation "I don't understand you, my husband" (490). Indeed, "Teresa's proverbial speech [can be seen] as part of an egalitarian discourse of domesticity that she shares with Sancho" (Ciallella 2007, 25), but there is no feminist emancipation here in the early seventeenth century.

But Teresa changes her tune in the splendidly humorous chapter 50 of the second part, where a page brings a letter to her and their daughter Mari Sancha (also called Sanchica) announcing that Sancho has in fact been named the governor of an *ínsula*. Their reactions are euphoric, with the gullible Teresa stating "By my faith, we're not poor relations anymore! We have a nice little governorship! And if the proudest of the gentlewomen tries to snub me, I'll know how to put her in her place!" (786). And then this, with the page, a priest, and a bachelor bearing witness:

> "O daughter, you certainly are right!" responded Teresa. "And all of this good fortune, and some even greater than this, my good Sancho predicted for me, and you'll see, daughter, how he doesn't stop until he makes me a countess; it's all a matter of starting to be lucky; and I've heard your good father say very often—and he loves proverbs as much as he loves you—that when they give you the calf, run over with the rope; when they give you a governorship, take it; when they give you a countship, hold on to it tight, and when they call you over with a nice present, pack it away. Or else just sleep and don't answer when fortune and good luck come knocking at your door!"
>
> "And what difference does it make to me," added Sanchica, "if they say when they see me so proud and haughty: 'The dog in linen breeches'... and all the rest?"
>
> Hearing this, the priest said:
>
> "I can't help thinking that everyone in the Panza family was born with a sack of proverbs inside; I've never seen one of them who isn't always scattering proverbs around in every conversation they have."
>
> "That's true," said the page, "for Señor Governor Sancho says them all the time, and even though many are not to the point, they still give pleasure, and my lady the duchess and my lord the duke praise them a good deal." (788–89)

Teresa bears witness to the fact that Sancho is particularly invested in proverbs, and then she quotes one of his favorite proverbs, "When they give you the calf, run over with the rope," which she applies in a series of specific variations with respect to her new role as a fine lady. And the daughter, in anticipation of her new, haughty social position, chimes in as a budding proverbialist by saying that it will not make a difference if people were to comment about "'[t]he dog in linen breeches' . . . and all the rest." The complete proverb states "The dog in linen breeches says how crude, how crude," which is aimed at the poor who for whatever reason prosper and then belittle their old friends. Little wonder that the astonished priest speaks of "the Panza family [being] born with a sack of proverbs inside" that they "always scatter around in every conversation." The page seconds this claim by pointing to "Señor Governor Sancho" citing them also "all the time" even though they might not be appropriate. There is no doubt that this scene is part of "the broadly comic strain of mockery, laughter, and slapstick that has its roots in popular tradition" (Martín 2002, 168).

But let us now take a closer look at Sancho Panza's bottomless sack of proverbs, those passages where he enumerates proverbs as a trademark of his rich rhetoric. Much has been said and written about the fascinating character of Sancho Panza, but Don Quixote, who in the novel knows his squire best, has perfectly well described this unforgettable figure:

> "Sancho Panza is one of the most amusing squires who ever served a knight errant; at times his simpleness is so clever that deciding if he is simple or clever is a cause of no small pleasure; his slyness condemns him for a rogue, and his thoughtlessness confirms him as a simpleton; he doubts everything, and he believes everything; when I think that he is about to plunge headlong into foolishness, he comes out with perceptions that raise him to the skies. In short, I would not trade him for any other squire." (674)

Earlier in the novel, Don Quixote says to Sancho: "Devil take you for a peasant! What intelligent things you say sometime! One would think you had studied!" (263). Sancho responds honestly, "By my faith, I don't know how to read" (263). And there is a similar dialogue later on between the knight errant and his squire:

> "Every day, Sancho," said Don Quixote, "you are becoming less simple and more intelligent."
> "Yes, some of your grace's intelligence has to stick to me," responded Sancho, "for lands that are barren and dry on their own can produce good fruits if you spread manure on them and till them; I mean to say that your grace's conversation has been the manure that has fallen on the barren soil of my dry wits; the time that I have served you and talked to you has been the tilling; and so I hope to produce fruits that are a blessing and do not go to seed or stray from the paths of good cultivation that your grace has made in my parched understanding." (527–28)

What a wonderful, earthy metaphor by the peasant Sancho, which has plenty of scatological humor in it by indirectly comparing Don Quixote's words to "manure." But the knight errant has a sense of humor, as the narrator explains in a most telling paragraph that relates to Sancho's vast proverb knowledge:

> Don Quixote laughed at Sancho's pretentious words but thought that what he said about the change in him was true, because from time to time he spoke in a manner that amazed Don Quixote, although almost always, when Sancho wanted to speak in an erudite and courtly way, his words would plummet from the peaks of his simplicity into the depths of his ignorance; the area in which he displayed the most elegance and the best memory was in his use of proverbs, regardless of whether or not they had anything to do with the subject, as has been seen and noted in the course of this history. (528)

It would have been a good idea for the narrator to mention in this statement, from the twelfth chapter of the second part, that this observation would not really hold true for the first part of the novel, which had appeared in print ten years earlier. The at least at times unwarranted stringing together of proverbs is much more prevalent in the sequel. What is true, however, for the entire novel is that when Sancho uses proverbs one or at most two at a time, they make perfect sense in their contexts as expressions of commonsensical folk wisdom (Hernández 1984, 219; Landa 2013, xviii–xix). His personality is based on "that sound empirical common sense, that spontaneous wisdom which goes by the name of mother-wit" (Madariaga 1934, 130). His character clearly stands out because of "his astuteness, his ability to turn situations to his material advantage, his self-confidence, his inconsequential loquacity, his refusal to be intimidated by superior social rank, and his habit of turning to the wisdom of popular proverbs to comment on situations" (Russell 1985, 79). It can rightfully be claimed that there is plenty of sensical "candor and ingenuousness encapsulated in his proverbs" (Finello 1994, 86). The individually cited "proverbs are utilized in a functional [and sensical] way" (Casalduero 1947, 88), and this "oral, traditional culture [of proverbs] is close to common sense and worthy of respect" (Durán and Rogg 2010, 102). And Don Quixote is quite willing to accept a singular proverb, since, after all, he also cites a proverb from time to time. It is only the amassment of them that vexes him, as anything that is overstated becomes tedious if not mindless. While it is true that Sancho's "salty language, bursting with life and filled with refrains and sayings that express a wealth of popular knowledge" (Vargas Llosa 2010, 67), appears throughout the novel, its presence is by no means superfluous as for the most part the proverbs and proverbial expressions are integral parts of the whole narrative.

In other words, the proverbs as used in isolated dialogues by both Don Quixote and Sancho Panza make sense, and they show that Sancho is by no means a simpleton but rather a wise fool with traditional wisdom on his side.

It is almost surprising that Don Quixote's characterization of Sancho Panza as someone who strings proverbs together has not become proverbial in its own right. Anybody who has ever read *Don Quixote* will remember the bottomless sack of proverbs that contains the squire's folk wisdom, which he amasses several times into proverbial cannonades. Doubtlessly Cervantes enjoyed assembling these minicollections of proverbs just as other authors did in Spain and elsewhere in Europe. In fact, there is a definite literary tradition of plays and poems that consist of basically nothing but proverbs strung together. Connecting traditionally cited proverbs or varied anti-proverbs, such texts can make perfect sense, or they are intentionally created to be perceived as nonsense (Mieder 1974; Abrahams and Babcock 1977; Mieder and Bryan 1996; Sobieski and Mieder 2005). While Cervantes is part of this tour de force phenomenon, he most likely also wanted to pay tribute to the incredible paremiographical work undertaken during the sixteenth century. There is no indication that he intended to parody this worthwhile activity, which showed "the triumph of rustic wisdom" (O'Kane 1950; Iventosch 1980, 22). The reason for Cervantes's or better Sancho's obsession with proverbs must be that they make the perfect linguistic and stylistic tool or signature for Sancho the peasant, who, by amassing the proverbs ad infinitum, becomes a figure of ridicule and at times humor. But there is a twist to this perception, for this alleged simpleton is actually quite wise or at least a wise fool, and even though he strings proverbs together, what most normal people wouldn't do, he actually makes sense of what some readers might perceive as nonsense.

As would be expected, numerous scholars have expressed their thoughts on Sancho Panza, "the conjuror of words [and proverbs]" (Stavans 2015, 69). But they have concluded too quickly or superficially that these strings of proverbs are humorous and show Sancho's foolishness. This misses the point, particularly because the strings of proverbs that Sancho ties together are usually related in meaning without being contradictory or nonsensical as has been suggested. There might be humor and even satire in running the mouth with proverbs, but that does not automatically indicate foolishness or stupidity. But here is a list of what scholars have said about Sancho's proverb salvos in chronological order:

> [. . .] gluttonous, brutal, and clownish to the point of not even understanding the proverbs which he piles up in a jumbled manner. (Menéndez-Pidal 1947, 50)

Sancho's cracks and proverbs are not very mirth provoking either in themselves or in their repetitious accumulation. [. . .] Sancho Panza's main characteristic is that he is a sackful of proverbs, a sack of half-truths that rattle in him like pebbles. (Nabokov [1951–1952] 1983, 13, 24)

Sancho's shallow and artificial application of these traditional, stereotyped "truths" [. . .] reveals Sancho's character. He strung these ritualistic phrases into conversation—often as malapropisms and traditional truths without organic coordination. (Raymond 1951, 134)

Specifically, I refer to his [Sancho's] abuse of proverbs and Don Quixote's criticism of this. [. . .] Sancho has the inborn wit and wisdom of the peasant but lacks formal education. A symptom of the former is his remarkable facility in proverbs, while his ill-judged use of them reflects the latter. (Riley 1962, 69)

Sancho could be said to display jester's wit—his knowledge of proverbs. His diffuse and inconsequential recitals of them—such torture to Don Quixote's educated mind—are primarily an aspect of his comic artlessness. Nonetheless, he claims that his memory for proverbs is his one intellectual resource. [. . .] Sancho can cite proverbs both as a form of verbal foolery and in order to substantiate his judicious reflections. (Close 1973, 350)

Sancho's use of proverbs is a burlesque derivative of a Renaissance appreciation for the oral vox populi. [. . .] Sancho's proverbs are sometimes mechanically linked in irrelevant concatenations. On these occasions, purely verbal associations control discourse, regardless of the topic presumably under discussion. (Rivers 1984, 116–17, 118)

There is even the view that Cervantes had a low opinion of "Spain's oral tradition, such as Sancho's proverbs. That is to say, he perceived them as [a] ridiculous and grotesque [. . .] falsification of history" (Gilman 1989: 93). But these views, which include such descriptors for Sancho's strings of proverbs as "jumbled," "half-truths," "ill-judged," "inconsequential," and "irrelevant," simply miss the point. There is definitely a method to Sancho's proverb obsession, and it is by way of his folk language that he defines himself as an individual just as Don Quixote and other characters do through their verbal communication (Mackey 1974, 51). And there can be no doubt that R. M. Flores is correct with this enlightening statement: "Sancho's use of proverbs has come to be regarded as the quintessential characteristic of his personality. The widespread belief, however, that he continually misuses them is quite mistaken. If one follows Sancho's train of thought, one soon sees that any one of the proverbs or sayings of a particular series is perfectly appropriate to convey Sancho's reaction and answer to whatever has provoked it" (Flores 1982, 117–18; see also Finello 1994, 87).

More recently, Thomas Hart came to the somewhat more guarded conclusion that "when Sancho cites several proverbs in rapid succession, most though usually not all of them emphasize the point he wants to make," also drawing attention to the important fact that "it is Sancho's ability to use proverbs effectively to support his argument that Don Quixote admires and envies" (Hart 2002, 46, 47). But it should be added that it takes Don Quixote considerable time until he learns to appreciate Sancho's lists of proverbs, which is clearly a folkloric sign of his becoming "sanchifed" as the novel progresses. It is true that "on several occasions, Don Quijote points out that Sancho is using proverbial language indiscriminately and out of context," but Frank Nuessel goes too far in stating that "the appropriate application of proverbial language in the second book of the *Quijote* is one of the ways in which Cervantes signals the *Quijotizacíon* of Sancho" (Nuessel 1999, 260). After all, Sancho's proverb applications whether citing one, two, three, or many more proverbs in succession are for all general purposes correct throughout. And, as will be shown by the following interpretations of the most pertinent proverb strings, Don Quixote is as wrong as modern scholars when he considers Sancho's proverbs inappropriate or indiscriminate. That these proverb accumulations can to some degree be considered humorous in the context of other verbal and gesticular communication by Sancho might well be the case, but there is sense in the nonsense of formulating such proverb strings. After all, it is not customary to speak in proverbs to that degree, unless, of course, one would want to compete with the great proverb stringer Sancho Panza.

The first part of *Don Quixote* contains just four relatively short proverb strings, but already the first one sets the tone for their frequent misinterpretation by scholars. Don Quixote, who at this early stage has absolutely no appreciation for Sancho's folk wisdom, and who refers to it as foolish and incongruous to the subject under discussion, leads readers and interpreters to the false conclusion that the four proverbs "If you buy and lie, your purse wants to know why," "Naked I was born, and naked I die," "To think there's bacon when there's not even a hook to hang it on," and "You can't put doors on a field"; and to a lesser extent the three proverbial expressions "to eat something with one's bread," "to be someone's own business," and "to stick one's nose into something," don't add up to making sense. But upon closer inspection they do, supporting Sancho's claim that he doesn't care about the talk circulating about Queen Madásima, that there might be nothing to it, and that it can't be stopped in any case:

> "I don't say it and I don't think it [what people say about Queen Madásima's virtue]," responded Sancho. "It's their affair and let them eat it with their bread; whether or not they were lovers, they've already made their accounting with God; I tend to my vines, it's their business, not mine; I don't stick my nose in; if you buy and lie, your purse wants to know why. Besides, naked I was born, and naked I'll die: I don't lose or gain a thing; whatever they were, it's all the same to me. And many folks think there's bacon when there's not even a hook to hang it on. But who can put doors on a field? Let them say what they please, I don't care."
>
> "Lord save me!" said Don Quixote. "What a lot of foolish things you put on the same thread, Sancho! What does the subject of our conversation have to do with the proverbs you string together like beads? If you value your life, Sancho, be quiet, and from now on tend to spurring your donkey and leave matters alone that do not concern you. And know with all five of your senses that everything I have done, am doing, and shall do follows the dictates of reason and the laws of chivalry, which I know better than all the knights in the world who have ever professed them." (191–92)

The actual problem is that Don Quixote does not understand the proverbial metaphors that lead him to brush Sancho's remarks aside as nonsense. He also does not realize that there is a bit of ironic ambiguity in Sancho's speech (Flores 1982, 118; Gorfkle 1993, 149–51; Hart 2002, 51). That is not to say that the loquacious Sancho would not have done better by curbing his proverb string somewhat. As it is, the bit of humor in all of this stems from the overdose of the proverbial language, but not from its incongruity.

The second string of proverbs appears in an exchange between Don Quixote and Sancho Panza, with the former actually starting the proverb duel. And now there is considerable humor here by Sancho responding to his master's proverb "First impulses are not in the hands of men," with the self-characterization that his first impulse is always to talk. Yet, he does not employ a proverb, and instead it is Don Quixote who cites the medieval Latin proverb "The jug (pitcher) goes to the fountain (well) so long until at last it breaks," which has been loan translated into European languages (Paczolay 1997, 287–91). But notice, he only quotes the first half, attesting to the general knowledge of the proverb by all strata of society. Of course Sancho understands its message as it relates to the danger of talking too much. But in ever so shrewd a proverbial way he leaves the judgment of his loquaciousness up to God by combining the two proverbs

"God is in heaven and judges men's hearts" and "God sees all the snares" to "God's in His heaven, and He sees all the snares"—a perfect proverbial defense:

> "I mean I didn't look at her [Dulcinea] so carefully," said Sancho, "that I could notice her beauty in particular and her good features point by point, but on the whole, she seemed fine to me."
>
> "Now I forgive you," said Don Quixote, "and you must pardon the anger I have shown you; for first impulses are not in the hands of men." "I can see that," responded Sancho, "just like in me a desire to talk is always my first impulse, and I can never help saying, not even once, what's on my tongue."
>
> "Even so," said Don Quixote, "think about what you say, Sancho, because you can carry the jug to the fountain only so many times . . . and I shall say no more."
>
> "Well," responded Sancho, "God's in His heaven, and He sees all the snares, and He'll be the judge of who does worse: me in not saying the right thing or your grace in not doing it." (256)

It is important to recognize here that Don Quixote knows and uses proverbs, that he is the one who initiates them in this instance, and that he obviously appreciates their communicative value, especially in his conversations with his peasant squire.

Sancho's proverb strings are not all directed at Don Quixote, as can be seen from his comments to a priest in which he first connects the proverbs "Where envy rules, virtue cannot survive" and "Generosity cannot live with miserliness" to expose the lies of this man of the church. And then, effectively leading into them with the introductory formula "what they say is true," he cites the proverbs "The wheel of fortune turns faster than a water wheel" and "Those who only yesterday were on top of the world today are down on the ground." There could hardly be a better way to tell the priest that his fortune in the world might very quickly change, hopefully for the worse:

> "Ah Señor Priest, Señor Priest! Did your grace think I didn't know you? Can you think I don't understand and guess where these new enchantments are heading? Well, you should know that I recognize you no matter how you cover your face and understand you no matter how you hide your lies. In short, where envy rules, virtue cannot survive, and generosity cannot live with miserliness. Devil confound it, if it wasn't for your reverence, my master would be married by now to Princess Micomicona and I'd be a count at least, because I expected nothing less from the goodness of my master, the Knight of the Sorrowful Face, and

THE PROVERBIAL LANGUAGE IN CERVANTES'S *DON QUIXOTE*   213

from the greatness of my services! But now I see that what they say is true: the wheel of fortune turns faster than a water wheel, and those who only yesterday were on top of the world today are down on the ground." (410)

The four proverbs in double sequences are absolutely appropriate, and doubling them up does not appear too much of an overkill in this situation with Sancho wanting to put the priest, quite courageously actually, into his place. This is solid proverbial rhetoric without any pun or wordplay, and there is also nothing particularly comical about it all.

The fourth and final accumulation of proverbs in the first part of the novel follows the previous set of proverbs with only one paragraph in between. Having been accused by the barber (a companion of the priest) of being "pregnant" with the lunacy and madness of his master Don Quixote, Sancho begins his response with the claim that he is not pregnant by anybody. This little absurd play with the word "pregnant" still appears quite funny to readers today. But the humor, perhaps also a bit sexual, gets lost once Sancho starts his proverb bombardment of the poor barber. He begins with the proverb "Each man is the child of his actions," thereby echoing Don Quixote's use of the variant "Each man is the child of his deeds" (37) very early in the novel. Whether Cervantes put this proverb into the mouths of both his major characters intentionally would be impossible to ascertain, but the fact remains that the knight errant and the squire both realize that they are the makers of their own fate and that they are responsible for their undertakings. Then Sancho couples the proverbs "There is more to life than trimming beards" and "There's some difference between one Pedro and the other" to point out that there are many different aspects to life and that all people are simply not alike. Next comes the proverbial expression "to throw crooked dice," with which Sancho accuses the barber of trying to convince him of the madness of his master. It might have been smart to stop here, because by adding the proverb "God knows the truth" he appears willing to accept the idea that Don Quixote might just be a lunatic. And he still does not cease the floor, closing his tirade with the proverb "Things get worse when you stir them," which also leaves the possibility of his master's madness wide open:

"I'm not pregnant by anybody," responded Sancho, "and I'm not a man who'd let himself get pregnant even by the king, and though I'm poor I'm an Old Christian, and I don't owe anything to anybody, and if I want ínsulas, other people want things that are worse; each man is the child of his actions, and because I'm a man I could be a pope, let alone the governor of an ínsula, especially since my master could win so many he might not have enough people to give them to. Your grace should be careful what you say, Señor Barber, because there's more to life than trimming beards, and there's some difference between one Pedro and the other. I say this because we all know one another, and you can't throw crooked dice with me. As for the enchantment of my master, only God knows the truth, and let's leave it at that, because things get worse when you stir them." (411)

It is almost surprising that Sancho does not conclude his deliberations with the proverb "Let sleeping dogs lie," which he knew very well, as can be seen from his statement "enough said, we'll let sleeping dogs lie" (532) in another situation later on. In any case, there is danger in getting carried away with strings of proverbs, but they are certainly not inconsequential or nonsensical.

The numerous discussions between Sancho Panza and Don Quixote in the second part of the novel begin in the seventh chapter, in which they talk about how Sancho would be paid for his renewed services as squire. Cleary his wife Teresa wanted to make certain of such payment as well, having told her husband proverbially to keep an eye on his master and then adding a string of three proverbs to it to underscore her advice. That makes plenty of sense, as Sancho recalls it to Don Quixote, but when he then states that "[a] woman's advice is no jewel, and the man who doesn't take it is a fool," the sense is utterly lost. No wonder that Don Quixote is enjoying all of this, since obviously he is glad that Sancho with his antifeminist proverb appears to speak against his wife's counsel:

> "Teresa says," said Sancho, "that I should keep a sharp eye on you, and there's no arguing against written proof, because if you cut the deck you don't deal, and a bird in hand is worth two in the bush. And I say that a woman's advice is no jewel, and the man who doesn't take it is a fool."
>
> "And I say that as well," responded Don Quixote. "Continue, Sancho my friend, go on, for today you are speaking pearls." (498)

There is plenty of irony or humor here, since if a woman's advice is no good, then why should someone who doesn't take it be a fool? Calling all of this "pearls" is also quite humorous, although Sancho does not recognize it at all. Instead, he reminds Don Quixote with the proverbs "Here today and gone tomorrow," "The lamb goes as quickly as the sheep," and "Death is silent" that death could come to him at any time, leaving his poor squire without any financial means. He is making good use of the "distancing property of proverbs" (Hart 2002, 50) here by avoiding to tell Don Quixote that he is afraid that his master might die before him:

"The fact is," responded Sancho, "that as your grace knows very well, we're all subject to death, here today and gone tomorrow, and the lamb goes as quickly as the sheep, and nobody can promise himself more hours of life in this world than the ones God wants to give him, because death is silent, and when she comes knocking at the door of our life, she's always in a hurry, and nothing will stop her, not prayers or struggles or scepters or miters, and that's something that everybody hears, something they tell us from the pulpit."

"All of that is true," said Don Quixote, "but I do not know where it is taking you." (498)

No wonder that Don Quixote is perplexed, getting Sancho to become a bit more direct with his argument for payment assurances without wanting to come across like a proverbial penny pincher. His three proverbs "A hen sits on her eggs," "A lot of littles make a lot," and "As long as you're earning you don't lose a thing" clarify matters:

"It's taking me to this," said Sancho. "Your grace should tell me exactly what salary you'll give me for each month I serve you, and this salary should be paid to me from your estate; I don't want to depend on anybody's favors, which come late, or badly, or never; may God help me to tend to my own business. The point is, I want to know what I'm earning, whether it's a lot or a little; a hen sits on her egg, and a lot of littles make a lot, and as long as you're earning you don't lose a thing. And if it should happen, and I don't believe or expect that it will, that your grace gives me the ínsula you promised, I'm not such an ingrate, and not such a pennypincher, that I won't want the rent from the ínsula to be added up and deducted from my salary pro rat." (498–99)

Finally Don Quixote understands what Sancho is driving at with his "countless arrows of proverbs," and then, quite unexpectedly, he tries himself at a string of three proverbs that include "If the pigeon coop has plenty of feed, it will have plenty of pigeons," "Fine hopes are better than miserable possessions," and "A good lawsuit is better than a bad payment":

"And [I] understood you so well," responded Don Quixote, "that I have penetrated to your most hidden thoughts, and I know the target you are trying to hit with the countless arrows of your proverbs. Look, Sancho: I certainly should have specified a salary for you if I had found in any of the histories of the knights errant an example that would have revealed to me and shown me, by means of the smallest sign, what wages were for a month, or a year, but I have read all or most of their histories, and I do not recall reading that any knight errant ever specified a fixed salary for his squire. I know only that all of them served without pay, and when they least expected it, if things had gone well for their masters, they found themselves rewarded with an ínsula or something comparable; at the very least, they received a title and nobility. If, with these expectations and addenda, you, Sancho, would like to serve me again, then welcome, but if you think I am going to force the ancient usage of knight errantry beyond its limits and boundaries, then you are sadly mistaken. Therefore, my dear Sancho, return to your house and tell your Teresa my intention, and if it pleases her and you to serve me without wages, *bene quidem*, and if not, we shall still be friends, for if the pigeon coop has plenty of feed, it will have plenty of pigeons. And remember, Sancho, that fine hopes are better than miserable possessions, and a good lawsuit [is] better than a bad payment. I am speaking in this manner, Sancho, so you may understand that, like you, I too know how to pour down rainstorms of proverbs. And, finally, I want to tell you, and I do tell you, that if you do not wish to accompany me without pay, and take the same risks I do, then God be with you and turn you into a saint, for I shall have no lack of squires more obedient, more solicitous, less uncouth, and less talkative than you." (499–500)

Sure, Don Quixote claims that he is employing these proverbs only so that Sancho can understand him better, but his statement "I too know how to pour down rainstorms of proverbs" cannot hide the fact that he is enjoying this proverbial contest with his squire. Being part of the Spanish culture of his time, he is obviously as aware of its proverb lore as anybody else (Raymond 1951, 118–31).

Sancho, however, is so full of proverbs that he even speaks to himself in proverbs, as in this soliloquy:

"Well now: everything has a remedy except death, under whose yoke we all have to pass, even if we don't want to, when our life ends. I've seen a thousand signs in this master of mine that he's crazy enough to be tied up, and I'm not far behind, I'm as much a fool as he is because I follow and serve him, if that old saying is true: 'Tell me who your friends are and I'll tell you who you are,' and that other one that says, 'Birds of a feather flock together.' Then, being crazy, which is what he is, with the kind of craziness that most of the time takes one thing for another, and thinks white is black and black is white, like the time he said that the windmills were giants, and the friars' mules dromedaries, and the flocks of sheep enemy armies, and many other things of that nature." (515–16)

The proverb "Everything has a remedy except death" expresses Sancho's optimism in looking for Dulcinea, and the following two proverbs are metaphorical expressions for the friendship relationship between Don Quixote and Sancho. Sancho even admits that he must share in some of the craziness of his master, who proverbially speaking "thinks white is black and black is white." But the three proverbs cited by Sancho make eminent sense and are used in serious reflection without any humor intended.

This is definitely also the case in the following sequence of proverbs where Sancho deals with the upcoming wedding of Quiteria and Camacho and the hope that things might still turn out well for Camacho's rival, Basilio. After all, "God gives the malady and also the remedy," "Nobody knows the future," "There are a lot of hours until tomorrow," and "In a moment a house can fall." He also makes good use of the widely disseminated proverbial expression "to rain while the sun shines" (Kuusi 1957) and the proverbial phrase "to drive a nail into fortune's wheel" to indicate that things might well change for the better. Love will eventually win out, as Sancho declares at the end of his comforting comments: "Love looks through spectacles that make copper look like gold, poverty like riches, and dried rheum like pearls."

> "God will find the cure," said Sancho, "for God gives the malady and also the remedy; nobody knows the future: there's a lot of hours until tomorrow, and in one of them, and even in a moment, the house can fall; I've seen it rain at the same time the sun is shining; a man goes to bed healthy and can't move the next day. And tell me, is there anybody who can boast that he's driven a nail into Fortune's wheel? No, of course not, and I wouldn't dare put the point of a pin between a woman's yes and no, because it wouldn't fit. Tell me that Quiteria loves Basilio with all her heart and all her soul, and I'll give him a sack of good fortune, because I've heard that love looks through spectacles that make copper look like gold, poverty like riches, and dried rheum like pearls." (579)

Don Quixote's negative response to Sancho "string[ing] together proverbs" is unwarranted and unfair, since Sancho expresses them with kindness and compassion: "'Damn you, Sancho, where will you stop?' said Don Quixote. 'When you begin to string together proverbs and stories, nobody can endure it but Judas himself, and may Judas himself take you. Tell me, you brute, what do you know of nails, or wheels, or anything else?'" And then comes Sancho's most telling reaction, claiming that it isn't his fault that people don't understand his proverbs, which ought to make perfect sense since there is no foolishness in them. Of course, Don Quixote insists on having the last word, but it is nit-picking and does not earn him favor with the reader:

"Oh, well, if none of you understand me," responded Sancho, "it's no wonder my sayings are taken for nonsense. But it doesn't matter: I understand what I'm saying, and I know there's not much foolishness in what I said, but your grace is always sentencing what I say, and even what I do."

"*Censuring* is what you should say," said Don Quixote, "and not sentencing, you corrupter of good language, may God confound you!" (579)

Scholars have looked at this particular proverb string quite positively, with R. M. Flores speaking of "the good sense ensconced in Sancho's string of proverbs" and justifiably pointing out that "Sancho's retort to this [Don Quixote's statement] goes straight to the point, and also stands as an answer to the general misconception that holds that Sancho often does not know what he is talking about and misapplies his sayings" (Flores 1982, 119, 120). On a more philosophical level, Laura Gorfkle has stated that in this case "Sancho's speech, more than the construction of a single argument or point of view, is an exploration of the problem of fortune, and of the manners in which good and bad fortune can combine and alternate" (Gorfkle 1993, 147–48; see also Hart 2002, 46–47).

This is not to say that Sancho never cites a proverb the wrong way, as when he changes the proverbs "Wisdom is better than wealth" and "A saddled horse is better than an ass covered in gold" to their opposites. But upon close reading it becomes clear that he does so with the definite purpose of showing how things are out of kilter. The two preceding proverbs about the worth of a person and the haves and have-nots are, on the other hand, rendered in their normal wording:

"You're worth what you have, and what you have is what you're worth. There are only two lineages in the world, as my grandmother used to say, and that's the haves and the have-nots, though she was on the side of having; nowadays, Señor Don Quixote, wealth is better than wisdom: an ass covered in gold seems better than a saddled horse. [. . .]"

"Have you finished your harangue, Sancho?" said Don Quixote.

"I must have," responded Sancho, "because I see that your grace is bothered by it; if you hadn't cut this one short, I could have gone on for another three days." (589)

Once again it is Don Quixote here who reacts so negatively to Sancho's proverbial loquaciousness, when there would actually be no reason for him not to agree with what Sancho has just said.

It is at times surprising that Sancho remains loyal to his master, who has so little understanding for his mouth running over with proverbs. One wonders

THE PROVERBIAL LANGUAGE IN CERVANTES'S *DON QUIXOTE* 219

how Don Quixote would have reacted to this self-characterization by Sancho via three proverbs, which is so very complimentary:

> "I'm the one who deserves it [an *ínsula*] as much as anybody else; I'm a 'Stay close to a good man and become one'; and I'm a 'Birds of a feather flock together'; and a 'Lean against a sturdy trunk if you want good shade.' I have leaned against a good master, and traveled with him for many months, and I'll become just like him, God willing; long life to him and to me, and there'll be no lack of empires for him to rule or ínsulas for me to govern." (666–67)

And what insight once again by Sancho in saying that he is ever more becoming like Don Quixote. What the latter is not realizing yet is that he himself is also becoming more like Sancho, even in his increased use of proverbs, which he appears to despise so much.

Talking about insight, here is a string of eight proverbs that Sancho introduces with "I may be a fool, but I understand the proverb that says, 'it did him harm when the ant grew wings.'" With this he begins a train of thought that it might perhaps be best if he were never to get his governorship, with one proverb after another stating that things are just fine and a change might not be good. And not to forget the wisdom of the last proverb, that "All that glitters is not gold":

> "If I were a clever man, I would have left my master days ago. But this is my fate and this is my misfortune; I can't help it; I have to follow him: we're from the same village, I've eaten his bread, I love him dearly, he's a grateful man, he gave me his donkeys, and more than anything else, I'm faithful; and so it's impossible for anything to separate us except the man with the pick and shovel [an allusion to death]. And if your highness doesn't want me to have the governorship I've been promised, God made me without it, and maybe not giving it to me will be for the good of my conscience; I may be a fool, but I understand the proverb that says, 'It did him harm when the ant grew wings,' and it might even be that Sancho the squire will enter heaven more easily than Sancho the governor. The bread they bake here is as good as in France, and at night every cat is gray, and the person who hasn't eaten by two in the afternoon has more than enough misfortune, and no stomach's so much bigger than any other that it can't be filled, as they say, with straw and hay [the actual proverb is 'Straw and hay and hunger's away'], and the little birds of the field have God to protect and provide for them, and four

varas of flannel from Cuenca will warm you more than four of *limiste* [a very fine cloth] from Segovia, and when we leave this world and go into the ground, the path of the prince is as narrow as the laborer's, and the pope's body doesn't need more room underground than the sacristan's, even if one is higher than the other, because when we're in the grave we all have to adjust and shrink or they make us adjust and shrink, whether we want to or not, and that's the end of it. And I say again that if your ladyship doesn't want to give me the ínsula because I'm a fool, I'll be smart enough not to care at all; I've heard that the devil hides behind the cross, and that all that glitters isn't gold, and that from his oxen, plows, and yokes they took the peasant Wamba to be king of Spain, and from his brocades, entertainments, and riches they took Rodrigo to be eaten by snakes, if the lines from the old ballads don't lie." (678–79)

And the duchess to whom Sancho addresses these remarks could not "help but marvel at Sancho's words and proverbs" (680), indicating that they made good sense to her. And when she instructs him to govern the vassals of his *ínsula* well, good Sancho cannot resist adding a few more proverbs and proverbial expressions:

"As for governing them well," responded Sancho, "there's no need to charge me with it, because I'm charitable by nature and have compassion for the poor; and if he kneads and bakes, you can't steal his cakes; by my faith, they won't throw me any crooked dice; I'm an old dog and understand every here, boy [the proverb says: 'You don't need here, boy, here, boy, with an old dog'], and I know how to wake up at the right time, and I don't allow cobwebs in front of my eyes, because I know if the shoe fits: I say this because with me good men will have my hand and a place in my house [the phrase means 'trust and confidence'], and bad men won't get a foot or permission to enter. And it seems to me that in this business of governorships it's all a matter of starting, and it may be that after two weeks of being a governor I'll be licking my lips over the work and know more about it than working in the fields, which is what I've grown up doing." (680)

Even though Don Quixote is not witness to these proverb strings, he has heard his share of them. Matters come to a breaking point in the forty-third chapter when he instructs Sancho to refrain from using them once and for all when taking over his governorship. While poor Sancho agrees to do so, he cannot help himself and immediately strings four proverbs together (Madariaga 1934, 181–83). Despairing at such verbal behavior, Don Quixote admits to Sancho that one proverb at a time is perfectly fine, but it is the absurd accumulation of them that he objects to so vehemently:

> "Sancho, you also should not mix into your speech the host of proverbs that you customarily use, for although proverbs are short maxims, the ones you bring in are often so far-fetched that they seem more like nonsense than like maxims."
>
> "God can remedy that," responded Sancho, "because I know more proverbs than a book, and so many of them come into my mouth at one time when I talk that they fight with one another to get out, but my tongue tosses out the first ones it finds, even if they're not to the point. But I'll be careful from now on to say the ones that suit the gravity of my position, because in a well-stocked house, supper is soon cooked; and if you cut the cards, you don't deal; and the man who sounds the alarm is safe; and for giving and keeping, you need some sense."
>
> "Go on, Sancho!" said Don Quixote. "Force the proverbs in, string them together one after another on a thread! No one will stop you! My mother punishes me and I deceive her! I tell you to avoid proverbs, and in an instant you have come out with a litany of them that have as much to do with what we are discussing as the hills of Úbeda. Look, Sancho, I am not saying that an appropriate proverb is wrong, but loading and stringing together proverbs any which way makes your conversation lifeless and lowborn." (734–35)

What is important about the four proverbs "In a well-stocked house supper is soon cooked," "If you cut the cards, you don't deal," "The man who sounds the alarm is safe," and "For giving and keeping, you need some sense" is that they have nothing to do with each other. Here Sancho is really just amassing proverbs at random to vex his master even more and to repay him for his constant complaints against his proverbs. As R. M Flores has observed: "This is the only instance I can find in which Sancho's proverbs are apparently not suited to the occasion. But in this passage Sancho is purposely misusing his proverbs to provoke and exasperate his master" (Flores 1982, 121). It definitely is true that "Sancho does not generally choose proverbs at random as Don Quijote charges" (Hart 2002, 52) a contention that scholars have too quickly accepted at face value.

One might have thought that Don Quixote and Sancho Panza would let things rest at this point, but Cervantes as the author goes on to let the two of them converse about paremiological concerns, turning chapter 43 into a unique metaproverbial discourse that "is richly laced with proverbs so that the two discursive modes, the proverbs and the meta-proverbial, illuminate each other

222 PROVERBS IN LITERATURE

sapientially as well as ironically" (Hasan-Rokem 2007, 195). Sancho begins with a statement rich in proverbs that is supposed to illustrate that he will make a good governor despite his lack of education. It is truly amazing how he ties the following eight proverbs together: "There is a remedy for everything except death," "When your father is magistrate, you are safe when you go to trial," "To go for wool and come back shorn," "When God loves you, your house knows it," "The rich man's folly passes for good judgment in the world," "Be like honey and the flies will go after you," "You are worth only as much as you have," and "You won't get revenge on a well-established man":

> "I know how to sign my name very well," responded Sancho, "because when I was steward of a brotherhood in my village, I learned to make some letters like the marks on bundles, and they told me that they said my name; better yet, I'll pretend that my right hand has been hurt, and I'll have somebody else sign for me; there's a remedy for everything except death, and since I'll be in charge of everything, I can do whatever I want; then, too, when your father's the magistrate . . . [you're safe when you go to trial]. And being a governor, which is more than being a magistrate, just let them come and they'll see what happens! No, let them make fun of me and speak ill of me: they'll come for wool and go home shorn; and when God loves you, your house knows it; and the rich man's folly passes for good judgment in the world; and since that's what I'll be, being a governor and a very generous one, which is what I plan to be, nobody will notice any faults in me. No, just be like honey and the flies will go after you; you're only worth as much as you have, my grandmother used to say; and you won't get revenge on a well-established man." (735)

Don Quixote's by now expected negative reaction to this proverb bombardment is swift and cruel, but, whether he notices it or not, he actually admits his inability to cite proverbs like Sancho. In fact, he would have to "labor like a ditchdigger" to come up with but one applicable proverb:

> "O, may you be accursed, Sancho!" said Don Quixote at this point. "May sixty thousand devils take you and your proverbs! For the past hour you have been stringing them together and with each one giving me a cruel taste of torment. I assure you that one day these proverbs will lead you to the gallows; because of them your vassals will take the governorship away from you, or rise up against you. Tell me, where do you find them, you ignorant man, and how do you apply them, you fool, when to say

THE PROVERBIAL LANGUAGE IN CERVANTES'S *DON QUIXOTE*   223

only one that is really applicable, I have to perspire and labor like a ditchdigger?" (735–36)

This triggers the classic response by Sancho in which he argues that his proverbs are his wealth and that four of them that he can right at that moment think of would, proverbially speaking, fit perfectly well, "like pears in a wicker basket." And then, subservient as he is to his master, he employs the traditional Spanish proverb "Golden silence is what they call Sancho," which includes his name to announce that he will try to refrain from speaking in proverbs forthwith:

> "By God, my lord and master," replied Sancho, "your grace complains about very small things. Why the devil does it trouble you when I make use of my fortune, when I have no other, and no other wealth except proverbs and more proverbs? And right now four have come to mind that are a perfect fit, like pears in a wicker basket, but I won't say them, because golden silence is what they call Sancho." (736)

Much has been made of the "Sancho" proverb (for other proverbs with this name see Jehenson and Dunn 2010, 137), which was current in a number of variants before Cervantes employed it in *Don Quixote* as a rather ironic self-characterization of his squire (Morel-Fatio 1882; Colombi 1989a; Sevilla Muñoz 1993, 359–61). It has been suggested that it is this very proverb in the sense of "Silence is golden" that might have led Cervantes to call the infamous squire Sancho Panza, with his last name referring to his small but rotund stature (Hasan-Rokem 2007, 189–90; Bizzarri 2015, 534–35). The paremiological insight of this discourse is, of course, that proverbs are not universally applicable, because this specific Sancho Panza is way too talkative, especially in his proverb bombardments.

In any case, Don Quixote—how smart is he really—takes the bait and asks Sancho for the four proverbs, thus actually taking over the role of an enabler by giving Sancho a chance to launch into yet another string of proverbs:

> "That Sancho is not you," said Don Quixote, "because not only are you not golden silence, you are foolish speech and stubborn persistence, but even so I should like to know which four proverbs came to mind just now that were so to the point, because I have been searching my mind, and I have a good one, and I cannot think of a single proverb."
>
> "Which ones could be better," said Sancho, "than 'Never put your thumbs between two wisdom teeth' and 'There's no answer to get out of my house and what do you want with my wife' and 'Whether the pitcher

hits the stone or the stone hits the pitcher, it's bad luck for the pitcher'? They're all just fine. Because nobody should take on his governor or the person in authority because he'll come out of it hurt, like the man who puts his finger between two wisdom teeth, and if they're not wisdom teeth but just plain molars, it doesn't matter; and there's no reply to what the governor says, like the 'Leave my house and what do you want with my wife.' As for the stone and the pitcher, even a blind man can see that. So whoever sees the mote in somebody else's eye has to see the beam in his own, so that nobody can say about him: 'The dead woman was frightened by the one with her throat cut.' And your grace knows very well that the fool knows more in his own house than the wise man does in somebody else's."

"That is not so, Sancho," responded Don Quixote, "for the fool knows nothing whether in his own house or in another's, because on a foundation of foolishness no reasonable building can be erected. Enough of this now, Sancho, for if you govern badly, the fault will be yours and mine the shame; but it consoles me that I did what I had to do and advised you with all the truth and wisdom of which I am capable: now I am relieved of my obligation and my promise. May God guide you, Sancho, and govern you in your governorship, and free me of the misgivings I still have that you will turn the entire ínsula upside down, something I could avoid by revealing to the duke who you are, and telling him that this plump little body of yours is nothing but a sack filled with proverbs and guile." (736)

As can be seen, Sancho takes the opportunity to enumerate three proverbs and even supplies explanations for them. Perhaps he forgot the fourth proverb (Hernández 1984, 220). But not to worry, he throws in the biblical proverb "See the mote in someone else's eye but not the beam in one's own" (Matthew 7:3) and adds the proverbs "The dead woman was frightened by the one with her throat cut" and "The fool knows more in his own house than the wise man does in somebody else's" for good measure. And it all fits! It's just that Don Quixote misses the points of the last three proverbs. He sees only Sancho's shortcomings and not his own; he is perhaps threatened by Sancho's proverb mastery, and certainly Sancho the fool knows more about his "fount of proverb lore and folk wisdom" (Sullivan 2005, 229) than Don Quixote. Galit Hasan-Rokem has discovered a definite pattern in these proverb duels between the knight errant and his squire: "Don Quijote confronts Sancho with the excess of proverbs and their inadequate integration in his speech. Sancho on the one hand insists on his right to use proverbs, on the other swears to improve the level of integration and thirdly promises to keep altogether quiet, all three positions being equally characteristically inconsistent and intermittent. Sancho's inconsistency is one of his vital, lifelike characteristics, in blatant contrast to the deadening intransience of his master" (Hasan-Rokem 2007, 195). What Don Quixote doesn't understand, and here lies much of the irony, is that Sancho, the wise proverb fool, actually turns out the winner in these confrontations. He might be using proverbs a bit too much, but he knows only too well what he is doing with this traditional wisdom.

There is yet another proverb string that will give Don Quixote a chance to pick on the proverbial Sancho. Having suggested that they become shepherds, Sancho imagines his daughter bringing them food out in the country. But since Sanchica is a beautiful maiden, he thinks that some shepherd might take advantage of her, bringing to mind the proverbs "To go for wool and come back shorn," "If you take away the cause, you take away the sin," "If your eyes don't see, your heart doesn't break," and "A jump over the thicket is better than the prayers of good men." As the reader contextualizes these proverbs with the young girl meeting a young shepherd in the open, they make good sense and leave the chance of a sexual encounter to the imagination:

> "Oh, how polished I'll keep the spoons when I'm a shepherd. What soft bread, what cream, what garlands, what pastoral odds and ends that, if they don't earn me fame as a wise man, can't help but earn me fame as a clever one! Sanchica, my daughter, will bring food up to our flocks. But wait! She's a good-looking girl, and there are shepherds more wicked than simple, and I wouldn't want her to go for wool and come back shorn; love and unchaste desires are as likely in the countryside as in the cities, in shepherds' huts as in royal palaces, and if you take away the cause, you take away the sin, and if your eyes don't see, your heart doesn't break, and a jump over the thicket is better than the prayers of good men." (901)

Don Quixote's negative reaction is quick and to the point, but while he wants "no more proverbs," he is now ready to admit that "any one of those you have said is enough to explain your thoughts." In other words, he is no longer arguing that Sancho's proverb strings make no sense! Relying on the proverbial expression "to preach in the desert" to express his dismay over Sancho's continued use of proverb accumulations after having been told repeatedly not to do so (Raymond 1951, 135), he underscores Sancho's "misbehavior" by way of the proverb "My mother punished me, and I deceive her." Although the metaphor of the proverb seems inappropriate regarding Sancho as a male, there probably is some humor in this feminization of the plump squire. Be that as it may, Sancho takes no offense but rather pulls in the proverb "The pot calls the kettle black" to confront his master with the undeniable fact that he, too, uses proverbs (Madariaga 1934, 183). That is true, of course, but Sancho overstates matters by claiming that his master "strings them together":

> "No more proverbs, Sancho," said Don Quixote, "for any one of those you have said is enough to explain your thoughts; I have often advised you not to be so prodigal in your proverbs and to restrain yourself from saying them, but it seems that is like preaching in the desert, and 'My mother punishes me, and I deceive her.'"
>
> "It seems to me," responded Sancho, "that your grace is like the pot calling the kettle black. You reprove me for saying proverbs, and your grace strings them together two at a time." (901–2)

As usual, Don Quixote insists on having the last word before suggesting that they drop the whole matter. He stresses once again that proverbs are fine if they, proverbially speaking, "fit [the context] like the rings on your fingers" and are not randomly and en masse "dragged in by the hair."

> "Look, Sancho," responded Don Quixote, "I say proverbs when they are appropriate, and when I say them they fit like the rings on your fingers, but you drag them in by the hair, and pull them along, and do not guide them, and if I remember correctly, I have already told you that proverbs are brief maxims derived from the experience and speculation of wise men in the past, and if the proverb is not to the point, it is not a maxim, it is nonsense. But let us leave this for now, and since night is approaching, let us withdraw some distance from the king's highway, and spend the night there, and God alone knows what tomorrow will bring." (902)

Don Quixote will just not let go of his idée fixe of Sancho applying proverbs nonsensically. Whether he likes it or not, he is wrong, and the careful reader is catching on, realizing that Sancho is making plenty of sense as the wise fool toward the end of their adventures. And Don Quixote cannot escape this folk wisdom either, as evidenced by his statement's proverbial conclusion "God alone knows what tomorrow will bring," which is a proverb definition of sorts for his squire. As if Sancho doesn't know what a proverb is!

Relatively close to the end of *Don Quixote*, one might have thought that Cervantes had had enough of these exchanges around proverbs between the knight errant and his squire. But in fact, just a few pages beyond the previous dialogue, he returns to this proverbial theme one more time in the next chapter, chapter 68. Sancho is finally standing up to his master, telling him that he just wants to sleep and be himself. As always, Don Quixote is not pleased and in his anger scolds his loyal squire by giving him hope for solitude with the personalized medieval Latin proverb "Post tenebras lux (see also Job 17:12). Understandably, Sancho responds by telling Don Quixote that he does not understand Latin and then goes on quite philosophically about the equality of all people, certainly when they sleep. But that reminds him of yet another proverb that he cites only indirectly, namely "Sleep resembles (is the brother of) death":

> "O unfeeling soul! O pitiless squire! O undeserved bread and unthinking favor that I [Don Quixote] have given to you and intend to give to you in the future! Because of me you found yourself a governor, and because of me you have hopes of becoming a count or receiving another equivalent title, and the fulfillment of those hopes will take no longer than the time it takes for this year to pass, for *Post tenebras spero lucem*."
>
> "I don't understand that," replied Sancho. "I only understand that while I'm sleeping I have no fear, or hope, or trouble, or glory; blessed be whoever invented sleep, the mantle that covers all human thought, the food that satisfies hunger, the water that quenches thirst, the fire that warms the cold, the cold that cools down ardor, and, finally, the general coin with which all things are bought, the scale and balance that make the shepherd equal to the king, and the simple man equal to the wise. There is only one defect in sleep, or so I've heard, and it is that it resembles death, for there is very little difference between a man who is sleeping and a man who is dead." (903–4)

Don Quixote, his anger passed, actually praises Sancho for this philosophical statement and pays him the ultimate compliment by acknowledging the truth of one of his proverbs. In other words, he is starting to talk like his squire, and that's a big change indeed. Sancho's response is in typical fashion once again exaggerated. After all, his claim that Don Quixote is now the one who strings proverbs together is not corroborated by his actual statement:

> "I have never heard you speak, Sancho," said Don Quixote, "as elegantly as now, which leads me to recognize the truth of the proverb that you like to quote: 'It is not where you were born but who your friends are now that counts.'"
>
> "Ah, confound it, Señor!" replied Sancho. "Now I'm not the one stringing proverbs together; they also drop two by two from your grace's mouth better than they do from mine, but between my proverbs and yours there must be this difference: your grace's come at the right time, while mine are out of place, but in fact they're all proverbs." (904)

Instead of asserting himself as a capable proverbialist, Sancho backpedals by declaring that his master uses proverbs correctly whereas he as the subservient squire does not have this ability. Don Quixote has succeeded in brainwashing him to this split viewpoint. At least Sancho winds up his response with the pronouncement that "in fact they're all proverbs!"

And now, very close to the end of the novel, Cervantes gives both of his heroes one more chance to go at each other proverbially. The reader might well have hoped that Sancho will finally stand his ground, but he instead appears to succumb to the wishes of his master one last time. Cervantes does not even let him utter his four proverbs "In delay there is danger," "Pray to God and use a hammer," "One 'here you are' is worth more than two 'I'll give it to you,'" and "A bird in the hand is worth two in the bush" directly but only lists them through indirect speech:

> Sancho responded that he would do as his master wished but would like to conclude this matter quickly, while his blood was hot and the grindstone rough, because in delay there is often danger, and pray to God and use the hammer, and one "here you are" was worth more than two "I'll give it to you," and a bird in hand was worth two in the bush. (924)

Don Quixote's predictable answer is "no more proverbs," and he can't resist plugging in a bit of superfluous Latin that he knows Sancho can't understand. Accusing Sancho of being up to his old tricks with proverbs is correct, but who is telling whom here to speak plainly? And, wouldn't the reader know and expect it by now, Don Quixote winds up by using the proverb "One loaf is the same as a hundred." The loaf of bread here becomes a metaphor for Sancho's proverbs, which, at least to Don Quixote, are all the same and should most certainly not be amassed.

> "By the one God, Sancho, no more proverbs," said Don Quixote. "It seems you are going back to *sicut erat* ['as it was before'—that is, 'up to your old tricks']; speak plainly, and simply, and without complications, as I have often told you, and you will see how one loaf will be the same as a hundred for you." (924)

Sancho's timid response—he doesn't even point out that Don Quixote just used a proverb—is perhaps disappointing on first reading: "'I don't know why I'm so unlucky,' responded Sancho, 'that I can't say a word without a proverb, and every proverb seems exactly right to me, but I'll change, if I can'" (924).

The modern reader might wish that the closing phrase "I'll change, if I can" were not there so that Sancho could insist that proverbs are his life and that

THE PROVERBIAL LANGUAGE IN CERVANTES'S *DON QUIXOTE*

it is his right as an individual to use them. But to be sure, nobody has ever argued with Sancho or for that matter with Don Quixote that a proverb or two in the right place at the right time is not appropriate. This communication by proverbial "indirection" (Weiger 1985, 22) is certainly an integral part of the novel's complex nature. It is only Sancho's strings of proverbs that are at issue and legitimately questioned. The message of such proverbs as "Moderation in all things" and "Nothing in excess" is absent in Sancho's mind, leaving the door wide open for satire, irony, and humor.

BIBLIOGRAPHY

This chapter was first published with the same title in *Proceedings of the Tenth Interdisciplinary Colloquium on Proverbs*, Tavira, Portugal, November 6–13, 2016, edited by Rui J. B. Soares and Outi Lauhakangas (Tavira, Portugal: Tipografia Tavirense, 2017), 15–51.

SPANISH EDITION

Cervantes Saavedra, Miguel de. (1605, 1615) 1947–1949. *Don Qvixote de la Mancha*. Edited by Rodolfo Schevill and Adolfo Bonilla. 10 vols. Madrid: Gráficas Reunidas.

FIRST ENGLISH TRANSLATION

1612–1620, Thomas Shelton
Cervantes Saavedra, Miguel de. (1612–1620) 1907. *The History of the Valorous and Witty Knight-Errant Don Quixote of the Mancha*. Translated by Thomas Shelton. Introduction by Royal Cortissoz. 4 vols. New York: Charles Scribner's Sons.

SIX MODERN AMERICAN ENGLISH TRANSLATIONS

1949, Samuel Putnam
Cervantes Saavedra, Miguel de. 1949. *The Ingenious Gentleman Don Quixote de la Mancha*. Translated by Samuel Putnam. New York: Viking Press.
1981, Joseph Ramon Jones and Kenneth Douglas
Cervantes Saavedra, Miguel de. 1981. *Don Quixote*. Translated by Joseph Ramon Jones and Kenneth Douglas. New York: W. W. Norton. Major revision of Miguel de Cervantes Saavedra, *The Ingenious Gentleman Don Quixote of La Mancha*. Translated by John Ormsby. 4 vols. New York: Macmillan, 1885.
1995, Burton Raffel
Cervantes, Miguel de. (1995) 1999. *Don Quijote*. Translated by Burton Raffel. Edited by Diana de Armas Wilson. New York: W. W. Norton.
2003, Edith Grossman

Cervantes, Miguel de. 2003. *Don Quixote*. Translated by Edith Grossman. Introduction by Harold Bloom. New York: HarperCollins.

2005, Tom Lathrop

Cervantes Saavedra, Miguel de. 2005. *Don Quixote*. Translated by Tom Lathrop. Newark, DE: LinguaText.

2009, James H. Montgomery

Cervantes Saavedra, Miguel de. 2009. *Don Quixote*. Translated by James H. Montgomery. Introduction by David Quint. Indianapolis: Hackett.

SECONDARY SOURCES

Abrahams, Roger D., and Barbara A. Babcock. 1977. "The Literary Use of Proverbs." *Journal of American Folklore*, 90, no. 358 (October–December): 414–29. Also in *Wise Words: Essays on the Proverb*, edited by Wolfgang Mieder, 415–37. New York: Garland Publishing, 1994. Rpt., Abingdon, Oxon., England: Routledge, 2015.

Bizzarri, Hugo O. 2003. "Los refranes en Cervantes." *Boletín Hispánico Helvético* 2: 25–49.

Bizzarri, Hugo O. 2015. *Diccionario de paremias cervantinas*. Alcalá de Henares, Spain: Universidad de Alcalá.

Bjornson, Richard, ed. 1984. *Approaches to Teaching Cervantes' "Don Quixote."* New York: Modern Language Association of America.

Bloom, Harold. (1994) 2001. "Cervantes: The Play of the World." In *Cervantes's "Don Quixote,"* edited by Harold Bloom, 145–60. Philadelphia: Chelsea House.

Bloom, Harold, ed. 2001. *Cervantes's "Don Quixote."* Philadelphia: Chelsea House.

Bloom, Harold, ed. 2005. *Miguel de Cervantes*. Philadelphia: Chelsea House.

Bloom, Harold, ed. 2010. *Miguel de Cervantes's "Don Quixote."* New ed. New York: Chelsea House.

Cantera Ortiz de Urbina, Jesús, Julia Sevilla Muñoz, and Manuel Sevilla Muñoz. 2005. *Refranes, otras paremias y fraseologismos en "Don Quijote de la Mancha."* Edited by Wolfgang Mieder. Burlington: University of Vermont.

Cárcer y de Sobíes, Enrique de. 1916. *Las frases del "Quijote": Su exposición, ordenación y comentarios, y su versión á las lenguas francesa, portugesa, italiana, catalana, inglesa y alemana*. Lérida, Spain: Artes Gráficas de Sol y Benet.

Casalduero, Joaquín. 1947. "The Composition of *Don Quixote*." In *Cervantes Across the Centuries*, edited by Angel Flores and M. J. Benardete, 56–93. New York: Dryden Press.

Cascardi, Anthony J., ed. 2002. *The Cambridge Companion to Cervantes*. Cambridge: Cambridge University Press.

Cassou, Jean. 1947. "An Introduction to Cervantes." In *Cervantes Across the Centuries*, edited by Angel Flores and M. J. Benardete, 3–31. New York: Dryden Press.

Ciallella, Louise. 2003. "Teresa Panza's Character Zone and Discourse of Domesticity in *Don Quijote*." *Cervantes* 23, no. 2 (September): 275–96.

Ciallella, Louise. 2007. "Quixotic Antecedents and Zones of Proverbial Tactics." In *Quixotic Modernists: Reading Gender in "Tristana," Trigo, and Martínez Sierra*, 24–30. Lewisburg, PA: Bucknell University Press.

Close, A. J. 1973. "Sancho Panza: Wise Fool." *Modern Language Review* 68, no. 2 (April): 344–57.

Cobelo, Silvia. 2009. "Historiografia das traduções do *Quixote* publicadas no Brasil: Provérbios do Sancho Pança." PhD diss., University of São Paulo.

Colombi, María Cecilia. 1989a. "Al buen callar llaman Sancho." In *Speculum historiographiae linguisticae*, edited by Klaus D. Dutz, 243–52. Münster, Germany: Modus Publikationen.

Colombi, María Cecilia. 1989b. *Los refranes en el "Quijote": Texto y contexto*. Potomac, MD: Scripta Humanistica.

Correas, Gonzalo de. 1627. *Vocabulario de refranes y frases proverbiales*. Madrid: Ratés. Rpt., edited by Louis Combet. Lyon: Institute d'Étude Ibériques et Ibéro-Américaines de l'Université de Bordeaux, 1967.

Cull, John T. 2014. "*Nunca mucho costó poco*: Una vez más sobre las paremias del *Quijote*." *Paremia* 23: 147–61.

Dunn, Peter N. 1984. "Getting Started: *Don Quixote* and the Reader's Response." In *Approaches to Teaching Cervantes' "Don Quixote*," edited by Richard Bjornson, 77–86. New York: Modern Language Association of America.

Durán, Manuel. 1974. *Cervantes*. New York: Twayne Publishers.

Durán, Manuel, and Ray R. Rogg. 2010. "Constructing *Don Quixote*." In *Miguel de Cervantes's "Don Quixote*," edited by Harold Bloom, new ed., 91–107. New York: Chelsea House.

Eisenberg, Daniel. 1984. "Teaching *Don Quixote* as a Funny Book." In *Approaches to Teaching Cervantes' "Don Quixote*," edited by Richard Bjornson, 62–68. New York: Modern Language Association of America.

Eisenberg, Daniel. 2006. "The Text of *Don Quixote* as Seen by Its Modern English Translators." *Cervantes* 26, no. 1 (Spring): 103–26.

Finello, Dominick. 1994. *Pastoral Themes and Forms in Cervantes's Fiction*. Lewisburg, PA: Bucknell University Press.

Flores, Angel, and M. J. Benardete, eds. 1947. *Cervantes Across the Centuries*. New York: Dryden Press.

Flores, R. M. 1982. *Sancho Panza Through Three Hundred Seventy-Five Years of Continuations, Imitations, and Criticism, 1605–1980*. Newark, DE: Juan de la Cuesta.

Gerhard, Sandra Forbes. 1982. *"Don Quixote" and the Shelton Translation: A Stylistic Analysis*. Potomac, MD: Studia Humanitatis.

Gilman, Stephen. 1989. *The Novel According to Cervantes*. Berkeley: University of California Press.

González Echevarría, Roberto, ed. 2005. *Cervantes' "Don Quixote": A Casebook*. New York: Oxford University Press.

González Martín, Vicente. 1997. "El refrán en la literatura española de los siglos XVI y XVII." *Paremia* 6: 281–86.

Gorfkle, Laura J. 1993. *Discovering the Comic in "Don Quixote*." Chapel Hill: University of North Carolina, Department of Romance Languages.

Hart, Thomas R. 2002. "Sancho's Discretion." *Bulletin of Spanish Studies* 79, no. 1: 45–53.

Hasan-Rokem, Galit. 2007. "Literary Forms of Orality: Proverbs in the Hebrew Translations of *Don Quijote*." *Proverbium* 24: 189–206.

Hatzfeld, Helmut. 1947. "The Style of *Don Quixote*." In *Cervantes Across the Centuries*, edited by Angel Flores and M. J. Benardete, 94–100. New York: Dryden Press.

Hayes, Francis Clement. 1936. "The Use of Proverbs in the *Siglo de Oro* Drama: An Introductory Study." PhD diss., University of North Carolina.

Hernández, José Luis Alonso. 1984. "Interprétation psychoanalytique de l'utilisation des parémies dans la littérature espagnole." In *Richesse du proverbe*, edited by François Suard and Claude Buridant, 2:213–25. Lille, France: Université de Lille.

Iventosch, Herman. 1980. "The Decline of the Humanist Ideal in the Baroque: Quevedo's Attack on the *Refrán*." *Mester* 9, no. 2: 17–24.

Jehenson, Myriam Yvonne, and Peter N. Dunn. 2010. "Discursive Hybridity: Don Quixote's and Sancho Panza's Utopias." In *Miguel de Cervantes's "Don Quixote,"* edited by Harold Bloom, new ed., 127–44. New York: Chelsea House.

Joly, Monique. 1996. *Études sur "Don Quichotte."* Paris: Publications de la Sorbonne.

Krauss, Werner. 1946. *Die Welt im spanischen Sprichwort.* Wiesbaden, Germany: Limes Verlag. Rpt. in an enlarged edition, Leipzig: Philipp Reclam Verlag, 1975.

Krauss, Werner. 1959. "Die Welt im spanischen Sprichwort." In *Studien und Aufsätze*, 73–91. Berlin: Rütten und Loening.

Krikmann, Arvo. (1974) 2009. *Proverb Semantics: Studies in Structure, Logic, and Metaphor.* Edited by Wolfgang Mieder. Burlington: University of Vermont.

Kuusi, Matti. 1957. *Regen bei Sonnenschein: Zur Weltgeschichte einer Redensart.* Helsinki: Suomalainen Tiedeakatemia.

Landa, Luis. 2013. "The Plebeian and the Cultivated Proverb in Miguel de Cervantes' *Don Quixote*." In *Textures: Culture, Literature, Folklore; For Galit Hasan-Rokem*, edited by Hagar Salamon and Avigdor Shinan, 1:225–35 (in Hebrew), 1:xviii–xix (English abstract). Jerusalem: Hebrew University of Jerusalem, Mandel Institute of Jewish Studies.

Lathrop, Tom. 2006. "Edith Grossman's Translation of *Don Quixote*." *Cervantes* 26, no. 1 (Spring): 237–55.

Mackey, Mary. 1974. "Rhetoric and Characterization in *Don Quijote*." *Hispanic Review* 42, no. 1 (Winter): 51–66.

Madariaga, Salvador de. 1934. *Don Quixote: An Introductory Essay in Psychology.* London: Oxford University Press.

Mal Lara, Juan de. 1568. *La philosophía vulgar.* 4 vols. Seville, Spain: Hernando Diaz. Rpt., edited by Inoria Pepe Sarno and José-María Reyes Cano. Madrid: Ediciones Cátedra, 2013.

Mann, Thomas. (1934) 2001. "Voyage with *Don Quixote*." Translated by Helen Tracy Lowe-Porter. In *Cervantes's "Don Quixote,"* edited by Harold Bloom, 13–45. Philadelphia: Chelsea House.

Martín, Adrienne L. 2002. "Humor and Violence in Cervantes." In *The Cambridge Companion to Cervantes*, edited by Anthony J. Cascardi, 160–85. Cambridge: Cambridge University Press.

McGrath, Michael J. 2006. "Tilting at Windmills: *Don Quijote* in English." *Cervantes* 26, no. 1 (Spring): 7–40.

Menéndez-Pidal, Ramón. 1947. "The Genesis of *Don Quixote*." In *Cervantes Across the Centuries*, edited by Angel Flores and M. J. Benardete, 32–55. New York: Dryden Press. Also in *Cervantes' "Don Quixote": A Casebook*, edited by Roberto González Echevarría, 63–94. New York: Oxford University Press, 2005.

Mieder, Wolfgang. 1974. "The Essence of Literary Proverb Studies." *Proverbium* 23: 888–94.

Mieder, Wolfgang. 1993. *Proverbs Are Never Out of Season: Popular Wisdom in the Modern Age.* New York: Oxford University Press. Rpt., New York: Peter Lang, 2012.

Mieder, Wolfgang, ed. 1994. *Wise Words: Essays on the Proverb*. New York: Garland Publishing. Rpt., Abingdon, Oxon., England: Routledge, 2015.

Mieder, Wolfgang, ed. 2004a. *The Netherlandish Proverbs: An International Symposium on the Pieter Brueg(h)els*. Burlington: University of Vermont.

Mieder, Wolfgang. 2004b. *Proverbs: A Handbook*. Westport, CT: Greenwood Press. Rpt., New York: Peter Lang, 2012.

Mieder, Wolfgang. 2006a. "From 'Windmills in One's Head' to 'Tilting at Windmills': History and Meaning of a Proverbial Allusion to Cervantes' *Don Quixote*." *Proverbium* 23: 343–418.

Mieder, Wolfgang. 2006b. *"Tilting at Windmills": History and Meaning of a Proverbial Allusion to Cervantes' "Don Quixote."* Burlington: University of Vermont.

Mieder, Wolfgang. 2009. *International Bibliography of Paremiology and Phraseology*. 2 vols. Berlin: Walter de Gruyter.

Mieder, Wolfgang. 2011. *International Bibliography of Paremiography: Collections of Proverbs, Proverbial Expressions and Comparisons, Quotations, Graffiti, Slang, and Wellerisms*. Burlington: University of Vermont.

Mieder, Wolfgang. 2014. *Behold the Proverbs of a People: Proverbial Wisdom in Culture, Literature, and Politics*. Jackson: University Press of Mississippi.

Mieder, Wolfgang. 2016. *"Stringing Proverbs Together": The Proverbial Language in Miguel de Cervantes's "Don Quixote."* Burlington: University of Vermont.

Mieder, Wolfgang, and George B. Bryan. 1996. *Proverbs in World Literature: A Bibliography*. New York: Peter Lang.

Morel-Fatio, Alfred. 1882. "Al buen callar llaman Sancho." *Romania* 11, no. 41 (January): 114–19.

Nabokov, Vladimir. (1951–1952) 1983. *Lectures on "Don Quixote."* Edited by Fredson Bowers. New York: Harcourt Brace Jovanovich.

Neumeister, Sebastian. 1994. "Geschichten vor und nach dem Sprichwort." In *Kleinstformen der Literatur*, edited by Walter Haug and Burghart Wachinger, 205–15. Tübingen, Germany: Max Niemeyer.

Nuessel, Frank H. 1999. "Linguistic Theory and Discourse in *Don Quijote*." In *Advances in Hispanic Linguistics: Papers from the 2nd Hispanic Linguistics Symposium*, edited by Javier Gutiérrez-Rexach and Fernando Martínez-Gil, 1:248–64. Somerville, MA: Cascadilla Press, 1999. Also in *Linguistic Approaches to Hispanic Literature*, by Frank Nuessel, 97–114. Brooklyn: Legas, 2000.

Núñez, Hernán. 1555. *Refranes o proverbios en romance*. Salamanca, Spain: Juan de Canova. Rpt., edited by Louis Combet, Julia Sevilla Muñoz, Germán Conde Tarrío, and Josep Guia i Marín. Madrid: Guillermo Blázquez, 2001.

O'Kane, Eleanor S. 1950. "The Proverb: Rabelais and Cervantes." *Comparative Literature* 2, no. 4 (Autumn): 360–69.

Paczolay, Gyula. 1997. *European Proverbs in 55 Languages with Equivalents in Arabic, Persian, Sanskrit, Chinese and Japanese*. Veszprém, Hungary: Veszprémi Nyomda.

Parr, James A., and Lisa Vollendorf, eds. 2015a. *Approaches to Teaching Cervantes's "Don Quixote."* 2nd ed. New York: Modern Language Association of America.

Parr, James A., and Lisa Vollendorf. 2015b. "The Instructor's Library." In *Approaches to Teaching Cervantes's "Don Quixote,"* 2nd ed., edited by James A. Parr and Lisa Vollendorf, 17–31. New York: Modern Language Association of America.

Quint, David. 2005. "Cervantes's Method and Meaning." In *Miguel de Cervantes*, edited by Harold Bloom, 277–99. Philadelphia: Chelsea House.

Raymond, Joseph. 1951. "Attitudes and Cultural Patterns in Spanish Proverbs." PhD diss., Columbia University.

Riley, Edward C. 1962. *Cervantes's Theory of the Novel*. Oxford: Oxford University Press.

Riley, Edward C. 1986. *Don Quixote*. London: Allen and Unwin.

Rivers, Elias L. 1984. "Voices and Texts in *Don Quixote*." In *Approaches to Teaching Cervantes' "Don Quixote,"* edited by Richard Bjornson, 113–19. New York: Modern Language Association of America.

Rosenblat, Ángel. 1971. "El refranero y el habla de Sancho." In *La lengua del "Quijote,"* 35–43. Madrid: Editorial Gredos.

Russell, P. E. 1985. *Cervantes*. Oxford: Oxford University Press.

Schipper, Mineke. 2003. *Never Marry a Woman with Big Feet: Women in Proverbs from Around the World*. New Haven, CT: Yale University Press.

Serrano-Plaja, Arturo. 1970. *"Magic" Realism in Cervantes: "Don Quixote" as Seen Through "Tom Sawyer" and "The Idiot."* Translated by Robert S. Rudder. Berkeley: University of California Press.

Sevilla Muñoz, Julia. 1993. "Fuentes paremiológicas francesas y españolas en la primera mitad del siglo XVII." *Revista de Filología Románica* 10: 357–69.

Sobieski, Janet, and Wolfgang Mieder, eds. 2005. *"So Many Heads, So Many Wits": An Anthology of English Proverb Poetry*. Burlington: University of Vermont.

Stavans, Ilan. 2015. *"Quixote": The Novel and the World*. New York: W. W. Norton.

Sullivan, Henry W. 2005. "The Two Projects of the *Quixote* and the Grotesque as Mode." In *Miguel de Cervantes*, edited by Harold Bloom, 225–41. Philadelphia: Chelsea House.

Suñé Benages, Juan. 1929. *Fraseología de Cervantes: Colección de frases, refranes, proverbios, aforismos, adagios, expresiones y modos adverbiales que se leen en las obras cervantinas*. Barcelona: Editorial Lux.

Thacker, Jonathan. 2015. "*Don Quixote* in English Translation." In *Approaches to Teaching Cervantes's "Don Quixote,"* 2nd ed., edited by James A. Parr and Lisa Vollendorf, 32–47. New York: Modern Language Association of America.

Vallés, Pedro. 1549. *Libro de refranes*. Zaragoza, Spain: Juana Millán.

Vargas Llosa, Mario. 2010. "A Novel for the Twenty-First Century." In *Miguel de Cervantes's "Don Quixote,"* edited by Harold Bloom, new ed., 57–68. New York: Chelsea House.

Weiger, John G. 1985. *The Substance of Cervantes*. Cambridge: Cambridge University Press.

Zurdo Ruiz-Ayúcar, María I. Teresa. 2014. "Recursos aplicados para la transmisión del componente cultural en traducciones de *La Celestina* y del *Quijote*." *Paremia* 23: 35–44.

9

"ALL ROADS LEAD TO 'PERVERBS'"

Harry Mathews's *Selected Declarations of Dependence* (1977)

It has long been a commonplace that proverbs are not at all such rigidly structured statements as older definitions of this verbal folklore genre have claimed. In fact, they are often varied for syntactical reasons, only their "kernel" element is cited (Norrick 1985, 45), or they are deliberately parodied or satirized by word substitutions or short additions that put their supposed wisdom into question. The frequently employed proverbs with their claim to truth quite literally encourage speakers and writers, in agreement with Johan Huizinga's concept of "homo ludens" (1938), to "play" with these preformulated and perhaps too often cited insights into life and existence (Röhrich 1967, 181). This tendency to alter traditional proverbs is nothing new and has been attested in written documents throughout the ages, with William Shakespeare being a master in the syntactical and semantic manipulation of proverbs. But the bard is by no means an exception, with Bertolt Brecht, for example, being a more modern author who delighted in contradicting proverbial wisdom (Mieder 1998). But no matter how striking the reformulation might be, it is the interplay of tradition and innovation that adds to the communicative effectiveness of such "anti-proverbs" (Mieder 2004b, 28, 150–53), as these games with proverbs have been called internationally (for numerous other designations in different languages, see Litovkina 2015, 326–27; Litovkina and Lindahl 2007).

In the following deliberations, I will concern myself with primarily one type of anti-proverb, namely the deliberate mixture of the halves of different proverbs to create sensical or nonsensical statements. The humorous or insightful creations go beyond the two traditional proverbs, but clearly it is part of the game to recognize the two old proverbs involved. An example might be the anti-proverb "Strike while the heart grows fonder," based on the two well-known proverbs "Strike while the iron is hot" and "Absence makes the heart grow fonder." It is important to note that such proverbial play is nothing new (Röhrich 1967, 183–84), with aphoristic writers quite often basing their texts on such proverbial scramblings (Mieder 1999). Collections of anti-proverbs from humor magazines, books of humorous one-liners, and the mass media are replete with such "fun" texts for the entertainment of the reader. In this regard I delight in mentioning two unique books in my International Proverb Archives both at the University of Vermont and in my extensive private library at my country home in Williston, Vermont. Günter Lux had the splendid idea in the former German Democratic Republic to publish the two fascinating illustrated books *Die Axt im Hause wird selten fett: Ein Smalcalda-Sprichwort-Bastelbuch* (1981) and *Morgenstund ist aller Laster Anfang: Sprichwörter zum Selberbasteln* (1987). They cite 206 and 256 German proverbs, respectively, with each proverb occupying one page in such a way that the page can be cut, leaving one half of the proverb on the top and the other half on the bottom. By flipping the pages, literally hundreds if not thousands of anti-proverbs can be constructed, some with new insights, others with absurd statements or absolutely senseless mutations.

Actually, this is meant to have some fun with overused proverbs. This is also the case with a proverbial present that the Swiss advertising agency Woodtli sent out to its customers as a New Year's present. It basically consists of a round cardboard disk with the first half of twenty-seven German proverbs inscribed on a turnable part of the disk, while the other proverb halves are inscribed on the outer circle. By turning the inner circle, a good number of anti-proverbs become visible. In a way, this game shows exactly what advertising copywriters do when they formulate catchy slogans based on proverbial structures to add some hidden authority to their messages (Mieder 1985, 37). But as the East German writer Franz Fühmann (1922–1984) reported in 1974, such a device is really not needed in order to add some proverbial life to a party. All that is needed is to divide proverbs into two halves and write them on the front and back sides of a small paper card. After mixing the cards, players draw two of them and read out the resulting anti-proverbs (Fühmann 1974, 224–25; Mieder 1985). And there really is no end to such play with proverbs. Thus, at a party in December 1979 in Burlington, Vermont, I came across a cocktail napkin with the inscription "Scrambled Sayings" and the following list of anti-proverbs based on proverb halves:

> All that glitters is the root of all evil
> No fool makes waste
> Money is not gold
> Haste before you buy
> Look like an old fool
> One man's drink is a dangerous thing
> A little learning is another man's poison

The seven traditional proverbs clearly are "All that glitters is not gold," "No fool like an old fool," "Money is the root of all evil," "Haste makes waste," "Look before you leap [changed to buy]," "One man's meat [changed to drink!] is another man's poison," and "A little learning is a dangerous thing." Whether one or more of these anti-proverbs contain any new wisdom is questionable, but the little napkin could very well have served as a conversation starter at the cocktail party!

What clearly is more interesting is that there are poets who have had their "fun" with scrambling proverbs. The German poet Fred Endrikat (1890–1942) titled one of his poems "Sprichwörter" (c. 1930), indicating right from the start that he is dealing with proverbs, with his readers quickly noticing that he is scrambling them:

> Man darf den Tag nicht vor dem Abend dankbar sein
> und soll das Schicksal nicht für alles loben.
> Ein Gutes kommt niemals allein,
> und alles Unglück kommt von oben.
> Die Peitsche liegt im Weine.
> Die Wahrheit liegt beim Hund.
> Morgenstund hat kurze Beine.
> Lügen haben Gold im Mund.
> Ein Meister nie allein bellte.
> Vom Himmel fallen keine Hunde.
> Dem Glücklichen gehört die Welt.
> Dem Mutigen schlägt keine Stunde.
> (Mieder 1990, 32)

Hansgeorg Stengel (1922–2003), another German poet, gave his tour-de-force poem the title "Extempore" (1969), perhaps thereby signaling that he is mixing up these proverbs without any particular plan. Somehow one is reminded of the games already described in which the proverbial chips can fall wherever they may:

> Wo man hobelt, kräht kein Hahn,
> grober Klotz ist halb gewonnen.
> Was sich neckt, ist alt getan,
> wie gebettet, so zerronnen.
>
> Blindes Huhn sieht mehr als zwei,
> steter Tropfen kommt von oben,
> Aug um Aug verdirbt den Brei,
> Ende gut ist aufgeschoben.

238   PROVERBS IN LITERATURE

Gottes Mühlen beißen nicht,
keine Rose hat zwei Seiten,
wenn sie auch die Wahrheit spricht.
Guter Rat krümmt sich beizeiten.

Frisch gewagt, fällt selbst hinein,
unrecht Gut will Weile haben.
Morgenstunde höhlt den Stein,
wer zuletzt lacht, liegt begraben.
(Mieder 1990, 113)

But this is not just a German phenomenon, as the quite modern poem "Symposium" (1995) by the Canadian poet Paul Muldoon (b. 1951) illustrates. He plays primarily with proverb halves, but he also includes a few proverbial expressions. The title of the poem seems to suggest the empty chatter that might take place at yet another cocktail party at a scholarly conference, where segments of sentences seem to fill the room without any cohesive message being expounded:

You can lead a horse to water but you can't make it hold
its nose to the grindstone and hunt with the hounds.
Every dog has a stitch in time. Two heads? You've been sold
one good turn. One good turn deserves a bird in the hand.

A bird in the hand is better than no bread.
To have your cake is to pay Paul.
Make hay while you can still hit the nail on the head.
For want of a nail the sky might fall.

People in glass houses can't see the wood
for the new broom. Rome wasn't built between two stools.
Empty vessels wait for no man.

A hair of the dog is a friend indeed.
There's no fool like the fool
who's shot his bolt. There's no smoke after the horse is gone.
(Sobieski and Mieder 2005, 173)

Careful reading of this unique sonnet (!) reveals that Muldoon actually breaks the mold of cutting proverbs into halves and randomly rearranging them. He only picks one of the proverb halves in each case and ignores the other halves. That is innovative enough, once again resulting in some statements that make some sense, but the poem in its entirety presents a chaotic picture of a gathering of unconnected voices.

What these remarks thus far have shown is that the intentional variation, manipulation, alienation, or perversion of proverbs is nothing new—not even the amassing of parts of proverbs into poems of sorts. This deliberate play with proverbs has been practiced by aphoristic writers for centuries, with Georg Christoph Lichtenberg, Friedrich Nietzsche, Karl Kraus, and Gerhard Uhlenbruck coming to mind as impressive German practitioners of this entertaining and thought-provoking art form, which is so prevalent that one can speak of a genre of "proverbial aphorisms" (Mieder 1999; Mieder 2010). It is well known, of course, that France has a long tradition of aphoristic writing as well, and so it should not be surprising that there has been a modern preoccupation with proverbial aphorisms—often as anti-proverbs—there as well. The French author, critic, and linguist Jean Paulhan (1884–1968) had kindled the interest of linguistically inclined intellectuals in proverbial matters with his intriguing essay "L'expérience du proverbe" ([1913] 1966), in which he explains how he learned to understand and use Malagasy proverbs while spending some time on the island of Madagascar. As he made progress acquiring knowledge of the native language, he realized that there was something missing, leading him to also master the proverbial language. He understood proverbs as signs that play an important role in verbal communication (Syrotinski 1989, 13–55). With this interest in proverbs in mind, the French surrealist Paul Éluard (1895–1952) even founded the short-lived journal *Proverbe* (six issues between February 1920 and July 1921), which published papers questioning the meaning of words and phrases by way of innovative manipulations and alienations (Baudouin 1970; Siepe 1977, 45). A few years after the experimental journal had folded, Éluard and his friend Benjamin Péret (1899–1959) published a small collection of "152 proverbes mis au goût du jour" (1925), which were not traditional proverbs but rather surrealistic one-liners based to a considerable degree on them—they played with proverbial language to create anti-proverbs. Here are but a few examples together with English translations by Ela Kotkowska (2004–2005):

Une maîtresse en mérite une autre. (no. 2)
One mistress deserves another.

Il faut rendre à la paille ce qui appartient à la pouter. (no. 5)
Render unto the mote that which is the beam's.

Quand un œuf case des œufs, c'est qu'il n'aime pas les omelettes. (no. 13)
If an egg breaks an egg, it must not like omelettes.

240 PROVERBS IN LITERATURE

While these examples somewhat make sense, there are also others in which the proverbial transformations appear to be without any rhyme or reason and are just arbitrary substitutions that render the underlying proverbs into surrealistic word combinations (Genette 1993, 53).

Be that as it may, this play with proverbs became an essential part of the production of the French avant-garde literary society Oulipo (Ouvroir de Littérature Potentielle), which was founded by Raymond Queneau (1903–1976) and François Le Lionnais (1901–1984) in 1960 in Paris. Its small group of members dedicated to experimental writing was committed to overcoming any type of structural or stylistic restrictions and created texts that pushed language to its very limits. They are by no means easy to comprehend (if at all), and they require active work on part of readers to decipher what often seems to make no sense. Above all, their usually short writings are a game to be enjoyed and to be meditated upon. They also show, of course, what can be done with language once any linguistic constraints are overcome. Warren F. Motte Jr. has described this fascinating modus operandi in the valuable introduction to his book *Oulipo: A Primer of Potential Literature* (1986):

Scriptor Ludens, Lector Ludens
The Oulipian text is quite explicitly offered as a game, as a system of ludic exchange between author and reader. [. . .] The key word is exploration [. . . , which] demands the reader's participation, refusing on behalf of the latter any possibility of passivity toward the literary text. [. . .] Thus, to the concept of potential writing corresponds that of potential reading. [. . .] Serious and playful intent are not mutually exclusive in the Oulipo's ludic spirit: they are, on the contrary, insistently and reciprocally implicative. [. . .] At its heart is the belief that play is central to literature and, in a broader sense, to the aesthetic experience; in this, Oulipians fervently concur with Johan Huizinga, who asserted that "all poetry is born of play," extending his argument from poetry to culture itself. (Motte 1986, 20–22)

This at times contrived play with language, which could involve writing texts where all words lack a certain vowel or where certain phrasal units are manipulated according to mathematical patterns, does in fact require active readers who might well be discouraged by this unconventional writing. Such experimentation can also involve texts that are based on "perverted proverbs" or in French *perverbes* (*proverbes pervertés*), a term that is sometimes used for the more common "anti-proverb" (Villers 2014, 236, 418).

In one of the consecutively numbered issues of *Bibliothèque Oulipienne*, which appeared as small pamphlets, Marcel Bénabou (b. 1939) has a bit of

HARRY MATHEWS'S *SELECTED DECLARATIONS OF DEPENDENCE*   241

"fun" with what he calls "Locutions introuvables" (undiscoverable, untraceable proverbial expressions). What follows is just one example of his playful method. The title "Les œufs et la poule" indicates the subject matter, and when he starts the first group of invented proverbial phrases with "Mettre tous ses œufs . . ." and the second group with "Tuer la poule . . .," his readers will most likely think of the well-known proverbial expressions "Mettre tous ses œufs dans le même panier" and "Tuer la poule aux œufs d'or." Juxtaposing these phrases with Bénabou's phrasal inventions along with accompanying definitions will doubtlessly result in humor and perhaps sometimes more than that:

> *Les œufs et la poule.*
> Mettre tous ses œufs en Espagne: s'entourer de précautions inefficaces.
> Mettre tous ses œufs en poupe: prendre de gros risques.
> Mettre tous ses œufs dans le plat: utiliser toutes ses ressources.
> Mettre tous ses œufs aux corneilles: tenter sa chance.
> Mettre tous ses œufs dnas le jardin de quelqu'un: être indiscret, s'imposer, être importun.
> Tuer la poule dans le plat: attendre le denier moment pur s'acquitter d'une tâche indispensable.
> Tuer la poule devant les boeufs: faire un exemple.
> Tuer la poule sur le feu: agier de façon précipitée.
> Tuer la poule dans la bergerie: agir avec dissimulation.
> (Bénabou 1990, 147)

About ten years later, Bénabou published another *Bibliothèque Oulipienne* pamphlet with the title *Rendre à Cézanne: Locutions se rapportant à un seul peintre* (1993), which clearly alludes to the proverb "Render unto Caesar that which is Caesar's." This time, he took standard proverbs and substituted key words with the names of famous painters and then provided interesting accounts to justify the substitutions. Here is one of the shorter ones:

> *Au pays des aveugles, les Brown sont rois.*
> Ford Madox Brown (1821–1893), proche des préraphaélites, est demeuré longtemps comme le modèle des peintres surévalués: méconnu la plupart des connaisseurs, mais porté aux nues par quelques ignorants. Il est juste cependant de noter que cette situation s'est aujourd'hui modifiée, et que Brown jouit désormais d'une reputation bien meilleure. (Bénabou 1993, 10–11)

This and other texts like it indicate that the "perverbes" can also be telling statements that become clear as one reads the accompanying texts, which show an impressive knowledge of art history.

Following this issue of *Bibliothèque Oulipienne* in the same year was François Caradec's (1924–2008) *105 proverbes liftés suivis de quelques proverbes soldés* (1993), of but thirteen pages. But there is an important two-page preface explaining that many of the old proverbs in proverb collections are not understood any longer today and that they need "un sérieux 'lifting'":

> Comment un jeune Français peut-il comprendre un précepte de saine morale tel que "Qui vole un œuf vole un bœuf," alors qu'il sait que les œufs se vendent généralement par boîtes de douze et qu' "il ne faut pa smettre la charrue avant les bœufs" alors que les charrues ne sont plus tirées par des bœufs, mais par les tracteurs? Ne comprendraient-ils pas mieux si on leur disait:

> > Qui vole un vélo vole un auto.
> > Il ne faut pas mettre la charrue avant le tracteur.

> Le langage cuit lui-même a besoin aujourd'hui d'être réchauffé au four à micro-ondes, et les proverbes d'être liftées. C'est ce que nous avons fait pour un certain nombre d'entre eux, en espérant que cet exemple sera suivi. (Caradec 1993, 6)

Caradec need not have worried, since this type of rejuvenation of traditional proverbs via their change to anti-proverbs is as popular today as ever in almost all modes of communication, especially in proverbial aphorisms, advertising slogans, newspaper headlines, memes, and websites. Here are but a few of his examples:

> L'homme ne vit pas seulement de pain Poilâne.
> Il ne faut pas réveiller le député qui dort.
> Les chiens aboient, la caravane du Tour de France passe.
> Autres temps, autres faits de société.
> La critique est aisée, mais l'Oulipo difficile.
> (Caradec 1993, 8–9, 13)

The last text is telling insofar as it is indeed easy to criticize the linguistic play of the Oulipians, but it is at times also quite difficult to decipher their innovative proverbial messages as sensible statements. But again, it deserves to be mentioned that such proverb manipulations are not as "new" as the members of Oulipo seem to think. What is of importance is that these French intellectuals play with proverbs just as people of all walks of life have done for a long time for various reasons, from mere linguistic play to serious and necessary changes of old proverbial wisdom as the worldviews of modern societies change. No wonder that new proverbs are becoming current as well, something to which paremiologists need to pay much more attention (Mieder 2012). Many of them did in fact start as anti-proverbs based on established proverbs and their structures, but in a relatively short time they can become new proverbs in their own right, as *The Dictionary of Modern Proverbs* (2012) edited by Charles Clay Doyle, Wolfgang Mieder, and Fred R. Shapiro can attest.

While the Oulipians were primarily French, there was one American in the group, namely the novelist, poet, essayist, and translator Harry Mathews. He was born on February 14, 1930, in New York City, attended Princeton University in 1949, transferred to Harvard in 1950, and graduated in 1952 with a bachelor's degree in music. He then moved with his artist wife Niki de Saint Phalle to Paris, but the couple divorced in 1960, having had two children, Laura (b. 1951) and Philip (b. 1955). He subsequently married the writer Marie Chaix, with whom he lived in Paris, Key West, and New York from 1972 until his death on January 25, 2017. After befriending the Oulipian Georges Perec (1936–1982) in Paris in 1970 (Mathews 2003, 86), he was, beginning in 1973, "for decades [the] sole American member of Oulipo, the quirky French literary salon where authors and mathematicians practice what they call constrained writing: forcing themselves to follow contrived formulas—for example, using specific words or leaving out certain letters" (Roberts 2017; see also Tillman 1989, 10–11). Applying intricate mathematical patterns to some of his literary constructions, he developed "Mathews's algorithm: a set of rules that, applied in a prescribed order to a set of data, produces a particular result, no matter what the data may be" (Mathews 2005, 183). He explained this method in great detail in his 1981 essay "L'algorithme de Mathews," stating that "from the reader's point of view, the existence in literature of potentiality in its Oulipian sense has the charm of introducing duplicity into all written texts" (Mathews 1986, 126; Mathews 2003, 301). Part of the reader's challenge or joy is to figure out the linguistic signs that Mathews employs in his playful or contrived texts. "He takes semiotics out of the seminar and makes it live as fiction. [. . .] Language, in all of its many-meaninged, ambiguous, tragicomic potential, is itself his subject matter" (Stonehill 1982, 107).

There is then no doubt that Harry Mathews was a "literary maverick" whose "intellectual games" with language result in a challenging "multiplicity and ambiguity" (Leamon 1993, ix). His strategies and games with language are enigmas for readers, who find themselves perplexed by the infinity of possible conclusions about what it all might just mean (Mottram 1987, 159–60). Most likely influenced by such French surrealists as Paul Éluard and Benjamin Péret and his fellow Oulipians, Mathews turned to proverbs in his collection of French poems published as *Le Savoir des Rois: Poèmes à perverbes* (1976), which was published as the fifth issue of *Bibliothèque Oulipienne*. The title signifies that he will be changing proverbs into "perverbes" or anti-proverbs. The permutational "game" that Mathews is playing in these poems is well explained by Warren F. Motte Jr., the well-informed author of *Oulipo: A Primer of Potential Literature* (1986):

> These texts are based on the principle of the "perverb" [the English spelling of *perverbe*], a form which juxtaposes the first part of a given proverb to the second part of another: most of the poems in *Le Savoir des Rois* consist of a series of perverbs, each constituting a verse. Several things become apparent, even from this skeletal description. The ludic aspect of the exercise is suggested by the name "perverb"; the latter in turn, granted its phonetic and graphic form, which truncates and juxtaposes the words "pervert" and "proverb," emblematizes the function to which it refers. That function is itself clearly combinatoric, and when an entire poem is composed of perverbs, a second-order combinatoric system is elaborated, insofar as the various half-proverbs may recur within the text according to a given pattern. Finally, the proverb is a privileged locus for transformational play.
>
> If proverbs do offer such a fertile field for transformation, it is undoubtedly because they are so easily recognizable. That is, a certain sort of transformation, one that explicitly points to itself as such, relies on the identification of the hypotext within the hypertext. In the case of the perverb, the hypotext is constituted by the two initial proverbs, the hypertext by the perverb which results from them. Proverbs are easily recognizable and, paradoxically perhaps, almost transparent semantically: through use, their semantic aspect tends to erode. This, too, can be exploited in transformation. (Motte 1987, 95)

But here then is an example of Mathews's permutational poetics based on perverted proverbs. It is called "Du mouvement des roses" and has as a two-line motto "On revient toujours / Malheureux en amour." These two proverb halves, based on the proverbs "On revient toujours à ses premières amours" and "Heureux en jeu, malheureux en amour," are repeated as leitmotifs in each of the twelve stanzas that contain numerous other fragmented proverbs. Its beginning goes like this:

> Jeux de mains comme les rivières dans la mer!
> Plaisir d'amour ne dure qu'un instant, et Dieu pour soi!
> L'amour ôte l'esprit à ceux qui en ont et rentre par la fenêtre.
> Dans le royaume des aveugles, à ses premières amours.

HARRY MATHEWS'S *SELECTED DECLARATIONS OF DEPENDENCE* 245

(Tant va la cruche à l'eau que bon mari.)
L'homme propose, malheuereux en amour:
L'enfer des femmes fait danser les marrons.
Savoir dissimuler? Chagrin d'amour dure toute une vie.
Jeu de mains fait danser les marrons:
Plaisir d'amour ne dure qu'un instant? Il rentre par la fenêtre!
L'amour ôte l'esprit à ceux qui en ont (et bonnet blanc),
Nature est mère à ses premières amours:
"A vaillant cœur, bon mari!"
Rien ne sert de courir, malheuereux en amour!
L'enfer des femmes, *c'est il se fait ermite*;
Quand le diable est vieux, chagrin d'amour dure toute une vie.
(Mathews 1976, 89)

And on and on it goes for ten more stanzas in this fashion without any particular rhyme or reason (Güell 1999, 263–64). It is not even clear what the title of this tour-de-force perverb poem is meant to signify, since roses do not appear anywhere. Or are "roses" here metaphors for proverbs that are moved around? As one begins to read this long text, the missing proverb halves are recalled, and one is eager to read on to discover them. Clearly Mathews is activating the reader to go on a paremiological trip of sorts. In any case, as one reads this long poem, one is perhaps reminded of standing in front of Pieter Bruegel's 1559 oil painting *Netherlandish Proverbs* in the Gemäldegalerie in Berlin with its minute illustrations of over one hundred proverbs and proverbial expressions (Mieder 2004a). Part of the "fun and games" is to identify as many of the proverbial scenes and their verbal background as possible (Dundes and Stibbe 1981), and this is what Mathews seems to be intending with his verbal collage of numerous halves of the French proverb repertoire.

With the other poems along these lines included in this book, Mathews certainly established himself as the "perverbes" poet par excellence. They obviously cannot be considered here in detail, but a literary-minded paremiologist with a solid command of the French language could still make a considerable research project out of this *Bibliothèque Oulipienne* publication. Suffice it to add a somewhat different proverb poem by Harry Mathews, which he titled "Insomnies" and included in his collection *Écrits français* (1990). It is composed of eight four-line stanzas, each with three lines beginning with "La nuit" and ending with "tous les chats sont gris." In this manner, the two halves of the proverb "La nuit, tous les chats sont gris" frame the rest of the messages, with the entire poem giving the impression that during insomnia everything is blurred into a grayish matter. And true to his proverbial method, a few random proverb halves also appear. The poem starts like this and continues for six more stanzas:

246 PROVERBS IN LITERATURE

La nuit, jeux de vilains;
La nuit, tous les vices;
La nuit, tout se remplace,
Plaisir d'amour ne dure qu'un instant, tous les chats sont gris.
La nuit, on jette l'écorce.
La nuit a ses premières amours.
La nuit fait danser les marrons—
L'amour ôte l'esprit à ceux qui en ont, et tous les chats sont gris.
(Mathews 1990, 343)

Such poems are isolated examples of Mathews's permutational art, which also spilled over into the prose texts and novels of this prolific writer (McPheron 1987), "well known in certain literary circles but largely unknown to the general reading public" (Leamon 1993, ix). This unfortunate situation is primarily due to the fact that most readers do not react favorably toward experimental literature like that practiced by the Oulipians and other modernist writers who set out to engage readers as active participants in their creations. Little wonder that Harry Mathews's quintessential "perverb" work, his novel (if one can call it that) *Selected Declarations of Dependence* (1977), remains quite neglected. Uninitiated readers opening this compendium of prose and poetry based to a large degree on perverted proverbs will most likely be perplexed, frustrated, confused, and more, but if willing to "stick with it" and take up the challenge of reading something truly unique, they will eventually be richly rewarded by this avant-garde, experimental, and permutational literary creation of close to two hundred pages. There is much to be discovered in Mathews's perverb creations based on "combined proverbs permuted until the mind is dizzied and the meaning transmogrified: 'Every cloud is another man's poison'; 'The road to Hell is paved with rolling stones'" (*Time* 1977, 67).

The reviews that appeared shortly after the 1977 publication of *Selected Declarations of Dependence* with the small Z Press in Calais, Vermont (republished in 1996 by Sun and Moon Press in Los Angeles) did not exactly help to spread the good word. Susan Shafarzek dedicated but ten lines to it, stating that the book "includes a novella and a collection of 'Proverbs and Paraphrases.' Mathews is one of the most interesting experimental prose writers in this country, and his work is not to be missed" (1977, 2488). The obvious question of "why?" is answered in a more telling review by A. Ross Eckler: "The book is based entirely on a group of 46 proverbs. Its first part contains a story written solely out of the words in the proverbs (a form of lipogrammetry), its second part supplies 106 brief anecdotes illustrating perverbs (respliced halves of proverbs, as 'the early bird gathers no moss'). As the perverbs and their anecdotes are randomly scrambled, the reader can have the fun of matching them up.

The book concludes with a clever parody of 'This Is the House that Jack Built' based on the words in the proverbs" (Eckler 1978, 49). This is quite to the point but fails to mention that poems also play a major role in this work. In a third review by an anonymous author, it is important to note that here the title of the book takes on somewhat of a meaning:

> Is this a New York School grammatical farce, replete with ripped-off proverbs and 80 camp "doggie" drawings differing only in value, not content? Yes and no. [Axel] Katz's dogs give away the game. Mathematical theme and variation is its name. Suppose the given were a structured repertoire of meaning (proverbs). Suppose they were randomly cut and pasted. What new fictions might result from the rearrangement of sense? Subtract, add, substitute, reveal. Mathews, poet and author of three novels, derives whole stories from a limited word structure. Experimenting with abstractions, he transforms narrative meaning and finally genre (fiction into poetry), demonstrating the shared dependencies between. (*Booklist* 1978, 1602)

Finally, there is David Lehman's longer review, which is part of his discussion of five literary works from the late 1970s. Stating that this book "has not yet received its critical due," he offers the following comments:

> Mathews is one of our great experimentalists, and *Selected Declarations of Dependence* is a magnificent feat of verbal gamesmanship, providing conclusive evidence of his ability to create a proliferation of texts from the least promising of origins, to harness the generative power of language through the agency of applied mathematical principles. The book's *donnée* is a set of well-worn proverbs, forty-six of them, that supply the "theme" for an apparently inexhaustible number of variations. Capitalizing on typos is one way of renewing a dead metaphor, as Mathews shows in such "Snips of the Tongue" as "The toad to help is paved with good intentions." A more reliable method involves the equivoque, an arcane form in which the first half of any given line couples with the second half of the following line. Mathews calls the results he comes up with "perverbs." (Lehman 1980, 147)

Realizing that his literary creations challenged readers accustomed to making sense of what they were reading, Mathews provided a helpful foreword to the 1996 edition of *Selected Declarations of Dependence* that agrees with what the earlier reviewers had said:

Selected Declarations of Dependence is based on a set of forty-six familiar proverbs, used and abused in various ways:

The forty-six proverbs provide the entire vocabulary of the opening story, "Their Words, For You."

The sections called "Perverbs and Paraphrases" explore the narrative implications of the crossed proverb or "perverb."

(Two suitable proverbs yield two perverbs—for example, "All roads lead to Rome" and "A rolling stone gathers no moss" supply, when crossed, the perverbs "All roads gather no moss" and "A rolling stone leads to Rome.") The perverbs that gave rise to the so-called paraphrases have been listed randomly in order to leave the pleasure of making appropriate connections to the reader. (Mathews 1996, 10)

Pleasure might also be substituted by anxiety or vexation, because the matchups of the paraphrases with the perverbs are to a certain degree unsolvable, forcing readers to put the book aside but maybe picking it up again later to find resolutions. This is what makes active readers as Mathews envisions them, as can be seen from his comment in an interview with Susannah Hunnewell in 2007: "The expectation is that books are supposed to reach conclusions that bring all things that have been going on to an end so the reader can stop thinking about them. I avoid conclusions, not just to frustrate readers but to make them realize that they're going to have to take the book for what it is—a piece of writing that exists on its own and whose essential interest is its process. Isn't that the way life is, after all? No conclusions, no escape, until the very end" (Hunnewell 2007, 86). Let me add here that I wish I had known about this statement when I first read this "perverb book," because it would have explained to me that I was supposed to feel unresolved!

Be that as it may, Harry Mathews also explains in this informative interview that in *Selected Declarations of Dependence* he gave himself "the task of writing a story using the one hundred and eighty-five words that were found in forty-six proverbs. This is a forbiddingly small vocabulary. It was hard to know what to do with them. Then I started putting words together and a few words would lead to a sentence and then eventually it became a sweet love story" (Hunnewell 2007, 83). Of course, he mentions nothing about the interspersed perverb poems, which appear to be created from random texts, placed helter-skelter among the prose. Yet again, if he intends to get his readers thinking and enjoying the mere play with these forty-six proverbs, then he certainly hits the mark. As Frederick Ted Castle has observed proverbially,

Left to itself, the mind and hand of Harry Mathews will make up a story often "out of the whole cloth," often taking a particular locution as a text,

HARRY MATHEWS'S *SELECTED DECLARATIONS OF DEPENDENCE*   249

or rather, of course, as a pretext. Harry might be able to write a whole book out of the phrase "out of the whole cloth"—I almost hesitate to suggest since he might take up the gauntlet and run with it. Indeed, as I often say, never count your chickens until your milk is spilt, a perversion of folk wisdom which is, needless to say, open to many a jibe and thrust. (Castle 1987, 119–20).

But enough of this, for the time has come to have a look at the forty-six proverbs that Harry Mathews selected for his absolutely unique book, one that undoubtedly deserves the Oulipian designation! Coy or sly as he is, he has not provided his readers with a list, and here then it is, in which I have arranged the proverbs alphabetically according to keywords:

1. A *bird* in the hand is worth two in the bush.
2. The early *bird* catches the worm.
3. In the kingdom (land) of the *blind*, the one-eyed is king (are kings).
4. Once *burned*, twice shy.
5. Render unto *Caesar* the things which are Caesar's.
6. Many are *called*, but few are chosen.
7. Lucky at *cards*, unlucky in love.
8. It's raining *cats* and dogs.
9. When the *cat's* away, the mice will play.
10. Every *cloud* has a silver lining.
11. Too many *cooks* spoil the broth.
12. Let the *dead* bury the dead.
13. The *devil* takes the hindmost.
14. Every *dog* has its day.
15. You can't teach an old *dog* new tricks.
16. Let sleeping *dogs* lie.
17. *East* is east, and west is west, and never the twain shall meet.
18. A *fool* and his money are soon parted.
19. Never look a *gift horse* in the mouth.
20. What *goes* up, must come down.
21. The *grass* is always greener on the other side of the fence.
22. You can lead a *horse* to water but you cannot make it drink.
23. Half a *loaf* is better than no bread.
24. *Look* before you leap.
25. *Man* proposes, God disposes.
26. One man's *meat* is another man's poison.
27. A *miss* is as good as a mile.
28. Great *oaks* from little acorns grow.

250 PROVERBS IN LITERATURE

29. You can't make an *omelet* without breaking eggs.
30. Any *port* in a storm.
31. It never *rains* but it pours.
32. The *road* to hell is paved with good intentions.
33. All *roads* lead to Rome.
34. *Rome* was not built in one day.
35. When in *Rome*, do as the Romans do.
36. *Six* of one or half a dozen of the other.
37. Red *sky* at night, sailor's delight; red sky in the morning, sailors take warning.
38. *Sticks* and stones may break my bones, but names will never hurt me.
39. A *stitch* in time saves nine.
40. A rolling *stone* gathers no moss.
41. Leave no *stone* unturned.
42. Never give a *sucker* an even break.
43. You can't *take* it with you.
44. *Time* and tide wait for no man.
45. Never put off till *tomorrow* what you can do today.
46. It's an ill *wind* that blows no good.

From a paremiological point of view, it would be of interest to know how Mathews came up with this list. It definitely includes well-known proverbs that belong to the paremiological minimum of English proverbs (Haas 2008), and it should be noted that he included such modern proverbs as "The grass is always greener on the other side of the fence" and "Never give a sucker an even break" (Doyle, Mieder, and Shapiro 2012). But it must be stated that "Six of one or half dozen of the other" and "Leave no stone unturned" are proverbial expressions. It is also surprising that Mathews included two "bird," two "cat," three "dog," two "horse," two "man," two "road," three "Rome," and two "stone" proverbs, because the repetitions of these nouns placed even more limitations on the different words from these proverbs that he could use in his "Their Words, For You" story. But all of this was, of course, his decision, and it can be assumed that the "their words" of the title refers to the words of the proverbs. Here then is the first chapter of this fascinating short novel, with the prose section made up of the words of the proverbs and the following poems being composed of proverb halves (scrambled or fused proverbs) called perverbs (Villers 2010, 12–13). One wonders how readers, uninitiated by the list of proverbs presented above, might have reacted to all of this:

Another morning, another egg. The sky was up early. It had rained all night: to you and me sleeping, the storm was a delight. In the east, morning clouds are building a kingdom of red and silver. Time for you to get up! Come into the kingdom of morning delight and come as king! Come into the omelet of morning delight, and come as egg!

You can't make an omelet without breaking half a dozen of the other. Take six eggs . . . Eggs are things—eggs were things: have an omelet. Have a little bread with it too. Cat! Come on Cat, you old dog, have little bread till it's bone time.

You're looking good today. What of going down the road to the port? No—you propose old-stone-gathering at the water side, and going into the water when the tide comes in.

You go with me down fences that teach the intentions of the men that dispose of the grass. A horse waits at a fence; another rolls on the grass, breaking wind. (Good for the horse—one should break wind when one has to, putting it off does no good.) At the side of the road dead grass is burning, old sticks and grass, burning silver in the morning. The road is a delight, with water on one side, oaks and grass on the other; and the grass leads away to another water. In the oaks you once gathered bird's eggs from moss.

From the road you can see the port, the old port paved with stones, paved with bones. Sailors gather in it at night, gathering on the night side of the port looking for the tricks and stitches of love.

> *God disposes*
>   *Red sky at night,*
> *Man proposes*
>   *Sailor's delight*

When the tide is coming in, sailors can drink and sleep. In the morning all leave on the early tide. Not all: a few go on sleeping.

> *All roads lead to good intentions;*
> *East is east and west is west, and God disposes;*
> *Time and tide in a storm.*
> *All roads, sailor's delight.*
> *(Many are called, sailors take warning:*
> *All roads wait for no man.)*
>
> *All roads are soon parted.*
> *East is east and west is west: twice shy.*
> *Time and tide bury their dead.*
> *A rolling stone, sailor's delight.*

"Any port" sailors take warning:
All roads are another man's poison.

All roads take the hindmost,
East is east and west is west and few are chosen,
Time and tide are soon parted,
The devil takes sailors' delight.
Once burned, sailors take warning:
All roads bury their dead.

All roads have a silver lining;
East is east and west is west in a storm;
Time and tide are as good as a mile.
East is east and west is west—sailor's delight.
(East is east and west is west, sailors take warning!)
All roads are worth two in the bush. (Mathews 1996, 12–16)

Reading just these pages, it becomes clear that Mathews presents an "ingeniously crafted language game, played out within carefully defined limits. [. . .] It is not life or reality or experience but language that creates the story" (Everman 1986, 465–66). Readers have to take the leap into this contrived world of words and halves of proverbs, perhaps best without looking for any definite answers to what it all is supposed to mean. Welch D. Everman, in his enlightening essay "Harry Mathews's *Selected Declarations of Dependence*: Proverbs and the Forms of Authority" (1987), provides as good an interpretation as possible, and before going on to some additional examples, I cite it here at some length:

> The source of Mathew's declarations is the proverb, that commonplace bit of conventional wisdom which seems to belong to no one and everyone. Proverbs are cultural clichés, secondhand language. In a sense, of course, all language is secondhand, but the proverb is a special case, because it is prepackaged. As a cliché, the proverb is a phrase or sentence that functions as a unit, as a sign in its own right, a sign that everyone understands immediately, without the need for thought and interpretation.
>
> But, of course, the proverb is a very special kind of cliché, for it bears within itself a formidable authority. Proverbs offer advice, but to use a proverb is not to speak with one's own limited authority. It is to speak with the authority of the entire culture which adopted the proverb as an expression of its collective wisdom. [. . .]

Mathews's explorations in *Selected Declarations of Dependence* are designed to maintain the discourse of proverbs but at the same time to undermine their collective authority by carefully dismantling them, perhaps in hopes of making them say something new. [...]

"Their Words, For You" is, indeed, a story built from the fragments of dismantled proverbs, and yet the words come together again and again on proverbial structures. The text generates many new proverbs, constructed from bits of old proverbs and sharing their traditional form but without their built-in authority. "Playing the fool is a delight fools cannot have." "Love disposes of cats and kings, but a good stitch never parts." Mathews also uses larger "pieces" [poems] of proverbs to create new proverbial combinations and permutations:

> In the kingdom of the blind, few are chosen.
> In the kingdom of the blind, sailors take warning.
> In the kingdom of the blind, unlucky in love.
> Many are called, but the one-eyed man is king.

These are declarations of dependence because the author and the texts depend on the words the culture has offered in its proverbs. In fact, *Selected Declarations of Dependence* is only a special case in the general field of writing which is always dependent on language as a given and, more particularly, on a given discourse within that language. (Everman 1987, 149–51)

These are insightful observations to be sure, but when Everman claims that Mathews's "text generates many new proverbs," he should better have spoken of "perverbs" or anti-proverbs. As is well known, some such new creations based on traditional proverbs and their structures can become new proverbs, but Mathews's texts would have to become much better known and more widely disseminated for that to occur with his playful inventions. And yet, Keith Cohen is correct in stating that when with some of these perverbs "a sudden revelation of possible profundity occurs, the result is hilarious, since one realizes that the perverb has been created entirely haphazardly. The aura of eternal verity hangs onto each segment, through a kind of proverb intertextuality, even though the words themselves are fairly ordinary" (Cohen 1987, 182).

While some of the "perverb" poems don't follow any discernible pattern except for fusing halves of proverbs randomly together, there are also poetic texts in which the same proverb half begins each stanza as a type of proverbial anaphora:

254   PROVERBS IN LITERATURE

> *Every cloud blows no good.*
>   You can't make an omelet in a storm.
>   *Red sky at morning waits for no man.*
>   *Time and tide gather no moss.*
>
> *Every cloud, sailors take warning.*
>   *"It never rains"?—twice shy.*
>   *It's an ill wind that has its day.*
>   East is east and west is west, but it pours.
>
> *Every cloud wasn't built in a day.*
>   All roads in a storm.
>   *Red sky at night, but God disposes.*
>   *Time and tide have their day.* (Mathews 1996, 18–20)

There are seven more stanzas along these lines to follow, with Mathews obviously delighting in the creation of these often senseless permutations. And yet, some of the perverbs do make sense under certain circumstances, showing that sense can come from nonsense in such linguistic games. What is not clear is why Mathews italicizes some of his perverbs and others not.

Another structural pattern that he employs in stanzas is starting lines one, two, and four with the same proverb half and line three with another proverb half, while the fifth line is completely different. Here are two of four stanzas of such a collage:

> *The early bird waits for no man.*
> *The early bird gathers no moss.*
>   *A bird in the hand is soon parted.*
> *The early bird gets what you can do today.*
>   Red sky at morning gets the worm.
>
> *The early bird is soon parted—*
> *The early bird is on the other side of the fence!*
>   *A bird in the hand is twice shy.*
> *The early bird leaves no stone unturned.*
>   A rolling stone gets the worm. (24)

Then again, Mathews might take the first half of the proverb "The road to hell is paved with good intentions" and compose a four-stanza poem in which all the lines begin with the same proverb half:

HARRY MATHEWS'S *SELECTED DECLARATIONS OF DEPENDENCE* 255

The road to Hell gets the worm.
The road to Hell gathers no moss.
The road to Hell leaves no stone unturned.

The road to Hell from little acorns grows.
The road to Hell is paved with rolling stones.
The road to Hell waits for no man.

The road to Hell takes the hindmost.
The road to Hell has its day.
The road to Hell spoils the broth.

The road to Hell has a silver lining:
The road to Hell wasn't built in a day.
On the road to Hell, do as the Romans do. (50–52)

But he might also take the two "horse" proverbs from his list of forty-six and arrange their first halves according to the same pattern, completing them with randomly selected proverb halves:

You can lead a horse to water without breaking eggs.
You can lead a horse to water, but do as the Romans do.
   A gift horse is always on the other side of the fence.

You can lead a horse to water and never the twain shall meet.
   You can lead a horse to water, but God disposes.
   Mighty gift horses from little silver linings grow . . . (70)

Finally, here are three nine-line stanzas that show the complexity of such tour-de-force proverb permutations with proverb halves. Each starts with "You can't make an omelet," and each has lines beginning with "One man's meat" and "Too many cooks" as well as two or even three lines starting with "Half a loaf." Each stanza also ends with the proverb half "spoil(s) the broth" as a leitmotif:

You can't make an omelet with good intentions:
Too many cooks are better than no bread.
One man's meat, as good as a mile,
Once burned, spoils the broth.
Too many cooks are worth two in the bush—
You can't make an omelet on the other side of the fence.

256 PROVERBS IN LITERATURE

Half a loaf is better than two in the bush—
Half a loaf in the storm!
It's an ill wind that spoils the broth.

You can't make an omelet—but few are chosen:
A fool and his money are better than no bread.
One man's meat gets the worm—
Look before you spoil the broth!
Too many cooks take the hindmost.
One man's meat is greener on the other side of the fence.
Half a loaf is better than no silver lining.
Half a loaf is better without breaking eggs:
Man proposes, and spoils the broth.

You can't make an omelet, and God disposes.
One man's meat is better than no bread.
One man's meat is worth two in the bush.
(Sticks and stones spoil the broth.)
Too many cooks, twice shy.
Half a loaf is better than the other side of the fence.
Half a loaf is as good as a mile.
Half a loaf has its day.
Many are called, but spoil the broth. (76)

As readers compare all of these perverbs, they will delight in discovering those that make at least some sense, for example "Look before you spoil the broth!," with its authoritative exclamation mark added to underscore its truth value. And yet, if I may say so, when the perverb narrative "Their Words, For You" with its poetic interludes comes to an end on page 85, readers most likely need a well-deserved break.

And yet, the second half of *Selected Declarations of Dependence*, with the title "First Derivations," confronts them with perhaps an even greater challenge. The verbal game of guessing (deducing) traditional proverbs from paraphrased statements is well established. I have played it at parties in Germany as well as the United States. Usually someone brings a list of the paraphrases, and people will try to come up with the proverbs behind them. Richard Lederer presents a section of examples in his book *The Play of Words: Fun and Games for Language Lovers* (1990, 219–23), with three typical examples being:

Integrity is the superlative strategy.
Proverb: Honesty is the best policy. (221)

Individuals who make their abode in vitreous edifices of patent frangibil-
ity are advised to refrain from catapulting petrous projectiles.
Proverb: People who live in glass houses should not throw stones. (222)

Refrain from enumerating the denta of gratuitous members of the
Equidae family.
Proverb: Don't look a gift horse in the mouth. (223)

The hidden proverbs are relatively easily found here, but Harry Mathews now
wants readers to discover his more complex perverbs behind his prose paraphrases (Loberer 1996, 2). He is kind enough to give an example at the beginning:

Perverbs and Paraphrases
"The sky was clear except for the fog rising to the east—fermentation
from the oak bog" is a *paraphrase* of the *perverb* "Every cloud from
little acorns grows." (Mathews 1996, 86)

But now the challenge starts, for this is not just reading perverbs any longer but
rather recalling those that fit certain paraphrases. Since honesty is the best policy,
let me admit that I had to give up eventually. Scholars who have tackled this text
have had the same reaction. Thus, Keith Cohen writes that "it is exceedingly
difficult to derive the original perverb from the paraphrases. One paraphrase
that I was able to decipher is 'Are acorns bitter?! Don't you remember when we
were camping and some fell in the soup?'—from 'Little acorns spoil the broth.'"
(Cohen 1987, 183). There are 106 paraphrase stories divided into four groups, each
followed by a list of possible perverbs to which they might be referring. That nar-
rows it down somewhat! In any case, here is one that Everman (1987, 151) solved:

He had won forty thousand francs at trente quarante, forty thousand
dollars at chemmy, and after the casino closed, forty thousand pounds
in a private poker game. Yet when I suggested he celebrate and have
some champagne, he did not even answer but raised his eyes to heaven
and cut the deck. (Mathews 1996, 110)
Perverb: Lucky at cards, but you can't make him drink. (122)

Daniel Becker (2012, 4) solved this one:

Two colossal representations of the Trinity had been raised on the Via
Appia Antica, the second immediately outside the city gates. (Mathews
1996, 136)
Perverb: Six of one lead to Rome. (144)

And here are three of the "perverbial" riddles untied by David Lehman (1980, 148):

> In ordinary circumstances his verboseness was less than dangerous. But compounded by a generous desire to share with his audience every detail of his money-making scheme, it produced a lecture so interminable that captain and officers fell asleep and failed to notice the clear portents of the ship's impending doom. (Mathews 1996, 108)
> *Perverb:* It's an ill wind that blows with good intentions. (122)

> In another version of the Polyphemus myth, the blinding with the lighted stake is part of the ritual enthronement of the Cyclops in his royal functions. (118)
> *Perverb:* Once burned, the one-eyed man is king. (122)

> Max smashed the truncheon across the bridge of my nose. Tony screwed the slabs sandwiching my right hand a notch tighter. They were approaching the point of permanent damage. I just kept grunting out the truth: I had spent thirteen hours with Phang, but there had been no way to administer the poison—in all that time he had not once raised to his lips as much as a glass of water or a cup of tea. (142)
> *Perverb:* Sticks and stones may break my bones, but you can't make him drink. (144)

May others try their luck at this vexing game, but as I said, I gave up after having solved only a few more of these perverbial conundrums.

For paremiologists, there is one more section in the book interspersed among all of this—perhaps to relax readers!—and that is "Snips of the Tongue" (124–28), where Mathews tries his hand at more traditional anti-proverbs that are simply formed by letter or word exchanges, or, as he would have it, by "snips of the tongue." Since there are not many, they are reproduced here entirely:

> Once burned, twice snide [shy].
> Every drug [dog] has its day.
> The road to help [hell] is paved with good intentions.
> Never pull [put] off tomorrow what you can do today.
> When in Rome, do as the Trojans [Romans] do.
> Half a loan [loaf] is better than no bread.
> Every crowd [cloud] has a silver lining.
> One man's meat is another man's person [poison].
> Look before you leave [leap].

A snitch [stitch] in time saves nine.
In the kingdom of the blind, the one-eyed man is kinky [king].
Too many cooks spoil the dwarf [broth].

These anti-proverbs are actually quite original, since with but one exception they do not appear in the largest collections of such intentional variations of proverbs. Mathews's "Never pull off tomorrow what you can do today" comes close to "Never pull off tomorrow what you can pull off today" from 1971 (Litovkina and Mieder 2006, 235), but his "Look before you leave" was recorded by me from a newspaper in 1981 (Mieder 1989, 274; Litovkina and Mieder 2006, 205). It is highly doubtful that the journalist was influenced by Mathews's anti-proverb from 1977, showing that polygenesis of such anti-proverbs does occur. But Mathews might have been surprised to learn in any case that his text is about twenty years older. We have recorded it in our *Dictionary of Modern Proverbs* as early as from 1958 on a poster urging drivers to be cautious when changing lanes: "Squeeze plays are preventable / Look before you leave" (Doyle, Mieder, and Shapiro 2012, 150).

In conclusion, let it be said that Harry Mathews's unique *Selected Declarations of Dependence* is a remarkable treasure trove of anti-proverbs, or "perverbes," as the French Oulipians and subsequently the French paremiologists like to call them. Manipulating traditional proverbs is nothing new, but Mathews created a literary work based on such intellectual play with them. It is a challenging book to be sure, but it is a delight to readers interested in play with language. It is a shame that the book has not received any attention from paremiologists thus far, and I hope that this introduction will change that. After all, the innovative transformations of traditional proverbs are part of cultural, folkloric, historical, and literary studies (Mieder 1987; Mieder 2008). Surely Harry Mathews would agree that "familiar proverbs, used and abused in various ways" (Mathews 1996, 10), continue to be part of oral and written communication in the modern world, and whether it is *homo ludens* or more specifically *scriptor ludens* or *lector ludens*, let's keep playing with proverbs while realizing that proverbs as such will undoubtedly continue to *play a role* in modern life.

BIBLIOGRAPHY

This chapter was first published with the same title in *Proverbium: Yearbook of International Proverb Scholarship* 36 (2019): 183–216.

Baudouin, Dominique. 1970. "Jeux de mots surréalistes: L'expérience du *Proverbe.*" *Symposium* 24, no. 4: 293–302.

Becker, Daniel Levin. 2012. "My Words Aren't Stones to Harm You but Fences to Make You Not Harm Me: On the Peculiar Generosity of *Selected Declarations of Dependence*." *Quarterly Conversation*, September 3. http://quarterlyconversations.com/my-words -arent-stones-to-harm-you-but-fences-to-make-you-not-harm-me.

Bénabou, Marcel. 1990. *Locutions introuvables*. In *La Bibliothèque Oulipienne*, 2:135–50. Paris: Éditions Seghers. First published in *Bibliothèque Oulipienne*, no. 25 (1984).

Bénabou, Marcel. 1993. *Rendre à Cézanne: Locutions se rapportant à un seul peintre*. *Bibliothèque Oulipienne*, no. 59.

Booklist. 1978. "Harry Mathews: *Selected Declarations of Dependence*." June 15, 1602.

Caradec, François. 1993. *105 proverbes liftés suivis de quelques proverbes soldés*. *Bibliothèque Oulipienne*, no. 60.

Castle, Frederick Ted. 1987. "Lies Like Truth: The Art of Harry Mathews." *Review of Contemporary Fiction* 7, no. 2: 119–27.

Cohen, Keith. 1987. "The Labors of the Signifier." *Review of Contemporary Fiction* 7, no. 3: 173–86.

Doyle, Charles Clay, Wolfgang Mieder, and Fred R. Shapiro. 2012. *The Dictionary of Modern Proverbs*. New Haven, CT: Yale University Press.

Dundes, Alan, and Claudia A. Stibbe. 1981. *The Art of Mixing Metaphors: A Folkloristic Interpretation of the "Netherlandish Proverbs" by Pieter Bruegel the Elder*. Helsinki: Suomalainen Tiedeakatemia.

Eckler, A. Ross. 1978. "The Literary Wordplay of Harry Mathews." *Word Ways* 11: 49.

Éluard, Paul. 1968. "152 proverbes mis en goût du jour au collaboration avec Benjamin Péret [1925]." In *Œuvres complètes*, by Paul Éluard, edited by Marcelle Dumas and Lucien Scheler, 1:153–61. Paris: Éditions Gallimard.

Everman, Welch D. 1986. "Harry Mathews." In *Postmodern Fiction: A Bio-Bibliographical Guide*, edited by Larry McCaffery, 464–67. Westport, CT: Greenwood Press.

Everman, Welch D. 1987. "Harry Mathews's *Selected Declarations of Dependence*: Proverbs and the Forms of Authority." *Review of Contemporary Fiction* 7, no. 3 (September–December): 146–53. Also in *Who Says This? The Authority of the Author, the Discourse, and the Reader*, by Welch D. Everman, 65–77. Carbondale: Southern Illinois University Press, 1988.

Fühmann, Franz. 1974. *Zweiundzwanzig Tage oder die Hälfte des Lebens*. Rostock, Germany: Hinstorff Verlag.

Genette, Gérard. 1993. "Kurze Parodien." In *Palimpseste: Die Literatur auf zweiter Stufe*, 47–59. Frankfurt am Main: Edition Suhrkamp.

Güell, Mónica. 1999. "La manipulación lúdica del refrán y de la locución en los trabajos de la Oulipo." *Paremia* 8: 261–66.

Haas, Heather A. 2008. "Proverb Familiarity in the United States: Cross-Regional Comparisons of the Paremiological Minimum." *Journal of American Folklore* 121, no. 481 (Summer): 319–47.

Huizinga, Johan. 1938. *Homo ludens: Proeve eener bepaling van het spel-element der cultuur*. Haarlem, Netherlands: H. D. Tjeenk Willink & Zoon. Also in English as *Homo Ludens: A Study of the Play-Element in Culture*. London: Routledge and Kegan Paul, 1949.

Hunnewell, Susannah. 2007. "Harry Mathews: The Art of Fiction, no. 191." *Paris Review* 49, no. 180 (Spring): 72–102. https://www.theparisreview.org/interviews/5734/the-art-of -fiction-no-191-harry-mathews.

Kotkowska, Ela, trans. 2004–2005. "Benjamin Péret and Paul Éluard: 152 Proverbs Brought Up to Date." *Chicago Review* 50, nos. 2–4 (Winter): 173–84.

Leamon, Warren. 1993. *Harry Mathews*. New York: Twayne Publishers.

Lederer, Richard. 1990. *The Play of Words: Fun and Games for Language Lovers*. New York: Pocket Books.

Lehman, David. 1980. "In the Cool Element of Prose." *Parnassus: Poetry in Review* 8: 137–51.

Litovkina, Anna T. 2015. "Anti-Proverbs." In *Introduction to Paremiology: A Comprehensive Guide to Proverb Studies*, edited by Hrisztalina Hrisztova-Gotthardt and Melita Aleksa Varga, 326–52. Berlin: Walter de Gruyter.

Litovkina, Anna T., and Carl Lindahl, eds. 2007. *Anti-Proverbs in Contemporary Societies*. Special issue, *Acta Ethnographica Hungarica* 52, no. 1: 1–285.

Litovkina, Anna T., and Wolfgang Mieder. 2006. *Old Proverbs Never Die, They Just Diversify: A Collection of Anti-Proverbs*. Illustrations by Olga Mirenska. Burlington: University of Vermont; Veszprém, Hungary: University of Pannonia.

Loberer, Eric. 1996. "*Selected Declarations of Dependence* by Harry Mathews." *The Complete Review*. https://www.complete-review.com/reviews/mathewsh/selectdd.htm.

Lux, Günter. 1981. *Die Axt im Hause wird selten fett: Ein Smalcalda-Sprichwort-Bastelbuch*. Illustrations by Ulrich Forchner. Leipzig: Messedruck.

Lux, Günter. 1987. *Morgenstund ist aller Laster Anfang: Sprichwörter zum Selberbasteln*. Illustrations by Bernd A. Chmura. Berlin: Eulenspiegel Verlag.

Mathews, Harry. 1976. *Le Savoir des Rois: Poèmes à perverbes. Bibliothèque Oulipienne*, no. 5. Rpt., Geneva: Éditions Slatkine, 1981.

Mathews, Harry. 1986. "Mathew's Algorithm." In *Oulipo: A Primer of Potential Literature*, edited by Warren F. Motte Jr., 126–39. Lincoln: University of Nebraska Press. Also in *The Case of the Persevering Maltese: Collected Essays*, by Harry Mathews, 301–20. Normal, IL: Dalkey Archive Press, 2003.

Mathews, Harry. 1990. *Écrits français. Bibliothèque Oulipienne*, no. 51. Also in *La Bibliothèque Oulipienne*, 3:337–68. Paris: Éditions Seghers, 1990.

Mathews, Harry. 1996. *Selected Declarations of Dependence*. With illustrations by Alex Katz. Los Angeles: Sun and Moon Press. First published, Calais, VT: Z Press, 1977.

Mathews, Harry. 2003. *The Case of the Persevering Maltese: Collected Essays*. Normal, IL: Dalkey Archive Press.

Mathews, Harry. 2005. "Harry Mathews." In *Oulipo Compendium*, edited by Harry Mathews, Alastair Brotchie, and Raymond Queneau, 183–84. London: Atlas Press.

Mathews, Harry, Alastair Brotchie, and Raymond Queneau, eds. 2005. *Oulipo Compendium*. London: Atlas Press.

McPheron, William. 1987. "Harry Mathews: A Checklist." *Review of Contemporary Fiction* 7, no. 3: 197–226.

Mieder, Wolfgang. 1985. "Spiel mit Sprichwörtern: In Memoriam, Franz Fühmann (1922–1984)." In *Sprichwörtliches und Geflügeltes: Sprachstudien von Martin Luther bis Karl Marx*, 33–39. Bochum, Germany: Norbert Brockmeyer.

Mieder, Wolfgang. 1987. *Tradition and Innovation in Folk Literature*. Hanover, NH: University Press of New England.

Mieder, Wolfgang. 1989. *American Proverbs: A Study of Texts and Contexts*. Bern: Peter Lang.

Mieder, Wolfgang, ed. 1990. *"Kommt Zeit—kommt Rat!?" Moderne Sprichwortgedichte von Erich Fried bis Ulla Hahn*. Frankfurt am Main: Rita G. Fischer.

Mieder, Wolfgang. 1998. *"Der Mensch denkt: Gott lenkt—keine Red davon!" Sprichwörtliche Verfremdungen im Werk Bertolt Brechts*. Bern: Peter Lang.

Mieder, Wolfgang. 1999. *Sprichwörtliche Aphorismen: Von Georg Christoph Lichtenberg bis Elazar Benyoëtz*. Vienna: Edition Praesens.

Mieder, Wolfgang, ed. 2004a. *The Netherlandish Proverbs: An International Symposium on the Pieter Brueg(h)els*. Burlington: University of Vermont.

Mieder, Wolfgang. 2004b. *Proverbs: A Handbook*. Westport, CT: Greenwood Press. Rpt., New York: Peter Lang, 2012.

Mieder, Wolfgang. 2008. *"Proverbs Speak Louder Than Words": Folk Wisdom in Art, Culture, Folklore, History, Literature, and Mass Media*. New York: Peter Lang.

Mieder, Wolfgang. 2010. *"Spruchschlösser (ab)bauen": Sprichwörter, Antisprichwörter und Lehnsprichwörter in Literatur und Medien*. Vienna: Praesens Verlag.

Mieder, Wolfgang. 2012. "'Think Outside the Box': Origin, Nature, and Meaning of Modern Anglo-American Proverbs." *Proverbium* 29: 137–96.

Motte, Warren F., Jr. 1986. *Oulipo: A Primer of Potential Literature*. Lincoln: University of Nebraska Press.

Motte, Warren F., Jr. 1987. "Permutational Mathews." *Review of Contemporary Fiction* 7, no. 1: 91–99.

Mottram, Eric. 1987. "'Elusions Truths': Harry Mathews's Strategies and Games." *Review of Contemporary Fiction* 7, no. 2: 154–72.

Norrick, Neal R. 1985. *How Proverbs Mean: Semantic Studies in English Proverbs*. Berlin: Mouton.

Paulhan, Jean. (1913) 1966. "L'expérience du proverbe." In *Œuvres complètes*, 2:101–24. Paris: Cercle du Livre Précieux.

Roberts, Sam. 2017. "Harry Mathews, Idiosyncratic Writer, Dies at 86." *New York Times*, February 2. https://www.nytimes.com/2017/02/02/books/harry-mathews-dead -author.html.

Röhrich, Lutz. 1967. *Gebärde, Metapher, Parodie: Studien zur Sprache und Volksdichtung*. Düsseldorf: Pädagogischer Verlag Schwann. Rpt., edited by Wolfgang Mieder. Burlington: University of Vermont, 2006.

Shafarzek, Susan. 1977. "LJ's Small Press Roundup." *Library Journal* 102: 2483–89.

Siepe, Hans T. 1977. *Der Leser des Surrealismus: Untersuchungen zur Kommunikationsästhetik*. Stuttgart: Klett-Cotta.

Sirota, André. 1998. "La langue du pervers de société ou le 'perverbe.'" *Cliniques Méditerranéennes*, nos. 57–58: 157–65.

Sobieski, Janet, and Wolfgang Mieder, eds. 2005. *"So Many Heads, So Many Wits": An Anthology of English Proverb Poetry*. Burlington: University of Vermont.

Stonehill, Brian. 1982. "On Harry Mathews." *Chicago Review* 33, no. 2: 107–11.

Syrotinski, Michael Frederick Joseph. 1989. "Reinventing Figures: Jean Paulhan and the Critical Mystery of Literature." PhD diss., Yale University.

Tillman, Lynne. 1989. "Harry Mathews." *Bomb Magazine*, Winter 1989. https://bombmagazine .org/articles/1989/01/01/harry-mathews/.

Time. 1977. "Science: Perverbs and Snowballs." January 10. https://time.com/archive/6648268/science-perverbs-and-snowballs/.

Villers, Damien. 2010. "Les modalités du détournement proverbial: Entre contraintes et libertés." *Modèles Linguistiques* 31, no. 62: 147–72.

Villers, Damien. 2014. *Le proverbe et les genres connexes: Domaines anglais et français*. Saarbrücken, Germany: Presses Académiques Francophones.

10

"BLACK IS BEAUTIFUL"

Hans-Jürgen Massaquoi's Proverbial Autobiography
Destined to Witness (1999)

Several decades ago, nobody could have foreseen that Black German studies would become an important subfield of *Germanistik* (Blackshire-Belay 1996; Nenno 2016). By now it has been ascertained that "there exists a wide range of texts by Black Germans that covers the colonial period through the Third Reich and up to the present. The proliferation of autobiographical texts by Black Germans and Germans of African descent—as well as by migrants from Africa—illustrates the heterogeneity of Black Germans' experiences" (Nenno 2019, 169). A particularly valuable autobiography is Hans-Jürgen Massaquoi's sizable *Destined to Witness: Growing Up Black in Nazi Germany* (1999a), which appeared simultaneously in German translation as *Neger, Neger, Schornstein-feger: Meine Kindheit in Deutschland* (1999b; 2006 as a film). The best seller recounts Massaquoi's birth in 1926 in Hamburg as a biracial child of a German mother and a Black father from Liberia who returns to Africa, leaving his wife and son to fend for themselves in a working-class neighborhood in that large city. Their struggle to survive Nazi Germany is described in numerous small chapters of two to three pages that are informed somewhat by the journalistic style that Massaquoi became accustomed to once he was established in the United States as the managing editor of the African American magazine *Ebony*. His troublesome survival at school with teachers and others mistreating him as a non-Aryan Black youngster, his strenuous attempt to fit in, his early romantic experience, his development into a skilled metalworker, and his survival during the catastrophic bombing of Hamburg in 1943 are all told in vivid language that includes plenty of Germanisms. After all, German was his native language, but by 1946 he had also learned some English and left for Liberia for two years in 1948. There, he met his father and other relatives, but once again was con-fronted with not quite fitting in as an Afro-German (Campt 2004, 8–9). At the age of twenty-four, his ardent wish of emigrating to the United States became

264

a reality with the help of relatives on his mother's side. And yet, his idealized image of America being the country of freedom and liberty was shattered as he experienced racism once again, wondering how he would ever find his identity. In due time his mother, whom he respected and adored to the point that his account "is more or less a love letter" to her (Nganang 2005, 235), joined him outside of Chicago and lived to see him become a respected and accomplished journalist who at his death in 2013 in Jacksonville, Florida, could look back at a remarkable life's journey that deserved and needed to be told.

The autobiography is thus divided into three parts. About three-quarters of the book (1–332) deals with his life and survival in war-torn Germany; his time in Liberia fills not quite a hundred pages (333–411); and his early experiences in the United States take up a mere thirty pages (411–43). Clearly, then, readers "are provided with the fascinating case of a mixed-race man, considered 'black' by the Nazi regime (and in the United States) seeking to survive and make his way to adulthood in one of the most racist and anti-black regimes that the world has produced" (Barkin 2009, 259). As he writes proverbially in the prologue: "As a black person in white Nazi Germany, I was highly visible and thus could neither run nor hide, to paraphrase my childhood idol Joe Louis" (Massaquoi 1999a, xii). Indeed, the famous boxer Joe Louis (1914–1981) supposedly first uttered "You can run but you can't hide" in 1946 with the meaning that evasion will not avert a defeat. Due to his popularity, it quickly became a common proverb in the United States (Doyle, Mieder, and Shapiro 2012, 221).

It took Massaquoi years to write his significant account. It began with a trip in early 1966 to his old hometown, Hamburg, as an aspiring staffer on *Ebony*, which resulted in a lengthy two-part account, "A Journey into the Past," with numerous illustrations, in the February and March issues (Massaquoi 1966). Just like a somewhat later autobiographical sketch (Massaquoi 1984), the *Ebony* piece contains several reminiscences of his socialization process that reappear in *Destined to Witness* (Walden 2004). In addition, colleagues and friends, notably Alex Haley of *Roots* (1976) fame, encouraged him to expand his memories into a full-fledged book. Frank Mehring explains that Massaquoi's "tricultural background, his racial encounters in Nazi Germany, Liberia, and the United States made him suspicious of the American dream of liberty, equality, and opportunity" (Mehring 2009, 66–69; Mehring 2014), and yet his second autobiography, published unfortunately only in its German translation as *Hänschen klein, ging allein . . . Mein Weg in die Neue Welt* (Massaquoi 2004), tells about his professional success—from rags to riches—as an American journalist (Mehring 2014, 275). From a sociolinguistic point of view it is interesting to note that he mastered both German and English eloquently with all their cultural nuances. While he clearly was not schizophrenic, he certainly had two mother tongues so to speak that make his autobiographies so special as he "wrestles with the vicissitudes of racial identity formation" (Hodges 2001, 54) as an Afro-German eventually living among African Americans in the United States. As Elaine Martin has observed so eloquently in her remarkable scholarly review of *Destined to Witness*: "This somewhat peripatetic life results in a revelatory juxtaposition of three different cultures, their attitudes toward race, and the author's complex identity shifts in accordance with an ever-changing milieu. [. . .] [H]e remains irrevocably an outsider, culturally, linguistically, and even physically. In the United States seeming and being are similarly at odds: he is taken for an American black, but neither of his parents is American, and English is not his native language" (Martin 2001, 91–92; see also Nganang 2005, 235). As Massaquoi states: "I kept being dogged by my old habit of not fitting in" (1999a, 261), and "I realized that I was still light-years away from feeling that I belonged" (413).

Speaking of language, Martin is an isolated literary critic who does at least in one sentence say something about Massaquoi's impressive linguistic register: "The narrative tone belongs to the tradition of oral literature, often using colloquial or clichéd expressions ('[he] hated my ten-year-old guts,' 'the ripe old age of 88,' 'in sunny California') as well as numerous phrases and short sentences in German" (Martin 2001, 94). Alexandra Lindhout in her otherwise revealing article on Massaquoi's autobiography as an "act of identity formation" also singles out Massaquoi's use of numerous German expressions but merely gives a few individual words as examples (Lindhout 2006, 3). And Frank Mehring in his otherwise superb analysis of Massaquoi's two autobiographies ignores any linguistic, folkloric, or phraseological matters altogether (Mehring 2014). And yet, Massaquoi's appealing and intriguing style is richly informed by his word choices, his allusions to folkloric matters, and his effective employment of German and English proverbs, proverbial expressions, and other phraseologisms. These materials are without doubt part of what makes his unique autobiography such a compelling narrative. Realizing that it contains 509 fixed phrases (645 counting 136 duplicates), it is clearly worthwhile to have a closer look at Massaquoi's proverbial style.

As one might expect, Massaquoi employs some of the standard Nazi vocabulary for titles and offices, but there are also colloquial German terms that come to him naturally, as they belong to his native language. These kinds of explanatory comments add much to this macaronic style, as the following contextualized examples show:

> Among the more intriguing neighborhood events was the occasional sighting of a siren-blaring police paddy wagon, nicknamed *Grüner August* because of its dark green color. (Massaquoi 1999a, 20)

MASSAQUOI'S PROVERBIAL AUTOBIOGRAPHY *DESTINED TO WITNESS*   267

My mother would invariably dress me up in my *Sonntagsanzug* (Sunday suit), and we would head outdoors. (23)

It was through the newsreels that I received my first, albeit lopsided, impression of the *Land der unbegrenzten Möglichkeiten* (land of unlimited possibilities), as the United States was called. (51)

I gave her my *Ehrenwort* (word of honor) and sealed my promise with a solemn handshake. German boys, it had been drilled into me from as far back as I could remember, never break their *Ehrenwort*, no matter what. (58)

"The Brown Bomber [the boxer Joe Louis] turned out to be a *Flasche*," another boy chimed in, using the derisive street term for "weakling." (117)

"What *um Himmels Willen* (in heaven's name) was on your mind when you decided not to show up for work as you had been ordered?" (223)

I thanked my good Samaritan who, in turn, wished me "*Hals und Beinbruch*" (neck and leg fracture)—a German expression for *Good luck*. (237)

"Anyone who has a problem with that is an *Arschloch* (asshole) and can go straight to hell." (418)

Massaquoi is also steeped in German folkloric references, which he picked up as a child. An especially interesting example early in the book is his description of a scene with his beloved African grandfather in prewar Hamburg:

There were even times when Momolu had my mother wake me up after I had already gone to bed because he wanted me to demonstrate my linguistic prowess to some African and German dinner guests. On such occasions, the old man would ask me to sing a German nursery song, such as "Hänschen Klein Ging Allein" (Little Hans Walked Alone), and I would be only too happy to oblige. For my trouble, I could bask in the adulation of the guests, who never failed to be impressed by the fact that not only did I speak accent-free German, but that I did so with unmistakably Hamburgian brogue. (14)

The memory of this song remained with Massaquoi for seventy years, and he used its beginning as the title of his second autobiography in 2004 to describe

268   PROVERBS IN LITERATURE

his life's story as an immigrant to the United States. But speaking of language, in his revealing chapter "Mistaken Identity" (233–37) he gets out of a scrape by communicating in solid German with a police lieutenant: "When I told him what had happened to me at the plant, he soon became convinced that, my brown skin notwithstanding, my unadulterated Hamburger dialect was unmistakably homegrown" (236). Speaking of color identity, his self-assured African aunt Fatima is a model for young Hans-Jürgen of accepting and dealing with his Blackness: "Tante Fatima, on the other hand, loved nothing more than being the center of attention, and deliberately dressed and acted in a way that made it impossible for her to be overlooked. Long before I made the discovery that black was beautiful, she wore an Afro so huge it would have aroused the envy of a Fiji Islander" (60). While Massaquoi does not draw any special attention to the proverb "Black is beautiful," it must have been on his mind when working on his autobiography. In fact, in the year of his birth Langston Hughes (1902–1967) had declared it the "duty of the younger Negro artist [. . .] to change [. . .] that old whispering 'I want to be White,' hidden in the aspiration of his people, to 'Why should I want to be white? I am a Negro—and beautiful.'" One year later in 1927, the first reference of the proverb appeared in a newspaper: Marcus Garvey (1887–1940), a Jamaican-born political activist and journalist, "made black people proud of their race. In a world where black is despised he taught them that black is beautiful" (Doyle, Mieder, and Shapiro 2012, 22). Perhaps Massaquoi had come across Hughes's statement, but no matter what, he most certainly was conversant in the slogan-turned-modern-proverb. It doubtlessly played a significant role in his decision to identify himself as an African American in due time.

It comes as a surprise then that Hans-Jürgen Massaquoi agreed to have the German translation of his autobiography appear with the title *Neger, Neger, Schornsteinfeger*, a stereotypical children's chant directed against Black people out of mischievous ignorance (in German folklore, the chimney sweep wears black clothes). At the end of his second autobiography, he explains the choice of the title of his first book as follows:

> Der Verleger von Scherz [Verlag]. Peter Lohmann, war so begeistert, dass er persönlich nach New Orleans kam, um mit mir die Einzelheiten des Projektes zu besprechen. Wir mussten uns vor allen Dingen einen Titel einfallen lassen, der in Deutschland funktionieren würde. Stundenlang zermarterten wir uns das Hirn, bis Lohmann schließlich vorschlug, mein Buch *Neger, Neger, Schornsteinfeger!* zu nennen, was mir in der Kindheit andere Kinder hinterher gerufen hatten. Zuerst war ich entsetzt. Das Wort „Neger" weckte in mir eine Fülle schmerzhafter Erinnerungen, und auch sein englisches Pendant *Negro* war bei Afroamerikanern in

den USA genauso unbeliebt. Doch Lohmann meinte, wenn der Titel mit Anführungsstrichen als Zitat kenntlich gemacht würde, wäre es nicht beleidigend, er würde sogar noch stärker veranschaulichen, was ich als Kind durchgemacht hatte. Da ich keine bessere Idee hatte, erklärte ich mich zögerlich einverstanden. (Massaquoi 2004, 256–57)

Peter Lohmann, the publisher of the Scherz Company, was so enthusiastic that he personally came to New Orleans in order to discuss the details of the project. Above all we had to come up with a title that would work in Germany. We racked our brains for hours, until Lohmann finally suggested to call my book *Neger, Neger, Schornsteinfeger*, something that other children called after me in my childhood. At first I was horrified. The word *Neger* awakened many painful memories in me, and its English equivalent *Negro* was equally disliked by African Americans in the United States. But Lohmann argued that if the title were made to be recognizable as a quotation by placing it within quotation marks, it would not be insulting. That title would even show more strongly what I as a child went through. Since I had no better idea, I declared somewhat reluctantly that I was in agreement.

The controversial title did indeed draw attention to the book and helped it on its way to becoming a best seller in Germany. But be that as it may, here is the heart-wrenching way he describes his first encounter with the racist expression, and it is well to remember that the black-clad chimney sweep in German folklore can also represent the devil (Röhrich 1991–1992, 3:1397–98; Rölleke 1993):

Instead of the friendly glances and flattering comments I had been used to, I suddenly drew curious, at times even hostile stares and insulting remarks. Most offensive to me were two words that I had never heard before and that I soon discovered were used by people for the sole purpose of describing the way I looked. One word was *Mischling*, which, after pressing Mutti for an explanation, she defined as someone who, like me, was of racially mixed parentage. The other word was *Neger*— according to Mutti, a misnomer as far as I was concerned, since she insisted that I was definitely not a *Neger*, a term that she applied only to black people in America. But street urchins, who were my worst tormenters, apparently did not know, or care, about such fine distinctions. As soon as they spotted me, they would start to chant, "*Neger, Neger, Schornsteinfeger* (Negro, Negro, chimney sweep)!" and they would keep it up with sadistic insistence until I was out of their sight. (Massaquoi 1999a, 18; also 37, 431, 433)

There is a fascinating, quite similar autobiographical account by the African medical student Martin Aku, who was confronted by the stereotypical expression "Neger, Neger, Schornsteinfeger" in the mid-1930s in Bremen:

> Nun war ich also in Bremen [aus Afrika angekommen]. Meine Träume verflogen, und an ihre Stelle trat die Wirklichkeit. [. . .] Auf der Straße versetzte meine Erscheinung die Leute in Aufregung. Finger deuteten auf mich, und unzählige Augen waren auf mich gerichtet, neugierig, mitleidsvoll. Die Kinder schrien hinter mir her: „Neger, Neger, Schornsteinfeger", und sangen noch andere Lieder dazu. Ich kam mir wirklich wie ein Weltwunder vor. Unter diesen Leuten als einziger Farbiger zu leben, dieses Bild Tag für Tag, wißt ihr, was das bedeutet für einen Menschen [. . .]? (Westermann 1938, 270–71)

> Well, there I had arrived in Bremen from Africa. My dreams vanished, and reality stepped into their place. [...] On the street my appearance put people into excitement. They pointed with fingers at me, innumerable eyes were directed at me, curious, sympathetic. The children screamed after me: "Neger, Neger, Schornsteinfeger," and also sang other songs along with it. I felt as if I were a wonder of the world [a prodigy]. To live among these people as the only Black person and to experience this picture every day, can you imagine what that means to a human being?

And there is also Karl Gengenbach's account from his youth, which begins with the expression followed by a linguistic "joke" and an explanatory comment:

> Neger, Neger, Schornsteinfeger
>   Weißer zum Neger: Du schwarz
>   Neger zum Weißen: Ich weiß
> Diesen Spruch habe ich als Junge immer wieder aufgesagt. Nach dem Krieg waren amerikanische Soldaten in Pforzheim stationiert und ein großer Teil davon schwarz. Diese Schwarzen waren für uns Neger. Das Wort Nigger kannten wir überhaupt nicht, das kam von den weißen Amerikanern. (Gengenbach 2016, 108)

> Neger, Neger, Schornsteinfeger
>   White man to a Black man: You [are] Black
>   Black man to a white man: I [am] white [*weiß* can mean "to know" or "white"]

I recited this verse again and again as a boy. After the war, American soldiers, of whom a considerable number were Black, were stationed in the city of Pforzheim. These Black men were Negroes for us. The word "nigger" we did not know at all; that came from the white Americans.

There is then no doubt that the expression was quite current some decades ago, and it is surprising that it has not been recorded in any scholarly collections. In any case, children being children, things changed in due time for the better for Hans-Jürgen Massaquoi, as he established friendships with other children: "Luckily, after a short time, the status and taunts became fewer as the novelty of my appearance began to wear off. Soon, some of the kids who had shouted the loudest became my closest pals. To my great relief, it seemed as if all of a sudden they had become oblivious to the visual differences that set us apart" (Massaquoi 1999a, 18). One is inclined to ask why some adults to this day have not learned to be blind to color and race. Why can people not be convinced "that true human decency is [. . .] simply a matter of the heart?" (419).

But here are a few more textual examples of Massaquoi's remembrance of the German folklore he had encountered as a child and student in Germany. The stereotypical names for chocolate pastries in the first statement remained part of German culture well into the 1960s (Yeo 2001, 119; Mehring 2014, 257) when they began to be sold under the innocuous term *Schaumküsse* (foam kisses):

Each time Tante Fatima came around, she insisted on taking me out to some nearby *Konditorei* for a pastry and whipped cream treat. [. . .] Neither of us was amused when at one *Konditorei* the waitress snidely suggested that we try some of the establishment's delicious *Negerküsse* (Negro kisses) or *Mohrenköpfe* (Moors' heads), two popular chocolate-coated pastries. (Massaquoi 1999a, 60–61)

The mere thought of being seen in the street with a violin case—that we kids contemptuously called a *Kindersarg* (children's coffin)—gave me the creeps. (74)

Ironically, among my favorite books during my formative years were those that dealt with the old Germanic legends of Siegfried, the fairest of fair knights, which provided much of the National Socialists' racial mythology. (80)

Dozens of young men carrying small swastika streamers marched up and down Salza's Hauptstrasse, shouting and rabble-rousing and singing

"Muss i denn zum Städtele hinaus," the traditional German farewell song. (90)

Mirror, mirror on the Wall. (91, chapter heading)

We would sing "Das Lied vom Guten Kamerad" (The Song of the Good Comrade), Germany's traditional military burial song. (96)

Somehow the scene reminded me of the conclusion of that old German fairy tale when the seven little goats dance with their mother around the well in which the big bad wolf has just drowned. (259)

But references to English folklore and classical mythology are also part of Massaquoi's writing style, which is steeped in cultural literacy. These allusions do not just appear as curiosities but are cited as parallels of his own situation:

When I reached the school and saw my mother's eyes light up as I presented her with my treasures—a couple of chocolate bars, some sardine cans, and a few bars of soap—I felt like Robin Hood must have felt when he robbed the rich to give to the poor. (250)

At one point I lost my grip on my suitcase and it slipped down the muddy hill, causing me to repeat part of my strenuous climb all over. It reminded me of the legendary King Sisyphus of Greek mythology, whom the gods condemned to push a huge rock to the top of a steep hill in Hades, only to have the rock slip from his grasp and roll back down the hill, forcing him to start his backbreaking labor over again. I recalled that Sisyphus, a former Mount Olympus insider, had offended the gods by cheating death, and wondered what I had done to suffer a similar fate. (378)

Turning to proverbial language, it might be appropriate to conjecture that Massaquoi had been introduced to it by his reading obsession, as he mentions in a two-page mini-chapter, "Books to the Rescue" (79–80): "If the relentless barrage of Nazi propaganda to which we were constantly exposed [as schoolchildren] failed to close my mind permanently, it was because of a childhood habit of mine that reached compulsive proportions. As soon as I had learned to read, my mother fostered my interest in books, and by the time I was eight years old, I had become hopelessly addicted to reading books—any books" (79).

Among other authors, he mentions having read Cervantes's *Don Quixote* with its amassments of proverbs (Mieder 2016) as well as works by Charles

Dickens (Bryan and Mieder 1997) and Mark Twain (West 1930), whose novels are replete with proverbs and proverbial expressions. Of course, journalistic writing is also often informed by proverbial phrases as catchy titles and as expressive metaphors throughout (Mieder 2004, 150–53). His predisposition toward phraseologisms of all types is apparent from the headings of some of his short chapters:

The Good Life at the Alster (Massaquoi 1999a, 12–16)
The New Kid on the Block (17–23)
Head Start (28–30)
Hitler Strikes Home (54–56)
Mutti's Inner Circle (83–85)
Making Ends Meet (88–89)
Life Goes On (145–48)
Forbidden Fruit (187–91)
The Beginning of the End (196–200)
Operation Gomorrah (201–7)
No Room at the Inn (242–47)
Free at Last! (250–61)
The Razor's Edge (262–64)
Home, Sweet Home (265–67)
Reconciliation in the Nick of Time (390–95)
In the "Home of the Brave" (411–30)

It is of interest to note how Massaquoi with an ironic twist superimposes well-known American expressions on his German predicament. Thus he employs "Free at Last!," which is based on an African American spiritual that was popularized by Martin Luther King Jr.'s use of the phrase at the end of his "I Have a Dream" speech of August 28, 1963 (Mieder 2010, 194–201), to describe the newfound freedom at the news of Hitler's death on April 30, 1945. Understandably, it is also in this passage in which Massaquoi describes overcoming his insider/outsider German identity (Nganang 2005, 235–37):

I was now "on the other side." It dawned on me that in one fell swoop I had ceased to be what I had always considered myself—a German. But somehow the thought didn't bother me. The Germans never let me fully share in their happy past. Now I didn't need any part of their miserable present. I concluded that I had reached a watershed in my life. I could sense that the pendulum of fate was swinging my way for a change and wondered what had taken it so long. For the first time in years I felt totally free of the paralyzing fear that my pride had never permitted me to admit to anyone, least to myself, but that had stalked me relentlessly by day and by night. It was not an ordinary kind of fear, such as the fear of being killed in a bombing raid or in a Nazi concentration camp. Instead it was the fear of being humiliated, of being ridiculed, of being degraded, of having my dignity stripped from me, of being made to feel that I was less a human being, less a man than the people in whose midst I lived. Suddenly, that fear was lifted from me like a heavy burden I had carried without being fully aware of it. (Massaquoi 1999a, 257–58)

With this significant watershed behind him, "Life goes on" (145–48), as the title of an earlier chapter expresses it proverbially. Thus Massaquoi's account of having found a basement abode in a bombed-out building for him and his mother gets the uplifting proverb title "Home, Sweet Home," even though it is infested with fleas and in no way represents the tender claim of the 1823 song with that title by J. H. Payne (1791–1852). Massaquoi might also have cited the proverb "Be it ever so humble, there's no place like home," which has its origin from that very song (Mieder, Kingsbury, and Harder 1992, 304). And finally, when Massaquoi, the "confirmed Americophile" (Massaquoi 1999a, 308), deals in the third part of his autobiography in but thirty pages with his life in the United States, he uses the partial line "The land of the free and the home of the brave" from Francis Scott Key's (1779–1843) "The Star-Spangled Banner" (1814; see Shapiro 2006, 424) as the title "In the 'Home of the Brave'" (Massaquoi 1999a, 411). There is some bitter disappointment as he experiences racism and discrimination, as he states later in that chapter by quoting the entire line from the national anthem: "I no longer felt the need to idealize the United States. For the moment, I felt terribly disappointed and betrayed regarding my view of 'the land of the free and the home of the brave'" (421). Earlier in his autobiography, he had made a similar observation: "It took me a while to psychologically digest my introduction to the American dilemma—America's inability, or unwillingness, to live up to its creed of 'liberty and justice for all'" (318–19). And yet, Hans-Jürgen Massaquoi did eventually find a positive identity:

After several years of paying dues, including journalism studies at two universities, things started to look up and fall into place. Ever so slowly, I began to see the light at the end of the long, long tunnel. I knew I had not only survived but succeeded when I went on my first major assignment for *Ebony*, to interview President [Ahmed] Sékou Touré of newly independent Guinea at the Libertyville, Illinois, home of UN Ambassador Adlai Stevenson. When the two world figures sat down for an animated chat with me, the "racially inferior" dead-end black kid from

MASSAQUOI'S PROVERBIAL AUTOBIOGRAPHY *DESTINED TO WITNESS* 275

Nazi Germany, it seemed to me that my coming to America had not been such a bad idea after all. (430)

In fact, as thousands of immigrants before and after him, Massaquoi learned to make his peace with his new homeland: "After scuffling and 'paying dues,' [. . .] I had found my American dream" (431) as a top-notch journalist with a wife and two sons in a nice neighborhood of Chicago.

The last two quotations from Massaquoi's autobiography reveal his proverbial style! The proverbial phrase "to pay one's dues" appears twice, but there are also three more such phrases: "to fall into place," "to be a light at the end of the tunnel," and "to be at a dead end." Such proverbial groupings are no rarity. In a chapter with the proverbial title "Head Start" (28–30), Massaquoi tells about the unexpected event of his childhood playmate Erika (when they were only four years old) exposing herself to him, getting the youngsters into obvious trouble: "Literally caught with her panties down by her nonplussed grandmother, Erika shifted into reverse and started to cry" (29). After this playful use of the proverbial phrase "to be caught with one's pants down," he ends his account with three additional proverbial phrases:

The lessons I gleaned from this traumatic interlude were (1) that there was a distinct anatomical difference between boys and girls, (2) that there was something about that difference that for some unfathomable reason made grown-ups uptight, and (3) that a girl could get a fellow into a whole lot of trouble. Having had my share, I decided to leave well enough alone and in the future to avoid girls like the plague. But the best-laid plans of men and mice sometimes go awry, so eventually did mine. (29–30)

Not only are the three proverbial phrases "to have one's share," "to leave well enough alone," and "to avoid like the plague" strung together here, but he adds the proverb "The best-laid plans of men and mice often go astray" to boot, assuring his readers with an ironic smile that he later learned to deal plenty well with the opposite sex.

Massaquoi's descriptions of his terrible experiences at school having to listen to racial slurs that at times elevated to physical aggression are especially disturbing, but these stereotypical insults are alleviated by the camaraderie that existed among the schoolchildren, who could not deny that their Black outsider had plenty of intelligence:

Even though I breezed through most subjects with customary ease, there were two subjects that gave me a run for my money—English and math. In math, I at least managed—by hook or by crook—to get a passing grade, mainly by convincing Tom Shark that I really tried. In English, on the other hand, I was completely over my head. Since I had joined the class of Frau Dr. Fink, the only teacher in the entire grade school with a doctorate, my progress in English had ground to a complete halt. (133)

Clearly Massaquoi enjoyed writing this passage, especially in light of the fact that English became a second "mother tongue" to him in due time. And, of course, he knows all the right five colloquial phrases to add expressiveness to his prose: "to breeze through something," "to give someone a run for his money," "by hook or by crook," "to be over one's head," and "to grind to a halt." The popular twin formula "by hook or by crook" (Gallacher 1970) reappears at the beginning of the proverbially entitled chapter "The Razor's Edge" (Massaquoi 1999a, 262–64), in which Massaquoi once again interweaves several proverbial phrases:

Nothing could convince me that things would not get better for me now that the Nazis were gone and the war was over. The latest setback was simply a reminder that nothing would be handed to me on a [silver] platter. But I was quite willing to do whatever it took to make things happen, although at the moment, I hadn't the foggiest idea what my options were. All I knew was that, if I could help it, I would never work in anybody's machine shop again. I was grateful to my mother, who had sacrificed to give me the opportunity of learning a trade, but after four years of growing calluses while risking life and limb with backbreaking labor amid lung-blistering stench and ear-shattering noise, I was more than ready for a change. By hook or by crook, I was determined to make the transition to the white-collar class; in what capacity, I wasn't quite sure. (262)

It is a bit surprising that Massaquoi does not include the word "silver" in his use of the proverbial expression "to be handed on a silver platter." In any case, he adds the phrases "to not have the foggiest idea," "to risk life and limb," and "by hook or by crook" to express the vicissitudes of his precarious situation, which he is determined to change to a meaningful existence.

The following example may well serve as a final example of such phraseological run-on comments. It is of special interest since it shows once and for all that Massaquoi is keenly aware of language as he is confronted with new American English idiomatic phrases:

I had begun to notice that Americans—especially the black Americans I had met—spoke a language that bore little resemblance to the one taught by my English teachers Herr Harden, Herr Neumann, and Frau Dr. Fink. When, at the urging of Smitty, I filled his colleague in on my life under Hitler, Slim was moved to interrupt from time to time with "I dig," "Can you beat that?," "Get a load of that," and "Ain't that a bitch?," none of which made a great deal of sense to me. (297)

There is no doubt that Massaquoi steadily relies on metaphorical expressions throughout his spellbinding account of survival as a biracial person in three countries in which he cannot escape the unfortunate reality of being a misfit no matter how hard he tries to fit into the social fabric riddled by racial prejudices. The following contextualized examples are representative of this stylistic modus operandi, with many more to be found in the attached index of proverbial texts that can unfortunately only be listed without context due to space restrains:

As a dyed-in-the-wool arch-Nazi, [school principal Heinrich] Wriede was on a constant alert to weed out anything that conflicted with his deeply entrenched conviction of German superiority. (71)

There were a few [teachers], who—sensitive to my particular plight [harassment]—went out of their way to make my life a little easier. Among the latter was Herr Schneider, a goateed man with erect, military bearing who taught us zoology, biology, botany, and, in a roundabout way, about the birds and the bees. (73)

When all of us agreed that at least five minutes had elapsed and there was still no sign of him [teacher Harden], we dispersed like rats leaving the sinking ship. (77)

Now the cat was out of the bag and I realized how [principal] Wriede had been setting me up. (103)

This relatively quick disillusionment with the HJ [Hitler Youth]—which, as a matter of sour grapes, I welcomed from the bottom of my heart—did not occur in my class alone but was manifest throughout my school and, I suspect, throughout the city and beyond. (104)

By the time I had reached my second apprenticeship year, I no longer considered working as hard and as long as a full-grown man such a harsh reality. It had simply become reality. Yet, even under those conditions, my life was not all work and no play. (159)

It had been drummed into our heads by our teachers that, in the Führer's National Socialist state, men ran the show with women as their helpmates. (171)

I always made sure to bring a buddy along as a decoy [on a date with his girlfriend Gretchen]. I reasoned that a threesome appeared like a more ambiguous, therefore less suspicious, relationship than a twosome. To make the deception work, I would always position myself in such a way as to lead the uninitiated observer to believe that I, not the decoy, was our trio's "fifth wheel." (172)

Looking at several dozen pairs of hostile eyes and realizing too late that he had opened the wrong can of worms, the soldier let go of my lapel. Thoroughly humiliated, he awkwardly moved to the exit. (227)

Nazi Germany had clearly and incontrovertibly reached the point when it desperately needed "the likes of me," not to *win* the war, but merely to buy itself a few days of time before it would be crushed by the Allied juggernaut. The shoe, I decided, was clearly on the other foot. (232)

"I'll cross that bridge when I get to it," I told myself. Fortunately, my luck held out again and the bridge remained uncrossed. (233)

Having been totally isolated from other non-Aryans, I had developed a false sense of security. Egon [a Jewish friend] made me realize that we were all in the same boat, and that at any moment the boat could be sinking. (239; Mieder 2005, 187–209)

Trying not to look like cats that swallowed the canary, we busied ourselves with furiously sweeping the garage floor. (249)

I was confident that in the new era of Allied occupation, my color would be less of an obstacle than it had been so far and that, one way or another, I would find a way to put bread on the table for my mother and myself. (272)

As a victim of Nazi racial hate, I, too, favored the approach of the Soviet troops, who, it was widely known, purged the Nazis in their zone of occupation with an unforgiving head-for-an-eye policy. But my orientation was too Western and my knowledge of and interest in dialectic materialism too vague for me to throw out the baby with the bathwater and abandon my American dream. (286; Mieder 1993, 193–224)

This "little white lie" [that his father was an American and not a Liberian], I had discovered, could make the difference between cordial acceptance as a brother and cold rejection as an unwelcome stranger. (316)

Cautioning us to hang on, he [an American army captain] floored the gas pedal and, to our great delight, the vehicle took off like a bat out of hell. (318)

My father promised to help me make up my educational deficiencies by having me attend college, perhaps in the United States. His words were music to my ears, and I intended to do everything I could to earn his continued support and trust. (357)

They [some young people] made me realize how much of my own youth I had lost struggling merely to survive. I also envied the way their careers, and often their future marriages, had been carefully arranged by their families while I had to keep flying by the seat of my pants. (363)

Eventually, I realized that perhaps I should be the one to extend the olive branch [to his father who had neglected him]. (390)

For me, however, it was utterly ludicrous that a nation that prided itself on its democratic traditions and looked down on the Nazis for their racial attitudes would segregate soldiers who served in the army and who were expected to fight the same enemy. Despite my misgivings, I learned to take the bitter with the sweet. (428)

Massaquoi had been warned by a friend that he "might never get used to that side of the 'American Way'" (412), but as his second autobiography about his successful personal and professional life in the United States shows, he did not acquiesce and joined the civil rights movement with word and deed as an engaged and responsible citizen. Reflecting on the two-thirds of his life spent in the United States, he writes at the end of his first autobiography with justified pride and measured humility:

There was no better way I could have repaid my mother for all she had done for me than to "make something of myself" and to present her with two grandsons, Steve Gordon and Hans Jürgen, Jr., who likewise have made something of themselves. Following Steve's graduation from Harvard Medical School and the enrollment of Hans at the University of Michigan Law School, nothing gave her more pleasure than to brag about "my grandson, the doctor, and my other grandson, the soon-to-be lawyer." As she always used to say, "Ende gut, alles gut." (443)

As the good son that he was, he gives his dear mother—who, once Hamburg was in the hands of the British occupation forces, had put her life into the hands of her dear son—the last word by quoting one of her favorite German proverbs:

> She surprised me by formally turning the reins of our small "family" over to me. "You are in charge now," she told me. "With this new British occupation, I don't know my way around anymore. So from now on, you make the decisions for us both." I was deeply touched and honored, and resolved to skipper our little boat as best I could. The question was, where could we go?" (264)

Indeed, they were together in the same familial boat, to cite the proverbial expression that appears some twenty-five pages earlier with its metaphor standing for the common fate of Massaquoi and other persecuted victims of Nazi Germany.

To a certain degree, Massaquoi's autobiography is also the biography of his mother, who is depicted as a gifted proverbialist throughout the book. Her proverbial prowess, more than the proverbs her son might have gleaned from reading Cervantes, Dickens, and Twain, appears on many pages of this lively account, with her last proverb, "Ende gut, alles gut," being only the crescendo of it all. As the following pages with numerous examples will show by way of German and English proverbs, Massaquoi's mother had a major influence on his magnificent book, with its many actual proverbs in addition to the multitude of proverbial phrases. It all starts early in the book in the chapter "The New Kid on the Block" (17–23) with its proverbial title. Having found "a tiny, one-room, cold-water, attic flat on the third floor of a tenement building" (17) for them, his working mother tries her best to raise her little boy:

> She was a kind and soft-hearted woman, who, although somewhat gruff in demeanor, never spanked me or in any way became physical when I stepped over the line. She didn't have to. For those not altogether rare occasions, she had a handy deterrent that never failed to do the trick. Intoning the old German proverb "He who doesn't listen must feel"

MASSAQUOI'S PROVERBIAL AUTOBIOGRAPHY *DESTINED TO WITNESS* 281

[Wer nicht hören will, muß fühlen], she'd reach into her broom closet
and fetch her notorious *Rute*, consisting of a bundle of thin twigs tied
together at one end, which, she claimed, Santa Claus had left behind for
precisely such occurrences. Just waving this vaunted instrument of may-
hem in my face was all she needed to do to make me return in a hurry
to the straight and narrow path of righteousness. (22–23)

Not only does this short paragraph include the three phrases "to step over
the line," "to do the trick," and "to be a straight and narrow path," but it also
contains the first example of his mother's rich repertoire of German proverbs
that Massaquoi cites in English. But he does not shy away from confronting
his English readers by often quoting proverbs in German to which he adds
the English translation in parentheses to ensure proper understanding. This
is the case in a scene in which his mother, who had lost her job, is asking for
support from an administrator who desires favors in return: "'I am positive
that I can arrange for you to get your job back,' he added with an encouraging
smile. 'You do understand, however, that I can't go out on a limb for a person with your—let's say—past without you showing me some cooperation.
Eine Hand wäscht die Andere. (One hand washes the other)'" (56). Here, it is a
despicable man who is using the internationally disseminated proverb from
ancient Rome (Paczolay 1997, 174–78) to coerce his mother into a quid pro quo
relationship, but she, "beginning to smell a rat about the size of the administrator" (Massaquoi 1999a, 56), will have no part of it. The proverbial expression "to smell a rat" is fittingly expanded here into a metaphor describing the
manipulative bureaucrat.

Doubtlessly Massaquoi had learned the proverb from his mother, and that is
also the case for the proverb "Man muß gute Miene zum bösen Spiel machen,"
which also exists in the form of the proverbial phrase "gute Miene zum bösen
Spiel machen," as appears in this next reference: "I made *gute Miene zum bösen
Spiel* (smiled in the face of adversity), to quote Mutti, and resigned myself to
the inevitable" (75). It is clear that Massaquoi recalled his mother's proverbial
speech throughout the many years that he was working on his autobiography. This brings to mind observations that the psychoanalyst Theodor Reik
(1888–1969), a student of Sigmund Freud, made in his article "The Echo of the
Proverb" (1939). Just like Massaquoi, he remembers how he heard proverbs
during his childhood and how they are recalled in later life:

In recalling those proverbs and phrases heard in early youth, the memory of the people who used them is easily evoked. Many beloved phan-
toms rise up from the shadowy past, and many hated ones as well. These
proverbs were uttered on various occasions by our parents, relations,

friends, and acquaintances, but most of them, by far, came from our grandfather. [. . .] Something said in passing often reappears after many years as an echo. The hoard of proverbs and idiomatic phrases overheard by us children [. . .] will return more and more frequently the older we grow. They demand that we should listen to them and obey them. What is their purport? To remind us of our childhood, or our parents and grandparents, who once upon a time pronounced them. (Reik 1940, 233–34, 238, 241)

There is no doubt that his mother's proverbs were deeply ingrained in Massaquoi's mind. This comes to the fore in a truly remarkable chapter, "Words of Wisdom" (Massaquoi 1999a, 81–83), which might just as well have been titled "My Mother's Proverbs" or "Mutti's Proverbs." It includes nine German proverbs cited in English translation, to which I have added the texts in their original language. They represent a testimony to Massaquoi's mother, whose proverbial wisdom helped shape her son's personality, and they appear to have been guideposts during his impressive life's journey:

Words of Wisdom
Of the many characteristics that defined my mother, one of the more pronounced ones was her incurable optimism. This was most apparent in her high expectations for me in spite of the dim outlook imposed by Nazi racial laws. Nothing could shake her conviction that, quite apart from race, I had exceptional potential and that some day—Nazis or no Nazis—I would make something of myself. [. . .] She convinced me that an engineering career would be within my reach, if only I reached hard enough. To encourage me to do just that, she would say, "If you want to become a hook, you'll have to start bending early" [Was ein Häkchen werden will, krümmt sich beizeiten].

[. . .] Instead of religious dogma, she had at her command an inexhaustible supply of proverbs, rhymes, and maxims to which she adhered. There was one for every occasion a person might possibly encounter in a lifetime—advice on how to manage money, how to treat friends, why it pays to be punctual, and on and on. It was a legacy from her mother, one she was determined to pass on to me. By the time I started first grade, I already knew that "lies have short legs" [Lügen haben kurze Beine], especially after having been caught in a lie. When she tried to teach me the benefits of a righteous life, she'd say, "A good conscience is a soothing pillow" [Ein gutes Gewissen ist ein sanftes Ruhekissen]. To instill modesty and politeness in me, she'd say, "With hat in hand, you can travel through the entire land" [Mit dem Hut in der Hand kommt man

MASSAQUOI'S PROVERBIAL AUTOBIOGRAPHY *DESTINED TO WITNESS* 283

durchs ganze Land]. To keep me from treating a school chum meanly, she'd warn, "If you dig a hole for others, you'll fall into it yourself" [Wer andern eine Grube gräbt, fällt selbst hinein]. When I seemed unappreciative of a money gift because it was smaller than I expected, she would remind me that "he who doesn't honor the penny doesn't deserve the dollar" [Wer den Pfennig nicht ehrt, ist des Talers nicht wert]. Although, unlike the Ten Commandments, they lacked divine endorsement, these little morsels of German folk wisdom have lost nothing of their validity since I became a man, something I've tried to impress upon my two sons. Today, nothing pleases me more than to hear them quote their *Omi* (granny) or me when making a point. [. . .]

Mutti loved to sing—anything from operatic arias to tunes from movies and operettas, folk songs and hit tunes from her youth. One of her frequent laments was that she didn't have a beautiful voice. That realization, while perhaps true, did not make her any less inclined to fill our apartment with songs, whether she was knitting, crocheting, or doing the laundry. "Where there's music, settle down," she would say, "for evil people have no songs" [Wo man singt, da laß dich nieder, böse Menschen haben keine Lieder].

Generous to a fault, Mutti would spare no effort to help a needy friend in distress. [. . .] She was a courageous, stubborn, and combative woman who didn't mind confronting anyone, high or low, who she felt had done her or me wrong. But if ever someone she had trusted crossed her in a major way, she would put that person out of her life for good with no possibility of reconciliation. She was of the opinion that "trash fights and trash makes up" [Pack schlägt sich, Pack verträgt sich].

Unbounded resiliency enabled her to get through the many ups and downs of her long life. Strong and determined, she used to quip, "Weeds don't perish" [Unkraut vergeht nicht], whenever someone noted her remarkable ability to bounce back from adversity.

Despite her outspokenness that spared no one, Mutti was well liked and, in turn, liked people. Frequently on weekends, our tiny attic was packed with her friends, mostly fellow hospital and factory workers, who gathered for a *gemütlichen Abend* (cozy evening) of talking, singing, laughing, eating, and coffee drinking, all of which were her favorite pastimes. (Massaquoi 1999a, 81–82; in the German translation with the title "Worte der Weisheit," Massaquoi 1999b, 100–103)

In addition to this unique proverbial collage, Massaquoi lets his mother expound proverbs throughout his book as he recalls her wise words of behavioral advice. There are a few paremiological studies that have looked at such proverbial traditions in American (Lindahl 2004; Newall 1994; Robinson 1991; Wienker-Piepho 1991), French (Chiche 1983), Jewish (Ben-Amos 1995; Lévy and Zumwalt 1990), Italian (Bornstein 1991; Filippini 1999), Portuguese (Marbot-Benedetti 1989), Russian (Fomina 2006), and Spanish (Chahin et al. 1999) family settings, usually attesting that wisdom is handed down from grandparents or parents to children (Mieder and Holmes 2000; Mieder 2017). Just as is evident from Massaquoi's recollection of his mother's frequent use of proverbs, these studies deal with family relationships, didacticism, ethics, socialization, tradition, transmission, values, and worldview (Mieder 2009). Hans-Jürgen Massaquoi with his African American wife and his two sons might have been especially interested in Dennis Folly's "Getting the Butter from the Duck: Proverbs and Proverbial Expressions in an Afro-American Family" (1982), Mary Page and Nancy Washington's "Family Proverbs and Value Transmission of Single Black Mothers" (1987), and Linda McWright's "African-American Mothers' Perceptions of Grandparents' Use of Proverbs in Value Socialization of Grandchildren" (1998). Finally, mention must also be made of Derek Williams's study "'Everything That Shine Ain't Gold': A Preliminary Ethnography of a Proverb in an African American Family" (2003), which looks at but one proverb with a particular dominance in a family. As is obvious, the proverb under discussion is an African American variant of the medieval European proverb "All that glitters is not gold" (Paczolay 1997, 125–30).

In any case, here are a few more contextualized references that show the effective use of proverbial language by Massaquoi's amazing mother, who as a single mother coped through years of hardship and raised her biracial son to be an exemplary person who respected, admired, and loved her to the end. In the first reference, his Mutti remembers her own mother, Massaquoi's grandmother, having employed the proverb as family wisdom:

> Like most German women of her generation, she avoided going into debt, convinced like her mother that *borgen macht Sorgen* (to borrow makes sorrow). Consequently, she categorically never bought anything on credit. (Massaquoi 1999a, 88)

> Even the corroborating testimony of my story by several of the perpetrators [the boys had launched paper gliders from the balcony during a church service] could not sway him [Pastor Ottmer] to let me off the hook. I remembered my mother's dictum, *Mitgefangen, mitgehangen* (caught together, hanged together). With 20/20 hindsight, I could see that she had been right. Even though I had not participated in the glider caper, I had put myself in the company of goof-offs on the balcony and thus gotten myself into a mess. (147)

Morris's [his Liberian brother] shack made our basement refuge in bombed-out Hamburg look inviting. I had trouble concealing my shock at the squalid conditions in which my brother had been living and shuddered at the thought of having to call this hovel my home. But I decided not to sound too negative. Besides, I had long ago learned from my mother that "in a pinch, the devil eats flies" [In der Not frißt der Teufel Fliegen]. (380)

Although I hadn't touched a lathe since I worked for Lindner A. G. in Nazi Germany, it took only a short while to feel at home behind the cranks and levers of the machine in front of me. My mother was right, *gelernt ist gelernt* (learned is learned). (417)

Massaquoi does not always mention his mother when citing a German proverb, but he almost definitely learned them from her. Here is a telling example in which he applies a well-known proverb to himself:

That evening I scrubbed and dressed with extra care in preparation of the adventure ahead. Whatever second thoughts cropped up in my mind, they were quickly dispelled by my hopeless state of anticipation. With near-fatalistic resignation, I invoked the old popular German proverb that holds—quite illogically, I think—that *Wer A sagt muss auch B sagen* (he who says A must also say B). I certainly had taken step A, and nothing could stop me from taking a crack at step B. If everything worked out according to my plan, today—July 31, 1941— would go down in history as the day when I learned the true meaning of making love. Much later I discovered that it was also the day on which *Reichsmarschall* Hermann Göring issued the first known written order for the murder of all Jews living under Nazi rule, an action he referred to as the *Endlösung* (Final Solution). (190)

Having been brought up with a barrage of German proverbs, Massaquoi developed his own fondness for proverbial wisdom and incorporated it repeatedly in his autobiographical narrative. But as an adult journalist living in the United States communicating in excellent oral and written English, he obviously built up his own repertoire of proverbs in that language. One is inclined to change the old proverb "Like father, like son" to the befitting anti-proverb "Like mother, like son." Right at the beginning, Massaquoi talks about his German grandfather and includes the proverbs "Charity begins at home" and "Last hired, first fired," with the latter being a modern American proverb having originated in 1918 (Doyle, Mieder, and Shapiro 2012, 121; Mieder 2019, 129):

While he [Hermann Baetz, his mother's father] felt no animosity toward the foreigners [Italian laborers], he was a patriotic German of simple principles, which included the firm conviction that charity begins at home. For years, several Italians had worked at the quarry when jobs were plentiful. But the unwritten rule had always been that they were the last to be hired and, if there was a shortage of jobs, the first to be fired. (Massaquoi 1999a, 6)

The proverb "Absence makes the heart grow fonder" appears quite differently twice in the autobiography, with the second text negating the proverb to describe Massaquoi's troubled relationship with his father, who had abandoned him and his mother. Together, these two proverb instantiations show clearly that proverbs exhibit polysituativity, polyfunctionality, and polysemanticity and that they are not necessarily cited in their traditional wording (Mieder 2004, 9):

Although I had become extremely sensitive about displaying affection and emotions in public since I entered school, I made an exception when I let my mother hug and kiss me to her heart's content. It was at that point that I discovered the old verity that absence makes the heart grow fonder. (Massaquoi 1999a, 66–67)

A flood of conflicting emotions took hold of me as I prepared to open the letter [from his father], the first tangible link in almost eighteen years with the man my mother had taught me to call *father* despite the fact that from the time he left us, while I was still a little boy, he had been largely a stranger to me. Time and absence had not made my heart grow fonder of him. If I felt anything about him, it was detached curiosity. (333)

But here are a few more examples of Massaquoi's effective and expressive integration of proverbs that underscore his trials and tribulations as a biracial youngster in Nazi Germany, as a young adult in Liberia, and eventually as an immigrant in America:

Herr Harden [his English teacher] was a fanatic practitioner of the "spare the rod and spoil the child" philosophy, and—backed by a system that condoned, if not encouraged, corporal punishment—literally made the rod the centerpiece of his pedagogy. As a result, he was the most despised and feared teacher on the Kätnerkamp faculty. He was also the first teacher who got a piece of my hide during my eventful eight-year elementary school career. (75–76)

Sometimes her [his mother's] methods of instilling values in me and indelibly impressing on my young mind that crime doesn't pay were as creative as they were effective. It didn't take me long to realize that her wheels of justice turned swiftly and inexorably. (87)

When a pupil referred to my scholastic and athletic abilities to refute [teacher] Dutke's contention that people of other than "Aryan blood" were both intellectually and physically inferior, Dutke dressed down the pupil for daring to disagree with him. He then lectured the class that my case was merely the exception that proved the rule, and suggested that whatever "normal characteristics" I displayed I had definitely inherited from my Aryan parent. (110)

Then, after suggesting that in every barrel of apples, there are a few rotten ones, he [school principal Wriede] continued, with a withering stare in my direction, that there would be some boys who, for one reason or another, would be found unworthy of the honor of wearing the uniform of a German soldier. For them, he said, he had only one piece of advice: to get out of Germany while they could. (129–30)

By an odd coincidence, shortly after I joined the boxing club, Hitler made boxing lessons an integral part of all schools' athletic curricula, since he was convinced that boxing built character and bolstered self-confidence. By the time the first boxing classes were taught in my class by a teacher who had to take a crash course in the sport's fundamentals, I was already an accomplished amateur boxer. Since in the land of the blind, the one-eyed man is king, I was hailed immediately as a boxing phenom. (137–38)

On the wall above the workbench was a large poster with an illustration of a blond Siegfried-type worker with rolled-up sleeves and bulging muscles, holding a heavy hammer in his right hand. ARBEIT ADELT (Work ennobles)! the poster claimed in large letters against the backdrop of a swastika flag. If the poster's intent was to inspire us, it had totally missed its purpose with me. All I could see in my immediate future was a lot of toil and drudgery and very little, if any nobility. (151–52; this is actually an anti-proverb of "Tugend adelt" and a clear sign of proverb manipulation by Nazi propaganda; see Mieder 1993, 225–55)

From the few times I had met Hans's parents, I had always assumed that they were just an ordinary working couple whose biggest adventure in life was watching their only child achieve victories in the boxing ring. But I soon learned never to judge a book by its cover. (Massaquoi 1999a, 157)

But since we had no role models by which to judge our performance, we "jitterbugged" to our hearts' content behind Herr Lucas's [the dance instructor's] back, and in the process proved beyond a shadow of doubt that ignorance is truly bliss. (180)

Following a brief "short-arm inspection" and rubdown with a dry towel [in a Hamburg brothel], she pulled out a fresh condom and, before I could say *Danke schön*, had me all suited up and ready to go. Without further ado she flung herself backward on the bed, spread her ample thighs, and reminded me in a querulous voice that time was money and that five marks didn't entitle me to spend all night. (187)

I decided to play hooky from my gig [as a musician] at the Alkazar the following day and instead return to the *Appleton Victory*. Hard times had long taught me to not pass up an opportunity to make hay while the sun shines. (302)

I now understood what he [his father] meant when he told me about the advantages of being a big frog in a little pond, like Liberia, versus the other way around. (369–70)

The wheels [of a demolished car], it appeared, had already been picked clean of tires by "salvagers," as was the interior of the van, which showed no trace that it had been loaded with rice. It reminded me of the old saying, "One man's meat is another man's poison." For the hungry bellies of the poor villagers of Ganta [in Liberia], my father's accident and several thousand pounds of rice must have been a welcome windfall. (392)

At least Karl [a childhood friend] was spared the indignity suffered by many German POWs who, upon their return home, found their wives had replaced them with an English or American soldier—true to the saying, "To the winner go the spoils." (442)

These selected references are ample proof of Hans-Jürgen Massaquoi's virtuosic employment of proverbs that he integrates in their traditional wording or in innovative alterations. At times he only cites them partially or merely alludes to them, as in "being a big frog in a little pond" cited above. *The Dictionary of Modern Proverbs* (Doyle, Mieder, and Shapiro 2012, 78, 64) lists two complete variants: "Better a big fish in a little pond (puddle, pool) than a little fish in a big pond (mighty ocean)" from 1903, and "It is better to be a big duck in a little puddle (pond) than a little duck in a big puddle (pond)" from 1934 (Mieder 2020, 199–200). To this can now be added Massaquoi's third variant, which in its entirety must be "It is better to be big frog in a little pond than a little frog in a big pond." In any case, as the attached index of proverbial texts shows, his autobiography, in addition to its intrinsic value as a personal account of survival and struggle for identity, is also a paremiological and paremiographical treasure trove.

Finally, then, it comes as no surprise that Hans-Jürgen Massaquoi, who "stuck it out in the United States and became a leading journalist after graduating from the University of Illinois" (Barkin 2009, 263), very appropriately cites the proverb "You can't go home again," which has become a modern proverb with its inception as the title of Thomas Wolfe's (1900–1938) novel published posthumously in 1940 (Doyle, Mieder, and Shapiro 2012, 123). It appears in the last chapter, "Germany Revisited" (430–36), in which Massaquoi recalls his visit to his original homeland in 1966 that resulted in the already mentioned two-part descriptive and reflective essay published in that year in *Ebony*. Having been forging a new existence for sixteen years by then, it must have been a heart-wrenching experience for him to fly to Frankfurt and then travel on to his native Hamburg. Here is but one lengthy paragraph of his moving account, with the proverb at its end:

> Visiting my former neighborhood on the north side of town, I stood stunned before a crate-littered vacant lot where on that memorable summer night twenty-three years earlier my home had been razed in an air attack. It seemed that the "[new economic] miracle" hadn't quite reached this point. Briefly, I paused at the site of the air-raid shelter where I had survived the crucial attack that had turned my neighborhood into an inferno. I remembered the charred corpses of the unfortunate people who had been unable to reach the shelter in time. On that site there now stood a spanking-new housing development with green play lots and children playing the same old games I had played as a little boy. As I watched them, I wished, somehow, that at least one of them would give me once again the old *Neger, Neger, Schornsteinfeger* routine, just for old time's sake. But either German children had changed, or I no longer rated. Like a latter-day Rip van Winkle, I walked the vaguely familiar-looking streets where once I had known just about every lamp-post, every tree, and every face, unrecognized by the people I met and recognizing none of them. For me, who had once been a celebrity of sorts in Barmbek [a suburb of Hamburg], whom everybody had known,

if not by name, certainly as *der Negerjunge*, it was an unfamiliar feeling. At that moment the full truth of Thomas Wolfe's famous assertion hit me: you can't go home again. (Massaquoi 1999a, 432–33)

Amazing, how Massaquoi experiences a strange longing to hear that children's rhyme "Neger, Neger, Schornsteinfeger" in a bizarre nostalgic moment, perhaps forgetting for an instant what a terrible stereotype it was. Surely, he had no intention to return to Germany, but one senses some love for it despite the horrors that had been brought to thousands of innocent people by way of the Holocaust and otherwise. By the mid-1960s he had found his identity as "an African American with deep German ethnic roots," as he described it in a letter from 2005 (Lindhout 2006, 4). America had been his dream, and it became the new homeland for him as a former Afro-German and his mother. Thus, indeed, there is plenty of truth in the proverb that "You can't go home again," but the old German proverbs appeared in Hans-Jürgen Massaquoi's life as echoes of the past and wisdom for the future.

NOTA BENE

I thank my colleague and friend Helga Schreckenberger from the University of Vermont for giving me Hans-Jürgen Massaquoi's autobiography as a Christmas present in 2020. The book means more to me as a German immigrant to the United States in 1960 than words can express. As far as my life as a paremiologist is concerned, *Destined to Witness* represents the best there is regarding proverbs as meaningful wisdom and worldview.

INDEX OF PROVERBIAL TEXTS

The following list of phraseologisms (proverbs, proverbial expressions, proverbial comparisons, twin formulas, idioms, and a few quotations), alphabetically arranged according to keywords, registers all 509 proverbial texts (645 counting 136 duplicates) with their page numbers from Hans-Jürgen Massaquoi's autobiography *Destined to Witness: Growing Up Black in Nazi Germany* (1999). An asterisk * identifies actual proverbs.

A
* *Wer A sagt muss auch B sagen* (he who says A must also say B) 190
To rest (sleep) in **Abraham's** bosom (lap) 380
***Absence** makes the heart grow fonder 67, 333

To be in the **air** 53
To clear the **air** 343
To not take no for an **answer** 83
To keep up **appearances** 281
To whet one's **appetite** 185
*There is at least one rotten **apple** in every barrel 129
To be the **apple** of one's eye 12
*ARBEIT ADELT (Work ennobles) 151
To charge an **arm** and a leg 183, 271
To give one's right **arm** for something 307
To twist someone's **arm** 374
To welcome with open **arms** 127, 135, 276, 337, 409
To be an *Arschloch* (asshole) 418
To be down on one's **ass** 232
To get one's **ass** whipped 218
To stick something up someone's **ass** 70
To be an **asshole** 303

B
To throw the **baby** out with the bathwater 286
To get someone off one's **back** 104, 263, 355
To keep off one's **back** 181
To turn one's **back** on someone 426
To be left holding the **bag** 251
To have a **ball** 375
To keep the **ball** rolling 415
To go **bananas** 50
To jump (get) on the **bandwagon** 104
To undergo a **baptism** of fire 234
To take off like a **bat** out of hell 318
To fight an uphill **battle** 271
Can you **beat** that? 297
To **beat** someone green and blue 115
To skip a **beat** 150
To buzz like a **beehive** 195
***Beggars** can't be choosers 115, 315
To be the **beginning** of the end 196
To have something under one's **belt** 426
To get the **best** of someone 131
To hope for the **best** 144
To make the **best** of something 202, 373

The **birds** and the bees 73, 259
Ain't that a **bitch**? 297
To pitch a **bitch** 320
To take the **bitter** with the sweet 428
***Black** is beautiful 60
To be a **blessing** in disguise 439
*In the land of the **blind**, the one-eyed are kings 138
To have something get into one's **blood** 155
Out of the **blue** 32
To be in the same **boat** 239
To miss the **boat** 79, 149
With **body** and soul 161
To be like a **bolt** of lightning 99
*Don't judge a **book** by its cover 157
To be in one's **book** 31, 357
To have written the **book** on something 283
To give someone the **boot** 175
To be at the **bottom** of the totem pole 426
*German **boys** don't cry 130
To rack one's **brain** 186
To put **bread** on the table 272
To give someone a **break** 182
To **breeze** through something 133
To shoot the **breeze** 175, 389
To cross the **bridge** when one gets to it 233
To beat around the **bush** 285, 301
To be smooth as a baby's **butt** 160
To be the **butt** of a joke 143
To **butter** someone up 331
*Let **bygones** be bygones 258, 387

C
To be a piece of **cake** 248
To be a wake-up **call** 327
To open a **can** of worms 227
To be quite a **card** 399
To play one's **cards** right 398
*You play the **cards** you are dealt 327
To build **castles** in the air 337
To let the **cat** out of the bag 103
To look like the **cat** that swallowed the canary 249

To play **cat** and mouse 330
To **catch** someone red-handed 329, 424
To throw **caution** to the wind 162, 183, 243
To hit the **ceiling** 217, 372
To add one's two **cents'** worth 164
To have a fighting **chance** 194
To jump at the **chance** 399
To play **charades** 326
***Charity** begins at home 6
To work like a **charm** 410
To be a reality **check** 326
To turn the other **cheek** 147, 402
To have the right **chemistry** 315
To get something off one's **chest** 379
To be **chicken** 177
***Children** should be seen and not heard 153
To be (in) the inner **circle** 83
To be in a **class** by oneself 75
To only have the **clothes** on one's back 277
To be too close for **comfort** 113
To not know whether one is **coming** or going 419
*A good **conscience** is a soothing pillow 81
   (translated German proverb: Ein gutes Gewissen ist ein sanftes Ruhekissen)
To keep one's **cool** 224
To be driven (pushed) into a **corner** 249, 330
To blow one's **cover** 198, 306, 317
To fall through the **cracks** xvi
To have to one's **credit** 188
To be up shit's **creek** 249
To give someone the **creeps** 74
***Crime** doesn't pay 87
To cry (shed) **crocodile** tears 29
To be a far **cry** from something 134, 218, 259, 318, 358, 396

D
To put a **damper** on something 112
To be a **damsel** in distress 280
To bring someone up to **date** 285, 289
To call it a **day** 240
The good old **days** 289
To have seen better **days** 273

294   PROVERBS IN LITERATURE

To be **dead** set against something 121
To not want to be seen **dead** with someone 105
To have a **deal** 149
To be in the lion's **den** 107, 324
To be left to one's own **devices** 17
Devil-may-care 51
*In a pinch, the **devil** eats flies 380
    (translated German proverb: In der Not frißt der Teufel Fliegen)
To roll the **dice** 421
To be a **dime** a dozen 273
To (not) imagine in one's wildest **dreams** 8
At the **drop** of a hat 239
To march to a different **drummer** 31, 369
To be a sitting **duck** 205
To take to something like a **duck** to water 9
To be an ugly **duckling** 167
To pay one's **dues** 400, 430

E
To grin from **ear** to ear 314, 387
To turn a deaf **ear** to something 437
To (not) be meant for someone's **ears** 154
To not believe one's **ears** 136
To be rough at the **edges** 416
To be a dead **end** 430
__Ende__ gut, alles gut (All's well that ends well) 443
To make **ends** meet 74, 88, 149
To be green with **envy** 104, 157
To be a necessary **evil** 6
To be the root of all **evil** 106, 197
*The **exception** proves the rule 110
To look someone in the **eye** 138
Without blinking an **eye** 17
To raise an **eyebrow** 305
To keep **eyes** and ears open 153
To make one's **eyes** pop 248
To not believe one's **eyes** 124

F
To get out of someone's **face** 244
Until being blue in the **face** 81, 423

*MASSAQUOI'S PROVERBIAL AUTOBIOGRAPHY *DESTINED TO WITNESS* 295*

Father knows best 351
To ruffle **feathers** 343
To get back on one's **feet** 362, 375
To land on one's **feet** 441
To sweep someone off their **feet** 11
To think on one's **feet** 287
To be **few** and far between 314
To be fit as a **fiddle** 419
To level the playing **field** 38
To keep one's **fingers** crossed 107
To be a **Flasche** (the derisive street term for "weakling") 117, 135
To not hurt a **fly** 153
To make a **fool** out of oneself 49, 77, 359
My **foot** 218
Free at last 250
    (based on a spiritual and popularized by Martin Luther King Jr.'s use of the
    phrase at the end of his "I Have a Dream" speech of August 28, 1963)
*Better a big **frog** in a small pond than a little frog in a big pond 370
To be a forbidden **fruit** 187, 288
We don't **fuck** with them, and they don't fuck with us 297, 298, 318, 427
To be **fun** and games 129

G
To play **games** with someone 327
To let the **genie** out of the bottle 79
To hang up one's **gloves** 138, 434
To get someone's **goat** 71
To be too **good** to be true 254, 310, 337
To get (have) **goose pimples** 122
*Ich lasse den lieben **Gott** einen guten Mann sein* (I let God be a good
    man) 145
To be sour **grapes** 104
To go (hear it) through the **grapevine** 95, 315, 332
To be caught off **guard** 287
To be a smoking **gun** 394
To hate someone's **guts** 109

H
Hals- und Beinbruch (neck and leg fracture) 237
To grind to a **halt** 133
Eine **Hand wäscht die andere* (One hand washes the other) 56

296 PROVERBS IN LITERATURE

One **hand** doesn't know what the other one is doing 427
To overplay one's **hand** 226
To get (put) one's **hands** on something 116, 280
To have one's **hands** full 345
To hold something in one's **hands** 150
To take something into one's own **hands** 38
To wash one's **hands** of something 433
To work one's **hands** to the bone 283
To engage in **hanky-panky** 161
To play **hardball** 217
*With **hat** in the hand, you can travel through the entire land 81
  (translated German proverb: Mit dem Hut in der Hand, kommst du durch
  das ganze Land)
To wreak **havoc** 250
*Make **hay** while the sun shines 302
From **head** to toe 266
Something raises its ugly **head** 437
To be over one's **head** 108, 133, 365
To drum into someone's **head** 171
To go to one's **head** 90
To walk with one's **head** high 112
To not make **heads** or tails out of something 269
From the bottom of one's **heart** 53, 104, 328
To have one's **heart** in something 315
To one's **heart's** content 178, 180
To put **heart** and soul into something 197
To smell to high **heaven** 305
To be **hell** on earth 198
To beat the **hell** out of someone 164
To catch **hell** 423
To go to **hell** 418
To have all **hell** break loose 204
To raise holy **hell** 182
To rest on one's lazy **hide** 132
With **hide** and hair 158
  (translated from German: mit Haut und Haar)
To have 20/20 **hindsight** 371
*Last **hired**, first fired 6
To be a **hit** 65
To go through without a **hitch** 69

MASSAQUOI'S PROVERBIAL AUTOBIOGRAPHY *DESTINED TO WITNESS* 297

*If you dig a **hole** for others, you'll fall into it yourself 81
  (translated German proverb: Wer andern eine Grube gräbt, fällt selbst hinein)
To be a **hole** in the ground 205, 206
To need like a **hole** in the head 414
***Home**, sweet home 264
To be a **home** away from home 318, 374
To drive something **home** 258, 425
To strike **home** 54, 92
*You can't go **home** again 433
To have done one's **homework** 168
By **hook** or by crook 133, 262
*If you want to become a **hook**, you'll have to start bending early 81
  (translated German proverb: Was ein Häkchen werden will, krümmt
  sich beizeiten)
To be (let someone) off the **hook** 147, 276, 293
To play **hooky** 302
To hope against **hope** 197, 293
*What is hot is **hot** and what's not is not 316
At the eleventh **hour** 253
to have the run of the **house** 12
The **hustle** and bustle 294

I
To be on thin **ice** 174
To break the **ice** 171, 356
To not have the foggiest **idea** 262
***Ignorance** is bliss 180
To add **insult** to injury 49
To be an **item** 155, 172

J
To hit the **jackpot** 371
To be a big **joke** 276
To be a **Judas** 331
To be noisy like in a **Judenschule** 102

K
To earn one's **keep** 149
To play for **keeps** 425
To **kick** oneself 188

298   PROVERBS IN LITERATURE

To be the new **kid** on the block 17
To treat someone with **kid gloves** 383
To **kiss** and make up 258
To **kiss** someone's behind 190
To **know** what one is talking about 83

L
The **land** of the free and the home of the brave 411, 421
The **land** of unlimited opportunities 8
    (translated from German: Land der unbegrenzten Möglichkeiten)
Land der unbegrenzten Möglichkeiten (land of unlimited possibilities) 51
To be the **land** of milk and honey 328
To be happy as a **lark** 275, 291
Last but not least 159, 281
To have the last **laugh** 260
To be in someone's **league** 133
*Gelernt ist gelernt (learned is learned) 417
To have a new **lease** on life 207
Tough as **leather**, swift as greyhounds, and hard as Kruppsteel 115
    (Hitler quotation)
Liberty and justice for all 319
To be a white **lie** 316
***Lies** have short legs 81
    (translated German proverb: Lügen haben kurze Beine)
***Life** goes on 145
To be (have) the good **life** 12
To hang on for dear **life** 303
To see the **light** at the end of the tunnel 430
To strike someone like **lightning** 337
To risk **life** and limb 194, 262
To go out on a **limb** 56
To be out of **line** 134
To step over the **line** 22
To be the weakest **link** in the chain 274
*He who doesn't **listen** must feel 22
    (translated German proverb: Wer nicht hören will, muß fühlen)
Get a **load** of that 297
To be **love** at first sight 160, 337, 415
To (not) press one's **luck** 310
To leave someone in the **lurch** 182

M

To have (got) it **made** 295, 299
To **make** something out of oneself 443
The **man** on the street 120
To hit (kick) a **man** when he's down 136
*To kiss a **man** without a mustache is like eating an egg without salt 423
To put something on the **map** 10
To lose one's **marbles** 150
To be the real **McCoy** 423
*One man's **meat** is another man's poison 392
To be dead **meat** 243
If this is so, I want to be called **Meier** 142
   (Hermann Göring quotation)
To have the **Midas** touch 246
*Gute **Miene** zum bösen Spiel machen* (smile in the face of adversity) 75
To be in one's right **mind** 167
To lose one's **mind** 281
To be a gold **mine** 410
To have fifteen **minutes** of fame 350
**Mitgefangen, mitgehangen* (caught together, hanged together) 147
Slow as **molasses** 339
***Money** doesn't grow on trees 50
To be right on the **money** 379
To get one's **money's** worth 280
To keep one's **mouth** shut 153, 332, 367, 382, 393, 400, 410
To be **music** to one's ears 357
To face the **music** 117
*Where there's **music**, settle down, for evil people have no songs 82
   (translated German proverb: Wo man singt, da laß dich nieder, böse Men-
schen haben keine Lieder)

N

To be the **name** of the game xiv, 177
To stick out one's **neck** 139
Neger, Neger, Schornsteinfeger (Negro, Negro, chimney sweep)! 18, 37 twice,
   431, 433
To get on one's **nerves** 94
Nichts für ungut (No offense meant) 181
To keep one's **nose** clean 216
***Nothing** lasts forever 94

300 PROVERBS IN LITERATURE

To declare something **null** and void 272
In a **nutshell** 435

O

To rise to the **occasion** 381
To have the **odds** against oneself 76
To extend an **olive** branch 390
To go into **overdrive** 196

P

To be (get) caught with one's **pants** down 29, 182
To have something down **pat** 69
To be a straight and narrow **path** 23, 148
To be at **peace** with oneself 435
As proud as a **peacock** 360
To be like two **peas** in a pod 429
*He who doesn't honor the **penny** doesn't deserve the dollar 82
 (translated German proverb: Wer den Pfennig nicht ehrt, ist des Talers
 nicht wert)
To get into a **pickle** 182
To paint a rosy **picture** 412
To see the big **picture** 104
To not hear a **pin** drop 426
To **pinch** hit 71
To smoke the peace **pipe** 79
To fall into **place** 430
To put someone in his **place** 36
To avoid like the **plague** 30, 94, 166, 297
*The best-laid **plans** of men and mice often go astray 30
To hand (be handed) on a silver **platter** 262
To be fair **play** 139
To be foul **play** 126
To take the **plunge** 184, 407
To come to the **point** 165, 395
To drive home a **point** 108, 127, 174
To earn brownie **points** 265, 384
To be in a **pressure cooker** 138
To pay the **price** 162
To keep a low **profile** 418
To beat someone to the **punch** 387
To be **puppy love** 134

Q

To be out of the **question** 381
To hurt someone to the **quick** 115
To **quit** while being ahead 157

R

Rain or shine 50
To take a **rain check** 169
Rank and file 234
To **rant** and rave 342
To smell a **rat** 56
The **rats** are leaving the sinking ship 77
To be the **razor's edge** 262
*You shall **reap** what you sow 267
To be thin as a **reed** 64
To give full **rein** to someone 251, 373
To turn over the **reins** 264
To get something on the **road** 309
To hit the **road** 312, 404
To be like **Robin Hood** who robbed the rich to give to the poor 250
*Spare the **rod** and spoil the child 76
To fiddle while **Rome** burns 80
*When in **Rome** do as the Romans do 405
To have no **room** at the inn 242
To show someone the **ropes** 242, 243, 248
To be **rough** and ready 160
To pull the **rug** from under someone 354
To give someone a **run** for his money 133
*You can **run** but you can't hide xii

S

To hit the **sack** 122
To play it **safe** 129
*Easier **said** than done 69, 161, 209, 214, 235
For old time's **sake** 433
To be a good **Samaritan** 237
From **scalp** to toes 193
To be a **scapegoat** 130, 236, 415
To make a **scene** 35
To be a *Schweinehund* 230
To even the **score** 269

By the **seat** of one's pants 191, 363

To be beyond a **shadow** of a doubt 180

To get a fair **shake** 431

To be the lion's **share** 267

To have one's **share** 30

To be a sinking **ship** 194

To (not) give a **shit** 287, 418

The **shoe** is on the other foot 232

To be a big **shot** 65, 90, 168, 174, 234, 413

To fall on someone's **shoulders** 146

To run the **show** 171

To be **sick** and tired 48, 200

To be on the safe **side** 116

To **sink** or swim 364

To be like **Sisyphus** pushing a rock up a hill 378

By the **skin** of one's teeth 225

To come out of the blue **sky** 210

To get a **slap** on the wrist 260, 276

To have something up one's **sleeve** 230

Slowly but surely 205

Sodom and Gomorrah 201

*You give (win) **some**, you take (lose) some 136

To be a **son** of a bitch 297, 354

Sooner or later 70, 172, 278, 353

*Borgen macht **Sorgen** (to borrow makes sorrow) 88

To be **spic** and span 396

To put one's own **spin** on something 180

To get back to **square** one 436

To be **squared** away 302

To be a **stab** in the back 53 twice

To set the **stage** 166

To be at **stake** 180

To **stand** tall 424

To have a head **start** 28

To **steal** someone blind 421

To watch one's **step** 314

To cause a **stir** 64

To keep someone in **stitches** 399, 415

To have in **store** for someone 131, 332

To be the lull before the **storm** 144

MASSAQUOI'S PROVERBIAL AUTOBIOGRAPHY *DESTINED TO WITNESS* 303

To talk up a **storm** 346
To be a two-way **street** 136
To be a **strike** against someone 434
To **strike** out 188
To be a quick **study** 389
To know one's **stuff** 132
Anything under the **sun** 360
In one fell **swoop** 257

T
To fit to a **T** 247
To master to a **T** 383
To turn the **tables** on someone 168
To make small **talk** 411
To be a hard **taskmaster** 136
To be armed to one's **teeth** 254
To come with the **territory** 162
To be the acid **test** 266
Thanks but no thanks 283, 401
To have second **thoughts** 190, 386
To make something **tick** 153
Long **time** no see 279
***Time** is money 187
To be (have) quality **time** 23
To be in the nick of **time** 77, 390
To give someone a hard **time** 321
To have a good **time** 310
To kill **time** 185
To (not) give someone the **time** of day 300
To be a **time bomb** 194
To be the **tip** of the iceberg 399
To step on **toes** 120
To weigh like a **ton** of bricks 191
To be **tongue** in cheek 419
To hold one's **tongue** 48
To fight **tooth** and nail 439
To throw in the **towel** 75, 93, 284
***Trash** fights and trash makes up 82
  (translated German proverb: Pack schlägt sich, Pack verträgt sich)
To give someone the royal **treatment** 411

304   PROVERBS IN LITERATURE

To do the **trick** 22, 181
To play **tricks** on someone 376
To put **two** and two together 108 twice, 198, 418

W
To be a **wallflower** 179
To test the **waters** 364
To make **waves** 341
To be on one's merry **way** 305, 313
To go out of one's **way** 73
To learn the hard **way** 129, 136
To look the other **way** 91, 107
To be the worse for **wear** 314
As dependable as the **weather** in April 280
***Weeds** don't perish 82
    (translated German proverb: Unkraut vergeht nicht)
To leave **well** enough alone 30, 439
To be the fifth **wheel** 172
To be clean as a **whistle** 270
*Um Himmels **Willen*** (in heaven's name) 223
To be in a no-**win** situation 56
To be a new **wind** blowing 67
To catch a second **wind** 185
To get **wind** of something 229
To be a **windfall** 392
*To the **winner** go the spoils 442
To be out of the **woods** 172, 225
To be dyed in the **wool** 71, 114, 313
To pull the **wool** over someone's eyes 48
To keep one's **word** 151
To put in a good **word** for someone 177
To speak the last **word** 110
To take someone by his **word** 1
To take someone's **word** for something 298
To not mince **words** 70
To be all **work** and no play 159, 194
To be (feel) on top of the **world** 387
To be a nervous **wreck** 150
*Ich weiss es wird einmal ein **Wunder** geschehn* (I know a miracle is going to
    happen) 197
    (actress Zarah Leander in the film *Die große Liebe*)

BIBLIOGRAPHY

This chapter was first published with the same title in *Proverbium: Yearbook of International Proverb Scholarship* 39 (2022): 173–223.

Barkin, Kenneth. 2009. "African Americans, Afro-Germans, White Americans, and Germans." Review of *Race After Hitler*, by Heide Fehrenbach, and *Witness to Destiny*, by Hans J. Massaquoi. *Journal of African American History* 94, no. 2 (Spring): 253–65.

Ben-Amos, Dan. 1995. "Meditation on a Russian Proverb in Israel." *Proverbium* 12: 13–26.

Blackshire-Belay, Carol Aisha, ed. 1996. *The African-German Experience: Critical Essays.* Westport, CT: Praeger.

Bornstein, Valerie. 1991. "A Case Study and Analysis of Family Proverb Use." *Proverbium* 8: 19–28.

Bryan, George B., and Wolfgang Mieder. 1997. *The Proverbial Charles Dickens: An Index to Proverbs in the Works of Charles Dickens.* New York: Peter Lang.

Campt, Tina M. 2004. *Other Germans: Black Germans and the Politics of Race, Gender, and Memory in the Third Reich.* Ann Arbor. University of Michigan Press.

Chahin, Jaime, Francisco A. Villarruel, and Ruben Anguiano Viramontez. 1999. "*Dichos y Refranes*: The Transmission of Cultural Values and Beliefs." In *Family Ethnicity: Strength in Diversity*, 2nd ed., edited by Harriette Pipes McAdoo, 153–67. Thousand Oaks, CA: SAGE Publications.

Chiche, Michèle. 1983. "Proverbes . . . et mon enfance embaume ma mémoire." *Cahiers de littérature orale*, no. 13: 159–61.

Doyle, Charles Clay, Wolfgang Mieder, and Fred R. Shapiro. 2012. *The Dictionary of Modern Proverbs.* New Haven, CT: Yale University Press.

Filippini, Giovanna. 1999. "Detti tramandati in una famiglia fiorentina." In *Proverbi, locuzioni modi di dire nel dominio linguistico italiano*, edited by Salvatore C. Trovato, 231–36. Rome: Editrice Il Calamo.

Folly, Dennis W. [Anand Prahlad]. 1982. "Getting the Butter from the Duck: Proverbs and Proverbial Expressions in an Afro-American Family." In *A Celebration of American Family Folklore: Tales and Traditions from the Smithsonian Collection*, edited by Stephen J. Zeitlin, Amy J. Kotkin, and Holly Cutting Baker, 232–41, 290–91. New York: Pantheon Books.

Fomina, Sinaida. 2006. "'Der Vogel freut sich über den Frühling und das Kind freut sich über seine Mutter': Familie im russischen Sprichwort." *Proverbium* 23: 135–68.

Gallacher, Stuart A. 1970. "By Hook or by Crook." *Proverbium* 15: 451–53.

Gengenbach, Karl. 2016. *Wahre Geschichten von damals und heute.* Norderstedt, Germany: Books on Demand.

Hodges, Carolyn. 2001. "The Color of Blood: Black German Writers and Racial Integration." *Synthesis: An Interdisciplinary Journal* 6: 51–64.

Lévy, Isaac Jack, and Rosemary Lévy Zumwalt. 1990. "A Conversation in Proverbs: Judeo-Spanish 'Refranes' in Context." *Proverbium* 7: 117–32. Also in *New Horizons in Sephardic Studies*, edited by Yedida K. Stillman and George K. Zucker, 269–83. Albany: State University of New York Press, 1993. Also in *Cognition, Comprehension, and Communication: A Decade of North American Proverb Studies (1990–2000)*, edited by Wolfgang Mieder, 255–69. Baltmannsweiler, Germany: Schneider Verlag Hohengehren, 2003.

Lindahl, Carl. 2004. "Proverbs Ever After: Proverbial Links Between the Märchen Diction and the Everyday Conversation of a Kentucky Mountain Family." In *Res humanae proverbiorum et sententiarum: Ad honorem Wolfgangi Mieder*, edited by Csaba Földes, 187–96. Tübingen, Germany: Gunter Narr.

Lindhout, Alexandra E. 2006. "Hans J. Massaquoi's *Destined to Witness* as an Autobiographical Act of Identity Formation." *COPAS: Current Objectives of Postgraduate American Studies* 7. https://copas.uni-regensburg.de/article/view/89/113.

Marbot-Benedetti, Claire. 1989. "La famille à travers les proverbes." In *Europhras 88: Phraséologie contrastive; Actes du Colloque International Klingenthal-Strasbourg, May 12–16, 1988*, edited by Gertrud Gréciano, 291–300. Strasbourg, France: Université des Sciences Humaines.

Martin, Elaine. 2001. "Hans J. Massaquoi, *Destined to Witness: Growing Up Black in Nazi Germany*." *Colloquia Germanica* 34, no. 1: 91–94.

Massaquoi, Hans-Jürgen. 1966. "A Journey into the Past," parts 1 and 2. *Ebony*, February, 91–99; and *Ebony*, March, 102–11.

Massaquoi, Hans-Jürgen. 1984. "Hans Massaquoi." In *"The Good War": An Oral History of World War Two*, edited by Studs Terkel, 496–504. New York: Pantheon Books.

Massaquoi, Hans-Jürgen. 1999a. *Destined to Witness: Growing Up Black in Nazi Germany*. New York: William Morrow.

Massaquoi, Hans-Jürgen. 1999b. *Neger, Neger, Schornsteinfeger: Meine Kindheit in Deutschland*. Munich: Fretz und Wasmuth.

Massaquoi, Hans-Jürgen. 2004. *Hänschen klein, ging allein . . . Mein Weg in die Neue Welt*. Bern: Scherz Verlag.

McWright, Linda Almond. 1998. "African-American Mothers' Perceptions of Grandparents' Use of Proverbs in Value Socialization of Grandchildren." PhD diss., Michigan State University.

Mehring, Frank. 2009. "'Bigger in Nazi Germany': Transcultural Confrontations of Richard Wright and Hans Jürgen Massaquoi." *Black Scholar* 39, nos. 1–2 (Spring–Summer): 63–71.

Mehring, Frank. 2014. "Afro-German-American Dissent: Hans J. Massaquoi." In *The Democratic Gap: Transcultural Confrontations of German Immigrants and the Promise of American Democracy*, 255–300. Heidelberg, Germany: Universitätsverlag Winter.

Mieder, Wolfgang. 1993. *Proverbs Are Never Out of Season: Popular Wisdom in the Modern Age*. New York: Oxford University Press.

Mieder, Wolfgang. 2004. *Proverbs: A Handbook*. Westport, CT: Greenwood Press.

Mieder, Wolfgang. 2005. *Proverbs Are the Best Policy: Folk Wisdom and American Politics*. Logan: Utah State University Press.

Mieder, Wolfgang. 2009. *International Bibliography of Paremiology and Phraseology*. 2 vols. Berlin: Walter de Gruyter.

Mieder, Wolfgang. 2010. *"Making a Way Out of No Way": Martin Luther King's Sermonic Proverbial Rhetoric*. New York: Peter Lang.

Mieder, Wolfgang. 2016. *"Stringing Proverbs Together": The Proverbial Language in Miguel de Cervantes's "Don Quixote."* Burlington: University of Vermont.

Mieder, Wolfgang. 2017. "'Little Pitchers Have Big Ears': The Intricate World of Children and Proverbs." *Children's Folklore Review* 38: 39–55.

Mieder, Wolfgang. 2019. *"Right Makes Might": Proverbs and the American Worldview.* Bloomington: Indiana University Press.

Mieder, Wolfgang. 2020. *The Worldview of Modern American Proverbs.* New York: Peter Lang.

Mieder, Wolfgang, and Deborah Holmes. 2000. *"Children and Proverbs Speak the Truth": Teaching Proverbial Wisdom to Fourth Graders.* Burlington: University of Vermont.

Mieder, Wolfgang, Stewart A. Kingsbury, and Kelsie B. Harder. 1992. *A Dictionary of American Proverbs.* New York: Oxford University Press.

Nenno, Nancy P. 2016. "Reading the 'Schwarz' in the 'Schwarz-Rot-Gold': Black German Studies in the 21st Century." *Transit* 10, no. 2: 1–6.

Nenno, Nancy P. 2019. "Terms of Engagement: Teaching the African Diaspora in German-Speaking Europe." *Die Unterrichtspraxis / Teaching German* 52, no. 2 (Fall): 167–71.

Newall, Venetia J. 1994. "A Tradition Bearer: Memories of My Grandmother." *Proverbium* 11: 189–96.

Nganang, Patrice. 2005. "Autobiographies of Blackness in Germany." In *Germany's Colonial Pasts*, edited by Eric Ames, Marcia Klotz, and Lora Wildenthal, 227–39. Lincoln: University of Nebraska Press.

Paczolay, Gyula. 1997. *European Proverbs in 55 Languages with Equivalents in Arabic, Persian, Sanskrit, Chinese and Japanese.* Veszprém, Hungary: Veszprémy Nyomda.

Page, Mary H., and Nancy D. Washington. 1987. "Family Proverbs and Value Transmission of Single Black Mothers." *Journal of Social Psychology* 127, no. 1: 49–58.

Reik, Theodor. 1940. "The Echo of the Proverb." In *From Thirty Years with Freud*, 228–41. Translated by Richard Winston. New York: Farrar and Rinehart, 1940. First published in *Life and Letters To-Day* 21, no. 21 (May 1939): 45–50; and 21, no. 22 (June 1939): 43–49.

Robinson, Herbert. 1991. "Family Sayings from Family Stories: Some Louisiana Examples." *Louisiana Folklore Miscellany* 6, no. 4: 17–24.

Röhrich, Lutz. 1991–1992. *Das große Lexikon der sprichwörtlichen Redensarten.* 3 vols. Freiburg, Germany: Herder.

Rölleke, Heinz. 1993. "Der Teufel als Schornsteinfeger: Anmerkungen zu einem Motiv der Volks- und Kunstliteratur." *Fabula* 34: 291–93.

Shapiro, Fred R. 2006. *The Yale Book of Quotations.* New Haven, CT: Yale University Press.

Walden, Sara. 2004. *Die Analyse der Sozialisation von Hans-Jürgen Massaquoi anhand von ausgewählten Aspekten.* Munich: Grin Verlag.

West, Victor Royce. 1930. *Folklore in the Works of Mark Twain.* Lincoln: University of Nebraska.

Westermann, Diedrich. 1938. *Afrikaner erzählen ihr Leben: Elf Selbstdarstellungen afrikanischer Eingeborener aller Bildungsgrade und Berufe und aus allen Teilen Afrikas.* Berlin: Evangelische Verlagsanstalt.

Wienker-Piepho, Sabine. 1991. "Sozialisation durch Sprichwörter: Am Beispiel eines anglo-amerikanischen Bestsellers." *Proverbium* 8: 179–89.

Williams, Derek A. 2003. "'Everything That Shine Ain't Gold': A Preliminary Ethnography of a Proverb in an African American Family." *Proverbium* 20: 391–406.

Yeo, Lacina. 2001. "'Mohr,' 'Neger,' 'Schwarzer,' 'Afrikaner,' 'Schwarzafrikaner,' 'Farbiger'— abfällige oder neutrale Zuschreibungen?" *Muttersprache* 111, no. 2: 110–46.

Proverbs in Culture

11

"YOU HAVE TO KISS A LOT OF FROGS BEFORE YOU MEET YOUR HANDSOME PRINCE"

From Fairy-Tale Motif to Modern Proverb

Since around the turn of the twenty-first century, literary scholars and folklorists Charles C. Doyle, Donald Haase, Maria Tatar, Hans-Jörg Uther, Jack Zipes, and myself, in a number of letters, have raised the question concerning the origin of the motif of a princess kissing a frog as it relates to the Grimms' fairy tale "The Frog King" (KHM 1; ATU 440), as well as the modern proverb "You have to kiss a lot of frogs (toads) before you meet your handsome prince." All of us have tried to solve this matter, with my friend Don finally writing to me on February 7, 2012: "It's still a mystery to me, but the kiss must have occurred first in one of the 19th-century English translations, don't you think?" This conjecture makes considerable sense in light of the fact that there is no kiss scene in the Grimms' tale. This also explains why much of the scholarship on the fairy tale is mute regarding the transformation of the frog into a prince by way of a kiss from a princess (Röhrich 1975; Röhrich 1991). In fact, a kiss is actually only mentioned in those studies that present modern parodistic adaptations of the fairy tale in prose or rhyme, but such compilations do not offer any explanations of where the kiss motif comes from (Mieder 1980; Röhrich 1979; Röhrich 1986a; Röhrich 1986b; Röhrich 2000). In my two encyclopedia articles on "The Frog King," I do mention the infamous kiss, but the more detailed research presented in the present chapter will show that my claim that in most English versions the frog is kissed by the princess is no longer maintainable (Mieder 2000; Mieder 2008). As it turns out, the matter with that kiss is much more complicated than scholars have assumed.

The most comprehensive study of "The Frog King" is Lutz Röhrich's detailed and richly illustrated book *Wage es, den Frosch zu küssen! Das Grimmsche Märchen Nummer Eins in seinen Wandlungen* (1987), whose catch title "Dare

311

to Kiss the Frog" must have surprised quite a few of his German readers. After all, they know of no kiss scene in the actual Grimm fairy tale! However, by 1986 the modern American proverb "You have to kiss a lot of frogs (toads) before you meet your handsome prince" had already been loan translated into German. And this resulted in a wave of often sexually motivated cartoons, comic strips, slogans, aphorisms, advertisements, and literary reworkings that eventually had its effect on the German fairy tale. Knowing that his German readers had started to link the new proverbial wisdom with the traditional fairy tale, thereby replacing the scene of the princess throwing the frog against the wall with her actually kissing it, Röhrich felt that his provocative title was perfectly reasonable. His truly remarkable book also gives at least a partial answer to the vexing question of how the kiss motif became associated with "The Frog King" fairy tale.

As expected, Röhrich reprinted the texts of the fairy tale as it is cited by the Brothers Grimm in their manuscript from 1810, in the first published version of 1812, and in the final rendering in the seventh edition of the *Kinder- und Hausmärchen* of 1857 (Röhrich 1987, 76–81). In all accounts, the disgusted princess grabs the ugly frog and throws him against the wall, thus liberating herself from his ever more demanding advances. The sexual undertones of this scene in the princess's bedroom are more obvious in a variant of the tale that the Brothers Grimm published as no. 13 of the second volume of their collection in 1815. Here, the frog sleeps at her feet for two nights in a row. The third evening the frog sleeps under her pillow, and when the princess wakes up in the morning, a handsome prince stands in front of her. In this case, it would indeed take little imagination to think that there actually was a kiss that brought about the transformation. Be that as it may, when the Brothers Grimm brought out the one-volume second edition of their fairy tales in 1819, they decided to keep the "wall-throwing" variant at the expense of the sexually more explicit variant, which in 1822 was relegated to a scholarly conceived volume of notes and variants (Rölleke 1980, 3, 15–19). Realizing that Wilhelm Grimm in particular modified the fairy tales from edition to edition so that they would be better fit for children, it is no surprise that the "pillow" variant was deleted from their canonized collection.

We will never know whether the Brothers Grimm came across a variant of "The Frog King" that contained a kiss scene, but such a rendering might well have been in circulation in their time. Two German folklorists have in fact collected dialect variants that include the kiss scene that Lutz Röhrich did not come across. In 1891, Ulrich Jahn published the fairy tale "De Koenigin un de Pogg'" (The Queen and the Frog), which he had recorded orally from an informant. Here, the frog explicitly requests a kiss from the princess, who in desperation covers her eyes with a cloth and puckers up (Jahn 1891, 31–34;

Volkmann and Freund 2000, 5–7). Another variant in a northern German dialect was recorded in 1897 with the title "Der Froschprinz" and published by Siegfried Neumann in 1971. Once again the frog asks the beautiful girl for a kiss, and when she indulges the creature, a handsome man stands in front of her (Neumann 1971, 154–56). And there is a third, East Prussian variant "De Kreet" (The Toad), which Hertha Grudde collected from oral tradition and published in 1931, in which a toad asks for a kiss. Even though the girl thinks she is going to die, she kisses the ugly creature, and, following a loud bang, a prince stands in front of her (Grudde 1931, 54–56; also in Röhrich 1987, 98–99).

A fourth, Pomeranian variant of "Der Froschkönig" collected in Poland and published in 1935 is also of much interest because it combines the kiss scene with the wall scene to a certain degree. Here, the princess wants to fetch water from a well for her sick father, but a large frog will not permit it unless she kisses him first. When she is afraid to do so, the frog suggests that she hold a handkerchief in front of her mouth so that she will not feel his cold wetness. Later, when the frog wants to sleep with her, she throws him against the wall, and in the morning she finds her handsome prince (Moser-Rath 1966, 53–56; also in Röhrich 1987, 104–7). Finally, there is also a versified and illustrated account, "Die beiden Schwestern" (The Two Sisters), from 1881 by the popular German author and artist Wilhelm Busch. In this case, a frog begs a young girl to kiss him. For the girl, the first kiss tastes just awful, but the green frog turns blue. The second kiss tastes already much better, and the frog takes on more colors and becomes larger. The third kiss is accompanied by loud noise as if cannons were going off. A large castle appears, and a prince stands in front of its door (Busch 1959, 5, 24–33; also in Röhrich 1987, 92–94).

What these variants with the kiss show is that fairy tale scholars should make much more use of other collections. The *Kinder- und Hausmärchen* of the Brothers Grimm is but one resource of many. Of course, it is not known whether they predate the year 1810, when Jacob and Wilhelm Grimm registered "The Frog King" for the first time. In fact, Hans-Jörg Uther is most likely correct when he observes that the transformation by way of a kiss appears in "Frog King" variants only toward the end of the nineteenth century (Uther 2008, 3). But there is something that is certain: they had very little, if any, influence on spreading the kiss motif across Germany or even beyond. It is very doubtful that German immigrants would have disseminated these variants in the United States, and the kiss motif in the Anglo-American tradition of the fairy tale must have a different origin. In fact, as will be shown, the popularity of the kiss scene in Germany today most likely also has nothing to do with these very little-known variants. But what these early variants from oral tradition do show is, of course, that the fairy tale might well have had a rather sexual beginning, which was pushed aside in later times as social mores changed and the fairy tales were not so much meant for adults any longer but rather for innocent children.

The concept of the transformative power of a kiss is, of course, well documented in mythology and folklore. Jacob Grimm refers to situations in which someone "in some disgusting shape, as a snake, dragon, toad or frog, has to be kissed three times" (Grimm 1888, 3, 969), and there are certainly many folk tales "that relate to transformation of Princes into beasts, and their release through woman's love, as the Frog Prince, and Beauty and the Beast. [. . .] It [the animal] can be released on one condition only—that a fair maid shall kiss it on the lips" (Baring-Gould 1910, 74). Röhrich also stresses the fact that variants other than that of the Brothers Grimm fall much more in line with the so-called animal bridegroom cycle of fairy tales, in which the princess must first show love in order to bring about the animal's transformation—she has to kiss the frog or at least let him sleep next to her for three nights (Röhrich 1987, 40). Little wonder that Hans-Jörg Uther, in his splendid revised edition of *The Types of International Folktales*, states that "in some variants the frog is disenchanted by means of a kiss, marriage, from being decapitated, etc." (Uther 2004, 1, 262; Jacobs [1894] 2002, 150–54). But while German scholars like Walter Scherf reduce their analysis of "The Frog King" to only the "wall-throwing" scene without any mention of the kiss variants (Scherf 1982, 133–38; Heindrichs 2000, 13–15), others have gone too far in overstating the prevalence of variants in which the transformation of the frog comes about by the princess's kiss. I have already admitted to having done so myself in my encyclopedia articles mentioned above, and D. L. Ashliman commits the same overgeneralization, although his precise comments regarding the kiss versus the wall variants are worth noting:

> In many instances the same tale type is told with different conclusions, indicating that individual storytellers have dared to mold stories to their own needs and views instead of always conforming to a received standard. Possibly the best example of this is offered by the various versions of "The Frog King" (AT 440). In most traditions the princess turns the frog into a prince by kissing him or by sleeping with him for three nights. In other words, she converts him by doing what *he* wants, by accepting him as he is. A minority position has also been recorded, the first tale in the Grimms' *Kinder- und Hausmärchen*. Here the princess refuses to allow the frog into her bed, but rather throws him against the wall, apparently intending to kill him. Precisely this self-assertive act, performed in direct violation of her father's will, converts the frog into a prince. (Ashliman 2004, 149)

Bruno Bettelheim, in his psychological interpretation of "The Frog King" from the Brothers Grimm collection, follows up his comments on the wall scene with a curious and definitely erroneous comment: "In most versions this [transformation] happens after the frog has spent three nights with her. An original version is even more explicit: the princess must kiss the frog while it lies at her side in bed, and then it takes three weeks of sleeping together until the frog turns into a prince" (Bettelheim 1976, 287). In a footnote, he refers to the Grimms' original manuscript from 1810 published in 1927 by Joseph Lefftz, but there is of course no kiss scene mentioned there! (see Lefftz 1927, 53–54).

Other generalizations about American versions abound. The text printed for advertising purposes on the dust cover of Röhrich's *Wage es, den Frosch zu küssen!* is also absurd, and I am certain it was not written by Röhrich himself: "But for Americans it would be unimaginable that the frog would be thrown against the wall: The wet kiss brings about the transformation, nothing else." In light of the fact that there were isolated German variants of "The Frog King" with a kiss scene, it seems odd to attach any special American notion to it. And yet, Maria Tatar in the intriguing annotations to her beautifully illustrated English edition *The Annotated Brothers Grimm* makes a somewhat similar claim: "Anglo-American versions have replaced the act of violence with a kiss, a symbolic gesture that has led to the widely disseminated maxim 'You have to kiss a lot of frogs before you meet your handsome prince'" (Tatar 2004, 10). And let me add a somewhat earlier observation by David M. Siegel and Susan H. McDaniel to this:

> The climactic scene in which the frog is thrown against the wall is changed in many English translations to the princess kissing the frog, resulting in his return to human form. Kissing does not appear in the original Grimm story and is not the version known to German youth. It is, however, the magical moment known best to American children, and the youth of many other Western societies. It is, in fact, an aphorism known to many young women, that one must kiss many frogs to find one's prince. (Siegel and McDaniel 1991, 559)

While I am obviously delighted that these scholars mention the modern "frog" proverb, let me react with the proverbial and somewhat cautionary phrase "hold your horses!" Not so fast, for things are usually not quite as simple as they seem.

First of all, it is correct that German youth hold steadfast to the "wall-throwing" variant. The Grimm editions on the market include only that variant, and searching through dozens of newer fairy tale books for children has not resulted in the discovery of any versions where a kiss takes place! Literary adaptations in the form of poems by such modern German authors as Franz Fühmann, Peter Grosz, Gerhard C. Krischker, Inge Meyer-Dietrich, and Frank Zwillinger all maintain the "wall-throwing" scene as well (Mieder 1983, 23–27; Mieder 2009, 116–17, 121–22), and this is also the case with short prose adaptations by Peter Heisch, Barbara König, Johann Friedrich Konrad, Karin Struck, and Heinrich Wiesner (Röhrich 1987, 129–31, 135–39, 142–45, 149–57; Mieder 1986a, 54–57, 59). All of this makes it very surprising that the "frog" proverb caught on relatively quickly in Germany.

But it is also not true that the kiss scene has become so very prevalent in the Anglo-American book market. The widely disseminated *Folk-Lore and Fable* anthology, edited by Charles W. Eliot in the Harvard Classics series and reissued numerous times in subsequent decades, includes a faithful translation of the Grimm variant with the princess throwing the frog against the wall (Eliot 1909, 49). The same is true for Brian Alderson's *The Brothers Grimm: Popular Folk Tales* (1978, 59) and Jack Zipes's *The Complete Fairy Tales of the Brothers Grimm* (1987, 4). But Amy Ehrlich, who adapted "The Frog Prince" for American children in *The Random House Book of Fairy Tales*, also writes: "No longer could she [the princess] bear it! Catching hold of the frog, she threw him with all her might against the wall. 'Now, will you be quiet, you ugly frog!' she screamed" (Ehrlich 1985, 99). And, as expected, Diane Goode provides an appropriate drawing of the princess hurling the frog against the wall. And wouldn't you know it, here are the final two stanzas of Gwen Strauss's poem "The Frog Princess" (1990) retelling the self-liberation of a woman:

> Three weeks
> the puffed up thing
> slept beside me.
> I dared not move
> or even breathe.
> In the dark, I watched it
> pant, a hollow smudge
> on my pillow.
>
> At last I slept and when I woke
> my hand touched him.
> Shock, then rage
> got me hurling him
> towards a wall; that's how I got
> my Prince to explode from frog.
> (Strauss 1990, 26)

FROM FAIRY-TALE MOTIF TO MODERN PROVERB   317

Having the frog sleep three times or even for three weeks on the bed brings
to mind the variant "Der Froschprinz" that the Grimms had included in their
collection in 1815, with the slight title change to "The Frog Prince."

As it happened, Edgar Taylor, as the first English translator of the *Kinder-
und Hausmärchen*, preferred this variant and included it eight years later in
his popular edition *German Popular Stories* (1823, 237–39), thereby spreading
a slightly more suggestive version as well as the more appropriate designation
of "Frog Prince" among English readers. Scholar Martin Sutton has traced the
history and importance of this translation, which has the frog sleeping on the
princess's bed for three nights: "[W]hen she opened it [her bedroom door],
the frog came in and slept upon her pillow as before till the morning broke: and
the third night he did the same; but when the princess awoke on the following
morning, she was astonished to see, instead of the frog, a handsome prince
gazing on her with the most beautiful eyes that ever were seen, and standing at
the head of her bed" (Taylor 1823, 209). Sutton did not need to occupy himself
with a possible kiss scene in his valuable study "A Prince Transformed: The
Grimms' 'Froschkönig' in English" (1990), but the frog sleeping on her pillow
might have led Anglo-American readers with an imagination to "dream" up a
kiss between the frog and the princess (Clouston 1890, 494). Be that as it may,
Sutton is absolutely correct in stating at the end that this variant conquered
the Anglo-American book market just as the variant with the "wall-throwing"
scene has done in translation. Iona and Peter Opie's well-received edition of *The
Classic Fairy Tales* (1974, 241–44) includes it with the title "The Frog-Prince,"
and Berlie Doherty's close retelling of "The Frog Prince" in her *Fairy Tales*
(2000, 191–204) for young readers holds on to this "pillow" variant: on the
third night, the princess

> put the frog on her snowy-white pillow. [. . .] The frog just gazed at her
> and gulped and blinked. And that night the princess dreamed of the
> deep, dark well and the red roses that trailed over its mossy walls, and
> woke up to such a strong scent of roses that she thought for a moment
> she was in the garden. She lay in her bed half awake and half asleep,
> watching the sun as it rose in the sky like a golden ball. "Princess," said
> a quiet voice, and she sat up startled. Standing by her bed was a young
> man with bright, smiling eyes. (Doherty 2000, 201–2).

The illustrations by Jane Ray add to the charm of this innocent account, where
there is once again no sign of any kiss.

So where does that leave us? Let's face it, the two Grimm variants of "The
Frog King" and "The Frog Prince" in German or English have clearly had no
influence on the spread of the "frog-kissing" motif. The same is true for the

318 PROVERBS IN CULTURE

few German variants that do include the kiss scene due to the fact that they never reached any noticeable distribution or currency in the modern age. And it is simply not true that variants of the fairy tale with a kiss scene have replaced these two Grimm variants. But I am happy to add a small and significant caveat! While no German fairy tale book of any type could be found that includes "The Frog King" with the kiss scene, I have finally, after years of searching, succeeded in locating two American children's books that do include such a scene. There is first of all Linda Yeatman's retelling of "The Frog Prince" in her *A Treasury of Bedtime Stories* (1981, 42–45), with illustrations by Hilda Offen. While she employs the title of the "pillow" variant, the transformation takes place the first night the frog spends in the princess's bedroom:

> "Oh, Frog," she exclaimed, "I suppose now you have come to sleep in my bed. Very well, a promise made has to be kept, my father says. You may sleep on the end of my bed."
> The frog, however, jumped on her pillow and sat there, cold and damp, waiting for the princess to get into bed. Reluctantly she edged under the covers.
> "Please kiss me," then croaked the frog.
> Now the princess did not want to break her word, nor did she want to kiss the frog. "If I do it quickly, that should be all right," she decided. As her lips touched the frog's smooth skin, she felt it change. Suddenly there before her was a handsome young man. (Yeatman 1981, 44)

A conundrum is Bill Adler Jr.'s plot summary of "The Frog Prince" in his pedagogical *Tell Me a Fairy Tale: A Parent's Guide to Telling Magical and Mythical Stories* (1995, 49–50): "She [the princess] had to allow the frog to eat off her plate, sit by her side, and sleep in her bed! In the beginning, she hated this. But she was won over by the frog's kindness and gentle manner. One day she kissed the frog. The frog turned into a handsome prince, released by the beautiful princess from a witch's curse." What printed version might Adler be summarizing here? Or is he simply letting his imagination go wild, as it were, by thinking of Yeatman's widely distributed retelling of 1981 but not remembering it in every detail?

In any case, here is my second treasure, namely "The Frog Prince" as retold by Wendy Wentworth and charmingly illustrated by Scott Gustafson in their children's book *Classic Fairy Tales* (2003, 94–103). It is based on Taylor's translation of the Grimm variant; at first it looks as if the princess will throw the frog if not against the wall then at least out of the room, but then she shows her kinder side and decides on her own (!) to kiss the frog:

So she picked up the frog with her finger and thumb, carried him upstairs, and put him in a corner, and when she had lain down in her bed to sleep, he came creeping up to her, saying, "I am tired and want to sleep as much as you. Pick me up, or I will tell your father."

The princess's patience with the frog was nearly at an end. In anger, she picked him up once more and was about to throw him through the doorway. Then, remembering her father's words, she stopped, and dropped him onto the pillow instead.

"Ahh," said the frog, as he snuggled down into the silken sheets, "don't you love sleepovers?"

The princess, pulling the covers over her head, curled up on the farthest edge of the mattress, with her back to the frog—and went to sleep.

And that is how it went for the next three days and nights. The princess did all the things that a princess usually did, but she was always accompanied by the little frog. But a strange thing happened during those three days after the princess had made her promise. The princess actually grew fond of the little frog.

On the evening of the third day, the strangest thing of all happened. Before blowing out the candle as they prepared to go to sleep, the princess leaned over and kissed the frog good-night.

In a twinkling, the frog ceased to be a frog at all. He became a handsome young prince with beautiful, kind eyes. (Wentworth 2003, 100, 102)

This represents indeed a marvelous retelling of the old fairy tale without any violence or disgust, but simply natural and innocent friendship leading to liberating love. And since we are dealing with miraculous fairy tales here, it should not be surprising that I can list a third modern version of "The Frog Prince" from Wendy Jones's recent retelling of the second Grimm variant in her *The Fairy-Tale Princess* (2012, 21–29) with wonderful illustrations by Su Blackwell:

On the third evening, the frog fell into the soup and that made the princess laugh. She carried him to her bedroom, where she washed and dried him. Then she placed him carefully on her pillow, blew him a kiss and said, "Goodnight."

In the morning, the princess awoke hoping that the frog might still be there. And he was! As the first rays of sunshine came through the window, the frog gave a huge leap to the end of the bed and as he landed, he turned into a handsome prince. (Jones 2012, 27–28)

This British children's version might not mention a real kiss, but it does show the beginning of true love, which can bring about transformations in magic fairy tales with their ever-present hope for a better world. But let me stress once again, there appear to be no such "kiss" retellings in German fairy tale books for children, and the three Anglo-American texts that I have found simply do not justify the generalization that especially American fairy tale books for the most part contain the kiss scene!

But that leaves us with that ultimate question that has bothered some of my fairy tale scholar friends and that has occupied me off and on for at least two decades—where does the predominance of the kiss scene in America come from, and how did it travel to Germany in the form of a loan translation of the proverb "You have to kiss a lot of frogs (toads) before you meet your handsome prince"? To answer this question in earnest, let me cite a few contextualized references about "kissing frogs" from the twentieth century that do not necessarily have any direct connection with "The Frog King" or "The Frog Prince." If this first text from a short newspaper account titled "Our Children" from around Christmastime 1925 were a reference to an extant variant of "The Frog Prince," that variant has yet to be found:

> No. I'm not a bit afraid of deceiving children by telling them the jolly old Saint [Santa Claus] is on the way. I've told them the broom stick is a prancing steed who will carry them up the clouds where the sun children frolic; I've told them the fairies dance on the tops of toad stools; I've shown them the enchanted frog asleep under his stone, waiting for the princess to kiss him. And it's been such fun. And it never cost me the faith of a child yet. Rather it brought it to me. (Patri 1925, 4)

This strikes me as if Angelo Patri as the author of the piece is telling us that he enjoys inventing far-fetched stories for children rather than relying on actual folk narratives. In any case, my second reference is a passage at the beginning of a chapter titled "The Inner World of Childhood" from Frances G. Wickes's psychological study of the same title (1927). While "The Frog Prince" fairy tale according to the Taylor translation is mentioned, the kiss comes into the picture only when the author refers to the tale cycle "Beauty and the Beast," where kisses do play a role:

> Here we may trace the analogy between this type of phantasy and the old fairy tale. The Frog Prince must be taken in the maiden's lap in his form of ugly frog. Beauty must kiss the Beast while he is yet a beast, and recognize the love and kindliness that has shone through his beastly outer self. It is only when we feel ourselves accepted as we really are, our whole selves with both the good and evil, that we can find true release

of our feeling selves. Through feeling ourselves acceptable to one whom we love we can also accept ourselves. (Wickes 1927, 174)

The third reference, from the British satirical magazine *Punch*, has the title "The Princess and the Toad" (V. G. 1935) and is the third one-page account in a series of "Impossible Stories." It is clearly based on "The Frog King," including even references to Dunkelheim, Germany. While it deals with an utterly homely princess, whose kiss does not transform the ugly toad into a prince, it is clearly an explicit though invented variant of the fairy tale in which the kiss plays a major role. But I doubt that this grotesque story is based on one of the German dialect variants of "The Frog King" mentioned above, and I assume that its author, V. G., most likely took the fairy tale and combined it with the kiss motif of the animal bridegroom cycle. Here are the most relevant sections (about one-sixth) of this invaluable reference:

> Once upon a time there was a Princess who was renowned for her bad looks. She was as plain as a pikestaff, whatever that may be, and no Prince in all the princedoms of the world would look at her. [. . .]
>
> So, the Princess, though ugly without, was lovely within; and it was therefore not astonishing that when she met a toad in her boudoir, or, as the Germans call it, her *Gelounge*, she gave orders to that it should be taken away and cared for and given food, drink and shelter. [. . .]
>
> [In a dream, her Fairy Godmother tells her that the toad is a prince and that to release him from his terrible spell he must be kissed. So she goes out to find the toad.]
>
> The Princess blanched. Could she kiss him or could she not? [. . .] "To-day," said the Princess, "I am going to kiss you. [. . .] I know that you are a prince in disguise and I am determined to release you from your cruel bondage so that you may be free again to go wherever you please. Come here!" [. . .]
>
> The Princess leant forward [. . .] and planted a kiss on the toad's forehead. [. . .] "Rise, Sir Prince!" cried the Princess, curtseying to the floor. [. . .] Nothing had happened. [. . .]
>
> The Princess and the toad are still living happily at Dunkelheim. They really get on admirably, as each thinks the other the ugliest creature in the world. [. . .] (V. G. 1935, 24)

That the mythological and folkloric motif of kissing an ugly animal to release a perfect human being from a spell comes almost automatically to mind when confronted by "The Frog King" or "The Frog Prince" fairy tale variants, can also be seen in a dance drama for schoolchildren that Truda Kaschmann adapted from the Grimms' fairy tale in 1937. The description of the little play reads in part as follows:

> The frog jumped out of the well, looking very ugly in his mask and cape, and did his frog dance of leaps, jumps, and rolls. [. . .] When the princess asked the ugly frog to give her the ball he showed her that he wanted a kiss before he returned the golden ball. Her dance of excitement followed. [. . .] The jester again tried to cheer the princess with a very funny dance. He made two of the maids of waiting kiss the frog, but the frog insisted upon a kiss from the princess! [. . .] The princess danced cautiously around the well. Although she was very much afraid, she finally kissed the frog courageously. He gave her the golden ball and immediately turned into a charming prince. (Myers et al. 1938, 309–10)

This is clearly a free adaptation and not taken from a possibly extant kiss variant of the fairy tale, and I would argue that the following excerpt from Angela Thirkell's novel *Love Among the Ruins* (1948) is also an intentionally altered remembrance of the Grimms' fairy tale:

> "Do you suppose," said Clarissa to Captain Belton, "that he is the frog prince?"
>
> She looked towards the frog, who had sunk into a kind of trance, broken from time to time by a lightning flash of his tongue as a mutton chop or a roast quail sailed past him disguised as an insect.
>
> Lucy Marling, remembering her Grimm, drew nearer.
>
> Captain Belton's mind went back to the day at Holdings when Clarissa found the remains of the gilded ball in the little pool.
>
> "King's daughter, fairest," he said to Clarissa, "let me eat from your golden plate and drink from your gold cup." [. . .]
>
> "You'll have to kiss the frog if he is to turn into a prince," said Leslie. [. . .]
>
> "Here he is," said Leslie, who by a masterly flank movement had captured the frog and bore him dripping to land. "Quick, Clarissa."
>
> Clarissa shrieked in a ladylike way and clung to Captain Belton's arm. The frog, remembering his grandmother's warning against allowing human girls to kiss one, as they were apt to turn one into a prince and one could never get back to the green slime of the pond, hit out with his hind legs, described a parabola in the air and dived under the lily pads. (Thirkell 1948, 249)

FROM FAIRY-TALE MOTIF TO MODERN PROVERB 323

These four texts from the first half of the twentieth century are figures of the imagination and are not based on a traditional folk narrative of a princess kissing an enchanted frog. I also very much doubt that they have had any influence whatsoever on the following two very modern literary references. In fact, it might very well be possible not only that they are once again allusions to the kissing of enchanted animals in general but, and this is more than likely, that they are influenced by the modern proverb "You have to kiss a lot of frogs (toads) before you meet your handsome prince." Here, first of all, is a frog-kissing scene from Gary Larson's *There's a Hair in My Dirt! A Worm's Story* (1998), albeit without his hilarious drawings:

> Harriet thought she saw something move in the tall grass near her feet. Dropping gracefully to her knees, she almost put her hand on a small slug that was wandering by. Recoiling in disgust, she cried, "Stay away from me, you slimy little thing!"
>
> And then, seeing the real object of her desire, she lunged forward and came up with her prize. "Hello, Mr. Frog!" she said, laughing. "Should I kiss you and see if you turn into a prince?"
>
> Fortunately for Harriet, she *didn't* kiss this little creature, for it wasn't "Mr. Frog" she was holding, but "Mr. Toad," and like most toads (and some frogs), this one packed a powerful, sometimes lethal, toxin in its skin. On the other hand, the slug slime was actually quite harmless, if perhaps a bit gooey.
>
> Kissing out of your species is not really recommended, Son, but if you have to, always choose a gastropod over an amphibian. (Larson 1998; on toxins, see Siegel and McDaniel 1991, 560–62)

The next text comes from the third chapter in E. D. Baker's juvenile novel *The Frog Princess* (2002), which is in part based on "The Frog Prince" but with the addition of the kiss scene and a wonderful twist, the young woman becoming a frog:

> "Gee," said the frog, looking flustered. "I don't know. All I asked for was a kiss."
>
> "You want a kiss? Fine! I'll give you a kiss. I'd rather kiss you than Prince Jorge any day!"
>
> I knelt on the ground at the edge of the pond. With a mighty leap, the frog landed on the ground beside me and puckered his lips.
>
> "Wait just a minute," I said, drawing back.
>
> The frog looked distressed. "You haven't changed your mind, have you?"

"No, no. it's just that . . . well, here." Fumbling in the small pouch attached to the waist of my gown, I found an embroidered handkerchief. I reached out and gently patted the fog's mouth clean. "You had dried fly feet stuck to your lips," I said, shuddering. "All right, let's try again."

This time the kiss went without a hitch. I leaned down, puckered my lips, and closed my eyes. [. . .] The frog's lips felt cool and smooth against mine. The sensation wasn't too unpleasant. It was what happened next that took me by surprise [her transformation into a frog!]. (Baker 2002, 27–28)

It is noteworthy that the Walt Disney animated musical fantasy comedy film *The Princess and the Frog* (2009) is loosely based on this novel for young readers, ingraining the act of kissing a frog once again into the minds of millions! Had Disney created an animated film based on "The Frog Prince" some decades earlier and added the kiss scene, we could today say that it was that film that spread the kiss motif everywhere. Alas, this was not the case!

But it was also not necessary, for by the third quarter of the twentieth century the frog-kissing motif had become quite ubiquitous in the United States, with Americans often simply assuming that the motif is present in "The Frog Prince" of the Brothers Grimm as well. Over the years I have collected numerous modern poems that rely on it, with Stevie Smith's appropriately titled book *The Best Beast* (1969) and its lengthy poem "The Frog Prince," which begins as follows, as my earliest find:

> I am a frog,
> I live under a spell,
> I live at the bottom
> Of a green well.
> And here I must wait
> Until a maiden places me
> On her pillow,
> And kisses me.
> (Smith 1969, 14)

Such poems as John N. Miller's "Prince Charming" (1969), Anne Sexton's "The Frog Prince" (1971), Phoebe Pettingell's "Frog Prince" (1972), Robert Graves's "The Frog and the Golden Ball" (1975), Robert Pack's "The Frog Prince (A Speculation on Grimm's Fairy Tale)" (1980), Galway Kinnell's "Kissing the Toad" (1980), and others followed suit (Mieder 1985, 23–42; Mieder 1987b, 13–22), with these well-known poets thinking that they are basing their modern interpretations of the fairy tale on the text from the Brothers Grimm.

This is also the case for cartoonists, who with their clever drawings and pointed captions play off an imagined variant of the fairy tale with the kiss scene, often adding a sexually rather obvious message. The illustrations usually show a beautiful woman (princess) and her relations with an ugly frog, with her kiss not succeeding in transforming the creature into a handsome man (prince). Even without the imagery, the following statements make it clear that kisses do not always result in transformative miracles, that they will not bring about the desired change:

"You call that a kiss?"
   (*Penthouse*, December 1978, 22)
"Thanks for the kiss, but I'm not the prince. A poacher got him."
   (*Field and Stream*, April 1979, 188)
"Any girl crazy enough to go around kissing frogs deserves what she gets."
   (*Playboy*, September 1978, 100)
"I started out looking for a prince, but now I just like to kiss frogs."
   (*Good Housekeeping*, January 1980, 186)
"A kiss would work wonders."
   (greeting card from Pen & Inc., 1981)
"I may kiss an occasional frog but never a turkey."
   (*Short Ribs* comic strip, *Bloomington (IN) Herald-Times*, December 15, 1981, 19)
"You kissed better when you were a frog."
   (*Good Housekeeping*, September 1984, 198)
"Kiss me! I don't smoke."
   (antismoking advertisement, *Muskegon (MI) Chronicle*, November 11, 1984)
"Do you have any stories where the princess kisses a frog, and he turns into a Beagle?"
   (*Peanuts* comic strip, *Burlington (VT) Free Press*, January 10, 1992, 5D)
"If you don't kiss him, how're you gonna know if he's a prince?"
   (*Dennis the Menace* cartoon, *Burlington Free Press*, October 22, 2003, 3C)

One could perhaps argue that poets, cartoonists, and copywriters for advertisements and greeting cards might want to reread "The Frog King" or "The Frog Prince" from time to time, but such a request is absurd, since the kiss-scene motif has established itself solidly in the mind-set of the general population.

In Germany, on the other hand, the "old" Grimm variant remains much more intact, with the kiss motif appearing in poems, prose, aphorisms, advertisements, headlines, cartoons, and greeting cards only toward the very end of the 1970s, clearly through the massive influence of the Anglo-American media. One of the earliest German-language examples is a political cartoon with the caption "Kiss me, and I change into a handsome Chancellor" (*Nebelspalter*, June 1979, 10), with a later reference being "Now I have already kissed more than a hundred frogs, but a prince was not among them!" (*Neue Post*, August 24, 1995, 64; for more references, see Mieder 1987a, 92–95; Mieder 2009, 115–41). Little wonder then that it also did not take long for the modern American proverb "You have to kiss a lot of frogs (toads) before you meet your handsome prince" to get established in translation in Germany. But is this relatively new proverb a remnant of "The Frog King" or "The Frog Prince" fairy tales as the Brothers Grimm recorded them? Not really! It most likely is not even based on a retelling of one of the variants that contains the kiss motif, since the earliest such variant found thus far appears only in 1981 in Linda Yeatman's *A Treasury of Bedtime Stories*.

It would rather be my educated conjecture that the proverb, while growing out of the general notion of beauty having to kiss the beast, was coined by members of the feminist movement during the 1970s. It should, of course, also be remembered that the proverb's message is quite different from that of the animal bridegroom fairy tale cycle. The folk narrative princess is not really out to find a suitable husband as such, but she is surprised to wind up with a prince. The proverb instead argues that men are in general no good, or at least that it takes a woman a lot of "disgusting" trials until the right man can be found! This is not to say that by now people conceive of a link, including folklorists like Maria Tatar (see above), Charles C. Doyle, and myself. After all, in 1993 I stated quite categorically, "This type of unromantic reflection also resulted in the reduction of this particular fairy tale to the new American proverb 'You have to kiss a lot of frogs before you meet a prince' and its variant 'Before you meet the handsome prince you have to kiss a lot of toads'" (Mieder 1986b, 263; Mieder 1993, 154). And this is what Doyle, Fred Shapiro, and I said about this proverb in our *Dictionary of Modern Proverbs* (2012), choosing as our paremiographical lemma the variant "You have to kiss a lot of frogs (toads) to find a prince," followed by a number of contextualized references: "Most often the proverb refers to the difficulty of a woman's finding suitable male companionship, but it can apply to other kinds of searches as well. The prevalence of the *toads* form of the proverb is surprising, given the fact that the popular tale to which it alludes is nearly always referred to as 'The Frog Prince'; perhaps, in the popular mind, toads better exemplify extreme unattractiveness" (Doyle, Mieder, and Shapiro 2012, 89). From what has been said, I find this latter formulation much more appropriate. In other words, the proverb is not so much a "reduction" of the fairy tale but rather an imprecise (!) "allusion" or reminiscence to it.

FROM FAIRY-TALE MOTIF TO MODERN PROVERB

Due to space limitations, we could only cite five contextualized references from between 1976 and 1980, having found the earliest printed variant in the *Coshocton [OH] Tribune* of February 10, 1976: "Before you meet your handsome prince, you'll probably have to kiss a lot of toads." Many more examples of this by now popular proverb from printed sources of all types (including headlines, slogans, cartoons, greeting cards, T-shirts, etc.) can be found in my International Proverb Archives at the University of Vermont, with new references being added constantly, among them also the variants "Before you discover your handsome prince, you have to kiss quite a few toads" (1977), "Before you meet the handsome prince you've gotta kiss a lot of toads" (1979), and "You've got to kiss a lot of frogs before you meet your handsome prince!" (1982). German references are included as well, of course, with the proverb in English appearing for the first time in a German collection of graffiti, slogans, and sayings in 1983 as "You must kiss many frogs before you'll find your prince" (Rauchberger and Harten 1983, 30–31). Another English text was registered in a collection of German graffiti from about twenty years later, attesting to the fact that the English language plays a considerable role in Germany as the international lingua franca: "You've got to kiss a lot of toads before you find your prince!" (Beck 2004, 42).

But the American proverb was quickly translated into German as well, with the earliest German reference found thus far appearing in a collection of similar one-liners in 1984: "Bevor du deinen Prinzen findest, mußt du eine Menge häßliche Frösche küssen" (Before you find your prince, you have to kiss a lot of ugly frogs; Glismann 1984). As with any new proverb that establishes itself, the new "frog" proverb is current in a number of variants in Germany: "Man muß viele Frösche küssen, bis man einen Prinzen gefunden hat" (One has to kiss many frogs, until one has found a prince; 1986), "Man muß viele Frösche küssen, bevor man einen Prinzen findet" (One has to kiss many frogs, before one finds a prince; 1988), "Bevor du einen Prinzen findest, mußt du viele Frösche küssen" (Before you find a prince, you have to kiss many frogs; 1990), "Wer einen Prinzen sucht, muß viele Frösche küssen" (Anyone who searches for a prince, has to kiss many frogs; 1991), "Du musst viele Frösche küssen, bevor ein Prinz dabei ist" (You have to kiss many frogs until a prince is found among them; 2000), "Man muss 1000 Frösche küssen, um einen Prinzen zu finden" (One has to kiss a 1,000 frogs, in order to find a prince; 2003), "Du musst schon eine ganz schreckliche Anzahl von Fröschen küssen, bis du endlich einen Prinzen findest!" (You really have to kiss an awful number of frogs until you finally find a prince; 2004), and "Wer einen Prinzen will, muss viele Frösche küssen" (Anyone who wants [to have] a prince, has to kiss many frogs; 2004) (Mieder 1990, 161–62; Mieder 2009, 115–41). A standard German form is slowly but surely developing, and there is no doubt that it belongs to quite a number of proverbs that have been taken over from the stock of American proverbs (see Mieder 2010, 285–340).

In conclusion then, there is no doubt in my mind that even though there are a few dialect variants of "The Frog King" fairy tale from the second half of the nineteenth century with a kiss scene, the by now widespread frog-kissing motif entered German culture only in the late twentieth century by way of the modern American proverb "You have to kiss a lot of frogs (toads) before you meet your handsome prince." Due to the incredible linguistic prowess and influence of the mass media, Germans as well as Americans and other native English speakers are superimposing the kiss scene onto the old fairy tale, even though I have not yet found a German version of the fairy tale that has exchanged the "wall-throwing" scene with a kiss. But as I have shown, in America the first rendering of the fairy tale with the kiss scene appeared only five years after the first recording of the proverb! But that this change is happening can be seen from a caption of a political caricature from 1983 that connects the "wall-throwing" motif with the one of the kiss: "[A]nd he [the West German politician Franz Josef Strauß] changed, without someone having kissed or thrown him against the wall, into a political prince from the East" (*Nebelspalter*, August 9, 1983, 7).

But here is the quintessential reference to prove my point. In a poster catalogue of German caricatures on the topic of Germany's unification, the following explanatory comment was added to a caricature of Chancellor Helmut Kohl from 1991 with the caption "Froschkönig verkehrt" (Frog King reversed): "In the German fairy tale of 'The Frog King,' the frog changes into a prince by way of a kiss of the princess. Here [in this caricature], in view of a (female) Michel [German stereotypical figure] (of the East), Chancellor Helmut Kohl turns from a rich prince back to a poor, ugly frog" (Keim 1992). There are obviously plenty of Germans who simply think that the kiss scene is in fact in the fairy tale by the Brothers Grimm! In fact, when Ulrich Freund asked Germans in 2000 how a frog can be changed into a prince, half of the respondents answered by a kiss, and the other half answered by the traditional thrust against the wall (Freund 2000, 23). My own ad hoc field research among Germans and Americans in 2012 showed that by now most informants think that it is the kiss by the princess that changes the frog into a prince. This is indeed a remarkable development, since the respondents include professorial types!

But for me, as a fairy tale scholar and paremiologist, all of this shows the cultural might of a proverb that came into being not as the reduction of a fairy tale but at best as an imaginative allusion to one of the most favorite fairy tales of them all. Of course, the prevalence of the kiss motif in most of the modern reminiscences or *Schwundstufen* (remnants) of the fairy tale in literature and the mass media is most likely also a form of a *Selbstberichtigungsprozeß* (process of self-correction; Röhrich 1987, 65; see also Anderson 1951, 3–5, 43–45)—a return perhaps to a very early original variant of "The Frog King" fairy tale in which the kiss was the original motif, pushed aside in later times in order to deemphasize the natural sexuality of the folk narrative.

BIBLIOGRAPHY

This chapter was first published with the same title in *Marvels and Tales: Journal of Fairy-Tale Studies* 28, no. 1 (2014): 104–26.

Adler, Bill, Jr. 1995. *Tell Me a Fairy Tale: A Parent's Guide to Telling Magical and Mythical Stories*. New York: Plume.

Alderson, Brian, trans. 1978. *The Brothers Grimm: Popular Folk Tales*. Garden City, NY: Doubleday.

Anderson, Walter. 1951. *Ein volkskundliches Experiment*. Helsinki: Suomalainen Tiedeakatemia.

Ashliman, D. L. 2004. *Folk and Fairy Tales: A Handbook*. Westport, CT: Greenwood Press.

Baker, E. D. 2002. *The Frog Princess*. New York: Bloomsbury.

Baring-Gould, Sabine. 1910. *Family Names and Their Story*. Philadelphia: J. B. Lippincott.

Beck, Harald, ed. 2004. *Graffiti*. Stuttgart: Philipp Reclam Verlag.

Bettelheim, Bruno. 1976. *The Uses of Enchantment: The Meaning and Importance of Fairy Tales*. New York: Alfred A. Knopf.

Busch, Wilhelm. 1959. *Das Gesamtwerk des Zeichners und Dichters*. Edited by Hugo Werner. 6 vols. Olten, Switzerland: Fackelverlag.

Clouston, W. A. 1890. "The Story of 'The Frog Prince': Breton Variant, and Some Analogues." *Folklore* (London) 1, no. 4 (December): 493–506.

Doherty, Berlie, ed. 2000. *Fairy Tales*. Somerville, MA: Candlewick Press.

Doyle, Charles Clay, Wolfgang Mieder, and Fred R. Shapiro, eds. 2012. *The Dictionary of Modern Proverbs*. New Haven, CT: Yale University Press.

Ehrlich, Amy, ed. 1985. *The Random House Book of Fairy Tales*. New York: Random House.

Eliot, Charles W., ed. 1909. *Folk-Lore and Fable: Aesop, Grimm, Andersen*. New York: P. F. Collier.

Freund, Ulrich. 2000. "Das Froschkönig-Märchen im therapeutischen Prozeß: Verwünschung und Verwandlung, Lösung und Erlösung." In *Der Froschkönig . . . und andere Erlösungsbedürftige*, edited by Helga Volkmann and Ulrich Freund, 18–32. Baltmannsweiler, Germany: Schneider Verlag Hohengehren.

Glismann, Claudia, ed. 1984. *Edel sei der Mensch, Zwieback und gut: Szene-Sprüche*. Munich: Wilhelm Heyne.

Grimm, Jacob. 1888. *Teutonic Mythology*. Translated by James Steven Stallybrass. 4 vols. London: George Bell and Sons.

Grudde, Hertha, ed. 1931. *Plattdeutsche Volksmärchen aus Ostpreußen*. Königsberg: Gräfe und Unzer.

Heindrichs, Ursula. 2000. "Die erlöste Erlöserin: Wie die Weltschönste zu sich findet; Anmerkungen zu KHM 1." In *Der Froschkönig . . . und andere Erlösungsbedürftige*, edited by Helga Volkmann and Ulrich Freund, 10–17. Baltmannsweiler, Germany: Schneider Verlag Hohengehren.

Jacobs, Joseph, ed. (1890, 1894) 2002. *English Fairy Tales and More English Fairy Tales*. Edited by Donald Haase. Santa Barbara, CA: ABC-CLIO.

Jahn, Ulrich, ed. 1891. *Volksmärchen aus Pommern und Rügen*. Norden, Germany: Diedr. Soltau's Verlag.

Jones, Wendy. 2012. *The Fairy-Tale Princess: Seven Classic Stories from the Enchanted Forest*. London: Thames and Hudson.

Keim, Walther. 1992. *German Michel—National Stereotype: The Cartoonists' View of German Unity; An Exhibition of the Institute for Foreign Cultural Relations*. Stuttgart: Heinrich Fink.

Larson, Gary. 1998. *There's a Hair in My Dirt! A Worm's Story*. New York: HarperCollins.

Lefftz, Joseph. 1927. *Märchen der Brüder Grimm: Urfassung nach der Originalhandschrift der Abtei Ölenberg im Elsaß*. Heidelberg, Germany: Carl Winter.

Mieder, Wolfgang. 1980. "Modern Anglo-American Variants of *The Frog Prince* (AT 440)." *New York Folklore* 6, no. 3 (Winter): 111–35.

Mieder, Wolfgang, ed. 1983. *Mädchen, pfeif auf den Prinzen! Märchengedichte von Günter Grass bis Sarah Kirsch*. Cologne: Eugen Diederichs.

Mieder, Wolfgang, ed. 1985. *Disenchantments: An Anthology of Modern Fairy Tale Poetry*. Hanover, NH: University Press of New England.

Mieder, Wolfgang, ed. 1986a. *Grimmige Märchen: Prosatexte von Ilse Aichinger bis Martin Walser*. Frankfurt am Main: Rita G. Fischer.

Mieder, Wolfgang. 1986b. "Sprichwörtliche Schwundstufen des Märchens: Zum 200 Geburtstag der Brüder Grimm." *Proverbium* 3: 257–71.

Mieder, Wolfgang. 1987a. "Grim Variations: From Fairy Tales to Modern Anti–Fairy Tales." *Germanic Review* 62, no. 2: 90–102.

Mieder, Wolfgang. 1987b. *Tradition and Innovation in Folk Literature*. Hanover, NH: University Press of New England.

Mieder, Wolfgang. 1990. "Aphoristische Schwundstufen des Märchens." In *Dona Folcloristica: Festgabe für Lutz Röhrich*, edited by Leander Petzoldt and Stefaan Top, 159–71. Frankfurt am Main: Peter Lang.

Mieder, Wolfgang. 1993. "Fairy-Tale Allusions in Modern German Aphorisms." In *The Reception of Grimms' Fairy Tales: Responses, Reactions, Revisions*, edited by Donald Haase, 149–66. Detroit: Wayne State University Press.

Mieder, Wolfgang. 2000. "The Frog King." In *The Oxford Companion to Fairy Tales*, edited by Jack Zipes, 173, 188. Oxford: Oxford University Press.

Mieder, Wolfgang. 2008. "Frog King." In *The Greenwood Encyclopedia of Folktales and Fairy Tales*, edited by Donald Haase, 1:390–92. Westport, CT: Greenwood Press.

Mieder, Wolfgang. 2009. *"Märchen haben kurze Beine": Moderne Märchenreminiszenzen in Literatur, Medien und Karikaturen*. Vienna: Praesens Verlag.

Mieder, Wolfgang. 2010. *"Spruchschlösser (ab)bauen": Sprichwörter, Antisprichwörter und Lehnsprichwörter in Literatur und Medien*. Vienna: Praesens Verlag.

Moser-Rath, Elfriede, ed. 1966. *Deutsche Volksmärchen*. Cologne: Eugen Diederichs.

Myers, Alonzo F., Louise M. Kifer, Ruth Clara Merry, and Frances Foley. 1938. *Coöperative Supervision in the Public Schools*. New York: Prentice-Hall.

Neumann, Siegfried, ed. 1971. *Mecklenburgische Volksmärchen*. Berlin: Akademie Verlag.

FROM FAIRY-TALE MOTIF TO MODERN PROVERB

Opie, Iona, and Peter Opie, eds. 1974. *The Classic Fairy Tales*. Oxford: Oxford University Press.

Patri, Angelo. 1925. "Our Children." *Youngstown (OH) Vindicator*, December 14.

Rauchberger, Karl Heinz, and Ulf Harten, eds. 1983. *"Club-Sprüche."* Hamburg: Verlag Hanseatische Edition.

Röhrich, Lutz. 1975. "Das *Froschkönig*-Märchen." *Der Schweizerische Kindergarten* 65: 246–50.

Röhrich, Lutz. 1979. "Der Froschkönig und seine Wandlungen." *Fabula* 20: 170–92.

Röhrich, Lutz. 1986a. "Der Froschkönig: Das erste Märchen der Grimm-Sammlung und seine Interpretation." In *Das selbstverständliche Wunder: Beiträge germanistischer Märchenforschung*, edited by Wilhelm Solms and Charlotte Oberfeld, 7–41. Marburg, Germany: Hitzeroth Verlag.

Röhrich, Lutz. 1986b. "Froschkönig." In *Enzyklopädie des Märchens*, edited by Kurt Ranke et al., 5:410–24. Berlin: Walter de Gruyter.

Röhrich, Lutz. 1987. *Wage es, den Frosch zu küssen! Das Grimmsche Märchen Nummer Eins in seinen Wandlungen*. Cologne: Eugen Diederichs.

Röhrich, Lutz. 1991. "Mit dem Froschkönig ins Bett." *Morgen* 15: 45–49.

Röhrich, Lutz. 2000. "Der Froschkönig: Rezeption und Wandlungen eines Märchens bis zur Gegenwart." In *Der Froschkönig . . . und andere Erlösungsbedürftige*, edited by Helga Volkmann and Ulrich Freund, 33–49. Baltmannsweiler, Germany: Schneider Verlag Hohengehren.

Rölleke, Heinz, ed. 1980. *Brüder Grimm: Kinder- und Hausmärchen; Ausgabe letzter Hand mit Originalanmerkungen der Brüder Grimm*. 3 vols. Stuttgart: Philipp Reclam Verlag.

Scherf, Walter. 1982. *Lexikon der Zaubermärchen*. Stuttgart: Alfred Kröner.

Siegel, David M., and Susan H. McDaniel. 1991. "The Frog Prince: Tale and Toxicology." *American Journal of Orthopsychiatry* 61, no. 4 (October): 558–62.

Smith, Stevie. 1969. *The Best Beast*. New York: Alfred A. Knopf.

Strauss, Gwen. 1990. *Trail of Stones*. New York: Alfred A. Knopf.

Sutton, Martin. 1990. "A Prince Transformed: The Grimms' 'Froschkönig' in English." *Seminar: A Journal of Germanic Studies* 26, no. 2 (May): 119–37.

Tatar, Maria, ed. 2004. *The Annotated Brothers Grimm*. New York: W. W. Norton.

Taylor, Edgar, trans. 1823. *German Popular Stories: Translated from the Kinder- und Hausmärchen*. London: C. Baldwyn.

Thirkell, Angela. 1948. *Love Among the Ruins*. New York: Alfred A. Knopf.

Uther, Hans-Jörg. 2004. *The Types of International Folktales: A Classification and Bibliography*. 3 vols. Helsinki: Suomalainen Tiedeakatemia.

Uther, Hans-Jörg. 2008. *Handbuch zu den "Kinder- und Hausmärchen" der Brüder Grimm*. Berlin: Walter de Gruyter.

V. G. 1935. "The Princess and the Toad." *Punch*, July 3.

Volkmann, Helga, and Ulrich Freund, eds. 2000. *Der Froschkönig . . . und andere Erlösungsbedürftige*. Baltmannsweiler, Germany: Schneider Verlag Hohengehren.

Wentworth, Wendy, ed. 2003. *Classic Fairy Tales*. Seymour, CT: Greenwich Workshop Press.

Wickes, Frances G. 1927. *The Inner World of Childhood: A Study in Analytical Psychology*. New York: D. Appleton.

Yeatman, Linda. 1981. *A Treasury of Bedtime Stories*. New York: Simon and Schuster.

Zipes, Jack, trans. 1987. *The Complete Fairy Tales of the Brothers Grimm*. New York: Bantam Books.

12

"THE WORD (AND PHRASE) DETECTIVE"

A Proverbial Tribute to *OED* Editor John A. Simpson

Ten years after John A. Simpson, lexicographer par excellence, coeditor with Edmund Weiner of the second edition of the famed *Oxford English Dictionary* (1989; online in 2000), and pioneer of the work on the third online-only edition (ongoing since 2000), published his acclaimed *Concise Oxford Dictionary of Proverbs* (1982), my colleagues Stewart A. Kingsbury, Kelsie B. Harder, and I edited our *Dictionary of American Proverbs* (1992). Having produced a proverb dictionary for Oxford University Press put Simpson in the role of judging whether our large project was worthy of the OUP imprint. I remember a meeting at the OUP office in New York City, where I had the opportunity to meet Simpson to discuss our collection project. We benefited from his suggestions and received his important stamp of approval. Our book appeared ten years after his own smaller collection, but I have never forgotten his support and help. Many years have passed since our encounter, and after having started his work at OUP in 1976, John Simpson brought his tenure there to an end in 2013. To occupy his keen mind, he has been working on the multifaceted language of James Joyce's *Ulysses*, leaving him time enough to write his fascinating scholarly autobiography *The Word Detective: Searching for the Meaning of It All at the "Oxford English Dictionary"* (2016). When I discovered this personal account, I read it with great interest as I remembered that I am indeed indebted to John Simpson. In order to put my appreciation into words, I offer this proverbial tribute to this great scholar in the form of a review of his very own proverbial language in his intriguing and revealing account of his dedicated work on the English language. I shall not be able to comment on every proverb or proverbial expression in the book, but the attached list of 260 phrases on 350 pages demonstrates clearly that his work on phraseological units rubbed off on his narrative style.

One might have thought that the positive reviews that his memoir received would include some comments on his language. After all, John Simpson

332

dedicated his entire professional life to the English language! But while bestowing plenty of praise on the content of the book, reviewers ignore Simpson's impressive writing ability. They do compare his book favorably with Simon Winchester's two excellent earlier books *The Professor and the Madman: A Tale of Murder, Insanity, and the Making of the "Oxford English Dictionary"* (1998), discussing James Murray, and *The Meaning of Everything: The Story of the "Oxford English Dictionary"* (2003). Simpson lists several other studies on the *OED* at the end of his book (2016, 343–46), but his account is quite different because of his expertise and experience as the modern chief editor. And there is also his personal journey, which includes his wife Hilary, a literary scholar, and his daughters Kate and Ellie. The latter beloved child has remained at the mental state of an infant without the ability of intelligible speech. John Simpson as the father finds touching words about Ellie on these pages, perplexed by the fate that he as a masterful linguist cannot relate to his daughter by way of words:

> Even if I can't communicate with her verbally, spending time with her reminds me that interaction isn't only verbal. Seeing her takes you into a corridor where communication fluctuates with the passage of time: sometimes stronger, sometimes weaker. When it's weak, it seems almost to vanish away, and you wonder if you will see it again. When it's strong, it's the most important thing there is. Wordless, but powerful. (339)

The memoir's reviewers are mindful of this painful but loving situation in the Simpson family (*Kirkus Reviews* 2016; Hitchings 2016), but they obviously zero in on John Simpson's invaluable role as the chief editor of the *OED* as of 1993. Lynne Truss in *The New York Times* summarizes Simpson's untiring work in the service of the English language as the modern lingua franca with these laudatory words:

> "The Word Detective" is a charmingly full, frank and humorous account of a career dedicated to rigorous lexicographical rectitude. [. . .] I doubt there has ever been a better account of how a person with a capacious brain sits down with a cup of tea and a pile of cards and sets about creating authoritative definitions. Throughout the text, Simpson inserts potted word biographies (apprenticeship, deadline, inkling) that illustrate both the complexity and the "excitement" of the work. It is astonishing that anyone could have done this taxing job, without a break, for over 35 years, especially while engaged in heaving and shoving the whole intractable project from its original state as a set of heavy (and instantly outdated) books toward being a lively interactive online tool. He is an absolute hero. (Truss 2016)

Simpson is indeed a lexicographical hero, who would be the first to admit that he was standing on the broad shoulders of James Murray, the editor of the original ten-volume *A New English Dictionary* (1888–1928), which evolved into the twenty volumes of the second edition with its more appropriate title *Oxford English Dictionary* (1989). Like Murray, Simpson never rested on his laurels and has remained a humble and unassuming yet progressive world-class lexicographer. Luiza Lodder offers an insightful description of Simpson's modus operandi in her review of his intriguing memoir:

> Simpson's memoir [is a] pleasant and cohesive account of his career and personal life. He writes with easeful grace, employing a humorous and conversational tone saturated with characteristically British self-awareness. Additionally, Simpson packs his narration with explanatory asides and parenthetical insertions, and renders his memories with light-hearted charm. [. . .] Although the self-deprecating humor is excessive at times, for the most part Simpson's recollections sparkle with immediacy and relatability. Unlike the executives at the Press or the Oxford dons with frightening credentials, Simpson retains his everyman sensibilities, and keeps the focus of the Dictionary and his memoir on what really matters: the words.
>
> This focus manifests itself in sections of bold text in which Simpson narrates the etymological twists and turns of a particular word used in the preceding paragraphs. By showcasing words like *serendipity, Aerobics*, and *bird-watching*, Simpson intends to show that "any word can have an interesting history, if you just take a few moments to look behind the scenes." These little lexicographical interludes will delight any reader who enjoys accumulating tidbits of learning and trivia. (Lodder 2016)

Lodder's review touches on Simpson's writing style, emphasizing such matters as "conversational tone," "immediacy and relatability," and "everyman sensibilities." This might well have led her to comment on Simpson's quite frequent employment of proverbial language, but she fails to mention this stylistic feature, which doubtlessly adds to the readability of his memoir.

A particularly interesting use of an old English proverb by Simpson was picked up by Henrik Bering in his review of the book: "From his stint as the editor of *The Concise Oxford Dictionary of Proverbs*, he will offer an early sixteenth-century proverb: 'The longest way round is the shortest way home' as especially pertinent to lexicographers, since 'language development isn't linear'" (Bering 2016). Throughout his book, Simpson emphasizes the fact that there are no shortcuts for lexicographical work, which always must include diachronic and synchronic aspects in dealing with words and phrases. His involvement with proverbs came about because Oxford University Press was interested in marketing a small proverb dictionary—a matter of "publishing politics" (Simpson 2016, 80) as Simpson calls it:

> Oxford had an *Oxford Dictionary of English Proverbs* [3rd ed., 1970, by F. P. Wilson]. However, in those days you shouldn't *just* have a full Oxford dictionary of any subject; it was also advantageous to have a *Concise Oxford Dictionary* on the same topic, and possibly even a *Little* one, too, if you thought the market wouldn't object. There is an element of publishing-by-numbers here, but it made sense: you might not want to buy the full weighty and complex version, but you might want its little sidekick. (80)

As a paremiologist I might argue that it would be a welcome move on the part of Oxford University Press to plan a fourth edition of the large proverb dictionary, but this desideratum appears to have found no interest whatsoever. In fact, after Simpson published his *Concise Oxford Dictionary of Proverbs* in 1982, he brought out an expanded second edition with the assistance of Jennifer Speake in 1992, followed by a third edition in 1998. The fourth edition of 2003 saw two major changes: John Simpson was no longer listed as coeditor, with Jennifer Speake being the sole editor from now on, and the title was changed to *The Oxford Dictionary of Proverbs*, an indication most likely that the large proverb dictionary from 1970 will not see a new edition. In the meantime, the sixth edition of the shorter collection appeared in 2015 under the editorship of Jennifer Speake as well, and it would not be surprising if there were another edition in due time. I might add that Elizabeth Knowles has also edited a less scholarly *Little Oxford Dictionary of Proverbs* (2009) for the popular market. Oxford University Press clearly has recognized that there is money to be made with proverb dictionaries.

In any case, in the early 1980s Simpson accepted the challenge of editing *The Concise Oxford Dictionary of Proverbs*, which gave him a break from his work on the *Supplement to the OED* (4 vols.; Burchfield 1972–1986). He really had little paremiological or paremiographical experience, but he took on the challenge and succeeded in bringing out a very useful and reliable proverb dictionary. He recounts his experience with proverbs on seven fascinating pages of his memoir (Simpson 2016, 80–86), which include some of the following observations:

> While working on the *Supplement to the OED* I had had little to do with proverbs, as we were predominantly dealing with the emergent vocabulary of the nineteenth and twentieth centuries, and most proverbs were

well and truly set in stone by then. Modern proverbs tend to have a long gestation period, beginning as quotations from known authors, and only gradually assuming the status of universal proverbs or maxims many years later, when the identity of the original author has been largely or completely forgotten. It's a moot point whether we should still call *If it ain't broke, don't fix it* (Bert Lance, US President Jimmy Carter's director of the Office of Management and Budget: 1977), or *Work expands to fill the time available* (Parkinson's Law—British naval historian C. Northcote Parkinson: 1955), quotations, or whether they have moved into the more abstract world of proverbs. Proverbs are pithy sayings that offer some general truth, by and large. Also, I had expressed no interest in proverbs over my time at the dictionary. (80–81)

Simpson valiantly devoted himself "to the unknown realm of 'old said saws' and proverbs" (81), without any prior paremiological training. Not surprisingly then, there are a number of problems with this statement. For one, the proverb "If it ain't broke, don't fix it" did not originate with Bert Lance in 1977, with numerous earlier references beginning in 1960 having now been registered (Doyle, Mieder, and Shapiro 2012, 80–81). Modern proverbs also have often rather short gestation periods due to the incredible influence of the mass media in all of its forms. It is also not true that the author is known for most modern proverbs (Doyle 1996; Mieder 2012; Mieder 2014). I also would not speak of "the more abstract world of proverbs," a better adjective perhaps being "general" (or indirect, metaphorical, etc.). But as John Simpson obviously realized during his work on this proverb dictionary, proverbial matters are as difficult to deal with as are individual words. The paremiographers and lexicographers have difficult tasks to master in order to give precise information. But Simpson faced the challenge and got into it, to put it colloquially:

And so I spent the next year, which expanded to eighteen months, writing out by hand—as you did in those days—the entire text of a *Concise [Oxford] Dictionary of Proverbs* [quite an achievement in that short time, with Wilson's 1970 dictionary providing a solid base, of course]. By the end I could speak fluently in "old said saws" and offer trite truisms on demand to anyone who approached me with a problem. One man may steal a horse, while another may not look over a hedge; a stern chase is a long chase; near is my shirt, but nearer is my skin; the best thing for the inside of a man is the outside of a horse (i.e., take some exercise); little pitchers (i.e., children) have large ears; bairns and fools should not see half-done work; if you lie down with dogs, you will rise up with fleas (a saying translated from the Roman sage Seneca); the looker-on sees more of the game. Proverbs were universal truths (or what passed as these), normally presented in sentence form. Some were abstract [in this case, this adjective fits] (of the "Hope springs eternal" variety), but many evolved from the home and hearth of the medieval peasant, and so their subjects were often homely subjects—cats, dogs, friends, the weather, churchgoing, food and drink. They were extraordinary, colourful, reassuring adjuncts to everyday conversation. (Simpson 2016, 82)

That's quite an enumeration of proverbs, although it is a bit surprising that Simpson chose rather archaic texts for the most part—perhaps because they need explanatory comments as to their origin and meaning in the dictionary itself. Of special interest for his writing style is his humorous tongue-in-cheek statement that after working so much on proverbs he could "speak fluently in 'old said saws' and offer trite truisms." No wonder that his memoir is replete with proverbial language!

As Simpson worked on abridging, correcting, and updating Wilson's massive *Oxford Dictionary of English Proverbs*, he came across a somewhat archaic proverb that in a nutshell could describe his detailed work as a lexicographer and short-time paremiographer: "I discovered that my favourite, the old and now almost-forgotten saw 'The longest way round is the shortest way home,' dated from the early sixteenth century, [had morphed] to 'The road to resolution lies by Doubt; The next way home's the farther way about' (where *next* is used in its etymological meaning of 'nearest'). It is a thought that applies to historical lexicography in spades, where you need constantly to remind people that the shortest way of doing something isn't necessarily the best way, and that there are advantages in being a little more considered" (85). Studying the intricate history of individual proverbs, Simpson became aware of the fact that he "should be looking not just for classical prototypes for English proverbs, but for the trail of development from Latin, say, into French or Italian, and then into English. As with words, the situation was much more complex than first meets the eye, but the final resolution is far more satisfying. The longest way round is the shortest way home" (85)

Numerous studies trace proverbs from Greek antiquity by way of Latin into the vernacular languages of Europe (Mieder 2009), and I might mention as an example my study, "'Big Fish Eat Little Fish': History and Interpretation of a Proverb About Human Nature" (Mieder 1987, 178–228, 259–68), which not only looks at historical texts but also discusses the meaning of the proverb in various contexts. Simpson chooses a proverb of a considerably more recent origin as an example, namely "When the cat's away, the mice will play," which had its start in medieval Latin, like so many other proverbs still employed today such as "Strike while the iron is hot" or "All that glitters is not gold." They were all translated verbatim into numerous languages, adding to the stock of common European proverbs (Mieder 2004, 9–13). But here is what Simpson writes:

> A good example of an expression that illustrates the mixed international heritage of proverbs would be *When the cat's away, the mice will play*. It's a typical old proverb, with imagery from the domestic environment, which is a hallmark of many old sayings. We know it in English from the early seventeenth century (Thomas Heywood's *Woman Killed with Kindness* [1607]). Even here it is offered as an "old proverb." In the absence of earlier English evidence, we can see, however, that the proverb existed in French from the early fourteenth century: *Ou chat na rat regne* ("Where there is no cat the rat is king [the rat rules]"). Maybe we are more squeamish than the French, and prefer mice to rats. (Simpson 2016, 85)

Admittedly, John Simpson is writing here for a general audience, but it would have been good to point out the medieval Latin origin of the proverb—"Dum deerit cattus, discurrens conspicitur mus" (When no cat is there, one can see the mouse running around)—which existed in a number of variants, as proverbs often do as they are handed down over time. But Simpson is wrong in thinking that the French text with the "rat" might have been the source for the English reference. The proverb has existed in French since the late twelfth century with a mouse: "Ou chat n'a, souriz i revelent" (Where there is no cat, the mice become playful), and numerous medieval French variants with "mouse" have been recorded (Paczolay 1997, 114–19; Singer and Liver 1995–2002, 6:452–54).

In any case, Simpson finishes his account of the challenging work on his *Concise Oxford Dictionary of Proverbs* with the following remarks, which show how the serendipitous request by OUP for him to compose this book resulted in his very much deserved advancement on the editorial staff of the *OED*. That he also relates his concerns about whether his manuscript would be judged worthy of publication shows the humility of this renowned scholar/editor:

> Before the proverb dictionary could be published, it had to survive an internal review. This turned out to be crucial to me and my prospects of promotion on the main *OED*. I was nervous about how my draft dictionary would be received. Oxford likes to criticize—on the principle that it is the making of good scholarship—but a bad review would be catastrophic. After a few months of anxious waiting, the review came in. [. . .] I was fortunately informed that I had got the thumbs-up [this phrase also appears on page 224], and the next thing I knew I was joining Ed [Weiner] in a more senior role [senior editors, to be precise] on

the *OED*. As a footnote, it's curious that the first major printed notice of the proverb dictionary appeared in the *Times Literary Supplement*, in the same issue as its (equally positive) review of [Simpson's wife] Hilary's book *D. H. Lawrence and Feminism*. Things were looking up. (Simpson 2016, 86)

With two books in their hands and a promotion at OUP, life indeed looked good for the couple, but there was more to be delighted about. A baby arrived with much joy, leading Simpson to one of his many comments that make his memoir such a reading pleasure:

In the same year in which the proverb dictionary was published (1982), things took an altogether different track at home: we had our first baby, Katherine Jane ("Kate"). Despite my rather curious job, we did all the usual, ordinary things: bringing the baby home very cautiously the first time, photographing her in her carry-cot, etc. Over time Kate hit all the right percentiles, fitted the right-sized clothes, and developed her eating habits just the way the books said she would. Later, Kate would come to argue with me about words, not appreciating that I was in fact the ultimate arbiter. Sometimes kids just don't realise. (86)

Their second daughter Eleanor ("Ellie") was born in 1990, and as already noted, she unfortunately has not developed mentally. The many pages dealing with her disability include the most touching statements in the entire book. They show how intelligent parents with superb linguistic abilities are confronted by a dear child without verbal or cognitive abilities. Tears are coming to my eyes again as I type just these few comments filled with love and understanding by John Simpson and through him by Hilary as well:

I desperately wanted her to speak, and to speak to her. There was a period of about eighteen months when we used to return home from work every day hoping to hear that Ellie had spoken her first word. It never happened. We'd look for signs of comprehension, and try to transmit ideas to her by action, tone, if not by speech. But it was no use. There *was* communication and comprehension happening, but it was at a very low level: she seemed to understand about five words. But was it even that? Was she just picking up on situations in which they be used ("car," "food," "drink"—not much else). Then at times she'd burst out laughing: it's always been clear that she has a quiet sense of humour. And she liked the colour yellow for some reason. [. . .] But nothing coordinated remained, nothing that could be a cognitive platform from which easy communication might develop. In the end, we found that gestures and tone—leading, guiding, directing, assisting—were all we could use, and we hoped that she was happy with our efforts. We were an excessively "wordy" family with a wordless newcomer in our midst: at times she dragged us into her silence, and we couldn't think how to help her. (260–61)

Despite all, there is much love in the Simpson family for Ellie to this day, and one can well imagine that Simpson's strenuous work on the *OED* was of help in dealing with the deep concerns about Ellie. Work can help to deal with pain and anguish, and writing his humane memoir in such telling words must also have given him comfort.

And work John Simpson did year after year as his autobiography makes clear on almost every page. There was so much to do to bring the not perfect multivolume dictionary up to date. Simpson expresses this fact with a very appropriate proverb in his introduction to the book: "Nothing, of course, is perfect. As I continued to work on the dictionary, I—along with many of my colleagues—became more and more aware of cracks in the wallpaper. Back then, the *OED* was a late nineteenth-century dictionary which had hardly changed in a hundred years. As editors, we were adding new meanings to it, but really it needed a complete overhaul and update" (xii). And with this first appearance of a proverb, John Simpson is on a proverbial roll without overburdening his readers with such folk speech, heeding the wisdom of such proverbs as "Nothing in excess" and "Everything in moderation." The attached list of all phraseological units reveals Simpson's colloquial style beyond any doubt, with the following discussion of at least some particularly telling examples of his narrative use of proverbial language illustrating that they serve a considerable communicative purpose.

Since this is a personal narrative, it should not come as a surprise that there are quite a few proverbial statements that employ the "I" pronoun. Early in the book, Simpson explains that he decided to respond to a job advertisement announced by OUP, giving his comment a metaphorical flavor by using a well-known proverbial expression: "The promised salary wasn't large—in fact it was only moderate—but in comparison with a student grant it suggested undreamt-of affluence. Eventually I decided to throw my hat in the ring" (6; there is another reference of this proverbial phrase on page 243). As he reflects on the possibility of a job interview, he employs another proverbial expression, which shows his reserved if not shy nature as well as his honesty with himself:

I was nervous about the interview—there were so many questions I could be asked to which I would not want to commit an answer. I think

A PROVERBIAL TRIBUTE TO *OED* EDITOR JOHN A. SIMPSON   341

I'm quite a slow learner. At least I don't like to commit myself until I know what I'm talking about. Given time I can usually work things out, but not necessarily right away. [. . .] I would just dry up, not wanting to commit myself and be wrong. I'm fine after a while—after I've had a chance to absorb things. But for those first crucial ten seconds of an interview I wouldn't put my money on me. (15)

But luckily the interview did take place, leading Simpson to the following proverbial observation: "Somehow I had survived those first ten seconds with the amiable chief editor [Bob Burchfield], but his deputy [John Sykes] saw through me immediately—or, as I like to remember, he formed the wrong and worst opinion of me from the moment he walked through the door. Furthermore, I suspect that he didn't like playing second fiddle to the chief editor in an interview for a post reporting to him" (21). This proverbially charged description of his OUP interview concludes with a fascinating reworking of a quotation from Shakespeare's *Julius Caesar* long turned proverb: "There is a tide in the affairs of men which, taken at its flood, leads on to fortune" (Mieder, Kingsbury, and Harder 1992, 595). By shortening this hopeful expression and adding to it the negative proverbial phrase of the game being up, Simpson is able to verbalize his impression that he had failed the interview: "There came a tide in the affairs of the interview when I knew the game was up, and I was ushered back out of the office, leaving both editors to discuss my prospective candidacy" (Simpson 2016, 22). Unfortunately his negative premonition proved to be correct, as he was informed a few days later that he had not made the cut this time.

But fortune did smile upon the young man when a month later he received a letter from OUP offering him an alternative job after all, which would change life for him and Hilary rather abruptly, as indicated by the triadic proverbial expression "lock, stock, and barrel." Add to this that the idea of moving to Oxford almost immediately was, proverbially speaking, sinking its teeth into him, it becomes clear that he would be married not only to Hilary but to OUP as well:

Once the new letter had arrived from Oxford University Press, Hilary and I had to decide whether to pack up our things lock, stock, and barrel and relocate almost immediately to Oxford. We talked about it. Hilary was happy to shift her research to Oxford, with instant access to the gargantuan holdings of the Bodleian Library, so she needed little convincing. I still toyed with the possibility of further medieval research [toward a never completed dissertation], but the idea of becoming involved in a major international language project based in Oxford was starting to sink its teeth into me. I'd always liked approaching things from odd angles: maybe dictionary work would be an intriguing outlet for my interest in language, literature, and historical research. Also, there were no other job offers available on our kitchen table that day. So, arguments in favour: more or less everything. Arguments against: we would have to move. (25)

One might well have expected that at this point of his narration Simpson would have cited Julius Caesar's proverb "The die is cast," but instead he comments proverbially on not finishing his graduate studies as he sets out on his lifelong lexicographical journey: "Soon another letter was on its way to OUP informing the powers to be that, even before I had my master's degree in medieval studies tucked under my belt, I would be 'delighted' to launch myself on the sea of historical lexicography" (25). This is quite the understatement by this accomplished champion of the *OED*, but this is his humble nature that becomes a leitmotif throughout his scholarly autobiography.

John Simpson certainly never blows his own horn on these pages. As his career advanced, he remained down to earth without showing off. This is obvious from such proverbial statements as "Without realizing it, I was bringing myself into the spotlight, and starting to etch out a future for myself" (69) and "I was beginning to make a faint appearance on the chief editor's radar as a prospect for the future" (70). When he was put in charge of the "New Words" project, he did not dominate the group of lexicographers, realizing that this was new lexicographical territory for him:

Running the New Words group didn't represent the future, but it gave us a breathing-space while we, and the University Press generally, thought about how we might work in the years to come. The group gave me my first opportunity to organize an area of the *OED*'s work from the ground up, and over the next few years my New Words colleagues and I lived very close at hand with the lexical changes to which the language was subject in the early to mid-1980s. I don't think I'd heard of a steep learning curve in those days, but I would have appreciated its meaning. (98–99)

The proverbial expression "to be (have) a steep learning curve" has become ever more popular in recent years, in light of the various electronic products that have become part of modern life.

Even after the second edition of the *OED* was published in 1989, Simpson did not rest on his laurels as he realized that there was much more to be done, notably bringing the famed dictionary into the computer age, accessible first on CD-ROM and now as a constantly updated online version. Instead of bragging about his accomplishments, he negates the proverbial expression "to be the be-all and end-all" in order to stress that the work on the *OED* must go on:

> For me, the *OED* was at last heading in the right direction. It wasn't that I thought the Second Edition was the be-all and end-all of lexicography. In truth, for me it was a mechanistic project—though tough and imaginative for all that. I wanted to see the text of the dictionary safely housed on computer so that we could start updating the *OED* comprehensively, rather than making piecemeal additions through supplementary volumes. It was, of course, still very uncertain. [. . .]
>
> But first of all, we had to get the dictionary on to a computer by 1989. If we couldn't do that, there was little point in trying to write a happy ending beyond. I thought of the project until 1989 as Phase One; Phase Two was our secret dream of what we wanted to do with the dictionary in the longer term. We thought perhaps we could engineer an *OED* redux—an *OED* reborn. If you wait long enough, most things make a comeback. (148–49)

The dream continues to be materialized with the constantly updated electronic version of the *OED* today. Thus the older versions of the dictionary are indeed reborn in a modernized way, even though it took a long time to get this ongoing project on track. John Simpson did well to summarize all of this with his statement "If you wait long enough, most things make a comeback," which most likely is based on the modern proverb "If you keep anything (wait) long enough, everything (it) comes (will come) back into style" (Doyle, Mieder, and Shapiro 2012, 243). Toward the end of his book, Simpson comes up with his ultimate proverbial understatement. To be sure, he is not a computer expert, but he shepherded the *OED* into becoming the modern online resource it is today. There really was no need for him to state: "I'm not always the sharpest knife when I come to new ideas" (Simpson 2016, 323). Let's just agree that the English language owes the world to this sharp guy, who as a lexicographer thought innovatively outside the box. That certainly is the path to new horizons in dictionary making, even if, as Simpson states, it might be "only a start, but the first step, as they say—to quote another trite proverb—is the most difficult" (326).

Of course, whether the lexicographical steps might be traditional or innovative, they are best accomplished by way of cooperative team efforts. John Simpson by no means accomplished the breakthrough advances of the modern *OED* by himself. This can easily be seen by his repeated use of the "we" pronoun, indicating that he surrounded himself with excellent lexicographers for whom he was a true team player. Mindful of the modern proverb "There is no 'I' in team" (Doyle, Mieder, and Shapiro 2012, 128), Simpson begins many proverbial statements with the collective "we." The results are emotive comments that add considerable expressiveness to the team spirit of the lexicographers among whom Simpson would best be described as "primus inter pares." Here are a few contextualized examples of this effective style of narration, showing the ups and downs of serious lexicographical work in which everybody has to work together for the common goal of the most complete and up-to-date dictionary possible:

> We had had to restrain the *Supplement* to its four volumes, and we had around four or five years to complete the task for publication before the 1980s ran out of steam (the fourth and final volume was published in 1986). (Simpson 2016, 87)

> Word selection wasn't really an issue, as we had drawn up rules and guidelines based on hard evidence and currency, which took any guesswork out of the whole process. We applied a rule of thumb that demanded that any term had to have existed over several years (we said five in the early days, and later modified that to ten); had to be documented in various genres (formal, technical, everyday, slang—not all of these for every word, of course); and had to be evidenced by at least five documentary examples in our card files. (104; the "thumb" phrase reappears on page 246)

> Did the Press owe the *OED* a living, or did the *OED* need to start earning its keep? The smart money was on option two, but we had our heads down, and some of us didn't notice that the world was changing. [. . .] It turned out that the future [of the computer] was opening up before our very eyes. (130)

> For the time, this was big data. And if we couldn't transfer this international interest in the dictionary into something that opened up the text [via the computer] to the masses, then we weren't worth the paper we were written on. (139)

> If we could pull it off [the computerization of the dictionary], then dictionaries would make a quantum leap to the benefit of both readers and editors. [. . .] We would be creating a massive, dynamic, and updatable language resource. (150)

> By now we were battling hell-for-leather to meet our regular and draconian deadlines for processing the text, and checking the proofs that were

rolling off the old-style printing presses to form the pages of the Second Edition [1989, twenty volumes in the print edition]. The full dictionary text existed on computer at this point, but it was only accessible internally, to *OED* editors. (176)

Just for a moment [at the publication of the twentieth volume of the second edition], we felt on top of the world. Over the previous five years we had commandeered the text of the dictionary from its old-style book form on to computer; we'd proofread it, added 5,000 new entries, and altered the pronunciation system; and we'd got it all to the point at which it could be published. Curiously, it was going to be published again as a book, and not (straightaway) as an electronic resource. We still had some work to do. (177–78)

We didn't tell them [the OUP Advisory Committee] how far we would move in the future, because the issue—for example—of citing web pages didn't exist. In due course we did open the floodgates even further, accepting evidence of the language from the Internet—from personal web pages, for example. (219–20)

With the ever-present deadline [for the online third edition of the *OED*] of the year 2000 looming, we needed to take serious action to recruit staff. [. . .] We did manage to bring into (or back into) the fold several colleagues willing to give it all a shot. But we still needed more hands on deck, and we needed them quickly. (242)

When we advertise for editorial posts, we have to be very careful not to open the net too wide. We did once, in the early days, and received over a thousand applications for three jobs. It's not worth the time spent reading through those applications. If the job is described in too open a fashion, you just encourage anyone who loves words, or who wants an excuse to extend their adolescence in Oxford, to throw their hat in the ring. (243)

It turned out that although we could extract remarkable swaths of historical material from the electronic databases, we sometimes needed the raw brainpower and ingenuity of a researcher to track a problem right down to earth: there was room for both research techniques. (279)

It would be nice to report that once the dictionary had gone online we could relax into automatic pilot, allowing the steady pendulum of progress to take the *OED* on its stately route through the alphabet. When we went online we were committed to updating and publishing at least 1,000 entries a quarter, but we wanted to get that up to 2,000 or 3,000 a quarter as quickly as possible. (304)

Alongside all of these plans for the future, we still needed to keep the editorial chariot on track, maintaining our production targets and publishing more and more of the dictionary online at each of our quarterly updates. We were progressing well through the alphabet by now, and we were producing remarkable entries, full of new and exciting information. Wherever the dictionary was going in the future, we knew we'd brought it through. (328)

These thirteen texts with their proverbial expressions are telling statements of the teamwork that John Simpson was involved in and guided as the time-honored *Oxford English Dictionary* went from traditional printed volumes to its constantly updated online version. Being a bookish person, I must admit that I still enjoy using the first and second print editions from time to time, but obviously I value what the online *OED* has to offer as the most comprehensive and up-to-date dictionary in the world, and for the lingua franca of the world to boot.

With such proverbial tidbits, Simpson succeeds in a truly lively and somewhat colloquial account of his life's work. In addition to writing about himself, he also speaks of his team in a personal way by employing the "I" and "we" pronouns. And there is a third stylistic feature in all of this, namely those statements in which he uses the pronoun "you." This enables him to speak to his readers and draw them into his amazing tale. As one of those eager readers, I had two wonderful experiences. The first came when early in the first chapter I discovered the name Richard Chenevix Trench (1807–1886), later archbishop of Dublin, who had bemoaned the fact in his lecture "On Some Deficiencies in Our English Dictionaries" (1857) at the Philological Society of London that the English language was lacking a scholarly historical dictionary (Simpson 2016, 7). I might add here that Trench was an incredibly prolific author, publishing his own poetry, anthologies, translations, and works dealing with history, the church, and philology. Among his philological books are *On the Study of Words* (1851), *English Past and Present* (1855), and *A Select Glossary of English Words* (1859). But he also published a still valuable book *On the Lessons in Proverbs* (1853). It went through seven editions during Trench's lifetime and several more later on, including a final edition with additional notes and a bibliography in 1905 with the slightly changed title *Proverbs and Their Lessons*. The publication history of this slim volume of less than two hundred pages is ample proof that it is an important and influential survey on the origin, nature, distribution, meaning, and significance of proverbs in the English-speaking world. It was my honor to edit a reprint of this book in 2003. Obviously I have been delighted for quite some time that a fellow paremiologist was instrumental in getting the ball rolling toward a superb dictionary that had its beginning with James Murray in 1879.

The other reading experience came in the second chapter, where Simpson writes: "The Philological Society had, very early in the life of the dictionary, invited American politician and man of letters George Perkins Marsh [1801–1882] to drum up support across the Atlantic. He was not entirely successful, but later efforts produced a steady influx of American English material. And as the dictionary grew in size and acclaim, more and more [American] readers became attracted to the work" (Simpson 2016, 34; for the American influence, see 112–13, 235–36). Marsh deserves a few more comments from me if alone for the fact that he was born in Woodstock in my beloved state of Vermont. But there is so much more to this incredible Renaissance man—a true gentleman and a scholar. He was not only a diplomat, having been appointed as the first US ambassador to Italy by President Lincoln in 1861 and holding this position to his death in 1882 (he is buried in the Protestant Cemetery in Rome). He is also considered the first American environmentalist, with his book *Man and Nature; or, Physical Geography as Modified by Human Action* (1864) being considered a classic in introducing the concept of a sustainable environment. More importantly for the English language, he is the author of the two massive volumes *Lectures on the English Language* (1860) and *The Origin and History of the English Language, and of the Early Literature It Embodies* (1862). I shall never forget the day when my wife Barbara and I discovered the two green volumes in a second-hand bookstore in Maine and acquired them for a mere two dollars each! He was an unbelievable polyglot linguist whose expertise included Icelandic, and he did considerable work in comparative linguistics. But there is more: while in Italy, he amassed a personal philological library of twelve thousand volumes, which at his death was donated to the library at the University of Vermont. When I arrived at Burlington in 1971, the librarian gave me a present that I read cover to cover: *Catalogue of the Library of George Perkins Marsh* (1892). These volumes are considered to make up one of the best collections in philology up through the nineteenth century in the United States, and it has been my privilege to have these books at my immediate disposal for the past forty-five years. And yes, the book on proverbs by Trench is among them!

I hope that I might be forgiven for these two digressions that are close to my heart. But let us return to our proverbial muttons, namely to the readers of Simpson's book and also to the readers who went through uncountable volumes of literature and other matters to excerpt references for the *OED*. The proverbial expressions "to play havoc with," "to put oneself in someone else's shoes," and "to stop someone in his/her tracks" add much metaphorical expressiveness to Simpson's explanation:

> "Reading" for the dictionary was all very well, and it helped to gather together a mass of material that might be useful in future years to the dictionary's editors, but it didn't do any good at all for my own ability to read. The process of reading text word by word, and then weighing up whether each word was worth carding for future reference, played havoc with my appreciation of literature. My estimate is that it would take the average person about five years of working on the dictionary and "reading" texts of all sorts before he or she came through the barrier and was able to read properly again.
>
> Put yourself in the reader's shoes: You are reading *Jane Eyre*, perhaps not for the first time, but you're enjoying it all over again. You've followed the narrative through its twists and turns. [. . .] What are the man-traps here for the budding lexicographer? Your growing lexicographical intuition stops you dead in your tracks. (Simpson 2016, 34–35; there is another reference on page 183)

Here is another example of how the use of the "you" pronoun pulls readers into Simpson's account. One can well imagine how readers might have a mental picture of digging themselves out of a proverbial hole: "He [classicist Philip Hardie] had a facility for knowing which entry in the *OED* was the exact counterpart to the entry you were struggling with, and which would therefore help in your attempt to dig yourself out of whatever lexicographical hole you were in" (76). Another telling example of this stylistic feature can be seen with the employment of the expression "to try one's hand at something":

> Although you might not be able to predict precisely which new words are just over the horizon, it is certainly possible to examine how new words arise, and to identify the general routes they take into English. If you do want to try your hand at prediction, you need to play the percentages—which means that you have to know two things: how words have been formed in the past, and which areas of the language are likely to generate new vocabulary. (113)

And on it goes with such short "you" proverbial comments as "and you can bet your bottom dollar," "but you didn't end up with a complete picture" (124), "but you get the idea" (135), and "that might stop you in your tracks" (183).

A PROVERBIAL TRIBUTE TO *OED* EDITOR JOHN A. SIMPSON 349

But I am not yet willing to be stopped in my tracks with this proverbial review. There are still at least a few contextualized examples of proverbial expressions to cite that exemplify John Simpson's captivating style. They add a great deal of emotive and metaphorical flavor to this erudite narrative with its personal touch:

> The Victorian editors had worked their fingers to the bone finding examples of everyday words. (31)

> Almost all the work on *red* had been edited by my old trainer, Lesley [Brown], and she was not one to leave any stone unturned. (60)

> If my first year at the *OED* had seemed to last for ages, as I concentrated on learning how to become an editor, the next few years—as we steered the *Supplement* project to a conclusion and finally brought the curtain down on old-style Oxford lexicography—seemed, in contrast, to rush by. (65)

> The *OED* doesn't just include the tip of the iceberg of language, but there are levels beneath the water that will be hard-pressed ever to make their way into the editing process. (71)

> It was simply a case of training, encouraging, and cajoling the junior editors to get through the requisite amount of work each week, and the *Supplement*'s final trajectory would be more or less in the bag. (87–88)

> There was a fly in the ointment. Despite the complexity of our work on the *Supplement to the OED*, I and others found ourselves becoming dissatisfied with the concept of supplementing—of adding lights and tinsel to the dictionary, rather than addressing the whole of the language all the way from the Anglo-Saxon period to the present day. (95)

> The *OED* was at the most alarming crossroads that it had seen for around one hundred years. Some senior members of the Oxford University Press and of the University of Oxford itself regarded the dictionary as a white elephant, and one that was stifling other exciting publishing projects. (133)

> If you wanted to, you could teach outside office hours, but that never appealed to me. There were enough other odd souls drifting around Oxford to pick up any additional teaching that the college or University

authorities offered, without upsetting the dictionary's apple cart. But as I had never regarded myself as a natural teacher, I chose not to take this route. (222)

Since the publication of the Second Edition of the *OED*, the whole project was becoming more visible to the public, and some companies had done their best to clamber on to the bandwagon of the dictionary's success. (291)

We couldn't go on field trips every day, but this one is a reminder of the value of paper-based research, conducted in conversation with an expert who can guide you through an archive. It is also a salutary reminder that even something in the *OED* may have been misinterpreted—that lexicographers should never accept anything at face value. Beware of relying simply on yourself or on the Internet. (297)

These texts all show Simpson's desire for the constant advancement of the *OED*, a most impressive and laudable commitment that he maintained for close to four decades. He even got involved in European language policies, bemoaning the fact that the study of foreign languages in Great Britain was not stronger:

The British are in general bad at learning foreign languages and the general concept of linguistic diversity, but I agreed with the multilingual objectives that EFNIL [the European Federation of National Institutions for Language] and the European Commission promoted: that state educational systems should promote the knowledge of two languages as well as the country's native tongue. It's just that dotting the *i*'s and crossing the *t*'s on a European document doesn't mean the British will play the game and sign on for language evening classes. (301–2)

Of course, Simpson is also aware of the fact that "most graduate programmes in the sciences [and business administration] in European universities are nowadays taught in English, and theses are predominantly written in English; major international companies in some countries—Germany, for example— use English as their internal company language. There are two sides to every question, as the old proverb wisely says" (298).

With all his professional commitments, it must be remembered that Simpson was not only married to his work on the *OED*. He also had a home life with a wife and two children. The two worlds needed to be balanced, and he could draw strength from both of them. But there were moments of frustration and anxiety as well, as can be seen from the following paragraph with the emotional reworking of the proverbial expression "to see the light at the end of the tunnel":

> As we entered the early 1990s, we embarked upon what I regarded at the time—and also in retrospect—as a dark phase of the project, which lasted perhaps for the first half of the decade. The Second Edition of the dictionary had been published to acclaim, but we had been working with our sights set so closely on this goal that we had completely overlooked the need to plan for—rather than just to expect—a future involving the comprehensive update to which computerisation was only the prelude. And my dark mood paralleled something of a dark period at home, as Hilary and I gradually realised that our younger daughter, Ellie, had severe developmental problems of the sort that no amount of funds, effort, care, support, or love would overcome. Not everything can have a happy ending, but at this point we were deep in a tunnel with no sign of light ahead. (207–8)

I remember the sadness that befell me when I read the last lines of this paragraph about the Simpson family. Of course, I also noticed John Simpson's appropriate use of the proverbial phrase to capture the family's anguish. It is not a cliché, and to be sure, love does prevail to this day.

Always being the historical/etymological lexicographer, John Simpson has integrated a number of word and phrase explications throughout his readable, entertaining, and enlightening book. In these scholarly "asides," the work on the *OED* as well as the *OED* itself come alive. I can imagine that many a reader would like to become a lexicographer at Oxford. I know well from my own studies of individual proverbs and proverbial expressions how much work goes into them, and Simpson as well as the *OED* must accomplish such tasks in a much-condensed space. In any case, Simpson's treatment of "hue and cry" (170–71), "to hit a brick wall" (172–74), "dribs and drabs" (201–2), and "to be a shaggy-dog story" (317–18) are an absolute delight for any phraseological sleuth. Being mindful of Simpson's splendid creation of the anti-proverb "An example is worth a thousand words," which is based on the internationally disseminated modern American proverb "A picture is worth a thousand words" from 1911 (Mieder 1993, 135–51; Doyle, Mieder, and Shapiro 2012, 196), let me cite his comments on the proverbial expression "by a long chalk" as an illustration:

> Phrases live and die through the amount of use they enjoy. In order to survive, they often need to leap from a small world into the big one. But they don't always jump continents. *By a long chalk* ("by far," "by a long

way") is an expression first recorded in 1840, just into the Victorian era. It is commonest in British English, with less evidence—for example—from Australia and New Zealand, and less still from America.

The phrase comes originally from the small world of bar-room games. If you were engaged in a long drinking session in a public house in Britain in the sixteenth century, the landlord might chalk up on a slate just how much you owed. In the seventeenth century, people found it useful to use chalk to keep the score in games (often also enjoyed in alehouses)—and each point you scored would be represented by a chalk mark. If you ran rings round your opponent in the game, then you'd win by a larger margin, or a "long chalk." So they say. (Simpson 2016, 314)

I am quite certain that Simpson had Thomas Chandler Haliburton's (1796–1865) satirical and humorous work *The Clockmaker; or, the Sayings and Doings of Samuel Slick of Slickville* in mind when he cited the year 1840 as the first recorded reference for the phrase. F. P. Wilson gives the years 1837–1840 with Haliburton as the earliest source in his *Oxford Dictionary of English Proverbs* (Wilson 1970, 113). However, Haliburton's *Clockmaker* was simultaneously published in 1836 by Joseph Howe in Halifax, Nova Scotia, and by George Routledge in London. The author used the phrase numerous times, but the first reference is: "[I]sn't this as pretty a day as you'll see between this and Norfolk; it whips English weather by a long chalk" (see Taylor and Whiting 1958, 64). The Halifax publication should not be a surprise, since Haliburton was born in Windsor, Nova Scotia, where he became a judge of the provincial supreme court. For now, the phrase's earliest written record is from Canada, and it remains to be seen whether an earlier occurrence can be found in Great Britain. Haliburton certainly liked it, but he is not necessarily the originator, and the phrase might well have come to Canada from England.

Enough of this, but it is a small illustration of how complex the search for the origin of a proverb or proverbial expression can be. In any case, Simpson also provides short comments on the modern expressions "the full monty" (Simpson 2016, 315) and "to be a couch potato" (291), with the latter adding some humor to it all:

At one point, the University Press's offices in Oxford were the object of a small demonstration by a potato company on behalf of their wards (the potatoes themselves). The argument—such as it was—ran along the lines that the *OED* was disrespecting the potato by including an entry for *couch potato*. Clearly, the demonstrators were people, not potatoes, as the potatoes were far too idle to get off their sofas in their own support. But things died down once the company had achieved whatever

A PROVERBIAL TRIBUTE TO *OED* EDITOR JOHN A. SIMPSON 353

publicity it was after. We fearlessly refused to budge from our position that people had the right to read an entry for *couch potato* in the *OED*, and we returned to our lairs wondering whether to seek revenge by downsizing our entries for *chip* and *spud*. (291)

Who would have thought that political correctness would get involved in this harmless but wonderfully descriptive phrase! But just think what the thought and language police could do when it comes to the sexual and scatological vocabulary that must be part of a truly comprehensive dictionary!? The astute Simpson does not dwell on such "taboo" words and phrases, but knowing that his readers want to know how the *OED* deals with this fascinating topic, he has included—wouldn't you know it?—the word "fuck." In fact, it receives major billing in an entire twelve-page section (226–37). It makes for great reading to see how this four-letter word has been treated by the *OED*. Not wanting to take the anticipation away from reading Simpson's splendid account, I shall reluctantly refrain from going into considerable detail here. Let me simply mention the "fuck" phraseology that is part of his learned exegesis: "tell whoever it is to go fuck themselves" and "fuck the bloody thing" (228), "fuck about, off, up" (235), "fuck around, over, with" (236), and the popular rhyming expression "to go fuck a duck" (236). Of course, I could add the modern disgusting proverbs "You don't fuck the face," "Fuck them and forget them," and "There is no such thing as a bad fuck" to this (Doyle, Mieder, and Shapiro 2012, 72, 89–90, 253–54; Mieder 2012, 184), and there is more! But let me give Simpson the last lexicographical word here:

One contemporary issue with *fuck* is whether it has lost, or will lose, its taboo status. That, like most other language change, would be something that happens over several generations. For one tier of society (by age, gender, ethnic background, national economic power, geographical location, social class, etc.) it will retain its power to shock, whereas for others it will tend to lose this. Words can become taboo (as *fuck* once did), or they can go the other way and enter the mainstream. Which one wins out depends on how our cultures move. Often the significant vector is age, and so as the generations pass, the meanings that the older members of society know and have clung to will disappear, and the younger strains of the language will assert themselves. But it doesn't have to be like that. The usage of a dominant economic power can influence the language of its less dominant cousins, and vice versa (Australians or others might be attracted to some American usages, such as the filter *like*, because of the attractions of the culture it represents, or the reverse may occur). Normally there's some conflict between a number of vectors, so you can't claim to know precisely what is going to happen. It's too complex for that. (236–37)

Indeed, complexity is the real thing when it comes to the study of the multifaceted aspects of language! John Simpson dedicated his professional life to the lexicographical documentation of the English language, and his name will forever be associated with the unsurpassed *Oxford English Dictionary*. I am not aware whether he has received a Doctor Honoris Causa from the University of Oxford, but if not, then he should definitely be honored in this fashion. The title of his memoir's last chapter, "Becoming the Past," has a melancholic tone to it, but Simpson is well aware that after thirty-five years with the *OED*, the end of his work had to come. He knows that much remains to be done, but he had "come to terms with that some years back" (329), as he puts it proverbially. And then, with typical humility, he relies on another fitting phrase to take his leave, as it were: "It seemed to me that the *OED* was entering a period of consolidation—without any radical changes on the horizon—and so it might be a good time to give someone else a chance to step into my editorial shoes. I hope I left it in good shape" (330). Indeed, everything is on track in keeping the *OED* going online due to his expertise, diligence, dedication, and "enthusiasm" (330). I like the last sentence of the book, thinking that my wife Barbara might say something similar about me as my own retirement is approaching: "Hilary says I'm just an ordinary bloke who's been lucky enough to do an extraordinary job. I suppose she's right. She usually is" (340). I am, of course, not putting myself on the same pedestal with John Simpson, and Barbara might well simply state that I have done a "good" job for my students and my paremiological work. John Simpson's shoes are a very special size and can't be filled by another person. He is a model for us all, and I am thankful that many years ago he helped me get my paremiological feet on the ground.

Proverbial references as they appear in the book:

p. xii: Nothing, of course, is perfect.
p. xiii: when I first set foot inside the *OED* offices.
p. 6: Eventually I decided to throw my hat in the ring.
p. 6: my experience was rock bottom.
p. 6: without needing to cross swords with scholars themselves.
p. 7: materials for a new English dictionary which would knock all of its predecessors into a tin hat or paper bag.
p. 7: To cut a very long story short.
p. 15: I wouldn't put my money on me.

A PROVERBIAL TRIBUTE TO *OED* EDITOR JOHN A. SIMPSON

p. 17: the air of a scholar searching austerely for wheat amongst chaff.

p. 17: but, truth to tell, the only one available.

p. 18: to put the academic world back on its axis.

p. 21: I suspect that he didn't like playing second fiddle to the chief editor.

p. 22: There came a tide in the affairs of the interview when I knew the game was up.

p. 23: who were more egg-headed and therefore more suitable than I was.

p. 23: Hilary didn't go into overdrive either.

p. 25: I had to decide whether to pack up our things lock, stock, and barrel.

p. 25: Oxford was starting to sink its teeth into me.

p. 25: even before I had my master's degree in medieval studies tucked under my belt.

p. 26: there wasn't all that much to write home about.

p. 27: as sharp as an icicle when it came to editing the dictionary.

p. 27: I came to look up to her as a dog looks up to his master.

p. 27: in the time it takes to make a pot of tea.

p. 28: it meant not rolling up your sleeves and tackling real editing until you'd been around the track with all sorts of ancillary tasks.

p. 30. The dictionary was starting to move with the times.

p. 31: the Victorian editors had worked their fingers to the bone finding examples.

p. 32: and you can bet your bottom dollar that they all came from my pen.

p. 33: it may be worth checking whether either of those celebrated first uses would pass muster today.

p. 34: The process of reading text word by word [. . .] played havoc with my appreciation of literature.

p. 34: Put yourself in the reader's shoes.

p. 35: Your growing lexicographical intuition stops you dead in your tracks.

p. 35: has been around since the dawn of time.

p. 36: in the form of whatever text they could lay their hands on.

p. 37: The editors were kindly, for the most part, and keen to show me the ropes.

p. 45: several other writers who were even then heading pell-mell towards oblivion.

p. 45: Others invariably see you through Oxford-tinted glasses, however different you think you are yourself.

p. 46: I felt it was our duty to be in at ground zero as this new vocabulary was arriving.

p. 51: In modern terms that is absolutely nothing, but it was a gold-mine back then.

p. 53: to let a breath of fresh air into the new *OED* in this way.

p. 54: Nowadays, leaving before the wedding lunch was over would probably put me beyond the pale.

p. 58: So the *OED* deserves a small pat on the head for knocking 63 years off the German world-record schedule.

p. 59: the work we conducted to research the history of the expression *the thin red line* [more on pp. 59–61].

p. 60: she was not one to leave any stone unturned.

pp. 60–61: But all was not lost.

p. 61: But this time it was John Bartlett who nearly came up trumps.

p. 61: Facts were dissolving like butter in a pan.

p. 62: The icing on the cake came a year or two later.

p. 65: finally brought the curtain down on the old-style Oxford lexicography.

p. 68: I regarded myself as the *OED*'s eyes and ears on the street.

p. 69: I amassed as many [. . .] magazines as I could lay my hands on.

p. 69: I was bringing myself into the spotlight.

p. 70. I was beginning to make a faint appearance on the chief editor's radar as a prospect for the future.

pp. 70–71: There were some eyebrows raised in the dictionary office.

p. 71: but they didn't generally stand the test of time.

p. 71: The *OED* didn't just include the tip of the iceberg of language, but there are levels beneath the water.

p. 75: This is a trap into which it is too easy for the lexicographical mind to fall.

p. 76: which would therefore help in your attempt to dig yourself out of whatever lexicographical hole you were in.

p. 77: I'd tell him the time of day when he needed it.

p. 78: If they are likened to foot soldiers marching to someone else's beat.

p. 80: wanted to float an idea about a future project that I might like to be involved in.

p. 81: I could see how my cards were marked.

p. 82: One man may steal a horse, while another may not look over a hedge.

p. 82: a stern chase is a long chase.

p. 82: near is my shirt, but nearer is my skin.

p. 82: the best thing for the inside of a man is the outside of a horse (i.e., take some exercise).

p. 82: little pitchers (i.e., children) have large ears.

p. 82: bairns and fools should not see half-done work.

p. 82: if you lie down with dogs, you will rise up with fleas (a saying translated from the Roman sage Seneca).

p. 82: the looker-on sees more of the game.

p. 82: the "Hope springs eternal" variety.

p. 83: it was plain wrong.

p. 85: I discovered [. . .] my favourite, the old and now almost-forgotten saw "The longest way round is the shortest way home."

p. 85: "The road to resolution lies by Doubt."

p. 85: "The next way home's the farther way about" (where *next* is used in its etymological meaning of "nearest").

p. 85: the situation was much more complex than first meets the eye.

p. 85: *When the cat's away, the mice will play.*

p. 85: *Ou chat na rat regne* ("Where there is no cat the rat is king").

p. 86: I had got the thumbs-up.

p. 87: we had around four to five years to complete the task for publication before the 1980s ran out of steam.

p. 87: Anything else would have to catch the next bus.

p. 88: the *Supplement*'s final trajectory would be more or less in the bag.

p. 88: The secret was to acknowledge that there are always at least two ways of doing something.

p. 90: to make sure the editors were all on track.

p. 91: It wasn't a dream job, as far as I could see.

p. 91: In no time at all I was handed the first instalment of yet another book with no plot.

p. 91: We pussyfooted along, exchanging courteous comments and responses.

p. 95: But this excitement came at a price.

p. 95: There was a fly in the ointment.

p. 96: It was only as the curtain fell on the final years of our work on the *Supplement*.

p. 98: what I selfishly regarded as the real thing.

p. 98: the dim prospect of an olive branch offered for the eventual revival of the full *OED*.

p. 98: if the cards fell in the right way.

p. 98: This, it goes without saying, became a matter of great interest.

p. 98: should the old warhorse ever survive.

p. 98: but it gave us a breathing-space.

p. 99: I don't think I'd heard of a steep learning curve in those days.

p. 99: So as not to miss a trick, we engaged in a correspondence.

p. 101: its associated vocabulary knocked on dictionary editors' doors for attention.

p. 104: We applied a rule of thumb that demanded that any term had to have existed over several years.

p. 106: but it was a child of its time.

p. 107: Selecting and defining words [. . .] can have many pitfalls.

p. 109: Plan A had fallen flat on its face.

p. 109: True to his word.

p. 110: We scratched our collective heads.

p. 112: We did a collective double-take when we heard that.

p. 112: a fearless, uncompromising lexicographer sticking his neck out.

p. 112: We had witnessed this assimilation of American English in previous decades ([. . .], or *to fly off the handle*).

p. 113: If you do want to try your hand at prediction.

p. 114: It goes without saying that they were [. . .] instantly forgettable.

p. 115: the economic strength of America pushed home this position.

p. 117: *OED* editors could see that there was more to *American* than met the eye.

p. 124: but you didn't end up with a complete picture.

p. 127: But the winds of change could penetrate even Oxford.

p. 130: or did the *OED* need to start earning its keep?

p. 130: The smart money was on option two.

p. 130: but we had our heads down, and some of us didn't notice that the world was changing.

p. 130: It turned out that the future was opening up before our very eyes.

p. 133: The *OED* was at the most alarming crossroads that it had seen for around one hundred years.

p. 133: the University of Oxford itself regarded the dictionary as a white elephant.

p. 134: In any case, our jobs were two halves of the same egg.

p. 134: to edge my way into that side of the project slowly.

p. 134: to get the project off the ground.

p. 134: so that it might in due course decide on whether to give us the official go-ahead.

p. 135: But you get the idea.

p. 135: but he also had his finger on the editorial pulse.

p. 137: we are actually looking at a mixed bag of words.

p. 139: We put the word around in Britain and internationally in our search for partners.

p. 139: or at least those in serious positions of power in the Press put the word around.

p. 139: then we weren't worth the paper we were written on.

p. 140: *Computer* (and its base, the verb *compute*) rings all the right bells for me.

p. 141: Once we had international partners on board.

p. 141: Tim Benbow (affectionately known as the Admiral), to keep us on track.

p. 141: without a director to keep them on the straight and narrow.

p. 141: I was enormously pleased when the news came down the line.

p. 141: but the right answer seemed to be "wait and see, and don't call an end to print publication straightaway."

A PROVERBIAL TRIBUTE TO *OED* EDITOR JOHN A. SIMPSON 359

pp. 141–42: my job was to call their bluff and to find the loose brick in the wall of obscurity they erected.

p. 142: It was rubber-stamped in gold when he asked me to turn out a few times in the [. . .] cricket match.

p. 142: I was at the edge of my competence.

p. 142: The Shark [. . .] tried to encourage us to put on a good show.

p. 143: he [. . .] lamented the loss of the windfall revenue that this Götterdämmerung of the *OED*'s heritage would precipitate.

p. 145: Promises like that have a short half-life.

p. 145: The Press had no stomach for other long-drawn-out supplements.

p. 145: there was a chance that the dictionary might just pull through.

pp. 147–48: We set about announcing the project [. . .] through [. . .] budget-free word of mouth. [The syntax of *word of mouth* is extraordinarily un-English; not surprisingly, it is a straight translation of the medieval Latin *verbum oris*, first recorded in English in the 1450s.]

p. 148: It wasn't that I thought the Second Edition was the be-all and end-all of lexicography.

p. 149: If you wait long enough, most things will make a comeback.

p. 150: If we could pull it off, then dictionaries could take a quantum leap.

p. 159: We revealed that Shakespeare was credited with augmenting the word-stock of English with [. . .] 146 phrases (*too much of a good thing*).

p. 159: There were two gentlemen who led the pack.

p. 170: When the *hue and cry* had died down, we wore T-shirts [more on pp. 170–71].

p. 171: my new responsibilities should have alarmed me to the core.

p. 172: sometimes they were just wrong and the computer hit a *brick wall* [more on pp. 172–74].

p. 173: (yes, there is no end to the twists and turns that a lexicographer can take).

p. 174: such as *banging your head against a brick wall* (known since 1697).

p. 174: coming up against a *brick wall* (an impenetrable barrier).

p. 175: when to put one foot in front of the other.

p. 176: By now, we were battling hell-for-leather to meet our regular and draconian deadlines.

p. 177: Just for a moment, we felt on top of the world.

p. 181: we were unused to sticking our heads out of our offices to talk about it [the *OED*] in public.

p. 182: We have the regional *poke*—a bag or sack, as in buying *a pig in a poke* (i.e., unseen)—in parallel with the standard *pouch*.

p. 183: That might stop you in your tracks.

p. 183: they were a little sorry and down-in-the-mouth that they didn't have their own historical dictionary of Japanese.

p. 184: the Japanese public, who thought that the best things come in old and dignified packages.

p. 186: was going to be put on hold.

p. 187: the other things will, at some point, fall into place.

p. 187: once a word like *lad* creeps into the limelight, it develops in ways we might not have expected.

p. 193: the *OED* needed to wait its turn.

p. 199: we would not be handed the future on a plate.

p. 199: not even *we* thought that the Second Edition was the end of the road, but that it was really only a new beginning.

p. 200: Researchers started to knock on our door, at first just in dribs and drabs [more on pp. 201–2].

p. 208: Not everything can have a happy ending, but at this point we were deep in a tunnel with no sign of light ahead.

p. 209: They would [. . .] loosen the institutional purse strings for us.

p. 209: and with luck decide to give the enormous update project the go-ahead.

p. 210: After three years in limbo, there was once again a palpable sense of excitement.

p. 214: The idea was that we could save ourselves from dipping even a toe in the murky waters of Anglo-Saxon.

p. 218: "They've been vetted, an' we're putting 'em through their paces" [quoting Rudyard Kipling].

p. 219: In due course we did open the floodgates even further.

p. 220: would benefit us and also benefit the dictionary in the long run.

p. 221: but I had been happy to remain on the other side of the fence.

p. 222: without upsetting the dictionary's apple cart.

p. 223: so we knew our place.

p. 224: If the committee liked what it saw, then it would give us the thumbs-up.

p. 225: taking it [the *OED*] by the scruff of the neck and forcing it into the twentieth (or, soon enough, the twenty-first) century.

p. 225: *Solvitur ambulando*, the Romans said: solving problems by practical experience.

p. 227: a figure to lend his academic weight to the inclusion of such a taboo term.

p. 227: Oxford was right there on the second bus.

p. 227: Once it had nailed the lid down on that sense.

p. 227: again tiptoeing rather gingerly round the issue.

p. 228: "tell whoever it is to go fuck themselves."

p. 228: "fuck the bloody thing."

p. 234: But Joyce, too, was a sign of the times—he wanted to write what people said.

p. 235: After that, we were in the realm of phrases and exclamations [. . .]. "Const. with various adverbs: *fuck about* [. . .]; *fuck off* [. . .]; *fuck up* [. . .]."

p. 236: the stock of expletives and colourful expressions we know today (*to fuck around, to fuck over*), and a phrase with a preposition, *to fuck with* (someone).

p. 236: phrasal verbs (*to fuck about*, etc.), exclamations and swearing ("go fuck a duck").

p. 240: we had high hopes for this candidate.

p. 242: We did manage to bring into (or back into) the fold several colleagues willing to give it a shot.

p. 242: But we still needed more hands on deck.

p. 243: we have to be very careful not to open the net too wide.

p. 243: you just encourage anyone who loves words [. . .] to throw their hat into the ring.

p. 246: We had several rules of thumb.

p. 246: that is just playing into our hands.

p. 253: Lexicography is a long haul, and you need to stay with it.

p. 254: They were the cream of the crop.

p. 254: Obviously we couldn't use all of them, but they were all on short odds.

p. 255: that would only cause problems down the line.

p. 255: it always left us on an up when the interview ended.

p. 256: the expression "poisoned chalice" was heard in the dictionary halls.

p. 256: whose job it was to steer the ship round any rocks that reared their ugly masses.

p. 257: we scratched our heads whenever the output seemed problematic.

p. 258: when the public thought they were probably writing to a brick wall in Oxford.

p. 259: Hilary and I took one day at a time, relied on our instincts.

p. 263: It's a rough ride, but [the letter] *B* doesn't throw anything unexpected at you.

p. 264: which does make it something of a handful.

p. 272: we were not going to pull this off by the year 2000.

p. 273: they should sit on both sides of the fence where scientific vocabulary was concerned.

p. 274: An example is worth a thousand words.

p. 279: we sometimes needed the raw brainpower and ingenuity of a researcher to track a problem right down to earth.

p. 282: Editors' ears were pricking up.

p. 289: even they could see that the wind was changing.

pp. 289–90: It was considered—by those in the know—that [. . .] we should concentrate on [. . .] subscriptions.

p. 290: who might not still be on the staff (through old age or infirmity) to see the fruits of their labour.

p. 291: some companies had done their best to clamber on to the bandwagon of the dictionary's success.

p. 291: that the *OED* was disrespecting the potato by including an entry for *couch potato.*

p. 293: Flavour of the Month [the title of chapter 12].

p. 293: we have the Illinois Association of Ice Cream Manufacturers to thank for the expression *flavor of the month* [more on pp. 293–94].

p. 297: who was accused of some hanky-panky [. . .] with a male friend.

p. 297: lexicographers should never accept anything at face value.

p. 298: There are two sides to every question, as the old proverb wisely says.

p. 298: The British government leaves the English language largely to itself, at least on the face of it.

pp. 299–300: *Faute de mieux,* as we say when we are trying to get out of a tight spot and don't want to involve the English language.

p. 301: (and so were on occasions prepared to let Britain off the hook).

pp. 301–2: dotting the *i*'s and crossing the *t*'s on a European document.

p. 302: the British will play the game and sign on for language evening classes.

p. 302: After several years of shadow-boxing.

p. 304: we could relax into automatic pilot.

p. 306: the engineers couldn't go back to basics to fix it.

p. 309: We didn't get the word willy-nilly from Paris or central France.

p. 310: If they start bending the rules.

p. 310: It's better and safer to err on the side of caution and conservatism.

p. 314: That wasn't what got him the job on the *OED* by a long chalk [more on p. 314].

p. 315: So we went back to square one.

p. 315: The sort of expression people might be interested in, apparently, was *the full monty.*

p. 316: there was a fighting chance that the public might turn up gold.

p. 316: The B.B.C.'s word hunt started to take shape.

p. 317: when she told us yet another shaggy-dog story about the origin of *shaggy-dog story* [more on pp. 317–18].

p. 317: we were all [. . .] prepared to throw it out the window.

p. 317: the expression first saw the light of day in a seaside town in East Anglia.

p. 319: We had found this sort of informal children's term hard to pin down.

p. 323: I'm not always the sharpest knife when I come to new ideas.

p. 326: It was only a start, but the first step, as they say—to quote another trite proverb—is the most difficult.

p. 327: It's something we need to work on, but we've travelled a little down that road.

p. 328: we still needed to keep the editorial chariot on track.

p. 329: I wouldn't see the update through to its completion, but I'd come to terms with that some years back.

p. 330: it might be a good time to give someone else a chance to step into my editorial shoes.

p. 330: You make the decision, and then you stick with it.

p. 331: Nonchalant, non-interventionist observation was the order of the day.

p. 333: that with my family there was sometimes less than meets the eye.

BIBLIOGRAPHY

This chapter was first published with the same title in *Proverbium: Yearbook of International Proverb Scholarship* 35 (2018): 223–62.

Bering, Henrik. 2016. "According to the OED . . ." *New Criterion* 35, no. 2 (October): 69.

Burchfield, R. W., ed. 1972–1986. *A Supplement to the Oxford English Dictionary.* 4 vols. Oxford: Oxford University Press.

Doyle, Charles Clay. 1996. "On 'New' Proverbs and the Conservativeness of Proverb Dictionaries." *Proverbium* 13: 69–84. Also in *Cognition, Comprehension, and Communication: A Decade of North American Proverb Studies (1990–2000),* edited by Wolfgang Mieder, 85–98. Baltmannsweiler, Germany: Schneider Verlag Hohengehren, 2003.

Doyle, Charles Clay, Wolfgang Mieder, and Fred R. Shapiro. 2012. *The Dictionary of Modern Proverbs.* New Haven, CT: Yale University Press.

Hitchings, Henry. 2016. "The Word Detective: A Life in Words, from Serendipity to Selfie by John Simpson." *Guardian,* November 3. https://www.theguardian.com/books/2016/nov/03 /the-word-detective-a-life-in-words-from-serendipity-to-selfie-by-john-simpson-review.

Kirkus Reviews. 2016. "The Word Detective by John Simpson." August 1. https://www.kirkus reviews.com/book-reviews/john-simpson/the-word-detective/.

Knowles, Elizabeth, ed. 2009. *Little Oxford Dictionary of Proverbs.* Oxford: Oxford University Press.

Lodder, Luiza. 2016. "Former OED Chief Editor's 'Word Detective' Makes for Compelling Reading." *PopMatters,* October 27. https://www.popmatters.com/word-detective-search ing-for-the-meaning-of-it-all-at-the-oxford-english-di-2495411358.html.

Marsh, George Perkins. 1860. *Lectures on the English Language.* New York: Charles Scribner.

Marsh, George Perkins. 1862. *The Origin and History of the English Language, and of the Early Literature It Embodies.* New York: Charles Scribner.

Marsh, George Perkins. 1864. *Man and Nature; or, Physical Geography as Modified by Human Action.* New York: Charles Scribner.

Marsh, George Perkins. 1892. *Catalogue of the Library of George Perkins Marsh.* Burlington: University of Vermont.

Mieder, Wolfgang. 1987. *Tradition and Innovation in Folk Literature*. Hanover, NH: University Press of New England.

Mieder, Wolfgang. 1993. *Proverbs Are Never Out of Season: Popular Wisdom in the Modern Age*. New York: Oxford University Press. Rpt., New York: Peter Lang, 2012.

Mieder, Wolfgang. 2004. *Proverbs: A Handbook*. Westport, CT: Greenwood Press. Rpt., New York: Peter Lang, 2012.

Mieder, Wolfgang. 2009. *International Bibliography of Paremiology and Phraseology*. 2 vols. Berlin: Walter de Gruyter.

Mieder, Wolfgang. 2012. "'Think Outside the Box': Origin, Nature, and Meaning of Modern Anglo-American Proverbs." *Proverbium* 29: 137–96.

Mieder, Wolfgang. 2014. "Futuristic Paremiography and Paremiology: A Plea for the Collection and Study of Modern Proverbs." *Folklore Fellows' Network Bulletin*, no. 44: 13–17, 20–24.

Mieder, Wolfgang, Stewart A. Kingsbury, and Kelsie B. Harder. 1992. *A Dictionary of American Proverbs*. New York: Oxford University Press.

Murray, James, ed. 1888–1928. *A New English Dictionary*. 10 vols. Oxford: Oxford University Press.

Paczolay, Gyula. 1997. *European Proverbs in 55 Languages with Equivalents in Arabic, Persian, Sanskrit, Chinese and Japanese*. Veszprém, Hungary: Veszprémi Nyomda.

Simpson, John A., ed. 1982. *The Concise Oxford Dictionary of Proverbs*. Oxford: Oxford University Press.

Simpson, John A. 2016. *The Word Detective: Searching for the Meaning of It All at the "Oxford English Dictionary."* New York: Basic Books.

Simpson, John, and Jennifer Speake, eds. 1992. *The Concise Oxford Dictionary of Proverbs*. 2nd ed. Oxford University Press.

Simpson, John, and Jennifer Speake, eds. 1998. *The Concise Oxford Dictionary of Proverbs*. 3rd ed. Oxford University Press.

Simpson, John A., and Edmund Weiner, eds. 1989. *Oxford English Dictionary*. 2nd ed. 20 vols. Oxford: Oxford University Press.

Singer, Samuel, and Ricarda Liver, eds. 1995–2002. *Thesaurus proverbiorum medii aevi: Lexikon der Sprichwörter des romanisch-germanischen Mittelalters*. 13 vols. Berlin: Walter de Gruyter.

Speake, Jennifer, ed. 2003. *The Oxford Dictionary of Proverbs*. 4th ed. Oxford: Oxford University Press.

Speake, Jennifer, ed. 2008. *The Oxford Dictionary of Proverbs*. 5th ed. Oxford: Oxford University Press.

Speake, Jennifer, ed. 2015. *Oxford Dictionary of Proverbs*. 6th ed. Oxford: Oxford University Press.

Taylor, Archer, and Bartlett Jere Whiting. 1958. *A Dictionary of American Proverbs and Proverbial Phrases, 1820–1889*. Cambridge, MA: Harvard University Press.

Trench, Richard Chenevix. 1853. *On the Lessons in Proverbs*. New York: Redfield. Rpt. as *Proverbs and Their Lessons*. London: George Routledge, 1905. Rpt. with an introduction by Wolfgang Mieder. Burlington: University of Vermont, 2003.

Truss, Lynne. 2016. "Why English Keeps On, Like, Totally Changing." *New York Times*, November 3. https://www.nytimes.com/2016/11/06/books/review/word-detective-john -simpson-words-on-the-move-john-mcwhorter.html.

A PROVERBIAL TRIBUTE TO *OED* EDITOR JOHN A. SIMPSON

Wilson, F. P. 1970. *The Oxford Dictionary of English Proverbs.* 3rd ed. Oxford: Oxford
University Press.

Winchester, Simon. 1998. *The Professor and the Madman: A Tale of Murder, Insanity, and the
Making of the "Oxford English Dictionary."* New York: HarperCollins.

Winchester, Simon. 2003. *The Meaning of Everything: The Story of the "Oxford English
Dictionary."* Oxford: Oxford University Press.

13

"INJUSTICE ANYWHERE IS A THREAT TO JUSTICE EVERYWHERE"

From Classical to Modern Law Proverbs

Not too long ago, my departed friend Dan Ben-Amos (1934–2023), always the scholar interested in the performance of folklore in context, recalled the following account in a letter to me of October 2, 2021:

> While I conducted field work in Benin, I was told that people engage in debates by using proverbs, each person tries to outsmart his opponent by using a better proverb. I asked a friend of mine to demonstrate it dramatically. He invited a friend, and they chose an imaginary point that was very realistic in Benin. In the imaginary dramatic scene, one of them began to build a house on an empty lot in the city, and the other argued that that was his lot and the builder had no right to build on it. You have to understand that in traditional society they did not have "ownership papers." They argued for about an hour. I recorded the scene, and at one point my friend got so excited that he moved away from the microphone. I asked him to get closer, and he later said, that by doing that I interrupted his "stream of proverbial thought" and he lost the debate. I know that you would like this dialogue for *Proverbium* but I'll have to finish the *Folktales of the Jews* project, before I can start working on that. Once it is done, you will be the first to know. It is really fascinating.

One day later I responded enthusiastically: "Your wonderful account reminds me of John Messenger's article 'The Role of Proverbs in a Nigerian Judicial System' [1959]." Both of us being obsessed with bibliographical references and enjoying exchanges in a sort of scholarly one-upmanship, we were quick to inform each other of related publications such as Olowo Ojoade's "Proverbial

Evidences of African Legal Customs" (1988), Idris Amali's "Proverbs as Concept of Idoma Dispensation of Justice" (1998), Jacob Arowosegbe's "Indigenous African Jurisprudential Thoughts on the Concept of Justice: A Reconstruction Through Yoruba Proverbs" (2017), and Lekau Eleazar Mphasha's "Just as European Courtroom Lawyers Use Previous Cases, Participants in Northern Sotho Argue with Proverbs Intended to Serve as Past Precedents for Present Actions" (2016). Indeed, as expected, such proverbial duels by lawyers, peppered with traditional proverbs of which some are based on customary law, have also been observed in medieval European societies. In fact, with Dan's scholarly work on the Grimms, we might well assume that he was aware of Jacob Grimm's keen interest in Germanic folk law, which he assembled and studied in his invaluable book *Deutsche Rechtsaltertümer* (1828; see also Mieder 1986), with his earlier essay "Von der Poesie im Recht" (1815) deserving to be a classic study of the poetic language of German law, which was to a large degree handed down orally in earlier centuries (Ebel 1975; Hueck 1999). In fact, based on Jacob Grimm's legal erudition and lasting influence, the brand of *Rechtsvolkskunde* (legal folklore) took hold in Germany and to a lesser degree elsewhere (Dundes Renteln and Dundes 1994). Following in his footsteps, later German scholars published impressive historical collections of legal proverbs that are unmatched in other languages, to wit Eduard Graf and Mathias Dietherr, *Deutsche Rechtssprichwörter* (1869); Leonhard Winkler, *Deutsches Recht im Spiegel deutscher Sprichwörter* (1927); and Ruth Schmidt-Wiegand and Ulrike Schowe, *Deutsche Rechtsregeln und Rechtssprichwörter* (1996). Numerous cultural, historical, and linguistic studies of German proverbial law have appeared after Grimm's original work, with this interest in both canonical and customary law expressed in proverbs not having waned in modern times (Cohn 1888; Elsener 1964; Kaufmann 1986; Osenbrüggen 1876; Weizsäcker 1956). Special note should be taken of Ruth Schmidt-Wiegand's essay about the relationship of literacy and orality regarding the complex nature of the transmission and dissemination of proverbs dealing with legal matters (Schmidt-Wiegand 2002). After all, there are quite a few law proverbs that have a classical Latin origin that survive today in Latin, as well as loan translations in numerous languages, in both written documents and oral communication. But there have also always been folk proverbs that become current in a particular language, during past centuries right up to the modern age.

Regarding law proverbs in the English-language tradition, it must be observed that paremiographical and paremiological interest has been rather limited. There really are no major collections to speak of, with Fred R. Shapiro's *The Oxford Dictionary of American Legal Quotations* (1993) and Elizabeth Frost-Knappman and David Shrager's *A Concise Encyclopedia of Legal Quotations* (2003) basically including interesting and perhaps quotable legal statements with but a sprinkling of proverbs. David Murray's statement of a good hundred years ago that "[t]here are many collections of English and Scottish proverbs, but the law proverbs have not been taken out separately" (1912, 54) is as true today as it was then. The picture is no better when it comes to general studies of legal proverbs—and there are plenty of them as well in languages other than English. All that can be said is that Archer Taylor, the unsurpassed doyen of proverb studies, comes to the rescue with his concise but superb chapter "Legal Proverbs" in his celebrated book *The Proverb* (1931, 86–97). Citing a number of examples, he states: "The apt quotation of a proverb will often turn the course of an argument, just as the citation of a precedent may win a case at law" (87). He also mentions that many vernacular law proverbs deal with property rights and mercantile affairs, stressing that many legal proverbs prove to be of Latin origin upon closer historical scrutiny (91–93). Taylor's friend Donald Bond followed suit with his essay "The Law and Lawyers in English Proverbs" (1935), stating: "In the standard collections of English proverbs one may find reflected almost every aspect of legal practice and tradition, with many of the Latin maxims paralleled in the homely wisdom of the folk" (724). In addition to well-chosen examples, he includes rather negative proverbs regarding the profession of the lawyer, such as "A good lawyer must be a great liar." Little wonder that the idea of the "tricky lawyer" has led Anna Litovkina to discuss various humorous or satirical anti-proverbs against lawyers in her article "'Where There's a Will There's a Lawyer's Bill': Lawyers in Anglo-American Anti-Proverbs" (2011; also in 2016, 122–38). In any case, Bond also published a second article, "English Legal Proverbs" (1936), with ample examples, claiming: "Perhaps no profession has contributed more to our proverbial stock than the law. Touching, as it does, so many aspects of human conduct and misconduct, it has had an unrivalled opportunity to enter into the experience of the plain man [folk]. No wonder, then that our popular speech reflects in so many ways the accumulated legal wisdom of the centuries" (935). Bond further says:

> Like the English language, English law may be regarded as the fusion of two great cultural forces—the Germanic "folk-laws" [. . .], and Roman law, as interpreted by the Norman conquerors. [. . .] From this fusion has developed a body of law [and] it is interesting to see how many of its basic principles find expression in the common proverbial wisdom of the folk. These proverbs correspond, on a popular level, to the Latin legal maxims of the learned, which represent the concentrated experience of generations of lawyers. (Bond 1936, 921)

Historically inclined legal scholars have done impressive work on the origin and wide dissemination of Latin law maxims, of which quite a few survive in their original language and in loan translations as well-established proverbs, having changed from learned legal to colloquial language (Schmidt-Wiegand 2002, 9). Herbert Broom has provided a voluminous *Selection of Legal Maxims* (1882), which lists Latin law maxims with rich annotations, including actual legal cases in which a proverb was used as part of the legal argumentation (see also Foth 1971; Liebs 1982; Williams 1985). Thus he discusses "Ignorantia juris non excusat" (Broom 1882, 252–67) in a fifteen-page section, citing it in Latin and its English translation "Ignorance of the law is no excuse," which is frequently cited today (Frost-Knappman and Shrager 2003, 149). Thomas Jefferson had an interesting take on this proverb in a letter of December 22, 1787: "Ignorance of the law is no excuse in any country. If it were, the laws would lose their effect, because it can always be pretended" (Shapiro 1993, 239, no. 9). For the proverb "Caveat emptor," Broom expands his discussion into an incredible forty-one pages (1882, 768–809) with case histories exemplifying its legal value, stating: "*Caveat emptor*—let a purchaser, who ought not to be ignorant of the amount and nature of the interest which he is about to buy, exercise proper caution" (768). This cautionary proverb remains in current use both in Latin and in the English variants "Buyer beware" and "Let the buyer beware." Regarding a proposed securities legislation, President Franklin D. Roosevelt changed the popular proverb to an anti-proverb during a press conference on March 29, 1933: "It applies the new doctrine of *caveat vendor* in place of the old doctrine of *caveat emptor*. In other words, 'let the seller beware as well as the buyer.' In other words, there is a definite, positive burden on the seller for the first time to tell the truth" (Roosevelt 1938, 96).

The proverbial claim that "silence gives consent" has been recorded in thirty-four European languages and goes back to the Latin "Qui tacet, consentire videtur" (Paczolay 1997, 430–32); it states that in legal and other deliberations, offering no response is tantamount to going along with what is being discussed (Foth 1971, 71–75; Krampe 1989). A more legalistic explanation states: "It is well settled that admissions may sometimes be implied from the mere silence of a party. Thus, the declaration made by one party to the other relative to the subject-matter in controversy, and *not denied* by him, are admissible as evidence for the former" (Bond 1936, 924). This might be clear enough, but it must be remembered that proverbs in general, and law proverbs as well, are not universal truths and are open to negation in certain contexts. In the case of the Latin proverb "In dubio, pro reo," which has not gained great currency in English as "When in doubt, rule for the accused" or "Give the accused the benefit of the doubt," one can well imagine the legal quarrels about its appropriateness in certain ambiguous cases (Frost-Knappman and Shrager 2003, 96; Holtappels 1965; Holzhauer 1978). At least jurisprudence has come up with the often cited proverb "Innocent until proven guilty" to protect people from being tried without proper evidence. It has been traced back to a fourteenth-century Latin source but appeared in English translation only at the beginning of the nineteenth century (Shapiro 2021, 658, no. 156). Of special interest is also the Latin law proverb "Necessitas dat legem," which once again has been translated into many languages, gaining currency in English as "Necessity knows no law." According to Archer Taylor, it "probably refers, not to necessity in a general sense, but to necessity forced upon one by the need of self-defence. In other words, *Necessity knows no law* means 'in defending one's self all means are legal'" (Taylor 1931, 91; Koller 2009). And yet, it is not necessarily easy to prove that dire need or self-preservation forced one to go against the law, but in a trial it could become a forceful and authoritative argument based on the long tradition of this proverb. In a bit of a slam against the finagling of lawyers, Benjamin Franklin wrote in his *Poor Richard's Almanack* of 1734: "Necessity has no law; I know some Attorneys of the name" (Shapiro 1993, 265, no. 1). Fifty years later, Abigail Adams, at any time the equal in intellectual prowess to her husband John Adams, second president of the United States, made tongue-in-cheek use of the proverb in a letter of July 6, 1784, showing that one can also have a bit of fun with a legal proverb:

> The door opens into the Cabbin [of the ship that was carrying Abigail to join her husband John in France] where the Gentlemen all Sleep; and where we sit dine &. We can only live with our door Shut. whilst we dress and undress. Necessity has no law, but should I have thought on shore; to have layed myself down to sleep, in common with half a dozen Gentlemen? We have curtains it is true, and we only in part undress . . . but we have the satisfaction of falling in with a set of well behaved, decent gentlemen. (Mieder 2005, 74–75; letter written on board the ship to her sister, Mary Cranch)

President Abraham Lincoln on the other hand had no choice some sixty years later during the Civil War but to write this miniscule message on August 27, 1862, to Governor Alexander Ramsay of Minnesota, who had asked to be allowed to postpone drafting new soldiers for the Union Army while there was fierce fighting between Native Americans and white settlers: "Attend to the Indian. If the draft can *not* proceed, of course, it *will* not proceed. Necessity knows no law. The government can not extend the time" (Mieder 2000, 152). One senses the frustration of this great president, with the war dividing the country resting heavy on his shoulders and mind. Of course, on a much lighter and humorous side, there are such modern anti-proverbs as "Necessity knows no law, and neither does the average lawyer" and "As a student in law school, they called him 'Necessity' because he knew no law" (Litovkina 2016, 130).

The idea of necessity having no law quite naturally leads to the Latin law proverb "Summum ius, summa iniuria," which has been translated into English as "Extreme Law is extreme injustice," "Extreme right is extreme wrong," "The extremity of law is the extremity of wrong," "Supreme law, supreme injustice," "Rigorous law is rigorous injustice," "Rigid justice is the greatest injustice," and so on, without gaining lasting proverbiality among the folk (Büchner 1957; Frost-Knappman and Shrager 2003, 151; Kornhardt 1953). No one less than Erasmus of Rotterdam included it in his unsurpassed collection *Adagia* (1500–1536), thereby spreading its message as a legal but also sociopolitical piece of wisdom. Presenting a short, scholarly treatise on its origin going back to Cicero, he writes: "Extreme right is extreme wrong means that men never stray so far from the path of justice as when they adhere most religiously to the letter of the law. They call it 'extreme right' when they wrangle over the words of a statute and pay no heed to the intention of the man who drafted it. Words and letters are the outer skin of the law" (Erasmus 1989, 244–45). The expression's various English translations during the sixteenth and seventeenth centuries have been registered as proverbs in collections, but their currency among lawyers appears to be in steady decline (Tilley 1950, 571; Wilson 1970, 235). The proverb basically states that an uncritical interpretation and application of the law and its purpose without considering the context might well lead to injustice. In other words, it is a cautionary proverb, warning that the application of the law to the letter can engender serious injustice. The proverb could well be applied to the extreme laws against abortion in some US states that cause serious harm to women in need of this operation. The English variant "The strictest law is the greatest oppression," cited in the *New-York Evening Post* in 1747 (Whiting 1977, 255), would fit this situation perfectly! One might imagine it being employed in a hearing at the Supreme Court of the United States, but that would assume that lawyers know the Latin proverb. Unfortunately, however, the study of Latin has not been a requirement for law students, or for medical students for that matter, for quite some time.

This leads to a final classical Latin law proverb, which continues to be cited as "Suum quique" in formal writing but is frequently cited as "To each his own." Thus the transcendentalist Ralph Waldo Emerson could title a short poem in 1834 with the Latin text to express the thought that while a farmer deals with what nature brings, he (Emerson) will follow his own intellectual concerns. In other words, may everybody act according to their own predicament:

> *Suum Quique*
> The rain has spoiled the farmer's day;
> Shall sorrow put my books away?
> Thereby are two days lost.

Nature shall mind her own affairs,
I will attend my proper cares,
In rain, or sun, or frost. (Mieder 2014b, 280)

In legal terms, the short proverb expresses the right of people to mind their own business and not to be deprived of their own property and privileges. Today it is often used to express the right to one's own ways of life. As such, it is innocuous enough in the many languages in which it is current in translation. This is also true for German, in which the proverb has gained positive currency as "Jedem das Seine." However, since it was crafted into the iron gate of the Buchenwald concentration camp during the Nazi period, the proverb is now avoided by most Germans (Brunssen 2010; Doerr 2000; Klenner 2002). This is, of course, also true for the proverb "Arbeit macht frei," which appeared on the iconic main gate of Auschwitz and cannot and should not be used any more today in the German language (Brückner 1998; Doerr 2000). This all indicates that proverbs can be misused in the most vicious ways. Proverbs are by no means sacrosanct, as numerous stereotypical proverbs against Jews, Roma, Native Americans, and other groups show (Mieder 1993, 225–55; Mieder 1997; Roback 1944).

With this being said, these deliberations can move on from law proverbs having originated in classical Latin to proverbs with a source in medieval Latin. They have been registered in Hans Walther's nine massive volumes *Proverbia sententiaeque latinitatis medii aevi* (1963–1986), and they are presented with loan translations into major European languages that appeared during the Middle Ages in the thirteen equally impressive volumes of Samuel Singer and Ricarda Liver's *Thesaurus proverbiorum medii aevi* (1995–2002). As one would expect, they contain medieval law proverbs, with today's extremely popular proverb "First come, first served" surprisingly enough being one of them. At first glance, one might not think that this short text could be based on a medieval customary law, but a historical investigation leaves no doubt about this claim. The proverb appears first in a twelfth-century medieval manuscript in Latin as "Qui capit ante molam, merito molit ante farinam" (Who gets to the mill first, rightfully grinds his flower first), with a number of variants following (Walther and Schmidt 1966, 4:134, 4:148; Singer and Liver 1999, 8:87). These early Latin texts emphasize that it is the legal right of the first farmer arriving at the mill to get served first, but by the time Erasmus registered the proverb in his *Adagia*, he already simply wrote, "Qui primus venerit, primus molet" (Erasmus 1992, 34, 134). His rendering once again influenced the proverb's appearance in the vernacular languages, with the German "Wer zuerst kommt, mahlt zuerst" being its precise translation with contextualized references reflecting its legal claim (Janz 1989, 89–93; Mieder 2016; Schmidt-Wiegand and Schowe 1996,

FROM CLASSICAL TO MODERN LAW PROVERBS

100). The Germans to this very day say "Who comes first, grinds first," with most people not realizing that they are citing an old mill proverb. In fact, young Germans at times write *mahlt* (grind) as *malt* (paints), clearly indicating that they are unaware of its origin. In fact, of course, arriving first and then painting first is utter nonsense! But then we all cite proverbs as linguistic formulas without much thought about their semantic origin.

In any case, the proverb's development in the English language went quite differently. Geoffrey Chaucer wrote in *The Wife of Bath's Prologue* (c. 1386): "Whoso that first to *mille* comth, first grynt." But some two hundred years later, Henry Porter cited the truncated version "So, first come, first served" in his *Two Angry Women of Abington* (1599), perhaps an early example of the predilection toward linguistic shortening that is so prevalent today (Mieder 2004, 43–45). During the next three centuries, the long version of grinding at the mill competed with this short text. However, with the grist mill disappearing over time, the elliptical variant took over to express the legal concept that whoever arrives first at a location has the commonsense right to be taken care of first. When people cite the proverb today, they probably are not aware of "First come, first served" being a legal proverb based on a customary law dating back to the Middle Ages. Yet the civil rights icon Martin Luther King Jr. seemed well aware of its legal implications when he cited it on March 15, 1956, in relation to the bus boycott being staged in the city of Montgomery, Alabama:

> For fourteen weeks a united Negro community, led by the clergy, has stayed off the Montgomery busses in a peaceful protest against injustice. With dignity and with the power of the human spirit we have sought to implement the American tradition of fair play. Our threefold demands are simple and moderate: courtesy from the bus drivers, seating on a first-come first-served basis, and employment of Negro drivers on busses transversing predominantly Negro neighborhoods. (Mieder 2010, 253)

But there is yet one more recent development in the long history of this by now internationally disseminated concise proverb that parallels the German linguistic misunderstanding mentioned above. Ever more young people, like my students, cite the proverb as "First come, first serve," dropping the "d" of the passive verb form. When I have pointed out to them that the notion that whoever arrives first, serves first, makes little or no sense, they usually shrug their shoulders and say that everybody knows that they are talking about being served first. To them, my grammatical and semantic concern is simply irrelevant. This development has gone so far that two of my paremiological friends in Germany have asked whether "First come, first serve" should be registered as a legitimate variant of "First come, first served" (Chlosta and Grzybek 1955,

74–75). But no matter, we all agree with its basic message and in most cases will insist on being served or getting our turn first in a queue if in fact we got there first.

The matter of contradictory proverbs is a well-established topic in proverb scholarship, with one of the most revealing couplets being "Right makes might" and its reversal, "Might makes right." While especially the claim of the second proverb with its unfortunate image of power winning out over justice is expressed in longer Latin maxims, it first appears in this distinct formulation in English in 1311. Its positive antipode "Right makes might" appears in Middle English a bit later in 1375 as "Rycht mayss oft the feble wycht" (Right often makes the feeble [man] strong). Over time, it developed into the shorter and more precise "Right makes might." Thus, William Shakespeare has "Right should thus overcome might!" in his *Henry IV, part 2* (1598), and there is also "Right is stronger than might" (1845). But strange as it might seem, it took Abraham Lincoln's emotional speech of February 27, 1860, in New York City to establish it as a well-known proverb. In the speech, he forcefully expressed his unwavering commitment to maintaining the Union and to keeping the ills of slavery from spreading. Toward the end of the speech, the president rose to an impressive oratorical crescendo with the threat of Civil War looming:

> Can we [. . .] allow it [slavery] to spread into the National Territories, and to overrun us here in these Free States? If our sense of duty forbids this, then let us stand by our duty, fearlessly and effectively. Let us be diverted by none of those sophistical contrivances wherewith we are so industriously plied and belabored—contrivances such as groping for some middle ground between the right and the wrong, vain as the search for a man who should be neither a living man nor a dead man—such as a policy of "don't care" on a question about which all true men do care. [. . .] Neither let us be slandered from our duty by false accusations against us, nor frightened from it by menaces of destruction to the Government nor of dungeons to ourselves. *Let us have faith that right makes might, and in that faith, let us, to the end, dare to do our duty as we understand it.* (Mieder 2000, 25–27)

Lincoln might have been influenced by a fascinating statement by his contemporary James McCune Smith, an African American intellectual and abolitionist, in his 1841 essay "The Destiny of the People of Color": "In overcoming the Institution of Slavery, we must by our conduct confute the doctrines on which it is based. One of these doctrines [is], that 'Might makes Right': because men have the power, therefore, they have the right to keep other men enslaved. [. . .] We are not in possession of physical superiority: yet we must overturn the doctrine 'might makes right,' and we can only do so by demonstrating that 'right makes might'" (Smith 2006). Lincoln returned four more times to this proverb in speeches during the fateful year of 1860, which has led some to consider him its originator when he in fact helped to popularize it as a just and fair proverbial doctrine. It continues to be cited with or without mentioning Lincoln, with former Israeli prime minister Menachem Begin, when he was an opposition member of the Knesset, giving his address before the Twenty-Fourth Zionist Congress in 1956 in Jerusalem the most appropriate title "Right Makes Might." Echoing his deeply admired predecessor Lincoln (as well as Begin), President Barack Obama in an "Address to the Nation" of 2009 also used the proverb, if not as a legal requirement then certainly as an ethical one: "America—we are passing though a time of great trial. And the message that we send in the midst of these storms must be clear: that our cause is just, our resolve unwavering. We will go forward with the confidence that right makes might, and with the commitment to forge an America that is safer, a world that is more secure, and a future that represents not the deepest of fears but the highest of hopes" (Mieder 2019, 273–78). There is no doubt that in its opposition to the unlawful proverbial maxim that "Might makes right," the humane proverb "Right makes might" expresses a lawful humane ideal. Together, the proverb pair reflects the vicissitudes of life with its struggle between right and wrong. John Mark Templeton did not include the proverb in his collection and discussion of two hundred proverbial *Worldwide Laws of Life* (1997) for people to adhere to in the course of their lives. Quite a few of them go back to ancient wisdom literature, appear in the texts of the major religions of the world, and are current as traditional folk proverbs. They provide a moral compass, for example the golden rule, "Do unto others as you would have them do unto you," which might not hold up in a court of law, just as "Right makes might" is not part of official jurisprudence. However, cited by a lawyer at the right moment during a trial, they could well persuade the jury to deliver an ethical judgment.

No persuasion is needed to convince people that their domicile is a private sanctuary, safe from unwanted or illegal intrusion. This almost immediately brings to mind the proverb "My house is my castle," for which Archer Taylor wrote yet another of his exemplary studies on the history of individual proverbs entitled "The Road to *An Englishman's House . . .*" (1965). The basic idea is related to the early medieval Latin maxim "Domus sua cuique est tutissimum refugium" (One's own house is the safest sanctuary), which appears in a legal tract of 1644 together with what appears to be a rather free English translation: "A man's house is his castle, et domus sua quique est tutissimum refugium." By now it has been established that this English text was already current in variants starting toward the end of the sixteenth century: "His house is his castle" (1581), "Our law calleth a man's house, his castle" (1588), and "The house to every man is to him his Castle and Fortresse" (1605); and as "A man's house is his castle" in English proverb collections published since 1639 (Mieder 2019–2020). Referring specifically to the English tradition of the proverb, Samuel Johnson wrote: "In London a man's own house is truly his castle, in which he can be in perfect safety from intrusion" (1775); and Charles Dickens came up with: "People maintain that an Englishman's house is his castle" (1837), repeating it three more times during the next twenty years (Bryan and Mieder 1997, 116). And yet, it has long been pushed aside by the less specific and more current shorter variant "A man's house is his castle." It comes as a surprise then that Taylor alludes to it in his article title and that Jennifer Speake in her *Oxford Dictionary of Proverbs* (2015, 93) cites it as the proverbial lemma. After all, the proverb has long enjoyed international distribution together with its close variant "A man's home is his castle" (Mieder, Kingsbury, and Harder 1992, 304). There is no doubt that the proverb expresses a legal right that also pertains to the idea that the police must present an official search warrant from a judge before being permitted to enter and search a home. This can be observed in popular detective shows on television, but I have yet to hear an actor say "My house is my castle" in trying to resist the police. Instead, there are plenty of humorous anti-proverbs that play with this valuable basic right, to wit "How many times must I tell you, Mildred? A man's office is his castle!" (1963) as the caption of a cartoon showing a man not wanting his wife to bother him at the office, and "A man's house is his castle—Let him clean it" (1978) as a message on a feminist T-shirt. Such texts are another indication that anything cited as repetitively as proverbs, quotations, and other formulaic statements tends to be parodied (Litovkina and Mieder 2006).

As one would suspect, there are plenty of law proverbs that do not have their roots in classical or medieval times. One of them has been traced back to 1616 in the two variants "Possession is nine points of the law" and "Possession is eleven points of the law" (Tilley 1950, 550). In fact, "many ingenious attempts have been made to formulate the nine (or eleven) 'points' which are necessary to a successful law-suit, but there is good evidence for assuming that this is other than a concrete way of saying that in a dispute about property possession, [there] is so strong a point in favor of the possessor that it outweighs nine, or eleven, or ninety-nine points that might legally be urged in behalf of some one else" (Bond 1936, 929–30). Nancy Magnuson Geise, my former student and now a lawyer in Burlington, has provided a superb analysis of this matter in her article "'Possession Is Nine-Tenths of the Law': History and Meaning of a Legal Proverb" (1999), which I published in *Proverbium*. Following a detailed enumeration of historical texts including both variants of the proverb, she agrees with Archer Taylor that the choice of the two numbers "refers merely to the ten or dozen conceived of as a unit; in that case we need not seek to discover what the points really are" (Taylor 1931, 94). In fact, attempts to define the various points border on the ridiculous, for example: "It is said that success in a lawsuit requires nine things: (1) money, (2) patience, (3) a good cause, (4) a good lawyer, (5) good counsel, (6) good witnesses, (7) a good jury, (8) a good judge, and (9) good luck" (Geise 1999, 111). Clearly this list is far removed from the property law that is being expressed in the proverb. In any case, the number eleven brings to mind such measured concepts as twelve inches, a dozen, twelve jurors, or even twelve apostles. The number nine can easily be understood as being one item short of ten in the decimal system. And this might well explain why today a third variant of the proverb that does not refer to points has become prevalent, namely "Possession is nine-tenths of the law." Following a long list of historical contextualized references since the late nineteenth century, Geise offers this convincing explanation: "Unable to have a clear idea of what the legal points are that the original proverb[s] could refer to, the proverb took on a more familiar form as a fraction: the implication of 'points' became superfluous" (Geise 1999, 111). This is splendidly expressed by the early American feminist Elizabeth Cady Stanton in a speech of February 26, 1891:

Our reform [of more rights for women] is not lifting up an inferior order, but recognizing the rights of equals [i.e., women and men]. It is more like two contending royal families for the crown and scepter, the right by blood to rule and reign, compelling man at last to share his liberty and power with the equals in virtue and intelligence and the ability to govern themselves. But man has the prestige of centuries in his favor, the force to maintain it, and he has the possession of the throne, which is nine-tenths of the law. He has statutes and Scriptures, and the universal usages of society all on his side. (Mieder 2014a, 249–50)

The struggle to get men off their pedestals was well fought by Stanton and her friend Susan B. Anthony. They became models for future generations of feminists fighting for their legitimate part of the law.

Speaking of the latter, let it be said that it was she who originated the slogan "Equal pay for equal work" on March 18, 1869, repeating it on October 8 of that year in her feminist journal *The Revolution*: "Join the union, girls, and together say *Equal Pay for Equal Work*" (Mieder 2021, 145; Shapiro 2021, 24, no. 2). She clearly saw this formulaic statement as a sociopolitical law, citing it in several later combative speeches, for example on July 29, 1897:

That is the whole question. Equal pay for equal work. There isn't a woman in the sound of my voice, who does not want this justice. There never was one—there never will be one who does not want justice and equality. But they have not yet learned that equal work and equal wages can come only through the political equality, represented by the ballot. (Mieder 2014a, 246)

Here, she couples the demand for salary equity between men and women with the call for the right of women to vote, which regrettably did not come about until the passing of the Eighteenth Amendment of the Constitution of the United States in 1918. Slowly but surely, Anthony's rallying cry evolved from revolutionary slogan to proverb by gaining wide distribution during the feminist movement in the 1960s and 1970s. President John F. Kennedy expressed his support for its message in a speech on November 8, 1961: "Well, I'm sure we haven't done enough [for equal pay for women]. I must say I am a strong believer in equal pay for equal work, and I think we have to do better than we're doing" (Mieder 2023, 229), with Barack Obama on August 28, 2008, in his acceptance speech for the US presidency, adding a future-oriented personal touch to his commitment to this invaluable proverb: "And now is the time to keep the promise of equal pay for an equal day's work, because I want my daughters to have exactly the same opportunities as your sons" (Mieder 2009, 279). By now the proverb has been loan translated into other languages, for example in French as "Un salaire égal par un travail égal" and in German as "Gleicher Lohn für gleiche Arbeit." Unfortunately, complete salary equity has still not been reached in the United States, even though a number of legislative acts have been passed to guarantee this proverbial law of fairness in the workplace, notably the Equal Pay Act, which Kennedy signed into law in 1963 requiring employers to provide equal pay for equal work regardless of gender. The Civil Rights Act signed by President Lyndon Johnson in 1964 expanded upon this by universally prohibiting wage discrimination. It comes as no surprise then that the socially minded Bernie Sanders, senator from the state of Vermont, titled one of the sections of his programmatic book *Our Revolution: A Future to Believe In* (2016) "Equal Pay for Equal Work" (Mieder 2019, 249–50). Thus the relatively new proverb, barely a century and a half old, has played an important role in the struggle for equitable employment without discrimination against gender, race, color, religion, or national origin (immigrants). Its acceptance as a basic human rights demand shows convincingly that proverbs are not merely innocuous bits of wisdom but that their messages can also contain legalistic strategies for significant social change.

To return to the issue of property rights, numerous folk proverbs based on the image of a fence come to mind. Such common proverbs as "A fence between makes friends more keen," "Love your neighbor, but do not pull down the fence," and "Good fences make good neighbors" (Mieder, Kingsbury, and Harder 1992,

206) are metaphors arguing that it is important for people to have some space for themselves and their property. They express a common sense of wisdom about human behavior, with the "good fences" proverb having had its start as a customary law. The earliest reference found thus far appeared in the *Vermont Gazette* of May 30, 1794 (personal communication from Fred Shapiro). It comes as no surprise that it might well have originated in the rural state of Vermont, since the borders of fields were originally marked by boulders found in the fields. While such fences were erected to keep cows from wandering off, they also became markers of property lines. In fact, the well-known Vermont poet Robert Frost wrote a celebrated poem, "Mending Wall" (1914), which describes how two neighbors act out the proverb "Good fences make good neighbors" by repairing the stone wall in the springtime:

> [. . .]
> I let my neighbor know beyond the hill;
> And on a day we meet to walk the line
> And set the wall between us as we go.
> To each the boulders that have fallen to each.
> And some are loaves and some so nearly balls
> We have to use a spell to make them balance:
> "Stay where you are until our backs are turned!"
> We wear our fingers rough with handling them.
> Oh, just another kind of outdoor game,
> One on a side. It comes to little more:
> There where it is we do not need the wall:
> He is all pine and I am all apple orchard.
> My apple trees will never get across
> And eat the cones under his pines, I tell him.
> He only says, "Good fences make good neighbours."
> [. . .]

True enough, there are no more cows even to be kept out, but the old Vermont farmer insists that a solid fence, erected by both neighbors, is a good idea for getting along. But hidden between this only too human proverb are legal implications. In older times, villages had so-called professional fence viewers to check on the proper maintenance of the commonly held fences between neighbors. A *New York Times* article, "Viewers of Fences" (1942), explains these customary law matters:

> "Good fences make good neighbors," goes an Old New England saying.
> So firmly convinced of this were early settlers that they chose fence

viewers to make sure that good neighborliness did not suffer from neglect. [. . .] The fence viewer was an arbiter of disputes, [. . .] simply a court of original jurisdiction to establish each man's obligation to maintain a joint fence. Their function was to settle a dispute before it got to the lawing stage. (Gould 1942)

In fact, the famed Supreme Court Justice Felix Frankfurter employed the proverb in his opinion regarding the separation between state and religion on March 8, 1948: "If nowhere else, in the relation between Church and State, 'good fences make good neighbors.'" This certainly is an example of the use of a well-known proverb as a metaphorical and thus indirect argument to make a legal statement. The proverb has been cited as a law proverb in numerous legal cases seeking to establish proper and fair relations between two parties (Mieder 2005, 233–37), and also on the international political scene, as remarks by then still senator John F. Kennedy on October 8, 1957, show: "A friendship such as ours [between Canada and the United States], moreover encourages healthy competition in international trade, it requires that neither take the other for granted in international politics. 'Good fences,' reads a poem by one of our most distinguished New England poets, Robert Frost, 'make good neighbours.' Canada and the United States have carefully maintained the good fences that help make them good neighbours" (Mieder 2023, 177).

The proverb also appeared repeatedly in the world press when Israeli prime minister Ehud Barak was discussing building a security wall to deal with the Israeli-Palestinian conflict, to wit the following statement in the *Jerusalem Post* of October 22, 1999:

Barak Mulls Border Fence Plans
Prime Minister Ehud Barak held a meeting yesterday with several of his ministers to discuss the ways and means of setting up a border fence between Israel and the future Palestinian entity. The prime minister has long advocated the creation of such a barrier, quoting often from the Robert Frost poem about how "good fences make good neighbors," and using grand hand motions to illustrate his belief that the best future for his land involves "us here—and them there." (Mieder 2005, 233–42)

With the popularity of this proverb, it is truly surprising that President Franklin D. Roosevelt did not cite it in his extemporaneous address, "The Golden Rule in Government," on August 26, 1933:

Many centuries ago, as you know, it was the principle of the old English common law—nearly 1,000 years ago, and its development has been constant and consistent—to be fair to one's neighbors and not do things that hurt them. In the old days, when there were only agricultural communities, it was unfair, for example, to our neighbors to allow our cattle to roam in our neighbors' land. We were told we had to fence in our cattle. [. . .] Now the extension of the idea of not hurting our neighbors is recognized today as no infringement on the guarantee of personal liberty—personal liberty to the individual. (Roosevelt 1938, 340–41)

In any case, while the "good fences" proverb has no direct claim as a law proverb, it most certainly contains the metaphorical wisdom of fair and legal behavior.

There are many other folk proverbs that reflect customary (also called folk) law concepts but that might not necessarily be of statutory law value or significance (Dundes Renteln and Dundes 1994, 1:1–4). Nevertheless, in the mind of the folk, they represent legal concepts that fit everyday situations, for example "The receiver is as bad (guilty) as the thief" (1623), stating that it takes two parties to commit theft; "One might as well be hanged for a sheep as a lamb" (1678), expressing that one might just as well go for a big crime rather than a little one; "Wretches hang that jury-men may dine" (1714), arguing against hasty and careless verdicts by juries (Doyle and Doyle 2007); "It is better that ten guilty persons escape than that one innocent suffer" (1765), pleading the case for the falsely accused person (Reiman and Haag 1990); "Finders, keepers" (1825), arguing for the right to keep what one has found without any obvious claim of another's ownership; and "You break it, you buy it" (1952), announcing that damaging something in a store results in having to purchase the item. There is also the quite old metaphorical proverb "Who bulls the cow must keep the calf" (c. 1505), which argues that the man is responsible for his illegitimate child (Tilley 1950, 125–26). Fatherhood was difficult to prove in former times, whereas today with DNA testing it is easy enough to identify the father of a child and to make him face his proper responsibilities. Many other old proverbs expressing legal concepts exist, but several have become outdated. This, however, leads to the interesting question of whether there are more modern proverbs that reflect the legal ideas of today's society.

Considering our modern litigious society's preoccupation with the law and lawyers, it should not be surprising that *The Dictionary of Modern Proverbs* (Doyle, Mieder, and Shapiro 2012) lists quite a few of them, including some rather disrespectful texts against the law profession: "Go to the devil for truth and to a lawyer for a lie" (1930) as well as the two related proverbs "We all hate lawyers except our own" (1992) and "We all hate lawyers until we need one" (1992), registered in one of the supplements (Doyle and Mieder 2020). All of this is somewhat reminiscent of the much older proverb claiming that "The law is such an ass" (1634), with the animal ass standing for "idiot." It was popularized by Charles Dickens in his novel *Oliver Twist* (1838) as "The law is a[n] ass" (Bryan and Mieder 1997, 185; Clapp et al. 2011, 153–57). As expected, there are quite a few proverbs that refer to criminals and crime, perhaps recalling the many detective and murder shows on television: "Crime doesn't pay" (1892), "A criminal (murderer) always returns to the scene of the crime" (1905), "The only crime is getting caught" (1940), "Don't do the crime if you can't do the time" (1957), and "It's not the crime but the cover-up" (1973). To a certain degree, these proverbs are cautionary or predictive claims. Of special interest is the proverb "Where there is no victim, there can be no crime" and its much shorter variant "No victim, no crime" (1971). This is based on the traditional proverb structure "No X, no Y," which is the basis of a large number of old and new concise proverbs (Mieder 2020, 12). Almost predictably, the proverb "No body (corpse), no crime" (1947) has been around for about seventy-five years as a judicial principle suffering from oversimplification. Of course, the extremely important three-word proverb "no means 'no'" (1980) is of utmost personal and legal importance. The entry in our *Dictionary of Modern Proverbs* cites it from an actual legal case:

> 1980 Court of Appeals of Wisconsin, *State v. Lederer* 99 Wis 2d 430 (decided 28 Oct. 436): "'No' means no, and precludes any finding that the prosecutrix consented to any of the sexual acts performed during the night." The proverb refers to the definitiveness of a woman's rebuff of sexual overtures. Of course, the clause is older in other uses (for example, as something a parent might say to a recalcitrant child). (Doyle, Mieder, and Shapiro 2012, 178–79)

There is a second, similar structural pattern "My X, my Y," sometimes varied to "Your X, your Y," which has served as the basis for modern proverbs expressing personal rights in relationships. *The Dictionary of Modern Proverbs* contains information on the following texts: "My game, my rules" (1963), "My money, my rules" (1975), "My house, my party" (1979), "My house, my rules" (1983), and "My party, my rules" (2003). They are also all current with the "your" pronoun, which transfers the rights to someone else. Of great importance is, of course, the modern proverb "My body, my choice" (1989), which had its relatively recent start as a feminist slogan. "The saying was originally used in reference to abortion rights, but it has sometimes been applied to sexual permissiveness, to suicide, and the refusal of certain medical interventions" (Doyle and Mieder 2020, 56).

And yet, laws must be obeyed, as is well expressed by the proverb "No man is above the law" (1734). President Theodore Roosevelt, in a speech on July 4, 1903, in Springfield, Illinois, expanded it ingeniously to the following statement: "No man is above the law and no man is below it; nor do we ask any man's permission when we require him to obey it. Obedience to the law is demanded as a right; not asked as a favor" (Shapiro 2021, 696, no. 13; Mieder 2021, 128). Appropriately dropping the limiting male designation and replacing it with "nobody," the proverb variant "Nobody is above the law and nobody is below it" has recently gained considerable frequency in the media, notably in legitimate reference to Donald Trump.

With this said, these comments on law proverbs can now turn to two final texts that deal with the ever-present contradiction between justice and injustice in human affairs. There is first of all the proverb "Justice delayed is justice denied," which was popularized by Prime Minister William E. Gladstone in a speech of March 16, 1868, in the British House of Commons. It had appeared earlier in the *Weekly Mississippian* newspaper on November 23, 1838, with even earlier precursors having been found in the mid-seventeenth century as "The delay of justice, is great injustice" (1646), and as "Justice delayed is little better than justice denied" (1815) in the early nineteenth century (Shapiro 2021, 327, no. 1). President John F. Kennedy cited the proverb in a speech of February 28, 1963, to vent his frustration about the slowness of judicial proceedings:

> Experience has shown, however, that these highly useful Acts of the 85th and 86th Congresses suffer from two major defects. One is the usual long and difficult delay which occurs between the filing of a lawsuit and its ultimate conclusion. In one recent case, for example, nineteen months elapsed between the filing of the suit and the judgment of the court. In another, an action brought in July 1961 has not yet come to trial. The legal maxim "Justice delayed is Justice denied" is dramatically applicable in these cases. (Mieder 2023, 201)

Applying the proverb to the fate of African Americans and their suffering under slavery, segregation, and discrimination, the great civil rights leader Martin Luther King Jr. had this to say in his famous "Letter from Birmingham City Jail" of April 16, 1963:

> We know through painful experience that freedom is never voluntarily given by the oppressor; it must be demanded by the oppressed. Frankly, I have never yet engaged in a direct action movement that was "well-timed," according to the timetable of those who have not suffered unduly from the disease of segregation. For years now I have heard the word "Wait!" It rings in the ear of every Negro with a piercing familiarity. This "Wait" has almost always meant "Never." It has been a tranquilizing thalidomide, relieving the emotional stress for a moment, only to give birth to an ill-formed infant of frustration. We must come to see

with the distinguished jurist of yesterday that "justice too long delayed is justice denied." We have waited for more than 340 years for our constitutional and God-given rights. The nations of Asia and Africa are moving with jet-like speed toward the goal of political independence, and we still creep at horse-and-buggy pace toward the gaining of a cup of coffee at a lunch counter. I guess it is easy for those who have never felt the stinging darts of segregation to say, "Wait." (Mieder 2010, 369–70)

But there is also the related statement "Injustice anywhere is a threat to justice everywhere" (1958), which King coined in his important book *Stride Toward Freedom: The Montgomery Story* (1958):

The racial issue that we confront in America is not a sectional but a national problem. The citizenship rights of Negroes cannot be flouted anywhere without impairing the rights of every other American. Injustice anywhere is a threat to justice everywhere. A breakdown of law in Alabama weakens the very foundations of lawful government in the other forty-seven states. The mere fact that we live in the United States means that we are caught in a network of inescapable mutuality. Therefore, no American can afford to be apathetic about the problem of racial justice. It is a problem that meets every man at his front door. The racial problem will be solved in America to the degree that every American considers himself personally confronted with it. Whether one lives in the heart of the Deep South or on the periphery of the North, the problem of injustice is his problem; it is his problem because it is America's problem. (Mieder 2010, 354)

Always the visionary champion for human rights, King repeated his slogan numerous times in his speeches and applied it to civil rights issues far beyond the United States, as in his lengthy interview with journalists of *Playboy* magazine, published in the January 1965 issue:

The world is now so small in terms of geographic proximity and mutual problems that no nation should stand idly by and watch another's plight. I think that in every possible instance Africans should use the influence of their governments to make it clear that the struggle of their brothers in the U.S. is part of a worldwide struggle. In short, injustice anywhere is a threat to justice everywhere, for we are tied together in a garment of mutuality. What happens in Johannesburg affects Birmingham, however indirectly. We are descendants of the Africans. Our heritage is Africa.

We should never seek to break the ties, nor should the Africans. (Mieder 2010, 355)

Martin Luther King's sententious claim has become so well known by now that it is cited with or without his name as its originator. In fact, it has become a proverb and has been registered as such in the *Dictionary of Authentic American Proverbs* (Mieder 2021, 111). As with the other proverbs with their legal messages mentioned in these deliberations, it, too, does not contain a reference to a specific law, but it is a humane law of life to act upon with compassion and humility. Martin Luther King said it best in repeatedly citing a statement from 1853 by the abolitionist Theodore Parker, which he rephrased as: "The arc of the moral universe is long, but it bends toward justice" (Mieder 2010, 210–13).

BIBLIOGRAPHY

Abbink, Jon G. 2017. "Traditional Ethiopian Legal Culture: Amharic Proverbs and Maxims on Law and Justice." In *Studies in Ethiopian Languages, Literature, and History: Festschrift for Getatchew Haile*, edited by Adam Carter McCollum, 3–20. Wiesbaden, Germany: Otto Harrassowitz.

Amali, Idris O. O. 1998. "Proverbs as Concept of Idoma Dispensation of Justice." *Proverbium* 15: 13–36.

Arowosegbe, Jacob O. 2017. "Indigenous African Jurisprudential Thoughts on the Concept of Justice: A Reconstruction Through Yoruba Proverbs." *Journal of African Law* 61, no. 2: 155–70.

Bond, Donald F. 1935. "The Law and Lawyers in English Proverbs." *American Bar Association Journal* 21, no. 11 (November): 724–27.

Bond, Donald F. 1936. "English Legal Proverbs." *Publications of the Modern Language Association* 51, no. 4 (December): 921–35.

Broom, Herbert. 1882. *A Selection of Legal Maxims, Classified and Illustrated*. 8th ed. Philadelphia: T. & J. W. Johnson.

Brückner, Wolfgang. 1998. *"Arbeit macht frei": Herkunft und Hintergrund der KZ-Devise*. Opladen, Germany: Leske und Budrich.

Brunssen, Frank. 2010. "'Jedem das Seine': Zur Aufarbeitung des lexikalischen NS-Erbes." *Aus Politik und Zeitgeschichte*, no. 8 (October 15): 14–20. https://www.bpb.de/themen /parteien/sprache-und-politik/42761/jedem-das-seine-zur-aufarbeitung-des-lexikali schen-ns-erbes/.

Bryan George B., and Wolfgang Mieder. 1997. *The Proverbial Charles Dickens: An Index to Proverbs in the Works of Charles Dickens*. New York: Peter Lang.

Büchner, Karl. 1957. "Summum ius summa iniuria." In *Humanitas Romana: Studien über Werke und Wesen der Römer*, 80–105. Heidelberg, Germany: Carl Winter.

Chlosta, Christoph, and Peter Grzybek. 1995. "Empirical and Folkloristic Paremiology: Two to Quarrel or to Tango?" *Proverbium* 12: 67–85.

Clapp, James E., Elizabeth G. Thornburg, Marc Galanter, and Fred R. Shapiro. 2011. *Lawtalk: The Unknown Stories Behind Familiar Legal Expressions*. New Haven, CT: Yale University Press.

Cohn, Georg. 1888. "Deutsches Recht im Munde des Volkes." In *Drei rechtswissenschaftliche Vorträge*. Heidelberg, Germany: Carl Winter.

Doerr, Karin. 2000. "'To Each His Own' (Jedem das Seine): The (Mis-)Use of German Proverbs in Concentration Camps and Beyond." *Proverbium* 17: 71–90.

Doyle, Charles Clay, and Clement Charles Doyle. 2007. "Wretches Hang That Jury-Men May Dine." *Justice System Journal* 28, no. 2: 219–39.

Doyle, Charles Clay, and Wolfgang Mieder. 2020. "*The Dictionary of Modern Proverbs*: Third Supplement." *Proverbium* 37: 53–86.

Doyle, Charles Clay, Wolfgang Mieder, and Fred R. Shapiro. 2012. *The Dictionary of Modern Proverbs*. New Haven, CT: Yale University Press.

Dundes Renteln, Alison, and Alan Dundes, eds. 1994. *Folk Law: Essays in the Theory and Practice of Lex Non Scripta*. 2 vols. New York: Garland Publishing.

Ebel, Wilhelm. 1975. "'Tausch ist edler als Kauf': Jacob Grimms Vorlesung über Deutsche Rechtsaltertümer." In *Festschrift für Hermann Krause*, edited by Sten Gagnér, Hans Schlosser, and Wolfgang Wiegand, 210–24. Cologne: Böhlau.

Elsener, Ferdinand. 1964. "'Keine Regel ohne Ausnahme': Gedanken zur Geschichte der deutschen Rechtssprichwörter." In *Festschrift für den 45: Deutschen Juristentag überreicht von der juristischen Studiengesellschaft in Karlsruhe*, 23–40. Karlsruhe, Germany: C. F. Müller.

Erasmus of Rotterdam. 1989. *Collected Works*. Vol. 32, *Adages I vi 1 to I x 100*. Translated by R. A. B. Mynors. Toronto: University of Toronto Press.

Erasmus of Rotterdam. 1992. *Collected Works*. Vol. 34, *Adages II vii 1 to III iii 100*. Translated by R. A. B. Mynors. Toronto: University of Toronto Press.

Foth, Albrecht. 1971. *Gelehrtes römisch-kanonisches Recht in deutschen Rechtssprichwörtern*. Tübingen, Germany: J. D. B. Mohr.

Frost-Knappman, Elizabeth, and David S. Shrager. 2003. *A Concise Encyclopedia of Legal Quotations*. New York: Barnes and Noble.

Geise, Nancy Magnuson. 1999. "'Possession Is Nine-Tenths of the Law': History and Meaning of a Legal Proverb." *Proverbium* 16: 105–24.

Gould, John. 1942. "Viewers of Fences." *New York Times*, February 8, 31. https://www.nytimes .com/1942/02/08/archives/viewers-of-fences.html.

Graf, Eduard, and Mathias Dietherr. 1869. *Deutsche Rechtssprichwörter*. Nördlingen, Germany: C. H. Beck. Rpt., Aalen, Germany: Scientia Verlag, 1975.

Grimm, Jacob. 1815. "Von der Poesie im Recht." *Zeitschrift für geschichtliche Rechtswissenschaft* 2: 25–99. Also in *Kleinere Schriften*, by Jacob Grimm, 6:152–91. Berlin: Ferdinand Dümmler, 1882.

Grimm, Jacob. 1828. *Deutsche Rechtsaltertümer*. Göttingen, Germany: Dieterich'sche Verlagsbuchhandlung.

Holtappels, Peter. 1965. *Die Entwicklungsgeschichte des Grundsatzes "in dubio pro reo."* Hamburg: Cram, de Gruyter & Company.

Holzhauer, H. 1978. "In dubio pro reo." In *Handwörterbuch zur deutschen Rechtsgeschichte*, edited by Adalbert Erler and Ekkehard Kaufmann, vol. 2, 349–58. Berlin: Erich Schmidt.

Hueck, Ingo J. 1999. "Dichtung und Rechtssprichwörter im Recht: Poetry and Proverbs in Law in European and German History." In *Interdigitations: Essays for Irmengard Rauch*, edited by Gerald F. Carr, Wayne Harbert, and Lihua Zhang, 723–30. New York: Peter Lang.

Janz, Brigitte. 1989. *Rechtssprichwörter im "Sachsenspiegel": Eine Untersuchung zur Text-Bild-Relation in den Codices picturati*. Frankfurt am Main: Peter Lang.

Kaufmann, Ekkehard. 1986. "Rechtssprichwort." In *Handwörterbuch zur deutschen Rechtsgeschichte*, edited by Adalbert Erler and Ekkehard Kaufmann, vol. 4, 364–67. Berlin: Erich Schmidt.

Klenner, Hermann. 2002. "Jedem das Seine." In *Schlagwörter und Schlachtrufe: Aus zwei Jahrhunderten deutscher Geschichte*, edited by Kurt Pätzold and Manfred Weißbecker, 2:327–32, 2:388. Leipzig: Militzke Verlag.

Koller, Michael. 2009. *Not kennt kein Gebot: Entstehung, Verbreitung, Bedeutung eines Rechtssprichwortes*. Münster, Germany: Lit Verlag.

Kornhardt, Hildegard. 1953. "Summus ius." *Hermes* 81, no. 1: 77–85.

Krampe, Christoph. 1989. "'Qui tacet, consentire videtur': Über die Herkunft einer Rechtsregel." In *Staat, Kirche, Wissenschaft in einer pluralistischen Gesellschaft: Festschrift zum 65; Geburtstag von Paul Mikat*, edited by Dieter Schwab, Dieter Giesen, Joseph Listl, and Hans-Wolfgang Strätz, 367–80. Berlin: Duncker und Humblot.

Liebs, Detlef. 1982. *Lateinische Rechtsregeln und Rechtssprichwörter*. Munich: C. H. Beck.

Litovkina, Anna T. 2011. "'Where There's a Will There's a Lawyer's Bill': Lawyers in Anglo-American Anti-Proverbs." *Acta Juridica Hungarica* 52, no. 1: 82–96.

Litovkina, Anna T. 2016. *"Do You Serve Lawyers and Politicians Here?" Stereotyped Lawyers and Politicians in American Jokes and Anti-Proverbs*. Komárno, Slovakia: Univerzita J. Selyeho.

Litovkina, Anna T., and Wolfgang Mieder. 2006. *Old Proverbs Never Die, They Just Diversify: A Collection of Anti-Proverbs*. Burlington: University of Vermont; Veszprém, Hungary: University of Pannonia.

Messenger, John C., Jr. 1959. "The Role of Proverbs in a Nigerian Judicial System." *Southwestern Journal of Anthropology* 15, no. 1 (Spring): 64–73. Also in *The Study of Folklore*, edited by Alan Dundes, 299–307. Englewood Cliffs, NJ: Prentice-Hall, 1965. Also in *Folk Law: Essays in the Theory and Practice of Lex Non Scripta*, edited by Alison Dundes Renteln and Alan Dundes, 1:421–31. New York: Garland Publishing, 1994.

Mieder, Wolfgang. 1986. *"Findet, so werdet ihr suchen!" Die Brüder Grimm und das Sprichwort*. Bern: Peter Lang.

Mieder, Wolfgang. 1993. *Proverbs Are Never Out of Season: Popular Wisdom in the Modern Age*. New York: Oxford University Press. Rpt., New York: Peter Lang, 2012.

Mieder, Wolfgang. 1997. *The Politics of Proverbs: From Traditional Wisdom to Proverbial Stereotypes*. Madison: University of Wisconsin Press.

Mieder, Wolfgang. 2000. *The Proverbial Abraham Lincoln: An Index to Proverbs in the Works of Abraham Lincoln*. New York: Peter Lang.

Mieder, Wolfgang. 2003. "'Good Fences Make Good Neighbors': History and Significance of an Ambiguous Proverb." *Folklore* (London) 114, no. 2 (August): 155–79. A longer version also in *Proverbs Are the Best Policy: Folk Wisdom and American Politics*, by Wolfgang Mieder, 210–43, 287–96. Logan: Utah State University Press, 2005.

Mieder, Wolfgang. 2004. *Proverbs: A Handbook*. Westport, CT: Greenwood Press. Rpt., New York: Peter Lang, 2012.

Mieder, Wolfgang. 2005. *Proverbs Are the Best Policy: Folk Wisdom and American Politics*. Logan: Utah State University Press.

Mieder, Wolfgang. 2009. *"Yes We Can": Barack Obama's Proverbial Rhetoric*. New York: Peter Lang.

Mieder, Wolfgang. 2010. *"Making a Way Out of No Way": Martin Luther King's Sermonic Proverbial Rhetoric*. New York: Peter Lang.

Mieder, Wolfgang. 2014a. *"All Men and Women Are Created Equal": Elizabeth Cady Stanton's and Susan B. Anthony's Proverbial Rhetoric Promoting Women's Rights*. New York: Peter Lang.

Mieder, Wolfgang. 2014b. *Behold the Proverbs of a People: Proverbial Wisdom in Culture, Literature, and Politics*. Jackson: University Press of Mississippi.

Mieder. Wolfgang. 2016. "Zur Diachronie des Sprichworts 'Wer zuerst kommt, mahlt zuerst.'" In *Historisch syntaktisches Verbwörterbuch: Valenz- und konstruktionsgrammatische Beiträge*, edited by Albrecht Greule and Jarmo Korhonen, 237–60. Frankfurt am Main: Peter Lang.

Mieder, Wolfgang. 2019. *"Right Makes Might": Proverbs and the American Worldview*. Bloomington: Indiana University Press.

Mieder, Wolfgang. 2019–2020. "'Mein Haus ist meine Burg'—'My House Is My Castle': Zur Überlieferung und Bedeutung eines Deutsch-englischen Sprichwörterpaars." *Kairoer Germanistische Studien* 24, no. 24: 99–112.

Mieder, Wolfgang. 2020. *The Worldview of Modern American Proverbs*. New York: Peter Lang.

Mieder, Wolfgang. 2021. *Dictionary of Authentic American Proverbs*. New York: Berghahn Books.

Mieder, Wolfgang. 2023. *A Rising Tide Lifts All the Boats: The Proverbial Rhetoric of John F. Kennedy*. New York: Peter Lang.

Mieder, Wolfgang, Stewart A. Kingsbury, and Kelsie B. Harder. 1992. *A Dictionary of American Proverbs*. New York: Oxford University Press.

Mphasha, Lekau Eleazar. 2016. "Just as European Courtroom Lawyers Use Previous Cases, Participants in Northern Sotho Argue with Proverbs Intended to Serve as Past Precedents for Present Actions." *Journal of Sociology and Social Anthropology* 7, no. 1 (January): 20–26.

Murray, David. 1912. "Proverbs." In *Lawyers' Merriments*, 47–59. Glasgow: James MacLehose and Sons.

Ojoade, J. Olowo. 1988. "Proverbial Evidences of African Legal Customs." *International Folklore Review* 6: 26–38.

Osenbrüggen, Eduard. 1876. *Die deutschen Rechtssprichwörter*. Basel, Switzerland: Schweighauser.

Paczolay, Gyula. 1997. *European Proverbs in 55 Languages with Equivalents in Arabic, Persian, Sanskrit, Chinese and Japanese*. Veszprém, Hungary: Veszprémi Nyomda.

Reiman, Jeffrey, and Ernest van den Haag. 1990. "On the Common Saying That It Is Better That Ten Guilty Persons Escape Than That One Innocent Suffer: Pro and Con." *Social Philosophy and Policy* 7, no. 2: 226–48.

Roback, Abraham Aaron. 1944. *A Dictionary of International Slurs (Ethnophaulisms)*. Cambridge, MA: Sci-Art Publishers.

Roosevelt, Franklin D. 1938. *The Public Papers and Addresses*. Vol. 2, *The Year of Crisis: 1933*. Compiled by Samuel I. Rosenman. New York: Random House.

Schmidt-Wiegand, Ruth. 2002. "Rechtssprichwörter im Gericht: Zum Verhältnis von Mündlichkeit und Schriftlichkeit in mittelalterlichen Rechtsquellen." In *Rechtssprichwort und*

Erzählgut: Europäische und afrikanische Beispiele, edited by Heinrich Scholler and Silvia Tellenbach, 9–24. Berlin: Duncker und Humblot.

Schmidt-Wiegand, Ruth, and Ulrike Schowe, eds. 1996. *Deutsche Rechtsregeln und Rechtssprichwörter: Ein Lexikon.* Munich: C. H. Beck.

Shapiro, Fred R. 1993. *The Oxford Dictionary of American Legal Quotations.* New York: Oxford University Press.

Shapiro, Fred R., ed. 2021. *The New Yale Book of Quotations.* New Haven, CT: Yale University Press.

Singer, Samuel, and Ricarda Liver, eds. 1995–2002. *Thesaurus proverbiorum medii aevi: Lexikon der Sprichwörter des romanisch-germanischen Mittelalters.* 13 vols. Berlin: Walter de Gruyter.

Smith, James McCune. 2006. "The Destiny of the People of Color." In *The Works of James McCune Smith: Black Intellectual and Abolitionist,* edited by John Stauffer, 48–60. New York: Oxford University Press.

Speake, Jennifer. 2015. *Oxford Dictionary of Proverbs.* 6th ed. Oxford: Oxford University Press.

Taylor, Archer. 1931. *The Proverb.* Cambridge, MA: Harvard University Press. Rpt. as *The Proverb and an Index to The Proverb.* Hatboro, PA: Folklore Associates, 1962. Rpt. as *The Proverb and an Index to The Proverb,* with an introduction, bibliography, and photograph of Archer Taylor by Wolfgang Mieder. Bern: Peter Lang, 1985.

Taylor, Archer. 1965. "The Road to *An Englishman's House . . .*" *Romance Philology* 19, no. 2 (November): 279–85.

Templeton, John Mark. 1997. *Worldwide Laws of Life: 200 Eternal Spiritual Principles.* Philadelphia: Templeton Press.

Tilley, Morris Palmer. 1950. *A Dictionary of the Proverbs in England in the Sixteenth and Seventeenth Centuries.* Ann Arbor: University of Michigan Press.

Walther, Hans, and Paul G. Schmidt. 1963–1986. *Proverbia sententiaeque latinitatis medii aevi: Lateinische Sprichwörter und Sentenzen des Mittelalters.* 9 vols. Göttingen, Germany: Vandenhoeck und Ruprecht.

Weizsäcker, Wilhelm. 1956. "Rechtssprichwörter als Ausdrucksformen des Rechts." *Zeitschrift für vergleichende Rechtswissenschaft* 58: 9–40. Also in *Ergebnisse der Sprichwörterforschung,* edited by Wolfgang Mieder, 67–86. Bern: Peter Lang, 1978.

Whiting, Bartlett Jere. 1977. *Early American Proverbs and Proverbial Phrases.* Cambridge, MA: Harvard University Press.

Williams, James. 1895. "Latin Maxims in English Law." *Law Magazine and Law Review,* 4th ser., 20, no. 297: 283–95.

Wilson, F. P. 1970. *The Oxford Dictionary of English Proverbs.* 3rd ed. Oxford: Oxford University Press.

Winkler, Leonhard. 1927. *Deutsches Recht im Spiegel deutscher Sprichwörter.* Leipzig: Quelle und Meyer. Rpt., Leipzig: Zentralantiquariat der Deutschen Demokratischen Republik, 1977.

PROVERB INDEX

A, 285, 290
Abraham, 290
Absence, 35, 90, 130, 199, 235, 286, 290
Accused, 369
Acorns, 257
Actions, 28
Advertise, 25
Advice, 214
Age, 34, 266
Air, 291, 355
Airs, 202–4
Alligator, 25
America, 80, 126, 172
Answer, 9, 132–33, 223, 291
Ant, 219
App, 33
Appearance, 291
Appetite, 291
Apple, 6, 23–24, 28, 50, 291, 350, 360
Apple cart, 350, 360
Apples, 287
April, 29
Arc, 385
Argument, 70
Arm, 291
Arms, 291
Around, 22
Ask, 8, 32, 75, 125–27, 175–77
Ass, 25, 291
Asshole, 267, 291
Atheists, 9, 170
Axis, 355

Baby, 23, 279, 291
Back, 133, 291
Bacon, 210–11
Bag, 291, 349, 354, 357–58
Bairns, 336, 356
Ball, 291, 347
Bananas, 291
Bandwagon, 291, 350, 362
Baptism, 291
Basics, 362
Bat, 279, 291
Battle, 291
Beat, 25, 277, 291, 356
Beauty, 29, 34–35
Bed, 27, 95
Beehive, 291
Beggars, 29, 291
Beginning, 122, 273, 291
Bells, 358
Belt, 291, 342, 355
Berry, 25
Best, 291
Bicycle, 32
Bird, 21, 23, 29, 33, 47, 214, 228, 238, 246, 249, 254
Birds, 216, 219, 277, 292
Bitch, 277, 292
Bitter, 279, 292
Black, 216, 217, 264, 268, 292
Blessing, 292
Blind, 241, 249, 253, 259, 287, 292
Blood, 292

Blow, 7, 82–83
Blue, 292
Bluff, 359
Board, 358
Boat, 9, 21, 157, 278, 280, 292
Body, 15, 35, 143, 292, 382
Bolt, 238, 292
Bone, 349
Book, 7, 28, 63, 288, 292
Boot, 292
Born, 227
Borrow, 284, 302
Bosom, 290
Bottom, 292, 354
Box, 21, 57, 343, 364
Boxing, 362
Boy, 78
Boys, 29, 292
Brain, 292
Brains, 269
Branch, 279, 357
Bread, 35, 56, 98, 105, 136, 159, 210–11, 219, 238, 251, 278, 292
Break, 15, 292, 381
Breeze, 275–76, 292
Brick, 359
Bridge, 278, 292
Broke, 336
Broom, 238
Brooms, 198
Buck, 74, 148
Burned, 249, 252, 255, 258
Bus, 357, 360
Bush, 292
Business, 26, 28, 33, 35, 74, 95, 210–11, 372
Butt, 292
Butter, 56, 284, 292, 305, 356
Buyer, 14, 369
Bygones, 292

Caesar, 241, 249
Cake, 9, 62, 175, 238, 292, 356
Cakes, 220
Calf, 205
California, 78
Call, 292

Called, 249, 253, 256
Camera, 29
Can, 4, 42, 85, 119, 159, 190, 278, 292, 388
Candle, 144, 169, 188
Canoe, 25
Cap, 70
Car, 33
Card, 292
Cards, 221, 249, 257, 292, 356–57
Castles, 292
Cat, 6, 13, 219, 277, 292–93, 337, 338, 357
Catch, 293
Cats, 249, 278
Caught, 284, 299
Cause, 225
Caution, 293
Cave, 22
Ceiling, 293
Cents, 293
Chalice, 361
Chalk, 13, 351–52, 362
Chance, 293, 362
Charades, 293
Charity, 9, 171–72, 285–86, 293
Charm, 293
Chase, 336, 356
Check, 293
Chemistry, 293
Chest, 293
Chicken, 201, 293
Chickens, 46, 249
Child, 8, 79, 111–12, 213, 357
Children, 293
Choice, 382
Circle, 273, 293
City, 25, 77
Class, 293
Cloth, 248–49
Clothes, 293
Cloud, 99, 246, 249, 254, 257–58
Come, 14, 29, 372–73
Comfort, 293
Coming, 293
Competition, 25
Conceal, 204
Conscience, 282, 293

PROVERB INDEX

Cooker, 300
Cooks, 249, 255–56, 259
Cool, 293
Coop, 215–16
Core, 359
Corner, 293
Corpse, 382
Cost, 129
Couch, 352–53, 362
Country, 9, 32, 75, 78, 80, 125–27, 146, 175–77
Cover, 293
Cow, 21, 91, 151, 381
Cracks, 293
Cream, 361
Credit, 293
Creek, 293
Creeps, 271, 293
Crime, 5, 25, 287, 293, 382
Criminal, 382
Crocodile, 293
Crossroads, 349, 358
Crow, 40
Cry, 293
Cup, 134
Curtain, 349, 356–57
Curve, 342, 357
Customer, 25
Cut, 341

Damper, 293
Damsel, 293
Date, 293
Daughter, 201
Dawn, 355
Day, 25, 80, 95, 255, 293, 361
Days, 293
Dead, 201, 249, 294
Deadline, 31
Deal, 294
Dealt, 35
Death, 214–15, 227
Deck, 214, 361
Deer, 22
Delay, 228
Den, 294
Desert, 225–26

Devices, 294
Devil, 113, 174, 220, 249, 252, 285, 294, 381
Diamond, 64
Dice, 213–14, 220, 294
Die, 342
Difference, 213–14
Dig, 277
Diligence, 26
Dime, 294
Ditchdigger, 222–23
Do, 5, 8, 37, 53, 81, 89, 92–94, 97–98, 102–4, 107, 109, 111, 136, 197, 375
Dog, 7, 32, 63, 65, 205–6, 220, 238, 249, 251, 258, 351, 362
Dogs, 31, 64, 103, 214, 242, 336, 356
Dollar, 80, 348, 355
Door, 360
Doors, 210–11, 357
Double-take, 358
Doubt, 369, 386
Dozen, 250–51
Dream, 31
Dreams, 294
Dress, 35
Dribs, 351, 360
Drop, 294
Drum, 347
Drummer, 294
Duck, 25, 284, 289, 294, 305
Duckling, 294
Dues, 274, 275, 294

Ear, 294
Earning, 215
Ears, 294, 361
Earth, 345, 361
East, 249, 251–52, 254
Eat, 29
Edge, 273, 276, 359
Edges, 294
Egg, 239, 355, 358
Egg-headed, 355
Eggs, 9, 99, 169, 170, 241–42, 250–51
Elephant, 29, 349, 358
End, 274–75, 280, 294, 343, 359–60
Ending, 351, 360

Ends, 273, 294
Enemy, 69
Enough, 114
Envy, 212, 294
Everything, 25, 216
Evil, 294
Exception, 287, 294
Excess, 229
Experience, 26
Eye, 204, 214, 224, 279, 294, 337, 357–58, 363
Eyebrows, 294, 356
Eyes, 107, 108, 225, 294, 344, 356, 358

Face, 281, 294, 299, 350, 358, 362
Facts, 5, 25
Fame, 299
Familiarity, 139
Farmer, 151
Father, 28, 144, 149, 222, 285, 295
Fear, 124–25, 128, 168
Feathers, 295
Feet, 32, 295, 354
Fellow, 25
Fence, 9, 140–42, 360, 361
Fences, 5, 15, 23–25, 49–50, 57, 142–43, 157, 379–81, 386–87
Few, 295
Fiddle, 295, 341, 355
Field, 295
Fight, 32
Finders, 28, 381
Finger, 358
Fingers, 295, 349, 355
Fire, 170
First, 14, 29, 372–73
Fish, 5, 21, 31, 41, 94, 197, 289, 337
Flaunt, 25, 33
Flavor, 362
Fleas, 336, 356
Flies, 222
Flood, 341
Floodgates, 345, 360
Flow, 25, 32
Fly, 295, 349, 357
Fold, 361
Folly, 222

Fool, 73, 224, 236–38, 249, 256, 295
Fools, 336, 356
Foot, 295, 354, 359
Footsteps, 367
Fortune, 205, 212–13, 217
Fountain, 102–3
Free, 7, 82–83, 273, 295
Freedom, 4, 7–9, 25, 73, 82–84, 129
Freedom fighter, 82
Friend, 7, 14, 25, 59–62, 64–70, 238
Friends, 34, 62–63, 65, 67–71, 216, 227
Frog, 288–89, 295, 328
Frogs, 4, 12, 33, 43, 54–55, 57, 311–12, 315, 320, 323, 326–27
Frown, 62
Fruit, 273, 295
Fruits, 362
Fuck, 295, 353, 360–61
Fun, 295

Gain, 106–7
Game, 33, 337, 341, 350, 356, 362, 382
Games, 295
Garbage, 33
Gauntlet, 249
General Motors, 80, 172
Generation, 138
Generosity, 212
Genie, 295
Gift horse, 249, 255, 257
Girl, 64, 202–3
Give, 31, 134–35, 228
Given, 127, 135
Glass, 9, 24, 179, 257
Glasses, 355
Globally, 10, 24, 52–53, 79, 180
Glove, 26, 35
Gloves, 295
Go, 22, 249, 358, 360
Goat, 295
God, 77, 83, 94, 132, 200, 212–14, 217, 221–22, 226, 228, 251, 256, 295
Gold, 6, 21, 44, 120, 198, 219–20, 237, 284, 307, 337, 355, 362
Gold-mine, 355
Good, 172–74, 295

PROVERB INDEX

Goose pimples, 295
Government, 7, 37, 73, 108, 114
Grapes, 277, 295
Grapevine, 295
Grass, 6, 28–29, 52, 57, 249–51
Grave, 26, 95
Ground, 358
Group, 78
Guard, 295
Guilty, 388
Gun, 295
Guts, 6, 25, 31, 266, 295

Hair, 111, 152, 226, 238
Half-life, 359
Halloo, 47
Halt, 276, 295
Halves, 358
Hand, 56, 112, 197, 220, 281, 295–96, 348, 358
Handful, 361
Handle, 358
Hands, 33, 113, 296, 345, 355–56, 361
Hanky-panky, 296, 362
Happen, 78, 84, 139
Hardball, 296
Harmony, 166–67
Haste, 236–37
Hat, 282, 296, 340, 345, 354, 361
Haul, 361
Have, 115
Haves, 218
Havoc, 296, 348, 355
Hay, 238, 288, 296
Head, 276, 296, 359
Heads, 238, 278, 296, 344, 358–59, 361
Heart, 33, 225, 277, 286, 288, 296, 347
Heat, 147
Heaven, 296, 304
Hell, 258, 267, 296, 344, 359
Hen, 215
Here, 228
Hesitate, 90
Hide, 296
Hindsight, 296
Hired, 32, 106, 285–86, 296
History, 27

Hit, 296
Hitch, 296
Hold, 360
Hole, 283, 297, 348, 356
Home, 78, 273–74, 289–90, 297, 337, 355, 357–58, 376
Homework, 297
Honesty, 256–57
Honey, 222
Hook, 27, 276, 282, 284, 297, 305, 362
Hooky, 288, 297
Hop, 46–47, 56
Hope, 94, 297, 337, 356
Hopes, 215–16, 361
Horn, 342
Horse, 218, 238, 249, 255, 336, 356
Horses, 6, 9, 49, 57, 73, 177–78, 190, 315
Hot, 297
Hounds, 238
Hour, 297
Hours, 217
House, 10, 14, 26, 37, 42, 73, 181–87, 190–91, 217, 221, 223–24, 247, 297, 375–76, 382, 388–89
Hue, 351, 359
Hunger, 201
Hustle, 297

I's, 350, 362
Ice, 297
Iceberg, 356
Icing, 356
Idea, 276, 297, 348, 356, 358
Ignorance, 14, 288, 297, 369
Impulses, 212
Indian, 30, 181, 190
Industry, 26
Injustice, 4, 14, 366, 371, 384
Innocent, 369
Insult, 297
Iron, 6, 21, 56, 149–50, 198, 235, 337
Item, 297

Jacket, 171
Jackpot, 297
Job, 357

396 PROVERB INDEX

Joke, 297
Journey, 138
Judas, 297
Judge, 98
Judgment, 104
Jug, 212
Jump, 225
Justice, 144–45, 160, 371, 383–85, 387

Keep, 297, 344, 358
Keeper, 82
Keeps, 297
Kick, 297
Kid, 273, 280, 298
Kid gloves, 298
King, 258, 287
Kings, 202–3, 249, 292
Kiss, 298
Kitchen, 147
Knee, 188
Knife, 343, 362
Know, 143, 298, 361
Knowledge, 110

Labor, 362
Lamb, 104, 214–15
Land, 267, 274, 298
Lark, 298
Las Vegas, 78
Last, 298
Late, 28
Laugh, 298
Laurels, 342
Law, 14–15, 370–71, 376–77, 381, 382, 386
Laws, 202–3
Lawsuit, 215–16
Lawyer, 368, 381
Laziness, 26, 95
League, 298
Leap, 344
Learned, 285, 298
Learning, 236–37
Lease, 298
Leather, 298, 344, 359
Leave, 275, 354
Leg, 202–4, 295

Lemons, 34, 90, 150
Letter, 371
Liberty, 82, 274, 298
Lie, 279, 298
Lies, 282, 298
Life, 4, 5, 25–26, 31, 34, 37, 75, 90, 101, 115, 150,
    213–14, 273–74, 276, 298
Lifetime, 202
Light, 134, 274–75, 298, 351, 360, 362
Lightning, 298
Limb, 281, 298
Limbo, 360
Limelight, 360
Line, 280–81, 298, 356, 358, 361
Link, 298
Lion, 169
Lips, 220
Listen, 280, 298
Littles, 215
Load, 277, 298
Loaf, 228, 249, 255–56, 258
Lock, 341, 355
Long, 343
Look, 90, 199, 236, 249, 256, 258–59, 355
Looker, 356
Lost, 356
Love, 32, 34, 75, 80, 197, 217, 253, 298
Luck, 202, 267, 298
Lunch, 31, 85
Lurch, 298

Main Street, 80–81
Maine, 78
Make, 279–80, 282, 299
Man, 5, 6, 15, 21, 29, 35, 56, 76, 78, 91, 95, 105,
    132, 135–36, 213, 219, 221–22, 236–37, 249,
    251, 256, 299, 336, 356
Manners, 31
Many, 108
Map, 299
Marbles, 299
McCoy, 299
Meat, 82, 91–92, 237, 249, 255–56, 258, 288, 299
Men, 5, 21, 25, 37, 43, 85, 100–101, 103, 108, 119,
    159, 191, 388
Mess, 284

PROVERB INDEX

Midas, 299

Might, 14, 37, 43, 69, 99, 119, 130, 374–75

Mill, 14, 29, 372

Mind, 143, 299

Mine, 299

Minutes, 299

Miracle, 304

Misery, 75

Misfortune, 219

Miss, 249

Mississippi, 77

Moderation, 229, 340

Molasses, 299

Money, 25, 29, 33, 80, 115, 236–37, 275, 299, 341, 344, 354, 358, 382

Monty, 352, 362

More, 28

Mortal, 151

Mote, 224, 239

Mother, 225–26

Mouse, 26

Mouth, 299, 359

Murderer, 382

Music, 279, 283, 299

Muster, 355

Muttons, 347

Nail, 217, 238

Naked, 210–11

Name, 267, 299

Necessity, 14, 28, 94, 370–71, 387

Neck, 299, 358, 360

Negotiate, 124–25, 128

Neighbor, 104, 137, 202

Nerves, 299

Net, 345, 361

Nick, 273

No, 35, 382

Nobody, 217, 383

Nose, 63, 202, 210–11, 238, 299

Nothing, 229, 299, 340, 354

Now, 83

Null, 300

Number, 32

Nutshell, 300

Oaks, 249, 251

Occasion, 43, 300

Odds, 300, 361

Offense, 299

Olive branch, 300

Omelet, 169–70, 239, 250–51, 254–56

One, 108

Opposites, 28

Order, 363

Ounce, 147

Over, 5, 25

Overdrive, 300, 355

Own, 21, 53, 56, 371, 385–87

Paces, 360

Pack, 359

Packages, 360

Pain, 34, 106–7

Pale, 356

Pants, 31, 275, 300

Papa, 149

Paper, 344, 358

Party, 382

Passion, 26

Past, 40

Pat, 300, 356

Path, 220, 300

Pay, 5, 25, 70, 101–2, 115, 146–47, 377–78

Peace, 130–31, 149–50, 166–67, 300

Peacock, 300

Pears, 223

Peas, 300

Pell-mell, 355

Pendulum, 273

Pennsylvania, 78

Penny, 29, 215, 283, 300

People, 7, 37, 73, 108, 114, 238, 257, 283

Perception, 76

Personal, 77

Persons, 381, 388

Pickle, 300

Picture, 6, 24, 51, 300, 348, 351, 358

Pig, 359

Pigeon, 215–16

Pilot, 345, 362

Pin, 300, 362

Pinch, 300
Pipe, 300
Pissed, 35
Pit, 197
Pitcher, 198, 223–24
Pitchers, 306, 336, 356
Pitfalls, 357
Place, 28, 205, 274–75, 300, 360
Plague, 275, 300
Plain, 321
Plans, 275, 300
Plate, 360
Platter, 276, 300
Play, 300, 373
Plunge, 300
Point, 300
Points, 300
Poison, 246
Political, 77
Politics, 43, 75–76, 119
Poor, 79, 81, 114, 124
Port, 250, 252
Possession, 14, 376–77, 386
Pot, 204, 225–26
Potato, 352–53, 362
Poverty, 95
Power, 76
Practice, 9, 28, 145–46
Prayers, 225
Preach, 225
Preaching, 226
Prevention, 147
Price, 33, 82, 129, 300, 357
Pride, 21
Problems, 360
Profile, 300
Promise, 110, 318
Promises, 141
Prophet, 197
Proverb, 38
Pull, 359, 361
Pulse, 358
Punch, 300
Puppy love, 300
Purse, 210, 211, 360

Purse strings, 360
Pussyfoot, 357

Quarrel, 54, 149–50
Question, 301
Quick, 301

Radar, 342, 356
Rags, 265
Rain, 25, 217, 250, 254, 301
Rain check, 301
Rank, 301
Rant, 301
Rat, 281, 301
Rats, 277, 301
Razor's edge, 301
Reap, 301
Receiver, 381
Reed, 301
Rein, 301
Reins, 280, 301
Remedy, 216, 222
Removes, 5, 25–26, 95
Required, 127
Requires, 135
Rest, 27
Revenge, 222
Rich, 79, 80, 114, 124, 272, 301
Ride, 361
Right, 3, 14, 37, 42–43, 69, 72, 85, 99, 119, 130, 133, 159, 307, 371, 374–75, 388
Righteousness, 133
Rights, 112–13, 172
Rings, 226, 352
Road, 138, 246, 250–51, 255, 258, 301, 337, 357, 363
Roads, 11, 57, 143–44, 248, 250–52, 254
Rod, 286, 301
Rome, 238, 250, 258, 301
Roof, 146–47
Room, 273, 301
Ropes, 301, 355
Rough, 301
Rubber-stamped, 359
Rug, 301

PROVERB INDEX

Rule, 344, 357, 361
Rules, 362, 382
Run, 25, 265, 275–76, 301

Sack, 301
Safe, 28, 301
Safety, 25
Said, 28, 301
Sailors, 253–54
Sake, 289, 301
Samaritan, 301
Sauce, 201
Saying, 357–58
Scalp, 301
Scapegoat, 301
Scene, 301
Score, 33, 301
Seat, 279, 302
Secret, 70
See, 169
Seeing, 82
Sell, 31
Sense, 221
Sex, 35
Shadow, 302
Shake, 302
Shape, 354, 362
Share, 275, 302
Sharp, 355
Sheep, 381
Ship, 153, 302, 361
Shirt, 171, 336, 356
Shit, 25, 31, 34, 302
Shoe, 220, 278, 302
Shoes, 107, 348, 354–55, 363
Shot, 54, 302, 345
Shoulders, 302
Show, 278, 302, 359
Sick, 302
Side, 302, 362
Sides, 350, 362
Sight, 90, 199
Sign, 360
Signs, 77
Silence, 223, 369, 387

Silver, 252, 255
Sin, 225
Sink, 302
Sisyphus, 302
Six, 250–51, 257
Size, 35
Skin, 302
Sky, 7, 238, 250–51, 254, 302
Slap, 302
Sleep, 227
Sleeping, 26, 95
Sleeve, 302
Sleeves, 113, 355
Sloth, 26, 95
Slowly, 302
Smelt, 35
Smoke, 238
Society, 124
Sodom, 302
Some, 302
Son, 302
Sooner, 302
Sow, 135–36
Space, 357
Spade, 30, 42
Speak, 5, 25, 74, 154
Speed, 33
Spic, 302
Spin, 302
Spot, 362
Spotlight, 342, 356
Square, 302, 362
Squared, 302
Stab, 302
Stage, 302
Stake, 302
Stand, 302
Start, 273, 275, 302
Statistics, 29
Steal, 302
Steam, 344, 357
Step, 138, 302, 343, 362
Stick, 363
Sticks, 250–51, 256, 258
Stir, 302

Stitch, 21, 259
Stitches, 302
Stomach, 219, 359
Stone, 60, 224, 248, 250–51, 254, 336, 349, 356
Stones, 246, 255
Stools, 238
Store, 302
Storm, 302–3
Story, 351, 354, 362
Straight, 281, 358
Straw, 219
Street, 303
Strike, 303
Strikes, 25
Strokes, 5, 22, 24, 41, 43, 53, 57, 90, 118
Struggle, 4, 42, 72, 76, 85, 96, 100, 119, 190
Study, 303
Stuff, 303
Style, 343
Succeed, 28
Success, 25, 34
Sucker, 250
Sun, 99, 197, 217, 303
Supper, 221
Swallow, 21, 197
Sweat, 98
Swoop, 273, 303
Sword, 105–6, 149
Swords, 131, 354

T, 228, 303–4, 343
T's, 350, 362
Tables, 303
Take, 250
Talk, 22, 25, 303
Tango, 6, 24, 32, 54, 149
Taskmaster, 303
Tastes, 91–92
Team, 343
Teeth, 223–24, 303, 341–42, 355
Tell, 216
Terms, 354, 363
Territory, 303
Terrorist, 81
Test, 303, 356
Texas, 77–78

Thanks, 303
Thief, 381
Thing, 31, 357, 359
Things, 29, 30, 139, 213–14, 360
Think, 10, 24, 52–53, 79, 180
Thoughts, 303
Thumb, 344, 357, 361
Thumbs, 223, 357, 360
Tick, 303
Tickee, 30
Tide, 5, 9, 154–58, 251, 341, 355, 388
Tiger, 151–53
Time, 24–25, 27, 34, 41, 45, 95, 110, 146–47, 250–52, 254, 288, 303, 355–57
Time bomb, 303
Times, 355
Tip, 303, 349, 356
Tiptoeing, 360
Toads, 12, 43, 54–55, 57, 311–12, 320, 323, 326–28
Today, 214–15
Toe, 360
Toes, 303
Tomorrow, 92, 250, 258–59
Ton, 303
Tongue, 247, 258, 303
Tooth, 303
Toothpaste, 31
Top, 212–13, 345, 359
Tough, 75
Towel, 303
Town, 78
Track, 343, 346, 354, 357–58, 363
Tracks, 348–49, 355, 359
Train, 33
Trap, 356
Trash, 31, 283, 303
Treat, 116
Treatment, 303
Trend, 70
Trick, 280–81, 304, 357
Tricks, 228, 304
Trumps, 356
Trunk, 219
Trust, 71, 75
Truth, 9, 133–34, 151, 355

PROVERB INDEX

Turd, 35
Turn, 238, 360
Twists, 348, 359
Two, 304

United States, 80
Universe, 385
Up, 361
Ups, 283, 344
Use, 29

Value, 350, 362
Ventured, 199
Vermont, 78
Vessels, 238
Victim, 15, 382
Victory, 24, 139
Vigilance, 7, 82
Village, 8, 43, 79, 84, 110–12, 117

Wagon, 25
Wait, 343, 358–59
Wall, 80–81, 351, 359, 361
Wall Street, 80, 81
Wallflower, 304
Want, 238
War, 127–28, 130
Warhorse, 357
Waters, 304
Watershed, 273–74
Waves, 304
Way, 4, 5, 42, 75, 83–85, 119, 159, 190, 277, 304,
    306, 337, 357–58, 388
Ways, 32, 43, 357
Wear, 304
Weather, 146, 304
Weatherwise, 26
Weeds, 283, 304

Week, 76
Weight, 360
Well, 304
Wheat, 355
Wheel, 212–13, 217, 278, 304
Wheels, 287
Whistle, 304
White, 216–17
Wife, 223–24
Will, 28, 368, 387
Willy-nilly, 362
Win, 25, 33, 304
Wind, 202, 250, 254, 256, 258, 304, 361
Windfall, 288, 304, 359
Windmills, 232–33
Window, 362
Winds, 358
Winner, 288, 304
Winooski, 77
Wisdom, 218
Wish, 144
Woman, 30, 32, 44, 120, 202–4, 214, 224,
    234
Wood, 238
Woods, 47, 304
Wool, 222, 225, 277, 304
Word, 122–23, 158, 267, 279, 304, 358–59
Words, 304, 361
Work, 53, 202–3, 278, 287, 291, 304, 336, 385
World, 151, 212–13, 304, 345, 359
Worm, 96–97
Worth, 93, 218, 222
Wreck, 304
Wretches, 381, 386
Wrong, 144, 357
Wrongs, 28

Zero, 355

ABOUT THE AUTHOR

Wolfgang Mieder is University Distinguished Professor Emeritus of German and Folklore at the University of Vermont, where he taught for fifty years and was the longtime chairperson of the Department of German and Russian. Among his many honors are honorary doctorates from the Universities of Athens, Bucharest, and Vermont. The author of well over a hundred books on fairy tales, folk songs, and legends, he is recognized internationally for his expertise in paremiology (proverb studies).

Printed in the United States
by Baker & Taylor Publisher Services